Iran, Israel, and the Jews

YESHIVA UNIVERSITY CENTER FOR ISRAEL STUDIES SERIES

❦

Yeshiva University Center for Israel Studies Publications
Academic Advisory Committee

Selma Botman
Shalom Carmy
Steven Fine
Joshua Karlip
Jill Katz
David Lavinsky
Zafrira Lidovsky-Cohen
Ronnie Perelis
Jacob Wisse

Iran, Israel, and the Jews

Symbiosis and Conflict from the
Achaemenids to the Islamic Republic

EDITED BY
AARON KOLLER & DANIEL TSADIK

FOREWORD BY *Steven Fine*
INTRODUCTION BY *Daniel Tsadik & Aaron Koller*

☙PICKWICK *Publications* · Eugene, Oregon

IRAN, ISRAEL, AND THE JEWS
Symbiosis and Conflict from the Achaemenids to the Islamic Republic

Yeshiva University Center for Israel Studies Series 1

Copyright © 2019 Wipf and Stock Publishers. All rights reserved. Except for brief quotations in critical publications or reviews, no part of this book may be reproduced in any manner without prior written permission from the publisher. Write: Permissions, Wipf and Stock Publishers, 199 W. 8th Ave., Suite 3, Eugene, OR 97401.

Pickwick Publications
An Imprint of Wipf and Stock Publishers
199 W. 8th Ave., Suite 3
Eugene, OR 97401

www.wipfandstock.com

PAPERBACK ISBN: 978-1-5326-6170-9
HARDCOVER ISBN: 978-1-5326-6171-6
EBOOK ISBN: 978-1-5326-6172-3

Cataloguing-in-Publication data:

Names: Koller, Aaron J., 1978–, editor. | Tsadik, Daniel, 1969–, editor. | Fine, Steven, foreword.

Title: Iran, Israel, and the Jews : symbiosis and conflict from the Achaemenids to the Islamic Republic / edited by Aaron Koller and Daniel Tsadik ; foreword by Steven Fine.

Description: Eugene, OR: Pickwick Publications, 2019. | Yeshiva University Center for Israel Studies Series 1. | Includes indexes.

Identifiers: ISBN: 978-1-5326-6170-9 (PAPERBACK). | ISBN: 978-1-5326-6171-6 (HARDCOVER). | ISBN: 978-1-5326-6172-3 (EBOOK).

Subjects: LCSH: Iranians—Antiquities. | Jews—Antiquities. | Judaism—History—Talmudic period, 10–425. | Achaemenid dynasty, 559–330 B.C. | Zoroastrianism—History. | Israel—Foreign relations—Iran.

Classification: DS135 .I65 2019 (print). | DS135 (epub).

Manufactured in the U.S.A.   NOVEMBER 27, 2019

Dedicated to Yaakov Elman of blessed memory

ניצחו אראלים את המצוקים וְנִשְׁבָּה ארון הקודש

Contents

Foreword / Steven Fine / ix
Introduction / Daniel Tsadik & Aaron Koller / xi
List of Contributors / xvii

PART 1: PRE-MODERN HISTORY

1. Negotiating Empire: Jewish Life and Jewish Theology under the Achaemenids / *Aaron Koller* / 3

2. Iranian Influence at Qumran:
Texts and Beliefs / *Miryam T. Brand* / 24

3. The Image of the Jews
in Zorastrian Literature / *Mahnaz Moazami* / 46

4. Digestion as a Means of Purification in Fourth-
and Fifth-Century Sources: A Rabbinic Conundrum
and an Avestan Problem / *Yaakov Elman* / 59

5. Fire Typologies in Zoroastrianism and in the Babylonian Talmud:
A Methodological Consideration / *Geoffrey Herman* / 108

6. Prophecy and the Prophecy of Moses in *Ḥovot Yehudah* by Rabbi Yehudah ben Elazar / *Shaul Regev* / 120

7. Preliminary List of Judeo-Persian Manuscripts at the Institute of Oriental Manuscripts of the Russian Academy of Sciences and at the National Library of Russia, St. Petersburg, Russia / *Vera B. Moreen* / 140

PART 2: MODERN CULTURAL HISTORY

8. Rabbi Menaḥem Shemuel Halevy, Hamadan, Persia—Jerusalem (1884–1940) / *Nechama Kramer-Hellinx* / 171

9. Iran 1972 Revisited in Memories, or In the Footsteps of the Deer / *Galit Hasan-Rokem* / 212

10. Iranian Jews' Ritual Objects / *Ruth Jacoby* / 231

11. The Binding of Isaac in the Work of Moshe Shah Miraḥi: A Persian-Jewish Folk Artist in Early Twentieth-Century Jerusalem / *Shalom Sabar* / 254

12. Iranian and Jewish: Becoming Iranian American Jewish / *Leah R. Baer* / 287

PART 3: MODERN POLITICAL HISTORY

13. The Symbolic Role of King Cyrus in Israel's Relationship with Iran / *Miriam Nissimov* / 311

14. Jews in the Pre-Constitutional Years: The Shiraz Incident of 1905 / *Daniel Tsadik* / 336

15. The Concept of Tyranny in the Anti-Israeli Discourse in Contemporary Iran / *Agniezka Erdt* / 367

Index / 405

Foreword

THE CENTER FOR ISRAEL Studies is dedicated to deepening Yeshiva University's longstanding relationship with the State of Israel. Our area studies approach to Israel, its land and peoples, brings together Yeshiva University's rich faculty, museum, and library resources to explore Israel in all of its complexities. Our work is expressed through diverse scholarship, publications, academic programs, museum exhibitions, public events, and educational opportunities.

In this spirit, I am most pleased to introduce *Iran, Israel, and the Jews: Symbiosis and Conflict from the Achaemenids to the Islamic Republic*. This marvelous volume is edited by my distinguished colleagues, Daniel Tsadik and Aaron Koller, and brings together a community of scholars of uncommon depth to explore one of the longest and most complex relationships between two peoples in the history of humanity. The twenty-five hundred years of "symbiosis and conflict" that have connected the Jewish and Iranian peoples are quite exceptional. This fascinatingly long span is a virtual laser beam through human history, and I am proud that our Center is the soil in which it has germinated.

Iran, Israel, and the Jews: Symbiosis and Conflict from the Achaemenids to the Islamic Republic began as a conference organized by the YU Center for Israel Studies in 2010. I thank Aaron, Daniel, and all of the authors for bringing this publication to fruition with this exceptional volume.

This volume inaugurates the **Yeshiva University Center for Israel Studies Series** in Pickwick Publications, an imprint of Wipf and Stock. This series will be a place to assemble and celebrate the riches of CIS academic conferences and projects. This is an exciting development, made possible by the Leon Charney Legacy Fund of the Center for Israel

Studies and The Michael Scharf Publication Trust of Yeshiva University Press. I thank Tzili Charney and Jeffrey Gurock for their support of this project, and of the people of Wipf and Stock for their congeniality and professionalism.

It is my hope that *Iran, Israel, and the Jews,* like all projects of the Yeshiva University Center for Israel Studies, will contribute broadly to the academic conversation on Israel, and also to a broad and excited readership within the Yeshiva University community, and beyond.

Steven Fine
Dean Pinkhos Churgin Professor of Jewish History
Director, Yeshiva University Center for Israel Studies
New York and Jerusalem

Introduction

DANIEL TSADIK AND AARON KOLLER

Eliz Sansarian wrote, "The Iranian Jews are the most researched non-Muslim religious minority in Iran."[1] Even if this statement is correct, scholarship on Iranian Jews is still sparse compared to the research conducted on Jews residing elsewhere. One can hardly speak of diverse approaches, different schools of historiography, or even major debates among the few scholars who address Iranian Jewry's past. Generally, scholars make no serious attempt to systematically juxtapose, connect, or contrast questions relevant to Iran's Jews and issues of broader Jewish significance. Absent also is detailed research on a variety of topics in most of the periods during which Jews lived in Iran, including on the daily life, women's position and on historical processes and socio-cultural developments. Several factors may account for these and other deficiencies, but the primary one is clearly the simple fact that we still do not possess data regarding various aspects of Jewish existence in Iran, without which no meaningful discourse can emerge in any field of research.[2]

However, the picture is not entirely a gloomy one. Academic conferences in the field of the Jews of Iran are convened every few years — in Jerusalem, Tel-Aviv, and New York, among other places. Answers to questions about the Jews' lives are given, new and sometimes forgotten fields of research are examined and re-examined. Thus, for instance, studies of Iranian Jewish relations during Sasanian times seem to be flourishing

1. Eliz Sanasarian, *Religious Minorities in Iran*, Cambridge Middle East Studies 13 (Cambridge: Cambridge University Press, 2000), 44.

2. Partly based on Daniel Tsadik, *Between Foreigners and Shi'is* (Stanford: Stanford University Press, 2007), 1.

as never before, and studies of nineteenth-century Iranian Jewry have greatly progressed, with two books published in recent years.³ Significantly, primary sources and private stories are gradually coming to light. It will suffice to mention some of the recently published memoirs, which shed light on aspects of life during twentieth century Iran; this includes Hakham Y. Shofet's *Khatirat* (2000), M. Ezri's *Mi Bakhem mi-Kol 'Ammo* (2001), H. Levi's *Khatirat-i Man* (2002), E. Khalili's *Yadi az Gudhashtah-ha* (2004), sections at N. Tefilin-Menashri's *Ve-Ahavti le-Re'ay Kamoni* (2005), H. Kirmanshachi's *Tahavvulat-i Ijtima'i-yi Yahudiyan-i Iran dar Qarn-i Bistum* (2007), M. Farivar's *Hadith-i Yak Farhang* (2007), E. Eshaqyan's *Hamrah ba Farhang* (2008), and F. Goldin's *Wedding Song* (2003) and *Leaving Iran* (2015).

Recent years witnessed scholarly attempts to sum up certain aspects of the Iranian Jews' lives, as well. Vera Moreen's In *Queen Esther's Garden: An Anthology of Judeo-Persian Literature* (2000) was followed by Houman Sarshar's edited volume of *Esther's Children* (2002), in turn to be followed by the Ben Zvi Institute Hebrew volume (2005) on the Jews of Iran in the nineteenth and twentieth centuries. The *Encyclopaedia Iranica* also published a series of entries on the Jews of Iran, which were later collected into the book *Jewish Communities of Iran* (2011). Despite the significance of such endeavors in sketching Iranian Jews' lives in broad lines, further detailed research is still imperative. In virtually all sub-fields relating to the Jews of Iran much can be still explored, and questions still await serious answers. Some of those questions are, it is to be hoped, addressed in the present volume.

The present book, *Iran, Israel, and the Jews: Symbiosis and Conflict from the Achaemenids to the Islamic Republic*, developed from the conference "Israel and Iran," which was convened by Yeshiva University on October 31, 2010. Some of the lectures delivered then are now presented in the book, while additional papers are included.

The present book consists of fifteen chapters, addressing aspects of Jewish-Iranian relations from antiquity to the early twenty-first century. The first five papers address the first thousand years of Jewish-Iranian interactions, which began in earnest with the Achaemenid conquest. Aaron Koller surveys Jewish political and cultural life during the period of the Achaemenids, and then focuses his attention on the theological challenge of the Persian empire: with such a successful political apparatus, where

---

3. Tsadik, *Between Foreigners and Shi'is*; David Yeroushalmi, *The Jews of Iran in the Nineteenth Century*, Brill's Series in Jewish Studies 40 (Leiden: Brill, 2009).

was God in running the world? Koller shows that Persian-era Jewish texts offer various views on this point, suggesting that it was a debated topic at the time. Miryam Brand then looks at the Dead Sea Scrolls, which were of course found in the Judean Desert, but which show centuries of accumulated influence from various cultures. Charting a careful methodological course, Brand looks in depth at the question of dualism, and shows that while there is undoubtedly influence from the Zoroastrian culture on Qumran thought, it is not a simplistic matter of borrowing, but something more subtle and complex—and that this is true for other examples, as well.

Turning to the way Persians perceived Jews, Mahnaz Moazami examines the discussions of Jews found in Zoroastrian literature. She finds that much of the polemical material against Jews was actually primarily for internal consumption, and served inner-Zoroastrian purposes of reinforcing doctrines and patrolling borders. On the other side, Yaakov Elman (of blessed memory) studies a particular legal issue: the status of "swallowed impurities." Bringing together philological, historical, and anthropological approaches to this legal question, Elman shows that the rabbis of the Talmud and the Zoroastrian sages were struggling with similar legal problems within their religious systems, and hit upon similar solutions. Rounding out this section, Geoffrey Herman looks at a talmudic text that has a patently obvious Zoroastrian background, but, against earlier scholars, Herman shows that this is again not simply a question of borrowing, but of influence that echoes within the borrowing culture in innovative ways.

Two papers treat the early modern period, from very different perspectives. Shaul Regev studies the fascinating seventeenth-century Persian-Jewish book Hovot Yehudah, written by R. Yehudah Ben El'azar. Besides its significance as one of the few Persian-Jewish books from the century, it is also inherently fascinating, with novel approaches to classic problems of Jewish thought, and an overt polemical purpose which leads the author to buttress his argumentation with citations from the Qur'an, for instance. Vera Moreen publishes here a catalog of the Judeo-Persian manuscripts in two major research collections in St. Petersburg. Most are nineteenth-century mss from Bukhara (although there is one tenth-eleventh-century manuscript), and were purchased by the great Karaite collector Abraham Firkowicz and the great orientalist Vladimir Alekseevich Ivanow. The genres preserved run the gamut from biblical interpretation through mishnah interpretation to poetry.

Beginning with chapter 8, we move to the modern era, and chapters 8 through 13 treat aspects of cultural and intellectual history. Nechama Kramer-Hellinx offers a contextualized biographical sketch of Rabbi Menaḥem Shemuel Halevy, which provides insight into Iranian-Jewish culture of the early twentieth century, and the reasons why and ways in which the center of this culture began to shift to Palestine and Israel in the following decades.

In a different vein, Galit Hasan-Rokem takes us along with her on a trip to Iran in 1972. Hasan-Rokem's illustrated personal account brings to life what pre-Revolutionary Iran was like through the eyes of an informed outsider. Drilling deeper into one aspect of that life, Ruth Jacoby studies the ritual objects of Iranian Jews now in museum collections in Jerusalem. The accoutrements of the Torah are particularly treated, as an initial foray into the study of Persian Jewish material culture. Shalom Sabar turns his attention to the artistic world, offering a close analysis and contextual analysis of a picture of the Binding of Isaac by Iranian-Jewish artist Moshe Shah Mizrahi, who lived in Jerusalem in the early twentieth-century. Finally, Leah Baer adds another culture to the mix, and studies the processes by which Iranian Jews in the United States navigated their very complex identities. Subtly describing the opportunities afforded by acculturation alongside the pressures to retain their earlier identities, Baer affords us insight into dynamics unique to this group, on the one hand, but also familiar to all immigrant groups, on the other.

The last section of the book deals with modern political history. Miriam Nissimov traces the figure of Cyrus the Great in the political discourse between Israel and Iran in the mid-twentieth century. Nissimov shows that the Iranians were generally keen to claim the mantle of Cyrus, the benign conqueror, and the Israelis were keen to remind the Iranians of the way in which Cyrus had positively shaped Jewish history. The image of Cyrus faded from Iranian, and therefore Israeli, discourse in the 1970s, however. Daniel Tsadik investigates the alleged improvement in the standing of Jews in Iran during the Constitutional years and the immediate run-up to the Constitutional Revolution. Combining a broad survey with a detailed study of one prominent incident in Shiraz, Tsadik concludes that the picture is complicated, with the Jews' standing rising to some extent, but the community also being subject to discrimination and even attacks, for political, religious, and economic reasons. Finally, Agnieszka Erdt traces the concept of "tyranny" in Iranian discourse about Israel. Erdt's analysis shows how an ancient Islamic concept has been re-deployed in modern times to conceptualize a new political and religious problem.

In sum, the papers cover the wide sweep of this long-lasting and multi-faceted relationship between two peoples and nations that have interacted for more than two millennia. While not a comprehensive history, this volume opens previously-underexplored areas of inquiry, and it is our hope that these will be picked up by other researchers and developed further. It is our further hope that the presentation of this volume as a whole will lead others to investigate the longue durée of this relationship, as well, for the details can only be fully understood as part of the rich tapestry.

Two of the chapters have been previously published. Tsadik's chapter was originally published in *Iranian Studies* 43 (2010) 239–63, available online: DOI 10.1080/00210860903543, https://www.jstor.org/stable/40646835, and Sabar's chapter appeared in Hebrew in *Minḥah le-Menaḥem: Qobeṣ Ma'amarim li-Khvod ha-Rav Menaḥem ha-Kohen*, ed. Hannah 'Amit, Avi'ad ha-Kohen, and Haim Be'er (Bene Beraq: ha-Qibbuẕ ha-Me'uẕad, 2008), 465–87. Both appear here with the kind permission of the copyright holders.

We are deeply indebted to our student Judah Kerbel, for his excellent work editing and indexing the manuscript. Because of the wide range of disciplines represented in the book, and the divergent traditions of these disciplines, we did not ask authors to adhere to a uniform strict transliteration system; instead, authors were given the option to choose their own style. We are also very grateful to K. C. Hanson, Daniel Lanning, and Matt Wimer at Wipf and Stock, for their thorough work on a complicated manuscript. We are indebted to Dr. Shana Strauch Schick for her editorial help with Yaakov Elman's article.

Additionally, we would like thank the different institutions and people who were involved in the planning of the 2010 Yeshiva University conference and in the production of the present book: Prof. Steven Fine, head of The Center for Israel Studies, offered tremendous assistance, from the outset, which was crucial for the successful completion of the conference and the book; Prof. David Berger, head of the Bernard Revel Graduate School of Jewish Studies at Yeshiva University; The Schneier Center for International Affairs, headed by Prof. Ruth Bevan, who continuously offered her highly significant support; and Prof. Jacob Wisse, head of the Yeshiva University Museum.

Finally, it is with heavy hearts that we dedicate this volume in memory of Yaakov Elman. Yaakov's contributions to our understanding of interactions between Jews and Persians in antiquity have profoundly altered the way scholars conceptualize those centuries, and will shape generations of scholarship to come. More importantly, he was a generous and kind human being, whose friendship and collegiality were treasured by colleagues around the world. He is already sorely missed, although it is some comfort that we are able to give voice to his work in this volume.

The Bernard Revel Graduate School of Jewish Studies and
Beren Department of Jewish Studies
Yeshiva University
New York

Contributors

Leah R. Baer is an independent scholar whose work focuses on the cultural and social heritage of the Iranian Jewish community. In 1978 while studying at the university in Mashhad, she visited the knisa. Her encounter with the Jewish community prompted an interest in their traditions as well as the influence of the dominant society on the ritual behavior of a minority population.

Miryam Brand holds a PhD in Bible and Second Temple Literature from New York University. Her book on the portrayal of sin in the Second Temple period (*Evil Within and Without: The Source of Sin and Its Nature as Portrayed in Second Temple Literature*) was published in 2013 and her commentary on the Book of Enoch was published as part of *Outside the Bible* in 2013. She is currently an Associate Fellow at the Albright Institute of Archaeological Research.

Yaakov Elman was the Denenberg Professor of Talmud at Yeshiva University, and a director of the Friedberg Genizah Project. He was the author of *Authority and Tradition: Toseftan Baraitot in Talmudic Babylonia* (1994), and many dozens of articles on all aspects of Talmudic studies and Jewish thought. His work inspired a generation of scholars to return to the study of the relationship between the Babylonian Talmud and Middle Persian culture and religions.

Agniezka Erdt has her PhD in philosophy from the University of Warsaw, and is currently working on a project devoted to the reception of ancient philosophy in the thought of Mulla Sadra. Dr. Erdt was awarded a Fulbright Program grant (University of Texas at Austin) and a scholarship at the University of Tehran. Her main areas of research include Shi'i philosophy, Qur'anic commentaries, and Iranian intellectual history.

Galit Hasan-Rokem is Max and Margarethe Grunwald Professor of Folklore and Professor emerita of Hebrew Literature, at the Hebrew University of Jerusalem, where she taught for over forty years. She has published numerous books and scholarly essays in Jewish folklore, Rabbinic literature and folklore theory, as well as three books of poetry in Hebrew and several volumes of poetry translations from Swedish into Hebrew.

Geoffrey Herman (Hebrew University of Jerusalem, 2006) is currently a member of the School of Historical Studies at the Institute for Advanced Study in Princeton. His research focuses on Babylonian Jewish history in the Sasanian era, and its neighboring religious and cultural world, and in particular, Jewish-Persian interrelations. The recipient of the Bertel and Eliezer Shimshon Rosenthal Prize for Talmudic Scholarship in 2015, he has been a Starr fellow at Harvard, a visiting professor at Cornell, and a researcher at Mandel Scholion (Hebrew University of Jerusalem). He is the author of *A Prince without a Kingdom: The Exilarch in the Sasanian Era* (2012); *Persian Martyr Acts under King Yazdgird I* (2016); and his edited volumes include, *Jews, Christians and Zoroastrians: Religious Dynamics in a Sasanian Context* (2014); and with J. L. Rubenstein, *The Aggada of the Bavli and Its Cultural World* (2018).

Ruth Jacoby studied in the Hebrew University Archaeology, where she wrote her M.A. thesis on cities on the Assyrian reliefs under Prof. Yigael Yadin, and then wrote her doctoral dissertation on the Torah pointer in the Persian world under Prof. Bezalel Narkiss. She was at the Center for Jewish Art, and was the deputy director of the center.

Aaron Koller is Associate Professor of Near Eastern and Jewish Studies, Yeshiva University. He is the author of *Esther in Ancient Jewish Thought* (2014), *The Semantic Field of Cutting Tools in Biblical Hebrew* (Catholic Biblical Association, 2013), and *Unbinding Isaac: The Aqeda in Modern Jewish Thought* (forthcoming). He has served as a visiting professor at the Hebrew University in Jerusalem, and held research fellowships at the Albright Institute for Archaeological Research and the Hartman Institute.

Nechama Kramer (Ben-Mashiach) is professor at Queens College. Her PhD is in Spanish literature, and she is the author of *Antonio Enríquez Gómez: literatura y sociedad en El siglo pitagórico y Vida de don Gregorio Guadaña* (1992) and many studies of Spanish Jewish literature. Dr. Kramer also participated in numerous sessions of the MLA and AATS, Sephardic studies committee. She is also the author of earlier studies of Rabbi Menahem

Shemuel Halevy, who is Dr. Kramer's great-grandfather, and she has translated some of his religious poetry.

Mahnaz Moazami is an Associate Research Scholar at Columbia University. She studied History of Religion at the Sorbonne University (France) where she earned her DEA and PhD degrees in a joint program in Comparative Anthropology of Religions (Africa, America, Mediterranean, Far East). Her publications include Wrestling with the Demons of the Pahlavi Widēwdād. Transcription, Translation, and Commentary (2014) and Zoroastrianism: A Collection of Articles from the Encyclopaedia Iranica, 2 vols. (2016).

Vera B. Moreen (PhD Harvard University) specializes in the history, literature, and art of Iranian Jews between the fourteenth and eighteenth centuries. Her latest book is *The Bible as a Judeo-Persian Epic: An Illustrated Manuscript of 'Imrani's Fath-nama* (2016). She has taught Islam and Judaism at Swarthmore, Haverford, and Franklin & Marshall Colleges.

Miriam Nissimov is a lecturer in Persian and Modern Middle Eastern History in the department for Middle Eastern and African History in Tel-Aviv University. Her research interests include the history of the Jewish communities in modern Iran as well as the social and cultural aspects of Iranian literature in the twentieth century.

Shaul Regev taught at Bar-Ilan University. He has published articles on Jewish thought in the period of the expulsion from Spain and later, in the Ottoman Empire and the Jewish Diaspora in the East. His previous books are: *Rabbi Israel de Kuriel: Sermons and Articles* (1992); *The Sermons of Rabbi Isaac Caro* (1996); *Rabbi Israel Najara: Mikveh Israel* (2004); *Oral and Written Sermons* (2010); *Rabbi Ezra Ha-Bavli Netivot Shalom (Paths of Peace)* (2010); *Rabbi Solomon Twena, Shema Shelomo* (commentary on Ecclesiastes), (2012); *Rabbi Sadakah Hussein, Abodat Hasedakah* (2017).

Shalom Sabar is Professor of Jewish Art and Folklore at the Hebrew University of Jerusalem. His research concentrates on the history of Jewish art from Biblical times to the present, and the rituals and material culture of Jewish communities in Europe and the lands of Islam. He has published numerous essays and reviews related to these topics. Among his books are *Mazal Tov: Illuminated Jewish Marriage Contracts, Jerusalem - Stone and Spirit: 3000 Years of History and Art, The Life Cycle of the Jews in Islamic Lands*, and *The Sarajevo Haggadah: History & Art*.

Daniel Tsadik is Associate Professor of Sepharadic and Iranian Studies at the Bernard Revel Graduate School of Jewish Studies, Yeshiva University. He is the author of *Between Foreigners and Shi'is: Nineteenth-Century Iran and Its Jewish Minority* (2007), and of *Jews of Iran and Rabbinic Literature* (forthcoming). A Fulbright Scholar, Daniel Tsadik received his PhD from Yale University.

PART 1

Pre-Modern History

1

Negotiating Empire
Living Jewishly under the Achaemenids in Persia and Palestine

AARON KOLLER[1]

THE ACHAEMENID EMPIRE AND ITS JEWS

Beginning from a small area of Fārs in southwestern Iran, the Persians under the leadership of Cyrus began expanding their territory in 550 BCE. Just over a decade later, they controlled all of southwest Asia, from the Levant and Anatolia in the west through Kyrgyzstand. How this was accomplished is "one of the great conundrums of Cyrus' rise to power."[2] The bulk of the territorial gains came in 539, when the Persians took over

---

1. I am indebted to my colleagues and friends Joseph Angel, Ari Mermelstein, and Shira Hecht for very helpful comments on earlier drafts. I am also indebted to comments by Larry Schiffman for clarifying certain ways in which the Qumran texts may be brought to bear on these issues. Finally, thanks to Daniel Tsadik and Steven Fine for inviting me to participate in the *Iran and Israel* conference, and to Daniel for his astute editorial suggestions in turning the oral version into an article.

2. Matt Waters, "Cyrus and the Achaemenids," *Iran* 42 (2004): 91–102 (quote from 92).

the Neo-Babylonian Empire. Having defeated the Babylonian armed resistance at Sippar, north of Babylon, the Persian army marched into Babylon and took it bloodlessly, as Cyrus narrates in his famous Cylinder.[3]

Among the populations inherited by Cyrus when he took over the Babylonian empire were Jews. A series of exiles in the late seventh and early sixth centuries had brought many thousands of Judeans to Mesopotamia and nearby areas. At this point, the vast majority of Jews lived in this region. The trauma of these events left its mark on the Jewish literature produced in the following century, including books such as Ezekiel.[4] During the Neo-Babylonian Empire, the Jews openly lamented their fate (cf. Psalm 137) and hoped for a restoration to the land of Israel (cf. especially Isaiah 40–55 and below).[5]

---

3. This text has often been held up as an ancient model of human rights and enlightened rule; this view is especially associated with the Shah of Iran, who often pointed to Cyrus as an Iranian ruler who spread human rights and religious tolerance throughout the world. This is a misreading of Cyrus' text and of the historical record. For a balanced discussion, see Josef Wiesehöfer, *Ancient Persia 550 BC—650 AD* (London: Tauris, 2006), 42–55, and Wiesehöfer's earlier polemic against the political use that has been made of Cyrus, "Kyros, der Schah und 2500 JahreMenschenrechte. Historische Mythenbildung zur Zeit der Pahlavi-Dynastie," in *Mythen, Geschichte(n), Identitäten: Der Kampf um die Vergangenheit*, ed. Stephan Conermann (Schenefeld/Hamburg: EB, 1999), 55–68. For the text and translation, see Hanspeter Schaudig, *Die Inschriften Nabonids von Babylon und Kyros' des Großen, samt den in ihrem Umfeld entstandenen Tendenzschriften: Textausgabe und Grammatik* (AOAT 256; Münster: Ugarit-Verlag, 2001). A good English translation by Irving Finkel is available on The British Museum's website (http://www.britishmuseum.org/explore/highlights/article_index/c/cyrus_cylinder_-_translation.aspx), and translations are available in recent anthologies of ancient Near Eastern texts as well.

4. For the "trauma" of the exile as seen in biblical literature, see Daniel L. Smith-Christopher, "Reassessing the Historical and Sociological Impact of the Babylonian Exile (597/587–539 BCE)," in *Exile*, ed. James M. Scott (Leiden: Brill, 1997), 7–36. For a broader view of the literature produced in response to the exile, see Jill Middlemas, *The Templeless Age: An Introduction to the History, Literature, and Theology of the "Exile"* (Louisville: Westminster John Knox, 2007).

5. Terminology is a problem that haunts this essay. According to many scholars, the term "Jews" is inappropriate for the Iron Age (prior to 586 BCE). Some have argued cogently that even through the era of the Second Temple, the appropriate term should be "Judeans" rather than Jews. A thorough discussion is Steven Mason, "Jews, Judaeans, Judaizing, Judaism: Problems of Categorization in Ancient History," *Journal for the Study of Judaism* 38 (2007): 457–512. I retain the term "Jews" here, because the contrast between the residents of Yehud—the Judeans—and their co-religionists throughout the Persian Empire—here called the Jews—is a fundamentally important one.

When Cyrus took over the empire, he allowed the peoples conquered by the Babylonians to return to their ancestral homelands, as he claims in his Cylinder text and as confirmed by the biblical accounts.[6] For obvious reasons, therefore, the ascent of Cyrus was hailed by some Jews as evidence of the hand of God in history.

Still, for most Jews, as for most people in the Babylonian heartland, the transition from Babylonian rule to Persian rule did not affect everyday life.[7] For some Jews, however, Cyrus' policies had an immediate effect, and they took the opportunity to move westward to their people's former homeland, which was now incarnated as the Persian province of Yehud.[8] The biblical prophets Haggai and Zechariah encouraged the construction of a new Temple, which was dedicated around 515 BCE. If there were hopes among the Judeans that this would inaugurate a profoundly new political era, these hopes were complicated, and ultimately disappointed, by reality.[9]

If we survey the Jewish world in the late sixth and early fifth centuries, we find Jews centered in three regions of the world.[10] Some Jews lived in Egypt; we have documentation from the Jewish garrison in the southern border town of Elephantine and evidence of Jews elsewhere as

---

6. For a skeptical view of the biblical narratives about Cyrus, see Amélie Kuhrt, "The Cyrus Cylinder and Achaemenid Imperial Policy," *Journal for the Study of the Old Testament* 25 (1983): 83–97. Most scholars, even skeptical ones, see the biblical claims as plausible, however; cf., e.g., Bob Becking, "'We All Returned as One!': Critical Notes on the Myth of the Mass Return," in *Judah and the Judeans in the Persian period*, ed. Oded Lipschits and Manfred Oeming (Winona Lake, IN: Eisenbrauns, 2006), 3–18.

7. See, for instance, the statement in Michael Jursa, *Neo-Babylonian Legal and Adminstrative Documents: Typology, Contents and Archives* (Guides to the Mesopotamian Textual Record 1; Münster: Ugarit-Verlag, 2005), 1. My thanks to Shalom Holtz for this reference.

8. Evidence for the existence of the province of Yehud in the late sixth and early fifth centuries comes from bullae stamped with the names of governors of the province; cf. Nahman Avigad, *Bullae and Seals from a Post-Exilic Judean Archive* (Qedem 4; Jerusalem: Hebrew University, 1976).

9. For a good discussion of the relevant textual evidence for such hopes, see Wolter H. Rose, *Zemah and Zerubbabel: Messianic Expectations in the Early Postexilic Period* (Library Hebrew Bible/Old Testament Studies 304; Sheffield: Sheffield Academic, 2000).

10. A good survey of Jewish history (social, religious, and intellectual) can be found in Mayer Gruber, "Judeo-Persian Communities, ii. Achaemenid Period," in *Encyclopædia Iranica* (http://www.iranica.com/articles/judeo-persian-communities- ii-achaemenid-period).

well.¹¹ (Egypt was not part of Cyrus' empire, but was conquered by his son and successor, Cambyses, in 525 BCE.) The textual remains from the Jewish community at Elephantine, including letters and legal documents, have been thoroughly studied, and the archaeology of the site has provided valuable information about the community, too.¹² According to most scholars, this community was heterodox, their religion and culture strongly the result of an Israelite substratum overlaid with influences from their Egyptian surroundings.¹³

Many Jews, presumably motivated either by socio-economic factors or by ideological considerations, now lived in Yehud. It is difficult to say what it meant to live "Jewishly" within Achaemenid Yehud. Attempts at reconstructing life are plagued firstly by a lack of data,¹⁴ and secondly by the irregularity of the data we do possess. Quantitatively speaking, the textual record seems substantial. We have the biblical texts of Ḥaggai, Zekhariah, Malakhi, the second half of the book of Isaiah, Ezra, Neḥemiah, Daniel, Esther, and Chronicles, all of which either date from the Achaemenid Period or describe it. Apocryphal books such as 1 Esdras, Tobit, and Judith may also be relevant to varying degrees,¹⁵ and some of the

---

11. For an accessible and thorough overview of these communities, see Joseph Mélèze Modrzejewski, *The Jews of Egypt: From Rameses II to Emperor Hadrian*, trans. Robert Cornman; foreword by Shaye J.D. Cohen (Philadelphia: Jewish Publication Society, 1995), 21–44. The fullest discussion is still Bezalel Porten, *Archives from Elephantine: The Life of an Ancient Jewish Military Colony* (Berkeley: University of California Press, 1968).

12 See Günter Dreyer et al., "Stadt und Tempel von Elephantine: 28./29./30. Grabungsbericht," *Mitteilungen des Deutschen Archäologischen Instituts. Abteilung Kairo* 58 (2002) 157–225.

13 Cf. Porten, *Archives*, for example; contra Paul-Eugène Dion, "La religion des papyrus d'Éléphantine : un reflet du Juda d'avant l'exil," in *Kein Land für sich allein; Studien zum Kulturkontakt in Kanaan, Israel/Palästina und Ebirnâri für Manfred Weippert zum 65. Geburtstag*, ed. Ulrich Hübner und Ernst Axel Knauf (Freiburg, Schwitzerland: Universitätsverlag, 2002), 243–54.

14. The quantitative gaps are dramatic and led to serious miscalculations by later readers trying to reconstruct Achaemenid history from biblical literature: Jewish tradition by the first century CE already had compressed the Persian period of Jewish history to a mere 34 years, rather than the 206 one would expect (539–333). While there may be numerous factors driving this miscalculation, the paucity of data is a necessary prerequisite for such a view. See Joseph Tabory, "התקופה הפרסית בעיני חז״ל," *Millēt* 2 (1984): 65–77.

15. The book of Tobit will be dealt with below; although it may not be a Persian-era composition, it purports to describe life in the eastern Diaspora, allegedly under the Assyrians but undoubtedly from a later perspective. The dating of Judith is also

other literature preserved in Qumran also may date to the Persian period. In particular, the Aramaic texts such as the Pseudo-Daniel literature (4Q242–244) and the court tales labeled 4Q550 may have circulated in Jewish circles far and wide for centuries.¹⁶

Even the basics of political history are difficult to reconstruct, however. The plentiful archaeological data from Palestine is surveyed masterfully by Stern,¹⁷ but it does not make for a narrative of the history.¹⁸ Sometimes, even when we do have good archaeological evidence, our ability to exploit it for historiography is confounded by the lack of textual data. For example, we know there must have been military action in around 475 BCE, since many sites show destruction levels dated to then, but in the absence of texts, we do not know who was fighting or why. Although our corpus of epigraphic remains from the period is also substantial and continues to grow, it, too, does not provide us with anything like a running historical narrative. Despite his 200-page survey of the evidence available, Ephraim Stern wrote: "Although the Persian period is relatively late from the archaeological standpoint, it is one of the most obscure eras in Palestine and its history remains practically unknown."¹⁹

The problem, in a nutshell, is that what we have is the equivalent of anecdotal evidence. From our sources we know of an event that occurred in the year 539 (Cyrus' proclamation), something that happened two decades later (the dedication of the Temple), and some things that happened half a century after that (the activities of Ezra and Neḥemiah in the 450s and 440s). But no attempt is made in any other surviving Jewish

---

uncertain. For a fourth-century date of Judith, see the studies of Michael Heltzer collected in his *The Province of Judah and Jews in Persian Times (Some Connected Questions of the Persian Empire)* (Tel Aviv: Tel Aviv University Archaeological Center, 2008), 31–70, and Edward Lipiński, "The Province Yehud and Jews in the Achaemenid Empire," *Studia Judaica* 12 (2009): 369–79, at 370–74. Although fascinating in many ways, the book of Judith will not be dealt with here, since it does not overtly deal with the issues which this paper focuses on.

16 See, for instance, Ursula Schattner-Rieser, *L'araméen des manuscrits de la mer Morte, I. Grammaire* (Instruments pour l'étude des langues de l'Orient ancien 5; Lausanne: Zèbre, 2004), 25. There is more that can be said here.

17. Ephraim Stern, *Archaeology of the Land of the Bible,* Vol. II: *The Assyrian, Babylonian, and Persian Periods, 732–332 BCE,* Anchor Bible Reference Library (New York: Dooubleday, 2001), 373–575.

18. For some of the problems, see David Biale, *Power & Powerlessness in Jewish History: the Jewish Tradition and the Myth of Passivity* (New York: Schocken, 1986), 18.

19. Stern, *Archaeology of the Land of the Bible,* Vol. II, 360.

text to narrate the broad sweep of the nation's history, as had been done earlier by the authors of Kings for the history of Israel in the Iron Age.

Regarding social history, the situation is even more difficult. The only evidence available for the situation in Yehud is the literary remains, particularly the biblical narratives. This corpus presents a skewed picture, however: it focuses our attention almost entirely on Jerusalem, and almost entirely on the group that produced these texts, the group associated with Ezra and Neḥemiah in the mid-fifth century BCE. If we inquire about interactions between the Jews of the texts and other groups, the dominant voice heard is that of the Ezra-Neḥemiah group, who demanded that social intercourse with anyone other than the Judean returnees from Babylonia be strictly circumscribed.[20] But we do have contrary evidence, preserved within the same texts, that their view was not the only one, and possibly not a very popular one; furthermore, there exists evidence from other biblical texts of a more open attitude towards acceptance of foreigners into the community.[21] Indeed, demographic evidence suggests that the isolationist approach of Ezra and Neḥemiah did not carry the day: the population of Yehud boomed over the following centuries, and some historians have argued that this growth can only be explained through large numbers of others joining the community.[22]

Still other Jews—by far the majority, in fact—remained in Mesopotamia and Persia proper. Our sources of information for these Jews and their communities are severely limited, however. In terms of their integration into society in ways other than geography, we have some evidence from the archive of the banker Murašu of the city of Nippur, dating from the second half of the fifth century BCE and first published in 1893.[23] Many Jews, identifiable by names such as Yehonatan and Ye-

---

20. Peter Ross Bedford, *Temple Restoration in Early Achaemenid Judah*, JSJ Sup 65 (Leiden: Brill, 2001), 32–33, denies the historicity of these accounts; cf. also Lisbeth S. Fried, "The House of God Who Dwells in Jerusalem," *JAOS* 126 (2006): 94–95.

21. Moshe Weinfeld, "The Universalist Ideology and the Separatist Ideology in the Period of the Return to Zion," *Tarbiz* 33 (1964): 228–242 (Hebrew).

22. For further discussion of the various views in Persian-era Yehud regarding the acceptance and exclusion of foreigners of various types, see Daniel L. Smith-Christopher, "Between Ezra and Isaiah: Exclusion, Transformation, and Inclusion of the 'Foreigner' in Post-exilic Biblical Theology," in *Ethnicity and the Bible*, ed. Mark G. Brett, Biblical Interpretation Series 19 (Leiden: Brill, 1996), 117–142.

23. For a full presentation of this archive and the socio-economic history that can be culled from it, see Matthew W. Stolper, *Entrepeneurs and Empire: The Murašu Archive, the Murašu Firm, and Persian Rule in Babylonia* (Istanbul: Nederlands

dayah, appear in this archive, and these amount to something between 3% and 8% of the names in the texts.[24] To be sure, many Jews, even Jews with strong Jewish identities, did not have names readily identifiable as Jewish. One thinks, for example, of Sheshbazzar and Zerubbabel, the leaders of the late sixth-century restoration, who bear Babylonian names; the characters Mordecai and Esther in the book of Esther also bear Babylonian (and, in Esther's case, possibly Persian), names.[25] The number of Jews in these texts is, therefore, likely higher.

On the basis of these economic texts, it can be concluded that by the late fifth century, at least some Jews had become fully integrated into Nippur economic life.[26] According to David Vanderhooft, this was not possible—or at least, possible only to a lesser degree—under the Neo-Babylonian Empire, but part of the Achaemenid policy was to encourage the participation of minorities in the bureaucracy in order to foster an atmosphere of loyalty.[27] The biblical book of Esther also depicts Jews such as Mordecai as playing a role in the Persian bureaucracy. We know that this is no mere literary conceit: a Jew, Abda-Yahu son of Barāka-Yāma, is identified as a Persian imperial tax collector (*dēku*) in a Persian-era cuneiform tablet.[28] On the other hand, for the most part, the Jews named in the texts we have did not rise far in the ranks: they were minor functionaries, not powerful members of the bureaucracy.[29]

Clearly, not all the Jews integrated, even in the most basic, geographical sense. A collection of cuneiform tablets published since 1999

Historisch-Archaeologisch Instituut, 1985).

24. See Michael David Coogan, *West Semitic Personal Names in the Murašu Documents*, HSM 7 (Missoula, MT: Scholars, 1975), and the studies by Ran Zadok, *The Jews in Babylonia in the Chaldean and Achaemenian periods in the Light of the Babylonian Sources* (Tel-Aviv: Mifal Hashichpul, 1976); *On West Semites in Babylonia during the Chaldean and Achaemenian periods: An Onomastic Study* (Jerusalem: Wanaarta, 1977).

25. For one suggestion about the name of Esther, see Ran Zadok, "Notes on Esther," *ZAW* 98 (1986): 105–110.

26. Cf. Michael D. Coogan, "Life in the Diaspora: Jews at Nippur in the Fifth Century B.C.," *BA* 37 (1974): 6–12.

27. David S. Vanderhooft, "New Evidence Pertaining to the Transition from Neo-Babylonian to Achaemenid Administration in Palestine," in *Yahwism after the Exile: Perspectives on Israelite Religion in the Persian Era*, ed. Rainer Albertz and Bob Becking, Studies in Theology and Religion 5 (Assen: Royal Van Gorcum, 2003), 219–35.

28. Joannès and Lemaire, "Trois tablettes cunéiformes," 27–28; see also Bedford, *Temple Restoration in Early Achaemenid Judah*, 47 n. 14.

29. Daniel L. Smith-Christopher, *A Biblical Theology of Exile*, Overtures to Biblical Theology (Minneapolis: Fortress, 2002), 69–70.

come from the community of āl-Yahūdu "the town of the Jews," which was apparently a Jewish town in the vicinity of Nippur.[30] This indicates that at least some Judean refugees lived in voluntarily segregated areas. Most Jews were distributed in multi-ethnic and multi-cultural regions, however. The onomastic studies of Ran Zadok showed that Judean exiles lived throughout southern Mesopotamia, as well as areas farther north and east (including Susa).[31] Thus, as Haman is quoted in the biblical book of Esther as saying, the Judean exiles were both "spread throughout the land" and "separated."

However, none of this really allows us to speak about what Jewish life was like in Achaemenid Mesopotamia and Persia. We have two types of evidence available: literary texts and "quotidian" texts.[32] The quotidian documentary texts have the advantage of not describing only the élites within society. Yet, these texts open such a limited window onto life that the evidence available is almost certainly not broadly representative. The literary texts, on the other hand, consist for the most part of meditations

---

30. Approximately half of the known tablets were published by Laurie E. Pearce and Cornelia Wunsch, *Documents of Judean Exiles and West Semites in Babylonia in the Collection of David Sofer*, Cornell University Studies in Assyriology and Sumerology 28 (Bethesda, MD: CDL, 2014). The publication of the rest has been announced, but has not yet occurred. Earlier discussions include: F. Joannès, and André Lemaire, "Trois tablettes cunéiformes à onomastique ouest-sémitique (collection Sh. Moussaïeff) (Pls. I-II)," *Transeuphratène* 17 (1999): 17–34; Ran Zadok, *The Earliest Diaspora: Israelites and Judeans in pre-Hellenistic Mesopotamia*, Publications of the Diaspora Research Institute 151 (Tel Aviv: Diaspora Research Institute of Tel Aviv University, 2002), 33–35; Kathleen Abraham, "West Semitic and Judean Brides in Cuneiform Sources from the Sixth Century BCE: New Evidence from a Marriage Contract from Āl-Yahūdu," *Archiv für Orientforschung* 51 (2005–2006): 198–219; Laurie Pearce, "New Evidence for Judaeans in Babylonia," in *Judah and the Judaeans in the Persian Period*, ed. Oded Lipschits and Manfred Oeming (Winona Lake, IN: Eisenbrauns, 2006), 399–411; W. G. Lambert "A Document from a Community of Exiles in Babylonia," in *New Seals and Inscriptions: Hebrew, Idumean, and Cuneiform*, ed. Meir Lubetski (Sheffield: Phoenix, 2007), 201–5; Kathleen Abraham, "The Reconstruction of Jewish Communities in the Persian Empire: The Āl-Yahūdu Clay Tablets," in *Light and Shadows—The Catalog -The Story of Iran and the Jews*, ed. Hagai Segev and Asaf Schor (Tel Aviv: Beit Hatfutsot, 2011), and 33–35 and 264–61 (sic).

31. See Zadok, *The Earliest Diaspora*, 29–45, 46–47.

32. The term "quotidian" for the texts that are produced in the course of daily life and allow us to reconstruct that life is drawn from the study of this type of text from a later period by Baruch Levine, "Quotidian Documents from the Judean Desert," in *The Dead Sea Scrolls at 60: Scholarly Contributions of New York University Faculty and Alumni*, ed. Lawrence H. Schiffman and Shani Tzoref, STDJ 89 (Leiden: Brill, 2010), 199–215.

on, and studies of, individual lives and individual issues. They come from the elites of society, and while these lives are explored in more detail, the figures involved cannot be taken as typical.

Neither of these bodies of evidence, then, allows us to fully explore what *ordinary* life was like. What was the social standing of the Jews? From another perspective, how did the Jews perceive themselves within Persian society, and how were they, in turn, perceived? We read in the Bible, for instance, of Neḥemiah, a high-ranking bureaucrat in fifth-century Susa, who felt a strong enough affiliation with the Jewish community in the province of Yehud that he convinced the king to re-assign him there. But were his sentiments commonplace? Did other Jews in Susa pay attention to the news out of Jerusalem? Is he unique in our literary corpus because he was unique, or because the vicissitudes of history bequeathed to us an erratic literary legacy? The preservation of his narrative means that certain groups found his story compelling,[33] but did the Jews back in Persia have a different view? Did they, like Neḥemiah, think of Yehud as their proper homeland? Perhaps they could have claimed, as some later Babylonian Jews did, that they were already dwelling in an ancestral homeland, and point to Genesis for evidence of Abraham's origins in Ur.[34] Unfortunately, the voices of Jews from the Achaemenid Empire are mostly mute.

This discussion highlights the basic point: it is not possible, given the available evidence, to produce any sort of serious description of *Jewish life* in the Achaemenid Empire. We can say some assorted things about *life for Jews*, but what it meant to live as a Jew, what it meant to live a Jewish life within the Achaemend imperial context of either the eastern Diaspora or Yehud, is not recoverable.[35] In short, when we as historians

33. The position that the canon is the product of the ideological forces that shaped it was strongly argued by Morton Smith, *Palestinian Parties and Politics that Shaped the Old Testament* (New York: Columbia University Press, 1971). My thanks to Ari Mermelstein for urging me to consider his arguments in this context.

34. The Bavli (b. Pesaḥim 87b) compares God's exile of the Jews to a husband who is angry at his wife, so he sends her "to her mother's home." This striking claim on the part of the Babylonian rabbis is discussed by Isaiah Gafni, *Land, Center and Diaspora: Jewish Constructs in Late Antiquity*, Journal for the Study of the Pseudepigrapha Supplements 21 (Sheffield: Sheffield Academic, 1997), 52–55.

35. Some recent essays show this clearly. Mary Joan Winn Leith devotes two paragraphs to the Jews in Babylonia in her survey of the history of Israel in the Persian period ("Israel among the nations: the Persian period," in *The Oxford History of the Biblical World*, ed. Michael D. Coogan [New York: Oxford University Press, 1998], 413–14), and Mayer Gruber concludes his essay on the subject of Iranian Jews in the

seek answers for the questions which most readily appeal to us—about daily life, cultural and religious values and practices, social realities and interactions, and so on—we find that the available evidence is not interested in providing answers.[36] The questions possible for other periods, earlier and later, because of the richer documentary remains, are simply not answerable for Persian period Jewish societies.[37]

SKETCHING RELIGIOUS HISTORY

Only glimpses of the social history of the Jews in the Achaemenid empire, then, can be sketched with the evidence currently available. Perhaps instead of imposing the questions we would like to ask on the available evidence, we should allow the available evidence to dictate the questions to be asked. Instead of asking questions about Jewish life as lived by the people, we will turn our attention to Jewish life as *thought* and *believed*. Since what we have available is religiously-oriented literature, let us now give up on the quest for a social historical perspective, and look instead for insights from the realm of ideas.

The literature reveals a range of views on central philosophical and theological issues, and it may be possible to discern within this literature differences between the Jewish cultures in the eastern diaspora and in Palestine (at least as imagined by those producing the literature). It should

---

Achaemenid period by terming it an "obscure period" ("The Achaemenid Period," in *Esther's Children: A Portrait of Iranian Jews*, ed. Houman Sarshar [Philadelphia: Center for Iranian Jewish Oral History in association with the Jewish Publication Society, 2002], 3–12).

36. Keith Whitelam, "Recreating the History of Israel," *JSOT* 35 (1985): 45–70, at 53–54, criticizes history which focuses on reconstructing lists of high priests but does not "investigate the situation of Palestine vis-à-vis the Persian empire, particularly changing trade patterns, or to outline changes in settlement patterns in Palestine as a result of the change in political hegemony." H. G. M. Williamson, "Early Post-Exilic Judaean History," in *Studies in Persian Period History and Historiography*, Forschungen zum Alten Testament 38 (Tübingen: Mohr/Siebeck, 2004), 9–12, defends "traditional" scholarship against these charges.

37. Recently, there was a bold attempt at a social history of Phoenicia in the Persian Period: cf. Vadim S. Jigoulov, *The Social History of Achaemenid Phoenicia: Being a Phoenician, Negotiating Empires*, BibleWorld (London: Equinox, 2010). Even Jigoulov's work remains at a far more general level of analysis than what is envisioned here; his achievement is in ascertaining the level of integration of the various Phoenician cities with one another and in the Achaemenid Empire as a whole, rather than how individuals or families negotiated the conflicting identities of "Phoenician" (and even "Sidonian") and "Persian."

be noted, however, that although a number of studies have explored the dynamics of the Homeland-Diaspora relations in this period,[38] one could well ask whether there really is any difference between "homeland" and "diaspora" when both are ruled by a foreign empire—indeed, the very *same* empire.[39] The upshot of the following discussion is that despite well-deserved skepticism on this point, there indeed seems to be some differences between homeland and diaspora, even in such circumstances.

In what follows, a number of ideologies found within the texts at our disposal will be surveyed. The texts to be discussed all have something to say about a fundamental issue: the role of God in the world. It is, I think, readily apparent why this was an important issue in a time when the people who considered themselves God's chosen ones found themselves scattered throughout the known world, negotiating lives ruled by forces which appeared powerful enough to challenge God himself.

Schematically, three views can be seen. According to one view, God acted through human monarchs, and therefore, working for the human monarchs was, indeed, a way of serving God in the world; this is the view of Ezra and Neḥemiah, for example. On a second view, God had withdrawn, and the world was now bifurcated: there was the present reality, in which chaos reigned, and a beatific reality in metaphysical existence elsewhere, in which divine order reigned. According to this view, truly religious people would focus their attention and energies on the

38. See the provocative arguments of Peter R. Bedford, "Diaspora: Homeland Relations in Ezra-Neḥemiah," *Vetus Testamentum* 52 (2002): 147-65, who argues that the community in Yehud remained dependent on the Diaspora, and the discussion in John Kessler, "The Diaspora in Zechariah 1-8 and Ezra-Neḥemiah: The Role of History, Social Location, and Tradition in the Formulation of Identity," in *Community Identity in Judean Historiography: Biblical and Comparative Perspectives*, ed. Gary N. Knoppers and Kenneth A. Ristau (Winona Lake, IN: Eisenbrauns, 2009), 119-45. Note the comments of Bustenay Oded, "Exile—Homeland Relations during the Exilic Period and Restoration," in *Teshûrôt LaAvishur: Studies in the Bible and the Ancient Near East, in Hebrew and Semitic Languages—Festschrift Presented to Prof. Yitzhak Avishur on the Occasion of His 65th Birthday*, ed. Michael Heltzer and Meir Malul (Tel Aviv-Jaffa: Archaeological Center Publications, 2004), 153*-160*, at 157* ("beyond the evidence and are even hazardous").

39. Martin Hengel influentially argued that in the Hellenistic period, there should not be a presumption of difference between Judaism in Palestine and Judaism elsewhere. See Hengel, *Judaism and Hellenism: Studies in Their Encounter in Palestine during the Early Hellenistic Period*, trans. John Bowden (Philadelphia; Fortress, 1974 [2nd German ed., 1973]), 103-6, for a summary statement of this position. While his methodological strictures and many of his insights are well taken, I think close inspection shows that there *were* differences among the various Jewish communities throughout the latter half of the first millennium BCE.

otherwordly existence and forsake the disarray of the present reality. This perspective is found in much of the Jewish apocalyptic literature. Yet a third view, found especially in the book of Esther, was that the world was somewhat chaotic, but could be—and had to be—navigated by human effort in order to ensure Jewish survival in this new order, since there was no alternative. Interestingly, it is this third view that proved the most difficult for the Jews living in Achaemenid Yehud to accept.

View 1: God Works through the King

Representing the first view—that there was a confluence of wills between the human monarchs and God—are first and foremost the Jews who returned to Yehud, both in the late sixth century and in the mid-fifth century, associated with the Ezra-Neḥemiah movement.[40] Of course, this type of thinking has roots in earlier Israelite thought. In the late eighth century, Isaiah claimed that Assyria was the rod of God's wrath,[41] and in the early sixth century, Jeremiah conceived of the Babylonians as the arm of God (see especially Jeremiah 25 and 27).[42] In the Persian Period, this

---

40. Sara Japhet, "Sheshbazzar and Zerubbabel against the Background of the Historical and Religious Tendencies of Ezra–Neḥemiah: Part 1," *ZAW* 94 (1982): 66–98, reprinted in and cited from Japhet, *From the Rivers of Babylon to the Highlands of Judah: Collected Studies on the Restoration Period* (Winona Lake, IN: Eisenbrauns, 2006), 53–84, at 59. Erich Gruen, "Persia through the Jewish Looking Glass," in *Jewish Perspectives on Hellenistic Rulers*, ed. Tessa Rajak, Sarah Pearce, James Aitken, and Jennifer Dines (Berkeley: University of California Press, 2007), 53–75, and elsewhere in his writings, has contested this point. He argues that Jewish literature generally is at best cynical and at worse hostile towards the Persians rulers and concludes: "The doltish Ahasuerus [of Esther] bears a close resemblance to the inept and occasionally ridiculous Achaemenids who people the pages of Ezra-Neḥemiah, 1 Esdras, Daniel 6, and the Greek additions to Daniel" (69). His readings seem overly cynical, however, and the authority of the king in Ezra-Neḥemiah seems to be depicted as appropriate and unquestioned.

41. See especially Baruch A. Levine, "Woe, Assyria, Staff of My Anger! (Isa 10:15)—Biblical Monotheism through the Interlational-Political Lens," *Eretz Israel* 27 (2003): 136–42 (Hebrew); Levine, "Assyrian Ideology and Israelite Monotheism," *Iraq* 67 (2005): 411–27.

42. For a nuanced discussion of this view in Jeremiah, with an excellent discussion which situates it within the theological positions found elsewhere, see Dalit Rom-Shiloni, "God and Man at War: Responses to the Destruction of the First Temple," in *War and Peace*, ed. Shlomo Avineri (Jerusalem: Merkaz Zalman Shazar, 2009), 1–11 (Hebrew), and at greater length, Rom-Shiloni, *God in a Time of Destruction and Exiles: Biblical Theology* (Jerusalem: Magnes, 2009). On this motif in Jeremiah 27–29 in

view is the most popular one in the biblical texts. It is clearly expressed in the discussion in Ezra and Nehemiah of the Temple: according to these books, the Temple was built at the behest of God, through Persian imperial decree and with Persian financial support.[43] It is also the view of the prophet whose words are preserved in Isaiah 44, where God speaks of Cyrus as "my appointed one" (משיחי).[44]

Although the situation in the book of Daniel is more complex, there, too, we find the view that the monarch, when deserving, is granted his power by God. Such a view is presented clearly in the very first verses of Daniel 1, where after reporting that Nebuchadnezzar laid siege to Jerusalem, the text claims that God handed victory, including some of the temple vessels, to him. Thus, the book claims from the very beginning that the king, powerful as he may appear, is a puppet of God.

Indeed, a major theme in the stories that follow is precisely this point, which is made in varying dramatic ways. Perhaps most poignant is the image of the king in Daniel 4, reduced to animal status because of his hubris and restored to his humanity (and his monarchy) only when he recognizes the power of God. Although the Daniel stories also mock the kings and seem to adopt a skeptical attitude towards their power, it is also clear that the stories take for granted their authority in the world—as long as they do not challenge God or those who serve him.[45] Chronologi-

---

particular, and the question of the relationship of these chapters to the rest of the book of Jeremiah on the one hand, and to Daniel (see the next paragraph) on the other, see Paul-Alain Beaulieu, "The Babylonian Background of the Motif of the Fiery Furnace in Daniel 3," *JBL* 128 (2009): 273–90, esp. 288–90.

43. This point is made by many; cf. for example, Japhet, "Sheshbazzar and Zerubbabel," and David L. Petersen, "The Temple in Persian Period Prophetic Texts," in *Second Temple Studies 1: Persian Period*, ed. Philip R. Davies, JSOT Sup 117 (Sheffield: Sheffield Academic, 1991), 125–44, at 131–32.

44. I am indebted to Ari Mermelstein for the significance of Deutero-Isaiah for this point.

45. For a more nuanced discussion of the image of the empire in the book of Daniel, see Sharon Pace, "Diaspora Dangers, Diaspora Dreams," in *Studies in the Hebrew Bible, Qumran, and the Septuagint Presented to Eugene Ulrich*, ed. Peter W. Flint, Emanuel Tov, and James C. VanderKam, Vetus Testamentum Supplements 102 (Leiden: Brill, 2006), 21–59. She concludes: "The author thus presents a nuanced examination of foreign laws that can be kept and foreign laws that should be abhorred . . . Even a sympathetic king, such as Darius (Daniel 6) may not be able to protect the community against those who hate and fear them—how much more so a king who despises them" (58–59). It should be emphasized (as Ari Mermelstein reiterated to me) that Daniel differs from the other books in its attitude towards the foreign king. This is a theme explored in great detail recently by Erich Gruen, who argued that many of the biblical

cally prior to the biblical story, the same perspective is apparently found in the Aramaic Jewish known as the Prayer of Nabonidus, which tells of the Babylonian king Nabonidus extolling the virtues of God because a Jewish exorcist was able to cure him of his physical maladies by encouraging him to worship God.

In all these texts, therefore, the king's power is recognized, but it is claimed that this immense royal power is actually subject to the will of God. The readers of these texts can therefore conclude that if the king is successfully wielding his power, it is at the pleasure of God that he does so. His actions then carry with them the divine imprimatur of legitimacy.

It is noteworthy that the voices in the early Achaemenid period that most vehemently argue this viewpoint come from the east. The stories of Daniel are likely of Mesopotamian origin, and Ezra and Neḥemiah themselves are from the eastern Diaspora. It is not surprising that the Jews of the east would adopt this perspective on history, since it is not only well-entrenched in earlier Jewish literature, but also precisely what the Persian kings themselves argued![46] Of course, there are differences: Darius in his Behistun inscription attributes his actions to Ahuramazda, whereas Ezra and the other biblical authors claim that it is the God of Israel who controls even foreign kings, thus subverting and co-opting the Persian ideology. The basic claim that the king's actions are the means by which the divine will is executed in the world, however, is both the view of the Persian propaganda and the view of some Jews, especially those close to the center of Persian power.[47]

Despite some deep rifts between Ezra and Neḥemiah and the populace in Jerusalem,[48] these leaders were at least partly successful in impos-

---

books were satirizing the imperial monarchs. For Daniel, this is undoubtedly true. See above, n. 38, as well as the second half of Gruen's *Diaspora: Jews Amidst Greeks and Romans* (Cambridge: Harvard University Press, 2002).

46. See James Bowitck, "Characters in Stone: Royal Ideology and Yehudite Identity in the Behistun Inscription and the Book of Haggai," in *Community Identity in Judean Historiography: Biblical and Comparative Perspectives*, ed. Gary N. Knoppers and Kenneth A. Ristau (Winona Lake, IN: Eisenbrauns, 2009), 87–117, at 106–7.

47. According to Elie Assis, the presence of God in Jerusalem in the late sixth century BCE was a point debated by Haggai and his audience: they feared/believed that God had abandoned them, and Haggai argued that he was present and awaiting a house. Cf. Assis, "To Build or not to Build? A Dispute between Haggai and His People (Hag 1)," *ZAW* 119 (2007): 514–27.

48. For which see especially Weinfeld, "The Universalistic Ideology and the Separatist Ideology." More recent discussions can be found in Joachim Schafer, *Priester und Leviten in achämenidischenJuda: Studien zur Kult- und Sozialgeschichte Israels*

ing their vision of Judaism. This may have been in part because of the power of their historiosophy: they saw divine action in the activities of the Empire—whom they, conveniently, represented.[49] In the following centuries, this view is presented in Jewish texts produced in Palestine, as well. Chronicles, for example, takes this approach to history, ending its narration of history (in its very last chapter) with the assertion that both the exile at the hands of Nebuchadnezzar and the restoration ordered by Cyrus were performed in fulfillment of the will of God.[50] More fundamentally, it has been argued that Solomon, the ideal Israelite king according to Chronicles, is described in that book in a way meant to be reminiscent of the Achaemenid kings.[51] I would suggest that the prerequisite to this depiction may well be that the Achaemenid kings—like Solomon—were seen to be God's chosen earthly rulers.[52] Thus, Ezra and Neḥemiah's vision of God's active role in the world, through the medium of the kings, is the one that dominates the last books of the Bible.

View 2: God Has Withdrawn from the World and Rules in Heaven

Other literature of the time, which also has roots in the east but flourished in the west, emphasizes an apocalyptic worldview in which the "real" world, the valuable world, is other than the present world. The early examples of the Jewish apocalyptic literature, such as the oldest parts of the Enoch literature, have strong roots in Mesopotamian culture.[53] It is

in persischer Zeit, Forschungen zum Alten Testament 31 (Tübingen: Mohr/Siebeck, 2000), and Peter Ross Bedford, Temple Restoration in Early Achaemenid Judah, Journal for the Study of Judaism Supplements 65 (Leiden: Brill, 2001), especially 10–27. Bedford argues that there were no serious conflicts.

49. For a similar view argued from a different perspective, see Vanderhooft, "New Evidence Pertaining to the Transition," 219–35.

50. Joseph Angel pointed out the relevance of 2 Chron 36 here to me.

51. For a thorough discussion of this argument, see Helen Dixon, "Writing Persepolis in Judah: Achaemenid Kingship in Chronicles," in Images and Prophecy in the Ancient Eastern Mediterranean, ed. Martti Nissinen and Charles E. Carter, Forschungen zur Religion und Literatur des Alten und Neuen Testament 233 (Göttingen: Vandenhoeck & Ruprecht, 2009), 163–94.

52. Interestingly, Solomon and the Persian king (Xerxes) are compared with regard to their power in the Babylonian Talmud (Megillah 11a–b). According to the dominant view there, the power of Xerxes was greater than that of Solomon.

53. That this literature is based on Mesopotamian traditions has long been noted; see, for instance, John J. Collins, The Apocalyptic Imagination: An Introduction to Jewish Apocalyptic Literature, 2nd ed. (Grand Rapids: Eerdmans, 1998), 46. For the issues

an open question where these motifs of eastern origin were put into their current literary contexts. Recent scholarship has tended to see the oldest parts of the literature itself as originating in Mesopotamia,[54] although there is no doubt that the texts as we have them are Judean in origin.

Combining Mesopotamian traditions, Biblical figures, and Jewish oral lore with a sharply dichotomizing approach to the world, this literature has a very different view of God's involvement in the world. It contends that divine justice and fairness exist in the world, but that these are restricted to the heavenly realms, which are still directly controlled by God. The earthly existence experienced mundanely has been ceded by God to mundane forces and so is unpredictable and hardly worth anything.[55]

One implication of this approach can be seen in the attitude towards the Second Temple adopted by some Jewish writers of the time. According to these writers, the construction of this Temple, which was initiated at the behest of a Persian king rather than an autonomous Davidic monarch, does not signal the end of the period of exile. Indeed,

---

involved and other views, see especially James C. VanderKam, *Enoch and the Growth of an Apocalyptic Tradition*, Catholic Biblical Quarterly Monograph Series 16 (Washington, DC: Catholic Biblical Association of America, 1984). VanderKam argues that the Astronomical Book (chapters 72–82) is likely eastern (102; and see the discussion on 91–106 and 189), but the AB is the least apocalyptic of the Enochic sources. For detailed discussions of the Mesopotamian backgrounds of the primary motifs in the early Enoch literature, see Helge S. Kvanvig, *Roots of Apocalyptic: The Mesopotamian Background of the Enoch Figure and of the Son of Man*, Wissenschaftliche Monographien zum Alten und Neuen Testament 61 (Neukirchen-Vluyn: Neukirchener, 1988), and Amar Annus, "On the Origin of Watchers: A Comparative Study of the Antediluvian Wisdom in Mesopotamian and Jewish Traditions," *Journal for the Study of the Pseudepigrapha* 19 (2010): 277–320. For a methodologically sound discussion of the dates of Enoch literature, see Gabriele Boccaccini, *Roots of Rabbinic Judaism: An Intellectual History, From Ezekiel to Daniel* (Grand Rapids: Eerdmans, 2002), 93–103, arguing for a fifth–fourth-century date.

54. See especially the work of Siam Bhayro, in his monograph *The Shemihazah and Asael Narrative of 1 Enoch 6-11: Introduction, Text, Translation and Commentary with Reference to Ancient Near Eastern and Biblical Antecedents*, Alter Orient und Altes Testament 322; Münster: Ugarit-Verlag, 2005), and in brief in his article, "Noah's Library: Sources for *1 Enoch 6-11*," *Journal for the Study of the Pseudepigrapha* 15 (2006): 163-77. See also Henry K. Drawnel, "Between Akkadian *Tupšarrūtu* and Aramaic ספר: Some Notes on the Social Context of Early Enochic Literature," *Revue d'Qumran* 24 (2010): 373-403. Drawnel argues that the Mesopotamian traditions were likely adopted directly by Jewish scholars trained in Babylonian scribal culture, although the materials may have been mediated by Aramaic tradents (see esp. p. 396).

55. See the discussion in Boccaccini, *Roots of Rabbinic Judaism*, 91–92.

the triumphant return of God to his city, which had been described by Ezekiel, was still expected.[56] According to these texts, the exile was actually *still in progress* even after 515, even though a Temple was technically was operating in Jerusalem.[57] The world as perceived by these authors was one that had been abandoned by God, and one could not now expect to encounter him there. For the time being, such encounters could only be had on other levels of reality; only in the future could God be expected to take control of the world again.

View 3: God Is Absent from, or Hidden in the World

The third view, that the world was chaotic but could be successfully navigated, was the viewpoint of the book of Esther. In my view, this is a Persian Jewish composition from late Achaemenid times, although this is an issue that cannot be discussed in detail here.[58] According to Esther, far from being God's earthly representative, the Persian king is a buffoon![59] He is incomparably powerful, capable of authorizing genocide with the simple impression of his ring, but this does not show that he is reflecting God's will. On the contrary, his power can be harnessed by anyone who learns how to manipulate the king and manipulate the system. In the story of Esther, the Persian Empire is a terrifying behemoth. It is

---

56. See Joseph Angel, *Otherworldly and Eschatological Priesthood in the Dead Sea Scrolls*, Studies on the Texts of the Desert of Judah 86 (Leiden: Brill, 2010), 102.

57. See Bradley C. Gregory, "The Postexilic Exile in Third Isaiah: Isaiah 61:1–3 in Light of Second Temple Hermenutics," *Journal of Biblical Literature* 126 (2007): 475–96, esp. 489–92, who discusses early texts such as Isaiah 61 and Ezra–Nehemiah, as well as later texts such as Daniel 9, 1 Enoch, T. Levi 16–17, and CD 1:5–11. See also the earlier study (regarding later literature) by Michael A. Knibb, "The Exile in the Literature of the Intertestamental Period," *Heythrop Journal* 17 (1976): 253–72.

58. That Esther's provenance is the eastern Diaspora (Mesopotamia or Persia itself) has long been the dominant view. See, for a sampling of references, Elsie R. Stern, "Esther and the Politics of Diaspora," *Jewish Quarterly Review* 100 (2010): 25–53, at 25 nn. 1–2. Stern herself suggests that Esther was written in Palestine as an imagination of what life might be like in the Diaspora. Her only argument in favor of a Palestinian provenance is the language, Hebrew, but this is a weak reed on which to lean. Another recent paper, by Jean-Daniel Macchi ("Le livred'Esther: regard hellénistiquesur le pouvoiret le monde perses," *Transeuphratène* 30 [2005]: 97–135), argues that the book is a later Hellenistic work from Egypt, reflecting back on the Persian Empire. For further discussion, see Koller, *Esther in Ancient Jewish Thought* (Cambridge: Cambridge University Press, 2014).

59. Gruen, *Diaspora: Jews Amidst Greeks and Romans* (above, n.43), 145–48.

terrifying not because it is evil; Ahasuerus is not portrayed as evil. It is terrifying because it is, at bottom, a soulless bureaucracy. If a genocidal madman happens to get the ear of the king, catastrophe may follow. But all is not lost. One must be prepared to outmaneuver; one must learn to navigate the bureaucracy and manipulate the behemoth if one is survive and thrive in a world such as this.[60] Reliance on God is not an option: the best-known fact about the Hebrew text of Esther—and a fact that is fundamental to understanding its politics—is that God is never mentioned. Within the world of the story, God does not exist.[61]

One can argue, I believe, that the book of Esther is strongly asserting views on many issues, which were consciously reactions to the opinions in circulation in many Jewish circles, but a detailed analysis of this possibility belongs elsewhere.[62] For the moment, it will suffice to say that Esther's politics are straightforward, if radical: the elite exiles must live in Susa, because it is only through their intervention in the upper echelons

---

60. It is not only the book of Esther that thus mocks the Persian king while standing in awe of his power. Steven Weitzman has analyzed the image of the king and the empire in 1 Esdras, and come to similar results. Both the book of Ezra and the book of 1 Esdras provide explanations for the return of the cultic vessels to the Jerusalem temple. But whereas the Ezra story the king is the originator of all beneficence and the Jews are merely the passive recipients, in 1 Esdras the Persian king plays a passive role. Indeed, not only does the story mock the king (as argued by Gruen, *Heritage and Hellenism*, 166–167), but also the mockery allows Zerubbabel to win the king's favor—and in the end the Jews *are* dependent on winning the king's favor (Weitzman, *Surviving Sacrilege*, 29–32).

61. The exact theological claims being made by the book of Esther are not so simply summarized. It is open to discussion if the book means to (a) claim that God is operating behind the scenes, (b) question whether God is actively playing a role, or (c) strongly asserting that God in uninvolved in the world. For the literary question of whether God was originally in the *text* of Esther, see recently Kristin de Troyer and Leah Rediger Schulte, "Is God Absent or Present in the Book of Esther? An Old Problem Revisited," in *The Presence and Absence of God: Claremont Studies in the Philosophy of Religion, Conference 2008*, ed. Ingolf U. Dalferth, Religion in Philosophy and Theology 42 (Tübingen: Mohr/Siebeck, 2009), 35–40.

62. In particular, I have in mind the issues of the centrality of Jerusalem, the return of the exiles to Yehud, the segregation of the Judean community from others, the significance of the Law, the use of Hebrew, and, most fundamentally, who was considered a loyal Judean. In *Esther in Ancient Jewish Thought*, I argue that on all of these issues, as well as other less central ones, the author of Esther is consciously and robustly responding to views found in other biblical and non-biblical books, and that therefore (a) the initial responses to the book of Esther were predictably negative, (b) it took a drastic change in political and social realities to make Esther canonical, and (c) the Rabbis, who inherited the same problematic book but now with canonical status, had to work hard to read it in ways that undermined much of its original radical nature.

of the Persian bureaucracy that the Jews everywhere—including Yehud itself—can be spared massacre and annihilation.[63] Jerusalem once was the center (Esther 2:7), but the center of power is now neither in Jerusalem nor in heaven, but in the halls of the Persian palace.

Perhaps not so surprisingly, we have indications that Esther received a rather cool reaction in Palestine. Esther is the only biblical book of which no copies were found at Qumran, which is not plausibly an accident.[64] Rather than assuming sectarian opposition to the book (which may also have existed), it seems likely that in this respect the sect of the Dead Sea Scrolls reflect the situation more generally in Jewish Palestine. After all, Esther prescribes a festival for all Jews without so much as paying lip service to the priests or other leaders in Jerusalem.[65] In Hasmonean times, the priests in Jerusalem issued a "revised and improved" edition of the book of Esther (now available as "Greek Esther," part of the Apocrypha), which corrected some of its many wrongs.[66] In their version of the story, God was now a major character in the story, intimately and actively participating in the events of history; Esther and Mordecai both offer long and heartfelt prayers; Esther expresses her deep sorrow at her predicament, trapped as she is in a foreign palace; Mordecai is re-cast as a prophetic dreamer in the mode of Joseph.

Besides all these issues, the fundamental worldview of the book may have also been deemed unacceptable by the Jews of Yehud. Support for the claim that this view propounded by Esther—that the world is unpredictable but it is all that we have—made it an objectionable book, comes from the apocryphal book of Tobit. This is a book likely produced in Palestine,[67] but it depicts life in the exile. For the author of Tobit, exilic

63. That Jerusalem was in danger is emphasized by Ramban (Nahmanides) in his commentary on the Bavli, beginning of Megillah: he argues, indeed, that the Jews in Jerusalem were *more* in danger than the Jews elsewhere, since he knows from the narratives of Ezra-Nehemiah that Jerusalem's walls were not completed until the reign of Artaxerxes.

64. For some comments, see Isaac Kalimi, "The Book of Esther and the Dead Sea Scrolls' Community," *Theologische Zeitschrift* 60 (2004): 101–6.

65. As a contrast, we know from the preserved letters that the Jews of fifth-century Elephantine had turned to the priests of Jerusalem for approval when they needed political and religious assistance.

66. This does indicate that there were readers of the book of Esther for whose benefit the priests wanted to improve it. Who these readers were and why the original, problematic version of the text wound up in the canon of the Hebrew Bible, is discussed more extensively in the monograph referred to above (n. 62).

67. The provenance of Tobit has long been debated. Jozef T. Milik, "La patrie de

life is fundamentally topsy-turvy. Amy-Jill Levine puts the perspective of Tobit nicely:

> In exile, dead bodies lie in the streets and those who inter them are punished; demons fall in love with women and kill their husbands; even righteousness is no guarantee of stability, as both Tobit and his nephew Ahikar (cf. 14:10) realize. In the diaspora, no immediately clear solid ground for self-definition exists.[68]

According to Tobit, life in the homeland presumably was different. The life described is an exilic malady—which, for the author, may have been all the more reason Jews should live in Palestine!

With Tobit's description of life in exile, the book of Esther would not disagree: life *is* unpredictable, full of reversals, subject to the whim of an erratic and irrational all-powerful monarch. The author of Esther would have only one quibble with Tobit's claim: he would say that is an accurate portrayal of life not just in exile, but *everywhere* under the Persians, even in the homeland. Indeed, according to Esther, the residents of Jerusalem, too, would have been massacred were it not for the heroism of the Persian Esther and Mordecai. Success *anywhere* is guaranteed not

Tobie," *Revue Biblique* 73 (1966): 522–30, argued that the book was originally Samaritan, but was later re-edited in Galilean pro-Jerusalemite circles. For recent cogent and important arguments that the book is from Eretz Israel, based on the legal traditions evident therein, see Devorah Dimant, "Tobit in Galilee," in *Homeland and Exile: Biblical and Ancient Near Eastern Studies in Honour of Bustenay Oded*, ed. Gershon Galil, Mark Geller, and Alan Millard, Vetus Testamentum Supplements 130 (Leiden: Brill, 2009), 347–59; "The Book of Tobit and the Qumran Halakhah," in *The Dynamics of Language and Exegesis at Qumran*, ed. Devorah Dimant and Reinhard G. Kratz, Forschungen zum Alten Testament 2/35 (Tübingen: Mohr/Siebeck, 2009), 121–43. See the discussion, which goes in a similar direction, in Joseph A. Fitzmyer, *Tobit*, Commentaries on Early Jewish Literature (Berlin: de Gruyter, 2003), 53–54; the discussion in John J. Collins, "The Judaism of the Book of Tobit," in *The Book of Tobit—Text, Tradition, Theology: Papers of the First International Conference on the Deuteronomical Books, Pápa, Hungary, 20–21 May, 2004*, ed. Géza G. Xeravits and József Zsengellér, Journal for the Study of Judaism Supplements 98 (Leiden: Brill, 2005), 23–40, is also valuable.

68. Amy-Jill Levine, "Diaspora as Metaphor: Bodies and Boundaries in the Book of Tobit," in *Diaspora Jews and Judaism: Essays in Honor of, and in Dialogue with A. Thomas Kraabel*, ed. J. Andrew Overman and Robert S. MacLennan, South Florida Studies in the History of Judaism 41 (Atlanta: Scholars, 1992), 105–17, at 105; see also 113–17. Cf. also Beate Ego, "The Book of Tobit and the Diaspora," in *The Book of Tobit—Text, Tradition, Theology: Papers of the First International Conference on the Deuteronomical Books, Pápa, Hungary, 20–21 May, 2004*, ed. Géza G. Xeravits and József Zsengellér, Journal for the Study of Judaism Supplements 98 (Leiden: Brill, 2005), 41–54.

by righteousness, but by good fortune and skillful negotiation of complex realities. Tobit may be conceived of as a Palestinian response to Esther: "That may be *your* life," Tobit may say, "but that's because you are in exile. Here in the Promised Land life works the way it is supposed to." I am not sure Esther would agree.

CONCLUSIONS

In concluding, it should again be emphasized that ideas traced here can only be said with certainty to represent the views of the elites who composed the literature discussed here. The beliefs and ideals of the masses cannot be discerned from this literature, which for the most part eschews descriptions of everyday life and focuses on the extraordinary. Thus, what can be said is that the literati among the Jews of Yehud were prepared to believe one of two things about God and the world. They were happy to be told that far from being absent in the world, God was operating through the medium of the Persian monarch. This actually solved multiple problems, since it explained the theological conundrum of God's retreat from the world while demoting the Persian king to the role of a puppet. The Judeans were also prepared to accept that the world as it stood was hopelessly corrupt, and that God had retracted his dominion to the heavens alone. Thus, the apocalyptic literature was attractive, as it posited that there was another world in which God reigned, and there would be a future existence in which the balance of right and wrong, good and evil, would be restored.

The radical cynicism of the book of Esther, however, found no readers in Jewish Palestine. This book argued that the world was without direction, and that the only way to make one's way through the world was to learn to navigate the system. The original text of Esther became popular (and indeed, canonical) only after circumstances had changed. Prior to that, it was alternately ignored, disputed, and corrected. The author of the original book may not have appreciated the attempts to reform his radicalism, but he may have smiled knowingly at the unpredictable turns that life and literature take.

2

Iranian Influence at Qumran
Texts and Beliefs

MIRYAM T. BRAND

FROM THE TIME THE Dead Sea Scrolls were discovered, their parallels to other ancient texts have intrigued scholars. In particular, researchers have noted similarities between Iranian thought and approaches found in the Qumran scrolls. While the parallels are striking, the manner in which Iranian ideas "influenced" the Qumran Community, and the degree to which such influence was even possible, remains a matter of debate. The present survey will explore some of these similarities, the difficulties that have been raised with the assumption of direct influence, and possible paths to influence from Iranian thought to Qumran texts.

DUALISM AND DECEIT: THE TREATISE OF THE TWO SPIRITS

Any survey of the similarities between Iranian texts and the Dead Sea Scrolls must begin with the *Treatise of the Two Spirits*, a focal point in the discussion of Zoroastrian influence at Qumran. The *Treatise of the Two Spirits* is a self-contained exposition on the origin of sin and the nature of divine omniscience found in both the Cave 1 and Cave 4 versions of the Community Rule (1QS III.13-IV.26 and 4QpapSc [4Q257] V-VI). While the *Treatise* was once thought to represent the theological basis of Qumran thought due to its central position in the Community Rule, recent scholarship has recognized that the Treatise is unusual and should be studied independently.[1] Nevertheless, the placement of the *Treatise* indicates that it was significant to the Qumran Community or, at the very least, to the redactor of the Community Rule.

Following an introduction (1QS III.13-18a) describing God's omniscience and foreknowledge (III.15-16), the *Treatise* describes the dualistic underpinnings of human ethics, as established by God himself (1QS III.18b-25a):[2]

> ... And he placed two spirits for him (man) in which to walk until the appointed time of his (God's) appointment, namely the spirits of truth and deceit. In a spring of light is the begetting of truth and from a well of darkness is the begetting of deceit. In the hand of the Prince of Lights (is) the dominion of all the children of righteousness; in the ways of light they walk. And in the hand of the Angel of Darkness (is) all the dominion of the children of deceit; and in the ways of darkness they walk. Due to the Angel of Darkness is the straying of all the children of righteousness; and all their sins, their iniquities, their guilt, and

---

1. For examples of the former view, see D. Dimant, "Qumran Sectarian Literature," in *Jewish Writings of the Second Temple Period: Apocrypha, Pseudepigrapha, Qumran, Sectarian Writings, Philo, Josephus*, ed. M. E. Stone, Compendia rerum Iudaicarum ad Novum Testamentum 2 (Assen: Van Gorcum, 1984), 533-36; L. H. Schiffman, *Reclaiming the Dead Sea Scrolls: The History of Judaism, the Background of Christianity, the Lost Library of Qumran* (Philadelphia: Jewish Publication Society, 1994), 149-50; and G. W. E. Nickelsburg, *Jewish Literature Between the Bible and the Mishnah: A Historical and Literary Introduction*, 2nd ed. (Minneapolis: Fortress, 2005), 139-40. Typical is Nickelsburg's statement (139): "This section spells out systematically the religious worldview that undergirds the lifestyle and rituals of the community." For the latter view, see the treatments of the *Treatise* in A. Lange, *Weisheit und Prädestination: Weisheitliche Urordnung und Prädestination in den Textfunden von Qumran*, Studies in Texts of the Desert of Judah 18 (Leiden: Brill, 1995), 121-43, NaN-8; E. J. C. Tigchelaar, *To Increase Learning for the Understanding Ones: Reading and Reconstructing the Fragmentary Early Jewish Sapiential Text 4QInstruction*, Studies in Texts of the Desert of Judah 44 (Leiden: Brill, 2001), 194-203; and L. T. Stuckenbruck, "The Interiorization of Dualism within the Human Being in Second Temple Judaism: The Treatise of the Two Spirits (1QS III:13—IV:26) in Its Tradition-Historical Context," in *Light against Darkness: Dualism in Ancient Mediterranean Religion and the Contemporary World*, ed. A. Lange et al., Journal of Ancient Judaism Supplements 2 (Göttingen: Vandenhoeck & Ruprecht, 2011), 161-67.

2. The translation of this passage is the writer's.

their iniquitous works (are caused) by his dominion, according to God's mysteries, until his period. And all their afflictions and the appointed times of their suffering (are caused) by the dominion of his hostility. And all the spirits of his lot cause the children of light to stumble; but the God of Israel and the angel of his truth help all the children of light . . .

The dualistic worldview that this passage portrays is one in which cosmic dualism (reflected in the realms of the Angel of Darkness and the Prince of Light) is responsible for social dualism, namely the division between the "children of righteousness" and the "children of deceit." This connection between cosmic and social dualism is not surprising in a Qumran context; a similar connection is made in liturgical curse texts against Belial and Melkireša found in the Community Rule, the War Scroll, 4QBerakhot (4Q286–290), and 4QCurses (4Q280).

More importantly for the tracing of influence, this passage presents the separation between the "children of righteousness" and the "children of deceit" as a function of the basically dualistic nature of the ethical underpinnings of creation. The spirits of truth and deceit that determine human actions until the eschatological age (*mw'd pqwdtw*) reside in the areas of light and darkness, respectively. These areas are ruled by the Prince of Lights and the Angel of Darkness. Each of these supernatural beings is given a share of humanity to lead. The dominion of the Angel of Darkness includes the "children of deceit" while the Prince of Lights reigns over the "children of righteousness." This explains why the wicked walk "in the ways of darkness" and the righteous walk in the "ways of light." In the redacted text as it stands, this passage serves to limit the freedom of human will. Despite this division between the wicked and the righteous, the righteous can and do sin (III.21b–22a). They do so, however, only as a result of the machinations of the Angel of Darkness, whose power is apparently not confined to his own subjects.

The two spirits of truth and deceit, their subordination to the Prince of Light and the Angel of Darkness, and their role as the source of all positive and negative qualities, are not typical of Qumran texts. The differences between the *Treatise* and other Qumran texts, as noted by Armin Lange, include the lack of sectarian terminology, the use of terms (including unique terminology for the forces of evil) that appear nowhere else in the Scrolls, and the absence of prominent Qumran themes.[3] The considerable differences between the *Treatise* and other Qumran texts in-

---

3. Lange, *Weisheit und Prädestination*, 127–28.

dicate that outside influences played a significant role in its composition. At the same time, the fact that it included ideas found elsewhere in the Community Rule, such as the opposition of truth and deceit, made it acceptable to the Rule's redactor.[4] As the present writer has argued elsewhere,[5] the heavily redacted *Treatise* actually combines a number of disparate views of sin found in other Qumran texts but adds terminology and ideas that are unusual for sectarian texts.

The possibility that this work was influenced by Iranian thought has long been a focus of discussion. As many scholars have noted, the "Two Spirits" described in the *Treatise* indicate Iranian, and specifically Zoroastrian, influence. Most prominent is the parallel between the *Treatise* and Yasna 30, in one of the Gāthās found in the Old Avesta.[6]

> 30,3 These (are) the two spirits (present) in the primal (stage of one's existence), twins who have become famed (manifesting themselves as) the two (kinds of) dreams, the two (kinds of) thoughts and words, (and) the two (kinds of) actions, the better and the evil. And between these two, the munificent discriminate rightly, (but) not the miserly.
>
> 30,4 and when these two spirits confront each other (to vie for a person), then (that person) decides (of what nature will be) the primal (stage of his existence): vitality and lack of vitality,

---

4. C. Hempel has noted that certain terminology and themes found in the Treatise are particular to the *Community Rule*; see C. Hempel, "The *Treatise on the Two Spirits* and the Literary History of the *Rule of the Community*," in *Dualism in Qumran*, ed. G. G. Xeravits, Library of Second Temple Studies 76 (London: T. & T. Clark, 2010), 102–20. She notes the opposition of truth (*emet*) and deceit (*avel, 'awlā*) found in 1QS V–IX and its Cave 4 parallels (but notes that the phrase "people of deceit" is not attested in the *Treatise*, where the term used is "sons of truth/deceit"); Hempel, "Treatise," 116-8. S. Metso has already noted that both the *Treatise* and 1QS IX.12–26 share the terms "chosen ones," "children of righteousness," and "people of the pit," among others; S. Metso, *The Textual Development of the Qumran Community Rule*, Studies in the Texts of the Desert of Judah 21 (Leiden: Brill, 1997), 137. Hempel has also noted the common allusions to Mic 6: 8 and Isa 26: 3 in 1QS IV.5, 1QS V.3–4, and 1QS VIII.2 (and their Cave 4 parallels). She concludes that such links led to the perceived suitability of the *Treatise* to the *Community Rule* and, consequently, to its inclusion in the *Rule*, while other links were introduced after the *Treatise* was already incorporated into the *Rule*; see Hempel, ibid., 118.

5. M. T. Brand, *Evil Within and Without: The Source of Sin and Its Nature as Portrayed in Second Temple Literature*, Journal of Ancient Judaism Supplements 9 (Göttingen: Vandenhoeck & Ruprecht, 2013), 269–73.

6. Translation of Yasna 30 is taken from Helmut Humbach, J. H. Elfenbein, and Prods O. Skjærvø, *The Gāthās of Zarathushtra and the Other Old Avestan Texts* (Heidelberg: Winter, 1991).

and (on the other hand) of what nature (his) existence will be in the end: that of the deceitful (will be) the worst, but best thought will (be in store) for the truthful one.

30,5 Of these two spirits, the deceitful one chooses to do the worst (things), (but) the most prosperous spirit, who is clothed in the hardest diamonds, (chooses) truth, as also (do those) who devotedly satisfy the Ahura with true actions, (Him), the Wise One.

30,6 The Daēvas do not at all discriminate rightly between these two (spirits). Because delusion comes over them when they take counsel, so that they choose the worst thought, therefore they gather with Wrath, with which the mortals sicken existence.

The spirits of good and evil that reside in humans are reminiscent of a number of passages in Zoroastrian literature.[7] However, a close comparison between these Gāthās and the *Treatise* reveal many essential differences, such as the emphasis on choice rather than predestination in Yasna 30, and the contention between the spirits over each individual (30 [4]). Human choice between the two spirits, whereby one establishes one's eventual fate, is considered central to Zoroastrian dualism.[8]

The similarities between the *Treatise* and Yasna 30 served as the focus of the earliest comparisons between Persian thought and Qumran texts. The first of these was conducted by David Winston in his well-known article, "The Iranian Component in the Bible, Apocrypha, and Qumran: A Review of the Evidence."[9] However, the contrast between the emphasis on divine determinism in the *Treatise* and the centrality of choice in the Gāthās could not be ignored. When comparing the *Treatise* and Yasna 30, Winston noted three characteristics of the dualism in the Treatise, only the first of which, in his estimation, could be found in the Gāthās: a monotheistic framework, a predestinarian outlook, and

---

7. On the spirits of good and evil see S. Shaked, "Qumran and Iran: Further Considerations," *Israel Oriental Studies* 2 (1972): 437–40.

8. See P. O. Skjaervo, "Zoroastrian Dualism," in *Light against Darkness: Dualism in Ancient Mediterranean Religion and the Contemporary World*, ed. A. Lange et al., Journal of Ancient Judaism Supplements 2 (Göttingen: Vandenhoeck & Ruprecht, 2011), 72–74.

9. D. Winston, "The Iranian Component in the Bible, Apocrypha, and Qumran: A Review of the Evidence," *History of Religion* 5 (1966): 183–216.

imagery of light and darkness. However, Winston found the missing elements in the "Zurvanite heterodoxy."[10]

The hypothesis that a "Zurvanite heterodoxy," or "Zurvanism," existed alongside "orthodox" Zoroastrianism is based on the idea that the Zurvan myth, which explains the origins of Ohrmazd (Ahura Mazda) and Ahriman (Angra Mainyu) as twin spirits begotten from the preexistent god of Time (Zurvan), formed the theological basis of an entire sect. This idea can be found in Muslim accounts of religious movements in the early Islamic world but was first adopted in Western scholarship by Friedrich Spiegel in 1863.[11] The subsequent discovery of Manichean Middle Persian texts, in which the chief god of the Manichean pantheon was sometimes called Zurvān, coincided with the discovery of the Antiochus I of Commagene inscriptions, which testified to the existence of a Greco-Iranian dynastic cult and connected human destiny to the concept of "boundless time."[12] These discoveries increased the importance given to Zurvanism in Western scholarship.[13] At the same time, the lack of any reference to Zurvanism in Zoroastrian sources, despite the fact that the myth of Zurvan is well known from Armenian, Syriac, Greek, and Arabic sources, led scholars to believe that Zurvanism had been considered a "heresy" vis-à-vis orthodox Zoroastrianism, and was therefore purged from surviving Zoroastrian texts.[14]

It was from this understanding of Zurvanism that Winston drew in his comparison between the *Treatise* and Yasna 30. Winston connected the predestination found in the *Treatise* with Zurvan's identity as "fate" in

10. Ibid., 202.

11 In F. Spiegel, *Érân, das Land zwischen dem Indus und Tigris. Beiträge zur Kenntniss des Landes und seiner Geschichte* (Berlin: Dümmler, 1863), 64, 366 and later in *Erânische Altertumskunde* (Leipzig: Engelmann, 1871), 2:175–87. The following summary of attitudes toward Zurvanism draws extensively from Albert de Jong's survey, "Zurvanism," in *Encyclopaedia Iranica*, Online Edition, March 28, 2014, http://www.iranicaonline.org/articles/zurvanism.

12. Mary Boyce and F. Grenet, *A History of Zoroastrianism III: Zoroastrianism under Macedonian and Roman Rule*, HdO 1.8.1.2.2 (Leiden: Brill, 1991), 332–34.

13. Jong, "Zurvanism."

14. See G. Widengren, "Primordial Man and Prostitute: A Zervanite Motif in the Sassanid Avesta," in *Studies in Mysticism and Religion Presented to Gershom G. Scholem on His Seventieth Birthday*, ed. E. E. Urbach, R. J. Zwi Werblowsky, and Ch. Wirszubski (Jerusalem: Magnes, 1967), 337–52. Based on three "Zervanite" texts within Iranian and Indian Bundahišn compositions, which according to Widengren's analysis are actually Avestan in origin, Widengren deduces a "special Zervanite part of the Sassanid Avesta, now lost."

the *Dadestan ī Menog ī Xrad*. Winston connected the *Treatise*'s imagery of light and darkness to Zurvan's characterization of his son Ohrmazd as "light and fragrant" and Ahriman as "dark and stinking" in the Armenian and Syrian recountings of this myth.[15]

The possibility of a connection between Zurvanism and the dualism of the *Treatise* was echoed in later scholarship.[16] However, the difficulties with this approach were evident to anyone who did not accept that Zurvanism was a separate system of thought. Shaul Shaked, in particular, convincingly argued that "Zurvanism" was never a separate sect of Zoroastrianism. Rather, the Zurvan myth was one among many varieties of the Zoroastrian cosmogony myth found in Sassanian Zoroastrianism.[17] Consequently, similarities between the *Treatise* and the Gāthās could not be separated from their essential differences by categorizing both similarities and differences as "Zurvanite." Shaked accordingly proposed another approach to the reflection of certain Zoroastrian ideas in Dead Sea Scroll texts, explaining the similarities as the result of internal Jewish developments that found their direction in an Iranian pattern already well-known to Jews of the period.[18]

Nevertheless, the striking similarity of the imagery in the *Treatise* to that in Yasna 30 begs further investigation. As de Jong has noted, this extends to the fact that in the *Treatise* the spirits are both cosmic entities and active within the human being.[19] The manner in which the two chief spirits change throughout the *Treatise*, first morphing from personified divine beings into abstract spirits responsible for every human trait and

15. Winston, "Iranian Component," 203.

16. See Boyce and Grenet, *History of Zoroastrianism*, 423-24. P. Alexander, in "Predestination and Free Will in the Theology of the Dead Sea Scrolls," in *Divine and Human Agency in Paul and His Cultural Environment*, ed. J. M. G. Barclay and S. J. Gathercole, Library of New Testament Studies 335 (London: T. & T. Clark, 2006), 33-35, raises the influence of Zurvanism as a possibility, but prefers to see the similarity with the Gāthās as the development of direct influence and the subsequent adaptation of ideas from the Gāthās to Judaism.

17. Shaul Shaked, *Dualism in Transformation: Varieties of Religion in Sasanian Iran*, Jordan Lectures in Comparative Religion Series 16 (London: School of Oriental and African Studies, University of London, 1994), 53.

18. S. Shaked, "Iranian Influence on Judaism: First Century B.C.E. to Second Century C.E.," in *The Cambridge History of Judaism*, ed. W. D. Davies and L. Finkelstein, vol. 1 (Cambridge: Cambridge University Press, 1984), 309.

19. Albert de Jong, "Iranian Connections in the Dead Sea Scrolls," in *The Oxford Handbook of the Dead Sea Scrolls*, ed. T. H. Lim and J. J. Collins, Oxford Handbooks (Oxford: Oxford University Press, 2010), 494.

then into leaders of opposing camps, is the result of a complex redactional history. Yet, the unusual nature of these spirits compared to other Qumran texts is evidence that their complex nature is not simply the result of editorial meddling.

As this writer has explored at length elsewhere,[20] the *Treatise* was likely adopted as a central piece of the Community Rule because it could be seen as merging a variety of beliefs regarding sin and evil that were popular at Qumran: the existence of Belial, an evil being who opposed either an angelic character (the Prince of Light/Michael) or God himself; the presence of a constant human inclination toward evil; and the idea that demonic spirits could influence one to sin "from the inside." While this variety of beliefs allowed the *Treatise* to be wholeheartedly adopted by the Qumran Community, the unique terminology and imagery found in the *Treatise* are not actually drawn from other Qumran texts and present clear evidence of outside influence.

In a forthcoming article, the present writer argues that the similarity between the *Treatise* and Yasna 30 is the result not of direct influence, but could be the result of Zoroastrian ideas and worldviews reaching Judeans through the influence of oral folklore on narrative texts.[21] These intermediary narrative texts then informed the Treatise, itself a patchwork of ideas regarding the origin of sin.[22]

Possible evidence of such a route of influence can be found in the *Visions of Amram* (4Q543–549). The *Visions of Amram*, which has been identified as a pre-sectarian text,[23] describes two figures arguing over Amram in a dream. They explain to him that together they rule over all humans, but one of these figures, Melki-reša, rules over darkness and the other (presumably Melki-ṣedeq, although his name has not been

---

20. Brand, *Evil Within and Without*, 257–74.

21. M. T. Brand, "Spirited Evil: Persian Influence and Its Limits in Qumran Texts," to be published in the conference volume for the Eighth Symposium of the Melammu Project, November 11–15, 2014.

22. Brand, *Evil Within and Without*, 270.

23. Mainly because Jubilees seems to draw on the Visions as a source; see E. Puech, *Qumran Cave 4.XXII: Textes Araméens, Première Partie: 4Q529–549*, Discoveries in the Judaean Desert 31 (Oxford: Clarendon, 2001), 285–87; and R. R. Duke, *The Social Location of the Visions of Amram (4Q543–547)*, Studies in Biblical Literature 135 (New York: Lang, 2010), 89–103. See also J. T. Milik's categorization of this text in "Écrits Prééssèniens de Qumrân: D'Hénoch À Amram," in *Qumrân: Sa Piété, Sa Théologie et Son Milieu*, ed. M. Delcor, Bibliotheca Ephemeridum theologicarum Lovaniensium 46 (Paris: Duculot, 1978), 91–106.

preserved) rules over light.[24] However, in contrast to the *Treatise*, in the *Visions of Amram*, Amram is given the choice as to who will rule him. (Whether this is a choice given to every human or only to the righteous Amram is unclear.)

The choice given to Amram in the *Visions* is more in keeping with the approach found in Yasna 30 and in the Gāthās in general than with the deterministic outlook of the *Treatise*. In particular, the account in the *Visions* parallels the conflict between the spirits in Yasna 30, which is resolved by the individual's choice between them. It seems likely, then, that oral narratives and folklore describing a conflict between two spirits who fight over each individual, for good and for evil, found their way to Judean circles and were imported into this narrative. From there the imagery of two spirits who rule, one in light and one in darkness, could easily have found its way to the Treatise, particularly given the predilection of the redactor of the Treatise for harmonizing the different views of sin found throughout Qumran literature.

Key to this discussion is the understanding of influence itself as the integration of ideas within a system that is already in place. When filtered through a system of thought that is already developed, or adjusted to reflect the social circumstances of its new context, an imported idea will naturally develop significant differences when compared to its source; such is the case regarding Iranian dualism.

DUALISM OUTSIDE OF THE TREATISE

Dualism is evident throughout the works of the Qumran Community and, in fact, is considered central to Qumran belief.[25] This dualism is particularly evident in the Community Rule (and in the *Treatise of the Two Spirits* found within it) and the War Scroll. The dualism of the Qumran Community can be found in the opposition of the "lot of God" (Qumran Community members) and the "lot of Belial" (nonmembers/the wicked, gentile enemies, and Belial's demonic minions); the opposition of the

24. This description of the *Visions of Amram* draws from parallel texts in 4Q543, 4Q544, and 4Q547 and another fragment in 4Q544 2 11–16.

25. Of course, as with most Qumran ideas, the degree of centrality has been a matter of dispute; see D. Dimant, "Dualism at Qumran: New Perspectives," in *Caves of Enlightenment: Proceedings of the American Schools of Oriental Research Dead Sea Scrolls Jubilee Symposium (1947–1997)*, ed. J. H. Charlesworth (North Richland Hills, TX: Bibal, 1998), 58–59.

"children of light" and the "children of darkness"; and the more general contrast between contradictory terms: truth and falsehood, light and darkness, and righteousness and sin. The War Scroll, in describing the apocalyptic battles between "children of darkness" led by Belial and the "children of light" led by the "Prince of Light" (the angel Michael), demonstrates the necessary limits monotheistic belief places on dualism: the battle on earth is not between Belial and God, but between Belial and an angel of equivalent rank.

The range of dualism found at Qumran is comparable to what we find in Iranian thought. As Gerard Gnoli has stated, Zoroastrianism "results from an elaborate analysis of the superhuman world divided between good and evil, virtues and vices, opposed forces that, like man, may belong to the world of truth or of falsehood."[26] A similar worldview is reflected in dualistic Qumran texts, where not only is Belial contrasted with the "Prince of Light," but the "lot of Belial," made up of both evil humans and demonic powers, fights with the "lot of God." Anyone who belongs to the "lot of God" is righteous by definition, while the "lot of Belial" must be evil.

However, there is a key difference between the dualism of Zoroastrianism and that central to Qumran texts (including those outside the *Treatise*): the prominence of choice in Zoroastrianism dualism. As noted above, according to Zoroastrian texts the individual must choose between belonging to truth or falsehood.[27] While the determinism of Qumran texts is not absolute, according to the Community Rule, one's standing among the righteous is determined through the casting of lots within the Community[28] while the War Scroll indicates that the lot of the "children of light" was determined by the casting of lots by God himself.[29]

This determinism is not as absolute as it initially appears. Even the initiation ceremony described in the introduction to the Community Rule, which pits the "lot of God" against the "lot of Belial," does not explain how these lots are to be determined and depicts a hypocritical member casting his *own* lot with that of Belial.[30] While this may indicate that Qumran dualism was not *completely* deterministic after all, it is still

26. G. Gnoli, "Dualism," in *Encyclopaedia Iranica*, ed. E. Yarshater, vol. 7 (Costa Mesa, CA: Mazda, 1996), 578.
27. Ibid.
28. E.g. 1QS VI.16.
29. See 1Q33 XIII.9–10.
30. See Brand, *Evil Within and Without*, 245–48.

far from the emphasis on choice within a strong dualistic framework found in Zoroastrianism.

Shaked has expressed reservations to the idea that choice—or to be more precise, freedom of choice—is central to Zoroastrianism. According to Shaked, while the Gāthās and the Younger Avesta contain verses in which the verb "to choose" or "to make a choice" is prominent, this does not imply freedom of choice any more than the statement that each of the two eternal spirits "chose" its own way indicates an act of deliberation on their part.[31] Rather, according to Shaked, "choice" in these texts indicates "whole-hearted adoption" of doing one's duty. A close parallel to this idea is found in the Damascus Document, which includes a narrative history of sinners that continually stresses the need to *choose* the commandments of God over one's own will, repeatedly using the verb *bḥr* to emphasize this choice.[32]

The combination of choice with duty is not surprising, whether in an Iranian or a Qumran context. It can be expected that a religious group or faith would require its adherents to take responsibility for their choices and actions. This is so even if, according to the group's worldview, the fact that one has joined the Community or accepted the faith indicates in retrospect that one was fated to be righteous.

Moreover, the fact that choice is emphasized specifically in the *nondualistic Damascus Document* dissociates it from the influence of Iranian dualism. Consequently, the emphasis on choice that can be found in specific Qumran rule texts as well as in the Iranian traditions represented in the Gāthās and the Younger Avesta is intriguing but not necessarily evidence of influence. It does, however, demonstrate that the dualism found at Qumran need not be divorced from Iranian influence and that parallel developments in both religions could allow Judaism to more easily draw from Iranian ideas while not swallowing them whole.

IRANIAN LOANWORDS AND "LOAN CONCEPTS"

Iranian loanwords, including (*a*)*sparaka* "buckler" and *nadan* "sheath" (in the *Genesis Apocryphon*),[33] *daxšta* "desert" and *naiza-ka, written *nzk*, "spear" (*Targum of Job*), *naḥšīr* "hunt" (*War Scroll*), *naḥšīrūta* "slaughter"

---

31. Shaked, "Iranian Influence on Judaism," 1:318–19.
32. Brand, *Evil Within and Without*, 75–82.
33. The word *nadan* also appears in 1 Chron 21:27.

(*Testament of Levi*), *šinab* "watering channel" (*Hodayot*), and *res*, spelled *r's*, a measure of distance (4Q373),[34] could have entered the Scrolls indirectly through previous Iranian influence on Imperial Aramaic.[35] During the Achaemenid period, Aramaic ingested a considerable number of Iranian loanwords due to the use of Aramaic as the official language of government throughout the Empire.[36]

In addition, Shaked has proposed that several otherwise unique words in the Dead Sea Scrolls are actually Iranian loanwords, namely 'wšy from *uš-* "ear of," *bdny* from Old Iranian **abidaēnā-* through Middle Iranian: "style, mode, form, ritual," and *pnbd* from *paywand* "connection, relationship, association" (etymologically derived from **pati-band*).[37] However, like the Iranian loanwords mentioned above, these words are not evidence that Qumran language resulted from more Iranian influence than in other Judean texts. The fact that these specific words are unattested elsewhere simply points to our lack of knowledge regarding the Aramaic and Hebrew of this period and the scarcity of texts with which to track linguistic developments.[38]

The word *raz*, first appearing in the biblical book of Daniel, is prominent at Qumran in a meaning somewhat closer to that of later Iranian texts. Rather than involving dream interpretation, it indicates a secret or mystery known only to a few.[39] While de Jong correctly notes the difficulty of tracing an actual linguistic connection with later Iranian texts,[40] it is nevertheless possible that the *concept* of mystery that lies behind the word *raz* was influenced by the Iranian worldview. Cultural and linguistic influence can frequently be found not merely in actual loanwords, but

---

34. See J. C. Greenfield and S. Shaked, "Three Iranian Words in the Targum of Job from Qumran," *Zeitschrift der deutschen morgenländischen Gesellschaft* 122 (1972): 38; J. C. Greenfield, "Aramaic ii. Iranian Loanwords in Early Aramaic," in *Encyclopaedia Iranica*, ed. E. Yarshater (Costa Mesa, CA: Mazda, 1987), vol. 2, 259.

35. J. C. Greenfield, "Aramaic ii. Iranian Loanwords in Early Aramaic," in *Encyclopaedia Iranica*, ed. E. Yarshater, vol. 2 (Costa Mesa, CA: Mazda, 1987), 256–59; Albert de Jong, "Iranian Connections in the Dead Sea Scrolls," in *The Oxford Handbook of the Dead Sea Scrolls*, ed. T. H. Lim and J. J. Collins, Oxford Handbooks (Oxford: Oxford University Press, 2010), 488.

36. Greenfield, "Aramaic ii."

37. Shaul Shaked, "Qumran: Some Iranian Connections," in *Solving Riddles and Untying Knots: Biblical, Epigraphic, and Semitic Studies in Honor of Jonas C. Greenfield*, ed. Jonas Carl Greenfield et al. (Winona Lake, IN: Eisenbrauns, 1995), 277–81.

38. See ibid., 281.

39. De Jong, "Iranian Connections," 488.

40. Op. cit.

especially in the meanings that loanwords or their cognates acquire as a result of cultural contact.

Such may be the case regarding the "loan *concept*" of spirit, or *mēnōg*. The semantic range of *rwḥ*, "spirit," in Second Temple texts reflects a significant broadening of biblical usage, although not a complete innovation. Thus, the use of *rwḥ* to denote an abstract quality, such as the spirits of truth and deceit in the *Treatise of the Two Spirits*, may have roots in biblical use, such as the *rwḥ mšpṭ* "spirit of justice," in Isa 4:4; 28:6; while the employment of *rwḥ* to denote a quality of the individual bestowed by the Divine such as the "spirit of long-suffering" in 4QBarkhi Nafshi (4Q435 2i.4–5) and the "spirit of knowledge" in the Hodayot (1QHa VI.25) most clearly developed from a similar use of *rwḥ* reflected in Isa 11:2. However, the more widespread occurrence of these meanings in the Dead Sea Scrolls, coupled with the extremely common use of *rwḥ* to denote demonic entities, may indicate an external influence on the word's semantic development and structure. Shaked notes that in late Pahlavi (Middle Persian) writings, the term *mēnōg* (commonly translated "spirit") represents at least three distinct notions: an abstract quality, such as truth or lack of truth; a quality or psychological urge operating within the individual person, such as a person's wisdom or generosity; or a personified entity (i.e., a divine or demonic power) that acts on the individual externally as well as operating on a cosmic scale.[41] While it is difficult to determine definitively whether the Persian use of *mēnōg* influenced the parallel use of *rwḥ* in Jewish circles, particularly as the written evidence in Pahlavi post-dates Second Temple writings significantly, the parallels are striking.

However, there are additional uses of *rwḥ* found in Second Temple texts, particularly those of the Qumran Community, that do not reflect Shaked's categories and may indicate a more general tendency to "load" the term *rwḥ* during this period. These include the use of *rwḥ* to denote human beings themselves;[42] a continuation of the biblical use of *rwḥ* to denote life or breath;[43] and the use of *rwḥ* to represent a quantifiable attribute that enables the categorization of the group member.[44] It is perhaps

---

41. Shaked, "Iranian Influence on Judaism," 317.

42. For example, *rwḥ bśr* "spirit of flesh" in the *Hodayot*; *rwḥ* in Hodayot VII.26; and *rwḥ htwʻh* "erring spirit" in Hodayot IX.24.

43. As in 4QDamascus Document (4Q272 1 ii.1), 4QInstruction (4Q418 126 ii.8), and 4QpseudoEzekielª (4Q385 2 7), in a paraphrase of Ezek 37: 9.

44. As in the Damascus Document (CD XX.24), the Community Rule (1QS IV.26),

a combination of this last Qumran use of *rwḥ* and the second meaning of *mēnōg* noted by Shaked, a psychological urge, that is behind the intriguing reference in the fragmentary *4QRebukes Reported by the Overseer* (4Q477 2ii.4): *hʿwn ʿmw wgm rwḥ pʾrh ʿm[w]* "the offence is with him and also a haughty spirit (is) with [him]."[45] In this reference, the member is rebuked for a "haughty spirit," which both denotes the urge that led to his "sin" and also allows the overseer to categorize him, at least temporarily, within the Community. Once again, just as intriguing as possible evidence of influence is the manner in which the Qumran community has evolved the meaning of *rwḥ*, without completely adopting the Iranian model.

ESCHATOLOGY AND THE PRESENT AGE

There is strong evidence that Zoroastrian thought influenced Second Temple Judaism eschatology in general, and Qumran eschatology in particular. In biblical books composed before the Babylonian exile, there is no mention of heaven and hell, besides the murky *šʾwl*, or of judgment following death, and no explicit mention of resurrection. These ideas, however, which appear to be ancient ones in the Zoroastrian tradition,[46] do appear in books written toward the end of the Second Temple period, following an extended period of Persian rule.[47]

At Qumran there is yet another level of similarity with Iranian ideas of the eschaton, namely, the belief that the current age is one given over to the rule of evil. At Qumran, the present age is distinguished by the "dominion of Belial," which will end only at the eschaton. The attempt to reconcile earthly evil with a benign deity finds a parallel in Iranian thought and theology. In both Zoroastrian and Qumran thought, the faithful interpret their current existence as one where evil forces may hold sway, whether these forces are led by Angra Mainyu or Belial. And, according to both, these forces will finally be curbed in the final age by the Deity.

---

and 4QFour Lots (4Q279 5 5).

45. Text and translation follow E. Eshel, "477. 4QRebukes Reported by the Overseer," in *Qumran Cave 4. XXVI: Cryptic Texts and Miscellanea, Part I*, Discoveries in the Judaean Desert 36 (Oxford: Clarendon, 2000), 480–81.

46. S. Shaked, "Eschatology I. In Zoroastrianism and Zoroastrian Influence," in *Encyclopaedia Iranica*, ed. E. Yarshater, vol. 8 (Costa Mesa, CA: Mazda, 1998), 569.

47. See ibid., 568.

However, there are important differences between the two theodicies. Despite similarities, the Qumran Community's approach reflects a more purely dualistic outlook, when comparing the current period with the eschaton, than does Zoroastrian thought. The idea that there is a period in which Belial is free to work his evil will among humankind can be compared to the characterization of the period preceding the eschaton in Zoroastrian thought; this is the "middle" period between creation and the eschaton, in which Ahura Mazda, the "Lord Wisdom," and Angra Mainyu, the "Evil Spirit," do battle on earth. Yet, the attitude in Qumran texts is both more absolute and far more pessimistic than extant Zoroastrian texts that describe the contemporary age. In most Qumran texts, the present age is not one in which Belial is merely free, but one in which he actually rules; hence the denoting of the present age as *mmšlt bly'l* "the dominion of Belial."[48] This contrasts with the characterization of the present period in Zoroastrian thought, which describes the existence of good *alongside* evil in the present age. In fact, in Iranian thought, this period is characterized not as evil, but as a "mixture" (*gumēzišn*) of good and evil. Despite these differences, the preordained period of evil in Qumran texts appears to be a development of Persian periodization that has been adjusted to reflect the social situation of the Qumran Community.

The impetus for the stark view of the present age in Qumran theology can be found in the Community's shared experience of persecution that is referenced throughout central Qumran texts. This experience is specifically associated with the "dominion of Belial," as in the Community Rule (1QS I.16–17):

> And all those who enter the rule of the *yaḥad* (i.e., the Community) shall be initiated into the covenant before God, to act according to all which he commanded and not to backslide because of any terror, dread, or persecution during the dominion of Belial (*mmšlt bly'l*).

This admonition provides a striking description of how the Community perceived the threats inherent in the situation of all those "initiated into the covenant before God." For the initiated, "terror, dread, or persecution" will become inevitable, and can be explained as the result of Belial's rule in the current age.

---

48. See 1QS I.18, II.19; 1Q33 (1QMil☒amah) XIV.9 par. 4Q491 (4QMil☒amah) 8–10 i.6 (and cf. 1Q33 XVIII.1); 4Q390 2i.4; see also 4Q177 1–4.8.

The introduction to the Damascus Document, which presents a less hostile view of those outside the Community, still adamantly connects the current age of evil— the dominion of Belial—to the rejection of the Community and its laws (CD IV.12b–19a):

> But during all those years, Belial will be set free amidst Israel, as God spoke through the hand of the prophet Isaiah, son of Amoz, saying, "Fear and a pit and a snare are upon you, O inhabitant(s) of the land" (Isa 24: 17). *vacat* Its interpretation concerns the three traps of Belial, of which Levi, the son of Jacob, said that he (Belial) entrapped Israel with them, and he made (lit., placed) them (the traps) before them (Israel) (as if) they were three types of righteousness. The first is unchastity, the second wealth, and the third defilement of the sanctuary. He who escapes from this is caught by that and he who is saved from that is caught by this ... (CD IV.12b–19a)

This passage describes Belial not as persecuting believers, but rather as tricking those outside the Community into believing that their own, illicit interpretation of the law is actually correct. The result, however, is similar to the situation depicted in the Community Rule. Both the Community and its laws are rejected by the masses during the period that Belial rules. In this way, the "dominion of Belial" denotes a period of persecution while also providing an explanation for the dismissal of the Community's laws and the isolation of the Community itself, blaming both dismissal and persecution on the scheming of a powerful and demonic presence.

Consequently, in Qumran thought, the present period is not merely a mix of evil and good as in Zoroastrianism: it is *pure* evil, but only within the fixed time that has been allowed Belial according to the mysteries of the Deity. The contrast with Zoroastrian thought, according to which the current age is a mix of good *and* bad, may be most easily explained by the unique situation and social reality of the Qumran Community. Zoroastrian concepts of the eschatological age necessarily morphed to better reflect the experience of Qumran sectarians.

THE PROBLEM OF INFLUENCE

The survey above demonstrates that, as often as Qumran texts indicate the influence of Iranian thought, more in-depth comparisons reveal substantial differences. For example, as explored above, while the dualism found at Qumran could be seen as evidence of influence, it is not paired with the emphasis on choice that characterizes the Gāthās. The "choice" to commit to the commandments of God is found in Qumran texts specifically in the Damascus Document, a non-dualistic text. Qumran eschatology reflects Iranian influence, but includes the belief in a present period distinguished by complete evil, not a mixture of evil and good. Other differences are subtler, such as the expanded use of the term *rwḥ* compared to *mēnōg*. Nevertheless, based simply on the evidence outlined in this article, it is difficult to deny that the Iranian worldview influenced Qumran thought. Yet, the question of how this influence could have transpired is not easily answered.

In fact, the possibility of direct influence of Iranian thought on Second Temple Judaism has been cast into doubt by more recent scholarship.[49] The tracing of Iranian influence at Qumran is made particularly difficult by the lack of textual evidence for Zoroastrian thought contemporary to the non-biblical Dead Sea Scrolls, which are dated from the second century BCE to the first century CE. Zoroastrian texts were transmitted orally and have survived only in much later writings dating from the Sassanian period (ca. 500–600 CE) and in Pahlavi translations dated even later during the Islamic period (in the ninth century CE). The fact that extant Zoroastrian texts were put into writing much later than the Second Temple period, while ostensibly reflecting much earlier oral traditions, means that a search for exact linguistic parallels between Iranian texts and the Dead Sea Scrolls would seem quixotic.[50] Tracing Iranian influence thus requires an examination of both the extant texts' faithfulness to their oral source and how such oral accounts could have reached Jews in the Second Temple period.

It is the latter issue in particular that has called the idea of direct influence of Zoroastrian texts on the Judaism of the Second Temple period into question.[51] While Shaked counseled that "circumspect use can be

---

49. See Skjaervo, "Zoroastrian Dualism," 89; Y. Elman, "Zoroastrianism and Qumran," in *The Dead Sea Scrolls at 60: Scholarly Contributions of New York University Faculty and Alumni*, ed. L. H. Schiffman and S. Tzoref, Studies on the Texts of the Desert of Judah 89 (Leiden: Brill, 2010), 91–98.

50. See the contrasting approaches of de Jong and García Martínez discussed below.

51. See Skjaervo, "Zoroastrian Dualism," 89. Elman, "Zoroastrianism and Qumran," 91–98. Elman has further proposed that many parallels between Zoroastrian thought and Qumran ideas are the result of a shared fundamentalist mindset as defined by R. J. Frey, *Fundamentalism*, Global Issues (New York: Facts on File, 2007).

made of the old layers of tradition preserved in the late Middle Persian, or Pahlavi, books,"[52] more recently, many scholars have argued that mere circumspection is insufficient. Specifically, the idea that old Avestan texts were somehow transmitted to Judeans in the Second Temple period is difficult to justify: the original languages of the Gāthās (both Old and Young Avestan) were barely understood in the late Achaemenid period, when Judeans were most clearly exposed to Iranian thought. Consequently, as Prods Oktor Skjaervo has argued, it is difficult to explain how Zoroastrianism could influence other religions except as the result of either observation of actual practices or discussions with others familiar with Zoroastrian beliefs.[53] This type of influence would not produce clear textual parallels with the Avestan texts themselves.

The result of these questions has been a wide range of approaches to the possibility of Persian influence on Qumran thought and a reluctance to claim a direct impact of Iranian thought on Qumran texts. In a recent article, Yaakov Elman and Shai Secunda have noted possible Persian influences on Judaism of the Hellenistic period, while entirely omitting Qumran and the Scrolls from their discussion.[54] Regarding the faithfulness of later written copies to the ancient oral source of Zoroastrian works, García Martínez leans on the side of the belief that later written versions are reliable.[55] García Martínez argues that probable influence can be shown if the influenced text under discussion shares a general idea as well as a concrete, specific detail (a "motif") with the influencing works,[56] while for influence to be *proven* there must be a "lexical

52. Shaked, "Iranian Influence on Judaism," 312.

53. Skjaervo, "Zoroastrian Dualism," 89.

54. Y. Elman and S. Secunda, "Judaism," in *The Wiley-Blackwell Companion to Zoroastrianism*, ed. M. Stausberg and Y. Vevaina, Wiley-Blackwell Companions to Religion (Oxford: Wiley Blackwell, 2015), 423-35. (An earlier version of the same article, generously shared by the authors, did include the Scrolls.) Citing previous work by Hintze, Hultgård and Shaked, Elman and Secunda's examples of Persian influence include the demon Asmodeus in the apocryphal Book of Tobit, the idea that treasures are stored up in heaven as reward for good deeds performed on earth, the personification of deeds that precede the deceased, and the fate of the soul immediately after death, which in their view have developed in conversation with Zoroastrianism. They also note Persian influence on Jewish messianism and the belief in bodily resurrection.

55. F. García Martínez, "Iranian Influences in Qumran?," in *Qumranica Minora I: Qumran Origins and Apocalypticism*, ed. E. Tigchelaar, Studies on the Texts of the Desert of Judah 63 (Leiden: Brill, 2007), 229.

56. Ibid., 230.

connection," such as a loan word or a clear translation.⁵⁷ García Martínez consequently finds that while there is considerable *probable* Iranian influence in the *Testament of the Two Spirits* and the *War Scroll*, the lack of a clear terminological parallel means that there is no way to be sure of such influence.⁵⁸

In contrast, in Albert de Jong's survey of Iranian influence at Qumran, de Jong argues against the possibility of finding either linguistic *or* literary connections. He notes that using Avestan texts such as the Gāthās is particularly problematic, as there is little evidence to suggest that these were ever used as a "source" to be consulted for religious information.⁵⁹ He prefers an approach that focuses on structural parallels while trying to answer the question of "why the sectarian texts from Qumran present so many *more* parallels with Iranian notions than the rest of Jewish literature."⁶⁰

SUGGESTED SOLUTIONS

The variety of questions raised regarding the possibility of influence is matched by the range of solutions that have been offered, including historical contexts, paradigmatic worldviews, and possible chains of transmission.

Historical Context

De Jong, while doubting that the Gāthās could have directly influenced any Jewish text, posits two possible "contexts" for the contact of Second Temple Jews with Iranian ideas. The first is the well-known interaction with the Persian Empire during the Achaemenid period (550–330 BCE) when Judea was "Yehud," a province of the Empire.⁶¹ The second, a less familiar historical context to those who search for points of interaction

57. Ibid., 232.

58. Ibid., 233–41.

59. De Jong, "Iranian Connections," 482; idem, "Religion at the Achaemenid Court," in *Der Achamenidenhof / The Achaemenid Court: Akten des 2. Internationalen Kolloquiums zum Thema "Vorderasien im Spannungsfeld klassischer und altorientalischer Überlieferungen" Landgut Castelen bei Basel, 23.–25. Mai 2007*, ed. B. Jacobs and R. Rollinger, Classica et orientalia 2 (Wiesbaden: Harrassowitz, 2010), 537–38.

60. De Jong, "Iranian Connections," 496.

61. Ibid., 485.

between the Jews and Iranian thought, is the rise of the Parthians in the third century BCE and their status as the most notable opponent of the Seleucids.[62] However, as de Jong notes, most of the interaction between Parthians and Jews (such as the installation of Antigonus in 40 BCE) took place later than the dates usually assigned to sectarian texts from Qumran.[63] (Dating of these texts ranges from the second to the first century BCE, but even the latest accepted dating is earlier than 40 BCE.) Moreover, the contact between Parthians and Jews centered on politics and war, neither of which is conducive for the transmission of religious hymns or philosophical approaches.

Finally, there is the question of Iranian settings in Jewish texts. Iranian settings were common in Hellenistic works in general, and most are strikingly similar to each other, indicating that these settings are merely imported "decor" rather than true evidence of influence.[64] But the Qumran non-sectarian text "proto-Esther" includes Iranian terminology that is not usually found in texts of Palestinian origin, and consequently, Shaked posits that this work may have been composed by Jews of the East who lived near the court.[65] If so, its survival in Judean context is significant, and indicates yet another means of the transmission of ideas between Iran and Judea.

The Fundamentalist Mindset

Elman has proposed that the similarities between Zoroastrian ideas and those found at Qumran is simply the result of a shared mindset: fundamentalism. For the purposes of his argument, Elman borrows from Peter Berger, who defines fundamentalism, first, by its cognitive style, the "uptight and militant" manner in which a fundamentalist affirms her belief, and second, by its conflict with traditional religion.[66] Elman also notes Rebecca Frey's more extensive definition, which includes nine characteristics, among them a concern about the decline of religion sparking a

---

62. Ibid., 486–87.
63. Ibid., 487.
64. De Jong, "Iranian Connections," 486.
65. S. Shaked, "Qumran: Some Iranian Connections," in *Solving Riddles and Untying Knots: Biblical, Epigraphic, and Semitic Studies in Honor of Jonas C. Greenfield*, ed. J. C. Greenfield et al. (Winona Lake, IN: Eisenbrauns, 1995), 281.
66. P. L. Berger, "Foreword," in Frey, *Fundamentalism*, v–vi.

defensive or protective attitude toward religious belief, dualistic "black-and-white" thinking, an apocalyptic view of history, and a belief in election or chosenness.[67] Elman's conclusion is that any resemblance between Qumran ideology and Zoroastrianism is due to a "similarity of cognitive style." However, Qumran predestinarianism, which contrasts with the Zoroastrian belief in choice, is connected to Qumran ideas of chosenness and the rigidity of Qumran belief, another result of the fundamentalist mindset.[68] According to Elman's approach, Iranian influence is negated and similarities between Iranian and Qumran texts are mainly coincidental, having the same fundamentalistic underpinnings.

Orality and Influence

In a forthcoming article,[69] the present writer has argued that the similarities between the *Visions of Amram* and Yasna 30 discussed above, which are far greater than those between the *Treatise* and the same Yasna, are due to the more facile transmission of ideas via oral folklore. The narrative setting of the *Visions of Amram* provides a clue to how certain Zoroastrian ideas could have made their way via shared stories to the Qumran Community, been modified to fit a monotheistic framework, however uncomfortably, and then included in central texts such as the *Treatise*. The oral transmission of folklore provides a more probable medium for communicating the ideas in oral Zoroastrian works and would allow for easier molding of these ideas to a monotheistic Qumran worldview.

CONCLUSION

While this survey is hardly the first and will certainly not be the last to trace Iranian influence at Qumran, it is hoped that it has added to the ongoing discussion. In particular, a survey of possible evidence of Iranian influence highlights just how new ideas are molded to suit the substrate of their new environment, allowing them to become an intrinsic part of a worldview which may not have been able to adopt these ideas in their "pure," original form.

67. Elman, "Zoroastrianism and Qumran," 95–96; Frey, *Fundamentalism*.
68. Ibid., 96–97.
69. Brand, "Spirited Evil."

The clearest example of this can be found in Qumran dualism, which apparently owes much to Iranian dualism, particularly the idea central to the *Treatise of the Two Spirits* that there is a conflict between two spirits, each ruling over light or darkness, who fight over the individual for good and for evil. Yet, the individual choice emphasized in the Gāthās is nowhere to be found in the *Treatise of the Two Spirits*. Rather, this dualistic idea has been transformed to support the generally deterministic outlook of the Qumran community.

The "dominion of Belial" reflects a similar adaption of an Iranian idea, that of an age before the eschaton in which evil is allowed to exist. In Qumran texts, unlike the mixture of good and evil that characterizes the present age in Zoroastrian thought, the sect must contend with a *purely* evil era in which Belial is allowed free reign. This modified idea better suited the self-perception of Qumran sectarian as a righteous group that, nonetheless, suffers continuous persecution and rejection.

The evidence of Iranian loanwords and concepts is inconclusive in that it cannot prove direct influence from Iranian ideas on Qumran theology or texts, but it may simply be the result of the adoption of Iranian words into Imperial Aramaic. Yet, given the Qumran community's propensity to tailor external ideas for its own needs, it may well be that the shift in the semantic range of *rwḥ*, "spirit," to denote abstract and individual qualities as well as evil demons reflects not only a development of biblical ideas but also the indirect influence of Iranian worldviews. Thus, Qumran dualism, eschatology, and fundamentalist mindset may owe much to their Iranian forebears, but in their final form they are undeniably "Qumranian."

While direct influence between Iranian texts and the Qumran scrolls remains unlikely, rejecting influence unequivocally is far too absolute given the complexity of the ancient world. This complexity obviates the need of providing a single "solution" to the problem of influence. It may well be that such influence resulted from a combination of contact with the Persian Empire during the Achaemenid period, immigration of Jews from the East, and oral folklore traditions, an influence considerably facilitated by similarities in the fundamentalist mindsets. In a world where "new" ancient manuscripts may yet be discovered, we can hope that some of the issues of Iranian influence at Qumran will one day be resolved. In the meantime, the gratification of pondering the numerous possibilities provides its own compensation to scholars of Iran and Qumran alike.

3

The Image of the Jews in Zoroastrian Literature

Mahnaz Moazami

Sasanian Iran was a poly-ethnic, pluralistic society. The empire extended over a large part of western Asia, far beyond the borders of modern Iran; it included the ancient lands of Mesopotamia, the areas of modern Afghanistan, and the Central Asian Republics. The dynasty lasted from the third to the seventh centuries CE.

During their reign, the majority of Iranians, that is, speakers of one of the Iranian languages living in the Sasanian Empire, were Zoroastrian. As a result, Zoroastrianism became the official religion of the empire. At the same time, and as implied above, the Sasanian empire stretched far beyond the Iranian-speaking world and was home to a variety of different peoples with different languages and religions. The Western part of the empire, for example, was populated by a large number of Aramaic-speaking Jews, Christians, Manicheans, and Mandeans.

The Sasanian era was a crucially formative period in the history of all these religious traditions. It was during these centuries that the Babylonian Talmud, the great compilation of rabbinic tradition, was compiled, codified, and redacted (220–500 CE); the Church of the East and its doctrines gradually took shape;[1] Manichaeism spread over both

1. I. Gillman and H. J. Klimkeit, *Christians in Asia Before 1500* (Ann Arbor: University of Michigan Press, 1999), 109–27.

the Iranian and Roman empires; and the Zoroastrian religious identity became more defined and clearly articulated.

The non-Zoroastrian communities living under Sasanian rule were granted a certain degree of freedom of worship. They were allowed to have their own court to deal with religious and communal disputes, and they had the right to collect their own taxes, in addition to the *pro capita* taxes they had to contribute to the Sasanian administration.[2]

In this Zoroastrian-dominated society, Jews coexisted peacefully with Zoroastrians, and there were even productive cultural exchanges. Anecdotes preserved in the Talmud point to cordial relationships between leading Jewish figures and Sasanian monarchs, especially the two Shapurs and the queen-mother of Shapur II (309–79 CE), Ifra Hormiz(d). The Sasanian monarchs respected their Jewish subjects not only on a personal or civil basis but also in matters of religion.[3]

An illustration of the way in which rabbinic sources describe this respect is a Talmudic passage (Taʿanit 24b) describing how, when Shapur wished to chastise the rabbi Rava for administering corporal punishment, Ifra Hormiz(d) defended Rava. She advised her son not to become involved with the Jews since "their God gives them whatever they ask of Him," a claim which then promptly received miraculous confirmation. She asked for rain in the summer season, and Rava prayed for mercy, and the rain poured down until the gutters of Mahoza emptied their contents into the Tigris.[4]

Another episode in the Talmud (Avodah Zarah 76b) offers an example of tactful courtesy in the encounter between Zoroastrians and Jews: while entertaining Mar Yehudah, King Shapur was careful to cleanse his knife by repeatedly plunging it in the earth before cutting a slice of fruit

---

2. See A. Christensen, *L'Iran sous les Sassanides* (Copenhague: Munksgaard, 1944) 38; D. Goodblatt, "The Poll Tax in Sasanian Babylonia: The Talmudic Evidence," *Journal of the Economic and Social History of the Orient* 22 (1979): 233–95.

3. J. Wiesehöfer, *Ancient Persia from 550 BCE to 650 AD* (London: Tauris, 1996), 216–21; Y. Elman, "Middle Persian Culture and Babylonian Sages: Accommodation and Resistance in the Shaping of Rabbinic Legal Tradition," in *The Cambridge Companion to the Talmud and Rabbinic Literature*, ed. Ch. E. Fonrobert and M. S. Jaffee, Cambridge Companions to Philosophy, Religion and Culture (Cambridge: Cambridge University Press, 2007), 165–97.

4. All Talmudic passages are cited from Soncino *Babylonian Talmud*, translated into English with Notes, Glossary and Indices under the editorship of Rabbi Dr. I. Epstein (available at http://halakhah.com/).

to offer his Jewish guest, thereby complying with the laws of *kashrut* regarding utensils that had been previously used for non-kosher food.

Although the truth of such anecdotal evidence cannot be verified, the very fact that Jews did tell such stories demonstrates their favorable view of the royal family.[5] In addition, at least one prominent rabbi, Rabbi Nahman, seems to have named one of his daughters after one of the founding queens of the Sasanian dynasty, Denag (Kiddushin 70b).

Despite these observations, from the Jewish point of view, harmony and peaceful co-existence did not always reign in the land. On the one hand, Yazdgird I (399-420) married Shoshendokht, the daughter of the Jewish *resh galuta*, or head of the Babylonian Jewry (Exilarch), and he showed tolerance and even favor to Christians and other minorities, gaining thereby the enduring sobriquet "the Sinner"[6] or "the Harsh One"[7] among the Zoroastrians. On the other hand, the reigns of Yazdgird II (439-57) and his son Peroz (459-84) in the fifth century signaled a reversal of policies:[8] there was systematic persecution directed at the Jews and concrete evidence of violations of their religious freedom, such as forbidding them to openly and publicly celebrate the Sabbath, the closure of Jewish schools, and the execution of some of their leaders.[9]

A Talmudic passage (Gittin 16b-17a) relates that Rabbah b. Bar Ḥannah was once ill, and Reb Judah and Rabbah went to his home to inquire about his health. During their visit, they asked him a question regarding divorce. He was about to answer the question when a Zoroastrian priest entered the home of Rabbah b. Bar Ḥannah and removed the lamp which was set before the host and his guests, supposedly because it was some Zoroastrian festival during which the lighting of fire was forbidden. At this point, Rabbah b. Bar Ḥannah commented ruefully on his life in Babylonia compared to that in Rome: "O All Merciful One! (Let us live) either in your shadow or in the shadow of the son of Esau," referring to

---

5. See Y. Elman, "Acculturation to Elite Persian Norms and Modes of Thought in the Babylonian Jewish Community of Late Antiquity," in *Neti'ot le-David*, ed. Yaakov Elman, Ephraim Bezalel Halivni, and Zvi Arie Steinfeld (Jerusalem: Orh.ot, 2004), 31–56.

6. Pahl. *bazakkar* as in J. Markwart, *A Catalogue of the Provincial Capitals of Ērānshahr*, ed. G. Messina, Analecta Orientalia 3 (Rome: Pontifical Biblical Institute, 1931), 67.

7. *dabr*; cf. ibid, 67.

8. Wiesehofer, *Ancient Persia from 550 BC to 650 AD*, 215–16.

9. J. Neusner, "Jews in Iran," in *The Cambridge History of Iran*, vol. 3/2, ed. E. Yarshater (Cambridge: Cambridge University Press, 1983), 915.

the period before the Zoroastrians came to Babylon and the period subsequent to their coming. In other words, living under the Sasanian rule was regarded as unbearable.¹⁰ But as Richard Kalmin points out, some of the measures taken by the Zoroastrian clergy against the Jews were not necessarily and primarily prompted by an urge to persecute them, but rather they represent ways in which the clergy of different persuasions strove to safeguard their own religious laws. The same tendency can be observed in the way the Jewish community sought to demarcate and secure their laws.¹¹

During the Sasanian era, Iranian nationalism was revived and buttressed in part through the formation of a centralized Zoroastrian religious organization, inseparable from the royal authority of the state. The high priest, Kartir, after an initial struggle to win over the patronage of Shapur I (240–72), overcame his opponent Mani and established Zoroastrianism throughout the empire. Kartir served five consecutive Sasanian kings and ordered four inscriptions that supply valuable information about that period.¹² Kartir, who was only a simple priest under the reign of King Shapur I, managed to wield great power under his successors. He proclaimed himself the restorer of Zoroastrianism in Iran and claimed, among other things, that "Throughout the realm, Jews (*yahud*), Buddhists (*shaman*), Hindus (*braman*), Nazoreans (*nazara*) and Christians, Baptists (*magdag*) and Manicheans (*zandig*) were struck down, idol temples were destroyed, and the lairs of the demons were ruined and turned into thrones and seats for the gods."¹³ It should be kept in mind that, apart

---

10. See R. Brody, "Judaism in the Sasanian Empire: A Case Study in Religious Coexistence," in *Irano-Judaica* II, ed. S. Shaked and A. Netzer (Jerusalem: Ben-Zvi Institute for the Study of Jewish Communities in the East, 1990), 56–57. The attitude of the Sasanians to their Jewish subjects differed widely from that of the comparatively tolerant Arsacids, who ruled Iran from circa 250 BCE to circa 226 CE. According to a Talmudic passage, the Babylonian Jews informed the third-century Palestinian patriarch Yehudah that although "They [i.e., Arsacids] are like the armies of the House of David, the Guebers [i.e., Sasanian Zoroastrians] are like the destroying angels" (Kiddushin 72a).

11. R. Kalmin, *Jewish Babylonia Between Persia and Roman Palestine* (New York: Oxford University Press, 2006), 130–38.

12. Three of the inscriptions are at Naqsh-i Rajab and Naqsh-i Rustam near Persepolis; the fourth is at Sar Mashad on an ancient highway between Susa and Persepolis, where he records the deeds of a mighty and eventful career and the multitude of titles bestowed on him.

13. P. O. Skjærvø, *The Spirit of Zoroastrianism* (New Haven: Yale University Press 2011), 238; D. N. MacKenzie, "Kerdir's Inscription," in *The Sasanian Rock Reliefs at*

for Mani, there is no evidence of actions against non-Zoroastrians during Kartir's tenure. The religious policy set out in Kartir's inscriptions was perhaps intended for internal consumption and designed to envisage an ideal plan, a guide for the future. It should be regarded as a literary construct based upon what the official religion of the land should prescribe, rather than taken as the outcome of direct observation of actual historical events, though the timing is significant. In the Sasanian Empire, several religious movements, including the official religion, vied with each other to attract adherents; Zoroastrians were challenged by members of other faiths over details and principles on which they differed.[14] In this context, Zoroastrian authorities felt compelled to draw up new restrictions, suppress rival religions, and attempt major changes in the multi-confessional society of the Sasanian period, thereby affirming their distinct social and religious identity.

Zoroastrian authorities also composed theological works, notably the *Dinkard*[15] (Deeds of the *Den*) and *Shkand Gumanik Wizar*[16] (Doubt-Destroying Exposition), which defended the articles of their faith against Christian, Jewish, Manichean, and Muslim attacks. The mention and inclusion of Muslims is a reminder that Zoroastrian literature was committed to writing only in the Islamic period, particularly in the ninth and tenth centuries CE, well after the Arab-Muslim conquest of Iran. This

---

Naqsh-i Rustam, Iranische Denkmaler, Lief. 13, Reihe II: Iranische Felsreliefs, I (Berlin: Wasmuth, 1989), 35–72, paragraphs 9 and 11. Ph, Gignoux, *Les quatre inscriptions du Mage Kirdīr: Textes et concordances,* Collection des sources pour l'histoire de l'Asie centrale pré-islamique II/I = Studia Iranica, cahier 9 (Paris: Association pour l'avancement des études iraniennes 1991); P. O. Skjærvø, "Kartīr," in *Encyclopaedia Iranica*, ed. E. Yarshater, vol. 15 (New York: Encyclopaedia Iranica Foundation, 2011), 608–28.

14. According to *Dinkard* Book IV, Shapur II (r. 309–379) held religious disputations to examine and investigate all utterances. D. M. Madan, ed., *The Complete Text of the Pahlavi Dinkard (Dinkard)*, 2 vols. (Bombay: Society for the Promotion of Researches into the Zoroastrian Religion, 1911), 413.2–8. M. Boyce, *Zoroastrians: Their Religious Beliefs and Practices* (London: Routledge & Kegan Paul, 1979), 118; M. Shaki, "The Denkard Account of the History of the Zoroastrian Scriptures," *Archiv Orientální* 49 (1981): 119.

15. *Dinkard* is one of the main Zoroastrian religious texts. It consisted of nine books, but the first, second, and part of the third book are no longer extant. The contents of the book, which is essentially a compilation, belong to different periods, but the final redaction took place in the ninth century.

16. J. de Menasce, *Une apologétique mazdéenne du IXe siècle: Škand-gumānīk vičār. La solution décisive des doutes*, Texte pazand-pehlevi transcript, traduit et commenté (Fribourg, Switzerland: Librairie de l'Université, 1945).

took place at a time when the pressure on Zoroastrians to convert to Islam was increasing and their clergy feared they could no longer preserve their traditions through oral transmission. In spite of their late production, the content of the Zoroastrian books reflects older tradition and concerns.

Jews and Judaism are subjects of several controversies in Zoroastrian literature.[17] In the *Dinkard*, Judaism is presented as an 'evil' religion, originating from Dahag (Av. *Azi Dahaka-*):

> "He (Dahag) made *orayta*,[18] the fundamental book of Judaism, and built Jerusalem in order to keep [the *orayta* ?] in it. Dahag first came to Abraham, the chief of the Jews, and from Abraham to Moses, whose bond is feeble, and whom the Jews hold as a prophet and a bringer of [their] faith, and took rest (?). He found Moses, and propagated the Jewish faith, and after that, this deceit[19] of the demons. Dahag liked to do harm to creatures, and saw the principle of evil religion in the pronouncement of Judaism. He caused decline in the Zoroastrian religion and Iran through heresy, he destroyed luminosity a second and third time in the world, through that [there came about] victory to the demons and corruption to the character of people, impurity and lying waste to the world, decline and evil to creatures, inversion, distress and hardship to the good, ascent, broadness, and kingship to the bad."[20]

---

17. The references to Jews in Zoroastrian literature have been studied extensively: J. Darmesteter, "Textes pehlevis relatives au Judaisme," *Revue des études juives* 18 and 19 (1889): 1–15; 41–56; L. H. Gray, "The Jews in Pahlavi Literature," in *Actes du XIVe Congrès International des Orientalistes* (Paris: Leroux, 1906), 177–192; J. de Menasce, "Jews and Judaism in the Third Book of the Dēnkart," in *K. R. Cama Oriental Institute Golden Jubilee Volume* (Bombay: K. R. Cama Oriental Institute, 1969), 45–48; M. Molé, *Culte mythe et cosmologie dans l'Iran ancient: Le problème zoroastrien et la tradition mazdéenne* (Paris: Presses universitaires de France, 1963); S. Shaked, "Zoroastrian Polemics against Jews in the Sasanian and Early Islamic Period," in *Irano-Judaica* II, ed. S. Shaked and A. Netzer (Jerusalem: Ben-Zvi Institute for the Study of Jewish Communities in the East, 1990), 85–104; A. F. de Jong, "Zoroastrian Self-Definition in Contact with Other Faiths," in *Irano-Judaica* V, ed. S. Shaked and A. Netzer, eds. (Jerusalem: Ben-Zvi Institute, 2004), 16–26; E. Ahdut, "Ha-Pulmus ha-Yehudi-Zoroastri ba-Talmud ha-Bavli" (Jewish-Zoroastrian Polemics in the Babylonian Talmud), in *Irano-Judaica* IV, ed. S. Shaked and A. Netzer, eds. (Jerusalem: Ben-Zvi Institute, 1999) 17–40 (Hebrew Section).

18. The Aramaic term for the Torah among Babylonian and Iranian Jews in the Sasanian period.

19. Deceit (*frēb*) announces the rule of evil and the author associates Moses with evil.

20. Shaked, "Zoroastrian Polemics against Jews in the Sasanian and Early Islamic

In the Avesta, Dahag is depicted as a three-headed giant of a dragon. He worshipped Anahita in the land of Baβri and Vaiiu in the inaccessible Kuuiri☒ta. The tradition has interpreted Baβri as Babylon and Kuuiri☒ta as the castle of Dahag in Babylon.²¹ According to *Dinkard* VII, with the aid of sorcery, Dahag had made many wonderful things in Babel, thus luring people into idolatry in order to destroy the world, but Zoroaster recited the words of the religion and successfully countered Dahag's design.²² *Dinkard IX relates that* Dahag possessed five defects: greed, want of energy, indolence, defilement, and illicit intercourse.²³ And in the *Dadestan-i Denig* (The Judgment of The *Den*), Dahag is said to have been one of the seven worst sinners ever; that is, those who are closest to the Evil Spirit himself.²⁴

In Zoroastrian literature, Dahag is generally identified as a non-Iranian. Different texts make him out to be a Babylonian, an Indian, a Jew, an Arab, or whatever specific modification best suits the immediate purpose and political context of its use.²⁵ In the *Dinkard*, Judaism is exhibited as the demonic power blended into the Iranian mythological conception. As S. Shaked has noted, the important point here is that

---

Period," 99; J. de Menasce, *Le Troisième livre du Dēnkart: Traduit du pehlevi* (Paris: Klinsksieck, 1973), 240; D. M. Madan, ed., *The Complete Text of the Pahlavi Dinkard* (*Dinkard*) (Bombay: Society for the Promotion of Researches into the Zoroastrian Religion, 1911), 239.

21. See P. O. Skjærvø, "AŽDAHA," in *Encyclopaedia Iranica*, ed. E. Yarshater, vol. 3 (London: Routledge & Kegan Paul, 1989), 191–99. J. Darmesteter, *Le Zend Avesta*, Annales du Musée Guimet, 3 vols. (Paris: Librairie d'Amérique et d'Orient Adrien-Maisonneuve, [1st ed. 1892–93, repr. 1960], *Yasht*. 5.29, vol. II, 375 and *Yasht* 15.19–21), 584.

22. *Dinkard Book VII*, 639.5–10; M. Molé, *La Légende de Zoroastre selon les textes pehlevis*, (Paris: Klinckieck, 1967), chap. 7.4.72.

23. *Dinkard Book IX*, 789. 15–18.

24. *Dādestān i Dēnēg*, The Pahlavi Codex K35 (Copenhagen: Levin & Munksgaard, 1934), chap. 71, 221.

25. During the World War II, Kimon Evan Marengo, the political cartoonist, on the suggestion of Mojtaba Minovi, created a cotemporary version of Dahag/Zahhak, portraying him as Hitler. The two snakes would represent Mussolini and Tojo, the Japanese commander-in-chief and prime minister, while the devil, who inspires Zahhak and is disguised as a cook in the *Shahnameh*, was to be portrayed as Goebbels. See V. Holman,"Kem's Cartoons in the Second World War," *History Today* (March 2002): 21–27; reference kindly provided by Mohsen Ashtiany.

Jewish mythology takes the place of the Iranian mythology concerning Dahag and becomes part of the religious history of the Iranian religion.[26]

The concept of monotheism in Judaism is criticized in several other passages of the *Dinkard* by citing the inconsistencies and contradictions that arise from a conception of a deity that is responsible for everything in the world, including evil:

> The existence [of the following] is impossible: if the ignorance of the ignorant and the sinfulness of the sinful, which are manifest in the material world, are [regarded as] mixed together with the wisdom of the wise and the virtuousness of the virtuous [and are considered to be] of one single source and origin, as is the doctrine of the Jews. For both wisdom and ignorance [to come] from one common source [is thus impossible]. Nor is one and the same person manifestly [both] wise and ignorant. That principle to which belongs ignorance, and the ignorant person himself, and to which belongs sinfulness, and the sinful person himself, is not the pure Bounteous Spirit, but the Evil Spirit.[27]

Dinkard V,[28] which includes the answers of Adur Farnbay i Farrokhzadan, the leader of the followers of the Good Religion, to Yakob son of Khalid and the book called Gemara (Pahl. *Simra*), is less hostile. In *The Dadestan-i Menog-i Xrad* (The Judgments of the Divine Wisdom), the wise man asks the spirit of divine wisdom about the various beneficial outcomes of the reign of each ancient ruler. About Lohrasp, the legendry Kayanian king, the spirit of the divine wisdom says that his contribution was that he had destroyed Jerusalem and dispersed the Jews.[29] Additionally, according to the Dinkard (5.1.4–5), he sent an army to Hrom (Rome) and Jerusalem with Boxt-Narse (Nebuchadnezzar) to eradicate the evil laws and deeds, as well as the demon worship of the Bani-Srayel.

Examples from the opposite side, criticizing the Iranian religion, are found in the Talmud and treatises of *halakhah*, *aggadah*, or exegesis, and later in the Geonic literature in the form of incidental and passing remarks. For example, there is the well-known theological dispute between

---

26. Shaked, "Zoroastrian Polemics Against Jews in the Sasanian and Early Islamic Period," 90.

27. *Dinkard* Book III, 173.4. Shaked, "Zoroastrian Polemics Against Jews in the Sasanian and Early Islamic Period," 96.

28. J. Amouzgar and A. Tafazzoli, eds., *Le Cinquième livre du Dēnkard* (Paris: Association pour l'Avancement des études iraniennes, 2000), 22–23.

29. A. Tafazzoli, ed., *Mēnōg ī Xrad* (Tehran: Tus, 1985), chap. 26:64.

an unnamed Magus and Amemar in Sanhedrin 39a regarding Zoroastrian dualism in which Amemar notes that the physiology of urination contradicts the Zoroastrian theology:

> "A magi once said to Amemar: From the middle of your [body] upwards belongs to Ormuzd; from the middle downwards, to Ahriman. The latter asked: Why then does Ahriman permit Ormuzd to send water through his territory?"[30]

In another anecdote, R. Joseph describes Persians as those who eat and drink like a bear, are corpulent like a bear, are overgrown with hair like a bear, and are restless like a bear (Kiddushin 72a). When R. Ammi saw a Persian riding he would say, "There is [goes] a wandering bear!" (Avodah Zarah 2b).[31] In the Zoroastrian classification of animals, the bear is an animal created by the Evil Spirit and its creation with some other evil creatures is attributed to the union of Jam, the mythical king of Iran and his twin sister Jami with demons.[32] Although the anecdote expresses the critical opinion of R. Joseph of the Persians, it also suggests that he was well-acquainted with Zoroastrian theology, since letting one's hair grow like a bear's alludes to disheveled hair, a physical feature of the demons.

An important Zoroastrian work, whose composition is available only in Pazand, that is, in Middle Persian transcribed into Avestan letters, with its very name hinting at its contents, is *Shkand Gumanik Wizar* (Doubt-Destroying Exposition). The book can be dated to the second half of the ninth century, and as the editor of the text, J. de Menasce, notes, Mardan-Farrokh has provided us with a work describing the theology and apologetics of Zoroastrian dualism in the latest stage of its historical development,[33] before its slow decline to become the religion of a small minority that it is today.

Shkand Gumanik Wizar contains the most sophisticated polemics against beliefs of other religions known in Zoroastrian literature. It can be

---

30. The passage is already addressed by E. Ahdut, "Ha-Pulmus ha-Yehudi-Zoroastri ba-Talmud ha-Bavli," in *Irano-Judaica* IV, 17–40.

31. Avodah Zarah 2b: "On the departure of the Kingdom of Rome, Persia will step forth. Why Persia next?—Because they are next in importance. And how do we know this?—Because it is written: *And behold another beast, a second like to a bear* [Dan. VII, 5] and R. Joseph learned [Kid. 72a] that this refers to the Persians."

32. *Bundahišn*, TD1, fol. 44r, 44v.; B. T. Anklesaria, *Zand-Ākāsīh: Iranian or Greater Bundahišn* (Bombay: Rahnumae Mazdayasnan Sabha), chap. 14B, pp. 136–37.

33. J. de Menasce, *Une apologétique mazdéenne du IXe siècle*, 14.

assigned to that same apologetic genre to which the first three preserved books of the *Dinkard* also belong. Here, however, reason dominates over myth, and the author's arguments are detailed and couched in rational terms.[34]

Its author, Mardan-Farrokh, presents himself as a seeker in quest of truth who, after a long search that had led him to study other religions, had finally realized that he could find what he was looking for in his own faith of Zoroastrianism. Given this context, the author's intention in writing the book is to demonstrate the truth and validity of the teachings of the Zoroastrian faith, as well as to evaluate the dichotomies and discrepancies inherent in other religious beliefs.

The contents of *Shkand Gumanig Wizar* indicate that the author was familiar with many parts of the Bible and with the apocryphal, pseudepigraphic, and *aggadic* literature; additionally, his knowledge of the Bible was probably derived from a Syriac version.[35] The book also demonstrates the close involvement of Zoroastrians with the religious ideas of other faiths and shows how the author had tried to defend the integrity of his own faith by exposing the inherent deficiency of others.

Two chapters in the book criticize aspects of Judaism. Chapter thirteen gives an account of the story of creation as told in Genesis. The chapter contains a long argument against the biblical conception of God, particularly as it is expressed in the narrative of the creation of light.[36] The author tries to show that the story of the creation of light as told in the Bible implies a dualistic[37] conception of God, and that the God of the Bible is inferior and less powerful than Ohrmazd.[38]

---

34. C. G. Cereti, *La Letteratura Pahlavi: Introduzione ai testi con riferimenti alla storia degli studi e alla tradizione manoscritta* (Milan: Associazione Culturale Mimesis, 2001), 79.

35. Interchange between Persian and Syriac literature, especially the eastern Nestorian branch of the latter, took place in the fifth-sixth centuries and continued into the ninth century. We know that Nestorian jurisprudence was under the influence of the Talmudic law. It is legitimate, therefore, to assume that Syriac writings formed the venue through which the knowledge of the Bible and Talmudic legends reached Mardan-Farrokh, who was one of the last defenders of Zoroastrianism. See de Menasce, *Une Apologétique Mazdéenne au IXe Siècle*, esp. 177–78.

36. de Menasce, *Une Apologétique Mazdéenne au IXe Siècle*, §§5–11, 183.

37. Zoroastrians consider that their religion was an ethical and essentially monotheistic religion.

38. Ibid., §§59–77, 185–87.

Another aspect criticized by Mardan-Farrokh is the duration of the act of creation: if God created everything ex-nihilo through the power of his Word, why did he need six days to do so?[39] And why did he create Adam and Eve, the Garden of Eden, and the Tree of Knowledge?[40]

Chapter fourteen focuses on what in Zoroastrian eyes appears to be the negative aspects of the omnipotent God of Judaism, such as His wrath and His vengefulness:

"I am Adonai who is vengeance-seeking and vengeance-repaying and I pay the vengeance of the seven generations through the children, and I never forgot the foundation of this vengeance."[41]

This chapter narrates a visit paid by Adonai to an ailing Abraham;[42] this seems to have been pieced together from different *midrashim*.[43]

Mardan-Farrokh uses doctrines from other faiths in order to argue for and bolster the superiority of Zoroastrianism. The book addresses the Zoroastrian community, and in particular those who might have been drawn to other doctrines then prevalent in Iran. It is a polemical argument in the service of theological exposition, rather than a devaluation of rival religions. Such arguments are amply attested to in the Middle Persian texts; for instance, chapter 288 of *Dinkard* Book III presents the ten pieces of malevolent advice of Dahag to mankind, as opposed to the ten good counsels of Jam in chapter 287. From the beginning, the law of Dahag is identified as the law of the Jews. Of the evil advices, number nine mentions the custom of castrating animals and of circumcising all male children as prescribed by the Jews; number ten is against the slaughtering of cattle according to Jewish rites, but none of these points is exclusively Jewish.[44]

Scholars have argued that polemical texts in the Zoroastrian religion were written in order to instruct and educate Zoroastrians and,

---

39. Ibid., §§92–105, 187–89.

40. Ibid., §§121–134, 191.

41. Ibid., §§4–8, 197; Adonai/Ādīnō, the Jewish God, derived from Hebrew 'Adonay.

42. Ibid., §§40–50, 199. Parallel to several midrashim. Gen 17:1: BR 48 and BM 86b. God's visit to Abraham after circumcision (Gen 18:1–20), etc.

43. J. de Menasce, *Une apologétique mazdéenne du IXe siècle*, 176–81.

44. Madan, ed., *The Complete Text of the Pahlavi Dinkard*, 297–98. See J. de Menasce, *Le Troisième livre du Dēnkart: Traduit du pehlevi* (Paris: Klinksieck, 1973), 284–85; Shaked, "Zoroastrian Polemics against Jews in the Sasanian and Early Islamic Period," 103.

perhaps, to prepare them for actual debates with those of other beliefs.[45] This intention would explain the largely stereotypical presentation of religious adversaries.

However, polemical texts are also forms of interreligious communication and provide insight into differing religious outlooks from a historical perspective. The content of Zoroastrian polemical writings, though admittedly one-sided as such polemics are by nature, nevertheless convey pertinent information regarding the position of each religious group in society. They describe both how Zoroastrians regarded the other religion in conflict, and the strategies with which they chose to engage in polemical discord. Moreover, they show how the religion represented itself through the genre of mythologized sacred history.

Further scrutiny of these texts suggests that the overriding motive behind the writings of the Zoroastrians about other faiths was not so much to lay charges against an adversary from another religion; rather, it was closely bound up with internal debates and the diverging opinions within the Zoroastrian religious community itself. Kartir's inscription is significant in this regard. He mentions among his achievements that he promoted the Zoroastrian religion and the good priests, and he honored them. "But the heretics and unbelievers among the clergy who did not adhere to the doctrine regarding the Zoroastrian religion and the rites of the gods—them I punished and I tormented them until I made them better."[46]

In the Sasanian period, the question of conversion was of primary concern and a recurring topic in the discussions of Zoroastrian scholars. It was of sufficiently grave concern to stimulate debates concerning the sin of apostasy. In Middle Persian texts, the punishment for those who had renounced Zoroastrian faith and converted to other religions is death, which gives a sense of the strong rivalries that existed during the Sasanian period between Zoroastrianism and other religions. The same texts argue that the merit of those who save others from apostasy is immense and they are much praised, blessed, and honored. Their righteousness is abundant and their way to the best existence is assured.[47]

---

45. See A. de Jong, "Zoroastrian Self-Definition in Contact with Other Faiths," 16–26.

46. MacKenzie, "Kerdir's Inscription," in *The Sasanian Rock Reliefs at Naqsh-i Rustam*, para. 16, text, 55 and trans. 58–59; see also Skjaervø, "Kartīr," 612 and 617.

47. *Dādestān ī Dēnēg*, The Pahlavi Codex K35 (Copenhagen: Levin & Munksgaard, 1934), chap. 41, 167.

For the Zoroastrian jurists and imperial authorities, conversion was a major factor weakening the fabrics of the faith, a problem that remained of serious concern to the court until the end of the dynasty. A passage in *The Letter of Tansar*, a text composed in the name of a priest from the reign of Adashir I, which describes the introduction of formal procedures for prosecuting cases of apostasy, illustrates these points:

> The king of kings has established a law far better than that of the ancients. For in former days, any man who turned from the faith was swiftly and speedily put to death and punished. The king of kings has ordered that such a man should be imprisoned and that for the space of a year, learned men should summon him at frequent intervals and advise him and lay arguments before him and destroy his doubts. If he becomes penitent and contrite and seek pardon of God, he is set free. If obstinacy and pride hold him back, then he is put to death.[48]

This leads us to conclude that Zoroastrian polemical texts often had an internal function, within a Zoroastrian community, and their main outcome was used to reinforce the belief of their audience and accentuate the positive Zoroastrian doctrine. They had also kept open the paths of dialogue in an empire with many cultures and many religions within its borders, instead of resorting to violence. Zoroastrian authorities recognized the place of other religions in Iran and regarded their institutions as necessary to the empire, a point that distinguished them from their Christian contemporaries in the Roman world. Buddhist, Christians, Jews, and others could flourish within the Zoroastrian ideological framework of the Iranian Empire as long as they did not violate Persian rules and withheld from challenging the superiority of the Good Religion.

---

48. M. Boyce, trans. *The Letter of Tansar* (Rome: Istituto Italiano per il Medio ed Estremo Oriente, 1968), 17/42.

4

Digestion as a Means of Purification in Fourth- and Fifth-Century Sources

A Rabbinic Conundrum and an Avestan Problem

Yaakov Elman

In the last generation a number of scholars have returned to examining the rabbinic literature of late antiquity in its relation to Graeco-Roman culture. They have placed particular emphasis on tannaitic texts, primarily the Mishnah, redacted in Roman Palestine and in the early third century. They have also considered, to a more limited extent, other texts such as the Tosefta and the exegetical midrashim, whose final redaction may have taken place in the two centuries following, and for some of the exegetical midrashim, perhaps even in Babylon.

However, the text, which, for Rabbinic Judaism, became the canonical and universally accepted interpretation of the Mishnah was the Babylonian Talmud (hereafter: the Bavli). Though tightly based on Palestinian materials, the Bavli represents an attempt of rabbis whose cultural context was not Graeco-Roman, but rather composed of a mixture of various elements of Middle Persian and other cultures, to interpret and apply the Mishnah as a guide to their religious lives.

The Bavli may thus be seen as an intercultural zone, in which several centuries of the Babylonian rabbis struggled with the task of domesticating a partly foreign import into a culture that had been, for more than seven centuries, dominated by Iranian mores. In some cases, time-honored Babylonian attitudes and customs simply coexisted with their Graeco-Roman imports, but in most cases an attempt was made to reconcile those mores to the system represented by the Mishnah with Babylonian ones, and, in particular, attitudes which owed much to the Zoroastrian background of their lives.

Three different responses may be detected in the Bavli to Iranian institutions. In some cases, the Rabbis adopted the Iranian practice unchanged; in other cases, they modified it to accord with rabbinic values and belief systems; in yet other cases, Iranian procedures were rejected entirely. Let me illustrate each with an example.

Two prominent rabbis, Rav (who is the one reputed to have brought the Mishnah to Babylonia) and R. Naḥman (whose father served as a scribe to Rav's colleague, Samuel), are reported to have publically contracted temporary marriages when away from home, in keeping with time-honored Iranian practices, without, it would seem, feeling the disjunction between that practice and the stricter rabbinic norms of Roman Palestine.[1]

In contrast, the Zoroastrian requirement of burying nail parings, which was accompanied by an elaborate ceremony involving burial and prayer, was stripped of its Zoroastrian theological/demonological associations, and was described as a public health measure (Nid. 17a).[2] On the

---

1. See my "Returnable Gifts in Rabbinic and Sasanian Law," in *Irano-Judaica VI*, ed. A. Netzer and S. Shaked (Jerusalem: Makhon Ben Zvi, 2008), 150–95; "Acculturation to Elite Persian Norms in the Babylonian Jewish Community of Late Antiquity," in *Neti'ot David*, ed. E. Halivni, Z. A. Steinfeld, and Y. Elman (Jerusalem: Orhot, 2004), 31–56; and "The Torah of Temporary Marriage—A Study in Cultural History," in *Festschrift for Maria Macuch* (Wiesbaden: Harrosowitz, in press).

2. See my "'He in His Cloak and She in Her Cloak': Conflicting Images of Sexuality in Sasanian Mesopotamia," in *Discussing Cultural Influences: Text, Context, and Non-Text in Rabbinic Judaism: Proceedings of a Conference on Rabbinic Judaism* at Bucknell University, ed. Rivka Ulmer (Lanham, MD: University Press of America, 2007), 129–64. For a general orientation on pollution in Zoroastrian life and theology, see Jamsheed K. Choksy, *Triumph Over Evil: Purity and Pollution in Zoroastrianism* (Austin: University of Texas Press, 1989), 80–84; for a recent edition of the primary Zoroastrian text on these matters, see Mahnaz Moazami, *Wrestling with the Demons of the Pahlavi Widēwdād: Transcription, Translation and Commentary*, Iran Studies 9 (Leiden: Brill, 2014), 390–97. This concern seems to have been more widely held; see Robert Parker, *Miasma: Pollution and Purification in Early Greek Religion* (Oxford: Clarendon, 1983), 293, 295. For a more general survey, see James George Fraser, *The Golden Bough: A Study of Magic and Religion* (n.p.: Floating, 2009), chapter 21, sects.

other hand, though the ceremony is described in an entire chapter of the Zoroastrian scriptural book on pollution and purification, the Vidēvdād (ch. 17), and was intended to prevent demons from using the nails as a weapon, there is no reason to believe that the rabbis had access to that book; even though it had been translated into Middle Persian, it was still, at that point, transmitted orally.

A third method of dealing with Iranian beliefs or practices was to reject them altogether. Thus, for instance, in Zevaḥim 92a, the third-century rabbi, Samuel, takes pains to uproot a Zoroastrian belief that was apparently accepted by his fellow townspeople:

א"ל שמואל לרב חנא בגדתאה: איתי לי בי עשרה, ואימא לך קמייהו:
נסכים שנטמאו, עושה להן מערכה בפני עצמן ושורפן.

> Samuel said to R. Hana of Baghdad: Bring me ten people and I will teach you in their presence: if drink-offerings were defiled, one makes a separate fire for them and burns them.

Samuel's point of in gathering ten people was to publicize his ruling. He utilizes the same practice in Bava Batra 142b:

אמר ליה שמואל לרב חנא בגדתאה: פוק אייתי לי בי עשרה, ואימר לך באפייהו: המזכה לעובר קנה.

> Samuel said to R. Hana of Bagdad: 'Go bring me a group of ten [people] and I will tell you in their presence [that] if possession is given to an embryo [through the agency of a third party], it does acquire ownership.'

Yet while the rule that an embryo can transfer inheritances while still unborn carried practical implications in Samuel's own time, the relevance of the first ruling is harder to understand. The Temple had been destroyed a century-and-a-half before, and no drink-offerings were being offered in Palestine, let alone in Babylon. What then was the point of taking such pains to give publicity to this particular teaching? This is where the Zoroastrian background becomes relevant. According to Zoroastrian teaching, fire is holy and must be preserved from pollution; indeed, polluting the fire is a sin deserving of death. It could not be used as a purifying agent, as it was in Jewish ritual—and that was what Samuel wanted to emphasize: fire could purify, and, indeed, drink offerings that

---

6–8, on the subjects of nail-parings and hair-clippings.

had been polluted could be purified by fire. Of course, if it was indeed this point that Samuel wished to publicize, we must assume the belief that a fire must not be fed with polluted substances was so widespread among the Jews of Neharde'a (an important commercial town on the Euphrates and Samuel's hometown) that Samuel had to take steps to uproot it.

It is important to remember that Zoroastrianism itself was not a static entity, but open to influences from all directions. Thus, in the fifth- and sixth-centuries, when Zoroastrian scholars, under pressure from Manichaeism and the more general "scriptural movement" described by Guy Stroumsa, began to write down the ancient Avesta after millennia of oral transmission, they had to devise a new alphabet; in doing so, they borrowed letters from the Armenian one.[3] The balance of this paper will be devoted to a more subtle example of the interplay of Zoroastrian, Graeco-Roman, and rabbinic thought. We will examine how the Bablyonian rabbis understood the mishnaic system of Roman Palestine on a matter of ritual law important both to the rabbis and to Zoroastrian dastwars (jurist authorities). It was one in which Graeco-Roman medical knowledge played an important part, and, moreover, where its influence can be attested at least half-a-century earlier in Zoroastrian sources than in Babylonian rabbinic ones.

CORPSES AND CARCASSES

Both Zoroastrianism and Judaism have elaborate systems of ritual purity bound up with corpses, carcasses, and menstruation. The latter topic has been dealt with by Shai Secunda, in a dissertation which he is revising for publication, and which deals in detail with the similarities and differences between the two systems.[4] In the following, I will deal with one particular aspect of the pollution caused by *nasā*, dead matter—that is, edible parts from a corpse or carcass nibbled on by an animal or bird, or, for that matter, a human. In Zoroastrian law, such dead matter remains polluting while in the animal's body, but its polluting power is mitigated either by ingestion, according to one view, or digestion, according to the

---

3. See Guy Stroumsa, *The End of Sacrifice: Religious Transformations in Late Antiquity* (Chicago: University of Chicago Press, 2009) 28–55; and H. W. Bailey, *Zoroastrian Problems in the Ninth-Century Books* (Oxford: Clarendon, 1971).

4. Samuel Israel. Secunda, "*Dashtana—'Ki Derekh Nashim Li'*:" A Study of the Babylonian Rabbinic Laws of Menstruation in Relation to Corresponding Zoroastrian Texts" (PhD diss., Yeshiva University, 2007); it is currently being revised for publication.

other. In contrast, the Mishnah seems to view the polluting potential of ritually impure substances within the interior of the body as nullified by that presence, without regard to the process of ingestion or digestion. However, the redactional voice of the Bavli views that nullification as tied up to the process of digestion—a process which is not explicitly mentioned in the Mishnah or the Tosefta in connection with the human body. Rather, נתעבל / נתעבלו denotes the decomposition of flesh in the grave (Mishnah Sanhedrin 6:6 and associated talmudic discussion in both Talmuds) or the burning up of limbs and fats on the altar (Tosefta Kippurim 2:11, Sifra Tzav 1:2:4 and 11, and associated passages in the Bavli such as Berakhot 26b). It well may be that its later use as designating digestion developed from this. However, *ʿikkul* does not appear in this sense in the Mishnah.[5] Moreover, digestion is not explicitly mentioned as a factor in texts dealing with the nullification of pollution, as it is in the later layer of the Bavli and in Zoroastrian texts of the fifth century.

This is particularly noticeable in Ḥullin 71a–72a, which discusses the apparent paradox of the body's interior, which seems to constitute a "neutral zone:" pollution within the body (*tumʾah beluʿah*, "swallowed pollution") does not cause pollution, but the pollution itself is not nullified, and so, if it is vomited out, it once again causes pollution. It is this paradox that the Bavli attempts to explain, and in that process we find two stages: one attributed to two fourth-century rabbis, Rabbah and Rava, who attempt to find scriptural and rabbinic sources for the paradox; and the second to the Bavli's fifth- and sixth-century redactors, who attempt to analyze the paradox in terms of the transformative powers of the digestive process. This attempt is similar, *mutatis mutandis*, to a somewhat earlier debate within the Zoroastrian elite which will be examined below. Moreover, both debates may be linked with the Galenic view of digestion as beginning in the mouth (with the action of saliva) and culminating in the intestines, as signaled through defecation. That is not to say that the Bavli's redactors were familiar, or even aware, of Galen's works. Yet the achievements of Greek medical thought were highly regarded in the Sasanian Empire, and though the texts and the details may not have been generally known, the basic idea that medicine was not only a field of

---

5. See Michael Sokoloff, *A Dictionary of Jewish Babylonian Aramaic of the Talmudic and Geonic Periods* (Ramat-Gan: Bar-Ilan University Press, 2002), 861b, s.v. עבל. Sokoloff renders it as "to consume, disintegrate," with a suggestion that it was derived from אכל.

study devoted to diseases and their cures, but also a study of physiology and anatomy, had certainly become common knowledge even earlier.[6]

The growing interest in bodily structure and processes is one of the aspects of Galen's work that can be seen as revolutionary. This had implications for understanding the process of digestion and, by implication, the extent to which undigested food would remain in the body. Thus, in his *On the Natural Faculties*, III.vii, Galen stressed the action of digestion in *altering* food:

> Thus, the stomach will subdue and alter its food, but not to the same extent as will the liver, veins, arteries, and heart.
>
> We must therefore observe to what extent it does alter it. The alteration is more than that which occurs in the mouth, but less than that in the liver and veins. For the latter alteration changes the nutriment into the *substance* of blood, whereas that in the mouth obviously changes it into a new *form*, but certainly does not completely transmute it. This you may discover in the food which is left in the intervals between the teeth, and which remains there all night; the bread is not exactly bread, nor the meat, for they have a smell similar to that of the animal's mouth, and have been disintegrated and dissolved, and have had the qualities of the animal's flesh impressed upon them. And you may observe the extent of the alteration which occurs to food in the mouth if you will chew some corn and then apply it to an unripe [undigested] boil: you will see it rapidly transmuting—in fact entirely digesting—the boil, though it cannot do anything of the kind if you mix it with water ... Now, the masticated food is all, firstly, soaked in and mixed up with this phlegm; and secondly, it is brought into contact with the actual skin of the mouth; thus it undergoes more change than the food which is wedged into the vacant spaces between the teeth.
>
> But just as masticated food is more altered than the latter kind, so is food which has been swallowed more altered than that which has been merely masticated. Indeed, there is no comparison between these two processes; we have only to consider what the stomach contains—phlegm, bile, pneuma, [innate] heat, and, indeed the whole substance of the stomach. And if one considers along with this the adjacent viscera, like a lot of burning hearths around a great cauldron—to the right the liver, to the left the spleen, the heart above, and along with it the

6. See for example, Samuel S. Kottek, "Alexandrian Medicine in the Talmudic Corpus," *Korot* 12 (1996–1997): 80–89, and see Meir Bar-Ilan, "Ha-Refuah be-Eretz Yisrael ba-Me'ot ha-Rishonot li-Sefirah," *Katedra* 91 (5759): 31–78.

diaphragm (suspended and in a state of constant movement), and the *omentum* sheltering them all—you may believe what an extraordinary alteration it is which occurs in the food taken into the stomach.

How could it easily become blood if it were not previously prepared by means of a change of this kind? It has already been shown that nothing is altered all at once from one quality to its opposite. How then could bread, beef, beans, or any other food turn into blood if they had not previously undergone some other alteration? And how could the faeces be generated right away in the small intestine? For what is there in this organ more potent in producing alteration than the factors in the stomach? Is it the number of the coats, or the way it is surrounded by neighbouring viscera, or the time that the food remains in it, or some kind of innate heat which it contains? Most assuredly the intestines have the advantage of the stomach in none of these respects. For what possible reason, then, will objectors have it that bread may often remain a whole night in the stomach and still preserve its original qualities, whereas when once it is projected into the intestines, it straightway becomes ordure? For, if such a long period of time is incapable of altering it, neither will the short period be sufficient, or, if the latter is enough, surely the longer time will be much more so! Well, then, can it be that, while the nutriment does undergo an alteration in the stomach, this is a different kind of alteration and one which is not dependent on the nature of the organ which alters it? Or if it be an alteration of this latter kind, yet one perhaps which is not proper to the body of the animal? This is still more impossible. Digestion was shown to be nothing else than an alteration to the quality proper to that which is receiving nourishment. Since, then, this is what digestion means and since the nutriment has been shown to take on in the stomach a quality appropriate to the animal which is about to be nourished by it, it has been demonstrated adequately that nutriment does undergo digestion in the stomach.[7]

This analysis of Galen's, which may have been based on dissection, but also of close observation of the digestive system, could easily have been done by non-medical scholars based on observation alone, especially if it had been suggested to them by someone familiar with Galen's work. And, indeed, there are interesting points of intersection. For

---

7. *Galen On the Natural Faculties, with an English translation*, Arthur John Brock, LCL 71 (Cambridge: Harvard University Press, 1916), 253, 255, 257.

example, Galen's reference to food between the teeth is paralleled in the discussion of eating in Ḥullin 103b, in which R. Yoḥanan (mid-third century, but in the Bavli's version) refers to that area of the mouth and which we will examine below. Again, Galen's counterposing of the alteration in the stomach to that in the small intestine may be paralleled in Ḥullin 71a, also to be discussed below.

Despite this general awareness of the digestive processes resulting from Galen's work, even on the part of rabbis who had not read it, the Mishnah (whose redaction was at best contemporaneous with Galen, who died in 216 CE) does discuss matters related to the structure of the human body. Its surprising omission of explicit mention of the process of digestion therefore requires notice, especially since, as a common human experience, we might expect the transformation of foodstuffs to feces to have been noticed and applied to the problem of nullification of polluted organic matter. Despite this consideration, however, neither the Mishnah nor the Tosefta provides a term that describes the process of digestion, at least explicitly. As noted above, neither the term *'ikkul* nor its verbal forms appear in either work. That is not to say that the rabbis were unaware of the digestion and its effects; no specialized medical knowledge was required for that! Rather, the *transformative* effects of digestion, stressed in Galen's discussion of the process, seem not to have factored into rabbinic discussions of the nullification of the polluting effects of ritually impure substances. By "Galenic," then, I refer to the view rather than the author; that is, the idea that digestion transforms the ingested substance in a way that modifies—or nullifies—its polluting potential, though Galen himself is hardly interested in ritual pollution. We must take seriously M. J. Geller's judgment that

> no rabbi in Babylonia, whether involved in medicine or not, read Galen or read his works . . . In my view, Babylonian rabbis learned their science from cuneiform tablets, either directly or indirectly. They studied science from local Babylonian scholars, who could still read cuneiform tablets for much longer than we think, probably as late as the 3rd century AD. So physicians in Babylonia did not know Galen and in a sense did not need Galen; they had inherited a very old and useful and reasonably effective classical system of medicine which had been studied and used in Babylonia for many centuries, namely Babylonian medicine. Even by the 3rd century AD diet or purging or emetics

and bloodletting were not, as far as we can tell, ever prescribed by physicians.[8]

Thus, we mention Galen merely as a convenient way of referring to a general awareness of the transformative powers of digestion in overcoming pollution. What is clear, at any rate, is that explicit mention of digestion does not appear in the Mishnah or Tosefta, or even the parts of both Talmuds that contain statements of third- and fourth-century named authorities. Instead, it first appears in the fifth-century redactional layer of the Bavli, as well as in the debate between two early fifth-century Zoroastrian authorities, Abarg and Mēdōmāh.

Consequently, Mira Balberg, in her recent analysis of mishnaic purity law, is free to suggest that the Mishnah's treatment of this paradox—that substances may be neutralized within the body but remain polluting when vomited out—reflects its view of the human body and self, without even mentioning the possibility of digestion as a factor:

> In the realm of impurity there is an implicit rupture between an active legal subject, whose aim is to maintain a state of purity, and the physical object he or she inhabits, which either passively contracts impurity from others or produces its own impurity. Indeed, the Mishnah's rhetoric regarding the management of impurity seems to suggest that, from the point of view of the subject, the body is yet another thing one owns to which one needs to attend, and that one's responsibility to purify one's own body is not fundamentally different from one's responsibility to purify one's own property ... At the same time, the Mishnah leaves little room for doubt that the body is not only something that one has but is also *what one is*. Completely devoid of a language that distinguishes body from soul or mind, and practically devoid even of a designated word for the body as such, the Mishnah knows no other way for a subject to proclaim that his body is impure except by saying "*I* am impure." The Mishnaic purity discourse thus assumes an identity between self and

---

8. M.J. Geller, "Hippocrates, Galen and Jews: Renal Medicine in the Talmud," *American Journal of Nephrology* 22 (2/3)(2002): 101–6; the quote is from p. 103. This statement is based on quite a bit of research; see his "An Akkadian *Vademecum* in the Babylonian Talmud," in *From Athens to Jerusalem: Medicine in Hellenized Jewish Lore and in Early Christian Literature, Papers of the Symposium in Jerusalem, 9–11 September 1996*, ed. Samuel Kottek, et al. (Rotterdam: Erasmus, 2000), 13–32, and M. J. Geller, "Akkadian Medicine in the Babylonian Talmud," in *A Traditional Quest: Essays in Honor of Louis Jacobs*, ed. Dan Cohn-Sherbock, Journal for the Study of the Old Testament Supplements 114 (Sheffield: JSOT Press, 1991), 102–12.

body, despite the notable awareness of the incongruity between the body's condition and the subject's will.[9]

This tension between the self and the body is mitigated by viewing the body as modular: "The rabbis construct a body that is both extremely fluid in terms of its boundaries and highly modular in terms of its constitution, and these two qualities critically define the way impurity as a bodily phenomenon is shaped in the Mishnah."[10] Thus, touch and consumption affect different areas of the body. Moreover, it is possible for an impure substance to cause impurity when swallowed, but not within the esophagus or stomach, as we shall see below in regard to Mishnah Miqvaot 10:8.

Balberg's point regarding the modular nature of the body may easily be illustrated by reference to Mishnah Ḥag. 2:5:

. . . אם נטמאו ידיו נטמא גופו.

. . . if one's hands became defiled, one's [whole] body is deemed defiled.

According to Balberg, this reflects the "early rabbinic non-dualistic worldview." However, she stresses that

> the identicality of the self and the body in the Mishnah is not only assumed by the rabbis but also constructed by them, through a variety of rulings that define the physical body through subjectivity."

She goes on to say that

> "every part of the mishnaic subject's body is something that he *has*, but not every part of his body is something that he *is*, something that he sees as an inseparable part of himself . . . .The rabbinic body is not of one piece, but consists of various components, which at times can be—in actuality or conceptually—detached from the bodily mechanism and seen as units unto themselves. Such is the case for bodily components that can be physically removed from the body, such as hair, nails, and saliva, but such is also the case for hands, which while not removable can be conceptually taken as independent units.[11]

---

9. Mira Balberg, *Purity, Body and Self in Early Rabbinic Literature* (Berkeley: University of California Press, 2014), 61–62.

10. Ibid., 52.

11. Ibid., 62.

We can thus understand her assertion that

> by introducing the revolutionary notion that impurity can be contracted also through *ingestion* of impure substances the rabbis integrated a whole new arena into the realm of bodily impurity, namely, the interior part of the body. If impurity, according to the rabbis, can *enter* the body, then the body is transformed from two-dimensional to three-dimensional: impurity can actually reside within it and not just "on" it.[12]

The notion of the three-dimensional nature of pollution already appears in Num. 19:14, where a tent and all within it becomes polluted when someone dies therein.[13] As Balberg notes, however, this does not appear in relation to pollution *within* a human body, at least within the Pentateuchal texts. Moreover, as Balberg proceeds to write, the concept of internal pollution, as we may call it, brings in its wake the problem of purification, among them the question of whether immersion is effective when the polluted substance resides within one's innards. And how do we regard such foodstuffs before they have been digested? Balberg goes on to note:

> A conceivable way for the rabbis to overcome these problems could have been to prescribe a fixed temporal time frame for ingestion, after which the impure substance could have been assumed to have passed through one's system, and to determine that after this time has passed the source of this impurity is no longer in the body. In fact, this is exactly what the rabbis did in the case of animals that swallowed impure substances and then died: they determined that the digestion process in different animals lasts about three days, and thereby determined that an impure substance swallowed by an animal can be safely assumed to have left its body after this period of time. However, in the case of humans, the rabbis devised a completely different solution to the problem of ingested impurity: they submitted that once the source of impurity has entered the body, it is no longer consequential in any way. In other words, they conceptually removed the interior part of the body from the map of bodily impurity.

12. Ibid., 63.

13. For a Zoroastrian parallel, see Prods Oktor Skjærø and Yaakov Elman, "Concepts of Pollution in Late Sasanian Iran: Does Pollution Need Stairs, and Does It Fill Space?," *ARAM* 26/1–2 (2014): 21–45.

> According to the Mishnah, even though the impure substance renders the entire body impure as it is being swallowed, once it can no longer be seen it has no bearing on the body . . .[14]

Below we shall examine a number of texts in the Mishnah and Tosefta which explicitly locate this neutral zone within animals as well, thus contradicting Balberg's "selfhood" thesis. However, an ancillary suggestion of hers, that pollution which is invisible and inaccessible with a body may be applied to these texts, and we shall do so. In the meantime, let us continue with Balberg's analysis vis-à-vis human bodies:

> The rabbis conceptually detached the interior part of the body from the realm of impurity because they did not consider it to be fully part of the self because the self has no access to it, neither physical nor sensorial access, nor, for the most part, cognitive access. Fundamentally conceiving of the human body as a multipart mechanism that can be divided and dismantled rather than one indivisible whole, the rabbis set the interior part of the body aside, thus allowing the physical body to become not only more manageable and governable in terms of impurity (since one need not worry about impurity that is contained beyond one's reach), but also more commensurate with what the subject tends to identify with himself, and what others identify with him.[15]

Thus, to apply Balberg's rationale to our problem: since the animal is not regarded as having a "self," the nullification of pollution within its body must depend on some other factor, which in Ohalot 11:7 is its presence within the body's interior. Balberg stresses the multipartite view of the human body, and Mishnah Miqvaot 10:8, which deals with humans, chooses an example of an *impure ring* rather than an organic substance to illustrate the neutralizing effect of this interior zone. It is thus clear that digestion is not a factor in regards to human beings. What then is the status of the dead matter within an animal's body before it has been digested?

Let us examine these texts, first the "ring" Mishnah of Miqvaot 10:8. Here the Mishnah deals with the case of someone *eats* ritually unclean food and, in the parallel cases, *swallows* a ring, a ritually unclean one and then a ritually clean one. The Mishnah does not deal directly with the basic case of one who swallows dead matter, but rather with the added

14. Ibid., 63–64. The example is taken from Mishnah Miqvaot 10:8.
15. Ibid., 66.

complications of immersing in a ritual bath and vomiting them out, in the first case, or of one who swallows a clean or unclean ring, enters a room in which a corpse is lying, and undergoes some of the purification ritual before vomiting, in the second. Most important from our point of view, it deals with swallowing inorganic matter that, by definition, cannot be digested. Here is Mishnah Miqvaot 10:8:

אכל אוכלים טמאים ושתה משקים טמאים טבל והקיאן טמאים מפני שאינן טהורים בגוף.

שתה מים טמאים טבל והקיאם טהורים מפני שהם טהורים בגוף.
בלע טבעת טהורה נכנס לאהל המת הזה ושנה וטבל והקיאה הרי היא כמות שהיתה.
בלע טבעת טמאה טובל ואוכל בתרומה הקיאה טמאה וטמאתו...

> If one ate unclean foods or drank unclean liquids, and he immersed himself and then vomited them up [before they had remained in the stomach long enough to be digested], they are still unclean because they did not become clean in the body [that is, unclean foods and liquids except for water cannot be purified by immersion].
>
> If one drank unclean water and immersed himself and then vomited it up, it is clean, because it became clean in the body [since unclean water can be purified by immersion].
>
> If a person swallowed a clean ring, entered a tent wherein lay a corpse, was sprinkled [with purification waters] the first time and the second time [as prescribed by Numbers 19:19], immersed himself, and then vomited it out, it remains as it was before [that is, clean].[16]—
>
> If a person swallowed an unclean ring,[17] he must immerse himself [because he was rendered unclean by contact with the ring before swallowing it], and thereafter may eat *terumah* [a certain priestly gift; since he may do so, he is not rendered un-

---

16. This thus proves that a swallowed clean matter cannot contract uncleanness. For had the ring suffered uncleanness when the man entered under the same roof as the corpse, at which time the ring was swallowed within him, it would not now when vomited forth be clean, for the immersion and purification of the man could be of no avail with regard to the ring.

17. It was rendered unclean by reason of its having been brought into contact with a corpse, in which case the ring, being of metal, assumed the same degree, and not a lesser degree, of uncleanness as the corpse itself (see Ḥullin 3a). This assumption is necessary since lower degrees of pollution do not affect humans; that is, if the rings had been polluted to a lower degree, they would not, in turn, pollute humans.

clean by the unclean ring, that is, in his body, thus proving that swallowed unclean matter cannot render the one who swallowed it unclean.] But if he vomited it out [after this immersion], it is still unclean and has rendered him unclean [through contact as a result of the vomiting].

The second relevant mishnaic source is Mishnah Ohalot 11:7. Though it deals with the effect of the dead matter "lingering" within the intestines of the animal, it does not employ the word *'ikkul*, "digestion." The second part of this Mishnah deals with a live animal, while the first part deals with a dead one. We will thus begin with the second part:

כלב שאכל בשר המת ומת הכלב ומוטל על האסקופה...
כמה תשהה במעיו?
שלשה ימים מעת לעת.
בעופות ובדגים כדי שתפול לאור ותשרף דברי ר' שמעון רבי יהודה
בן בתירא אומר בעופות ובדגים מעת לעת.

[With regard to] a dog which had eaten the flesh of a corpse, had [subsequently] died and [whose body] was lying across the threshold [of a house] . . .

How long should [the uncleanness] have remained in its entrails [before the dog had died and the meat would have become digested and its pollution therefore nullified]?

Three whole days.

[As concerns] fish or birds, as long as [it takes for the uncleanness] to fall in the fire and be consumed, so said R. Shimon; R. Judah b. Bathyra says: In the case of fish or birds, twenty-four hours.

This rendering is taken from the Soncino translation, while its footnotes have been incorporated to some extent in the bracketed comments.[18] I would like to call particular attention to the interpretation embodied in the comment "[before the dog had died and the meat would have become digested and its pollution therefore nullified]." The Mishnah does not actually mention digestion, but rather stresses the polluted substance's "lingering" (*shoheh*) within the intestines (*me'av*) of the dog. The implication seems to be that the impurity remains in the dog's body

---

18. All translations of Mishnah and Babylonian Talmud are taken from the Soncino Press edition published under the editorship of Rabbi I. Epstein, *The Babylonian Talmud Translated into English, with Notes, Glossaries and Indices* (London: Soncino, 1948), with minor alterations by myself.

while being digested—the emphasis is not so much on digestion as on its *continued presence*, as Balberg emphasizes. It is not the digestive process that nullifies the pollution, but its passing out of the body of the animal—defecation.

This is not a quibble, for, as noted above, there is a debate in late antique Zoroastrian sources between those who view *ingestion* as mitigating the power of dead matter that has been swallowed by a bird or other animal, and those who prefer to consider that mitigation as signaled by defecation, following the completion of the digestive process, which is indeed mentioned explicitly in this text. The power of digestion in the Bavli may thus be "post-Galenic," while the Mishnah, whose redaction is conventionally dated to 220 CE, reflects a "pre-Galenic" view.

In the fifth and sixth centuries, the Bavli does report bloodletting, another "Galenic" tactic, although it retrojects it to earlier times (see b. Ta'an 25a, for example). In this case, it also attempts to reconfigure the Mishnah's neutral zone so as to include something of the effects of digestion, in contrast to the Zoroastrian view which saw internal pollution as only modified by ingestion, or not until digestion. But before we get there, let us continue with our review of the mishnaic views.

MISHNAH AND TOSEFTA

Let us now turn to the first half of Ohalot 11:7:

הכלב שאכל בשר מת, ומת הכלב ומוטל על האסקופה, ר"מ אומר:
אם יש בצוארו פותח טפח - מביא את הטומאה, ואם לאו - אינו מביא
את הטומאה, ר' יוסי אומר: רואין מכנגד השקוף ולפנים - הבית טמא,
מכנגד השקוף ולחוץ - הבית טהור, רבי אלעזר אומר: פיו לפנים - הבית
טהור, פיו לחוץ - הבית טמא, מפני שטומאה יוצאה דרך שוליו, רבי
יהודה בן בתירא אומר: בין כך ובין כך הבית טמא

> If a dog ate the flesh of a corpse and died, and lay upon the threshold [with its mouth pointed into the house]: R. Meir says. If its neck was one handbreadth wide, it brings the uncleanness [into the house, since the width of the neck is one handbreadth wide [even though it is not one handbreadth of space but consists of flesh, vertebrae, arteries etc.] the uppermost side of the neck overshadows as a 'tent' the uncleanness, and seeing that the 'tent' extends into the house it thus directs the uncleanness in]; and if not, it does not bring in the uncleanness [for a space

with one of its dimensions less than a handbreadth cannot be regarded as a tent with regard to uncleanness; see Ohalot 3:7].

R. Yose says. We must see [where the uncleanness lies]: if it [that is, that part of the dog in which the dead matter happens to be] lies opposite the lintel and inwards [that is, the inward side of the lintel, so the house overshadows the dead matter], the house is unclean [presumably, even though the dog's neck was not one handbreadth wide, for the uncleanness concealed within breaks through, so that the house overshadows the uncleanness.]; but if [the dead matter within the dog] lies opposite the lintel and outwards, the house is clean.

R. Eleazar says. If its mouth lies inside [but the dead matter within the dog's body is outside the house], the house remains clean; but if the mouth lies outside, the house is unclean, because the uncleanness would pass out of the dog by way of its lower parts [and therefore one may regard the uncleanness in the dog as extending along the lower parts of the animal (for by this way it would have been evacuated) into the house].

R. Judah b. Bathyra says. In all circumstances [that is, whether the neck was one handbreadth wide or not, and whether the actual uncleanness lay on the inside of the lintel or not, and whether the mouth of the dog lay inside or not] the house is unclean.

While R. Judah b. Bathyra does not explain the basis for his ruling, the others do, and though they differ in the exact mechanism, all view the body of the dead dog as a zone of *transmission* which *directs* the pollution within the dog's body into the house. In other words, the internal space of the dead dog is no longer capable of neutralizing the pollution; instead, it directs it into the house. With its death, visibility ceases to be a factor. We will return to the issue of visibility below; meanwhile let us examine the first part of Mishnah Ohalot 11:7, which does not explicitly refer to digestion, but rather to the time the dead matter *lingers* (*shoheh*) within the dog's innards (*me'av*), and, presumably, the time after it leaves—that is, after defecation. The time of "lingering" presumably refers to the time that digestion takes place, but the term is not employed.

The question then arises as to why the Mishnah goes on to discuss the length of time the polluting substance remains in the body of various species of animal (see above), if there is no difference in the status of the dead matter before or after pollution? Maimonides in his Mishnah commentary *ad loc.* rules in accordance with R. Judah b. Bathyra in regard to the 24-hour digestion period for birds and fishes; not surprisingly, medieval and modern commentators on the Mishnah follow him. But no one explains why the Mishnah goes on to discuss digestion altogether, if internal placement alone neutralizes pollution. Again, this mishnaic text then leaves the matter of internal pollution undecided in regard to live animals; it was this lacuna that the Bavli attempts to fill by proposing a number of arguments in favor of the neutrality of the interior space of both animals and humans.

Moreover, while this Mishnah deals with defining the length of time of the lingering, it does not deal directly with the status of the corpse-matter *after* it has been swallowed but *while it is* in the body of the animal. Indeed, neither the word "swallow," nor the words "digest" or "digestion" appears in this text at all.

Nevertheless, the Tosefta, which is now structured as a loose commentary to the Mishnah, recognizes a category of *belu'im*, "swallowed [matter]," a term that does not appear in the Mishnah. However, controversy has raged over the Tosefta's date, with Shamma Friedman suggesting that it was the source of many mishnaic texts, while Ḥanokh Albeck dates it in its current form as post-talmudic.[19] In any case, the two relevant toseftan texts are not mentioned in the Bavli, even though the Talmud elsewhere does deal with Mishnah Ohalot 11:7 in regard to the case of a dead dog (Ḥullin 16a); elsewhere it alludes to the matter of a dog's slow digestive process in one late zoological observation (Shabbat 155b). But, once again, digestion is not mentioned explicitly in the Tosefta, even though it has devised a term for swallowed matter. The text is from the Zuckermandel edition of the Tosefta, based on the MS Erfurt of Tosefta Ohalot 12:3, and clearly relates to the mishnah we have examined above, Ohalot 11:7, however we construe the relationship between Mishnah and Tosefta:

כלב שאכל בשר המת ונכנס לבית הבית טהור שכל הבלועין באדם
ובבהמה בחיה ובעופות טהורין

הקיאן הבית טמא מת
אם שהה במעיו עד שהוא חי שלשה ימים מעת לעת הבית טמא
ובעופות ובדגים מיד
ר' יהודה בן בתירה אומר בדגים מיד ובעופות מעת לעת ר' אלעזר
אומר משם ר' יהודה בן בתירה זה וזה מעת לעת:

---

19. For a discussion of the various views, see my *Authority and Tradition: Toseftan Baraitot in Talmudic Babylonia* (New York: Yeshiva University Press, 1994), 1–5. It is possible to reconcile the two views, but such an attempt would take us too far afield.

> [If] a dog ate flesh of a dead [body] and entered a house, the house is ritually pure, for all internal (lit., "swallowed") [corpse-matter] in a human, domesticated or wild animal, [or] in birds are ritually pure.
>
> [If the dog] vomited them out, the house is unclean with corpse-pollution.
>
> If [the flesh] remained in [the dog's] innards for precisely three days while [the dog] was alive, the house is ritually unclean[20] [during those three days], and in regard to birds and fish, [it is] immediately pure, [since digestion is apparently assumed to be immediate for them].
>
> R. Judah b. Bathyra says: In regard to fish, immediately, [but] in regard to birds, precisely twenty-four hours. R. Eleazar says in the name of R. Judah b. Bathyra: In both cases, precisely twenty-four hours.

The third paragraph presents a problem. As Lieberman notes, Raavad's commentary has "clean," which would eliminate the contradiction between the first and second paragraphs.[21]. If we accept the reading of MS Erfurt and the Raavad ("clean"), the second paragraph is redundant; what then is the difference between the two cases? On the other hand, if we accept the reading "unclean," it is contradictory: the first paragraph then presents the principle of neutral space, while the third may refer to nullification by digestion. But once again, digestion is not explicitly mentioned. The dog is described as "eating," and though the verb "swallow" (בלע) does not appear, Tosefta here employs a category unknown in the Mishnah, that of "swallowed [corpse-matter]"—that is, interior pollution that does not pollute. *Belu'im* thus serves as a quasi-conceptual term for a species of potentially polluting matter, which nevertheless does not pollute. In doing so, it explicitly contradicts Balberg's thesis in regard to animals in the Mishnah, and, as we shall see, serves as a precursor to the Bavli's redactional view that the interior of *both* human and animal bodies are neutral in regard to impurity.

It may be that the redactor attempted to supplement the teaching of the first paragraph, which mirrored the Mishnah's principle of interior pollution, with the later recognition of digestion as a factor, but the result

---

20. See the discussion in the body, immediately below.

21. Saul Lieberman, *Tosefet Rishonim*, III–IV (New York: Jewish Theological Seminary, 5759), 130 *ad* lines 37/38. This rule would be confirmed by Mishnah Zavim 2:3, as well as Tosefta, ed. Zuckermandel, p. 660, lines 18 and 25, as well.

is a contradictory jumble, which, in any case, is never mentioned in the Bavli.

Finally, there is Tosefta Kelim 6:12, another toseftan source which deals with our issue more directly, but again does not appear in the Bavli. This source suggests again that ingestion only neutralizes (Hebrew *matzil*, lit., "saves") a polluted substance within the digestive tract (*belu'im*, "things swallowed") from causing the one swallowing it to be ritually impure.[22] The implication is that ingestion *neutralizes* the meat's polluting effect but does not *nullify* it:

> שלשה דברים מצילין באהל המת הבלועין וצמיד הפתיל ואוהלין יש
> בבלועין שאין בצמיד פתיל ואוהלין יש בצמיד פתיל ואוהלין שאין
> בבלועין הבלועין מצילין על הטהורין מלטמא [ומצילין על הטמאין
> מלטמא צמיד פתיל ואוהלין מצילין על הטהורין מלטמא][23] ואין מצילין
> על הטמאין מלטמא הבלועין אין מיטמאין במשא הזב וצמיד פתיל
> ואוהלין מיטמאין במשא הזב החמת והכפישה שנפחתו במוציא רימוני
> אף על פי שבטלו מתורת הכלים מצילין באהל השרץ:

> Three things save [things from becoming unclean] in the tent [in which there is] a dead body: swallowed things, a sealed clay container and tents [within the larger tents]. Swallowed things and [secondary] tents have [additional characteristics] that do not [apply] to sealed clay containers and [secondary] tents, [and] sealed clay containers and [secondary] tents have [characteristics that do not apply] to swallowed things. Swallowed things save clean things from becoming unclean [and save unclean things from making (other things) unclean. Sealed

---

22. MS Erfurt and the *editio princeps* of Tosefta Kelim, Bava Qamma 6:12 read "swallowed [substances] neutralize (lit., 'save') pure [substances] from becoming impure, but do not neutralize (lit., 'save') impure [substances] from causing pollution [to those who swallow them]," but this text is universally emended to remove the "not," which runs counter to much rabbinic teaching, which implies that impure substances or objects that are swallowed by humans or animals do not cause pollution while the swallower is alive. For the purposes of this paper, it is safer not to rely on a disputed text, and so I shall not pursue the argument that this reading is authentic. However, if this reading is authentic, it would suggest that there was perhaps a Palestinian tradition that resembled the Zoroastrian rule, at least in part. However, if the emended text is correct, the question arises as to why it was ignored by Rabbah or the Bavli's redactors when they came to discuss the issue (see below). See *Sidrei Toharot*, p. 97a, where the author suggests that Sifra Shemini 7:7, which attempts to derive this teaching from Lev 11:33, is only an *asmakhta*, an "authoritative association" but not a full derivation. This would explain why it was not used in Ḥullin 71a–b or Niddah 42b–43a, where one would expect it. The Tosefta text, Kelim 6:12, will be presented below.

23. For the restoration, see Lieberman, *Tosefet Rishonim*, III–IV, 22 *ad* l. 5.

clay containers and (secondary) tents save clean things from becoming unclean], but do not save unclean things from making [other things] unclean. Swallowed [things] do not become unclean with [the uncleanness associated with] a *zav* carrying it, but [things within] sealed clay containers and [secondary] tents do become unclean with [the uncleanness associated with] a *zav* carrying them. A skin-bottle and a basket that were damaged [so that] they would release objects the size of] pomegranates—even though they are no longer useable as containers will save [objects within them] from [pollution] caused by overhanging a dead creeping thing.

This source refers to internal neutralization, and not digestion at all. Indeed, the issue does not at all become a focus for discussion in the Yerushalmi, the Talmud of Roman Palestine, even though, as we have seen, the issue of internal nullification does appear in both the Mishnah and in Tosefta, both Palestinian compilations. There is no Yerushalmi on the whole order of Holy Things (or Purities) except for part of Niddah, but there are enough passages dealing with such matters scattered throughout the Yerushalmi for an interested redactor to have included such a discussion somewhere. Apparently, the need for such a discussion was not felt by the third and fourth centuries.

Given the theoretical nature of the issue, this is hardly surprising. What *is* surprising is the interest it aroused among the Babylonian rabbis, since Babylonia was a place in which Levitical purity laws never applied.

This seems to be another example of the phenomenon documented by Leib Moscovitz: the Babylonian rabbis were indeed interested in conceptual issues more than their Palestinian colleagues, and the Bavli contains such discussions where the Mishnah, Tosefta and Yerushalmi do not. Moreover, if we loosen Moscovitz's definition of "conceptual" as requiring that the concept be "creative and quasi-philosophical," and allow for the development of legal and ritual concepts in the Bavli, we will understand such an interest; we will also begin to appreciate the significance of the existence of an entire Bavli order of Holy Things and the absence of such a Palestinian order.

In addition, I would add yet another factor into this cultural mix: a corresponding interest on the part of Zoroastrian scholars in the same issue. However, before we turn to that issue, let us examine Balberg's case for the importance of the issue of visibility in considerations of internal pollution.

In her discussion of the issue of visibility, she points to other areas of the body whose susceptibility to pollution depends on visibility:

> As a rule, whatever is located in what the rabbis call "a hidden place" (*bet ha-starim*), both in human bodies and in inanimate objects, is inconsequential in terms of impurity. This inconseqentiality manifests itself in two ways: first, if a source of impurity is located in an invisible place, it does not convey impurity; and second, whatever is located in an invisible place does not constitute a "barrier" in ritual immersion, that is, it does not obstruct the direct contact between body and water that is required for purification . . . . The centrality of visibility in the mapping of bodily impurity is manifested not only in mishnaic discussions on impurity contracted from external sources, . . . but also in impurity generated by one's own body.[24]

These include scale disease, where the Mishnah excludes areas that are "protected" from skin abnormalities, including the insides of the eye, ear, nose and mouth, wrinkles, the head and the beard, among others. Balberg notes that two considerations govern these exclusions: the affected area must be considered "skin" (and therefore nails are excluded) and the areas must be visible.

Balberg has thus suggested three reasons or methods of nullification of impurity in living human beings: the sense of selfhood, visibility, and the passage of pollution from the body, or defecation. We have seen that the latter two apply to animals as well as humans. We will now examine a fourth means: digestion. This means, though not mentioned explicitly in the Mishnah, is discussed in the Bavli, in a passage which is also the *locus classicus* for the discussion of *tum'ah belu'ah*, "swallowed pollution." In order to do so, it will be helpful to examine a passage touching on the matter in a Zoroastrian text of the fifth century, the Pahlavī Vidēvdād (hereafter PV), which is a Middle Persian translation and commentary on a text from the Zoroastrian scripture, the Avesta. The opening of the fifth chapter deals with pollution carried by scavengers. Consumption of meat from the dead or dying is the province of animal predators or scavengers; humans, and especially Jews and Zoroastrians, will only eat meat from properly-slaughtered animals. This is also the assumption of the Zoroastrian scholars: PV 5.1–3 deals with animals—wolves, dogs, birds, and flies—that would nibble meat from a corpse. All of these are scavengers.

24. Ibid., 66.

Balberg's thesis would then account for the disjunction between animal and human interiors in relation to the purity laws. Consequently, animal interiors are not "neutral zones" for impurity.

Instead, "objective" factors must be found to determine whether or not this dead matter within an animal's body will propagate pollution, and that is what the Mishnah does. The "objective" factor is the length of time between ingestion and digestion, and does not depend on perception. Balberg prefers to consider the end-time of this process as the point when the "the impure substance could have been assumed to have passed through one's system, and to determine that after this time has passed the source of this impurity is no longer in the body." This is presumably the time of defecation. As we shall see, the Bavli's redactors consider the time of *digestion* to be pertinent. And now, turning to the Zoroastrian discussion referred to above, we will find parallels in a dispute between Abarg and Mēdōmāh, two Zoroastrian authorities of the early fifth century— that is, the time during which the Babylonian rabbis turned to discussion of conceptual matters—debating whether ingestion or digestion is the crucial moment in mitigating the polluting power of dead matter. Abarg considers the time of *ingestion* to be the crucial moment at which dead matter—*nasā*—becomes *hixr*, "dry dead matter," and thus less polluting, and Mēdōmāh considers the time of defecation. Moreover, it is likely that this debate took place in the early fifth century, and thus before the great work of the Bavli's redaction got underway.[25] It is thus not impossible that the Bavli's understanding of the role of digestion in nullifying impurity came from the surrounding Zoroastrian culture. This is not to say that the redactors were aware of this Zoroastrian debate, but rather that the awareness of the role of digestion was, so to speak, "in the air."

THE VIDĒVDĀD

The Zoroastrian scriptural book on pollution and purification, the Vidēvdād, was composed in a semi-poetic Young Avestan style in the early first millennium BCE. It has a predilection for triads; in the case with which we will be concerned, it describes a bird polluting a tree branch by vomiting dead matter on it, defecating on it, or "sprinkling" on it, a term which may refer to the bird's combination of urine and feces.

---

25. See Alberto Cantera, *Studien zur Pahlavi-Übersetzung des Avesta*, Iranica 7 (Wiesbaden: Harrossowitz, 2004), 207–20, esp. 219–20.

The original discussion is not as interested in the bird's status as it is on the effect of this vomited or defecated dead matter on the tree branches that are being cut and gathered for the fire—and all fire is to some extent sacred in Zoroastrian thinking. If the dead matter is then deposited on the branch, the branch becomes polluted, and the pious Zoroastrian who wishes only to feed the fire will transgress a cardinal sin—polluting the fire by (unknowingly) feeding it with polluted firewood. Zoroaster asks Ohrmazd whether this heinous but inadvertent sin makes that pious Zoroastrian into a sinner; Ohrmazd asserts that this is not the case, since if one were to be considered guilty for an inadvertent sin, no matter how heinous, the road to Paradise would be blocked for all. The ancient Avesta is not interested in the status of the dead matter, but solely in the theological/ethical matter just noted. In Zoroastrian thought, then, internal pollution is not nullified by its presence in the interior of the animal's body, but either by ingestion or digestion.

Onto this dialogue is grafted a debate between two fifth-century dastwars, Abarg and Mēdōmāh, as to how and when the ingested dead matter becomes less polluting—that is, when *nasā* ("dead matter") becomes *hixr* ("dry dead matter"). The debate is recorded in the Pahlavī Vidēvdād 5.1–4, and concerns a principle enunciated in PV 8.34, "dry does not pollute dry," which suggests that the *hixr* may perhaps no longer transmit impurity to the branch, depending on how "wet" the branch is. Thus, a theological issue has been transmuted into a ritual one. The two dastwars disagree in regard to the status of the dead matter between ingestion and digestion; according to Abarg, ingestion has converted the *nasā* to *hixr*, "dry dead matter," while according to Mēdōmāh, it is still *nasā* until it is completely digested and passes out of the bird's body by defecation. The texts and translation are from the recent edition of PV by Mahnaz Moazami,[26] with some modifications based on an earlier rendering by Prods Oktor Skjærvø. The bracketed words are redactional glosses:

> 5.1 (A) mard ēdōn bē widerēd abar andar ān zofr rōstāg [ay zofrīh az kōf ast kē ēdōn gōwēd ay pad kār ī dēn gōwēd] (B) ān murw ul wazēd az ān ī buland gar abar ō ān zofr rōstāg (C) abar ān kirb frāz xwarēd ōy rist mardōm (D) ān murw ul wazēd az an zofr rōstāg abar ō ān buland gar (E) abar ān wan wazēd ī saxt [čiyōn wan ī wādām] narm [čiyōn wēd naft] (F) abar ān wāmīd — Abarg hixr guft Mēdōmāh nasā] abar ān rīd [hixr]

26. Mahnaz Moazami, *Wrestling with the Demons of the Pahlavi Widēwdād: Transcription, Translation and Commentary* (Leiden: Brill, 2014), 122–25.

ud abar paššinjīd [hixr].

5.1 (A) A man, thus, dies there, in a deep riverbed [depth (measured) from the mountain.]

There is one who says thus: The meaning is: ("profound") with respect to the works of the *dēn* [that is, religious tradition— YE] (B) A bird flies up there from the high mountain to the deep riverbed. (C) It eats from that body, that of the dead man. (D) That bird flies from the deep riverbed to the high mountain. (E) It flies up on that tree, a hardwood tree [like the almond tree] (or) a softwood tree [like the addle-willow]. (F) It vomits on that (tree). [Abarg said: *hixr*, dry dead matter; Mēdōmāh said: *nasā*, (wet) dead matter]; it defecated on it [*hixr*]; It sprinkled on it [*hixr*].

5.2 (A) mard ēdōn frāz rawēd az ān zofr rōstāg abar ān buland gar (B) abar ān wan rawēd kū ōy murw [Avestan:] *auui. dim. vaṇta*. kadār ataxš rāy ēsm xwāhēd (C) abar ān zanēd [pad bun] abar ān brīnēd [tāg tāg] abar ān tāšēd [Avestan: *dāiiata dāitiia.pairišti*] abar pad ān abrōzēnd ātaxš ī ohrmazd pus (D) kadār ōy ast tōzišn.

5.2 (A) A man thus goes forth there, from the deep riverbed to the high mountain. (B) He goes to that tree on which that bird had vomited, seeking firewood for the fire. (C) He strikes on it [on the trunk]; he cuts into it [the branches]; he cuts it down [*dāiiata dāitiia.pairišti*]. [Avestan quotation:] "Place it [on the fire] when it has been lawfully examined!]" With it (people) light the fire, the son of Ohrmazd. What is the penalty for it?

5.3 (A) u-š guft ohrmazd kū nē ān ī sag-burd nē ān ī way-burd nē ān ī gurg-burd nē ān ī wād-burd nē ān ī maxš-burd nasuš mard nē āstārēnēd kū wināhgār nē kunēd tā rēman ōh kunēd

5.3 (A) Ohrmazd answered: Neither carried by the dog, nor carried by the bird, nor carried by the wolf, nor carried by the wind, nor by the fly, dead matter causes a man to sin [it does not make a man sinful, though it makes it impure].

5.4 (A) agar-iz awēšān nasā kē sag-burd way-burd gurg-burd wād-burd maxš-burd nasuš mard āstārēnīdar būd hēnd [kū wināhgār ōh būd hēnd] (B) pad tēz-rawišnīh [kū ēd zūd būd hē] ān ī man harwisp axw īastōmand zad-xwāstār ī ahlayīh [kū-šān rāh ī kār ud kirbag zad ēstād hē] (C) xrōsišn-dād ō ruwān [kū-šān ruwān az garōdmān xrōstag ud xwistag būd hē] tanāpuhlīgān [kū margarzān bawānd] pad frahistīh [az wasīh] awēšān nasā kē abar ēn zamīg widerēnd

5.4 (A) (For) if these corpses, carried by the dog, carried by the bird, carried by the wolf, carried by the wind, and carried by the fly, were to cause a man to sin [they would become sinners] (B) right away [this would have happened soon (after death)], my entire material world would have been seeking the destruction of righteousness [the path to duty and good deeds would have been blocked to them.] (C) Howling would have been given to that soul [their souls would have been howled and chased from Paradise]; everybody would be a *tanāpuhl* sinner [would have been a sinner deserving of death], because of the great amount [due to the excessiveness] of these corpses of those who die on this earth.

Ohrmazd's underlying motivation is to make a life of religious good works and purity possible, that is, to build leniency into the system of pollution and purification. As it happens, Balberg has pointed to the same tendency in the Mishnah, as in the following, from Mishnah Toharot 3:6:

חרש שוטה וקטן שנמצאו במבוי שיש בו טומאה הרי אלו בחזקת
טהרה וכל הפקח בחזקת טומאה וכל שאין בו דעת להשאל ספיקו
טהור

> A deaf person, a mentally inept person (*shoteh*), and a minor who were found in an entry way in which there is impurity, are held to be pure; and all mentally capable persons (*kol ha-piqeah*) are held to be impure.
>
> Whoever has no mind to be asked, his doubt is pure (that is, will be considered pure in a case of doubt).

Balberg has two important observations to make on this text:

> This ruling is highly counterintuitive, but it is this very counterintuitivity that indicates how invested the rabbis were in making purity a tenable goal. If persons and animals who cannot be responsible for avoiding impurity and who cannot be held accountable for their state of impurity were considered to be perpetually impure, as would have been the predictable ruling based on the premises we have examined throughout his chapter, then one's ability to maintain oneself and one's immediate environment in a state of purity would be significantly compromised. Through this overarching ruling the Mishnah does not dismiss the possibility that those who cannot give an account of their actions have in fact encountered a source of impurity, but it allows one to ignore the ever-present potential of impurity that children and animals harbor, thus making the pursuit of purity more feasible.

The second mishnaic principle I will mention here pertains to cases of doubtful impurity in public as opposed to private domains. According to this principle, in a case of doubt regarding the contractions of impurity in a public domain, the ruling will be that the person or object in question is *pure*, whereas in a case of doubt regarding the contraction of impurity in a private domain, the ruling will be that the person or object in question is impure.[27]

The relevant rabbinic text is m. Toharot 6:4:

כל שאתה יכול לרבות ספיקות וספק ספיקות ברה"י טמא בר"ה טהור

However many doubts and doubts about doubts that one can multiply, a condition of doubt in a private domain is deemed unclean, and in a public domain it is deemed clean.

And, *mutatis mutandis*, the same principle operates in PV 5.4:

(S) rāh ud dar ī deh jōy hamēšag āb ka-š nasā abar mad wehān ud pōryōtkēšān pad hamkār be hilišn az ān be dar ī bēdom
    (S) When the dead matter has reached the gates of the village and the stream of running water, the faithful and teachers of the Mazdayasnian religion should allow (the use of the gate) for the same work; (this also applies to) the furthermost gate.

The tendency toward leniency on the part of Abarg may be seen in another decision of his, this one reported in a ninth-century Middle Persian text, Šayāst nē Šayāst 2.73–74, here in a recent, as-yet unpublished edition by Oktor Skjærvø:

2.73 ramag-ēw kē gōspand-ēw andar kē-š nasāy xward estēd
    ud wēšāg-ēw kē draxt-ēw andar kē nasāy andar gumēxt estēd [K20 57r/111]
    ud esm-dān-ēw kē esm-ēw tāg andar kē čarbišn andar gumēxt estēd
    Abarg guft
    ēw ramag ud wēšāg warōmand kerdan nē šāyēd ud esm a-kār o
    2.74 dar-ēw kē nasāy-ēw padiš pahikōbēd
    pad dar ī deh ud šahrestān ham-dādestān būd hēnd kū pad ham-kār [M51 69/166] bē hilišn
    pad dar ī bēdom jud-dādestān būd hēnd
    ud Gōgušasp guft ay pad ham kār bē hilišn čē šāyēd

27. Balberg, 43–44.

ud Sōšyans guft ay nē šāyēd
pad ābārīg dar ham-dādestān būd hēnd kū nē šāyēd o
2.73 (As for) a herd in which there is a sheep that has eaten a dead thing,
and a wood in which there is a tree containing a dead thing,
and a firewood-container in which there is a piece of firewood containing fat,
(about these) Abarg said: The implication is that it is not appropriate to make the herd and wood (a case of) "being in doubt" (and so needing testing), but (all) the firewood is useless.
2.74 (As for) a door/gate that a dead thing touches: about the gate of a village or town they agreed that it should be left to be used as before, about the outermost gate they disagreed:
Gōgušasp said: The implication is that it should be left (as such) because it is (considered) appropriate.
Abarg said: The implication is that it is not (considered) appropriate.
About the other doors, they were agreed that it is not appropriate.

Both systems—the Zoroastrian and the rabbinic—faced similar problems, and solved them in similar ways. In order to make highly complex systems of pollution and purification viable in everyday life, leniencies had to be built in to the system, and that is precisely what was done. The tendency of pollution is to spread, by contact or other ways, thus impairing the pious worshipper's path to holiness or righteousness. Public domain is by definition the greater part of an individual's geography, and must be protected from impurity as much as possible, and this is what is accomplished by the principle that doubtful pollution in such spaces are resolved leniently. As for the second Zoroastrian case, since the biblical/rabbinic system did not allow for domestic animals becoming polluted in such a way, there was no need for such leniencies.

As we will see, neutral internal space also presented a problem. Neutralization, after all, is not the same as nullification, and the impurity which had been neutralized in the body regained its polluting power when vomited up. In such scenarios, another process of purification would be desirable; digestion, once its nullifying power was recognized, provided that. For the Zoroastrians, the transformation was partial, from *nasā* to *hixr*, so that the dead matter, though polluted in itself, could not transfer the pollution any further, while for the rabbis, it was total.

Let us now return to PV 5.4:

Commentary:

> (D) abarg guft ay ēn pursišn pad hixr ud wizīr pad nasā bē kard čē ka-š xward way hixr
>
> (E) mēdōmāh guft ay ēn pursišn pad harw dō ud wizīr pad nasā bē kard čē tā gugārēd way pad nasā (F) pad harw dō čāštag hamdādestān būd hēnd kū ka-šān pad ān ī grāy kard ā-š pad ān ī xwārtar kard bawēd
>
> (D) Abarg said: This question was asked regarding the dry dead matter and (what is) the decision as to dead matter; for when the bird has eaten something, (what comes out) is dry dead matter (E) Mēdōmāh said: This question was posed regarding both (that is, *hixr and nas*ā), and (what is) the decision as to dead matter; for it is dead matter until (the bird) digests it. (F) They agreed that, by both teachings, when they have committed the heavy (sin), then one has (also) committed the lighter (sin).[28]

In other words, the eight or nine levels of sin in the Zoroastrian system (which were later enumerated in Šāyast nē Šāyast chapter 1) must be considered not as *discrete levels of individual sin*, but as a *continuum*. If one commits a sin of a higher level, he has *also* incurred the sum of the sins up to and including the level of sin he incurred in the present instance. Whether this rule, expressed by PV's redactors, is actually historically accurate regarding the original views of Abarg and Mēdōmāh cannot be determined, but it was one way in which the redactor could delimit an area of agreement between Abarg and Mēdōmāh. The motive for this seems to be that since both were *pōrtyōkešān*, early orthodox teachers, the redactor felt unable to decide between their differing views. The most he could do was to outline an area in which there was no disagreement. As talmudists are well aware, this mind-set was shared by the rabbis, and plays a major role in the form that that Talmud was to take. "*Hamdādestān*" has its direct parallel with the talmudic "*ve-shavin*."

The redactor's linkage of this dispute with Avestan exegesis is also important for understanding the place of PV within late antique intellectual history. Abarg and Mēdōmāh were debating how to ground these principles in the Avestan text. As presented in PV, the debate was twofold: Granted that *nasā* within the body (of a human or animal) retained its polluting power, was this power modified by its presence within the body, or, more precisely, by digestion? Again, even if we grant this point,

---

28. Moazami, 122–23.

the question might then have arisen as to whether this issue could be resolved by reference to an Avestan text. Clearly, the redactor of PV 5.1–4 considered this possibility to be likely, and attempted to explain this dispute as related to Avestan interpretation. Nor is this merely a matter of speculation. Guy Stroumsa has shown that there was a "scriptural movement" within several of the religions of Western Asia: Christianity, Manichaeism, Zoroastrianism, and Judaism.[29] That the Avesta is quoted or referred to in PV some 35 times is not as important as the fact that here, as well as in other places such as 6.5D-E or 6.9A-C, prominent dastwars such as Sōšāns, Kay Ādur Bōzēd, Abarg, Mēdōmāh and Gōgušnasp—and the redactor—devote effort to grounding their views in the Avestan text, as I have demonstrated elsewhere.[30]

The implications of this aspect of PV are significant, since we now have some reason to believe that the dispute between Abarg and Mēdōmāh in PV 5 did not represent a radical break with a mimetic priestly tradition, but was instead part of an ongoing attempt to define its parameters—an attempt that perhaps began in the early Sasanian period, and thus perhaps represents the beginning of an intellectual engagement with the Avesta.[31]

This passage also reveals an important stage in Avestan exegesis. Both Abarg and Mēdōmāh based themselves on the Avestan text, but neither they nor the redactors felt the need to provide a full interpretation of all three ornithological processes: vomiting, expelling and sprinkling.

29. See Stroumsa, *The End of Sacrifice*, 28–55.

30. See my "Toward an Intellectual History of Sasanian Law: An Intergenerational Dispute in Hērbedestān 9 and Its Rabbinic Parallels," in *The Talmud in Its Iranian Context*, ed. Carol Bakhos and Rahim Shayegan (Tübingen: Mohr-Siebeck, 2010), 21–57, and "The Other in the Mirror: Iranians and Jews View One Another: Questions of Identity, Conversion and Exogamy in the Fifth-Century Iranian Empire," in *Bulletin of the Asia Institute* 19 (*Festschrift* for Oktor Skjærvø), 15–26, and 20 (2009), 25–46. In the next century, in a super-commentary on PV, Zand ī Fragard Jud-Dēw-Dād (ZFJ), only refers to the Avesta some 21 times, which may reflects its tendency to downplay the exegetical aspect ("midrash halakhah") of PV, though it is still present to an extent in ZFJ. For an overview of this important text, see the entry of Yaakov Elman and Mahnaz Moazami in the internet version of the Encyclopedia Iranica, s.v. Zand ī Fragard Jud-Dēw-Dād, http://www.iranicaonline.org/articles/zand-fragard-jud-dew-dad. Whether this reflects a more general tendency requires more research.

31. Moazzami and I go into this issue in our paper in the forthcoming *Festschrift* for Moshe Bernstein, "The Quantification of Religious Obligation in Second Temple Judaism—and Beyond." This quantification is part of a "scholasticization of religious law" in late Sasanian Zoroastrianism, which mirrors a similar process in late Second Temple Judaism, both proto-rabbinic and sectarian.

This is in contrast to what Shai Secunda has found in regard to other texts; in particular, Secunda has shown that the redactor of PV interpreted PV 16.1 so that each synonym describing menstrual flow referred to a different color, just as here in 5.1D he carefully identified hardwood and softwood trees.[32] Note also that he provided both a literal and an allegorical interpretation for 5.1A:

> 5.1 (A) A man, thus, dies there, in a deep riverbed depth (measured) from the mountain.
> There is one who says thus: The meaning is: ("profound") with respect to the works of the *dēn* [that is, religious tradition—YE].

The word "deep" describing the riverbed is interpreted both as "depth (measured) from the mountain," and "profound with respect to the works of the *dēn*."

Furthermore, a century later, in ZFJ, this form of interpretation, which we may call "statutory construction," is applied to a dispute between Sōšāns and Kay-Ādur-Bōzēd, and serves, as does *ham-dādestān* in our passage in PV, to limit that area of dispute. Here is one example of this device, courtesy of Mahnaz Moazami. In ZFJ, aside from the redactor, we also have comments by a later commenter, who prefaces his remarks with *az man*, "in my opinion":

> [1.20] [438:8] dar ī srāy. ka-š nasāy abar rasīd čiyōn
> ēdōn čiyōn Sōšāns guft nē šāyēd.
> ēdōn čiyōn Kay-ādur-bōzēd guft šāyēd:
> az man bē agar srāy ān kē-š kadag-xwadāy dahlīz ēk ēdōn bawēd čiyōn. dar ī ganj ud šabestān.
> agar srāy az ān ī kadag-xwadāy 2–dahlīz ud dar ī . dahlīz abāz ō ēk āwurd ēstēd bē ō dar ī deh ud ān ī šahrestān handāzišn:
> (As to) the door of a house, if dead matter reached it. How is it?
> Thus, as Sōšāns said, it is not proper.
> Thus as Kay-Ādur-Bōzēd said, it is proper.
> In my (opinion), if the house is that (in which) the householder has one portico, then it is like the door of treasure houses and private apartments (i.e., useless);
> If the house is that (in which) the householder has two porticos, and their doors are directed (lit., brought) towards each

---

32. Secunda dissertaton; see his commentary *ad* PV 16.1.

other (lit., one), (then) it should be considered (like the) door of the village and that of the city (which can remain in place).

Here Az Man, as we may call him, a later commenter on ZFJ, reconciles the two earlier opinions by suggesting that they are referring to two different cases: one in which there is one portico, and one in which there are two, which perhaps constitute a public space and therefore more lenient rules apply, as we saw above. This form of statutory construction, familiar to talmudists as the talmudic *oqimta*, is not common in Pahlavi texts, but its very appearance is noteworthy.

Finally, there is yet another aspect of this passage that is enlightening as to the intellectual climate of late Sasanian intellectual history: a turn to conceptualization. This turn, as we noted above, typifies some developments in the intellectual history of the Bavli. Later on in the passage, Gōgušnasp, a senior contemporary reputed to be the teacher of Mēdōmāh,[33] raises the following issue, and gives an answer which reveals another important development in late Sasanian religious thought:

> (L) Abarg guft ay ka andar warg) gumēxt estēd hamag a-kar Gōgušnasp guft ay ōh gugārd dārišn
>
> (L) Abarg said: When (fat) is mixed in a leaf, (the entire firewood) is unsuitable for use. Gōgušnasp said: It should be considered as "digested."[34]

By referring to fat mixed in the leaf (however that is construed) with animal "digestion," Gōgušnasp converts the word *gūgard* from a physiological process to a legal/ritual one, similar to the rabbinic development of *balua'*, "swallowed," to *balua'* as a technical term for "internal" (see above). Fat on a leaf cannot be digested, of course, but it can be *considered* as digested and its pollution moderated in a ritual sense. If the fat is *nasā*, at some point it becomes *hixr*, and is thus no longer *a-kār*, forbidden for use.

Thus, it should be noted that *a-kār* is exactly equivalent to the rabbinic *asur ba-hana'ah*, a substance that is not only forbidden to be eaten, but also one from which it is forbidden to derive benefit. This is clear from ZFJ 457: *nān ud gōšt ka poxtag ayāb brištag xwardīg a-kār bē ō sag dahišn* —"bread and meat when prepared or roasted is forbidden for use,

---

33. See Cantera, 212.
34. Moazami, 124–25.

it should be thrown to a dog." It is also evident in ZFJ 458.2–3, *xwarišn ī sāxtag andar se gām* (3) *a-kār pad kār ī mardōmān nē šāyēd ō sag dahišn*, where *a-kār* is defined as *kār ī mardōmān nē šāyēd ō sag dahišn* —"cooked food within three paces is forbidden for use—it is not fit for the use of people, it should be thrown to a dog." This is equivalent to the biblical verse in Exod 22:30, referring to meat forbidden for human use: "Do not eat the meat of an animal torn by wild beasts; throw it to the dogs."

Needless to say, if "fat in the leaf" can be figuratively "digested," this implies that literal digestion can nullify pollution.

BAVLI ḤULLIN 71a–72a

We now turn to the *locus classicus* of the rabbinic discussion of internal pollution in the Bavli: Ḥullin 71a–72a, which contains the statements of two Babylonian rabbis of the fourth century, and a number of redactional arguments which recast those statements into the discourse of digestion and nullification. In so doing, it also recasts, by implication, the mishnaic discussion of "lingering" into one that relates directly to the effect of digestion on pollution. Since *'ikkul* does not appear in reference to digestion in the Mishnah, Tosefta or the Yerushalmi, the absence of references to these sources in this passage becomes less puzzling.

Thus, to review for a moment: Tosefta Ohalot 12:3 deals with the case of a live dog that has swallowed some dead matter; if the dog vomits it out, the house it had entered is polluted; however, if precisely three days have passed since he had ingested the dead matter, allowing time for the dead matter to pass out of the dog's body as feces, the house is not polluted (though there are problems with the reading). However, Tosefta, like the Mishnah, does not single out digestion as the necessary factor in nullifying the impurity. This suggests that Balberg's thesis, that it is the dead matter's invisibility and inaccessibility within the dog's body (rather than digestion *per se*) that is the operative factor, is correct. This passage describes the dog as eating and subsequently refers to the dead matter as "swallowed" (*belu'im*) and thus ingested, but still does not refer directly to any transformation of the dead matter.

In contrast, the redactors of the Bavli and the Zoroastrian scholars refer to the transformative power of ingestion or digestion, quite in the spirit of Galen. I therefore suggest that it was this Galenic view, or something like it, that turned the debate from visibility to transformation/ingestion/digestion in rabbinic literature.

It is tempting to claim that the same process underlies the Zoroastrian texts, and that the fifth-century debate between Abarg and Mēdōmāh also reflects Galenic influences. Unfortunately, we do not have earlier versions of the dispute on the Zoroastrian side in order to trace its history in that literature. But, as for rabbinic thought, neither the third-generation rabbi, Rabbah, nor the fourth-generation Rava refer to digestion in their discussion of the neutral zone of internal pollution. In the case of Rava, since the mishnaic text he cites, Miqvaot 10:8, refers to non-organic rings which cannot be digested, his understanding of internal pollution cannot be based on digestion. And even if we accept the scriptural proof provided for Rabbah as his own rather than that of the redactors, it is clear that ingesting the dead matter right before sunset will not leave any time for digestion. All references to digestion in this passage are thus clearly redactional, and reflect, as does PV 5.1–3, the penetration of Galenic, or quasi-Galenic, medicinal knowledge into the Sasanian Empire's cultural orbit.

Mishnah Kelim 8:5 (cited above), which discussed a rooster which swallowed a dead creeping thing and then fell into the airspace of an oven, seems to be lurking in the background of Rabbah's statement. And Rabbah's statement, in turn, set the agendum for the rest for Ḥullin 71a–72a—that is, just as a dead *sheretz* (creeping thing) that has been swallowed by a rooster which fell into a clay oven does not pollute the oven, so too, ritually clean substances that fell into that space do not become polluted. Here, then, is the Bavli:

אמר רבה: כשם שטומאה בלועה אינה מטמאה, כך טהרה בלועה אינה מיטמאה

טומאה בלועה מנלן? דכתיב: "והאוכל מנבלתה יכבס בגדיו," מי לא עסקינן דאכל סמוך לשקיעת החמה, וקאמר רחמנא טהור? ודלמא שאני התם דלא חזיא לגר?....נהי דלא חזיא בפניו, שלא בפניו מיחזיא חזיא ליה.

> Rabbah said: Just as an unclean object that has been swallowed cannot render [something else that had been swallowed] unclean, so a clean object that has been swallowed cannot be rendered unclean [within a person's body].
>
> [The redactors investigate the reason for Rabbah's statement:] Whence do I know this [about] internal uncleanness?—For it

is written, "And he that eats of the carcass of it shall wash his clothes" (Leviticus 11:40). Does this not apply even though he ate of it [only] a short while before sunset [since Scripture does not specify a time]? And yet the Pentateuch says that he becomes clean [immediately after sunset,—that is, he does not become unclean by virtue of the undigested food within him].

Perhaps there it is different, for the reason that it is no longer fit for a human being [as implied by Deuteronomy 14:21; but where it is fit for human consumption, it can become ritually impure] ...Even so, granted that it was not fit for a human being if it was swallowed [and disgorged] in his presence, it is however fit for a human being if it were not swallowed in his presence. [The redactors then mention a secondary dispute between two Palestinian authorities of the early third century, which need not detain us.]

Two arguments for the contention that interior space neutralizes pollution are presented. First, Rabbah presents an argument from analogy: just as internal pollution does not pollute further, so too ritually clean substances do not become polluted. Note that he takes for granted the rule that "swallowed polluted items" do not pollute, as we might expect, since it can be supported from the mishnaic and toseftan texts reviewed above, though they are not cited.

Instead, a rather forced interpretation of Lev 11:40 is proposed, and appended to Rabbah's remark. Taking the biblical text very literally, it produces a boundary condition in which internal pollution is immediately nullified, thus proving that swallowing it is what nullifies its pollution. That is, a *scriptural* interpretation is provided rather than a *rabbinic* source, in accordance with the "scriptural movement" pointed out by Guy Stroumsa, as noted above—and the passage in PV takes the same route. This concern for the scriptural grounding of rabbinic teachings is far more typical of the fourth-generation than the third-generation Rabbah, and there are sociological reasons for that, as I have shown elsewhere. First, let us examine the intellectual profile of the two.

The method of interpretation of Lev 11:40 by a border-line condition is prefaced by the question: "Does this not apply?" (*mi la asiqinan*). This question appears some 33 times in the Bavli. While 19 of them are redactional (Shab. 90b; Suk. 25a; Ḥag. 34a; Yev. 24a, 109a; Ket. 102b; Naz. 62b (twice); Sot. 29b; Git. 51a; Qid. 33a, 51b, 64b; BM 32b, 80b; Shev. 5b; AZ 47a; Zev 56a; Ḥul. 33b), most of the others are by scholars associated with Rava or his school: his teacher R. Naḥman (Yev. 17a), Rava himself (Shab. 84b, BM 88b, Zev. 94a), his student, R. Papa (Ber. 11a, 16a, perhaps Naz. 37a, and in Men. 9b, in a remark of R. Yosef b. Shmai'ah to R. Papa), and R. Ashi (Shab. 2b, 18b-19a, BB 29a); only one, Shab. 93b, occurs in an exchange with Ulla, and is therefore anchored in a third-generation source. Finally, one other, BM 88b, is attributed to R. Ammi, a Babylonian who immigrated to Palestine. Thus, it is likely that it is Rava who proposed this interpretation.

This brings us to a familiar problem to talmudists: distinguishing Rabbah from Rava. As Shamma Friedman has shown, early manuscripts did not clearly distinguish between the names Rava and Rabbah; both are contractions of Rav Abba, but spelled slightly differently. Rava is spelled with a final *aleph*, while Rabbah is spelled with a final *heh*, an artificial distinction.[35] In any case, in this instance the manuscripts are divided, but two of them—Hamburg 169 and Vatican 122—have Rava with an *aleph*, that is, the later Rav Abba, while Munich 95, Vatican 121 and 123b have Rabbah with a *heh*. As expected, the Soncino printing of 1489 has the latter reading, as does the standard Vilna edition. However, in the light of the fact that arguments of the form "do we not apply this text?" are overwhelmingly employed by Rava's associates, I suggest that we must prefer the reading of Hamburg 169—generally considered a very reliable witness—and Vatican 121.

The result is that it is Rava who addresses the problem of providing either a scriptural or rabbinic source for Rabbah's analogy. This too is typical of Rava's methodology.

As noted above, there is another reason to attribute this interpretation to Rava. Elsewhere, I have demonstrated in detail Rava's analytical approach to biblical exegesis;[36] the twelve midrashim attributed to Rabbah are fairly literal, with two exceptions in which he applies a method pioneered by the first-generation authority Samuel.[37] There are 58 attrib-

---

35. Shamma Y. Friedman, "Ketiv ha-Shemot "Rabbah" ve-"Rava" ba-Talmud ha-Bavli," *Sinai* 110 (5752): 140–64.

36. "Rava ve-Darkei ha-Iyyun ha-Eretz Yisraeliyyot be-Midrash ha-Halakhah," in Y. Gafni, ed., *Merkaz u-Tefutzah: Eretz Yisrael veha-Tefutzot bi-Ymei Bayit Sheni, ha-Mishnah veha-Talmud* (Jerusalem: Merkaz Shazar, 2004), 217–42.

37. For Rabbah: Shab. 82b (*di-khetiv*), and Pes. 38a–b, Suk. 2a, Ned. 67a–70a-b, Sot. 15b, BQ 46a, BB 115b (twice), Zev. 92b, Ar. 15b, 26b), at least two of which are really to be attributed to Rava [BB 115b, twice, see Pes. 54b]) for *qera*, and one which applies Samuel's method of temporal retrojection in Sanh. 60a/Sot. 15b. It is true that

uted to Rava,[38] many of which are pioneering and part of his program of systematic omnisignificance, as I have shown. Of those which fall outside that program, ten are nevertheless more adventurous than those attributed to Rabbah.[39] As noted above, the "do we not apply this text?" argument is typical of Rava's associates. It should also be noted that Friedman considers the doubtful cases to be those in which the attribution is given to Rabbah.

There is a reason for this disparity; apparently, between the time of Rabbah in Pumbedita and Rava in Maḥoza/Ctesiphon, the "Scriptural movement" described by Guy Stroumsa in his 2009 book, which affected Christianity, Manichaeism and Zoroastrianism, also reached Rava in Maḥoza. That is, there was a new emphasis on the scriptural roots of these religions. It is true that Stroumsa found himself unable to explain the rabbinic emphasis on the "Oral Torah" and the Mishnah, but I had already called attention to Rava's scriptural interests and their social grounding, in a paper delivered in 2003 and published in 2007.[40] Maḥoza was a suburb of the Persian winter capital of Ctesiphon, the home of a higher acculturated Jewish community, along with a similar Christian community. Moreover, as I have shown, the Jewish community included people highly skeptical of rabbinic authority, and one argument that Rava used was that the rabbis controlled the authoritative interpretation of Scripture.

In any case, it is clear that neither Rabbah nor Rava connected internal neutrality with the nullification accomplished by digestion, and that applies to the scriptural interpretation of Lev. 11:40 as well, since there is no time for digestion to have taken place. The neutralization or even nullification must be due to the ingestion and/or the inaccessibility of the

---

Rava employs this in Pes. 54b and BB 115b, but that is merely a manifestation of Rava's wide-ranging exegetical program.

38. Ber. 20b, 60a, 63a; Shab 24b–133a, 153b; Eruv. 66b, 57a; Pes. 54a, 83b, 85b; Yom. 53a, 71a (twice); Meg. 2b, 17a, 20b; Suk. 43a; MQ 8a; Yev. 8a, 23a; Ket 33a [=40b=Ar. 15a]; Naz. 19b, 36a, 45b, 58a, 61a; Git. 48b; Qid. 5a, 50b; BQ 22b, 25b, 67b, 71a, 88a, 90a, 101a, 111a; BM 47a; BB 12b, 109b, 111b, 113a, 120a; Sanh. 84a [=Zev 23b], 97a [in the name of his teacher, R. Naḥman]; AZ 8a; Hor. 9a, 11b, Zev 9a, 43b, 94a, 107b; Ḥul. 22b, 91a; Bek. 10b, 12b, 26b, 53b, 56a; Tem. 5b, [twice], 6a [twice], 10a, 25b; Ker. 17b, 24b, 26a [twice].

39. Ber. 60a, 63a; Yev. 8a; Ket. 33a=40b=Ar. 15a; Naz 58a, 61a; Git. 48a; Qid. 50b; BQ 22b, 67b.

40. See my "The Socioeconomics of Babylonian Heresy," *Jewish Law Association Studies* 17 (2007): 80–126.

impure substance, *a la* Balberg. This then suggests that the redactional intervention here differs in its view of digestion from the one we shall examine below.

However, there is another possibility. As we shall see, the redactional explanation below distinguishes two stages of digestion, that "above" and that "below," with the one "below" having greater power. "Below" clearly refers to the intestines. "Above" might refer to the stomach (as in the Galenic argument above), or perhaps to the mouth, where the teeth and saliva begin the digestive process. And, as my student Meir Rubin pointed out in detail in a paper inspired by an earlier version of the current one,[41] the Bavli had at its disposal a second-generation dispute (as it appears in the Bavli) between R. Yoḥanan and R. Shimon b. Laqish on whether it is "enjoyment of the gullet" or "enjoyment of the belly" that defines consumption of food. Here is the passage, with the rendering of the Soncino translation except for slight changes; as usual, the relevant footnotes have been incorporated into the bracketed material:

אמר ר"ש בן לקיש: כזית שאמרו - חוץ משל בין השינים, ורבי יוחנן אמר: אף עם בין השינים.

אמר רב פפא: בשל בין שינים - דכולי עלמא לא פליגי, כי פליגי - בין החניכיים, מר סבר - הרי נהנה גרונו בכזית, ומר סבר - אכילה במעיו בעינן.

אמר רבי אסי אמר רבי יוחנן: אכל חצי זית והקיאו, וחזר ואכל חצי זית אחר חייב, מ"ט - הרי נהנה גרונו בכזית.

בעא רבי אלעזר מר' אסי: אכל חצי זית והקיאו, וחזר ואכלו, מהו? מאי קא מיבעיא ליה? אי הוי עיכול אי לא הוי עיכול, ותיבעי ליה כזית! אלא, אי בתר גרונו אזלינן אי בתר מעיו אזלינן, ותפשוט ליה מדרבי אסי! רבי אסי גמריה איעקר ליה, ואתא ר' אלעזר לאדכוריה, והכי קאמר ליה: למה לי חצי זית אחר, לימא מר בדידיה, דאיכא למשמע מינה תרתי, שמעינן מינה - דלא הוי עיכול, ושמעינן מינה - דהרי נהנה גרונו בכזית! אישתיק ולא א"ל ולא מידי, א"ל: מופת הדור, לא זימנין סגיאין אמרת קמיה דרבי יוחנן, ואמר לך: הרי נהנה גרונו בכזית.

---

41. "What Role Does Digestion Play in the Rabbinic Definition of 'Eating'?"

R. Shimon b. Laqish said: The quantity of an olive's bulk of which they [the Rabbis] have spoken [as constituting consumption—YE] does not include that which is between the teeth. [This and the subsequent cases until the end of the chapter apparently refer to all prohibited substances. According to R. Shimon b. Laqish a person is liable only if he swallowed a whole olive's bulk, i.e., this quantity entered his stomach, but not if he put an exact olive's bulk into his mouth, for in the process of mastication some of the substance would certainly adhere between the teeth and this cannot be reckoned together with the amount swallowed]. R. Yoḥanan said: It includes even that which remains between the teeth.

Said R. Papa: As to that which remains between the teeth they certainly do not disagree [that is, all hold that it cannot be reckoned together with that which has been swallowed, for neither the gullet nor the stomach has derived any enjoyment therefrom]; they disagree only as to that which remains in the palate and tongue. One [R. Yoḥanan] maintains [that he is liable], since his gullet has derived enjoyment from a whole olive's bulk; the other [R. Shimon b. Laqish] maintains [that he is not liable, because] there must enter his stomach the full amount which constitutes "eating."

R. Assi said in the name of R. Yoḥanan: If a person ate one half-olive's bulk [of a forbidden substance] and vomited it out, and then [that is, within the period of time it takes to eat a half-loaf of the size of four (according to Maimonides, three) ordinary eggs,] ate another half-olive's bulk, he is liable. Why? Because his gullet has derived enjoyment from an olive's bulk.

R. Assi said in the name of R. Yoḥanan: If a person ate one half-olive's bulk [of a forbidden substance] and vomited it out, and ate another half-olive's bulk, he is liable. Why? [It is] because his gullet has derived enjoyment from an olive's bulk.

R. Eleazar enquired of R. Assi: What is the law if a person ate one half-olive's bulk [of a forbidden substance], vomited it forth and then ate it once again?

[Let us see], what was his real question? If the question was whether it [that is, what has been vomited out] is considered as digested food or not, then he might have put the question with regard to a complete olive's bulk [that is, if a person ate an olive's bulk of a forbidden substance, vomited it out, and swallowed it again, would he be liable twice or once only?]; and if the question was whether we regard [eating from the enjoyment of] the gullet or [from the enjoyment of] the stomach, then he might have solved this himself from R. Assi's statement above [in the preceding passage where R. Assi expressly states that the main factor of eating is the enjoyment of the gullet]?

[Actually,] R. Assi had forgotten the tradition [he had received from R. Yoḥanan], and R. Eleazar came and reminded him of it in the following manner [R. Eleazar himself was not in doubt at all about the law, but he put the case before R. Assi in the form of a question in order to remind him in the most respectful manner of the decision given by R. Yohanan.]: 'Why speak of another half-olive's bulk [which the person swallowed after he had vomited out a half-olive's bulk]? The Master could have dealt with the same [half-olive's bulk], by which two results would have been established, namely, we would have learned from it that it [that is, that which was vomited out] was not considered as digested food, and we would also have learned from it that [one is liable if only] the gullet had derived enjoyment from an olive's bulk.' He remained silent and made no reply at all. Thereupon he [R. Eleazar] said to him, 'O wonder of the generation! Did you not often say this [that he is liable even in the case of the same half-olive's bulk] before R. Yoḥanan and he agreed with you saying: "His gullet has in fact derived enjoyment from an olive's bulk."[42]

Note the redactors' efforts to determine the physiological meaning of "enjoyment of the gullet" and "enjoyment of the stomach." However, the word that Soncino renders as "his stomach" is *me'av*, which should rather be translated as "his innards," that is, the intestines. Whether the intestines include the stomach or not is here irrelevant, since it is clear that the redactors counterpose the "gullet" (*garon*) to the intestines (*me'ayim*). It is at least arguable that the redactors of Ḥullin 71a would similarly counterpose "above" and "below" in the same manner. If so, it would suggest that the Bavli's redactors conceptualized the human digestive system using the same distinction as their somewhat earlier Zoroastrian colleagues: it consists of the organ of ingestion (the mouth) and also the organ which produces the greater part of the digestive process (the intestines, including the stomach).

Still, the fact that saliva hardly does more than initiate the process of digestion explains why Resh Laqish opted for it as the primary organ of "enjoyment" or "benefit," and thus *hana'ah* here has the meaning of "enjoyment" rather than "benefit:" the emphasis is on the pleasure or enjoyment one receives from ingesting the food, rather than the feeling

---

42. Bavli Ḥullin 103b.

of satiation after digestion. R. Yoḥanan, in contrast, opts for the latter, at least according to the Bavli. It is significant, however, that in the Palestinian version of the debate—both disputants were Galileans—it is the "enjoyment of the palate" (*hana'at ḥiqo*) that is stressed by R. Shimon b Laqish, while the "innards" do not appear in the Yerushalmi passage at all. Moreover, it should be remembered that the debate here (as in the Bavli) centers not on pollution, but on how and under what circumstances one who ingests a limb torn from a living animal is culpable, since in the case of this prohibition, the emphasis is on a "limb" rather than the usual "olive's-bulk" that determines culpability in matters of consumption of forbidden substances. Here is the relevant part of the Yerushalmi passage:

ר' [יוסי] או' לחברייא. הוו ידעין דאיתפלגון ר' יוחנן ור' שמעון בן לקיש. אבר מן החי שחלקו ואכלו. דברי הכל פטור. מה פליגין. בשחלקו בפיו ואכלו. ר' יוחנן עבד פיו כלפנים. רבי שמעון בן לקיש עבד פיו כלחוץ. אמרין ליה. את מה אמר. אמ' לון. אנא אמרי לכון. הרי עולם פליגין ואתון אמרין אכן. אין כיני אפילו חלקו בחוץ ואכלו יהא חייב. למה. דרך אכילה היא.

ר' בא בר' מלל בעי. כזית מצה (שא) שחלקו בפיו ואכלו. תפלוג'... דר' יוחנן ור' שמעון בן לקיש. אמ' ר' יוסי ביר' בון. בכל מקום לא נהנה חיכו כזית.[43]

R. [Yose][44] says to the Colleagues: You should know that R. Yoḥanan and R. Shimon b. Laqish dispute [the issue of] a limb torn from a living animal which has been divided and eaten [and so each part consists of less than a "limb"]. Both agree [that the one who consumes these parts] is not culpable. When do they disagree? When it is divided in the mouth and eaten, R. Yoḥanan considers his mouth as within [the body], [and] R. Shimon b. Laqish considers his mouth as without. They [=the Colleagues] asked him: And you, what [do you say]? He said to them: I report to you that great scholars dispute, and you ask me such a thing? Yes, this it is: Even [if] it was divided without and eaten, he should be culpable: Why? It is the usual manner of eating [that is, dividing a meal into bite-size portions].

R. [A]ba b. R. Melel asked: is an olive-bulk of matza which has been divided in his mouth and eaten [likewise the object of] of dispute between R. Yoḥanan and R. Shimon b. Laqish? Said R.

---

43. The text reflects that of *Talmud Yerushalmi*, Nazir 6:1 (54d) as published under the auspices of The Academy of the Hebrew Language, Jerusalem, 2001, with an introduction by Yaakov Sussman.

44. Name restored by Qorban ha-Edah *ad loc.*

Yose b. R. [A]bun: Everywhere [the issue concerns the question of whether] his palate has enjoyed an olive's-bulk [of food].

For the Yerushalmi, the issue is taste and whether the divided limb is considered inside or outside the mouth of the one consuming it, since in the ordinary course of eating one divides a portion of food with his hands; for the Bavli, it has become a matter of digestion, and thus the dispute has been transformed as between one who stressed the action of the mouth or hand versus one who stressed the action of the mouth or the intestines. As for Abarg and Mēdōmāh, the essential issue is the *transformation* of the dead matter; according to Abarg, once that transformation begins, that is sufficient to transform *nasā* into *hixr*, while Mēdōmāh requires a full transformation, which is signaled by defecation. Thus, while the later Iranian sources (that is, the Bavli and the Pahlavi book) stress ingestion and digestion, the Yerushalmi stresses ingestion alone.

Likewise, in both Ḫullin 103b and 71a, the redactors attempt to understand earlier sources in terms of their referents in the new Galenic digestive scheme. Once again, we may understand why in the passage below, Rava, in the first half of the fourth century, quotes a Mishnah in regard to *inorganic* polluted matter that has been swallowed. It would seem that for him digestion was not the issue; the interior of the body itself nullifies pollution without any other process intervening. The mishnaic view still stood.

The Bavli's redactors, however, widen their inquiry to the question of whether *animal* ingestion follows Rabbah's rule regarding human ingestion. It is important to note—once again—that the Mishnah regarding a dead dog which had ingested some corpse matter before its death, or the rooster that fell into an oven of Kelim 8:5, are not cited here; the redactional argument was not sparked by that earlier rabbinic source, but by their own concerns. Moreover, they preferred a logical argument over appealing to the authority of an earlier rabbinic text. This concern may have been prompted (at least in part) by the intention to counter the Zoroastrian view that substances ingested by animals could still be polluting. It should be stressed that the logical arguments in this passage are also redactional, and thus date from the latter half of the fifth century at the earliest. This would also accord with Babylonian skepticism of rabbinic authority, which dated back to the previous century, and may have been instanced by the growth of the Karaite movement.[45]

---

45. See my "Acculturation to Elite Persian Norms in the Babylonian Jewish

After an *a fortiori* argument for the notion that the interior of the body is a neutral zone that protects ritually pure objects from becoming impure, the redactors turn to discussing the differences between "upper interiors" and "lower interiors," and thus bring digestion into the debate:

אשכחן בלוע דלמעלה, בלוע דלמטה מנלן?

קל וחומר: ומה למעלה שאינו עושה עיכול - מציל, למטה שעושה עיכול - אינו דין שמציל?

כלום עושה עיכול למטה אלא על ידי מעלה!

אפי' הכי, עיכול דלמטה רב.

אשכחן בלוע דאדם, בלוע דבהמה מנלן?

קל וחומר: ומה אדם שמטמא מחיים - מציל בבלוע, בהמה שאינה מטמאה מחיים - אינו דין שתציל בבלוע?

מה לאדם - שכן צריך שהייה בבית המנוגע, תאמר בבהמה - שאינה צריכה שהייה בבית המנוגע! בהמה, דאינה צריכה שהייה בבית המנוגע למאי הלכתא - לכלים שעל גבה, אדם - נמי לא בעי, דתנן: הנכנס לבית המנוגע וכליו על כתפיו, וסנדליו וטבעותיו בידיו - הוא והן טמאין מיד, היה לבוש כליו, וסנדליו ברגליו, וטבעותיו באצבעו - הוא טמא מיד, והן טהורין, עד שישהא בכדי אכילת פרס - פת חטים ולא פת שעורים, מיסב ואוכל בליפתן.

We have thus learnt the law regarding uncleanness swallowed from above [that is, through the mouth], but whence do we know that it is so even when the uncleanness was swallowed from below? [That is, the unclean matter was inserted into the body from below via the rectum. It must be, says Rashi, that it was inserted by a tube so that the unclean matter did not come into direct contact with the body of the person. It must further be explained that this action was performed a little before sunset, as above.]

[We would know this] from the following *a fortiori* argument. If in the upper part of the body where no digestion [of food] takes place [the fact that it is swallowed] prevents [the unclean matter from conveying uncleanness], how much more so in the lower part where the actual digestion takes place!

But digestion takes place below only if the food comes from above! —

Community of Late Antiquity," in *Neti'ot David*, ed. by E. Halivni, Z. A. Steinfeld, and Y. Elman (Jerusalem: Orhot, 2004), 31–56.

Even so, the fact that digestion takes place below is a stronger point [in the argument; so that the *a fortiori* reasoning holds good].

We have now learnt the law regarding uncleanness swallowed by man, but whence do we know it with regard to uncleanness swallowed by an animal? [We know it] from the following *a fortiori* argument: If in the case of man, who is capable of conveying uncleanness while alive, the fact that it is swallowed prevents [the unclean matter from conveying uncleanness], how much more so is it in the case of animals, which are incapable of conveying uncleanness while alive, that the fact that it is swallowed prevents [the unclean matter within from conveying uncleanness]!

Before moving on to the rest of the passage, I must at least mention one other redactional use of the word *'ikkul*. It appears in Menaḥot 69a-b, where a problem propounded by Rava's senior colleague, Rammi b. Ḥamma, is converted into a query on the power of digestion:

בעי רמי בר חמא: פיל שבלע כפיפה מצרית והקיאה דרך בית הרעי, מהו? למאי? אילימא למבטל טומאתה, תנינא: כל הכלים יורדין לידי טומאתן במחשבה, ואין עולין מטומאתן אלא בשינוי מעשה! לא צריכא, דבלע הוציו ועבדינהו כפיפה מצרית, מי הוה עיכול, הוה ליה [סט עמוד ב] ככלי גללים ככלי אדמה ואין מקבלין טומאה, דאמר מר: כלי אבנים וכלי גללים וכלי אדמה - אין מקבלין טומאה לא מדברי תורה ולא מדברי סופרים, או דלמא לא הוי עיכול?

Rami b. Ḥama raised the question. What is the law if an elephant swallowed an osier basket and passed it out with its excrement? In what connection does the question arise? If you say with regard to the annulment of its uncleanness [that is, the basket was unclean before it was swallowed, and it is suggested that now it should be regarded as clean, having divested itself of its uncleanness], but we have learnt it: All articles are rendered susceptible to uncleanness through intention. [The intention of a person to use an article in its present state for some purpose (even though the article normally serves another purpose and for that purpose the article is not yet complete) makes it susceptible to contract uncleanness. E.g., a hide is normally used for the making of shoes, so that before it is made into shoes it will not contract uncleanness. If, however, a man intended to use the hide, as it is now, for a mattress or a table cover, it thereby becomes susceptible to contract uncleanness] and divest themselves of their uncleanness only by an act which changes them!

[An article that is already unclean loses its uncleanness only if its structure has changed; e.g.. if it is broken. (Mishnah Kelim 25:9, Bavli Shabbat 52b, Sukkah 13b, Qiddushin 59a). In the case in question, since the basket is unchanged it still retains its uncleanness.] –

The case must be that it swallowed twigs and [the twigs when passed out] were made into an osier basket, and the question is: are [the twigs] regarded as 'digested' so that now [what is made from them is accounted] [69b] as a vessel made from cattle dung or from earth, which does not contract uncleanness. For the Master has stated: Vessels made from stone, from cattle dung or from earth do not contract uncleanness, either by Biblical or by Rabbinical law [Shabbat 58a; see Kelim 10:1]; or perhaps they are not regarded as 'digested' [so that the basket can contract uncleanness]?

Once again, the question of digestion is raised by the redactors.

Returning to Ḥullin 71a–72a, the Bavli's redactor(s) now introduce Rava's suggestion, and create a virtual dialogue (in the modern sense) between him and Rabbah—a dialogue that could never have occurred due to both chronological and geographical reasons. In this part of the passage, there is no question of digestion, since the case is of a dead fetus in the womb, and so the issue can only be one of a neutral interior—but one which the dead fetus still imparts uncleanness while still in the body, at least to a midwife who touches it. In response, Rava suggests that this pollution is rabbinically ordained in case the fetus protrudes its head outside the birth canal. In the roughly parallel case in PV 5.45, a woman gives birth to a still-born baby and is thereby polluted; what the rule would be while the fetus is yet unborn is not clear, though presumably, if it were dead, the woman would be polluted. Rava then provides a mishnaic support for Rabbah's statement, but since we have passed from considerations of digestion, we need not pursue the argument in detail. As we stressed above, rings are inorganic and cannot be digested. We will thus concentrate on the first part of the passage:

אמר רבא: תרוייהו תננהי; טומאה בלועה תנינא, טהרה בלועה תנינא.
טומאה בלועה, דתנן: בלע טבעת טמאה - טובל ואוכל בתרומתו,
הקיאה - טמאה וטמאתו. טהרה בלועה תנינא, דתנן: בלע טבעת
טהורה, ונכנס לאהל המת, והזה ושנה וטבל והקיאה - הרי היא כמה
שהיתה, כי קאמר רבה כגון שבלע שתי טבעות, אחת טמאה ואחת
טהורה, דלא מטמיא לה מטמאה לטהורה. [עב עמוד א] והא עובר
וחיה, דכשתי טבעות דמו, וקא מטמא לה עובר לחיה!

אמר רבה: שאני עובר, הואיל וסופו לצאת.

אמר רבא: עובר - סופו לצאת, טבעת - אין סופו לצאת?

אלא אמר רבא: פומבדיתאי ידעי טעמא דהא מילתא, ומנו - רב יוסף; דאמר רב יוסף אמר רב יהודה אמר שמואל: טומאה זו אינה מדברי תורה, אלא מדברי סופרים.

מאי אינה מדברי תורה אלא מדברי סופרים? דלא תימא אליבא דר' עקיבא דאמר: עובר במעי אשה - טמא, אלא אפי' לר' ישמעאל דאמר: עובר במעי אשה - טהור, גזרו בה טומאה מדרבנן.

מאי טעמא?

אמר רב הושעיא: גזירה שמא יוציא ולד ראשו חוץ לפרוזדור. אי הכי אשה נמי! אשה מרגשת בעצמה. ותימא לה לחיה! טרידא...

    Rava said: But we have [already] learned both these rules [in a mishnaic text]:[46] We have learned the rule concerning swallowed unclean matter, and we have learned the rule concerning swallowed clean matter. Concerning swallowed unclean matter we have learned the following Mishnah (Miqvaot 10:8): If a person swallowed an unclean ring,[47] he must immerse himself [because he was rendered unclean by contact with the ring before swallowing it], and thereafter may eat *terumah* [a priestly gift; since he may do so, he is not rendered unclean by the unclean ring, that is, in his body, thus proving that a swallowed unclean matter cannot render unclean.] But if he vomited it out [after this immersion], it is still unclean and has rendered him unclean [through contact as a result of the vomiting].

    And concerning swallowed clean matter we have learnt the following Mishnah (Miqvaot 10:8): If a person swallowed a clean ring, entered a tent wherein lay a corpse, was sprinkled

---

46. What, then, is the point of Rabbah's teaching? This is, as noted above, a redactional question. Rava himself perhaps only intended to suggest an alternative source for the rule. However, in the end, he decides, on the basis of the statement by R. Joseph, Rabbah's successor at Pumbedita, that this form of uncleanness is a rabbinic enactment and not biblical at all.

As to why Rava chose this Mishnah to prove that internal pollution does not pollute the person or any ritually clean swallowed substance, rather than other texts (such as Kelim 8:5 or Ohalot 11:7), it would seem that this proof was more efficient, since it served to prove both points.

47. It was rendered unclean by reason of its having been brought into contact with a corpse, in which case the ring, made of metal, assumed the same degree, and not a lesser degree, of uncleanness as the corpse itself (see Ḥullin 3a). This assumption is necessary since lower degrees of pollution do not affect humans; that is, if the rings had been polluted to a lower degree, they would not in turn pollute humans.

[with purification waters] the first time and the second time [as prescribed by Numbers 19:19], immersed himself, and then vomited it out, it remains as it was before!⁴⁸

[The redactor responds:] Rabbah had in mind the case where a person swallowed two rings, one clean and the other unclean, [and he teaches that] the unclean ring will not render the clean ring unclean.⁴⁹

[72a] But is not the case of the fetus and the midwife [of our Mishnah] similar to two rings [since both the fetus and the hand of the midwife can be seen as "swallowed" in the womb]? And nevertheless the fetus renders the midwife unclean [while you maintain that internal pollution is nullified]! [Why then derive it from Miqvaot?]

Rabbah [could have]⁵⁰ replied, "It is different in the case of the fetus because it must eventually come out [and is therefore not considered "swallowed"]!"

Rava retorted:⁵¹ The fetus [you say] must eventually come out; and must not the ring also eventually come out [but of course it is not Rabbah who introduced the case of the rings, so this question could not have been directed to him]?

Rava therefore replied: The 'Pumbedithans' (by which R. Joseph, who succeeded Rabbah in Pumbedita, is meant) know the reason for it. For R. Joseph said in the name of R. Judah who said it in the name of Samuel: This uncleanness [of the midwife] was not imposed by Biblical law but by decree of the Scribes.

---

48. That is, clean, thus proving that a swallowed clean matter cannot contract uncleanness. For had the ring suffered uncleanness when the man entered under the same roof as the corpse, at which time the ring was swallowed within him, it would not now, when vomited forth, be clean, for the immersion and purification of the man could be of no avail with regard to the ring.

49. This is a special case that could not so readily have been inferred from the cases stated in the above quoted teachings from Miqvaot. For it might have been suggested that the reason for the ruling in those two cases was that the contact between the ring and the person was made in the secret parts of the body, and such contact is not considered contact for the purpose of contracting or conveying uncleanness. In the case, however, where two rings were swallowed and both now lie in the secret parts, the argument of secret contact cannot apply for it is as though they are together in a chest, when one would certainly render the other unclean. Rava, however, by stating his view that even in the case of two rings, one cannot render the other unclean, strikingly informs us that the ground for the rulings in the Mishnah is that the matter is swallowed, and for that reason, it cannot contract or convey uncleanness.

50. Following MS Munich 95, since it is likely that the two never met.

51. Or rather, he could have retorted.

> Why is it said 'was not imposed by Biblical law but by decree of the Scribes'?
>
> So that you should not say that our Mishnah agrees [only] with R. Akiva who holds that a [dead] fetus while yet in the womb of its mother is unclean [and accordingly the midwife is by Biblical law rendered unclean by reason of contact with the fetus, for a swallowed unclean matter can convey uncleanness; the mother, however, remains clean because the uncleanness touches her in her secret parts and this does not render her unclean]; for indeed it is even in accordance with R. Ishmael who holds that the [dead] fetus while yet in the womb of its mother is clean, yet here the uncleanness [to the midwife] was imposed by Rabbinic decree. Why?
>
> R. Hoshaia said: As a precaution lest the fetus protrude its head beyond the ante-chamber [in which case, according to all views, the midwife would become unclean by Biblical law, for the fetus is by the protrusion of its head regarded as born].
>
> Then this should apply to the mother too [that is, this Rabbinic decree should apply also to the mother, to render her unclean as well]!—
>
> The mother would feel it [that is, that the head had emerged].
>
> Then she might tell the midwife of it?
>
> She is too distraught …

Above I called attention to the need for leniency in systems of pollution in order to allow for the orderly rounds of life, religious and secular. By declaring the pollution of a dead embryo to be of rabbinic enactment, Rava has done just this in this case. This is similar to the declaration of the transformation of dead matter to dry dead matter in PV 5.1–4. However, for Rava, who based his proof on Mishnah Miqvaot 10:8 in regard to inorganic matter, it is clear that "lingering" did not yet have the transformative power of digestion. It therefore remained for the redactors of the Bavli to resolve the problem of regenerating pollution when the neutralized pollution had been vomited up. While not contravening the Mishnah's decision, the redactors did provide a means of full nullification, one that the neutralizing power of internal pollution did not provide, but digestion did.

This brings us to another important point which will draw our investigation of digestion into the broader sphere of what we may call rabbinic and Zoroastrian nominalistic legislative policy. In the Mishnah, invisibility and inaccessibility were modes of neutralizing pollution. Recognizing the transformative powers of digestion added another mode, thus adding another entry onto the ledger of leniency. Recognizing digestion as a mitigating factor acted in the same way for the Zoroastrian dastwars. Though we cannot go into the further applications of this principle at this time, let me call attention to an important insight that Shamma Friedman provided us in his book on Tosefta: nullification of *ḥametz* by intention in the Bavli was yet another means by which the Bavli's redactors added a lenient mode into the laws of Passover.[52] This innovation, like Rava's emphasis on intention in areas that the Mishnah did not consider, may have been fostered by the Zoroastrian emphasis on good thoughts.[53]

In sum, my essential argument is not that the redactors of the Bavli, or that Abarg and Mēdōmāh, were aware of Galen's works, or other Graeco-Roman medical works, but that the transformative nature of digestion, and its consequent relationship to nullification of pollution, became an object of interest and discussion in the wake of the influence of those works. In the case of the Bavli, the mishnaic doctrine of neutral internal space was already in place, and could be explained or expanded by the action of digestion. In the case of PV, we have no way of ascertaining the views that preceded the debate between Abarg and Mēdōmāh, but since Abarg and Mēdōmāh lived in the first half of the fifth century, the debate between them most likely took place half-a-century before the redactional era of the Bavli really began.[54] It may thus be that this item of Graeco-Roman medical information came to the Bavli's redactors through more local sources. Of course, in the heterogeneous multi-ethnic and multi-religious environment of the Sasanian Empire, the redactors would have had other sources of information. Further research is needed

---

52. See Shamma Y. Friedman, *Tosefta Atiqta: Masekhet Pesah Rishon, Maqbilot ha-Mishnah veha-Tosefta be-Tzeruf Mavo Kelali* (Ramat Gan: Bar Ilan University Press, 2002), 333–47.

53. See, provisionally, my "Hercules Within the Halakhic Tradition: A Response to Ronald Dworkin," *Dinei Yisrael* 25 (2008): 7*–42*, and Shana Strauch-Schick's dissertation, "Intention in the Babylonian Talmud: An Intellectual History" (Ph.D. diss., Yeshiva University, 2011). The dissertation is being revised for publication; I, too, hope to return to this issue on another occasion.

54. See n.24 above.

to determine the exact mix of cultural elements that went into the formation of the redactional layer of the Bavli.

5

Fire Typologies in Zoroastrianism and in the Babylonian Talmud

A Methodological Consideration[1]

GEOFFREY HERMAN

THE ELABORATE CULT OF fire among the ancient Persians belongs to the earliest strata of Zoroastrian religious writings, and is a central component of the entire religious system of Zoroastrianism. Fire temples were ubiquitous, and fire altars typically feature on Zoroastrian coins, as well as on many seals,[2] as their dominant and foremost icon. Fire was, in fact, one of the most distinctive and noticeable aspects of the Zoroastrian faith throughout the Sasanian era.

---

1. A version of this paper was presented at the conference, The Halakhah: An Unchanging Canon? On the Halakhah in Changing Circumstances, 16–18 May, 2016, Ben-Gurion University of the Negev. I thankfully acknowledge discussing the matters of this paper with my friend, Prof. Dan Shapira of Bar-Ilan University.

2. Indeed, coins that reveal the image of the god, Ādur, are known, apparently, from the fourth century. Priests recite the daily prayers before fire. The careful preparation and tending of fires, maintenance of their purity, are basic to religious practice—certainly in post-Achaemenid times. The popularity of the worship of the god of fire, Ādur, is also suggested by the prosopographical record of Persians in this period.

Persian veneration of fire was also well known throughout the ancient world,[3] and this was no less true for the Jews living in the Sasanian Empire. Indeed, the Zoroastrian notions of the sanctity of fire may have impinged upon the Jews of Babylonia, as suggested in an anecdote related in *b. Gittin* 16b-17a concerning a *ḥabar* (magus) who seized the burning lamp from before a company of rabbis.[4] Elsewhere in the Babylonian Talmud, the legal question of providing wood or other items that would serve a fire temple is addressed.[5]

The centrality of fire in the Persian milieu may have also left its mark on Jewish tradition in other ways. I have proposed elsewhere that the manner in which the festival of Ḥanukkah was marked underwent a tremendous transition in Babylonia in the course of the Sasanian era. This is evident, in particular, with regard to the ritual kindling of the candles in all its detail, and the fixing of the central discussion on Ḥanukkah in the second chapter of Tractate Shabbat, which deals with the materials that can be used for the preparation of Sabbath candles. This shift, I have suggested, is inspired by the centrality of fire worship among the Persians.[6] In this paper, I would like to consider further how the centrality of fire worship among the Persians may have affected the Jews inhabiting the Persian empire. I shall start by casting our vision back to a historiographical episode from the very beginnings of the comparative research of Persia and Israel. This will provide an opportunity to address some issues of methodology, and will furnish a broader understanding of how religious cultures might affect one another.

---

3. On the classical sources see Albert De Jong, *Traditions of the Magi: Zoroastrianism in Greek and Latin Literature* (Leiden: Brill, 1997), 343–50.

4. See b. Ned. 62b. On this, see, especially, E. S. Rosenthal, "For the Talmudic Dictionary—Talmudica Iranica," in *Irano-Judaica*, ed. S. Shaked (Jerusalem: Ben-Zvi Institute, 1982), 38–41.

5. B. San. 74b; b. Shab. 45a. On these traditions, see Rosenthal, "For the Talmudic Dictionary," 41, 58–59. For the Geonic discussion of this tradition see, R. Brody, "Zoroastrian Themes in Geonic Responsa," *Irano-Judaica* IV (1999), 182–86.

6. For the details see G. Herman, "Religious Transformation between East and West: Ḥanukkah in the Babylonian Talmud and Zoroastrianism," in *Religions and Trade: Religious Formation, Transformation and Cross-Cultural Exchange between East and West*, ed. P. Wick and V. Rabens (DHR; Leiden: Brill, 2013), 261–82.

SCHORR AND KOHUT

The question of who was the first to identify what was claimed to be a stunning parallel between two sources, one Zoroastrian and the other from the Babylonian Talmud, is hard to determine, since both scholars, Joshua Heschel Schorr and Alexander Kohut, announced their discovery at almost the same time, about 150 years ago: Schorr in his journal, *HeḤalutz*, in the Hebrew year 5625 (1865); Kohut, in his doctoral dissertation on angels and demons in Judaism and their relation to Persian religion, that appeared in print in Leipzig in 1866.[7] While strictly speaking, Schorr's publication appeared first, Kohut appended to the end of his book a *Nachtrag* in which he declares that his book had been completed and ready for the press at the time when Schorr's journal reached him.[8]

Both had, in fact, drunk from the same source. Exactly two years previously the monumental volume by Friedrich Windischmann, *Zoroastrische Studien*, had appeared in Berlin (posthumously), and it contained the first full translation of *Bundahišn*, a Middle-Persian anthology of traditions focusing on cosmogony which was redacted in the ninth century.[9]

For Schorr, this parallel offered the ultimate proof of what he had tirelessly labored to demonstrate: "Even the stubborn cannot maintain within himself the lie and deny that just as I have claimed, it is indeed

---

7. Hehalutz 7 (1865): 48–49; A. Kohut, *Über die jüdische Angelologie und Dämonologie in ihrer Abhängigkeit vom Parsismus* (Leipzig, 1866): 32–33. See, too, Shelomo Rubin, *Paras Vihuda* (Podgorze, Poland: Wettstein, 1909), 97–98, but he sought to demonstrate the dependence of the Kabbalah on Zoroastrian veneration of fire.

8. Kohut, *Angelologie*, 96–105. He also questioned the academic quality of Schorr's work with a little more condescension than fully justified. While his afterword devoted some ten pages to detailed critique of particular aspects in Schorr's work, it did not relate to the sources discussed here.

9. This composition has reached us in two versions: an Indian and an Iranian one. The scholars who have discussed this parallel in the context of the Jewish source were only familiar with the Indian version, while the Iranian version is generally held to be earlier and more authentic. See Carlo G. Cereti, *La Letteratura Pahlavi*, Mimesis, 2001, 87–105. Maria Macuch, "Pahlavi Literature," in *The Literature of Pre-Islamic Iran—Companion Volume I: A History of Persian Literature*, ed. ed. Ronald E. Emmerick and Maria Macuch (New York: Tauris, 2009), 137–39; Dan D .Y. Shapira, "Pahlavi Fire, Bundahishn 18," *ARAM* 26 (2014): 127–49. Shortly afterwards appeared the edition by Ferdinand Justi, *Der Bundahesh* (Leipzig, 1868). An additional source of relevance, also from the ninth century, is the *Anthology of Zadspram*, which provides similar material to the *Bundahišn*.

so."¹⁰ What he had intimated, in fact, repeatedly in the volume, was that post-exilic Judaism, and rabbinic Judaism in particular, had borrowed considerably from Persian religion, in both Halakha and Aggada.¹¹ Kohut, too, was not far from this view, but in this particular case he had not made far-reaching claims, satisfying himself with merely pointing out the parallel in support of a local matter within his volume.¹²

The next scholar to relate to these sources was the French Jew, James Darmesteter, in the very first issue of *Revue des études juives* in 1880. He evoked Kohut's study, alone, and, with his expertise in Iranology, conducted a thorough comparison between the Zoroastrian and talmudic sources.¹³ The parallel sources concern the taxonomy of fire. In this paper I shall ask whether that which was considered an impressive parallel 150 years ago still impresses us, and what conclusions we might reach from it today.

TAXONOMIES OF FIRE

The talmudic source, from b. Yoma 21b, is as follows:¹⁴

ת"ר: שש אשות הן:
יש אוכלת ואינה שותה
ויש שותה ואינה אוכלת
ויש אוכלת ושותה
ויש אוכלת לחין כיבשין
ויש אש דוחה אש

10. "גם המתעקש לא יוכל לעשות בנפשו שקר ולהכחיש כי כאשר אמרתי כן הוא".

11. On this tendency with Schorr, see, in brief, Ezra Spicehandler, "Joshua Heschel Schorr—The Mature Years," *Hebrew Union College Annual* 40–41 (1969–1970): 521. He hints at the need for a full examination and reassessment of Schorr's work on Persia.

12. It is not without interest to the concerns of this paper that few of the other parallels that Kohut addressed in his volume have withstood the test of time.

13. James Darmesteter, "Les six feux dans le Talmud et dans le Bundehesh," *REJ* 1 (1880): 186–96. Some of Darmesteter's other studies of parallels between Jewish and Zoroastrian religion appear less compelling and have found few followers. See, e.g., his brief suggestions of correspondence in James Darmesteter, *The Zend Avesta*, Part I, *The Vendîdâd* (New York, 1898), III, lvii–lx.

14. The source is presented according to the Vilna printed edition of the Talmud. There is little variation between this version and the other textual witnesses of this source.

ויש אש אוכלת אש

"יש אש אוכלת ואינה שותה" - הא דידן.

"שותה ואינה אוכלת" – דחולין

"אוכלת ושותה" - דאליהו, דכתיב (מלכים א יח לח) ואת המים אשר בתעלה לחכה

"אוכלת לחין כיבשין" – דמערכה;

"יש אש דוחה אש" – דגבריאל;

"ויש אש אוכלת אש" - דשכינה. דאמר מר: הושיט אצבעו ביניהם ושרפן.

The Rabbis taught: There are six fires:
There is that which consumes but does not drink;
and there is that which drinks but does not consume;
and there is that which consumes and drinks;
there is that which consumes wet as dry;
and there is fire that repels fire
and there is fire that consumes fire.

There is that which consumes but does not drink—this is our own (fire);
that which drinks but does not consume—of the sick;
that which consumes and drinks—of Elijah, as it is written: "and [the fire] licked up the water that was in the trench" (1 Kings 18:38);
that which consumes wet as dry—of the altar
fire that repels fire—of Gabriel
fire that consumes fire—of the Divine Presence (*Shekhina*), as the master said: "he stretched forth his finger between them and burned them."

This source consists of a *baraita*, which provides us with a typology of fires, in Hebrew, followed by an Amoraic explanation. The explanation, partially in Aramaic, includes examples, scriptural citations, and proof-texts from elsewhere in the Babylonian Talmud. Thus, the mention of Gabriel is an intertextual reference to a story that appears in *b. Pesaḥim* 118a–b concerning the angel Gabriel who saves Azaria, Hananya and Mishael from the furnace of Nebuchadnezzar; and "of the *Shekhina*" relates to an account of the creation of man appearing in *b. San* 38b.

The Zoroastrian source from the *Bundahišn* is presented here in translation:[15]

---

15. The translation is based, with very minor changes, on Shapira, "Pahlavi Fire," 127–37.

1. It says in the Avesta, namely: 'five kinds of fire were created, [the fire *Bərəzī Sawang*, the fire *Wohu-Friiān*, the fire *Urwazišt*, the fire *Speništ*]:

2. the *Bərəzī Sawang* is the fire blazing before the Lord Ohrmazd;

3. the *Wohu-Friiān* fire, meaning the good propagator/confessor, is that which is in the bodies of men and cattle/animals;

4. the *Urwazišt* fire is that which is in plants;

5. the *Wazišt* fire is that which is in the cloud[s], which confront (the *dēw*) Spenjruš in the battle;

6. the *Speništ* fire, meaning the bountiful, is that which is in use in the world and it is also in the *Wahrām* fire.

7. Among these five fires, one consumes both liquid and substance, as that (fire) which is in human bodies [that it would be created in the stomach, whose (the fire's) function is to digest substance and liquid.

One consumes liquid, but not substance, as that (fire) which is in plants, which lives and flows by means of liquid.

One consumes substance, but not liquid, as that (fire) which is in use in the *gētīg* material world, and also as the Wahrām fire.

One consumes neither liquid nor substance, as the Wazišt fire and the *Bərəzī Sawang* (fire), and that (fire) which is inside the earth, mountains and other things.

Schorr and Darmesteter sought to demonstrate how the parallels between the two sources are precise and almost perfect. They assumed there was a direct relationship between the two, and the task set before scholarship was to determine which came first. Darmesteter, as those before him, maintained that the talmudic source was secondary. It is artificial, as it combines types of fire—the altar fire, fever, the Shekhina fire, which are fixed—with one-time occurrences or historical events, such as the fires in the case of Elijah on Mt. Carmel and the angel Gabriel. Darmesteter argued that the contradiction between the expectation created through the general formulation—"six fires"—that is, categories, and the unique nature of some of them, indicates that we are dealing with a secondary reworking of the material.

With the Zoroastrian sources, in contrast, the presentation of six fires exists in an earlier source than the *Bundahišn*, the Avestan *Yasna*,[16] and the continued categorization makes good sense in a Zoroastrian context. Darmesteter maintained that the value of the parallel was not limited to what it could tell us about Judaism and Zoroastrian influence

---

16. Y 36. For the details see Shapira, "Pahlavi Fire," 138–39.

upon it, but also that it presents us with the possibility of dating the Zoroastrian source itself.

Towards the end of his article, Darmesteter offered two conclusions: one for Judaism and the other for Zoroastrianism. For Judaism, the parallel proves that Zoroastrianism impacted upon Palestinian Judaism. Since we are dealing with a *baraita*, a source composed in Palestine, the parallel implies that the influence of Zoroastrianism was felt not only through direct contact with the Jews of Babylonia, in the Talmudic era, but also in Palestine in the time of the Mishna. A rabbi such as the second-century CE R. Natan the Babylonian, he surmised, might have brought the Persian tradition over when he migrated to Palestine.

There were also implications for Zoroastrianism. While the final redaction of the *Bundahišn* occurred in the ninth century (although scholars believe it is ultimately based upon earlier material), if the *baraita* is based on a citation from the *Bundahišn*, one could date at least one text found in the *Bundahišn* to the second century.

If modern scholars would accept the parallel here, they would probably be more receptive to Darmesteter's second conclusion than his first, but with a minor adjustment. The identification of the talmudic source as an authentic *baraita* is problematic. The fact that this *baraita* lacks any Palestinian parallel, precise or hazy, or other clear signs of a Palestinian provenance, in addition to the fact that the "explanation" evokes other *Babylonian* traditions, as mentioned earlier, supports treating the Talmud's list of fires as a "Babylonian *baraita*," not to be dated back to the Tannaitic era. Indeed, the only rabbinic parallel is from the *Midrash Abba Gurion*, which is viewed as a relatively late source and is certainly secondary to the Talmud.[17] Thus, this supposed talmudic parallel to the *Bundahišn* would belong to the post-Tannaitic era. It might still benefit Iranologists a little, but probably not surprise them, to date a tradition appearing in the *Bundahišn* prior to the final redaction of the Babylonian Talmud.[18]

---

17. *Midrash Abba Ben Gurion*, in ספרי דאגדתא על מגלת אסתר, ed. S. Buber (Vilna: Romm, 1886), 4. The reference to the six types of fire appears in the course of a debate between Nebuchadnezzar and the three youths, where the youths respond to the threat of the furnace, expounding the types of fire in the possession of God. Its secondary nature is evident, among other reasons, from the fact that it uses the example of the three youths in the furnace to describe one of the kinds of fire. On this work see Binyamin Oelbaum, "Midrash Abba Gurion on Esther," Ph.D. diss., Ramat Gan, 2011.

18. One should observe that we would now have *another* tradition from the *Bundahišn* echoed in the Babylonian Talmud. A series of recent publications from

One might, however, wonder about exactly how close these two sources really are. In our case we might be dealing with a commonplace, a precise but meaningless parallel. Fire features often in the Bible and in rabbinic literature, from the burning bush until the burning Torah scrolls around Ḥanina b. Teradyon. So, would our comparison pass the test set by Samuel Sandmel in his famous article from 1962 on "Parallelomania?"[19] Is due attention paid to the differences as well as the similarities?[20] Significantly, while these 19th century scholars were expressly seeking to undermine the uniqueness of Judaism, they were not advocating a broad comparative religion approach, which would have underlined the fact that fire is common enough in any and every culture and religion. Instead they were arguing for a special relationship between Judaism and Zoroastrianism—a relationship that emerged out of apparent closeness.[21]

However, since it is unlikely that *every* culture might imagine for itself diverse types of fire, precisely five or six in number, and organize them in accordance with their appetite, there is clearly something shared here, which cannot be the result of happenstance. The least one could

---

the pens of Dan Shapira and Reuven Kiperwasser have pointed to another literary unit from the *Bundahišn*, in the field of mythology, attested, with certain reworking, in the Talmud. See, for example, Reuven Kiperwasser and Dan D. Y. Shapira, "Irano-Talmudica II: Leviathan, Behemoth and the 'Domestication' of Iranian Mythological Creatures in Eschatological Narratives of the Babylonian Talmud," in *Shoshannat Yaakov, Jewish and Iranian Studies in Honor of Yaakov Elman*, ed. S. Secunda and S. Fine (Leiden: Brill, 2012), 203–35.

19. S. Sandmel, "Parallelomania," *Journal of Biblical Literature* 81 (1962): 1–13. He was not opposed to the very use of parallels in scholarship and did not reject their potential to contribute to the study of religion, but he was concerned over exaggeration and the lack of precision employed when marking parallels. Among the distinctions he wished to underline was that between what he termed "true" and "untrue" parallels. Untrue parallels are fragments devoid of their inner context. They appear to be parallels from a distance, but upon closer inspection within the inner context of the tradition, this is not the case. There are also true, "precise" parallels, as he describes them, but they are totally meaningless. For example, references to the Bible in the writings of various ancient Jewish and early Christian sects. All of these sects know Scripture and have an interest in interpreting it, particularly when there is a particular interpretative problem evident in the text. Therefore, one need not be surprised when, on occasion, diverse groups interpret in a similar way. This, then, has little to teach us.

20. A concern emphasized by Jonathan Z. Smith, in *Drudgery Divine: On the Comparisons of Early Christianities and the Religions of Late Antiquity* (Chicago: University of Chicago Press, 1990).

21. The extent of this closeness can be questioned, particularly in light of the fact that these scholars did not introduce a clear differentiation between Jewish sources that were the product of Sasanian Babylonia and those from Palestine, or the Bible.

say is that we perceive here a common way of expressing the experience of fire. This might, perhaps, be seen to be further supported by another source, M35, lines 21–36, which is a Parthian Manichaean fragment from the Turfan collection. It was published by Walter Henning in 1943, and reads as follows:[22]

> Like unto the way in which the fire, with powerful wrath, swallows the world and enjoys it, like unto the way in which this fire that is in this body, swallows the exterior fire that is (lit. comes) in fruit and food, and enjoys it [thus the Great Fire swallow both the fires . . .].

This fragment would appear to share a number of the assumptions found in the Talmud, and in particular, in the Zoroastrian sources. We have here fire within the human body, fire within plants, and fire that consumes fire. The three sources, the Talmud, the *Bundahišn*, and this source, all stem from a Sasanian milieu, which may be why there is a similarity in the way they perceive and describe fire.

Sandmel had called for examining perceived parallels in light of the sources' inner contexts. We shall do this, briefly, first with the Zoroastrian source. It can be divided into three parts. Its first part is a list of the five types of fire; next, there is a description of the nature of fire in each and every case; and, finally, we have a categorization in accord with water and food. Significantly, however, the order differs in this third part, and does not relate to all of the categories outlined earlier.

The attempt to fit the categories of fire into a straightjacket of water and food, then, does not encompass all the categories listed earlier, and therefore seems a little forced. One suspects that the notion of fire as consuming and drinking had an independent existence, perhaps outside of Zoroastrianism, and that the preexisting taxonomy was grafted upon it. This Zoroastrian tradition, then, reveals signs of a number of stages of development and transmission. Only at the last stage does the list relate to appetite.

The *Bundahišn* does not represent the earliest stage in the Zoroastrian engagement with fire, or even its taxonomy. As mentioned, an earlier list appears in the Avestan *Yasna*. Indeed, the development of multiple fires may well have been the product of scholastic interpretation or misinterpretation of these older texts.[23]

---

22. Henning, "Book of Giants," *BSOAS* 11 (1943): 71–72.
23. As argued recently by Dan Shapira. See "Pahlavi Fire". He also proposes the

Apart from the source we have mentioned specifically, the pertinent chapter of the *Bundahišn* also gathers many detailed traditions relating to a mythology of diverse fires and the locations of their temples. We hear of fire borne on the mythological ox through the sea, of the fire Gushnasp that was seated upon a horse and struggled against the forces of evil, and of much more. The unique distinction of fire in Zoroastrianism evidently and predictably engendered an impressive mythology. So while the reorganization of the categories according to appetite is actually the least unique to Zoroastrian religion, it is hardly a surprising development to encounter given the intensive engagement of Zoroastrianism with fire.

And what of the context of the talmudic source? The talmudic source appears towards the end of the first chapter of tractate Yoma. Surrounding it are additional reflections on the topic of the altar fire and smoke in the temple. This concentration of traditions on this topic is of interest in itself. The discussion there is primarily "Babylonian," and not a direct continuation of topics dealt with explicitly in the Mishna or *ad loco* in the Jerusalem Talmud. It therefore provides evidence of the innovative and distinctive Babylonian rabbinic perspective.

A Tannaitic tradition concerning "ten miracles that occurred in the temple" is brought on b. Yoma 21a-b, and appended to it is this addition, presented as a *baraita*:[24] "Rain never extinguished the fire of the wood of the altar and the smoke of the altar. Even if all the winds in the world come and blow on it, it cannot be moved from its place . . ."[25] After a diversion, the Talmud hones in on the subject of the smoke of the altar. It challenges the earlier tradition with a less authoritative one, introduced with the vague formula "the master said" (אמר מר), by listing five attributes associated with the altar fire, including that it does not have smoke. This tradition states as follows: "Five things are said concerning the fire of the altar: it lies down as a lion, and it is as clear as the sun, and it is tangible, and it consumes wet as dry; and it does not bring up smoke."[26] This contradiction is resolved by distinguishing between fire brought to the altar by a common person (הדיוט) and Divine fire which descends

---

impact of Zoroastrian fire interpretation on Manichaeism. See ib., 144–46.

24. On this addition, cited with the 'ten things' in *m. Avot* 5:5 see J. N. Epstein, *Introduction to the Mishnaic Text* (Jerusalem: Magnes, 2000), 2.965.

25. מעולם לא כבו גשמים אש של עצי המערכה ועשן המערכה אפילו כל הרוחות שבעולם באות ומנשבות בו אין מזיזות אותו ממקומו

26. חמשה דברים נאמרו באש של מערכה רבוצה כארי וברה כחמה ויש בה ממש ואוכלת לחין כיבשין ואינה מעלה עשן

from heaven. Next, the statement that the fire "lies down as a lion" is challenged by a *baraita* that recalls the fire of the altar "lying down as a dog." This perceived contradiction is resolved by the distinction between the first and second temples.[27] Next is the *baraita* we discussed above, after which appears discussion on the *baraita* cited earlier, which comments regarding the smoke of the altar: "Even if all the winds in the world come and blow on it, it cannot be moved from its place."[28] Thus, the aforesaid *baraita* on the categories of fire, far from constituting an isolated discussion here, is, in fact, part of a broader motion to thematically engage the place of fire in the temple cult, the heart of Jewish tradition. Putting two and two together, it would seem that the Persian milieu spurred the Babylonian rabbis to examine more closely those phenomena in Judaism that connect to fire, and perhaps even to encroach upon notions familiar to the Zoroastrians.

What can be said now of the "impressive parallel" from 150 years ago? We have two traditions before us. The *Bundahišn* links various types of fire to Zoroastrian tradition, and the b. Yoma links various types of fire to Jewish tradition. That which is parallel is the very concept of a typology of fire and its presentation in terms of food and drink. For this there is no need of shared written sources, or very close religious contact. In fact, none of the explicit religious formulations in the Zoroastrian sources appear in the talmudic source. Yet we are still dealing with a shared direction, and this deserves our attention.

My claim, then, is that in a Persian environment, such as Sasanian Babylonia, notions central to Persian religion would probably leave their mark—the Jew would be inclined to read his own heritage differently. He would surely oppose fire worship, but would nevertheless gather for

---

27. This is part of a broader tendency evident in the Babylonian Talmud to maintain and emphasize that the second temple was deficient with respect to the first.

28. One should mention additional traditions in the Talmud, especially from tractate Yoma, that emphasize the fire of the altar. In b. Yoma 46b, the fourth chapter of the tractate ends with a Babylonian discussion on the prohibition to extinguish the fire of the altar. See, too, the discussion in b. Zevaḥim 61b on "the fire that descended from the heavens in the days of Moses did not do away until Menashe came and removed it . . . Rav Papa said: it acted as a guest—sometimes here, and sometimes there." This is based on a citation from Sifra (*Nedava* 5:10, *Sifra on Leviticus* ed. Louis Finkelstein [New York: Jewish Theological Seminary of America, 1983], vol. 2, p. 44), with the Babylonian Rav Papa commenting on it. Suggestive is also the phrase בשום נור דאדליק בשום סק מסוק בשום ענני אישתא in an incantation bowl text (Schøyen 15) composed in Babylonian Jewish Aramaic. Fire features frequently elsewhere within the incantation bowl corpus.

himself its sparks. He would be interested in the fire of the altar in the Jewish temple, and relate wondersome miracles about it. Even when lacking explicit signs of religious influence, it is not coincidental that a given tradition emerges here, precisely, and only, in the Babylonian Talmud. To seek the primary testimony, as earlier generations have done, is perhaps superfluous. It is, however, imperative to recognize that in the Sasanian realm, and specifically there, fire would seem to have been on everyone's mind.

6

Prophecy and the Prophecy of Moses in *Ḥovot Yehudah* by Rabbi Yehudah ben Elazar

Shaul Regev

R. Yehudah ben Elazar (RIBA), who lived in the seventeenth century, wrote most of his *Ḥovot Yehudah* (Duties of Yehudah) in Persian, with the exception of the book's epilogue, which was written in Hebrew.[1] This is one of the few books that we have from seventeenth century Iran, and it sheds light on the state of Jewish religious and philosophical literacy in Iran at that time. In the next centuries, learning steadily declined to the point where the Iranian Jews of the nineteenth century were completely dependent upon Babylonian Rabbis.[2] As early as the eighteenth century, there is evidence of ties between the Jews of Iran and Babylon, as can

---

1. Amnon Netzer translated the book into Hebrew, allowing it to be read by the general audience that does not read Persian. He also added an extensive prologue covering the author's biography, the main points of his religious philosophy, and his source materials. See: Y. Ben El'azar, *Ḥovot Yehudah*, ed. and trans. A. Netzer (Jerusalem: Ben Zvi, 1995).

2. S. Regev, "The Relations between Iranian and Babylonian Jews," in *Iranian Jewry*, ed. S. Regev (Ramat Gan: Bar-Ilan University Press, 2017), 57–69; D. Tsadik, "Jews of Iran and Rabbinical Literature: Preliminary Notes," *AJS Perspectives* (Fall 2010): 14–16.

be seen from allusions and reports by R. Ezra the Babylonian,[3] who was apparently sent from Iraq to the cities of Iran in some rabbinic capacity, preceding the well-known commission of emissaries from Palestine who were sent to the cities of the Diaspora to collect donations and to serve as spiritual authorities during their stay there.[4]

As mentioned, *Hovot Yehudah* was mostly written in Judeo-Persian. Perhaps this is the reason for our limited knowledge on the dissemination of learning among Iranian Jews in the late Middle Ages. The Persian language was not a language of international use, and, therefore, the literature written in this language was not well known to Jewish scholars in other communities. Although we know from the book's epilogue that the author knew Hebrew, the fact that the book was not written in Hebrew, the language of the religious literature of this period, is indicative that the book was apparently designated for internal use by Iranian Jewry rather than for widespread Jewish consumption. Apparently, the author's main intention was to strengthen the Jewish affiliation and faith of his contemporaries and locale in light of the strong influence of other religions, specifically Islam. There were many repeated attempts by Muslim sages to convert the local Jews to Islam and the existing predilection, mostly among the younger members of Iranian Jewry, to accede to this pressure and convert.[5] This, perhaps, is the reason that the book's subject is the principles of Jewish belief, although this was not one of the primary topics in the Jewish philosophical literature of seventeenth century and thereafter.

3. S. Regev, *Rabbi Ezra Habavli Netivot Shalom* (Or-Yehuda, 2010), Introduction.

4. A brief overview on Jewish emissaries to Iran and Jewish passengers that passed there, see: E. Neumark, *Masa' be-erets ha-kedem* (Jerusalem: Epshtayn1947), 12–21. A. Ya'ari, *Sheluhey Eres Israel* (Jerusalem: Mosad Harav Kook, 1951), 381–82; 455–56; 487–88; and more.

5. See Netzer in: Y. Ben El'azar, *Hovot Yehudah*, 13–17. W. J. Fischel, "The Jews in Mediaeval Iran from the Sixteenth to the Eighteenth Centuries; political, economic, and communal aspects," *Irano-Judaica* 1(1982): 276–83; idem, "The History of Persian Jew during the Sefevid dynasty," *Zion* 2(1937): 282–87; V. Moreen, "A Seventeenth-Century Iranian Rabbi's Polemical Remarks on Jews, Christians, and Muslims," in *Safavid Iran and Her Neighbors*, ed. M. Mazzaoui (Salt Lake City: University of Utah Press, 2003), 160. D. Yeroushalmi, "Jews of the Ottoman Empire and the Jewish Communities of Iran in the Nineteenth Century: Background and Trends," *Sefunot* n.s. 8(23) (2003): 246–48; I. Ben-Zevi, *Mehqarim u-meqorot* (Jerusalem: 1966), 335; A. Levy, "Sources for the Research of the Persian Jews in 18th and 19th Century," in *Hagut Ivrit Be-Artzot Ha-Islam* (Jerusalem: Bialik, 1981), 315–26.

Discussions on the principal tenets of the faith have been at the focus of discussions since Maimonides, especially in the fourteenth and fifteenth centuries. In his commentary on the Mishnah, in the tenth chapter of tractate Sanhedrin (chapter Ḥeleq), Maimonides set down the Thirteen Principles of Faith. Since then, many have challenged the number of principles: Some sought to add to this number and others wished to narrow them down.[6] Preoccupation with this topic was widespread during the fourteenth and fifteenth centuries, whether attacking or defending Maimonides' tenets. One of the latest scholars to deal with this topic was the MABIT (R. Moses b. Yosef di Trani) in sixteenth-century Safed, who accepted Maimonides' Principles of Faith and identified their sources. Thereafter, this topic is almost never discussed, with the exception of an isolated few, such as R. Shim'on Aharon Agasi, who wrote a booklet on the topic in late nineteenth-century Baghdad.[7]

THE PRINCIPLES OF FAITH

R. Yehudah b. Elazar's pre-occupation with the principles of faith in 17th century Iran is, on the one hand, exceptional, especially since it was written in Persian, which underlines its unique designation. However, a redefinition of Judaism with the goal of strengthening religious belief was perhaps warranted in light of the pressure to convert to Islam and Shabbetai Zevi's influential messianic movement in the Diaspora,[8] which ended in the latter's conversion to Islam. A. Netzer assumes[9] that R. Yehudah's father himself converted to Islam; it is possible that he was forced to do so and it is also possible that he later returned to Judaism. Either way, this event undoubtedly left a strong impression on his son, R. Yehudah. Perhaps the latter was also forced to convert with his father along with other members of the community. Therefore, the need to strengthen the faith and establish its basic tenets seems more than natural.

---

6. M. Kellner, *Dogma in Medieval Jewish Thought* (Oxford: Liverpool University Press, 1986).

7. Sh. Agasi, *Qunṭres Yesode ha-Torah* (Jerusalem: 1976).

8. G. Scholem, *Shabbetai Zevi and the Shabbetaian Movement During his Lifetime* (Tel Aviv: Am Oved, 1987). M. Benayahu, "Sabbatian Liturgical Compositions and Other Documents from a Persian MS.," *Sefunot* 3–4 (1960): 7–38.

9. Netzer ibid n.1, p. 15.

One of R. Yehudah's surprising sources is the Qur'an.[10] In several places in his discourse, he supports his statements with verses from the Qur'an, although similar proof is available in the Bible.[11] Apparently, the use he makes of Muslim literature is also designed to serve the polemical orientation of his statements. In contrast to Maimonides, whose polemical orientation when determining the Principles is veiled and not openly expressed, the polemical orientation of R. Yehudah is obvious and explicit. His use of verses from the Qur'an and other Muslim sources[12] is proof of this disposition.

R. Yehudah b. Elazar's professed purpose in writing his book is not a polemical one; he directs his book to serve internal objectives, to guide and instruct his people. According to R. Yehudah b. Elazar's declared purpose, composing the book was meant to guide believers to intellectual perfection. He thus followed the Aristotelian philosophers, but mostly Maimonides, who considered the unique essence of mankind to be intelligence, which distinguishes man from the other unintelligent species. However, clearly not everyone can reach perfection, especially perfection in divine wisdom (= metaphysics), by studying all the wisdoms. Therefore, he discussed principles and fundamentals that should bring the reader to a minimum level, through which one may attain perfection. In his opinion, knowing the Principles of Faith is the minimum for what is called knowledge and wisdom:

> Divine wisdom is like an endless sea and a vessel with no end; nobody can fathom its purpose, all the more so to put it into writing and express it in human language, especially so for one with a dearth of knowledge or with some unknown teacher. Since this servant (the author) is lower than the lowliest, lesser than the least, and poorer than the poorest, Yehudah b. R. Elazar (may his soul be bound up in the bond of everlasting life), saw and knew that people in his time do not acquire wisdom, especially the principles of the faith, that their knowledge and belief which lead to everlasting life and immortality of the soul, so the author paid attention to this matter as indispensable, for all people, both the eminent as well as the simple people. Not everyone is capable of understanding the rules and details in the

---

10. V. Moreen, "Polemical Use of the Qur'an in Two Judeo-Persian Texts," *Irano-Judaica* 4 (1999): 203–13.

11. *Ḥovot Yehudah*, 320 para. 10 n. 7; the verse is in Exod 33:18–20.

12. See the list in H. Y. pp. 547.

books dealing with this subject in the Holy Language [Hebrew], and all the more so to understand their details and nuances.[13]

Two points in this paragraph should be stressed. First, the passage does not specifically mention the Jewish people as the subject, but rather the perfection of all mankind, "for all people." The term he used can refer to all mankind, but based on context, it probably refers to the common Jewish people. Only later does the second reservation appear, which is the possibility of understanding Hebrew; this is the reason he does not write his book in Hebrew but in the vernacular. To some extent, one can say that R. Yehudah intends his book to be universal and not specifically Jewish, although most of his sources are Jewish rather than non-Jewish ones and it is written in Judeo-Persian. Still, since the book's second purpose is polemical, his goal is to display the superiority of the Jewish religion over other religions, and specifically Islam, which is his immediate challenge. Consequently, he hardly mentions Christianity, since it was irrelevant to his purpose.

As is well known, in the introduction to Chapter Ḥeleq, Maimonides lists the Thirteen Principles of Faith. This number was not accepted by most of the Jewish scholars in later centuries. Some even attempted to interpret this number symbolically. R. Yehudah also does not accept this number, but his explanation of this number is unique and was perhaps appropriate for his contemporary culture of superstition. In his opinion, this number has a negative association, as it encompasses bad luck, and, therefore, one must distance oneself from it. According to R. Yehudah, Maimonides used this number intentionally to demonstrate that Jews who believe in God have nothing to fear from planetary influences, and they overcome any bad luck. "If the Israelites will religiously observe and worship God out of love, they will not be under any planetary influence and the Evil One will depart from them."[14]

The principles that R. Yehudah lists are not identical to those presented by Maimonides or any of the latter's opponents. R. Yehudah lists only four principles, although the remainder of Maimonides' Principles of Faith are included in the explanations, added as clarifications. However, they are not equal in status to the principles, branches, or roots [clauses] of other principles; they are only explanations and exegesis. R. Yehudah divides his principles into articles that have the status of primary

13. Ḥovot Yehudah, introduction, 274.
14. Ibid., 283.

principles, and then into chapters, which are explanations of the "Gates" and are not equal in status to the principles. He explains his method thus:

> I saw a need to elucidate the principles of faith in the best manner in order that the sons of Yehudah (= the Jews) will understand them, each according to his ability, and be thankful of the worship of the blessed Creator. I amended and collected the words of the earliest and latest sages in brief, and presented the Principles of Faith in an article. The "branches" that Maimonides (of blessed memory) considered to be Principles, I listed in a "gate." The other branches I added to the "chapters."[15]

R. Yehudah defines Maimonides' Principles of Faith as branches, and in his opinion, some are equal in status to principles, and others are equal in status to branches of principles. As mentioned, Maimonides does not distinguish between principles and branches. This distinction only appears later in the 14th and 15th centuries in critiques of Maimonides and his method by individuals such as R. Joseph Albo in his work, *Sefer ha-'Iqarim*. Thus, the design underlying R. Yehudah's division is unclear. R. Yehudah is probably alluding to the branches that are fundamental to the three principles listed in the Mishnah in Chapter Ḥeleq, according to which one can classify Maimonides' Principles of Faith into groups. According to Maimonides, the remaining principles have the same degree of importance. R. Yehudah, however, creates two levels for Maimonides' principles: principles and branches.

Neither does R. Yehudah follow Maimonides' path in defining faith. Maimonides defines faith as true knowledge of a particular thing, and when that knowledge is identical with the thing, one can say that faith exists. When that knowledge is not identical to that thing, then belief is non-existent and is false.[16] Although preliminary belief may exist, it is of another class and is mostly dependent upon emotion, which means it is not true faith. R. Yehudah offers a different definition for faith. In his opinion, faith is not applicable to something that can be known but only to something that cannot be proven or known by reason. Anything that is knowable and provable cannot come under the definition of faith.

> The definition for faith is belief in something invisible or in some future situation the prophet announces before they are realized, or opinions that are not possible in nature but become

---

15. Ibid., 278.
16. Maimonides, *Guide of the Perplexed* 1, 50.

possible by divine miracle by a righteous prophet, such as the splitting of the Red Sea, etc. It is required that such situations described as faith stem from the word by the blessed Creator, or that people learn them from the true Torah or by exegesis of the verses. That is to say, they should not be attributed to man.[17]

Another stipulation that he presents for the concept of faith is that things that come under the definition of faith are connected to God, God's words, or to the Torah. Additionally, all these articles should be such that they engender a person's success and spiritual perfection, which is the person's spiritual redemption. By this, R. Yehudah narrows the realm of faith to divine consciousness and excludes stories and legends that have no intellectual benefit.

R. Yehudah divides his book into articles, gates, and chapters, aside from the prologue and epilogue. The articles are equal in status to principles; the gates are equal in status to branches; and the chapters effectively explain and emphasize what is stated in the gates. In other words, according to R. Yehudah's method, there are four Principles of Faith. They are: 1. The existence of God. 2. Prophecy. 3. A heavenly given Torah. 4. The resurrection of the dead. R. Yehudah constructs his concept of the Principles on the Aristotelian concept of the four causes, which are: Material, Efficient, Formal, and Final. The principle of the existence of God corresponds to the Efficient cause; heavenly Torah corresponds to the Material cause, since it contains the secrets, allusions, and letters by which the cosmos was created; prophecy is the Formal cause; and the resurrection of the dead is the Final cause.[18]

Below I focus on the second principle—prophecy, with special reference to Mosaic prophecy.

PROPHECY

According to R. Yehudah, mankind has an essential need for prophecy[19] and the prophets belong to a class of leadership that is critical for world order since man is naturally a social being. Man needs society for his

---

17. *Ḥovot Yehudah*, 280.

18. Ibid., 286.

19. On prophecy in Jewish thought see H. Kreisel, *Prophecy: The History of an Idea in Medieval Jewish Philosophy* (Dordrecht: Kluwer Academic, 2001).

existence, and, therefore, he needs leaders to establish rules for society and government. In R. Yehudah's opinion, the prophets had a threefold role:

1. They are part of the local leadership whose purpose is to enact regulations and social order that lead to physical, social, and economic success. Therefore, the prophets belong to the ruling class.

2. In addition to social organization, the prophets individually lead society with the aim of bringing individuals to spiritual perfection and success. They teach individuals to achieve spiritual redemption and everlasting life.

3. The prophets bring the word of God to the people and guide them in deeds and commandments that bring them to perfection and bring them closer to God.

Therefore, in his opinion, divine wisdom requires sending the prophets so that Man knows how to fulfill God's laws and how to conduct the matters of the world correctly according to the divine order. In his opinion, sending the prophets is the product of divine grace and wisdom. The prophets cannot be universal but are unique to each people and nation. While any prophet may prophesize to several nations, he directs to each one its own distinct prophecy. The needs of each nation are different; therefore, each requires guidance that is uniquely relevant to it. R. Yehudah likens the prophets to farmers: farmers cannot be satisfied with knowledge of basic facts but must match the plants to the quality of the soil and climate. Each site and climate has its own type of flora and requires unique methods. One cannot transfer an agricultural method from one area to another without a preliminary examination of its suitability. The same applies to the prophets. Each prophecy is intended and appropriate for a specific people and is not necessarily suitable for another. Since one of the prophet's roles is to provide individual and national guidance designed to generate success and redemption, his guidance must match the unique requirements of the trainees.[20]

Undoubtedly, this argument is part of the hidden or overt polemic with Islam, an example of which can be found in other Jewish sources from Muslim countries.[21] R. Yehudah intends to counteract the constant

---

20. *Ḥovot Yehudah*, 381.

21. *Bustan al-akul*, trans. and ed. Rabbi Y. Qafih (Halichoth 'Am Yisrael, Kiryat Ono: 1984); R. Keiner, "Jewish Isma'ilism in Twelfth Century Yemen: R. Nethanel ben

pressure imposed upon the Jews to achieve salvation by embracing the Islamic faith. Salvation is personal, and it is a function of fulfilling the religion's commandments and following the course outlined by God. Each nation received its own prophets who outline the appropriate path for them. At this stage, without entering into the debate of whether Muhammad was a true prophet or not, conversion from one religion to another is not a good transition because each religion is appropriate for the nation to which the prophet was sent and not for all nations. The prophet offers guidance and exclusive instruction for the specific nation to which he was sent and is not appropriate for other nations. The prophet addresses and takes into consideration the unique requirements of each and every nation and cannot offer a universal religion. The principle of prophecy is that it is a specific mission with a specific target and is not a universal mission.

> Just as it is natural that agriculturists need to know which seeds are suitable for each type of soil, and what method is suitable for each type of seed, including their quality and quantity, so too does the prophet need to consider the quality and quantity of each nation's character and needs.[22]

According R. Yehudah's method, there are two classes of prophecy. The first class is natural prophecy. This prophetic method springs from the prophet's own initiative; after studying and learning, the prophet gains rational perfection and devotion to the active intellect.[23] Such a person becomes "God's confidant" and can enact regulations, rules and laws, which are instructions for justice and social perfection for his people. R. Yehudah's description of such a prophet is similar to Maimonides' method for achieving prophecy, for he too holds that the natural path is the result of the future prophet's initiative and efforts. According to Maimonides, however, sometimes, negative divine intervention withholds prophecy from those whom God does not wish to achieve prophecy or

---

al-Fayyumi," *JQR* 74 (1984): 249–66.

22. *Ḥovot Yehudah*, 381.

23. N. Arieli, "Prophecy as a Challenge to Reason," *Daat* 2–3 (1978): 49–65; H. Kreisel, "Sage and Prophet in the Thought of Maimonides and His Follower," *Eshel Bersheva* 3 (1986): 149–69; A. Altmann, "Maimonides and Thomas Aquinas: Natural or Divine Prophecy?" *AJS Review* 3 (1978): 1–19. E. Goldman, "Rationality and Revelation in Maimonides' Thought," in *Maimonides and Philosophy*, ed. S. Pines and Y. Yovel, International Archives of the History of Ideas 114 (Boston: Nijhoff, 1986), 15–23.

become prophets.[24] Although R. Yehudah also believes that this is one of the paths to prophecy, he does not call these individual prophets "God's confidants."

The second class of prophecy is more similar to classic prophecy, which is the candidate's divine selection without any previous preparation on his part. In fact, a careful examination of R. Yehudah's discussion shows that this second class of prophecy operates in the same method as the first. This prophet also must be educated and have a perfected, intelligent soul in order to prophesize. However, this class of prophecy is initiated by God and is subject to God's influence in applying the divine plenitude in the form of the wisdom and knowledge that cause the prophet to be an active intellect.

> The other type of prophecy is when the blessed Creator essentially pours over him (the man) the wisdoms and forms of those found with the perfection required by the speaking spirit after its separation.[25]

According to R. Yehudah, it is impossible for a soul yet encased in the material body to merit union with God or with the angels or the active intellect because this corporeal material cannot unite with perfect spirituality. Therefore, for the sake of such a union, a temporary separation of the spirit is caused to allow the individual to receive the divine plenitude or prophecy, after which the spirit returns to the body. In order for this action to take place, the spirit must attain physical perfection as well as the level of spiritual perfection. According to the first class of prophecy, prophecy is a voluntary action on the candidate's part, while in the second class of prophecy, prophecy is controlled by God's initiative. In fact, this second path is not far removed from Maimonides' approach to prophecy. The difference between the two views is the source of initiative. Maimonides requires the initiative of man, while R. Yehudah allows for godly intervention.

The difference between these two classes of prophecy is similar to the difference between philosophy and religion. The first is a philosophical concept of prophecy, which is union with the active intellect, the source of knowledge. In this case, it concerns a class of knowledge that

---

24. On Maimonides' prophecy, see Kreisel, *Prophecy*, 148–315. Also see H. Kreisel, "Maimonides' View of Prophecy as the Overflowing Perfection of Man," *Daat* 13 (1984): XXI–XXVI.

25. *Ḥovot Yehudah*, 382.

by nature may be grasped by the intellect, but the intellect has no way of acquiring them. The title of the prophet is not a precise one for this case, and it would be more appropriate to call him a "sage" or a "philosopher." Therefore, in R. Yehudah's opinion, this method requires the prophet to prepare for and initiate the prophecy. Such a prophecy, if it comes, can be a continuous prophecy and not a singular event. Examples of personalities who acquired prophetic knowledge through this path of receiving prophecy were what are known as *benei ha-nevi'im*—School of Prophets; namely, people who had some natural preparation for prophecy and went to study it with special teachers who were prophets themselves.

The second method involves a religious conceptualization of prophecy, namely, communication/connection with God or with his angels from whom the prophet receives his knowledge. This knowledge is outside the realm of human knowledge. Such knowledge is the knowledge that brings spiritual success to the believer. The operative significance between these two approaches is that the first receives prophecy for himself and can share with others those revelations revealed to him, while the second receives a prophecy for all and is obligated to convey these revelations to everyone. He cannot withhold his prophecy, and a prophet who does so is liable for punishment by death.[26] Such a prophet does not require preparation, for the prophetic plenitude pours over him without any previous preparation or by his previous knowledge. This class of prophecy is usually a singular event and not continuous. R. Yehudah places into this class all the biblical personalities who had a divine revelation but did not seem to be worthy of prophecy. Among the prerequisites for prophecy of this class is morality and honesty.

> Prophecy lacking in natural preparation is conditional upon two prerequisites: Firstly, that he shall not be an evil-doer, with low and disgusting vices, stupid, foolish, an adulterer, and a criminal. Such a person is a stranger, is called evil, and is not worthy of prophecy. Secondly, a person lacking natural preparation is only allowed prophecy for a temporary need.[27]

Sometimes, people receive this prophetic plentitude even if they are not entirely worthy of it, if the world so requires. So, for example, in his opinion, not all those who prophesized in the times of the Judges were worthy of receiving the prophetic plenitude according to the above

---

26. Sanhedrin 89a.
27. Ḥovot Yehudah, 383.

stated prerequisites, but since their service at that time was important for national salvation, they received this plenitude. Jephtah, for example[28], was unworthy of having prophetic plenitude come upon him. However, in his time he was the only one who could organize an army and go to war against the Ammonites in order to save Israel. Therefore, he received the prophetic plenitude allowing him to be victorious in war and redeem Israel.

Singular prophecy enables R. Yehudah to resolve the many questions involving prophecy by individuals who do not appear to be worthy of prophecy and by animals who are reported in the Bible as having some reaction following a divine command or the sight of an angel. Examples include kings such as Elimelekh, who were not descendents of Abraham, who had some type of revelation.[29] In R. Yehudah's opinion, this revelation was part of a just dream rather than a prophetic revelation. Such individuals did not merit prophetic plenitude even in the nation's hour of need, but they received a just (prophetic) dream designed to save the forefathers.

R. Yehudah explains the reactions of the she-ass and the fish that swallowed Jonah[30] as actual, physical reactions to some hidden stimulus, designed to allow them to fulfill a specific role. The fish is forced to expel Jonah because of discomfort or "dyspepsia," which took place soon after Jonah's prayer. God caused the fish to expel Jonah but did not orally command it to do so. The first action is the fish's natural one, similar to reactions in other creatures that expel their food if it is unsuitable for them. The second action of command is the conscious prophetic action. The fish, according to R. Yehudah, could not perform such an activity, not even according to the second approach to prophecy that bestows divine plenitude without preparation.[31]

This was also the case with Balaam's ass.[32] The ass did not see the angel standing in the path with a drawn sword but it apparently saw a real sword being drawn, something that instills fear in animals. Furthermore, the ass' speech is not speech in the full sense of the word; meaning, it is not a result of thought but from the angel placing her own words into the

---

28. Judg 11.
29. Gen 20:3–7.
30. Jonah 2:1.
31. *Hovot Yehudah*, 384.
32. Num 22:28–30.

ass' mouth without the latter's knowledge or understanding. This action by the ass is designed to fulfill two purposes. The first is to inform Balaam of the cause of the events. The second, and more important purpose, is that it informed Balaam that he does not have absolute control over his own mouth but rather is subject to God's rule that places the words in his mouth for him to pronounce. Just as the ass had no control over its speech and the speech took control of her, so too Balaam has no control over speech, but the speech has control over him. This is what Balaam does indeed say to Balak, "I cannot say what I want to say but only what God puts into my mouth." R. Yehudah uses this argument in a literal manner.

> The ass' opening her mouth and speaking were not from knowledge, and she was not trained to do this, but the angel placed and arranged the words in her mouth so that Balaam would know that his own mouth is not under his control when he could ordinarily curse as he wished according to his inclination, but it was in God's control, for he can make the dumb speak and the accomplished speaker become a dumb stutterer.[33]

A third level for communication/connection is the level of the Holy Spirit. While this is a level lower than prophecy, all prophecy includes the Holy Spirit. This level is for those who merit a level above that of the ordinary person, even an intellectual. At this level, the individual is able to receive visions similar to those visions in a prophecy but yet are not full prophecy.

An additional level for divine communications is that of the *bat qol*—the divine voice [lit. small voice or whisper]. The divine voice is a type of hidden voice heard in someone's ear, instructing him to act in a certain manner or to say certain things. The divine voice comes only to those who are worthy of it, even though recipients are unaware of the process. The divine voice might be some verse that is uttered by someone without forethought or previous preparation and touches on some specific situation. In the Talmud,[34] we find the divine voice stating such verses mostly by innocents who are unaware of the situation and pronounce the first verse that comes to their mind, which is generally attributed to the situation at hand. Adults standing in the vicinity of this innocent are able to draw conclusions that refer to the situation. As said before, the babe

---

33. *Ḥovot Yehudah*, 384.
34. Ḥagiga 15b; Gittin 68a.

does not know why it stated the verse, but the moment it is pronounced, the verse is considered the solution to a problem or an instruction that applies to the situation at hand. According to R. Yehudah, the babe's sudden pronouncement of a verse is an example of divine inspiration that causes him to choose that verse: On the innocent's part, the choice of the verse is casual, but as far as divine Providence is concerned, it is intentional. This class of inner voice is irrational and not understood. It has a divine source even though the recipient is unaware that its source is divine.

Prophets must have several attributes and performs several preparations before they are ready to receive prophecy:

1. Natural Preparation: The prophet needs to be physically perfect both in his outer appearance as well as in his inner characteristics and virtues. This actually represents the divine selection of the prophet even before his birth, as it is said, for example, about Jeremiah. The creation of one born with perfect form allows the individual to perfect himself through study and education.

2. Educated Intellectual Perfection: The prophet must be sagacious with perfect knowledge. Therefore, one who is physically ready will find learning and intellectual preparation easier. According to R. Yehudah, the prophets established special study halls where students who wished to attain prophecy were taught and prepared. This is the concept of the "sons of the prophets" or "band of prophets" that appears in the Bible.[35]

3. A Man of Law and Faith: Torah knowledge is one of the instruments for attaining prophecy. Consequently, prophets cannot come from the nations of the world since they are without Torah. The nations of the world can produce fortunetellers should they perfect their intellect and have a strong imagination.[36]

4. Additional characteristics of prophets are wisdom, valor, and wealth—of course, one who is happy with his lot, one who is not dependent upon others, and one who is not covetous. Another argument that R. Yehudah cites concerning wealth is that people will listen to him, since people generally do not pay heed to the poor and

---

35. 1 Sam 10:8; 2 Kgs 4:1; 2:3.

36. *Hovot Yehudah*, 386–88. Also see Maimonides, Guide 2, 32; Maimonides, *Mishneh Torah*, Yesodei Ha-Tora (Laws of Principles of the Torah), ch. 7.

wretched. He must be a person of humility and patience and one who distances himself from honor and prestige.[37]

According to R. Yehudah, it is self-understood that no prophet from the nations of the world can prophesize to Israel because such a prophet is not associated with the Torah and obviously cannot fulfill the prophet's role of guiding Israel in observing the commandments. Similarly, such a prophet cannot force them to convert or offer another religion to them, since they are bound to the Jewish faith they received at Mount Sinai. Clearly, these words were aimed as part of the polemic against Islam that was trying to convert the Jews.[38]

These preparations concern only prophets of the first class and not those of the second class who are selected by God without any preparation. Maimonides' influence upon R. Yehudah is evident, yet the differences are also apparent. In Maimonides' writings, we find none of the explicit conditions for learning the Torah and Law that R. Yehudah added. On the other hand, according to Maimonides, the power of imagination is necessary for prophets, while R. Yehudah only mentions this in connection with the nations of the world and not with the Jewish people.

THE PROPHECY OF MOSES

The singularity of the Mosaic prophecies[39] occupies an important place in the Jewish-Muslim debate during the Middle Ages.[40] Maimonides lists Moses' prophecy as one of the Principles of Faith together with the principle that the Torah will not be changed as part of the polemic against Islam.[41] In his *Guide for the Perplexed*, Maimonides cites the unique quality

37. *Ḥovot Yehudah*, 386–87.

38. Ibid., 388.

39. A. H. Ivry, "The Image of Moses in Maimonides' Thought," in *Maimonides*, ed. A. Ravitzky (Jerusalem: Merkaz Zalman Shazar, 2008), vol. 2, 481–97; D. R. Blumenthal, "Maimonides' Intellectualist Mysticism and the Superiority of the Prophecy of Moses," *Studies in Medieval Culture* 10 (1977): 51–67; M. Kellner, "Maimonides and Gersonides on Mosaic Prophecy," *Speculum* 52 (1977): 62–79.

40. Bat-Sheva Garsiel, "Moses and his Mission in the Qur'an," in *Moses the Man— Master of the Prophets*, ed. M. Hallamish, H. Kasher, H. Ben-Pazi (Ramat-Gan: Bar-Ilan University, 2010), 303–19.

41. D. J. Lasker, "Tradition and Innovation in Maimonides' Attitude towards Other Religions," in *Maimonides*, ed. A. Ravitzky (Jerusalem: Merkaz Zalman Shazar, 2008), vol. 1, 79–94.

of Moses' prophecy as a prophecy that borders on the miraculous and, in contrast to all other degrees of prophecy, does not constitute an attainable degree of prophecy.[42] R. Yehudah follows Maimonides in stressing that Moses' prophecy is unique and differs from the prophecy of all the other prophets before and after him. In his prologue to Moses' prophecy, R. Yehudah says:

> Know that one of the necessary beliefs of the Principles is that you know and believe that the prophecy of Moses our Teacher obm (of blessed memory) was the most noble and superior in relation to the prophecy of all the other prophets.[43]

In the opening sentence, R. Yehudah immediately alludes to the ulterior polemic against Islam by defining Moses' prophecies as the most superior of all the prophecies and prophets that came before and after him. This superiority also determines the Torah's superiority over all the other possible doctrines, since one can infer the level of the mission from the level of the emissary. In other words, we infer the Torah's superiority from Moses' superiority. Moses is the best of the human species and he is "head to all the early and later prophets."[44] R. Yehudah notes that Moses is also praised for his ability to detach himself from his corporeal body. Three such incidents are mentioned, each for a period of forty days and forty nights. It is R. Yehudah's understanding that the duration of Moses' stay on Mt. Sinai was intentional and not the result of the Golden Calf. According to R. Yehudah, Moses' stay on the mount was interrupted twice, forcing him to descend: once to deliver the tablets and a second time to announce that they were forgiven. This is not as it is written that Moses had to remain on the mountain only forty days and forty nights and the additional days were a result of the incidents. According to R. Yehudah, Moses' planned stay on the mountain was for a full one hundred and twenty days. R. Yehudah especially stresses that his descent from the mountain was not for the purpose of eating and drinking. This condition of isolation and corporeal severance accompanied Moses for his entire

---

42. *Guide for the Perplexed* 2, 35; *Yesodei Ha-Tora* 7, 6; *Commentary of the Mishnah*: Introduction to *Pereq Ḥeleq*, 7th principle. On the various stages of prophecy see Guide 2, 45. H. Kreisel, "The Prophecy of Moses Our Master in Medieval Jewish Provencal Philosophy—Natural or Supernatural?," in *Moses the Man—Master of the Prophets*, ed. M. Hallamish, H. Kasher, H. Ben-Pazi (Ramat-Gan: Bar-Ilan University, 2010), 179–203.

43. *Ḥovot Yehudah*, 391.

44. Ibid.

life, from the time of the Revelation at Sinai and thereafter. His descents to the people were performed for the people's needs and not for his own.[45]

R. Yehudah, following Maimonides, lists four differences between Moses' prophecy and the prophecies of all the other prophets. They are:

1. Immediacy. Moses spoke face to face with God, while other prophets prophesied through mediators (i.e., the angels).

2. Clarity. Moses received the prophecy as clearly as in a vista seen on a clear day, while the other prophets received it in various manners through a dream.

3. Resilience. The other prophets were afraid and debilitated when they prophesized, while Moses exhibited no change.

4. Continuity. With Moses, the prophecy was continuous, while the other prophets were dependent upon God's will. Prophecy was given only after much preparation.[46]

According to R. Yehudah, all these differences stem from the singular nature of Moses' prophecy, which was essentially different from that of all the other prophets. Moses' prophecy was a direct intellectual connection with the active intellect without any use of imaginative power, while all the other prophets needed to use their imaginative powers. Maimonides explains the prophetic process as plenitude that pours from God via the active intellect that acts first upon the intellect and then upon the imaginative power. As the imaginative power becomes stronger, the influence becomes brighter and clearer, and this is reflected in the different degrees of prophecy. Maimonides considers Moses' prophecy as a special prophecy that is independent of this process. It is something of a miracle; namely, a special level that is neither intended for nor attainable by any of the other prophets but is reserved for Moses alone.[47] This uniqueness is explained by R. Yehudah as another mode of receiving the prophecy without interposing the imaginative power but by connecting directly to the intellect.[48] R. Yehudah bases this difference between Moses' prophecy and the other prophets on Kabbalist literature.[49] Moses knew

45. Ibid., 391–92.
46. Ibid., 392–93.
47. Maimonides, *Guide for the Perplexed* 2, 35.
48. Ḥovot Yehudah, 393.
49. RIBA mentions the Kabbalistic book *Sefer Shefaʻ ṭal* by Shabtai Sheftel Horoyits as his source. On Moses in Kabbalistic literature see M. Hallamish, "The Image of

the secret of God's name, and so with its aid he could reach God, whereas the other prophets did not share this secret. R. Yehudah finds allusions to this interpretation in the writings of R. Nissim [Ra"N],[50] who disagreed with Maimonides. He notes that if one carefully examines Maimonides' writings, this also appears to be his opinion as well. Perhaps this is his attempt to present a united opinion on this important topic despite its controversy.

On the uniqueness of Moses' prophecy, which is directly from God and without intermediaries (i.e., the angels), R. Yehudah finds allusions in two other stories associated with Moses. One is the affair of the Golden Calf. As mentioned, as a result of the Golden Calf, Moses is informed that thereafter, God will express his leadership through an angel and not directly to Moses. Moses responded by refusing to accept this degradation in the terms of his leadership, and he requests that God continue to communicate directly as before. R. Yehudah deduces from this that Moses' leadership of Israel was effected through this direct link that he received from God and not through an angel. If leadership had already been conveyed through an angel, there would have been no reason for Moses to view the announcement as a worsening in terms. Leadership by an angel meant that from thereafter, he would receive the prophecy via an angel, whereas up until then he received the prophecy and leadership directly from God.

The second incident in the Torah supporting the difference between the prophecy of Moses and that of the other prophets is the series of statements made by Aaron and Miriam against Moses. They claim that they are also prophets and that God spoke to them as well. God's reply was that their prophecy was in a vision while God spoke to Moses directly, face to face, which implies direct prophecy rather than prophecy through an intermediary.[51]

The uniqueness of Moses' prophecy is also expressed in his ability to delegate to others, causing them to prophesize. However, what especially characterizes Moses' prophecy, according to R. Yehudah, is the continuity of the prophecy over time. This caused Moses to have an especially strong body, and he is the only person worthy of being called a "man of God."

Moses in Kabbalistic Thought," in *Moses the Man—Master of the Prophets*, ed. M. Hallamish, H. Kasher, H. Ben-Pazi (Ramat-Gan: Bar Ilan-University, 2010), 359–80.

50. Nissim ben Reuben Gerondi, *Shenem 'Asar Derashot*, Jerusalem 1974, 4th sermon.

51. *Ḥovot Yehudah*, 394–395.

> Moses our Teacher, obm, was above all the prophets, for at all times he was ready to receive prophecy. He had no impediments and had no need for seclusion, for the glory was within him and was never detached from the godhead.[52]

THE VISION OF THE BURNING BUSH

The vision of the bush, according to R. Yehudah, was the turning point in Moses' prophecy. Although we have no information about the level of Moses' prophecy before the vision of the bush, according to R. Yehudah, Moses was already at some level of prophecy and rose to his high level of prophecy after this incident.[53] Apparently, he considers Moses' leadership activities, even those performed when he was in Egypt and afterwards, as part of his prophetic expression, for as we saw, the prophets were part of the ruling class. At the vision of the bush, Moses received the prophetic plenitude upon his intellect, which remained with him for the rest of his life. This plenitude also poured into him physical powers that subsequently allowed him to perform all his roles and effectively cancelled all his corporeal needs. In this, R. Yehudah differs with Maimonides. According to Maimonides, the vision of the Bush prepared Moses to be a prophet and to accept his first mission, and only at the revelation at Mount Sinai did Moses attain his special level of prophecy. Until that moment, Moses was similar to all the other prophets who needed to prove the truth of their mission through omens. During and after the Revelation at Sinai, Moses did not need to prove the truth of his mission through an omen. R. Yehudah does not address the evidence needed to prove Moses' prophecy, but as previously mentioned he raises Moses to his unique degree of prophecy from his first mission and the vision of the Bush. According to R. Yehudah, in contrast to Maimonides, there is no development in prophecy, and the prophet does not rise in levels of prophecy. Every prophet that attains prophecy is, in fact, a prophet, and there is no difference between any of the prophets, with the exception of Moses. The difference between prophets is whether they attained their prophecy through intellect or through divine will alone.

---

52. Ibid., 397.
53. Ibid., 395.

SUMMARY

Despite R. Yehudah's great reliance upon Maimonides, he does not accept Maimonides' opinion on all issues, and he expresses different opinions—in his approach to the Principles, to prophecy in general, and to Mosaic prophecy in particular. R. Yehudah's approach to prophecy is a mid-way position between the traditional approach, according to which God prophesizes to man, and that of Maimonides, according to which one prepares oneself for prophecy and can attain it naturally. R. Yehudah believes that there are two types of prophecy: On the one hand, there is prophecy that requires preparation, as Maimonides says, and this is the degree to which an individual's prophecy remains fixed as long as he continues to prepare for it. There is also prophecy that is God's selection. Such prophecy is singular and is not continuous. R. Yehudah differs from Maimonides in his belief that Moses reached his degree of prophecy at the Vision of the Bush and not at Mount Sinai.

R. Yehudah does not expressly refer to the polemic against Islam, despite several allusions.[54] One of the forms of argumentation that R. Yehudah emphasizes repeatedly is that the only prophet from the nations of the world was Balaam, and even then, his prophecy was not actually prophecy but a mission similar to a type of prophecy. Thus, the issue of Mohammad's prophecy is averted. R. Yehudah repeatedly supports his statements on Moses' prophecy with verses from no other than the Qur'an, rather than from any of the existing Jewish sources. He did so to demonstrate that Islam was supposedly in agreement with the view of Judaism.

---

54. D. Tsadik, "Polemics between Shi'ites and Jews," in *Encyclopedia Iranica*, web edition; V. Moreen, ibid. n.5, 157–68.

7

Preliminary List of Judeo-Persian Manuscripts

at The Institute of Oriental Manuscripts of The Russian Academy of Sciences and at The National Library of Russia, St. Petersburg, Russia

VERA B. MOREEN

INTRODUCTION

IRANIAN JEWRY'S INTELLECTUAL LEGACY is still an underexplored area of Jewish and Iranian studies. It is largely preserved in Judeo-Persian manuscripts, most of which are scattered in major libraries throughout the world.[1] Cataloging the collections is an introductory and important step toward the study of these manuscripts. Two major collections have

---

1. See Vera B. Moreen, *Catalog of Judeo-Persian Manuscripts in the Library of the Jewish Theological Seminary of America*, Études sur le judaïsme médiéval 63 (Leiden: Brill, 2015), 4–6.

been cataloged so far,[2] a third one is nearing completion,[3] and a couple of smaller collections are also wholly[4] or partially[5] catalogued.[6]

Scholars know that the major libraries of Russia can boast of phenomenal manuscript and incunabula collections of Hebraica and Judaica.[7] Among them there are two significant collections of Judeo-Persian manuscripts that are still largely unknown. The Institute of Oriental Manuscripts has 29[8] and the National Library of Russia (both in St. Petersburg) has 17 Judeo-Persian manuscripts. These collections were formed primarily through the separate acquisitions of Abraham Firkowicz (1786–1874) and later, especially, through Vladimir Alekseevich Ivanow's (1886–1970) trip to Bukhārā in 1915 on behalf of the Asiatic Museum of the (Imperial) Russian Academy of Sciences (St. Petersburg; incorporated into the Institute of Oriental Studies (IOS) in 1930).[9] Except for the rudimentary list prepared A. A. Freiman in a publication dating from 1918,[10] and the very brief notice by I. I. Ginsburg in 1936,[11] I am not aware that anyone has looked closely at and identified in greater

---

2. In addition to the above, see Amnon Netzer's *Otzar kitve ha-yad shel yehude Paras be-Makhon Ben Tzvi* ['Manuscripts of the Jews of Persia in the Ben Zvi Institute'] (Jerusalem, 1985).

3. That of Israel's National Library is being prepared by Dr. Efraim Wust.

4. Joseph Rosenwasser, "Judaeo-Persian Manuscripts in the British Museum," *Handlist of Persian Manuscripts, 1895-1966*" (London: 1968), updated by Vera B. Moreen, "A Supplementary List of Judaeo-Persian Manuscripts of the British Library," *British Library Journal* 21 (1995): 71–80.

5. Ezra Spicehandler, "A Descriptive List of Judeo-Persian Manuscripts at the Klau Library of the Hebrew Union College," *Studies in Bibliography and Booklore* 8 (1968): 114–36.

6. For references to other Judeo-Persian manuscript explorations, see the Bibliography in Moreen, *Catalog*.

7. For a unique overview of the Russian holdings, see S. M. Iakerson, *Evreiskie sokrovischa Peterburga* ['Jewish Treasures of St Petersburg'], 2 vols. (St. Petersburg, 2009).

8. This number differs from the count (31) in my *Catalog*, where I included Ms. A 73 and counted Ms. 1682 twice because they appeared on the lists of both libraries.

9. Even if the manuscripts do not so specify, they are almost all from Bukhārā.

10. "Spisoky rukopisey priobritenikhi dlia Aziatekago Muzeya Rosiskoi Akademii Nauki V. A. Ivanovimi vi Bukhari vi 1915 g. ['Liste des manuscrits acquis pour le Musée Asiatique de l'Académie des Sciences de Russie VI série], 1918), 12 (1918): 1279–82.

11. "Kratkii obzor evreyskogo fonda rukopisnogo otdela Instituta Vostokvedenia Akademii Nauk, SSSR ['Brief Survey of the Hebrew Manuscripts of the Institute off Oriental Manuscripts of the Soviet Academy of Scienes'], *Bibliografia Vostoka* 10 (1936): 125–30.

detail the contents of these manuscripts. I saw the manuscripts in 1989 during a short visit to St. Petersburg, at which time I was provided with typed sheets with the most cursory shelf numbers and identifications. Since I had only limited time perusing the two collections, and at the time possessed relatively little knowledge of Judeo-Persian manuscripts, my own notes remained incomplete, falling short in particular in describing the manuscripts' physical appearance, at times not identifying individual poems fully, and occasionally providing no incipits, only headings. Regrettably, I have never been able to return to see the collections, and even if I could have, they were then (and probably still are) poorly foliated (a task that belongs to the local librarians), so my notes may not have been improved by much. Given these shortcomings, I hesitated for a long time to publish my notes. I changed my mind for two reasons. First, my knowledge of Judeo-Persian manuscripts matured and expanded considerably over the years, and second, contact with Dr. Irina F. Popova, Head of the Department of Manuscripts and Documents at the Institute of Oriental Manuscripts, reinforced the impression that such a publication would be useful.

The Judeo-Persian manuscripts in both Russian collections date largely from the nineteenth century with certain notable exceptions. First and foremost of these is ms. D 35 (1682; Firkowicz I), which dates from the tenth or eleventh century.[12] One ms. (C 77) bears the date 1617, and four manuscripts date from the eighteenth century: A 7 (1732); A 98 (1776); A 111 (1778), and A 24 (1780). As a comparison with existing catalogs and lists indicates, many of the items in the two Russian collections are identical with those found in other Judeo-Persian manuscripts. This reinforces the finding that Iranian Jews were attached to a fairly well established and "popular canon" of Persian, Hebrew, and Judeo-Persian literature. As was the case with most Hebrew manuscripts, most Judeo-Persian manuscripts were also copied by owners for their private perusal. At least two manuscripts (A 98 and A 111) were copied by (?) and belonged to Ya'qov b. Mullāh Shelomo b. Mullāh 'Abdullāh b. Mullāh Eliyahu b. Mullāh Qandīn b. Mullāh 'Ināyat, an individual from what it would appear to have been a distinguished family. Interestingly, some works of European provenance have also found their way into the IOM's collections of Judeo-Persian manuscripts. Among them are ms. A 116,

---

12. Thamar E. Gindin, *The Early Judaeo-Persian Tafsīrs of Ezekiel: Text, Translation, Commentary* (Vienna: Verlag der Österreichischen Akademie der Wissenschafte, 2007–).

Sefer shoshannat Ya'qov ['The Book of the Rose of Jacob'] by Jacob b. Mordecai of Fulda (fl. 17th cent.), a Hebrew work of chiromancy and astrology; ms. A 195, a fragment of sermons and eulogies from *Siyaḥ ha-Sadeh* ['Musings of the Field'] by Eliezer ☒ayyim b. Abraham (d. 1916), and a fragment from *Simkhat ha-Regel* ['The Joy of the Three Festivals'] by ☒ayim Joseph David Azulay (d. 1806) in the same ms., as well as ms. C 77, a fragment from Isaac Meir Dick's (1814–1893) Hebrew book *ha-Oreaḥ* ['The Visitor'] about Moses Montefiore's visit to Vilna in 1846. Their presence testifies to the fact that Bukhārā (and Iran) had increasing contact with world Jewry, especially in the nineteenth century.[13]

NB. The numbering of the manuscripts in the descriptions below follows the typed lists provided to me, and they are followed by the (shelf?) numbers I found in the manuscripts. In most (but not all) cases, I was able to determine identification with Freiman's (F) list. In addition, whenever possible, I indicate the presence of the same items in Netzer's and my own catalogs (N and M respectively); in the latter, more extensive bibliography about various items can also be found.

NB* This list omits ms. 73 included on IMO's list as its contents are entirely in Hebrew and of Italian provenance.

I. INSTITUTE OF ORIENTAL MANUSCRIPTS

MS A1 (N 1627/620)

Miscellanea (F=620)
Persian, Judeo-Persian, and Hebrew (Eliyahu Kohen b. David Irani) poems. Bukhārā. 94 leaves. Fols. 3r-4v, 26v-29r, 32r-87v are blank. Fol. 26v: 26 Nisan, yr? Acquired by IOM 1915.

1. Fol. 1r: a poem by Eliyahu Kohen b. David Iranī
   Heading (only):

   אין שירה אז אני איליהו כהן בן דוד אראני הסת...

2. Fol. 2r: A Hebrew quatrain by Eliyahu Kohen b. David Iranī about determining the gender of an unborn fetus preceded by a table of prognostication on the same subject.

---

13. See David Yeroushalmi, *The Jews of Iran in the Nineteenth Century: Aspects of History, Community, and Culture*, Brill's Series in Jewish Studies 40 (Leiden: Brill, 2009), Section VIII.

Incipit (after the table):

לידע אים אישה הרה...

3. Fol. 5r-26r: a Hebrew tale interspersed with some Persian (Bukhārān) vocabulary.
   Incipit:

הבט וראה הרשעם שעשו נבאלה במותם...

4. Fol. 26v: in pencil:

תאריך כ'ו ניסן נושת

אסתר...

5. Fol. 29v-30v: a poem by Ḥāfiẓ (d. ca. 1389/90).
   Heading:

ג'"זלי כ'גה חאפיס

   Incipit:

בגוג"א דבר זי דרדת ג"י...

6. Fols. 31r-31v: a Judeo-Persian poem.
   Incipit (refrain):

בכי גויים...

7. Fol. 88r: ledger accounts?
8. Fol. 89r: a Hebrew poem by Israel Najara (d. 1625) (N, M).
   Heading:

שירה סימן ישראל

   Incipit:

יושב שמי שחק בנה חצרותי...

9. Fol. 89v: a bilingual (Hebrew and Judeo-Persian) poem by Benjamin b. Mishaʾel [Amīnā; (d. after 1732)] (N, M)
   Heading:

שירה ית' סימן בנימין

   Incipit:

בשם עליון אשבח ברינה...

10. Fol. 90r: a bilingual (Hebrew and Judeo-Persian) poem by Shabbatai (N, M)
    Heading:

    ר'ת סימן שבתי

    Incipit:

    שדי פדני שמע אמרתי...

11. Fol. 91v-94r: explanations of Passover rituals mostly in Hebrew with some Judeo-Persian (N, M).
    Incipit:

    קדש ורחץ כרפס יחץ...

MS A6 (N 1627/619)
Miscellanea (= F 619)

Hebrew and Judeo-Persian poems. 39 leaves. Fols. 32v-34v, 36r-39v are blank. Various hands. Fol. 1r: owner: Yitzḥaq b. Mullāh Avraham Shoḥet (also given as Yiṣhaq Barukh b. Mullāh Avraham). The ms. has a small, elongated format. The cover is embossed and decorated, golden cardboard. Acquired by IOM in 1915.
Headings (only):

אתחיל לכתוב שירות בעזרת האל קורא דורות...

זה דסתך אזני י צחק בן מ'ו אברהם שוחט...הצעיר יצחק ברוך בן מ'ו אברהם

1. Fol. 2v-4v: A Hebrew poem by Israel Najara (d. 1625) (N, M)
    Heading:

    סימן ישראל בר משה בר לוי

    Incipit:

    יצא למלוך מבית סורים...

2. Fol. 4v-5r: An Aramaic poem by Siman Ṭov [Melamed; 'Ṭuvyah' (d. 1823 or 1828) (N, M)
    Heading:

    פזמון נאה ומשובח שחבר הרב סימן טוב

Incipit:

טס מטע מזוזרזים...

3. Fol. 4v-11v: an Aramaic and two Hebrew poems by Israel Najara (d. 1625). (N, M)
   Heading:

מי ישראל

Fol. 4v: Incipit:

חצבי לנהרא דמיא...

Fol. 7v: Incipit:

ידידי רועי מקימי ...

Fol. 8v: Incipit:

ירום ונישא גבה מאד...

4. Fol. 12r-20r: an anonymous Judeo-Persian didactic, peroration on what constitutes evil and misdeeds.
   Fol. 12r: Incipit:

אגר גרדש אין ג"רך ג"י אייד בר דר מא...

5. Fol. 20v-30v: poems by Ḥāfiẓ (d. 1389/90).
   Fol. 20v: Incipit:

בול עג'ב הא בין כימן בר יזדן...

6. Fol. 30v-31r: a Judeo-Persian poem by Bābāī b. Luṭf (fl. 17th cent.) (N, M)
   Fol. 30v: Incipit:

יא אליא יא אליא...

7. Fol. 31v-32r: a Judeo-Persian *mukhammas* by Yūsuf Yahūdī (d. 1788?)
   Fol. 31v: Heading:

מוכ'מס מ'ו יוסף

Fol. 31v: Incipit:

ביכון כארי כ'ודא דאיים...

8. Fol. 35r: same as A1, # 2.

9. Fol. 35v: the beginning of a Judeo-Persian poem.

Fol. 35v: Incipit:

עאשיקאן הר ג'נב מושתאקי...

MS A7
Miscellanea

Hebrew and Judeo-Persian poems. First 16 pages and fols. 71v-108v are blank. 108 leaves. Page size: 11 x 17.5 cm. Colophons: Fols. 47r: 5492 [1732]; 69r: Friday, 12th of Adar [no year]. Owner: Yitzḥaq b. Eliyahu. Inventoried by IOM in 1935 as #7.

1. Fols. 1r-47v: *Azharot* of Benjamin b. Mishaʾel [ʿAmīnā' (d. after 1732)]. (N, M)

    Heading:

    תפסיר אזהרות אז פרמודהי ה'מ השלום מ' בנימין בן ה'מ מישאל

    Incipit:

    כ'דאוונדא הר דו עאלם...

2. Fols. 47v-57r: Hebrew poems by Israel Najara (d. 1625) followed by Judeo-Persian translations. (N, M)

    Fol. 47v: Incipit:

    אזמרך אלוהי כל יצורים...

    Fol. 49r: Heading:

    תפסיר אזמרך

    Incipit:

    מדח גויים תורא יא חאלק דהר...

    Fol. 51v, 57r: Headings:

    ר'ת ישראל

    Fol. 57r: Incipit:

    תפסיר גיפתהי איצחק אסואני

    Fol. 57v: Incipit:

    קדרת בנמא אי שאה עאלם...

3. Fols. 70r-71r: Hebrew poems.

MS A 11 (N 1627/1055)
Miscellanea (=F 1055)
Hebrew and Judeo-Persian poems. 86 leaves. Same good hand throughout the ms. Fol. 86v: colophon: Nisan, 5639 [1879]. Bukhārā. Copyist (and owner?): Eliyahu b. ha-Mullāh Menashe. Acquired by IOM in 1915.

1. Fol. 1r: a Hebrew poem.
   Incipit:

   ואניביי אעליזה...

2. Fol. 1v: a Hebrew poem.
   Heading:

   שירה ר'ת ניסים

3. Fol. 2r: a Hebrew poem by Israel Najara (d. 1625).
   Heading:

   שירה ר'ת ישראל

4. Fol. 2v: a Hebrew poem by Aharon bar Ḥasin.
   Heading:

   ר'ת אני דוד בר אהרון חסין

5. Fol. 38v-48r: Hebrew poems, some with alternating lines of Judeo-Persian translation.

6. Fol. 48r: a Hebrew poem by Israel Najara. (N, M)
   Heading:

   שירה ר'ת ישראל

   Incipit:

   יבוא דודי לגן עדנו...

7. Fol. 49r: a Judeo-Persian poem (probably a translation of #6?).

8. Fol. 50r: a Hebrew poem.

9. Fol. 50v: a Judeo-Persian poem by Benjamin b. Misha'el ['Amīnā' (d. after 1732)]. (N, M)
   Incipit:

   כ'דאוונדא תויי מכבר בבאטן...

10. Fol. 58r-62r: a bilingual (Judeo-Persian and Hebrew) poem to be recited after Havdalah.
    Incipit:

    אלהא אז תו רחמאני...

11. Fol. 73r-76v: an Aramaic poem.

12. Fol. 77r-8rv: Hebrew poems.

13. Fol. 84r-86v(?) a Hebrew poem.
    Heading:

    נפלאים על סדר אלפא ביתא

MS A 14 (N 1627/1030)
Miscellanea (= F 1030)
Hebrew and Judeo-Persian poems. 9 leaves. Fols. 6r-9v are blank. Acquired by IOM in 1915. Inventoried in 1935 as # 14.

1. Fol. 1r: a Hebrew poem. (M)
   Incipit:

   ואני ביי אעלוזה...

2. Fol. 1r: a Judeo-Persian translation of a Hebrew poem by Israel Najara (d. 1625). (N, M)
   Incipit:

   רוז ברוז גויים שוכר מן בנדה...

3. Fol. 3v: two Hebrew poems by Israel Najara each one followed by a Judeo-Persian translation. (N, M)
   Fol. 3v: Incipit:

   יהלל ניב שפתינו...

   Fol. 3v: Incipit:

   מדח גוייד לבאני מא...

   Fol. 4r: Incipit:

   שחקים יצרו ידיו...

   Fol. 5r (?): Incipit:

   בקדרת ערש כרד מווג'וד...

MS A 24
Miscellanea
Two narratives on Jewish martyrdom. 89 leaves. Several hands. Inventoried by IOM in 1935 as 24. Two colophons: a. fol. 82r: Copied in memory of by Mullāh Khudāydād ha-Kohen; b. Copied by Kohen b. Mullāh Ḥayim Jāmulā in 5640 [1780] in the town of Sansan? (סנסן?)

1. Fol. 1r-82r: *Qiṣṣa-yi haft barādarān* ['The Story of the Seven Brethren'], also known as *Muṣībat-nāma* ['The Book of Calamity'], based on the famous rabbinic tale 'Miriam and Her Seven Sons,' by the Judeo-Persian poet 'Imrānī (d. after 1536). (N, M)
   Fol. 1r: Incipit:

   בנאם קאדר קדרת נמודאר...

2. Fols. 82v-89v: a versified narrative of the martyrdom of Yiṣḥaq Kamāl.[14] (M)
   Heading:

   ועתה אתחיל לכתוב ספר יצחק כמאל

   Incipit:

   בנאם כ'אסי או אג'''אז כרדם...

MS A 26 (N 1627/711)
Miscellanea (=F 711)
Hebrew and Judeo-Persian poems; *Khodāydād*. 124 leaves; fols. 43r-49v and 78r-84r are blank; poorly foliated. Acquired by the IOM in 1915. Inventoried in 1935 as #26. Colophons: fol. 26v: a *ghazal* copied in 5574 [1814]; fol. 124r: *Khodāydād* was copied by Nissim Saghirah ('the small'), between Tues. and Thurs. of Av [no year], for Mullāh Natan'el (?).

1. Fol. 1r: fragment of a Judeo-Persian poem.

   ...שויד הם דיואנה...

2. Fol. 1r-25v: Hebrew poems by Israel Najara (d. 1625).
   Heading:

---

14. Vera B. Moreen, "Yiṣḥaq-i Kamāl—A Martyr in Bukhārā," in *The Festschrift Darkhei Noam: the Jews of Arab Lands,* eds. C. Schapkow, S. Shepkaru, A. Levenson (Leiden: Brill, 2015).

PRELIMINARY LIST OF JUDEO-PERSIAN MANUSCRIPTS 151

שירה סימן ישראל

3. Fol. 25v-34r: Hebrew poems by Israel Najara with alternating Judeo-Persian strophe translations.

4. Fol. 34v: a Hebrew poem in honor of Rabbi Me'ir Ba'al ha-Nes.
   Heading:

שירה לכבוד רבי מאיר בעל הנס

5. Fol. 35v-37r: an alphabetical Hebrew poem in honor of Rabbi Shim'on bar Yoḥai.
   Heading:

שיר מיועד ע"ד א"ב לכבוד התנע האלאקי רבי שמעון בן יוחי

6. Fol. 38v-40r: a Hebrew poem in praise of Elijah.
   Heading:

שבח אליהו הנביא

7. Fol. 40r-42r: a Hebrew poem by David b. Ma'min. (N, M)
   Incipit:

מפי אל מפי אל תתברך ישראל...

8. Fol. 42v: a Hebrew poem in honor of Simḥat Torah.
   Heading:

שירה נאה לשמחה תורה

9. Fol. 50r-71r: Judeo-Persian transcriptions of classical Persian poems by Ḥāfiẓ (d. 1389/90, Jāmī (d. 1492), Rūmī (d. 1273), Sa'dī (d. 1291), and others.

10. Fol. 54r-54v: a Judeo-Persian poem by Yūsuf Yahūdī. (1788?)
    Heading:

גפתהי יוסוף יהודי

11. Fol. 71v-77v: a verse narrative in Judeo-Persian (Bukhārān vocalization) about an Arab sage and a girl.
    Heading:

הקאית פירי ערב ודוכ'תר

12. Fol. 85r: an alphabetical Judeo-Persian poem in praise of Elijah. (M)

   Heading:

   שירה זה שבח אליאהו הנביא מיוסד ע״ד א״ב

   Incipit:

   אלאהא אן תו רחמאני...

13. Fol. 85v-105: some poorly copied Judeo-Persian poems.

14. Fol. 105r-124r: a complete copy of the historical Bukhārān *masnavī Khodāydād* by Ibrāhīm b. Mullāh Abū'l Khayr (?). (N, M)
    Incipit:

   [יכי] רוזי אזין רוזי כ׳ודאוונד...

15. Last two pages: a rudimentary list of first line of some *ghazals*.

MS A 49
Miscellanea (=F 717)
The Story of Eldad ha-Dani in Judeo-Persian. *Khodāydād* by Ibrāhīm b. Mullāh Abū'l Khayr (?). 41 leaves. Inventoried in 1935 as # 49. Small square format and embossed leather cover.

1. Fol. 1r-32r: The Story of Eldad ha-Dani in Judeo-Persian. (N, M)
   Heading:

   הכאיתי ה׳ה׳ר אלדד

2. Fol. 32r-41r: *Khodāydād* by Ibrāhīm b. Mullāh Abū'l Khayr (?). (N, M)
   Heading:

   שיר קיצה שעירי כ׳וידד

   Incipit:

   יכי רוזי אז רוזי כ׳ודאוונד...

MS A 58
Miscellanea (=F 752?)
Musībat-nāma ['The Book of Calamity'], also known as *Qisse-yi haft barādarān* ['The Story of the Seven Brothers'], based on the *midrash* of

'Hannah/Miriam and Her Seven Sons' and *Asarah haruge malkhut* ['The Ten Martyrs of the Kingdom'], based on the famous rabbinic tale of the same title, both by 'Imrānī. 76 leaves. Inventoried in 1935 as 58. Colophon: fol. 76r: copied and completed on Friday, Rosh Ḥodesh Av 5576 [1816] by Eliyahu b. Yiṣḥaq.

1. *Musībat-nāma* ['The Book of Calamity'] by 'Imrānī (d. after 1536). (N, M)

    Caption title:

    אג״אז דאסתאן משיבת נאמה...מערפת מ. עמראני

    Incipit:

    דלא בגריי כי רוז מאתם אמאדי...

1. Fol. 46v-76r: *Asarah haruge malkhut* ['The Ten Martyrs of the Kingdom'] by 'Imrānī (d. after 1536). (N, M)

    Heading a:

    אם אשכחך ירושלים

    Heading b:

    אג״אז מרשיה עשרה הרוגי המלוכה

    Incipit:

    אלא אי פאך דין ופאך דאמאן...

    אם אשכחך ירושלים תשכך ימיני מרשיה פרסי עשרה הרוגי המלכות אז

    כלאם מ. עמראמי

    Incipit:

    ואניסת כה קיסר אישאן רא בבהאנה מכירת יוסף...

MS 98
Miscellanea
Midrash *Aliyat Moshe le-marom* ['The Ascension of Moses'], also known as *Ke-tapuaḥ be-'aṣe ha-ya'ar* ['Like an Apple among the Trees of the Forest']; a Judeo-Persian rendering of the *'Aqedah* by 'Abbās Judah Samuel; a Hebrew *baqqashah*; a Judeo-Persian rendering of *Keter Malkhut* ['The Crown of Kingship'] by Solomon b. Gabirol; a short Hebrew prayer; scribbles. The same hand as ms. A 111. Small format, 104 leaves; folios

size: 16 x 10.5 cm. Colorful, embossed leather (?) cover. 1904. No. 1483. Ad. 1904/51. Fol. 1v: recording of a death: Mullāh b. Mullāh ʿAbdullāh b. Mullāh Eliyahu b. Mullāh Qandīn Mullāh ʿInāyat in Bukhārā in Tamuz, 5586 [1826]. Fol 102 v: colophon: [copiyist/owner?] Yaʿqov b. Mullāh Shelomo b. Mullāh ʿAbdullāh b. Mullāh Eliyahu b. Mullāh Qandīn b. Mullāh ʿInāyat, 5536 [1776].

1. Fol. 3r-33v: Midrash *ʿAliyat Moshe le-marom* ['The Ascension of Moses'], also known as *Ke-tapuaḥ be-ʿaṣe ha-yaʿar* ['Like an Apple among the Trees of the Forest']. (N, M)
   Heading:

   מדרש מעשה מ'ר'ע'ה

   Incipit:

   כתוב כתפוח בעצי היער...

2. Fol. 34r- 52r: a Judeo-Persian rendering of the *ʿAqedah* by ʿAbbās Judah Samuel. (N, M)
   Incipit:

   עת שערי רצון להפתח...

3. Fol. 52r-57r: a Hebrew *baqqashah* for Yom Kippur.
   Heading:

   זה הבקשה אומרים בליל כפור

   Incipit:

   כל נדרין וחרמין...

4. Fol. 57v-102v: a Judeo-Persian rendering of *Keter Malkhut* ['The Crown of Kingship'] by Solomon b. Gabirol (d. 1058). (N, M)
   Caption title:

   בשם אל עוזר דלים אתחיל לכתוב תפסיר כתר מלכות...

5. Fol. 103 r: a short Hebrew prayer.
6. Fol. 104r: scribbles.

MS A 105
Miscellany (=F 410)

A Judeo-Persian poem by Joseph b. Isaac. *Muṣībat-nāma* ['The Book of Calamity'], also known as *Qiṣṣe-yi haft barādarān* ['The Story of the Seven Brothers'], based on the rabbinic tale of 'Hannah/Miriam and Her Seven Sons,' by 'Imrānī. *Khodāydād* by Ibrāhīm b. Mullāh Abū'l Khayr (?)Ibrāhīm b. Mullāh Abū'l Khayr (?). A Judeo-Persian poem by Yiẓḥaq Kamāl. Bukhārā. Acquired by IOM in 1915. Green, embossed cover with Arabic writing. 60 leaves. Fol. 23r: Copied by Mashiaḥ b. Aharon Masʿī on Wednesday, 28 of Adar, 5615 [1855].

1. Fol. 1r-2v: a Judeo-Persian poem by Joseph b. Isaac. (N, M)
   Heading:

   תוחיד בדרגהי רבי ג׳ליל אז נזמי מוולנא יוסף בן מוולנא יצחק

   Incipit:

   בנאמי קאדירי קדרת נמודאר...

2. Fol. 3r-60v: *Muṣībat-nāma* ['The Book of Calamity'], also known as *Qiṣṣe-yi haft barādarān* ['The Story of the Seven Brothers'], based on the rabbinic tale of 'Hannah/Miriam and Her Seven Sons,' by 'Imrānī (d. after 1536).
   Caption title:

   בשם אל עוזר דלים

   כתאבת מוסיבת נאמה...הפת פסראן מרים

3. Fol. ?- 17r. No. 2 above is interrupted by *Khodāydād* by Ibrāhīm b. Mullāh Abū'l Khayr (?). (N, M)
   Caption title:

   ביידי כ׳וידאת כי הסת דאניד

   Incipit:

   יכי רוזי אז רוזי כ׳ודאוונד...

4. Fol.? -23r. No. 2 above is interrupted by a Judeo-Persian poem by Yiẓḥaq Kamāl (see above, ms. A 11) (M)
   Caption title:

   ביידי יצחק כמאל הסת

   Incipit:

   בנאמי כ׳אסי או אג׳״אז כרדם...

MS A111 (N 1627/644)
Miscellanea (=F 644)
Prayer for the evening of Yom Kippur. A Judeo-Persian rendition of *Keter Malkhut* ['The Crown of Kingship'] by Solomon b. Gabirol. 8 leaves. Simple, embossed leather cover. The same hand as ms. A 98. Fol. 8r: Colophon: copied by Ya'qov b. Mullāh Shelomo b. Mullāh 'Abdullāh b. Mullāh Qand[īn?] b. Mullāh 'Ināyat b. Mullāh Eliyahu on Sunday, 18th of Kislev 5538 (1778). Acquired by IOM in 1915. Inventoried in 1935 as # 111.

1. Fol. 1r-8: prayer for the evening of Yom Kippur.
   Heading:

   ערבית ליל כפור

   Incipit:

   כל נדרי...

2. Fol. 8r-?: a Judeo-Persian rendition of *Keter Malkut* ['The Crown of Kingship'] by Solomon b. Gabirol (d. 1058). (N, M)
   Caption title:

   תפסיר כתר מלכות

   Incipit:

   בשם אל עוזר דלים...

MS A 116
Prognostication
Sefer shoshannat Ya'qov ['The Book of the Rose of Jacob'] by Jacob b. Mordecai of Fulda (fl. 17th cent.), a Hebrew work of chiromancy and astrology. 39 leaves; small format; black cardboard covers. The name (perhaps the owner?) "Ya'qov b. Mordekai Mi[mi?]gorshi" appears on the typed list of the IOM. (N)
   Caption title:

   ספר שושנת יעקוב

   Incipit:

   שושנת יעקוב

   פרק ראשון

סימני היד כתיב בזווהר...

MS A 121 (N 1627)
Miscellanea
A fragment (missing the incipit?) of a Hebrew rhymed prose text on the ʿAqedah. *Tafsīr-i ʿAqedat Yiṣḥaq* ['Translation/Commentary of the Binding of Isaac'] by Benjamin b. Misha'el ['Amīnā'] (d. after 1732) or by ʿImrānī (d. after 1536). 17 leaves; very small format. Acquired by IOM in 1915. Inventoried in 1931 as # 121.

1. Fol.1r-3r: a fragment (missing the incipit?) of a Hebrew rhymed prose text on the ʿAqedah.
   Incipit:

   עוקד אמר לשרה כי...

2. Fol. 3v-17v: *Tafsīr-i ʿAqedat Yiṣḥaq* ['Translation/Commentary of the Binding of Isaac'] by Benjamin b. Misha'el ['Amīnā'] or by ʿImrānī. (N, M)
   Heading:

   תפסיר עקדת יצחק

MS A 124 (N 1627)
Tafsīr-i ʿAqedat Yiṣḥaq ['Translation/Commentary of the Binding of Isaac'] by Benjamin b. Misha'el ['Amīnā'] or by ʿImrānī (possibly a continuation of ms. A 121 above). 16 leaves; very small format. Acquired by IOM in 1915. Inventoried in 1935 as 124. (N, M)

MS A 129 (N 364)
A fragment (missing the incipit) of *Ardashīr-nāma* ['The Book of Ardashīr'] by Shāhīn. 205 [199] leaves; 16.5 x 10.00 cm. Same, even hand throughout. Lovely, embossed leather cover. On p. 1, the inscription "Von Dr. Yahudah 1904 N. 364" is visible as well as the fact that this ms. was purchased in Bukhārā by Eliyahu Kohen b. David Kohen. Inventoried in 1935 as # 129.

Fol. 6r-205v: a fragment (missing the incipit) of *Ardashīr-nāma* ['The Book of Ardashīr'] by Shāhīn (fl. 14th cent.) (N, M)
Incipit (first legible lines):

אנהא כי במווג'זען יגאנה...

158   IRANIANS AND JEWS

MS A 133 (N 409; = F 409)
A Judeo-Persian rendition of *Keter Malkhut* ['The Crown of Kingship'] by Solomon b. Gabirol. 35 leaves. Acquired by IOM in 1915. Inventoried in 1935 as # 409. Colophon: Fol. 35v: copyist David b. Laya (sp?) Ḥakham Eliyahu Bavli in Bukhārā, in the month of "Zīv" ('Splendor,' that is, Iyyar) 5614 [1854].

Fol. 1r-35v: a Judeo-Persian rendition of *Keter Malkhut* ['The Crown of Kingship'] by Solomon b. Gabirol (d. 1058). (N, M)
   Heading:

אתחיל לכתוב כתר מלכות בעזרת האל...

   Incipit:

נפלאים ג״י עג׳איבאתי הסת...

MS A 136 (N 1627)
Miscellanea (= F 752)
Judeo-Persian poem by Yosef b. Yiṣḥaq. *Muṣībat-nāma* ['The Book of Calamity'] by ʿImrānī (d. after 1536). 76 leaves. Acquired by IOM in 1915. Inventoried in 1935 as # 136. Bukhārā.

1. Fol. 1v-7r: a Judeo-Persian poem by Yosef b. Yiṣḥaq. (N, M)
   Heading:

תוחיד בדרגאיי רבי ג׳ליל אז נזמי מולנא יוסף בן מולנא יצחק

   Incipit:

בנמי קדירי קודרת נמודאר...

2. Fol. 7v-73v: *Muṣībat-nāma* ['The Book of Calamity'] by ʿImrānī (d. after 1536).
   Heading:

אז גפתהי מולנא עמראני

   Incipit:

דילא בגרי כי רוז מ[א]תם אמד...

MS A 142
Miscellanea
Indeterminate prose contents; missing incipit and end. Ms. very damaged. Inventoried in 1935 as #142.

MS A 152
Miscellanea

Magic spells and remedies. Tales in Judeo-Persian from *Sefer Ben Gorion*, also known as *Jospippon* by Joseph ben Gorion (compiled in the 10th century), purporting to be about Jesus but about other subjects as well. *Sefer Harakhal (?)* 55 leaves; very damaged. Acquired (?) by IOM in 1906 as #423. Inventoried in 1935 as #152.

1. Fol. 1r-24r: magic spells and remedies.

2. Fol. 24v-47v: tales in Judeo-Persian from *Sefer Ben Gorion*, also known as *Jospippon* by Joseph ben Gorion. (M)
    Caption title:

אלה תולדותיו וסיפוריו של ישי הנוצרי כמו שנדרשי בספר בן גוריון אתחיל

לכתוב בלשון פארסי

Incipit:

דר רוזגראן אישאן בוד מרדי אז נסל דויד המלך...

3. Fol. 48r-55r: a fragment (?) from *Sefer Harkhal (?)* expounding in Judeo-Persian prose the ten occurrences that will precede the coming of the Messiah.
    Heading (?):

עסרה דברים

MS A 155 (N 424)
Mishnah

A Hebrew copy with word-by-word Judeo-Persian translation of the mishnaic tractate *Zeraʿim*. Small format; old, damaged brown leather covers. 127 leaves Acquired (?) by IOM in 1906 as #424. Inventoried in 1935 as #155. Colophon: Āghā-yi b. Mullāh Moshe b. Mullāh Avraham b. Mullāh Shabbatai. (M)

Caption title:

כסי עתא דישמיא

סדר זרעים מסכת ברכות ופרקיו ט׳פרק רישון

Incipit:

מאמתי אז כי עמוד עמד...

MS A 159 (N 1627)
Miscellanea (= F 879)
Hebrew poems of Israel Najara (d. 1635) interspersed with Judeo-Persian translations(?).17 leaves. Small format; lacking a cover; in a large, untutored script. Acquired by IOM in 1915–1916. Inventoried in 1935 as #159. Bukhārā.

Incipit:

יחיב חכמתא לחכימין...

MS A 192 (N 1627/617)
Miscellanea (= F 617)
Judeo-Persian and Hebrew poems. 10 leaves. Small format and poor hand, similar to MS A 159. Acquired by IOM in 1915. Inventoried in 1935 as # 192.

MS A 194 (N 1627)
Miscellanea
Medical remedies. A fragment of sermons and eulogies from *Siyaḥ ha-Sadeh* ['Musings of the Field'] by Eliezer Ḥayyim b. Abraham (d. 1916). A Judeo-Persian poem on the ʿ*Aqedah* by? Followed by a seal containing the names "Mullāh Raḥamim b. Ḥakham Eliyahu ʿOfer Bavli in the town of Bukhārā for (?) Shimʿ[ayin]on b. Ḥakham Eliahu ʿOfer." *Khodāydād* by Ibrāhīm b. Mullāh Abūʾl Khayr (?). Rules of Hebrew grammar and writing written/composed (?) in Isfahan. A fragment from *Simkhat ha-Regel* ['The Joy of the Three Festivals'] by Ḥayim Joseph David Azulay (d. 1806). A Hebrew fragment of a kabbalistic text. No. of leaves?; divided in fascicles. Colophon: at the end of Pt. V (fascicle IV): "in the year 5500 [1740]"; copied in Mashhad on Monday . . . 5628 [1868]. Acquired by IOM on October 13, 1915. Bukhārā.

1. P. 1: Medical remedies.
   Incipit:

   אנקרדיא כה נאלעסת אז ג'הת פאלג'...

2. Pt. I (fascicle I): medical remedies and medicinal plants.

3. Pt. II (fascicle II): a fragment of sermons and eulogies from *Siyaḥ ha-sadeh* ['Musings of the Field'] by Eliezer Ḥayyim b. Abraham (d. 1916).

Caption title:

ספר שיח השדה

4. Pt. III (fascicle III): a Judeo-Persian poem on the *'Aqedah* by .... (?).
   Incipit:

ביגוינד זכרי מן רוזי מחשר...

5. Pt. IV (in fascicle III): *Khodāydāvd* by Ibrāhīm b. Mullāh Abū'l Khayr (?) (N, M)
   Caption title:

ביידי כ'וידד ג" נ'ע

   Incipit:

יכי רוזי אז רוז כ'ודאוונד...

6. Pt. V (in fascicle IV): rules on Hebrew grammar and writing written/composed (?) in Isfahan.
   Heading:

המימסת דקדוקים כה דר ספאהאן נוישתה שודה

   Incipit:

בדאנך תהריר ותקדיר תפסיר תורה...

7. Pp. 4–18v (?):. a fragment from *Simkhat ha-regel* ['The Joy of the Three Festivals'] by Ḥayim Joseph David Azulay (d. 1806).
   Caption title:

מספר סמחת הרגל

8. Pp. 1–9 (?): a Hebrew fragment of a kabbalistic text (?)

MS A 294
Miscellanea (= F 714?)
Judeo-Persian explanatory notes on part of the Haggadah. Judeo-Persian tales (?). 42 leaves; small format; fol. 15r-15v are blank; damaged; poorly bound; dark brown leather cover with closing tongs.

1. Fol. 1r-14r: Judeo-Persian explanatory notes on part of the Haggadah.
   Heading:

אינסת שרח גאל קדש ורחץ ומעני הגדה

2. Fol. 16r-42v: Judeo-Persian tales (?)
   Incipit:

נאם אדם זנדה אסת והמה באר י מי תואנד כרדן...

MS D 35 (N 1682)

Judeo-Persian commentary on the Book of Ezekiel from the library of Carl Salemann. 113 leaves; in several scripts. N. 1682 (101). The date 5461 [1701] is provided on the typed sheet, but this important ms. is one of the earliest Judeo-Persian biblical commentaries and dates from the 10th or the 11th century (see n. 11 above). Fol. 113v: "Die collation beendet nachs 23/24 11//8/9 III 1901 C. S."

Heading (Latin): "Comentarius Judaeo-Persicus in Ezechielis librum e codice collectionis alterae Firkovicii."

MS C 40
Miscellanea

Sefer sharḥ-i Shāhīn Torah (Mūsa-nāma) ['Shāhīn's Book of Commentary on the Torah (the Book of Moses)'] by Mowlānā Shāhīn. A Judeo-Persian panegyric in praise of Moses. 271 leaves; restored but missing some folios; last pages very damaged. Inventoried in 1964 as #758. On the first page, Dr. Yahudah states that Shāhīn wrote this composition in Shiraz or Kashan in 1639 (Seleucid era, corresponding to 1327 C. E.), corresponding to the Hebrew date 5088 [1327/1328], and that he wrote the composition on Genesis [known as *Bereshit-nāma*] thirty years after this [1357/8] ..., signed, "Von Dr. Yahuda 1904 N. 365, Add. 1904/35" A copyist or owner's (?) name: fol. 124v and others: Shimʿon b. ☒akham Eliyahu S/sofer" ; Colophons: a. fol. 270r: 5521[(1860)/1861], corresponding to the Seleucid date 2172 [1860], followed by וחשוב זמן בחיבור עד עת נהיה תקליוס5536 [1776] שנים. b. fol. 271v: Samarqand, copied by Mullāh Shemuel b. Yosef ha-rofe ['the physician'], in 5310 [1550!], which does not correspond with the Hebrew letters also provided: אתתסא לטטחת (!)

1. Fol. 1r-271v: *Sefer sharḥ-i Shāhīn Torah (Mūsa-nāma)* ['Shāhīn's Book of Commentary on the Torah (the Book of Moses)'] by Mowlānā Shāhīn (fl. 14th cent.). (N, M)
   Caption title:

כתאב שרח שאהין תורה אז נזם וכלאם מולאנא שאהין עליה אל סלאם

Incipit:

אבתידא דר תוחיד אלאה תעאלא פרמאייד פרשת ואלא שמות

בנאם קאדר ברין ודאנא...

2. Fol. 2r-2v: a Judeo-Persian panegyric in praise of Moses
Caption title:

דר מדח כלים אלאה עליה אל סלאם פרמאייד

Incipit:

כלים אלאה כה הסת או גוהר פאך...

MS C 43

A fragment (missing the incipit and the end) of *Sefer sharḥ-i Shāhīn Torah (Bereshit-nāma)* ['Shāhīn's Book of Commentary on the Torah (the Book of Genesis)'] by Mowlānā Shāhīn. 98 leaves; large format; damaged leather cover; first folios very damaged. Fol. 99r: scribbles in French and the signature "Eyoub Machiah." Fol. 99v: owner: Mashia☒ b. ha-Mullāh Yi☒aq.

First legible line:

דד ודים [דאם] אז זין נאגה בג'סת...

MS C 77
Miscellanea (=F 1054)

A fragment of *Shāhzādah va-ṣūfī* by Elisha b. Samuel ['Rāghib'] composed in 1684. A short Hebrew treatise dealing with the weekly Torah readings for the Sabbath and holidays. Hebrew proverbs (?). Twelve chapters from the Book of Daniel. A Hebrew commentary on a kabbalistic text. Hebrew *kinnot* for Tesha' b'Av and other occasions. A short treatise on Hebrew grammar and a short list of Hebrew-Persian words. A fragment from Isaac Meir Dick's (1814–1893) Hebrew book *ha-Oreaḥ* ['The Visitor'] about Moses Montefiore's visit to Vilna in 1846. Accounts. A fragment of a Judeo-Turkish text. Lists and accounts. Judeo-Turkish texts. 66 leaves poorly collated. Many folios seriously damaged. A variety of scripts. Copyist: fol. 8v: 5377 (?) [1617] (?). Copyist: fol. 64r (?): Shelomoh Siman ☒a'ir Balkh (?) Berakha Kohen ha-Zaken z"l.

1. Fol. 1r-66v (but interspersed with items below): a fragment (missing the incipit and much of the text) of *Shāhzādah va-ṣūfī* by Elisha b. Samuel ['Rāghib']. (fl. 17th cent.) (N, M)
    First legible line:

    תרא ת'אני נבאשד אין יקינסת...

2. Fol. ? A short Hebrew treatise dealing with the weekly Torah readings for the Sabbath and the holidays.
3. Fol.? Hebrew proverbs?
4. Fol.? Twelve chapters from the Book of Daniel.
5. Fol. ? A Hebrew commentary on a kabbalistic text.
    Heading:

    וזה פירוש המרכבה מעשה

6. Fol.? Hebrew *kinnot* for Tesha' b'Av and other occasions.
    Heading:

    סדר תשע באב

7. Fol. ? A short treatise on Hebrew grammar and a short list of Hebrew-Persian words.
8. Fol. ? A fragment from Isaac Meir Dick's (1814–1893) Hebrew book *ha-Oreaḥ* ['The Visitor'] about Moses Montefiore's visit to Vilna in 1846.
    Heading:

    האורח

9. Fol.? A fragment of a Judeo-Turkish text.
10. Fol.? Lists and accounts.
11. Fol.? Judeo-Turkish texts.

NATIONAL LIBRARY OF RUSSIA[15]

MS I 39 (Firkowicz)
A large, damaged fragment (missing the incipit and the end) of a Hebrew commentary on Isa. 6 and other prophets; resembling or part of MS I 40 below. 109 leaves.
    Heading:

פירוש הר״ג (?) ז״ל על ספר ישעיהו

חזון ישעיהו

MS I 40 (Firkowicz)
A large, fire damaged fragment (missing the incipit and the end) of an unvocalized Hebrew copy of the *haftarot* (?). 129 leaves.

MS I 41 (Firkowicz)
A fragment (missing the incipit) of a Judeo-Persian commentary/translation on Jer. 70 leaves. Col.: Fol. 70v: "at the end of the 18th, beginning of the 19th year of the year . . .?"
    Heading:

פירוש הבב״ג (?) על ס׳ ירמיה

MS I 42 (Firkowicz)
A fragment (missing the incipit and the end) of a Hebrew commentary on the Book of Job. 51 leaves. Very damaged; lovely script.
    A title page:

פירוש הרי עשר לרבן...

פירוש הבב״ג (?) על ס׳ ירמיה

MS I 50
A complete copy of Shahīn's *Sefer Sharḥ-i Shāhīn Towrah [Bereshit-nāma]*. 220 fols. Several hands. Original leather cover. (N, M)
    Incipit:

פי תוהיד סבהאני ותעאלה

---

15. The numbers on the following manuscripts were provided to me on a typed sheet, which labelled them as either just "evr." ('Hebrew,' 'Jewish') or "evr.-arab." ("Judeo-Arabic"). Mss. I 39, I 40, I 41, and I 42 are specified as being part of the Firkowicz collection.

בנאם אן כה גיתי רא בנא כרד...

MS I 70
The Judeo-Persian *Aqedat Yiṣḥaq* by ʿImrānī (d. after 1536). 12 leaves; small format. Fol. 12r: Copyist: Yonathan b. Mullāh Moshe Kohen.
Caption title:

אין עקדת יצחק עת שערי רצון להתפתח

Incipit:

אי ישראלאן ברסיד וקתי אן...

MS I 75
The colophon (fol. 87r) identifies this complete (?) copy as *Sefer agron* ['The Book of Lexicon'], but it is also known as *Sefer ha-meliṣah* ['The Book of Rhetoric'] by Solomon b. Samuel of Urgench (Uzbekistan) composed in 1339. It translates and explains circa eighteen thousand Hebrew, Aramaic, Greek, and Persian words and expression of the Bible, Talmud, and Midrash into Judeo-Persian and Turkish. 87 leaves. In an excellent script. Colophon: Fol. 87r: copied by Shelomoh bar ha-Rav Shemuel and completed on Rosh-Ḥodesh Tamuz 5651 [1891] in Gurganj [Turkmenistan] for his own use. (N, M).
Caption title:

ספר האגרון בלשון פרסי

Incipit:

צנטפי (?) ולא אחזיק לשפכי חזקה כרד...

MS I 76
An additional fragment of I 75 above? 15 leaves.

MS I (?) 215
Twelve loose leaf pages of Judeo-Persian poetry in several hands, some are transcriptions of *ghazal*s by Saʿdī (d. 1291) and Ḥāfiẓ (d. 1389/90). P. 1: Copyist or owner (?): Yaʿqov Iliyaziyaoff [misidentified as "Iliyaev" on the typed sheet]. P 12: 1888.

MS I 218
A fragment of a Judeo-Persian commentary/translation from Exod.((?) and some Talmudic fragments. In very poor condition. Unfoliated.

MS 4605
A fragment of a Judeo-Persian commentary/translation of Gen. 27 leaves. 25.3 x 18 cm.

Incipit:

בשם אלהי עולם

ברכי נפשי את יי...

MS 4606
A fragment (missing the incipit and the end) of a Judeo-Persian commentary/translation of Deut. 15 leaves. Restored.

MS 4607
A fragment (missing the incipit and the end) of a Judeo-Persian commentary/translation of Gen. 4 leaves. Restored.

MS 4608
A very damaged fragment of a bilingual (Hebrew and Judeo-Persian) commentary/translation of Kings (1 or 2?) and Jer. 3 leaves. Restored.

MS 4609
A fragment of a Judeo-Persian commentary/translation of 1 Kings. 7 leaves. Restored.

MS 4610
A fragment of a Judeo-Persian commentary/translation of Isa. 4 leaves. Restored.

MS I 4611
A short fragment of a Judeo-Persian *tafsīr* (commentary/translation) of the Book of Jeremiah.
Fol. Fol. 1r: Incipit:

פ״ת נבואת יכפניה (?) ואת המשתחוים על הגגית לצבא השמים...

MS 1682
See above, IOM A 1682.

PART 2

Modern Cultural History

8

Rabbi Menaḥem Shemuel Halevy, Hamadan, Persia—Jerusalem (1884-1940)[1]

NECHAMA KRAMER-HELLINX

RABBI MENAḤEM SHEMUEL HALEVY, also known as Mollah Menaḥem and Monsieur Menaḥem, was born in Hamadan, Persia, in 1884, to a respected rabbinical family that traced its lineage back at least 10 generations.[2] He spent his childhood and youth in Hamadan, preparing himself for the day he would return to Palestine, or Biblical Zion. As an

---

1. As Rabbi Menaḥem was born before 1935 when the name Persia was changed to Iran, and since he uses Persia and Persian in his speeches and writing, I will accordingly use Persia and Persian in my references to the country and nationality when commenting on his writing. Previous scholarship about Rabbi Menaḥem includes my articles: "The Genealogy of Rabbi Menaḥem Shemuel Halevy of Hamadan (Iran) [Part I]," *Esti: Revue de Genealogie et d'Histoire Sefardes*, 30, 8 (September 2005): 9-18; "Life and Contirubion for the Cause of Zion of Rabbi Menaḥem Shemuel Halevy of Hamadan (Iran) [Part II]," *Esti: Revue de Genealogie et d'Histoire Sefardes*, 32, 9 (March 2006): 3-9; "Rabbi Menaḥem Shemuel Halevy's Poetry [Part III]," *Esti: Revue de Genealogie et d'Histoire Sefardes*, 34, 9 (September 2006): 6-9; "Envoy of the Sephardim: Rabbi Menaḥem Shemuel Halevy: Zionist, Peacemaker, Poet, 1884-1940," *International Sephardic Journal* 2.1 (2005/5765): 213-26; "Ha-Rav Menaḥem Sheumuel Halevy: Me-Hamadan she-be-Paras li-Yerushalayim," AB"A 6 (2012): 115-54.

2. Rabbi Menaḥem Halevy is my maternal grandfather. Some of the information introduced here was told and retold by my family and close friends of the Halevy family.

individual who lived through tumultuous times and whose life is relatively well documented, a study of this figure can shed light on the broader circumstances of Jewish life in Persia, particularly in Hamadan, in the early twentieth century, as well as the forces that brought many of them to the land of Israel.

FIGURE 1

Alliance Francaise. Rabbi Halevy is at the top left.

We begin the story with the Halevy family.[3] The available genealogical information of Rabbi Menaẖem Shemuel Halevy's family starts with his grandfather Mordechai Halevy (1820–1858), the rabbi of the Jewish congregation of Kermanshah, Persia. Responding to Islamic laws that forbade Jews from holding certain positions within Muslim society, Mordechai Halevy, like many of his Jewish compatriots, became a traveling merchant, wandering from village to village and selling a variety of merchandise in order to earn his livelihood and sustain his family. Ben Hanania describes this dejected way of earning ones livelihood:

---

3. Daniel Tsadik, *Between Foreigners and Shi'is: Nineteenth-Century Iran and its Jewish Minority* (Stanford: Stanford University Press, 2007). This is an imperative reference for a detailed history of the era; Daniel Tsadik, "Foreign Intervention, Majority, and Minority: The Status of the Jews During the Latter Part of Nineteenth Century Iran (1848–1896)" (PhD diss., Yale University, 2002), 294–326; Haideh Hashim, "Jews of Iran in the Qajar Period: Persecution and Perseverance," in *Religion and Society in Qajar Iran*, ed. Robert Gleave (New York: Routledge Curzon, 2005), 293–310; Janet Afary, "From Outcasts to Citizens: Jews in Qajar Iran," in *Esther's Children: A Portrait of Iranian Jews*, ed. Houman Sarshar (Philadelphia: Jewish Publication Society, 2002), 139–92.

> The residents of the Jewish City [Kermanshah] earn their bread by venturing into the villages as fabric dyers, sellers of haberdashery, doctors and pharmacists, without having an idea about this profession, and as writers of amulets against evil spirits. At times, these ill-fated are robbed going to the villages or returning from them, and consequently, they lose all their merchandise and are left naked and barehanded. And their life work goes down the drain. And in order to save themselves from imprisonment, they adopt the Muslim religion and abandon their wives and children in poverty and famine.[4]

In 1858, while on the road collecting debts from clients, Rabbi Mordechai Halevy was poisoned. He died, leaving his family fatherless and financially ruined. Rabbi Mordechai left behind three sons and a daughter: Eliyahu, Shemuel, Yair and Dina. The first born, Eliyahu Ben Mordechai Halevy, was a spiritual man. In 1859, Eliyahu traveled to The Holy Land, where he was ordained as a rabbi, by the famous Rabbi Yaakov Shaul Elyashar (1817–1906), with the purpose of taking over the place of his deceased father, Rabbi Mordechai Halevy.[5] Unfortunately, as soon as Eliyahu returned to Persia, he succumbed to the plague that ravaged the country and died. He had no children from his young wife, who happened to be his cousin, and following the religious guidelines of *yibbum*, "levirate marriage" (Deut 25:5–10), she was given as a bride to his younger brother, Shemuel.

Rabbi Shemuel Mordechai Halevy (1846–1918), Rabbi Menaẖem Halevy's father, was only thirteen years old when he married his cousin, the widow of his brother Eliyahu. Eventually, Shemuel went to Tehran, where he studied and was ordained as a rabbi, a judge, a teacher, and later served the Hamadani Jewish congregation. Years later, he traveled to Paris, France, to study medicine. For the first twenty-four years of his marriage, until he was 37 years old, Rabbi Shemuel and his wife did not have any children. In the tradition of the time, in order to continue the family line, he married another lady, Rachel Bat-Shemuel, from a highly

---

4. Joshua Ben H̱anania, "The Situation of the Iranian Jews, Fifty Years Ago" (according to reports by Mr. Yitzchak Bassan from the Ki'ach organization), *Mahberet* (Elul, 5715 / 1955): 141; see as well, Azaria Levi, "Yehudei Paras BeYerushalyim," *Kivunim* 27 (Jerusalem, 1985), 136 (in Hebrew); Daniel Tsadik, "Introduction," in *Between Foreigners*, 9–11.

5. Rabbi Yaakov Shaul Elyashar was appointed *dayyan* in Jerusalem on 1853. In 1869, he became head of the *Beth Din*. In 1893, he became the *Rishon LeZion*, or Sephardi chief rabbi of Palestine.

respected Hamadani family of medical doctors. While in Paris, Shemuel was notified that his first-born infant, Menaẖem, had died in Hamadan. Shemuel returned immediately to Hamadan and in 1884/תרמ"ד, he fathered his second son, who was also named Menaẖem (which means "the one who consoles"), the main protagonist of this paper. In all, Shemuel fathered 4 children who survived infancy: Menaẖem (1884–1940), Yaakov (1890–1968), Yocheved (1893–1980), and Yoseph (1900–1954).

As a judge and rabbi of the Jewish congregation in Hamadan, Shemuel established his own *yeshiva, Minḥat Shemuel* ("the offering of Shemuel"), and served as its principal. His children Menaẖem and Yaakov were educated in this yeshiva in Jewish and rabbinical studies. However, Shemuel also aspired to create a Jewish school in Hamadan, following the model of the *Alliance Israélite Universelle*. In the *Tenth Annual Report of the Anglo Jewish Association*, dated 1880–81, it is noted that Mr. Halévy from Hamadan, the "celebrated Jewish traveler," made a suggestion and inquiry about opening a Jewish School in Hamadan, in spite of the fear that the "fanatical Mahomedan neighbours [sic]" would interfere adversely in the creation of the school. It was agreed that the school, if and when established, would provide secular as well as religious instruction:

> The Association, adopting a suggestion made by the celebrated Jewish traveler, M. Halévy, now made inquiries into the practicability of forming a Jewish school at Hamadan. In a reply, forwarded by the heads of the Hamadan congregation, it was stated that the Community had appointed a committee of twenty-three members to attend to the subject of organizing a school, but they pointed out that owing to the recent famine the resources of the congregation had been completely drained, and they appealed to the Council for assistance to acquire a conveniently situated plot of ground for a school-house, which at the outset would be attended by 150 boys. They also mentioned that in consideration of the isolated and unprotected position of the Jewish Community, it would be necessary to obtain from the Government of the Shah an order to deter their fanatical Mahomedan neighbors from interfering with the management of proposed Jewish school. The Jews agreed that any school established under the auspices of the Anglo-Jewish Association should afford secular as well as religious instruction.[6]

---

6. *The Tenth Annual Report of the Anglo-Jewish Association in connection with the Alliance Israélite Universelle* (London: 1880–81 [5640–5641]), 38–39.

That vision materialized later, in 1900, when a branch of the *Alliance Israélite Universelle de Paris* was established in Hamadan, by its first principal Isaac Bassan. Rabbi Shemuel enrolled his children in the school so that in addition to their Jewish studies, they could become worldly-wise, learning French and western subjects, while he taught Hebrew and Torah studies there. Following the enlightened tradition of the family, his daughter Yocheved, as well, was later instructed both in French and Jewish education.

Shemuel was respected by the Muslims who called him *Nabi Samuel*, the Prophet Samuel. It was told by the family and other Hamadani elders that during the drought that devastated Hamadan, the Muslim population prayed for rain, but their prayers were not answered. Rabbi Shemuel intervened, gathered his congregation and called for general fasting. He took a Torah and led his people to the burial shrine of Esther and Mordechai. From there, they walked to the Jewish cemetery, where, with his stunning voice, he chanted the prayer of *Seliḥot* (forgiveness). The rain started falling and nurtured the thirsty earth. From that day on, in spite of their abhorrence and contempt for the Jews, designated by them as *najes* (impure), the Shi'is showed reverence for Shemuel, and called him *Nabi Samuel*.[7]

Isaac Bassan, the Alliance emissary from Europe, who became the first principal of the *Alliance Israélite Universelle* in Hamadan, writes in his report of 1902 about the persecution the Jews underwent by the Shi'is. He recounts that Mollah Rabbi, the chief Rabbi of Hamadan—Rabbi Shemuel—was admonished by the Aqa Shaykh Muhammad Hassan Bahari, who forbade the Jews from wearing nice clothes and silk belts, or they would face severe castigation. Rabbi Shemuel ordered work stoppage of his congregation, and with twenty representatives of the community approached Isaac Bassan asking him to intervene on their behalf with the authorities.[8] Consequently, the Persian authorities sent emissaries of good will to placate the Jews, asking them to return to work and to be reassured that no harm would be done to them. This served as a warning, though for a brief time, for the Shi'is to watch their steps with the Jews.

By all accounts, Rabbi Shemuel Halevy was a compassionate man who had never turned away a person in need, be it a Muslim, a Christian,

---

7. These anecdotes, repeated in my mother's family, were told to me by her nephew, Ezra Ben-Elyiahu (1906–1998), and by Hamadani elderly men who also lived in Jerusalem, who were children at the time this event took place.

8. Yehoshua Ben Hanania, "Matzav Yehudei Paras ..." 141.

or a Jew. Accordingly, he instilled in his offspring the spirit of their ancestry; uprightness and human empathy toward their fellow men as if they were their immediate extended family. Consequently, his children were benevolent humanitarians, dedicating their lives to helping the needy.[9] As a progressive, pragmatic person, Rabbi Shemuel understood the need of being an integrated part of the universe; thus, in addition to Jewish studies, he insisted on also educating children, women, and elders with a Western education and open-mindedness. When he died in 1918 (5677), at the age of 72, he received great honors from both Jews and Muslims.

Yair, Rabbi Mordechai Halevy's youngest son, was a travelling merchant, voyaging between Russia and Hamadan, like his father Mordechai before him. He died in 1899; his son, David Halevy, was then 13 years old. David was born in 1886, and he, too, in the tradition of his grandfather and his father, became a merchant of expensive garments. However, like many from Hamadan of this era, David converted to the Baha'i faith. Later, he converted back to Judaism when he wished to marry a Jewish woman. According to his children, though, he remained a Baha'i in his heart until his death. David's son was first named Zion, but David changed it to Cyrus so he would not bear a Jewish name. Zion Cyrus visited Israel in 1952, and found his father's cousin, Rabbi Yaakov Halevy, Menaẖem's younger brother. Wishing to pray *kaddish* for his father David, who had died in 1951, Zion went with Rabbi Yaakov Halevy to the synagogue named for Rabbi Menaẖem, the *Beit Menaḥem* synagogue in the *Bucharim* neighborhood of Jerusalem.[10]

As a child in Hamadan, Rabbi Menaẖem Shemuel Halevy received his Jewish education in his father's Yeshiva *Minḥat Shemuel* and simultaneously attended the Alliance Israélite Universelle, where he acquired knowledge of French and western education.[11] Additionally, he attended a public school in Hamadan, where he majored in Education. He was

---

9. When I was 22 years old, Rabbi Yaakov Halevy, Mollah Menaẖem's brother, met me and told me that I had to follow the family's tradition, and become a social worker in order to help the needy among us.

10. The synagogue Beit Menaẖem was inaugurated in 1953; my father, Shimon Ben-Mashiach, was in charge of the establishment of the synagogue, with the aid of Rabbi Yaakov Halevy. The event was attended by Rabbi Yitzchak Isaac Halevy Herzog, Ashkenazi Chief Rabbi of Israel, and Rabbi Ben-Zion Meir Chay Uziel, Rishon LeZion, the Sepharadi Chief Rabbi of Israel.

11. Nechama Kramer-Hellinx, "Envoy of the Sephardim: Rabbi Menaẖem Shemuel Halevy: Zionist, Peacemaker, Poet, 1884–1940," *International Sephardic Journal* 2 (2005): 213–26.

a gifted young man, and in 1904, at the age of 20, he was appointed as a teacher of French and Hebrew in the *Alliance Israélite Universelle* of Hamadan. In 1910, became the principal of the school, a position he maintained for twelve years.[12] At the same time, he taught French in a public school and privately tutored some children of the Muslim elite. In spite of his young age, Mollah Menaḥem headed the Jewish congregation of Hamadan and fought for equal civil rights for the Jews. His influence reached high places in the authorities, and thus, on many occasions, he saved many of his brethren from imprisonment, torture, and even death. As the "Shepherd" of the Jewish community, he educated children and adults in the religious, political, and nationalistic love of their homeland, Zion. Moreover, he insisted on teaching elders and youth, boys and girls, the Hebrew language and respect for the Torah. He was adamant regarding the importance of Hebrew as a communicative tool among Jews and an imperative tool for the comprehension of the sacred Bible and prayers.

Ezra Shoshani, who in the 1920s was a youngster, remembered and revered Rabbi Menaḥem as a cantor, orator, and a leader of the congregation in Hamadan who commanded great respect. Shoshani recalled how the Rabbi would attract the public to the synagogue where, from the pulpit, he would read the current events from the Israeli newspaper *Do'ar HaYom* (edited by Ze'ev Jabotinsky) and simultaneously translate it, along with the *Haftarah*, into Farsi. The names Jerusalem and Israel fascinated and stirred the congregation. Shoshani also recalled that on November 2, 1917, Rabbi Menaḥem announced the Balfour Declaration from the pulpit, and the congregation burst into tears, while thanking God for returning to them their fatherland. Even the Muslims came to congratulate the Jews for receiving a homeland.[13]

Rabbi Menaḥem founded the *Ḥevrat Me'orerei Yeshenim* (Organization for Awakening the Dormant) in Hamadan to return the "lost" souls

---

12. "Hamadan," in *Encyclopedia Judaica*, vol. 7 (Jerusalem: Keter, 1972), 1219–20; Giora Pozailov, *Chachmeihem Shel Yehudei Iran Ve Afghanistan* [Wisemen of Iran and Afghanistan] (Jerusalem, Sifriat HaMoreh HaDati, 1995), 123–34 (in Hebrew); Mordecai Cohen, ed., *Perakim Betoldot Yehudei Hamizrach*, vol. V [Chapters in the History of the Jews of the East] (Jerusalem: Misrad Hachinuch Vehatarbut, 1981), 262–65 (in Hebrew). Amnon Nezer, *The Jews of Iran* (Tel Aviv: Bet Koresh, World Center of Iranian Jews in Israel, 1988), 66.

13. *Me Iran u-mi-Makadonia le Yerushalyim: Sipureihen shel mishpahot ben-Eliyahu and Menaḥem* [From Iran And Macedonia to Jerusalem: Stories of Ben-Elyiahu and Menaḥem families] (ed. Ben-Zion Yehoshua; Jerusalem: Zur Ot Printer, 2002), 10–11.

who had suffered forced conversion to Islam and Baha'ism, back to the arms of Judaism.

Rabbi Halevy as the director of the Hevrat Me'orerei Yeshenim.
He is in the front middle, wearing black.

In addition, he was one of the founders of *Ḥovevei Yeshurun* (Lovers of Jeshurun). Both societies celebrated the Hebrew Language and the Zionist sentiments of love for the Promised Land as dictated by the Torah and preached, along the lines of the Mizrachi organization, the value of "the Land of Israel, for the people of Israel, according to the Torah of Israel."[14] Simultaneously, Rabbi Menaẖem established and headed local foundations to collect funds for building the Homeland of our forefathers, Israel: *Keren Hayesod, Keren Hageula,* and *Keren Kayemet LeYisrael.* He even sent a significant amount of the collected money to the Zionist Union in London.

Mollah Menaẖem had a political vision for his congregation, and thus he maintained rapport with non-Jewish societies, as well as with Jewish ones. He gained the esteem and respect of the various foreign authorities who came one after the other to Persia—Turks, Russians, British, and French—and he was even well received by the Persian Shah, Ahmed.

14. The Mizrachi Organization was founded in Vilnius in 1902, by Rabbi Yitzchak Yaacov Reines as a Zionist religious organization with adherence to the Torah. Their motto was "The Land of Israel, for the people of Israel, according to the Torah." It was the first religious Zionist movement.

The Balfour declaration on November 2, 1917, motivated Menaḥem to establish a branch of the Zionist Union in Hamadan. Being an enlightened educator, he also established a Zionist branch for Jewish women and established as well an alumni organization for the *Alliance Israélite Universelle*, whose dictum centered on carrying out the yearning for Israel. Moshe David Gaon praises the Rabbi for his hard work and positive inspiration on his congregation. He also recalls Rabbi Menaḥem's writings against the Baha'is, in a book named *Me'orer Yeshenim*, subtitled, "a collection of articles and speeches against the Baha'i faith." Gaon admires the dedication the Rabbi employed in order to eradicate the hold of Baha'ism on the confused Jewish converts. He also quotes the letters of recommendation the Rabbi received from the British consul in Hamadan and another recommendation from the Jewish Hamadani community board.

> While a Rabbi, he established the organization "Lovers of Yeshurun" and another society named "Awakening the Dormant" that had the objective to fight against the Baha'i faith. To accomplish the goals of this society, he dedicated great efforts by arranging lectures on Saturdays, as well as extensive edification sessions in the synagogues. He was successful in strengthening the frail hands. He also established the organization of Ki'ach [*Kol Israel Haverim*] students, and he was elected by the Jews as representative to the municipality and the national government ... Established a branch of the Zionist union in Hamadan ... Close to this time, he also served as a secretary in the Turkish consulate and in the chamber of commerce nearby in Hamadan.[15]

As the representative for the Jewish community in the local municipality during the First World War, he even petitioned and received aid from Europe for the impoverished Jews. His zeal and love of Zion echoed in his weekly sermons and influenced many Persian Jews in Hamadan, who had earlier abandoned the Jewish faith to return back to Judaism and even to settle in Israel.[16]

---

15. Moshe David Gaon, *Yehudei HaMizrach BeEretz Israel*. vol. 2 [The Eastern Jews in the Land of Israel] (Jerusalem: Dfus Azriel, 1937), 334–35 (in Hebrew).

16. Similar testimonials regarding Rabbi Menaḥem's devotion to his people and his causes are found in Reuben Kashani, *Yehudei Paras, Buchara Ve Afghanistan* [The Jews of Iran, Bukahara and Afaghnistan] (Jerusalem: Ahva, 2001), 42 (in Hebrew); *Encyclopedia Judaica*, Vol. 7: 1220; Reuben Kashani, *Kehilot Hayehudim BeParas* [The Jewish Congregation in Iran] (Jerusalem, 1980), 11, 24 (in Hebrew); Hanina Mizrachi, "Harav Menaḥem Levy, Z"L," *Hed Haḥinukh*, 6–7, Shevat 22 (1940): 144. A student of

Rabbi Menaḥem exerted a tremendous amount of energy combating the Baha'i faith and the attraction it had for Hamadani Jews to convert.[17] It is told in the family that some followers of the Baha'i Faith sent an assassin on Yom Kippur eve of 1922 to kill Rabbi Menaḥem as he left the synagogue. When encountering the Rabbi face to face and looking into his eyes, the assassin's hands started trembling as he realized that he was in front of a divine person. He confessed his evil mission to the Rabbi and advised him to flee Persia, because other assassins would follow to complete the task. This motivated him to travel sooner than planned to Palestine with a number of his congregation's families.

Rabbi Menaḥem's, Moshe Nehmad, representing the Hamadani congregation in an obituary (Moshe Nehmad, "Rabbi Menaḥem Halevy, Blessed Memory: Seven Days to His Demise," *Haboker* [February 6, 1940]), recalls his importance in general and his ability to persuade the converts to return to their forefathers' religion: "Many recall with praise, even today, his deeds and his success in every endeavor: His many lobbying appeals to the local authorities, the Turks, the Russians, and the British, that came one after the other to Iran; the financial and food assistance he obtained for the Jewish congregation that had suffered during the years of the last war [1st World War]. He organized, in his time (this doesn't make sense—please clarify), and headed the "Lovers of Zion" movement, in Hamadan, and many of the young men, who had assimilated, at that time, into the Baha'i Faith, returned to Judaism and became good Zionists."

17. Rabbi Menaḥem's family knows of an Arabic manuscript of his entitled "Mizan El Hak: A Critique of the Bah'ai Faith"; I have not been able to locate it. Rabbi Menaḥem lists all his published works and manuscripts at the end of his book *Mordechai VeEsther BeShushan HaBira*, and one of them is indeed "Mizan El Hak." Some of his writings were placed in carton boxes and given to his brother to guard and some were left with his children. Rabbi Menaḥem's daughter, Shoshana, and her husband, Shimon, kept some of his papers at home, and only later donated one notebook, still in Manuscript, to Ben-Zvi library in Jerusalem. A number of writers recall his fierce fight against conversion to Baha'ism and Islam; see Moshe D. Gaon, *Yehudei Hamizrach*, 334–35; Amnon Nezer, *The Jews of*, 67; Azaria Levy, 134; see as well Mordecai Cohen, 265.

FIGURE 3

נולד אלול תרמ"ד — נפטר שבט ת"ש
המדן ירושלים

Rabbi Halevy

Rabbi Menaẖem was distinguished as a powerful orator whose words captivated his audience. He directed his fervor straight to their hearts, with emotive religious vernacular as well as erudite worldly evidence. Hanina Misrahi, a writer and one of the leaders of the Persian community in the 1940s, describes the Rabbi's celebrated speaking aptitude:

> In Rabbi Menaẖem, of blessed memory, there was a fine blending from Jewish wisdom and European culture. In his sermons, he interwove and embroidered as a superb artist all the sublime and the loftiness of our sages' wisdom, of blessed memory, to one wonderful, attractive and, absorbing embroidery. He knew to tie in the words of the Rambam very nicely with the words of the Talmudic sages, sermons and compilations, and to intertwine at times in them quotes and proverbs from the beautiful literature of the West. With fiery religious speeches and with mighty power of a par excellence speaker, he knew how to captivate his large public and to bring them into sublime religious ecstasy. Dead silence reigned in the assembly of his congregation

when Rabbi Menaḥem Levy, blessed be his memory, expressed his uplifting sermons.[18]

As his father before him, Rabbi Menaḥem stressed the need for acquisition of European languages as a mode of communication with the non-Jewish world that protected the Jews at that time from Shiʻa Islam. Moreover, he well understood the importance of being the Jewish congregation's representative to the Municipality of Hamadan, and as such, to actively participate in the Persian government. At the beginning of the 20th century, the Persian Jews had enlisted the help of France and England to protect them from the wrath and hatred of their Muslim neighbors. However, being isolated in Hamadan, quite a distance from Tehran, they encountered odious attacks, both verbal and physical, without any intervention by the local governing administration. In spite of his spiritual nature, Rabbi Menaḥem found himself at times fighting with his fists against Muslim thugs. When, in 1910, Menaḥem and his brother Yaakov learned that a group of Muslims were going to desecrate the Jewish cemetery, they rushed to the cemetery to prevent the desecration, and as a result, both were attacked ferociously and injured gravely by Muslims. The two brothers were disrobed and were shamelessly marched half-naked through the streets, while being assaulted verbally and corporally by the mob. They were on the verge of being lynched. At the last minute, their lives were spared, when the governor recognized Rabbi Menaḥem as the private tutor of his daughters. The Bulletin of the *Alliance Israélite Universelle* of 1911 describes the attack inflicted on Menaḥem and his brother Yaakov at the hands of the Shiʻite soldiers:

> Mr. Jacob was assaulted . . . under the pretext that he was dressed in a European manner, he was undressed . . . beaten up mercilessly and dragged accompanied by vociferation of the mob until the governor's residence. Jacob's brother, Mr. Menaḥem [Ha] Levy, our Hebrew professor, having heard that his brother was

---

18. Hanina Misrahi, "Rabbi Menaḥem Halevy, Blessed Be His Memory," *Hed Haḥinukh*, 6–7 (15 of Shevat, 1940): 144 (in Hebrew). See also the reminiscences of Reuben Kashani, "HaMatif VeHamekonen HaGadol [The Great Preacher and Mourner]," *Yom Shishi* [23 Tamuz, 5748, 8–July-1988]: 15 [in Hebrew]) 48 years after the Rabbi's death: "I will never forget the lamentations he read in the eve of *Tisha B'Av*, with a Persian melody saturated with pain and sadness. Who didn't cry when hearing his words while sobbing about the destruction of the Temple and the exile of the *Shekhina* [Divine Presence]? Looking back . . . one could say: He, who did not hear Rabbi Monsieur Menaḥem mourning the *Ḥurban* [the Temple destruction], did not hear mourning in his life."

maltreated by the mob, ran to his help . . . In the blink of an eye, Mr. Menaḥem was disrobed of all his clothes . . . The soldiers then took aim at our professor and attacked him with the butts of their rifles. Mr. Menaḥem was dragged half nude for half an hour, under the chants of the crowd and the double blows by the soldiers . . . where he found his brother Jacob, half dead . . . Our two unfortunate young men were unconscious. Their faces and bodies were full of wounds, and they complained of strong internal pains. The governor recognized Mr. Menaḥem, who gave French lessons to his two daughters. He could hardly recognize the professor of his children in the lamentable state in which he was brought in front of him.[19]

In 1892, a zealous Shi'i Muslim, Akund Mullah Abdullah Burujirdi Hamadani had ordered violence against the Hamadani Jews and pillage of their property. Moreover, he issued edicts proclaiming religious intolerance of the Jews, whom he tried to convert en masse to Islam.[20] The two choices given to the Jews were conversion or death. Due to intervention by Great Britain, Mulla Abdullah was transferred to Tehran, and, eventually, after further intervention by International elements, the abuse subsided, to a certain extent.[21] Nevertheless, even though the open religious discrimination decreased, the total disregard for Jews remained rather evident.[22] The founder and first principal (1900–1904) of the Alliance Israélite Universelle in Hamadan, Yitzhak Bassan, reports in 1900 about the religious bigotry, persecutions, and indignity that the Jews endured at the hands of the Shi'is. The *Bulletin* further asserts that the circumstances that the Jews of Hamadan faced were reminiscent of the dark Middle Ages. The report recounts how in previous years, if two people had testified that a Jew spoke to a Muslim lady, or heard him speaking negatively of the Muslim faith, the whole Jewish congregation suffered and had to pay heavy fines. Almost all the attacks on the Jews were organized by the *Mujtahids*, or Shi'i religious scholars.

19. *Bulletin de L'Alliance Israélite Universelle* (Janvier, 1911), 69–70.

20. Daniel Tsadik, *Between Foreigners*, 155–77; Haideh Sahim, "Jews of Iran in the Qajar," 293–99; Hanina Misrahi, *The History of the Persian*, 47; Janet Afary, "From Outcasts to Citizens," 139–92.

21. *Bulletin de l'Alliance Israélite Universelle* (January 1892): 48–54 (lists the 22 prohibitions by Mullah Abdullah).

22. *The Twenty-Third Annual Report of the Anglo-Jewish Association in connection with the Alliance Israélite Universelle* (London: 1893–1894, 5653–5654): 17–18.

The report describes the circular red badge of shame the Jews had to wear at the level of the chest, and the forced conversion of Jews, who, from fear had to flee Hamadan and go to Tehran or Baghdad, where they could have returned to Judaism. Furthermore, it describes how many Jews were forced to convert, thereafter appearing as Muslims in the streets and at work, but acting as Jews in the privacy of their homes. The Muslim clergy, aware that the *Alliance* could report this misconduct against the Jews to the government in Tehran, went softer on the Jews, for a brief time.[23] Bassan comments, as well, on the subject of *Najasah*, impurity, that prevented the Jews from even handling the merchandise they wished to purchase, be it food, shoes or clothes. This definitely calls to mind the Spanish Inquisition in its darkest days, charging Jews and their descendants for lacking *Limpieza de Sangre* 'purity of blood.'[24] There were but brief points in time when the Jews' rights were partially restored in Hamadan. Nevertheless, the anxiety and fear of future abuse were always present with the Persian Jews.[25] Rabbi Menaẖem gathers the evidence of these historical events pertaining to the history of his family and his congregation and records it by composing a narration, or rather a traditional Hamadani Legend of Mullah Abdullah, in his book *Mordechai VeEsther BeShushan Habirah*.[26]

In 1923, when the atrocities against the Jews became intolerable, Rabbi Menaẖem Halevy, along with Shlomo Cohen Tzedek, the famous Zionist from Tehran, decided to publicize the violence directed against the Jews of Persia. They reached out to the 13th Zionist Assembly in London to plea for help for the Persian Jews by writing and signing a memorandum on behalf of The Zionist Union of Persia and The Committee of

---

23. *Bulletin de L'Alliance Israélite Universelle* (Paris: deuxième série, No 25, 1900): 72–89; Yehoshua Ben H̱anania, "Matzav Yehudei Paras," 141–43.

24. About Limpieza de sangre, see Albert A. Sicroff, *Les controverses des Statuts de 'Pureté de sang' en Espagne du XVe aux XVIIe siècles* (Paris: Didier, 1960).

25. *Encyclopedia Iranica*, 616–18; Ben Hanania, 141–43; Tsadik, *Between Foreigners*, 17–25.

26. *Mordechai VeEsther BeShushan HaBira* by Rabbi Menaẖem Halevy, son of Rabbi Shmuel Halevy (Jerusalem: Dfus HaTehia, 5692 / 1932). The book is a chapter from *Divrei Yemei Israel BeParas, MiḤatimat HaTalmud Ad HaYom HaZeh*. (Account of the History of Israel, in Persia, from the Conclusion of the Talmud, Until These Days). The book *Mordechai VeEsther BeShushan HaBira* contains a chapter about Customs: Legends related to the place; Legend of the Malkosh; Legend of Mulla Husein; Legend of Mulla Abdollah. It contains, as well, a poem, *Mrosh Mekadmei Eretz*, and a list of the Rabbi's published and unpublished books.

Persian Jews in Israel. Rabbi Menaḥem describes the ambience of hate and fanaticism of Shiʿa Hamadan, along with the plight and predicaments of the Persian Jews, maltreated and victimized by the hand of the Shiʿis. The memorandum depicts, in strong words, the plight of the Persian Jews, "descendants of the Babylonian exile." It tells about blood libels, false accusations, deprivation of civil and social rights, murders out in the open, and economical strangulation. It laments that any libel could provoke pogroms against the Jews, even in the Metropolis of Tehran. It describes the influence of the Shiʿi priests, who incite the people against the Jews, strangulating them economically and spiritually.

FIGURES 4–6: Report to the World Zionist Congress on the Persian Jews

FIGURE 4

תזכיר

מאת יהודי פרס

אל הכנסיה הציונית הי"ג

ירושלם, תרפ"ג

REPORT

OF THE SITUATION

OF THE PERSIAN JEWS

TO THE 13th

ZIONIST CONGRESS

JERUSALEM 1923

Printed by R. H. Cohen, Jerusalem

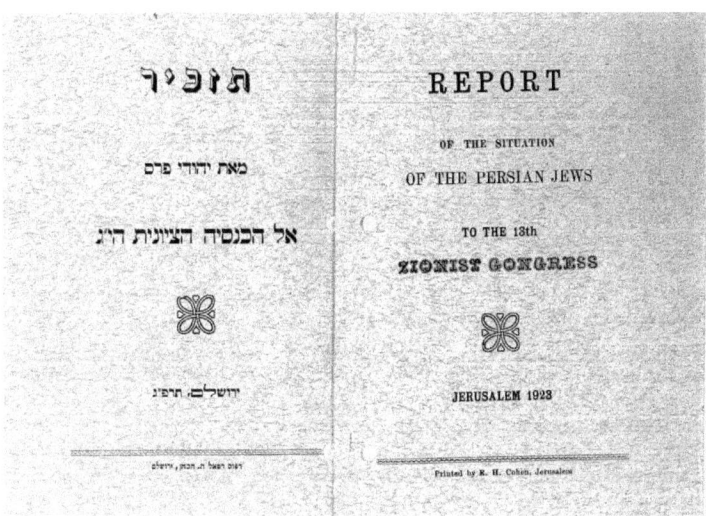

FIGURE 5

תזכיר
מאת יהודי פרס
אל הכנסיה הציונית דו"ג

כנסיה מאד נכבדה !

בשעה גדולה זו לעם ישראל, בשעה שכל קברניטי האמה מתכנסים למועצה הסתורית זו לנטול את אבני הנגף מעל דרך העם ולמצא את הדרכים לגאלתו, בשעה זו של גלוי כחירת הנרדמים של העם העתיק להצלת עצמיותו המיצאת את בטויה בדברי נביאינו, בשעה מסתוררן זו באים עליכם אלפי נדחי האמה מפרס, צאצאי אלה שעמדו בראש הבונים בזמן שיבת ציון מבבל, להגות לפניכם על צרותיהם לאין קץ, מאז דרכה רגליהם על אדמת פרס ולבקש מכם לבוא גם לעזרתו.

אחים יקרים !

רדיפות נסיון, שלילת כל זכיות אזרחיות וחברתיירת עלילות נתעבות, רציחות לעיני השמש, מסגר בתוך תחום מושב בודד, מחנק נפשי וכלכלי, כל אלה לוו את יהודי פרס בדרכם הארוכה במשך אלפי שנות נלוחם עד היום הזה, למרות רממשלה הקונסטיטוציונלית, למרות העזרה המוסרית של צירי

— 3 —

FIGURE 6

ו. אלף (1000) לי"מ לצרכי חנוך בעד ילדי יהודי
פרס.

ז. למנות את בא כח היהדות הפרסית בתור פקיד
באחד המשרדים של ההנהלה הציונית שינהל את
ה"ענפים האמורים לעיל תחת השגהתה ד"העליונה
של ההנהלה הצינית.

צירים נעלים!

היהדות הפרסית מלאה בטחון גמור כי הכנסיה הנכבדה
תתחשב עם הדרישות הצודקות של יהודי פרס ובמליאורתה
אחיהן תראה ברכה רבה באלמנט היהודי ד"פרסי בבנין
ד"ארץ ובתחית האמה.

בשם ההסתדרות הציונית   בשם וועד הכללי לעדת יהודי פרס
בפרס   בירושלם

שלמה כהן צדק   רב העדה:
מנחם ש. לוי   רחמים מלמד הכהן
                    הנשואים:
                    חנינא מזרחי
                    רפאל חיים כהן
                    עזרא שושני

The memorandum tells of forced conversion in Mashhad where the Jews could only follow the Mosaic Law in secret; of the sign of disgrace Jews had to wear in Shiraz and Yazd; of Jews chased out of their homes with just a pack of their belongings on their shoulders; and of murders in daylight in Hamadan. It complains of decrees prevalent in Persia against the so-called impure Jews, befitting of the Middle Ages. It describes the forceful haircut and shaving of side burns afflicted on Jewish men in public. As a consequence of the social and religious intolerance, many Persian Jews wish to return to the land of their forefathers. The memorandum demands the Congress for help both against the oppression and for obtaining entrance permits for the Persian Jews to the Holy Land where, with some help, they could participate in agriculture and construction. It states that in spite of the intervention of the European countries, the atrocities still persist. Rabbi Menaẖem wished to stop this malice and eradicate it before his Persian brethren would be obliterated from the face of the earth, either through death or through conversion to either Islam or the Baha'i faith. There are four additional signatures on the memorandum from the Iranian Jewish Committee in Jerusalem: Raẖamim Melamed Hacohen, H̱anina Mizrachi, Rafael H̱ayim Cohen, and Ezra Shoshani.[27] To feel the indignant hurt of the Rabbi, it's imperative to read the memorandum.

> To the XIII Zionist Assembly
> Highly honored Assembly!
> At this important time for the People of Israel, time when all the leaders of the Nation gather for an Historical Council in order to remove the obstacles from the path of our people and to find the means for its salvation; at this time of rediscovery of the dormant powers of the ancient nation to rescue its identity, found in the expressions of the prophets; at this mysterious time, thousands of our Nation's deportees arrive here from Iran; they are the descendants of those who stood at the head of the founders, during the return to Zion from Babylon; they address you to bemoan their interminable misfortune, since the minute they set foot on the land of Persia, and to ask you to come to their aid.
> Dear brethren;
> Shameless persecutions, denial of civil and social rights, hideous defamations, murders under the sun, lock-up within the boundaries of an isolated settlement, spiritual emotional and economical strangulation, all these have accompanied the Jews of Persia, during thousands years of their exile to our days. In spite of the constitutional government, in spite of the moral support of the Western States, in spite of the economical awakening in the Eastern Nations to enlightenment and freedom, one false meaningless intrigue, by whoever suffices to cause pogroms even in a metropolitan like Tehran. There is no need to stress the venomous influence of the religious clerics, those religious deities in the Shi'i countries, that every utterance from their mouth finds a strong echo in the heart of the masses. There are no words to describe the numerous exploits of these Sheiks who set the masses against the Jews, since they are Jews, with slander and despicable vilification . . . Spiritual torments of the forced converts . . . disgracing patches . . . Jews evicted from their homes and properties with their packages on their shoulders and wondering sticks in their hands . . . Murders in broad daylight without protest or grievance. Ask the people of Hamadan! Decrees from the Middle Ages, in all its terror, oppress the Jews of Iran. It is forbidden for a Jew to touch any object he buys, since he would defile and contaminate it. A Jew cannot venture

---

27. The original document, in the form of a small book, is in the Central Zionist Archives, Jerusalem Israel. Folder: J 1/12/2 (in Hebrew).

outside to the market when it rains, since he may contaminate the sacred Muslim by his touch; it's forbidden for a Jew to ride a horse; it's forbidden to him to grow hair and with rough hands they would cut his sideburns, under the sun. God Almighty! Civil and social suffocation, wherever he tries his hand!

Rabbi Menaḥem persistently searched for ways to rescue Persian Jews, particularly of Hamadan, in particular, from their predicament. Realistically, he realizes the hindrances in defeating the Shi'is within Persia. Thus, in addition to appealing to the XIII Zionist Assembly in London, he pleads with the Zionist administration in Jerusalem to facilitate the immigration of Persian Jews to Israel. He is aware that many Persian Jews were denied visas to the Holy Land, mostly due to their poverty. He is troubled by what he considers unfair bias and disregard for his people. Thus, in 1923, Rabbi Menaḥem asks that a meeting be held in Jerusalem between the representatives of the Zionist administration in Jerusalem and representatives of Persian Jewry to deal with the obstacles of immigration from Persia to the Promised Land.

At that meeting, Rabbi Menaḥem understood that he had to awaken the consciousness of the Zionist administration in the Holy Land and to bring to their attention the fact that his people had been besieged by abuse, indifference and animosity. He used any manipulative method possible to make his audience feel culpability and empathy for the dreadful circumstances of his constituency. Here again, Rabbi Menaḥem paints verbally the intense description of the predicament of the Jews in Persia since shortly before First World War to the present. His speech is a vivid historical portrait.

> The economic state of the Jews of Persia prior to the war [World War I] was more or less good, since all the commerce was in their hands, and they were happy with their fortune. The war and its aftermath caused deterioration of their condition and decline in their financial state. I was the president of the Zionist Union in Hamadan known as *Shushan Habira*, and also a Rabbi and a merchant, and there was hardly anyone happier than me ... Now the situation changed ... economic downfall and poverty reign ... Before the War, when the Jews felt oppression or distress, they asked the various consulates [European] for help and they protected them, mainly the British and the American ones. Now, their influence has dwindled and the Jews are foreseen for annihilation. Your brethren in Persia are found in an enclosed courtyard, without possibility of escape. They have no money

> ... the decrees multiply from day to day, that which causes life to be difficult and denigrating. The Jew is forbidden to go out on a rainy day, prohibited from riding a horse and wearing fine clothes ... He, who lends a Muslim a sum of money, has no hope of recovering it. And upon demanding his money, the borrowers would kill him ... The whole congregation is in danger. 80,000 Jews of Persia are being obliterated due to this distress ... the majority were merchants. There are among them a small number of craftsmen like: tailors, shoemakers, carpenters, silversmiths, etc. but it is difficult for them to maintain their trade; a tailor holding the fabric contaminates it and the Muslim is forbidden from wearing this article of clothing; the shoemaker stitches shoes with a thread, and he, indeed, contaminates the leather, and the Muslim is prohibited from wearing the shoe ... they would not participate in agriculture, since a Jew indeed could buy a terrain and plough and seed it but was not allowed to harvest, since the Muslims might eat the fruit of his labor ... They steal and pilfer everything, and the Jew is left with his hands empty. In Hamadan, the city of my residence, people who became impoverished in this way, within a month, have committed suicide. Here comes the day when there will be no memory from the 80,000 Jews of Persia.[28]

Rabbi Menaḥem declares that those wishing to come to Palestine are not looking for monetary handouts, since they would rather die than accept welfare. It is true that there are paupers among them, but all have self-respect and strong will to work hard and to support their families. Since the committee is not too enthusiastic about opening the way for the Persian Jews, Rabbi Menaḥem insinuates bitterly that there is discrimination against Persians. He also states that due to disillusion with the Holy Land, many Hamadani Jews adapted Baha'ism.

> The national movement is intertwined with the Religious movement in Persia. There are many of our brethren who believe in the doctrine of Sheik Bahá Aladin Afendi [Abdu'l-Bahá eldest son of Bahá'U'lláh born 'Abbás Effendí] who died in Haifa ... great number converted since they declared that the redemption expectation of Israel is a deceiving notion. Over twelve years, I fought against this notion through speaking and writing, in order to overcome them and avert them from their erring way. On Saturdays, I would preach to them and translate *Doar Hayom* to

---

28. The document containing the minutes of the meeting is found in the Central Zionist Archives, Jerusalem Israel. Folder: S15/ 20974 (in Hebrew).

them, so that they might believe in and be knowledgeable about of the existence of the nationalistic movement.

He proudly reports that many of the 250–300 Persian Jews who arrived in Israel are teachers, scientists, and intellectuals who are alumni of the Alliance, speaking seven or even eight languages. Despite this, the rabbi suggests starting agricultural settlements for them on Keren Hakayemet land. He is aware that it might be difficult, but as all commencements are difficult, they would get used to it eventually, working the earth with self-respect. With 50 pounds, he says, one may buy a cow and some chickens and survive from the fruits of the earth. When the committee members start arguing and doubting, the rabbi belittles them, telling an allegorical anecdote about an ailing man nursed by the priest who told him marvelous stories of the ever after. "The sick man complained, 'Why do I need the ever-after when I have not yet enjoyed this world?' This is the impression that your answers leave."

After continued negotiation, Rabbi Menaḥem lost his patience, realizing that the committee had no notion of the urgency of the dire situation. Annoyed by their cold business-like manner dealing with the lives of his congregation, the Rabbi bursts out sarcastically and bitterly:

> Nothing can stand in the way of good will. If all the great individuals, like Christopher Columbus and alike were to reflect on the difficulties and obstacles of materializing their objectives while thinking about the same thing days and nights, then they would not have commenced or created a thing. On one hand, it's bad, and on the other hand, it's bad as well, and there is no clear way for us. What shall we do? We shall take the hoe in our hands and will dig our own graves.

The shocking figurative description of morbidly using a hoe for digging a grave rather than for agriculture, and the sarcasm in which it was presented, shamed the committee into allowing him to investigate localities fit for settlements.

A few months later, 24 of Tishrei, 1924, Rabbi Menaḥem, apparently feeling anxious that things were not moving fast enough, sent a letter through his secretary, his brother Yaakov, on behalf of the General Committee of Persian Jews in Jerusalem, reminding them that they are still awaiting a positive response from *Vaad HaLeumi* for the Jews Of

Palestine and from the 13th Zionist Assembly in London to solve the problems of his people.²⁹

In an unpublished Hebrew manuscript of Rabbi Menaẖem entitled "A History of the Jews in Persia, from the completion of the Talmud until Today," found in the Ben Zvi library in Jerusalem, the Rabbi describes some of the cities where Jews lived and events that took place there. It is clear that much of what he reports was lore reported to him second- or third-hand, and perhaps even derivative of other written reports. It is a remarkable document, nonetheless, and he writes with an air of great authority. In his description of Shiraz, he relates that the Jews were threatened and later manipulated into converting to Islam.³⁰

> The Ghetto is found in a pitiful state: small houses, lacking air, sun and healthiness. Around three hundred houses serve more than a thousand families in very narrow streets. In many streets, it is impossible for two people to walk together unless in a row, and many diseases, such as typhoid, diphtheria, varicella [chickenpox], are found, mainly in children. The Jews have lived in Shiraz since antiquity, and there are headstones from 1,200 years ago. There are ten synagogues in the city and four public bathhouses because in all Persian cities, it is forbidden for a Jew to enter a Muslim bathhouse, and the converse, as well. And one of these synagogues was known with respect and praise among the Jews and Muslims due to a legend told about it . . . Seven hundred years ago, there were two competing congregations in Shiraz, and at the head of each congregation stood a religious judge (*Dayan*) . . . One of the judges named Abual Hasan, who was a butcher, sold the harvest of the ingathering of his congregation during few months and when this was revealed on the eve of Rosh Hashanah, his congregation lost trust in him and they joined the second congregation. The vain shepherd, upon seeing himself alone and abandoned, converted his religion and adopted Muhammad's faith. In a week, he managed to ignite the Muslims against his Jewish brothers; denouncing them saying that during their prayers they blaspheme and vilify the Shi'i

---

29. Found in the Central Zionist Archives, Jerusalem Israel. Folder: J1/12/2 (in Hebrew).

30. The manuscript bears the title דברי ימי ישראל בפרס, מזמן חתימת התלמוד עד היום and is found in Ben Zvi Library in Jerusalem (Number 1024; bulletin 1902, written in Rabbi Menaẖem's handwriting, library number 635939). I transcribed it, since most researchers who tried reading it encountered it to be illegible; difficulties due to the rabbi's peculiar handwriting and his habit of mixing in some writing in Persian, French, and other languages.

religion. The Muslim mob became incensed when they heard these accusations, and there was a strong attack against the Jews during Yom Kippur in the synagogues. The elders of the congregation risked their lives and went to plead before the Sheikh. The only way he gave them to save their souls was to convert and to enter as a group into the Muslim faith. The Jews, obviously, could not withstand death, and without exception converted unanimously, on Yom Kippur during the Ne'ilah prayer. But this Faith was from the mouth outwardly, and in their hearts they remained faithful to the Mosaic Faith. This lasted barely one year; for close to the anniversary on 6th Ḥeshvan, the convert Abual Hasan became sick and died. Minutes before his death, he knew that God's hand had stricken him and he wanted to redeem what he had damaged a year ago. He gathered his confident Muslim zealots who believed in his faith in Muhammad's teaching and swore to them that his claims against the Jews had been false and that he had concocted them and that the Jews were innocent of all crimes. These were his last words, and he died, acquiring his afterlife world in an hour. Immediately, the great Sheikh announced an order that any Jewish convert had the right to return to the Jewish Faith if so he wished. The news of the great Sheikh's order was disseminated swiftly in the city and a great number of the converts returned to Judaism the same day before nightfall ... A small number, who descended into the gates of sin, didn't want to return [to Judaism] and their offspring are called until these days *Jadid Al Islam*.[31] And in every family, there are one or two who benefitted personally, taking advantage of absent heirs, due to the Islamic law that offers the convert to Islam the inheritance, even though he had no kinship and in spite of the existence of real and close descendants (pp. 1–4).

In 1923, Rabbi Menaḥem concluded that he had done all he could to instill the love of Zion in his congregation and combat the Shi'is. He decided it was time to take his widowed mother Rachel, his parents-in-law, his wife Monavar Chanom (Rivka), daughter of Taus and Aziz Biajri, and their two infant girls, Esther (1921–2006) and Shoshana (1922–1986), to the Promised Land. Although some members of the Hamadani community felt abandoned by their "spiritual shepherd," other families joined him, and they set out on the long road, traveling through Iraq and Syria

---

31. Most of the converts from Mashad were *Anusim*, forced converts. They were called Jadid Al Islam, New Muslims.

in caravans. Many of the families had small children or elderly parents, or both.

FIGURES 7–10: Essay on the Tomb of Mordechai and Esther

FIGURE 7

בהנ"י.

מצבת
מרדכי ואסתר
אשר בעיר (שושן) המדאן (פרס)

המנהגים השיכים לה והאגדות הנשמעות עליה
עם הערות וביאורים מצד המחבר.

מאת
הרב מנחם בכה"ר שמואל הלוי

ירושלים תרצ"ב.

FIGURE 8

תמונת הקבר של מרדכי ואסתר בשושן הבירה

התא הימני
אשר נתרחב מחדש

הכניסה לחדר
הראשון והחיצוני

החדר השני והפנימי
אשר ממעל למצבות.

כל הזכויות שמורות
Printed in Palestine

דפוס „התחיה" ירושלים.

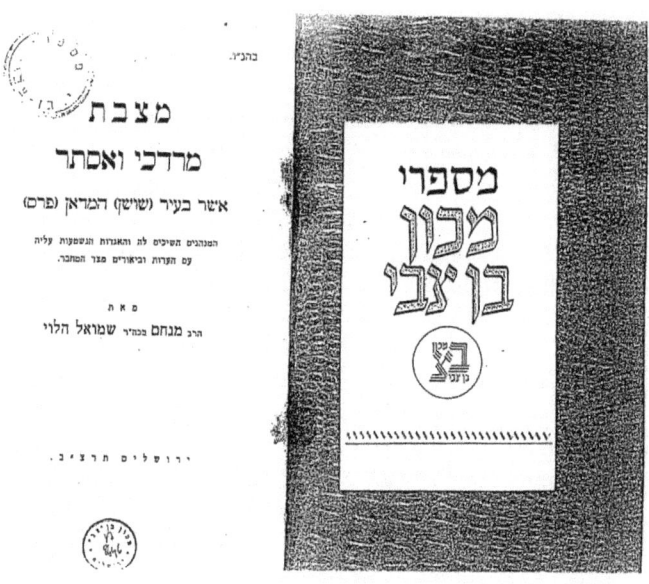

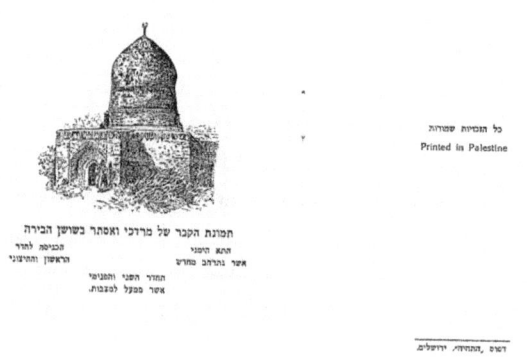

FIGURE 9

ספרי המחבר

ב ד פ ו ס :

א. זמירות ישראל.
ב. תרגום תפילת יוצר לשבת. בשפה הפרסית.
ג. תרגום מי כמוך של ר׳ יהודה הלוי על מגלת אסתר. בשפה הפרסית. בחרוז.
ד. מרדכי ואסתר בשושן, בעברית.

ב כ ת ב י ד :

א. זה ינחמנו על החומש.
ב. כתנות אור על הש״ס. פלפולים בהלכה ואגדה.
ג. לקוטי שושן על מקומות הקדושים אשר בפרס.
ד. דברי ימי ישראל בפרס. מזמן חתימת התלמוד עד היום.
ה. תרגום הובת הלבבות בשפה הפרסית.
ו. Les souvenirs de mon enfance בצרפתית על מקומות העתיקים בפרס.
ז. אידיאולוגיה על ספרי יצדי תאפיס׳ עמד־חיאם ומג׳לסי.
ח. אמאקן אל מוקדסה. מקומות הקדושים. בשפה הערבית.
ט. מיזאן אל חק. בקורת נגד האמונה הבהאית. בשפה הערבית.

FIGURE 10

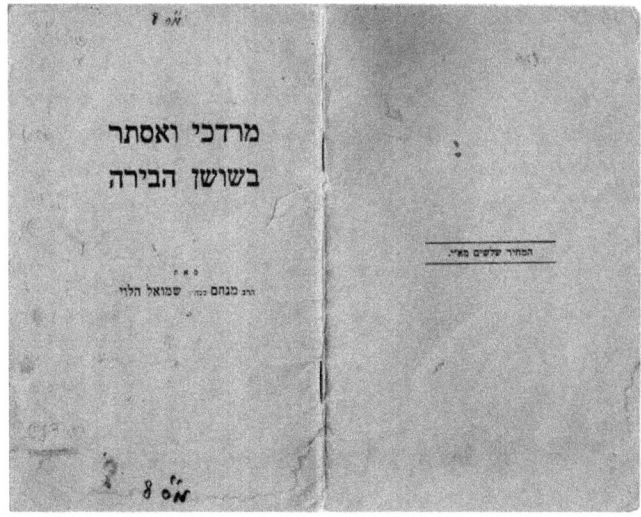

Organizations and individuals who stayed behind considered the Rabbi to be the official Persian Jewish representative to Palestine, who would open the doors to the Promised Land for his people. On 2nd of

196 IRANIANS AND JEWS

Adar, 5683/1923, he received a letter in Hebrew from ⊠ai ben Moshe (חאי בן משה):

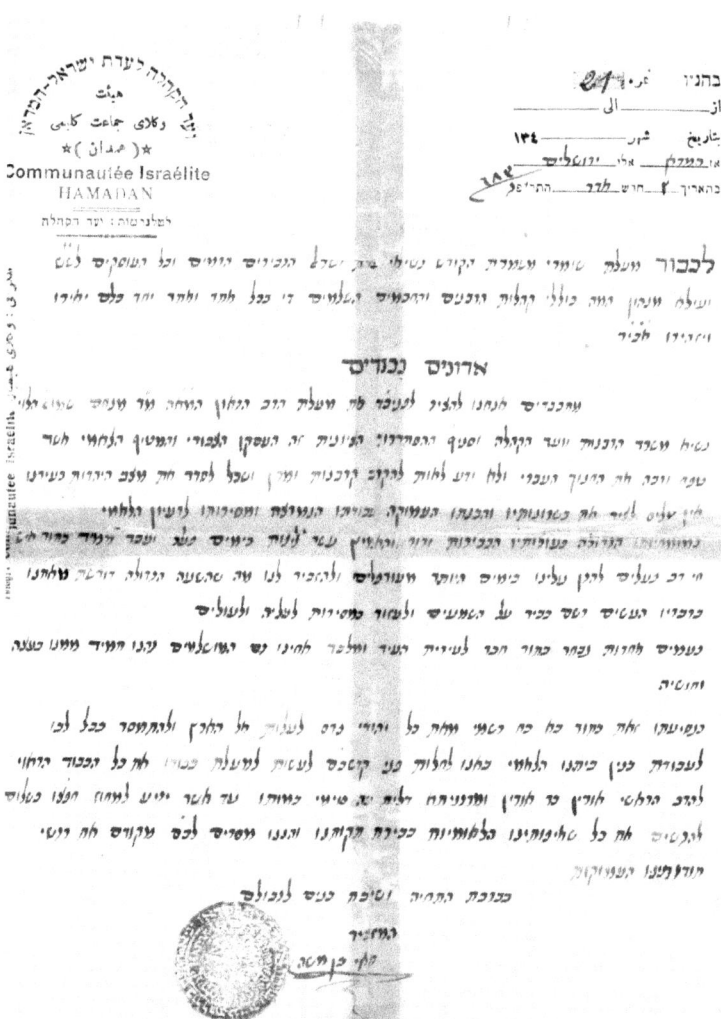

FIGURE 11

Letter from Hai ben Moshe on behalf of Rabbi Halevy

Respected Gentlemen,
    We are honored to introduce to you his highness the learned Rabbi Mena⊠em Shemuel Halevy, the president of the rabbinical office, the congregation committee, and the Zionist

Union branch. He is a public worker and national preacher who nurtured and increased Jewish education and never tired from sacrificing himself, using his energy and intelligence, to fix the situation of the Jews in our city [Hamadan]. There are no words to describe his talents, his understanding, his work, his deep loyalty for the national cause. With his great expertise and his daring spirit he functioned and worked always, day and night ... to protect us in these cloudy days, and he reminded us what is demanded of us at this time ... thus, help dependably the immigration and the immigrants.

He was often elected as a member to the municipality of our city, and in addition to our brethren, the Muslim too benefited from his advice and insight.

In this journey as an official representative for all Iranian Jews, to immigrate to Israel and dedicate with all his heart to the work of building our national home. We came to request from your holiness to aid his honor with all due respect deserving for a chief Rabbi ... until he arrives to his destined place in peace to fulfill all our national expectations in the capital of our hopes, and we extend our deepest gratitude ahead of time.

With the blessing of rebirth and returning the children to their homeland [Jeremiah 31:16].

The Secretary,
Hai Ben Moshe[32]

The Committee of the Jewish Congregation in Hamadan, as well, wrote a letter in Hebrew (dated January 22, 1923) presenting him as the head of the congregation and as an ardent Zionist who spread Zionism amongst the people:

---

32. My family possesses the original document and intends to give this and all original historic documents in our possession to an appropriate library or archive, after I finish the book I am writing about the life, literature and achievements of Rabbi Menaẖem Shemuel Halevy. Many of the documents, books, letters, photographs, and publications have already been given to the Ben Zvi Institute in Jerusalem.

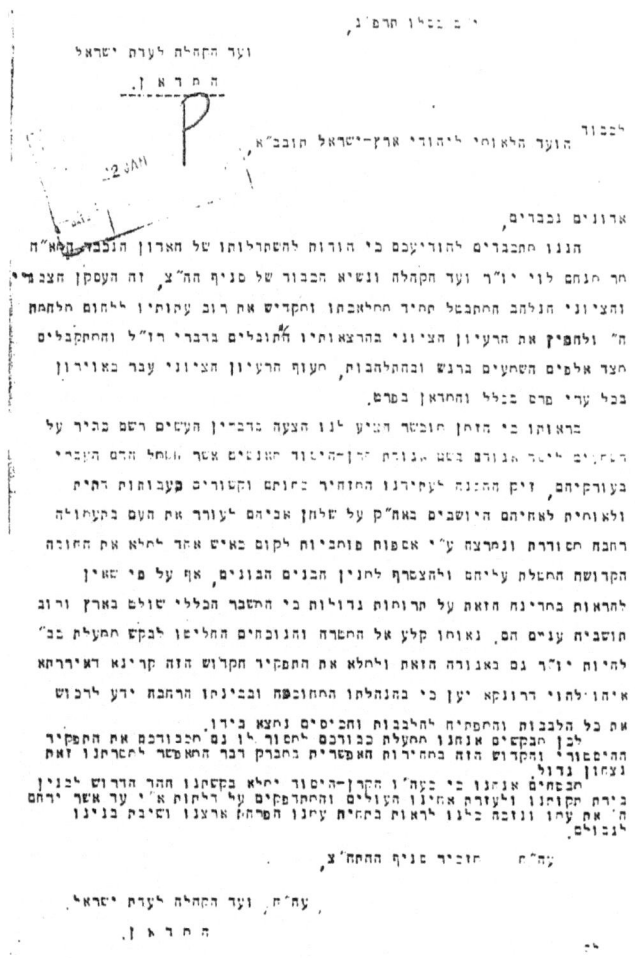

Letter from the Committee of the Jewish Congregation
in Hamadan on behalf of Rabbi Halevy

We are honored to inform you that thanks to the honorable Sir Menaẖem Halevy, the chairperson and president of the congregation, the public agent and the enthusiastic Zionist who always renders his work and dedicates most of his time to fight God's wars and to spread the Zionist ideology, through his speeches, spiced with the maxims of our sages and are welcomed with enthusiasm and emotions by thousands of listeners, the flight of the Zionist ideology took off like an airplane throughout all the cities in Persia in general and in Hamadan in particular . . .

Therefore, we request from your highness to render him respect for his historical and sacred concern too, as soon as possible in a telegram, which will allow great success for our goals.

We promise that with the help of God, *Keren Hayesod* will accept our requests, the needed resonance, in order to build our expectations and help our brethren who immigrate and knock on the doors of Israel, until God will take pity on his people and we all will triumph to see the rebirth of our people, flowering of our country and the return of children to their homeland [Jer 31:16].

The Persian Board of Education and Culture of Hamadan, as well, provided him with a recommendation letter, in Farsi, Dated 28 KAOS 1301 (1923):

FIGURE 13

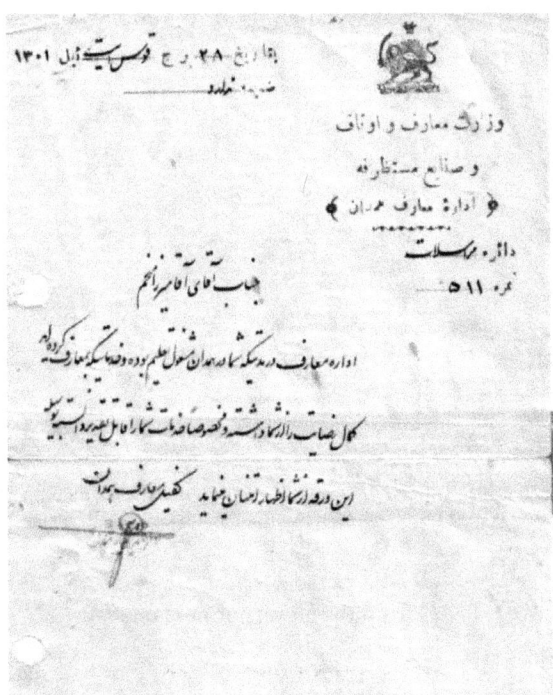

Letter from the Persian Board of Education and Culture in Hamadan

While you lived in Hamadan you worked devotedly for the Persian Department of Education and Culture. Your performance is worthy of commendation. You deserve our gratitude and respect for your accomplishments. We express our gratitude from the lines of this letter.

Signed, Kefil Matbet, Hamadan, the Principal of the Department of Education

The Governor of Hamadan representing The Interior Department of Hamadan gives him the following letter:

FIGURE 14

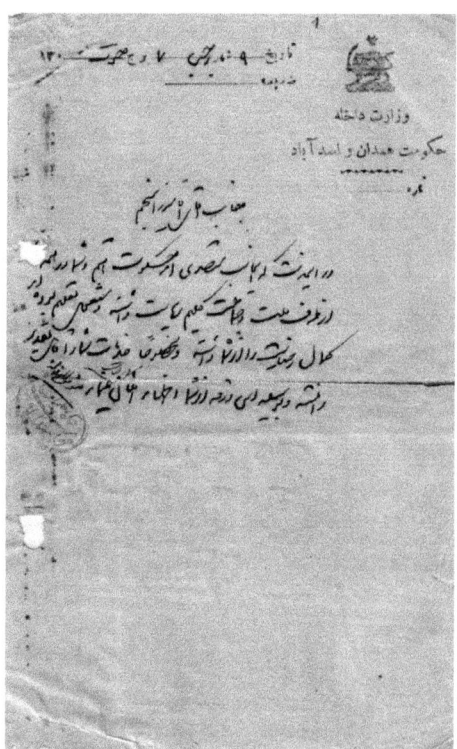

Letter from the Governor of Hamadan

Department of the Interior, Government of Persia, In the City of Hamadan and Azadabad

9 Rajah 7 [sic] Hut (Pisces) 1300; [February- March of 1923]

Honorable Mirzah Menaḥem,

During the time that I served as the local governor of Hamadan, I noticed that you dedicated your efforts for the Education and Culture of the Persian Jews. I commend you and especially appreciate your deeds for the sake of your people and congregation. From the lines of this letter, I thank you from the bottom of my heart, and with great admiration.[33]

Signed by, Governor of Hamadan, Muvathagh al Dawlah

Armed with these recommendations, Rabbi Menaḥem immigrated to Israel through Iraq and Syria and headed a caravan of many families, among them old people, youth, women and toddlers. In Baghdad, the Rabbi received yet another letter from The Iranian Consulate:

FIGURE 15

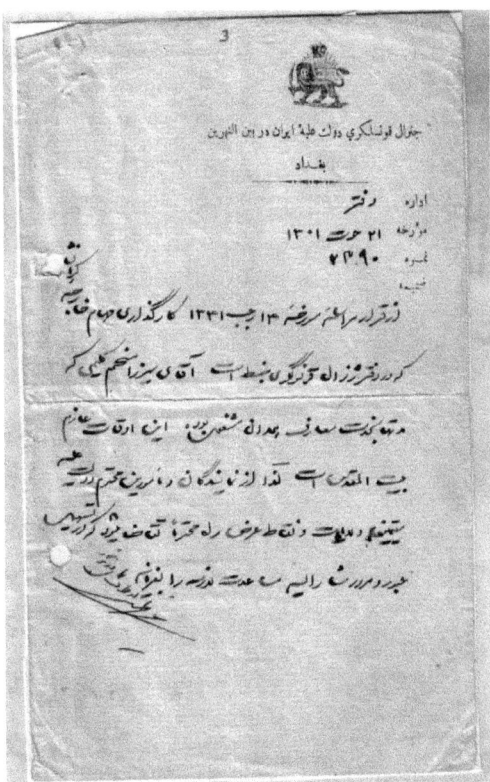

Letter from the Iranian Consulate on behalf of Rabbi Halevy

33. The letter is written in Farsi.

General Consulate of Iran in Mesopotamia [Iraq], Bagdad

21 Hut 1301 [march 1922], no. 2390

As is recorded in The Review books of the Foreign Department in Kermanshah, Rabbi Mirza Menaẖem [H]Levy served for many years in the Department of Education Hamadan. These days, the aforementioned is getting ready to journey to Eretz Israel, and, thus, I request from all the respected representatives and ambassadors of the Persian Government along the roads through which he might cross, to do everything in your power to facilitate his trip.

Please extend him your full cooperation. Signed, Persia's Consul in Baghdad.[34]

Before the departure from Hamadan, the three brothers, Menaẖem, Yaakov, and Yoseph, had sold their father's property and divided the revenue among them. The document attesting to the sale and division is an example of the way in which these documents were worded and written, in both horizontal and vertical directions as well as in a semicircle fashion. It declares that Mirza Yaghub (Yaakov), Mirza Yusuf [Yoseph] and Mirza Menaẖem, have made a deal regarding the sale of their father's house. They came into agreement about the contents as well:

---

34. The letter is written in Farsi.

FIGURE 16

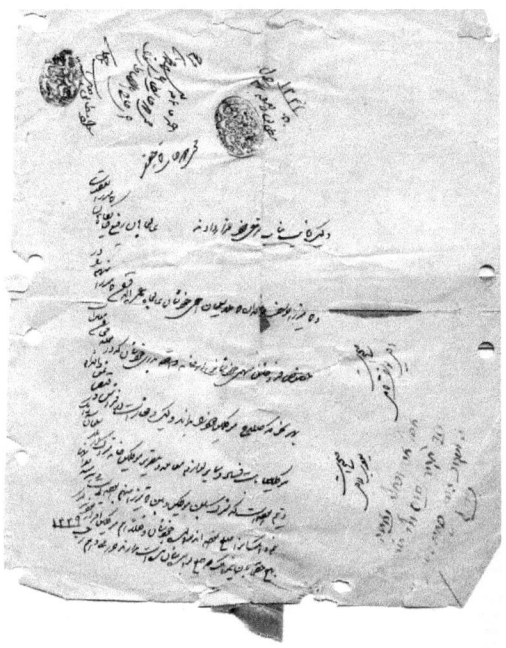

Document attesting to the sale of the Halevy home

Signed: Mohamad. Seal of Qajar
Signatures of Yusuf Levi and Yaghub Levi

The comments in Hebrew on the right bottom side deal with the witnesses to the transaction.

There follows another document, with both seals of Qajar and that of Rabbi Menaḥem. Here Yoseph signs his property to his wife, Nane-hJan, daughter of BabaJan and she transfers the property to Mousa and Mirza, her grandchildren. As a matter of fact, Yoseph who was born in 1900 was not married yet and definitely didn't have grandchildren. This demonstrates that these legal transactions were done fictitiously in order to be able to sell the property to Jewish families and have some money for the road, rather than have their property confiscated by any Shi'i who desired it. Rabbi Menaḥem is aware that if their property would be placed for sale, the Muslims could have tried to take ownership or pay minimal sum. In his unpublished manuscript, he describes how the Muslims have the habit to take over properties of Jews in Shiraz.

FIGURE 17

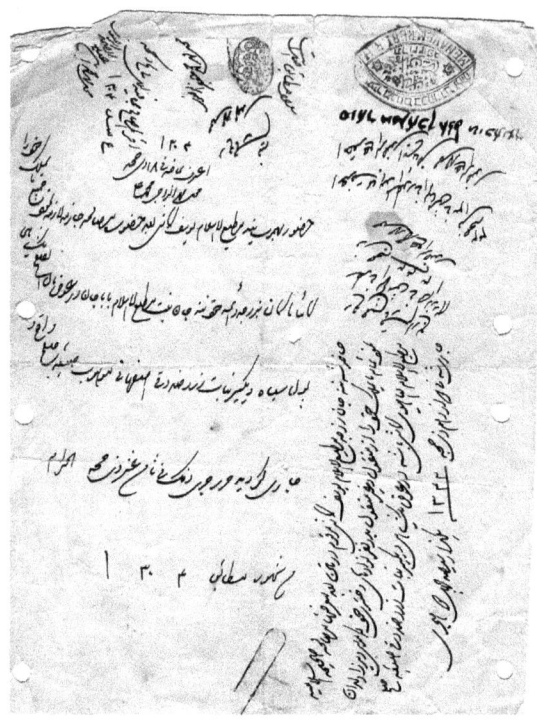

Deed of transfer of real estate, with seals of Qajar and Rabbi Halevy

After the long journey, the caravan arrived in the Holy Land, and their sense was that they had participated in the biblical promise of *Shivat Zion* ("the return to Zion"). They were received warmly by their family members who had preceded them, and they began new lives in Zion.

As soon as he arrived in the Holy Land, Rabbi Menaḥem was appointed to be one of the leaders of the Persian congregation there. He headed the Persian congregation and became a leading member of *Vaad Ha-Sephardim* ("The *Council of the Sefaradim*") and the *Histadrut Haluzei Ha-Mizrachi* ("Federation of the Oriental Pioneers") of Jerusalem. He was befriended by the chief rabbis of Israel, the Sephardic Jacob Meyer and the Ashkenazic Isaac Herzog. He was drafted by numerous organizations to teach, lecture, lead, and travel. In 1924, the *Vaad Ha-leumi* ("The National Council") of the Jews of the Holy Land Palestine appointed him a justice of the peace and judge in the Hebrew court of Jerusalem. His charisma led to many trips to various countries on behalf of different organizations to attract Jews to the land of Israel as well as to collect funds for the Jews there. He was sent as an envoy by *Keren Hayesod* ("The Foundation Fund"), Mizrachi, and B'nai Brith, to Aden (Yemen), Aram Naharyim (Mesopotamia), Beirut (Lebanon), Sidon, India, Egypt, Burma, China, Damascus (Syria), and Egypt.

In Jerusalem, he established a school for poor children of the Bukharan community, and—despite the protests of other rabbinic leaders—allowed girls to sit with boys in his school, believing that education was the only way to save the people. He insisted that his own children become teachers, as well. He established a Hamadani synagogue in the same courtyard in Jerusalem as the Mashadi synagogue, with whom he enjoyed warm relations. Surprisingly, he allowed his youngest daughter to wear athletic shorts in exercise classes; less surprisingly, his children reported never seeing him angry.

His last trip took him to India, where he met with Gandhi, who had a negative assessment of the Jewish people establishing themselves in Palestine. A letter from Rabbi Meir Berlin, world president of Mizrachi, written in Hebrew and dated February 3, 1939, thanked Rabbi Menaḥem for establishing a Mizrachi branch in Bombay, and acknowledging the importance of his meeting with Gandhi. Berlin expressed the hope that the meeting would change Gandhi's mind:

> It is imperative to take your meeting with Gandhi as greatly important. It seems that the Muslims captured him in their net, and the negative comments he published lately about the Land of Israel and about the Jews were widely reported around the whole world. Thus, your meeting with him is of great importance. Maybe your honor would have the power to change his mind to our favor. We are waiting to hear full details about the meeting.

Rabbi Menaḥem tried to change Gandhi's negativity, but to no avail. While the details of the meeting are lost, Rabbi Menaḥem told his older son Ḥayim that the meeting caused him deep anguish, as he could not understand why the people of Israel were treated in such as harsh manner.

This trip to India, in 1939, affected his fragile health negatively, and upon return, he felt exhausted and worn out.

Rabbi Halevy with the Magen Hasidim community in Bombay

He did want to teach his students about the world and about India, and at this point met Dr. A. I. Brauer, a Mizrachi activist, who watched him rushing to school, still bitter from his experience in India. According to Brauer, the rabbi looked sick but insisted on attending to his students. Just a few weeks later, Brauer wrote an obituary for Rabbi Menaẖem, remembering him as "a teacher who never rested." He recalled his visits to Rabbi Menaẖem's unique school:

> Here we found an exceptional teacher who did not ask for much. He minimized his needs and he was satisfied with a meager salary. He admitted many students to his classes and worked many hours. He worked day and he worked night, he worked in the winter and he worked all summer long, without vacation. He was a teacher, a principal, a secretary and a custodian, everything all at once. He went from success to success and improved and became perfect like the mare that did not need any more food for substance. And thus, it happened to him what happened to the mare—he succumbed and fell under the weight of his work ... I saw his school full and overflowing with impoverished children during the vacation days. They sat close to each

other, on unstable benches, 50–60 of them, of different ages, all in one class. The teachers rested during the vacation, and the yoke of work was left for Rabbi Menaḥem Shemuel Halevy, who served as a principal and custodian, as well... The teacher who never rested in his lifetime is resting now forever.[35]

Rabbi Menaḥem died in his sleep on January 29, 1940. He left behind students who adored him, rabbinic colleagues who respected him, and a congregation who could not believe that their shepherd had abandoned them. Left without the head of the family were Monavar Chanom, an impoverished widow, and 5 orphans: Esther (1921–2006), Shoshana (1922–1986), Ḥayim (1926–2005), Shimon (b. 1929), and his youngest, Meyer (b. 1935).[36]

Rabbi Menaḥem Halevy believed that he had witnessed the biblical "Return to Zion" (*shivat Zion*) in his lifetime. "Redemption, forgiveness, hope, and salvation," was his ideology. He saw the return of Jews from around the world to the city of Jerusalem as the fulfillment of biblical promises, and he expected that with the nation of Israel back in its homeland, wars against other nations should cease, and, as predicted in Ezekiel, God will not allow aggression against Israel. The nation of Israel would set root in the Holy Land like a flower and will bloom forever.

Rabbi Menaḥem lived only 17 years in the land of Israel. A rabbi, social worker, judge, ambassador, fundraiser, a husband, a father; yet he had time to write, create poetry, and to record historical events in the life and strife of the Persian Jewry.

---

35. Dr. A. I. Brauer, "Moreh Shelo Shavat: Leftirat Hamoreh Harav Menaḥem Shemuel Halevy Blessed Memory" [A teacher who did not rest: Passing of Menaḥem Shemuel Halevy, Blessed memory], *HaAretz*, February 6th, 1940 (in Hebrew).

36. My mother, Shoshana Ben-Mashiach, who was pregnant, named her second child, Nechama, after him.

FIGURE 19

Death notice of Rabbi Halevy

Thousands of people attended his funeral, and he was eulogized by leading men from the broader community: Chief Rabbis Ben-Zion Meyer Hai Uziel and Isaac Herzog, judges, professors, presidents and members of Mizrachi, representatives of the department of education and teachers union, members of the National Committee (*Ha-Va'ad ha-Le'umi*), and Sephardic committee, journalists. The most significant attendees at the funeral were the many students who received instruction under him. Every newspaper carried obituaries mourning his death and detailing the contributions and sacrifices he had made for his people. It rained heavily during his funeral in the cold winter streets of Jerusalem, adding to the chill in the heart of his family, who lost their father at the age of 54 years, and the community of Persian and Oriental Jews who lost their spiritual leader.

FIGURE 20

Rabbi Halevy's funeral

In his poem *Shivat Zion* ("the return to Zion"), Rabbi Menaḥem expresses his deepest love for Zion, his soul mate, home, mother, daughter, and bride. Zion is the biblical land promised to the Israelites by God. His love for Zion was political, nationalistic, and religious. It is the Promised Land from where the people of Israel were exiled and to where they were promised to return. His love for Zion is expressed with verses employed in Jewish Liturgy, from the prophets, and the Psalms, weaving them together to depict his sentiments and longings for the motherland. For him, Persia is the exile depicted by the biblical prophets. The suffering and intolerance toward the Persian Jewry parallels the laments of the Jews on the banks of Babel. The biblical deliverance of the Israelites to return to the Holy Land parallels the immigration of the Persian Jewish congregation to modern day Zion, and its heart Jerusalem.

Shivat Zion שיבת ציון
How beautiful upon the mountains of Zion;
Voice announcing to the impoverished nation;
Arise and depart from Zion;
To spring of fresh water Zion.

Nobles of nations have gathered,
As fleeting cloud so are they;
Your steps to me so beautiful;
Arise and let's ascend to Zion.

I made haste and did not delay,
My hope was not in vain;
To return to my homeland,
The tower of David is the city of Zion.

Longing and wishing my soul,
To reside in the courts of holiness;
To sacrifice the bread, offering by fire,
The day when the savior arrives at Zion.

To bring out the prisoner from the prison,
Set the sickle, for the harvest is ripe;
The bud withers the grass fades,
Awake, put on your strength, O Zion.

And the days of your mourning shall be ended,
Enlarge the place of your tent;
And God will be your king,
Chant and rejoice, O daughter of Zion.

Long live Mizrachi within his people.
As long as the sun, Yinon his name;
He will Plant the choicest vine in his vineyard,
The people who remain in Zion.

APPENDIX: WRITING OF RABBI MENAḤEM HALEVI

Zemirot Israel, [Hymns of Israel] by Menaḥem, First Born to Shmuel Halevy, Blessed be his Memory (Hamadan, Iran: Branch of the Zionist Union in Iran, 5681–1921). It was published with the help of the Zionist Union of Persia-Hamadan, containing 8 poems about Zion in Hebrew and transliteration to Persian in Hebrew letters. The book begins with the full 10 stanza version of Tikvateinu by Imber, written in Persian translation but in Hebrew letters.

Mordecai Ve Esther in Shushan Habirah (1932), describing the grave site of Mordecai and Esther and narrating many traditions and legends of the Persian community (1932), in Hebrew. The author states that this published book is the first chapter of the manuscript, *The History of the Jews of Persia since the completion of the Talmud until Today*. The book describes customs, legends related to the place, the legend of the Makosh, the legend of Mulla Husein, the legend of Mulla Abdalla, and a poem *Me-rosh Mekadmei Eretz*.

Tafsir Mi Kamocha, a commentary in Persian about Yehuda Halevi's poem, followed by a poem about Hadassa/Esther, bilingual, Hebrew/Persian (1924).

A poem for a Bar Mitzvah, printed after his death.

His manuscripts:

History of the Jews in Persia from the completion of the Talmud until today (I am currently working on transcribing this very interesting manuscript)

Les Souvenirs de mon Enfance, in French about ancient places in Iran

Amkan El Muqqadasa Religious Sites in Arabic

Mizan El Hak, Criticism of the Bahai religion, in Arabic

Zeh Yenachameinu about the Humash

Kutnot Or about the *Mishna*: Commentaries to *Halacha* and *Hagada*

Compiliation of Shushan on religious sites in Persia

Translation of *Hovat HaLevavot*, in Persian

Ideology of the books of *Saadi Hafit Amar-Hyiam and Megalsi* Translation of *Yotzer* LeShabat prayer in Farsi

9

Iran 1972 Revisited in Memories
In the Footsteps of the Deer

GALIT HASAN-ROKEM

> When we walked on the fire path
> East of the wood on the hill
> A young deer fled among the trees
> And left behind green silence.
> —GALIT HASAN-ROKEM, *Voice Training* (Hebrew), Tel-Aviv, 1998, p. 9

Dedicated to the memory of:
Elisheva Erez, Amnon Netzer,
Hadassah Salomon Romano, Sarah Sorour Suroudi

IT WAS THE END of a long trip that began in Jerusalem, via Sweden to Yugoslavia (yes those were the times), around Greece, then a short trip to Bulgaria and by train from Thessaloniki to Istanbul. The Istanbul episode began with the outcry of the newspapers that met us when we disembarked the train from Sofia. The newspapers were incomprehensible for those illiterate in Turkish, but pictures speak louder than a thousand words. It was September 1972, and the newspaper showed the horror of the massacre of Israeli sportsmen at the Munich Olympic Games. After some hesitations we decided to stick to the initial plan and take the regular bus on the route from Istanbul to Teheran. The four-day trip of over two thousand kilometers (almost thirteen hundred miles) was interrupted by three nights at roadside hotels. We hasted on a way overlooking Ankara from afar, hurried through Sivas, stopped in Erzincan to "talk" with young boys who made some money by weighing anybody curious and generous enough and ate delicious bake wares. In Erzurum, horse and carriage took us to view the beautiful double minarets of the Seljuk madrasa and a local festival. Later at night, we experienced the special conditions of the easternmost NATO post in the region: at 10:00 pm, all lights went out, some played with transistor radios to find Radio Yerevan, famous for its Soviet propaganda broadcasts, the cause for much mirth, and the source for a special sub-genre of jokes told all over the English speaking world.

The method for enforcing speed limits on the circling roads of East Anatolia was fascinating. Interspersed hundreds of kilometers apart were small posts in which the driver could fill in the hour of his arrival with a pencil in a small assigned booklet. Apparently, someone traveled and checked the books and checked that the intervals were long enough to prove that speeding laws were obeyed. To our great joy—we were young and unwise—a short distance from one of these stations, the driver stopped on the roadside and guided us to an earthly paradise of fruit trees—a veritable *boustan*—with mineral water flowing down the rocks. And then he raced to the next station, calmly filling in the hour proving the slow pace of his ride.

Most of the other people on the bus were Iranians returning home. I don't remember any Turkish travelers on their way to visit Iran. Foreigners were scarce on this $30 voyage (the train was just $10, however, without stops for the nights). Not counting the driver, three people remain vivid in my memory. An Armenian woman often sat next to me, sharing stories about her good relationship with her many Jewish neighbors in Teheran. It was "them" and "us," the Armenians and the Jews—and the Muslim majority. The two others were an odd couple: he was a tall, blond German in his mid-twenties, who carried with him a good sized pick and nothing much more. When asked what he intended to do in Iran, he said that he would climb the holy mountain Damavand and then continue to Afghanistan. Someone then told a rumor about a person who had gone on that route and slept outdoors with a group of people, ending up with somebody else's head on his shoulder in the morning. Tales that travelers tell. The young woman, who seemed to be the companion of the German fellow and conversed with him in his language, was a daughter of Tehran. She was a deeply believing Communist, counting the days of Shah Mohammed Reza Pahlavi with hope, probably not imagining in her worst nightmares who would succeed him. I have often conjured up her image in my memory, her playful shining black ponytail, the gray skirt ending a hand's breadth above her knees. Was she able, like the revolution, to transform one belief to another, or did she end up suffering much and losing her freedom? And what was her name?

FIGURE 1: MT. ARARAT

FIGURE 2: MT. ARARAT AND AUTHOR

The most spectacular sight on the road east of Lake Van is the towering presence of Mount Ararat. I was hooked at first sight and asked the driver to stop to get a good picture. But the mountain kept growing more majestic the further east we were moving, so I asked him to stop again. And again several times. It must have been at least seven (formulaic, sacred number) stops to catch the Ararat, to embrace the myth. Like the Damavand for the Iranians, the Ararat is sacred and numinous for the Armenians. For me, however, above all, the imagery of the mountain of Noah's Ark and the white dove was most meaningful. My folklorist's heart swelled with joy when one of the people on the bus recounted quietly of a personal encounter with a man who had, with his own eyes, seen, high up on the mountain, both a fossil of the dove and a piece of wood from the Ark.

After the mountain had disappeared from our eyes, the bus entered a new state of mind: we were coming closer to the Iranian border. And then clutshh . . . .a bloody hand on the front window of the big bus. Freddie and I silently feared the worst, with the pictures from Munich still on our retinas. But the fears were soon wiped away by the information that this was simply the border crossing sacrifice. Every time the regular bus between Istanbul and Teheran crossed the border between the two states, a lamb was sacrificed and a "hamsa," the blooded hand, was stamped on the front window of the bus to ensure safe passage. Consequently or not, having passed through Tabriz and Qazvin, the bus arrived, its driver's sometimes reckless driving notwithstanding, in one piece in Teheran.

Unlike the road from Istanbul to Teheran that somehow remains imprinted in my mind almost hour after hour, the two weeks in Iran itself remain in my memory in a non-linear form, almost as a part floral part geometrical pattern elaborately woven into a carpet. This is how I shall share them.

We were carrying along guide books and advice acquired from relatives and friends who had served in an economic UN mission in Iran, and a few Iranians in Jerusalem had shared their expertise. We still daily acquired new knowledge from locals who gladly helped us to design our trip. We were accompanied by a friend from Jerusalem, the librarian Hadassah Romano, who had arrived by plane from Tel-Aviv, bringing her own list of travel goals.

First, there was Teheran, a bustling metropolis with great boulevards (Elizabeth Boulevard . . .) and highrises into which the power and wealth of oil wells was channeled. On the other hand, climbing up the streets leading to the lush and affluent neighborhood of Shemiran, we saw women with their heads covered—which was then not the dominant style among women in Tehran—washing their babies in the waters of the open sewer like canals of less fortunate parts of the city. It was then that it occurred to us that the revolution that our friend on the bus had foreseen could not be too remote.

There were the museums housing the crown jewels and art from all periods. And there was the sad memorial ceremony at a Jewish school of Tehran (or was it one of the synagogue) a week after the Munich massacre, in the presence of the ambassador of Israel. The atmosphere in the ceremony was heavy and subdued. The representatives of the mostly affluent Jewish community in Iran, counting its beginning more or less from the Exodus of the Israelites from Egypt, seemed to receive invisible seismic vibrations of danger. On another day, on one of our walks, we asked about the location of the Israeli embassy, and many were able to guide us, but when we arrived we realized that there was no plaque identifying the building's status.

A carpet merchant in an elegant shop in the center of the city received us with a smile and gladly accepted the presence of my small tape-recorder. "A ewe among seventy wolves," he said, not feeling the need to add more details. The proprietor of Beroukhim Booksellers in downtown Teheran welcomed us and proudly showed his rich selections. He also told us about Serah the daughter of Asher's tomb in Pir Bakran outside of Isfahan and the annual Nu Rouz festivities and sold me two copies of the much cherished Persian-English Proverbs by Solayman Haim (lived ca. 1887–1970; publishing date of the volume 1956). One volume was for the proverb collection library of my beloved teacher Professor Matti Kuusi in Helsinki (who received it from me on my next visit to him), one for own multilingual library of proverb collections (today at the Folklore Research Center of the Mandel Institute of Jewish Studies at the Hebrew University of Jerusalem).

We took the bus from the central bus station of Teheran to Isfahan. On the way, we stopped outside the city wall of Qom. It was my first experience of being prohibited to enter on the basis of religious affiliation—no non-Muslims in the holy city. Then, we spent hours on the bus, where a young man distributed *limu* (lime) halves and glasses of water to the passengers.

FIGURE 3

Author in the shadow
of the Great Mosque of Isfahan

FIGURE 4

Madrasa in Isfahan

Isfahan is all I had always imagined, and much more. A true 1001 Nights décor. The architecture of abstract thought interlaced with meticulous concreteness of description. The huge mosques and the beautiful madrasas. Tiles, mosaics, and wooden ceilings. Gardens. The music room in the royal palace with its ingenious acoustic devices. The once polo field turned into a pool. The building named "Eighty Pillars"—forty of which on land, the other forty reflected in the adjacent pool—the absolute reality of the imagined.

FIGURE 5

The Great Mosque of Isfahan

FIGURE 6

The music room at the Royal Palace of Isfahan

FIGURE 7

Church (?) in Isfahan

FIGURE 8

Isfahan, a reflection

When we asked the Jewish receptionist at the luxurious Shah Abbas Hotel how to reach the synagogue for the Yom Kippur services, he warned us not to go there in the dark, and took us to see the royal suite and suggested that we photograph ourselves sitting on its couches. In the evening we went to listen to a professional singer of tales reciting the

Shahnameh (Book of Kings). I tacitly activated the tape-recorder on my knee. After twenty minutes of performance, his gaze caught me and he walked towards me pointing with his staff at the tape-recorder. Nervous that he would destroy my machine I hid it in the bag, but he clarified in body language that he wanted to listen to the recording. Isfahan, city of reflections: we listened together with the few other tourists to my recording of the professional singer's Shahnameh performance in the fragrant garden of the Shah Abbas Hotel.

FIGURE 9

The epic singer at Shah Abbas Hotel

A Jewish person in the suq provided an exact description of how to travel to Pir Bakran (according to the Muslims a saint and a mystic whose grave is there). This person told a folktale in which the beautiful Serah was pursued by the enamored Shah Abbas until God, in his wisdom and mercy, turned her into a beautiful gazelle, who then disappeared into the nearest cave. People who come on pilgrimage to Serah's grave walk to the cave and call after her koo-koo-loo, and that has become the name of the cave.

FIGURE 10

View in the direction of the Kookooloo cave

FIGURE 11

Serah Bat Asher's tomb/Pir Bakran cemetery

A foundational legend of the Jews of Isfahan that we were told shared the midrashic motif of Serah's magical prowess by which she was able to raise the lead casket of Joseph from the bottom of the Nile with a myrtle branch, so that the Israelites could fulfill his last wish to leave Egypt with them. During the desert wandering, the legend continues, Serah and some others with her did not join the others to cross the Jordan to Canaan, but rather continued all the way to Isfahan. And this is why the Jews of Isfahan have been there all the generations from the establishing of the Peacock Throne of the ancient Akhmenid kings of Fars.

FIGURE 12

Cemetery

The cemetery was dry and empty, leaving us to imagine its moments of glory when people—alternately Jews and Muslims—fill it with celebration and devotion.

Back in Isfahan, we visit the Khaju Bridge, borne up by its magnificent thirty-three arches, go to the market, and buy a huge nomadic carpet in orange and green that we instantly dislike. In the evening, we go to a restaurant and have Fasanjan. The Palestinian waitress' curiosity about our Israeli passports that we thoughtlessly flaunt makes some of us panic in the evening, and we call the embassy in Teheran. Their brusque order telling us to instantly pack and fly home sobers us and we sleep peacefully through our last night in the glorious city. The next day, the bus takes us further south to Shiraz. Our travel companion, Hadassah, has prepared a surprise; through her archeology contacts, we are invited to sleep at the local historical museum! The Kajari drapes ensured another calm night. Next day we are off to tour the city of roses and nightingales and poets. I remember a soft wind, but maybe it was in the lines of poetry inscribed in various public spaces such as the monumental tombs of Hafiz and Saadi. I don't remember having seen poets being honored with such tombs anywhere else in the world. Much later, I learned that lines of Saadi's poems are often used by Iranians, including Jews, as proverbs, as witnessed by recordings from oral tradition at the Proverb Research Project at the Folklore Research Center mentioned above.

In the *suq* of Shiraz, we were able to trade the huge orange-green carpet we bought in Isfahan for two lovely small Qashqai rugs in mixed woven and embroidered technique, still adorning the walls of our home in Jerusalem. They were pleasantly familiarized by our meeting on one of the roads with Qashqai nomads who had similar ones covering their saddles.

FIGURE 13

Takht-e-Jamshid/Persepolis

FIGURE 14

Author at Takht-e-Jamshid

FIGURE 15

The horses of Takht-e-Jamshid

FIGURE 16

Author's spouse at Takht-e-Jamshid

From Shiraz, we toured some memorable sites. In September, 1972, the ancient Akhmenid capital Takht-e-Jamshid (Persepolis in Greek) still housed the luxurious tent village that had been erected to host the dignitaries that had come a year earlier to celebrate the 2500 year jubilee of the consecutive monarchy of Iran. One might now ponder how much the almost obscene wastefulness of those festivities hastened the downfall of the object of celebration. But the long stone relief rows of Akhmenid dignitaries with fanciful hairdos and the artfully, lovingly carved horses on high pillars, some of which had fallen to the ground, silently witness the passing of centuries. We may only hope that in this case, national pride of ancient roots may prevent religious fervor from destroying the horses of Takht-e-Jamshid—Jamshid's Throne. Somewhat further away from Shiraz, we visit the tomb of the great eagle Cyrus, whose proclamation to return the Babylonian Jews to their ancestral land set the pattern for the Balfour Declaration in the context of a modern empire. Next to the grave was a stela inscribed with multiple orthographies. I was moved by the square Aramaic text on that stela and the ability to almost peruse some of the text. Three years later, I would be initiated to the secrets of ideograms and parallel scripts of the languages of Sasanid Persian in a class taught by Professor Shaul Shaked himself, sharing the room with such as luminaries Professors Eliezer Shimshon Rosenthal, Jonas Greenfield, and Joseph Naveh, may they all rest in peace. In addition to growing up in a multi-lingual environment, my daughter, Na'ama Rokem—whom I was then expecting—scholar in her own right, may have been inspired by the multiple translation exercises in that class.

FIGURE 17

Tomb of Cyrus in Pasargadae

FIGURE 18

Zoroastrian Temple in Naqsh-e-Rustum

On another day, a couple of hours of travel in a taxi on unpaved, stony roads brought us from Shiraz to Bishapur where monumental cliff reliefs represented Sasanid kings, Shapur, and Bahram, as well as Mithra gods. I knew Shapur was powerful and a dreamer, from his appearances in the Babylonian Talmud, but the mega-dreams that he had materialized to adorn the cliff sides of this desert city in South Western Iran were an astonishing surprise.

FIGURE 19

Naqsh-e-Rustum, Royal cliff relief

FIGURE 20

Naqsh-e-Rustum

FIGURE 21

Bishapur, Mithra and King Shapur (according to the local guide), author

Flying back from Shiraz to Teheran, I was subjected to my very first manual body check by and Iranian police woman, as a result of a recent airplane hijacking that had occurred on a flight between Iran and one of the states of the southern Arabian peninsula. Who knew then how many such bodychecks would meet us in airports around the world.

FIGURE 22

The Paykan and a distant view of Mt Damavand

Back in Teheran, we rented a Paykan, the Hillman product that was produced in Iran between 1967 and 2004 and of which everyone back then was immensely proud. We took the mountain road via the ski resort of Abali, with the Demavand towering over us, part of the time driving above and in the midst of clouds. On the northern slope of the mountain range, rich rice fields and fruit orchards welcomed the traveler. The city of Babolsar on the shore of the Caspian Sea at the mouth of the river Babol was a big and busy place. I remember the happy moment when I returned to Babolsar with the itinerant textile merchant in Dorit Rabiniyan's brilliant first novel (Hebrew 1995; translated as "Persian Brides"). But that was literally an entire life later. We drove westward along the coast to the resort town of Ramsar with many luxury hotels, and among them, one where the Shah used to stay, and found a smaller one. It was as I was eating a roasted fish skewer on the Caspian shore at Ramsar that I felt the first vague unrest in my belly that proved to be the earliest outward communication of my oldest son, Amitai, the beautiful, gifted boy who spent some invisible stages of his formation on Iranian soil, and whom we bitterly lost in a hiking accident in the Israeli Aravah in 1990.

From Ramsar, the Paykan rolled us to Hamadan. The first thing we saw there was carpets on the road that we had to drive over after having seen all the other cars do so. We had heard that some merchants do this to "antiquate" their new carpets; this was the first time we saw it with our own eyes. This is the city of the great scholar Ibn Sina and his tomb is a revered site. Our goal was the tomb of Esther and Mordechai, and as soon as we mentioned that we came from Jerusalem, we were warmly welcomed by the Jewish keepers of the site, although it was Sukkoth. The place was in exemplary shape, adorned with sumptuous carpets, and the yard was surrounded by a new iron fence, all in small Magen David design. I recently checked the website of the city of Hamadan and it said that the structure is "a tomb believed by some to hold the remains of Esther and Mordecai," and the fence has been replaced by one made of straight iron bars.

FIGURE 23

Hadassah Salomon and author at the Tomb of Esther and Mordekhai in Hamadan

FIGURE 24

Evening in Kermanshah

West of Hamadan lies Kermanshah, close to the border of Iraq. We had a strange feeling of approaching the great unknown, the utterly unapproachable. This is land of the Kurds, as is Hamadan. The women in this village were more liberally dressed than village women in other parts of Iran that we had visited, but of course, this village was not as modernized as those in Tehran, just more liberated and equal. I bought a thick silver chain in Kermanshah to have something of the local women's taste with me. On our way back, between Kermanshah and Hamadan, was yet another treasure of Sasanian Iran, Taq-i-Boustan, housing a lively masterful relief describing a royal hunting scene in a high grass landscape. The victorious king riding aloof, the hapless deer disappearing in the thicket sure to be caught.

FIGURE 25

Taq-i-Bustan

At the airport, on our way to the El Al flight back to Tel-Aviv, we entered the duty free shop, collecting some last bits of Iran to take along, perhaps pistachios. The young woman at the counter heard us speak Hebrew and asked, "Which language are you speaking?" When we had identified our language, she said: "Our kingdom was destroyed many centuries ago." I asked: "What was your kingdom?" "Assyria," she replied. I asked her to say something in her language, whereupon she answered in pure Babylonian Aramaic: "I want to drink". "You speak like the Talmud," I said half to myself, half to her.

10

Iranian Jews' Ritual Objects*

RUTH JACOBY

THE JEWS OF IRAN belong to one of the oldest Jewish diasporas. The first Jews came to Iran between the eighth and sixth centuries BCE, in the Assyrian and Babylonian exiles, respectively. In later centuries, Jews settled all over the country—in cities, villages, and small towns.[1] Throughout the ages, Iranian Jews paid visits the Holy Land, while cases

---

* This article is based on finds documented in Israel by the Center of Jewish Art of the Hebrew University of Jerusalem. The objects originated in synagogues of Iranian Jews all over Israel and in various collections of museums and private collectors, including the collections of the Israel museum in Jerusalem, the Eretz Ysrael museum of Tel-Aviv, the collection of the Haberman Institute in Lod, the Gross family collection, Lindver collection and others.

The survey and research of Iranian Jewish ritual objects started only in the 1980s. By then, many of the objects that were brought from Iran were already lost, while others were damaged and discarded and new items took their place. Some were made by artists who originated from Iran and produced objects as similar as they could to the original ones. Still, despite of all this, enough material is available to get a reasonably good picture of the ritual objects of the Jews in Iran mainly in the first half of the twentieth century.

Only lately a list was published of places where Jews were living. The list composed by Amnon Netzer includes over 250 names and refers to a long period—from the beginning of Islam in Iran to the present. See A. Netzer, "Yishuvei ha-yehudim be-Iran be-haluka le-Mehozot," in *The Jewish Communities of the East: Iran*, ed. Haim Saadoun (Jerusalem: Makhon Ben Zvi, 2005), 33. Another list is in: Tsion Ezri, "Arba Kanfot Paras u Madai," *ABA* 3 (2009): 74-93 (Hebrew).

of Iranian Jews immigrating to Palestine are known mostly from the end of the nineteenth century onward. A wave of relatively wealthy Jews made their way to the Holy Land at the beginning of the twentieth century via Iraq and the Syrian desert. This was a dangerous and treacherous route, and most of these people got to Jerusalem penniless and with hardly any belongings.[2] In the years that followed the creation of the state of Israel in 1948, most immigrants were poor people and members of the Zionist youth movements.

These immigrants did not bring many ritual objects with them, a fact which makes it difficult to get a full picture of what was used in their homeland of Iran. Furthermore, most of the immigrants were from a low socioeconomic class and mainly from small, remote Iranian locales. As a result, they usually had very few possessions and even fewer ritual objects. They were poor and the quality of whatever they managed to take with them was in accordance. Bearing this background in mind, the following essay will survey some of the major ritual objects used by the Jews of Iran.

The Torah scroll is the central and most precious religious object in the synagogue. It is kept in a special niche or cupboard—the Ark—called *heikhal* (היכל) and is separated from the prayer hall by a curtain—the *parokhet* (פרוכת). For its protection, the Torah scroll itself is put in a wooden case, which was decorated as elaborately as the means of the community could afford.

THE ARK'S CURTAIN (*PAROKHET*)

Any fabric is fit to serve as curtain. Two types of material were, nevertheless, common in Iranian synagogues: simple printed cotton cloth and carpets. The most elaborate Ark curtains were made of expensive carpets. In many cases, a cloth or metal plaque bearing a dedication was attached to the carpet. The example presented here is actually a typical Muslim prayer carpet with a mosque's lamp illustrated in its center. When used as an Ark curtain, it was put upside down, and on the lamp, covering most

---

2. David Yeroushalmi, "*Yoṣ'ei Iran be-Yisrael me-ha-Aliyot ha-Rishonot 'ad Yameinu*," in *Edot-Edut le-Yisrael: Exile, Immigration, Absorbtion, Contribution, and Acculturation*, ed. Avshalom Mizrahi, Aharon Ben-David (Netanya: Association for the Development of Society and Culture, 2001), 27–51.

of it, was a pink shiny piece of cloth embroidered by a blue dedication inscription dated 1945 (fig. 1).³

FIGURE 1

Reuse of a Muslim prayer rug as a Torah curtain.

The printed Ark curtain belongs to a group of common block-printed textiles, not necessarily Jewish. For Jewish use, a Hebrew inscription and typical Jewish motives, such as the Shield of David and the seven branched candelabrum (*menorah*), were used together with other general, common motifs like the cypress tree, flowers, floral medallions, and birds (fig. 2).

---

3. The inscription on the Torah Ark curtain reads: קלה/הפרכת הזאת נדבת/מ' מאיר רחמים הכהן/ הי"ו/ לעילוי נשמת אמו מ'/פרי בת ב אמם ז"ל/נפטרה ל' מנחם אב ה/תש"ה/ ת'נ'צ'ב'ה'

FIGURE 2

Torah curtain with East European motifs.

On this particular Ark curtain, which bears the date 1948–1952 and was made in Tehran, we find the popular representation of a "Shiviti-Menorah" amulet, which has become very popular in Jewish communities worldwide.[4] This usage is a fine example of Eastern European influence on the Jewish decorative world in Iran. The shape of the candelabrum with its entangled arms is typical to Eastern European countries, as is the shape of the two Tablets of the Law bearing on top a European shaped crown.[5]

4. This kind of Shiviti-Menorah was first found in Italy in the end of the fourteenth century and spread all over the Jewish world along with Kabbalistic texts. See E. Juhasz, *The "Shiviti-Menorah," A Representation of the Sacred Between Spirit and Matter* (Ph.D. thesis: Hebrew University in Jerusalem, 2004), 21, 37 (Hebrew).

5. For the *menorah*, see paper-cut from East Europe, as in: G. Frankel, *The Art of the Jewish Paper-cut* (Israel, 1983) (Hebrew), 21, 37, 51. For the Tablets of the Law and the crown, see R. Jacoby, *"Etzba" and "Kulmos," The Torah Pointer in the Persian World* (Ph.D. thesis: Hebrew University in Jerusalem, 2004), 89–90 and vol. 2, plate 24.

Nowadays, many of the Ark curtains are a modern mix, mainly influenced by European Ark curtains, dark red or blue velvet with an embroidery of Jewish motifs such as lions, Yakhin and Boaz—the two pillars of the Temple, the Tablets of the Law, the Shield of David, the Menorah, flowers, and a dedication inscription.

TORAH CASES (תיקים לתורה)

The Torah cases containing the scrolls are kept in the Torah Ark. They are made of wood and covered by different materials like metal sheets (silver or some cheaper metal); others are covered by cloth of different qualities, leather, or, in some cases, the polished wood (fig. 9). Their inside is upholstered by colored cotton cloth (fig. 3).

FIGURE 3

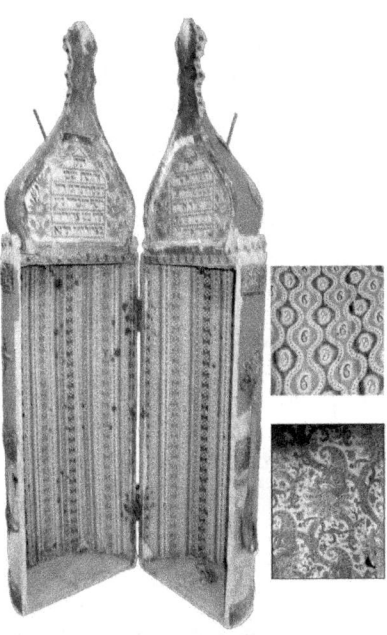

Open Torah case covered inside by colored cloth
and an inscription at its top.

The cases are cylindrical or prism-shaped. Their appearance reminds one of the shape of typical buildings in the Muslim environment, such as minarets, tombs, and other towers in city gates and palaces (fig. 4).⁶

FIGURE 4

Iranian mosque, citadel and tomb.

The phenomenon of ritual objects imitating architectural shapes is quite known, especially in small objects like Hanukah lamps, Torah finials, and spice containers.⁷ It is also known from various box-like shapes in religious use, such as a fine silver box in the Dome of the Rock in Jerusalem in which—according to Muslim tradition—three hairs of Muhammad's beard are kept,⁸ or a cupboard-like box from a mosque in Dirband which contains a Quran (fig. 5).⁹

---

6. See O. Schwartz-Beri, "The Silver Craft of the Jews of Kurdistan," *Pe'amim* 25 (1985) (Hebrew): 104–22. esp. 110.

7. See Benjamin H. Migdalei Besamim 'Masoret Zurat Haamigdal Bekufsaut Lebsamei Havdala, H . Benjamin, *Towers of Spice: The Tower- Shaped Tradition in Havdalah Spiceboxes*, Catalogue no. 224, The Israel Museum, Jerusalem, 1982; S. Landau, *Architecture in the Hanukkah Lamp*, Catalogue no. 186, The Israel Museum, Jerusalem, 1978.

8. This box stands at the south-western corner of the Rock. See E. Schiller *The Dome of the Rock and Foundation Stone* (Jerusalem, 1976), 59–60. This silver box was donated by Sultan Ahmet I in 1609.

9. I am indebted to Boris Khaimovitch for providing me with this photo.

FIGURE 5   FIGURE 6

Muslim containers of holy objects.

Flat-topped silver coated and decorated Torah case.

The cases can be divided into two different types according to the shape of their top. One has a flat top, and the other an onion-shaped one and an apex. They differ, as well, in the number of short staves for the finials attached to the tops: some have just two staves while others have up to six. Both types can be found in Jewish communities all over Iran. In general, the Torah cases with the onion-shaped tops are more common in western Iran, while the flat-topped ones are more common in the east of the country. Iran is part of a wider Persian-speaking world,[10] and one finds similar types in the Jewish communities in the east, such as in Afghanistan, Uzbekistan, and Azerbaijan.

---

10. The Persian world includes the countries that once used to be under Persian rule.

FIGURE 7

Simple flat-topped Torah case with a nail-heads decoration.
A detail—hook decorated with figures of hens.

1. Flat-topped Torah Cases

One very elaborate flat-topped case from the end of the nineteenth century originates in Yazd (fig. 7). It is prism-shaped, covered with a delicately flower-decorated silver sheet with six short staves for the *rimonim* (Torah finials). Two of these are actually the upper part of the Torah staves, around which the Torah inside the case is rolled. The other four only serve to hold the finials decorating the case. This fine artwork is one of the few surviving examples of high quality ritual objects used in some of Iran's synagogues.[11]

Another flat-topped case (fig.7) also from a rather large community, Shiraz, represents the work of poorer but very imaginative artists. This is a wooden brown-red leather-coated cylindrical case, in which the attaching metal nails form a decorative design of geometrical forms. The three metal-cast hooks that close this case at its front are shaped like hens (Fig.7). This case is "dressed" in a fancy green and gold cloth "coat" trimmed by muslin and ribbons used to tie its front. A colored kerchief is tied to each of its two staves, around which the Torah is rolled. These are dedications of the worshipers, mainly women.

2. Onion-shape topped Torah Cases

The onion-shape topped Torah cases are in the style typical in Iraq, which is most likely the origin of the type used in Iran. In Iraq, the majority of the cases were made in Baghdad, famous for its craftsmen in that field. The difference between the Iraqi and Iranian cases is mainly the material used for covering the wood and the decorative design. In Baghdad, it was usually silver sheets or parts of rectangular silver sheets decorated in a repetitive floral motive.[12]

---

11. For this case, see B. Yaniv, *The Torah Case, Its History and Design* (Jerusalem, 1997) (Hebrew), 160.

12. For more about the Baghdadi Torah cases, see ibid., 77–101

FIGURE 8   FIGURE 9

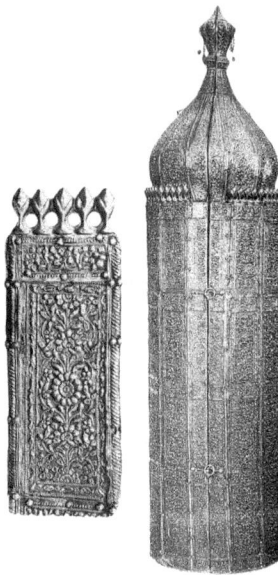 

Silver onion-shape topped Torah case.   Wooden onion-shape topped case with mirrors.

Not many examples of this kind of Torah case were found in Iran (fig.8).[13] Most of the Iranian communities could not afford a case like this and tried to produce ones that would give a rich impression with fewer expenses. The local artists were very creative and found various ways in form, color, and material to upgrade the look of the cases. An example (fig.9) of imitating the shiny impression of silver and of a division into rectangulars bearing a decorative design is a case with cut out "window"-like, elongated forms and with shiny mirrors inserted into them. Another effort was an imitation of the shape of the upper part of the Baghdadi case, which is decorated with a floral rim of buds, with red or blue beads between them. In the Iranian cases, the buds' form is sawn at the upper edge of the wooden case, and a row of holes under them represents the beads (fig. 10). To strengthen the impression of a rich decoration, especially attractive nails, with round or flower-shaped heads, were used. However, their functional purpose was fastening the covering material to

---

13. See Yaniv, *The Torah case*, pl. 16, p. 172.

the wood. This was accomplished by either using the shape of the *boteh*[14] or a geometric form. In some Torah cases, cheap colored metal strips and roundels on simple cloth (fig.11) were used as decoration, while in others, colored sheets of cheap metal. In many cases, the colored design was influenced by the local carpets (fig.12).

FIGURE 10   FIGURE 11

Wooden anion-shaped topped case.

Onion–shape topped case made of cheap materials.

14. An almond or cypress shaped design, which is very popular in Persian art, it is also called paisley. See Anton Felton, *Jewish Carpets: A History and Guide* (Woodbridge, UK: Antique Collectors' Club, 1997), 130.

FIGURE 12

Onion-shape topped case painted to imitate a rug's design.

APEX (ציצה)

An exceptionally fine silver apex of an onion-shape topped Torah case (fig. 14) is kept in the Israel Museum's collections. It is decorated by leaves, flanking pairs of birds and a faced-sun—finely carved, nicely proportioned, and well placed on the object. Its origin and date are not known. However, owing to its quality, motifs, and style, it may be attributed to an early period, perhaps the eighteenth century.

Some Torah cases, finials, and Torah pointers were made by a silversmith named Ivas Emuna,[15] who hailed from Shiraz in the 1950s. He continued to produce in Israel the same objects in the same style and as he did in Iran.[16] On one of the decorated finials he made, we find pairs of birds flanking a flower (fig.14). The comparison of the apex of fig. 14 and the above stresses the quality of each of them—the simplicity of Ivas Emuna and the delicacy of the earlier object.

---

15. His name is carved on one of the objects he made (Sc. 109/18 in the index of Jewish Art of the Hebrew University in Jerusalem).

16. About Ivas Emuna, see R. Jacoby, *"Etzba'" ve "Kulmos,"* 45–47.

FIGURE 13

FIGURE 14

Apex and some details of its design.

Finial decorated by birds (made by Ivas Emuna).

The sun bearing a human face is a well-known ancient non-Jewish Iranian symbol, which later developed into one of the symbols of 'Ali - the first Shi'ite Imam. One finds this with other symbols of 'Ali, such as the hand, on many artifacts, for example on the door of Sha'ab el Ammer mosque in Tabriz.[17] This symbol appears frequently on Jewish objects, such as marriage contracts (*ketubbah*) from Isfahan, where the sun with a human face is peeping from behind a lion (fig.15).[18] The sun and lion are part of the artistic vocabulary of the Persian world, also found on amulets and on Afghani Torah pointers[19] (fig. 16).

The fine apex mentioned before has pendants shaped like a bird with drop-shaped bells. Pendants in various forms decorate the Torah finials

17. See R. Beny, *Persien* (Luzern & Frankfurt, 1976).

18. See S. Sabar, *Ketubba, Jewish Marriage Contracts of the Hebrew Union College Skrible Museum and Klau Library* (Philadelphia, New York: 1990), 334–335. S. Sabar, *Mazal Tov: Mazal tov: illuminated Jewish marriage contracts from the Israel Museum collection* (Jerusalem: Israel Museum, 1993), 117.

19. For this image on a Judeo-Persian Talismanic Textile, see R. Shani, "A Judeo-Persian Talismanic Textile," *Irano-Judaica* IV (1999), 251–87. For a discussion and more examples, see Jacoby, "'*Etzba*'" ve "*Kulmos*," 95. The faced sun behind a tiger/lion decorates one of the main gates in the Registan of Samarkand from the fourteenth century.

as well. They serve as decoration, but mainly as a means of attracting the attention of the worshippers in the prayer hall to the fact of the Torah is being taken out of the Ark or being put back in, when, according to the Law, everybody present had to stand up to honor the Torah.

FIGURE 15

Upper part of a marriage contract from Isfahan.

FIGURE 16

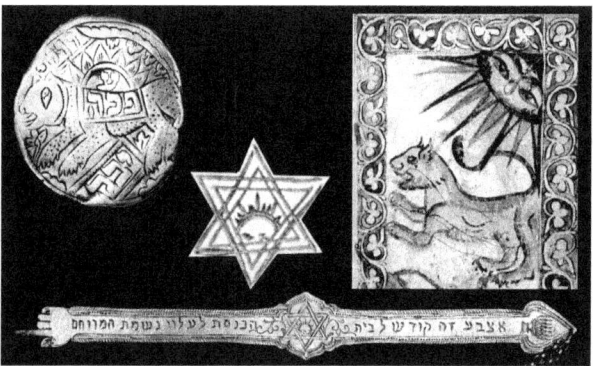

Lion and human faced sun on a Jewish amulet,
manuscript and a Torah Pointer.

FINIALS (רימונים)

We possess a big variety of finials coming Iran (fig. 17). Many of their shapes are influenced by the rich Persian art surrounding them. Many of these have an apex, which was decorated by various shapes that could have been an inspiration to the Torah finials.

As already mentioned, the finials were put on small staves made of wood or metal, and these were put on the upper part of the Torah case, whether flat or onion-shaped. There are two basic types of shapes of the finials: bulky and flat. The lower part of both types is hollow in order to enable putting them on the small staves. The bulky ones vary in proportions and form, from round, almost ball-shaped to elongated with a round or pointed top (fig.16). Some of these bear a dedication inscription on their body or foot. The other group, that of flat finials, includes single and double *boteh* (paisley) shaped, rectangular ones, round ones that encircle a Shield of David with the word Zion (ציון) in its center, those that look like a cut-out Shield of David, or others shaped in the form of hands. In some of these flat finials, some text—a blessing or a quotation from the Torah—written on paper or parchment is enclosed by the metal frame of the finial or engraved on the metal (fig. 17). In a case in which there are more than two finials, there are usually six—four bulky ones and two flat ones, which are called crowns.[20]

To the best of my knowledge, the hand-palm shaped finials are exclusive to the Jews of Iran. No wonder, since palm-shaped artifacts are one of the most common shapes in Shi'ite religious items and can be seen in everyday life. A major religious custom in Shi'ite Islam is the 'Ashura procession, which takes place on the tenth day of the month of Muharram. This procession commemorates the killing of Hussayn, the third Shi'ite Imam during the tragic defeat of the Shi'ites to the Sunnites at the battle of Karbala in 680. In the same battle, Hussayn's stepbrother, Abbas son of 'Ali, also died, and his arm and palm were cut off by the enemy. This made the hand a kind of a symbol of that event. The hand thus appears on these processions in the form of banners ('Alam) in many variations: in metal on a stave or painted on cloth banners (fig.18). Additional symbols were given to the palm, such as the five fingers standing

---

20. See B. Yaniv, "Content and Form in the Flat Finials from Eastern Iran and Afghanistan," *Pe'amim* 79 (1999): 96–128.

for the five pillars of Islam, the first five Imams of the Shi'ites, and other meanings attributed in Islam to the number five.[21]

FIGURE 17

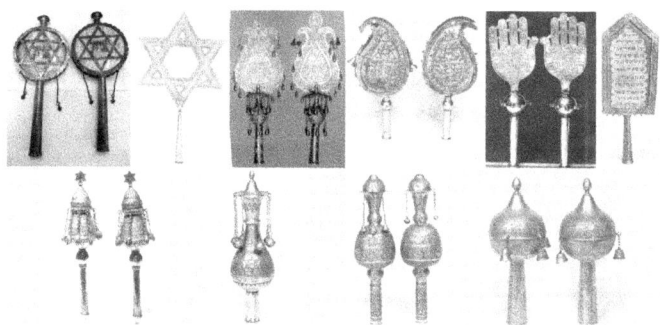

Iranian finials of various shapes.

FIGURE 18

Shi'ite Ashura procession carrying hand shaped banners.

In the Jewish context, palm-shaped banners were used in a similar way on the Ziaras (holy pilgrimage).[22] I am acquainted with three objects

21. For more examples, see, R. Jacoby, *"Etzba" and "Kulmos,"* 56.
22. Such as the ziara to the Tomb of the prophet Ezekiel in Keffil not far from

of that kind, and on two of them is engraved *"kaf yad"* i.e. palm (כף יד) (fig.19).[23] These *kaf yad*s, which have a similar shape and usage in both religions, can point to a link between the other objects in Jewish Iranian use bearing the shape of a palm, such as the Torah pointers and amulets (fig. 21).

Karbala, in today's Shi'ite area of Iraq.

23 The three objects in fig.19 and their inscriptions are (from right to left) :1.The Sassoon family estate (No. 31in the Sotheby's catalogue of 25 and 27 October 2000, Tel Aviv). The inscription on the center of the palm reads: "/הקדישו הבחור "יוסף עבדאל אלייהו/ לכבוד אדונינו/יחזקאל הנאבי זכותו/יגין בעד[ינו] אמין and on the fingers 1827) "שנת/התקפז /ליצירת/עולם").

24 In the Wolfson Museum collection, Hechal Shlomo, Jerusalem. The inscription is on the center of the palm- "מתנה בת הר יוסף יצחק יוסף הי / זה הכף התנדבו אותו מרים" (לכבוד אדונינו רבי מאיר/בה"נס זיע"א/מאנדלי ר"ח טבת התרנ"ו) 1896
Mandalie is a quarter in Bagdad in Bagdad with a synagogue bearing this name .
3.Museum Eretz Ysrael collection No .MHEJ 545 9. (Thanks to Nitza Bahrouzi for the permeation to publish this object). The inscription which appears on the fingers reads: "זה הכף/הקדישה/אותו ס'[ינירורה] בזנה/כתון מב"ת (מנשים באהל תבורך) אשת הר" That on the center of the palm: בעל הנס" זיע"א (זכותו תגן עלינו אמן)) לכבוד אדונינו רבי "מאיר/בה/נס
ם]/לרפואת בתה שרה/ יאריך ימיה בטיב/ושנותיה בנעימי"
About the use of these objects as banners by Jews, we learn from evidence given by Mrs. Kaflawy, the daughter of the caretaker of Ezekiel's tomb. The evidence is from the period before 1928, when she left her village. She mentions *"Kaf-Yad,"* made of silver, or even of gold, which were put on staves carrying cloth banners and stuck onto the door of the tomb (Ben-Yaacob Abraham, *Holy Tomb in Babylon* [Jerusalem: 1973], 38–94, in Hebrew). This custom is known from Shi'ite tombs such as the tomb of the Allawian family in Hamadan (end of twelfth to beginning of the thirteenth century). See fig.20.

FIGURE 19

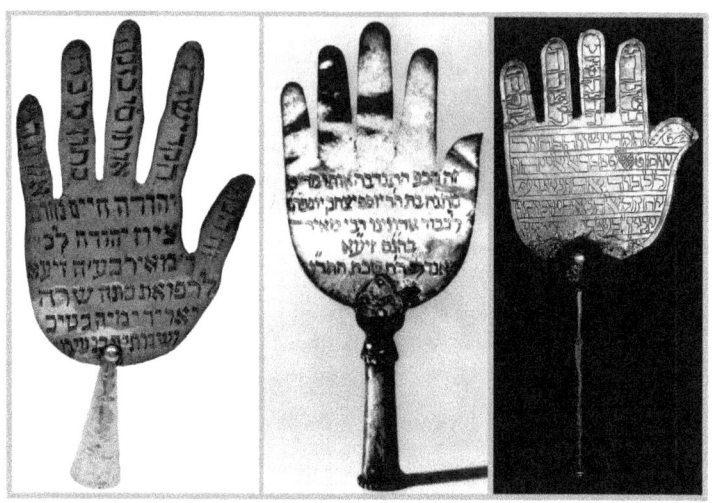

*kaf yad*s

FIGURE 20

A hand shaped statue on a Shi'ite tomb.

FIGURE 21

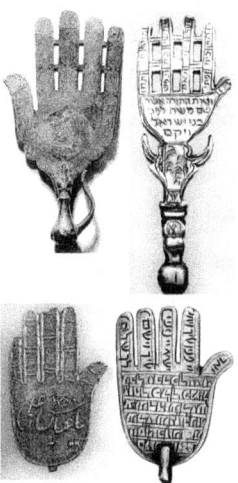

Similarity of a Shi'ite banner and a Persian Torah
pointer and a Shi'ite and Jewish amulets.

The palm shape used as an amulet against the evil eye has a very old history, even a pre-historic one.[24] It is also very common in North Africa where it is called *ḥamsa*.[25] However, in spite of the general similarity in shape, the North African palm and the Shi'ite one derive from different traditions; the first comes from the belief that it scares the evil eye, and the other from the tradition of 'Ali's arm that was cut off in the battle of Karbala.

TORAH POINTERS (ידיים לתורה)

The Torah pointer is not considered a holy ritual object, in spite of its "close touch" with the Torah scroll. It is accepted as a practical item used for pointing at the place to the reader of the Torah.[26] As it is a small item, it gets easily lost, and thus a limited number of typical Persian pointers have been discovered. Those can be divided into two: the Iraqi elongated, oval-shaped pointers and the palm-shaped ones (fig.22). The last group

---

24. See Rivka Gonen, "The Open Hand: On the North African Hamsa and Its Sources," *Israel Museum Journal* 12 (1994): 47–56.

25. See S. Sabar, "Judaization of the Hamsa," *Mahanaim* 14 (2002): 193–203.

26. See R. Jacoby, *"Etzba"* and *"Kulmos,"* 11–14.

has a wide straight-end, which is not very practical to point with since its edge is usually wider than a single word. Nevertheless, it seems to be the most common shape. This could probably be explained by the influence of the Shi'ite environment, and the hand of that shape is taken from the Shi'ite Alam-banners. Here, the wish to keep the local traditional shape is stronger than the practical side.

On some other pointers from the Persian world, such as Afghanistan, one finds a type of decoration technique known as "hidden animals"—such as birds and fish surrounding a flower—on the wide part of the pointer. These are not noticed at first sight; one has to "discover" them (fig.23).[27]

The different pointers represent the three major trends of the ritual objects in Iran: the main central Iranian local Shi'ite influence, the western Iraqi influence, and that of Eastern Bukhara.

FIGURE 22

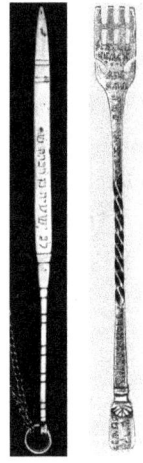

The two kinds of Torah pointers typical to Iran.

FIGURE 23

"Hidden" decoration of fish and birds on a Torah pointer.

INSCRIPTIONS

Script is not used as a decorative element on Jewish Persian ritual objects, although it is one of the important elements of the surrounding culture.

27 On this phenomenon, see R. Jacoby, *"Etzba" and "Kulmos,"* 79–80.

Some inscriptions do appear on Jewish objects; however, they are usually informative and not decorative, as they include details about the donor, in whose honor it was given along with some Biblical verses relevant to its use.[28] In some cases, a wish is added, such as a request for a male child.[29] On some small objects, such as the Torah pointers, one finds the Priestly Benediction, which is common on amulets, and this was perhaps also one of the uses of the pointers.

An interesting phenomenon is the warning inscription admonishing one who may potentially steal, sell, or take the Torah out of the synagogue without permission, and all the curses that will fall upon him if he violates.[30] The fact that these inscriptions are not rare shows stealing from the synagogue could be part of everyday life.

Some of the inscriptions were written in the script of a Torah, most probably by an expert who planned their placing. These were placed on the Torah case outer side, around the top and bottom of the metal sheet, which covered the case, or on two small metal plaques near the opening of the Torah case. In the onion-shaped cases, an inscription was placed inside the upper part of the case. It was written on paper or parchment and decorated on each side by colored flowers (fig.3). On small objects, such as finials and pointers, the inscriptions were seemingly added after the object and its decoration had already been finished and the inscription had to be squeezed into empty spaces. Consequently, the letters were uneven and not very legible.

Although the material is rather scarce—and from a limited time span—there is enough evidence to form a picture of the ritual objects used mainly by the lower social-economic classes. One can detect the influence of ritual objects of the neighboring Jewish communities, the effect of local non-Jewish art and artistic traditions, or even specific Iranian symbols that were incorporated in the decoration of the Jewish objects. But what is most characteristic of the "poor man's art" is the imagination and innovation in using whatever was available to create impressive and beautiful objects. The richest variety is found in the shapes of the Torah finials. These are relatively small, not too expensive to acquire, very decorative, and noticed by the whole community when in use. A perfect object to donate and receive the honor of giving the finials.

28   Like Leviticus 26, 46, which is mentioned when the Torah is read.
29. See Yaniv, *The Torah Case*, 228.
30. See some examples, Yaniv, 219.

The wealthier Jews and their synagogues must undoubtedly have owned some high-quality objects, which may have been made by Jewish or other silversmiths. However, most of these objects did not reach Israel. They got lost on the way or were taken by the immigrants to other countries. It is most likely that a rich array of ritual objects can be found in the new communities (as, for example, Los Angeles), although it is not clear how much the local craftsmen stuck to the old, original traditions of the Iranian synagogues. Actually, hardly any research has as yet been carried out concerning Jewish Iranian material culture.

ACKNOWLEDGMENTS

The Center for Jewish Art, The Hebrew University of Jerusalem: Fig.1–Sc 455; fig.6—Sc 38.3; fig.7—Sc 470.1; fig 8.—Ohel Moshe Jerusalem; fig.14—426; fig.16—Sc 008 (pointer);in fig.17—Sc 6, Sc 470,Sc 38, Sc 38; fig.21 - up-right; fig. 22—Sc 518.19,

The Israel Museum, Jerusalem: Figs.3 and 10—145/3; fig.9—145/37; fig.11—145/34; fig.13—147/204

The Gross family collection, Tel-Aviv: Fig.2; fig 17 - up left, low second on the right; fig. 21—lower right; fig.23.

Boris Khaimovitch: Fig. 5—right.

Private collection: Fig.16 up right

Sources of other illustrations:
Fig.5 see Schiller Eli, *The Dom of the Rock and the Foundation Stone* (Jerusalem, 1976), 5
Fig.12 right—Nemati P. *The Splender of Antique Rugs and Tapestries*, (New York, 2001), p.84, Fig. 42.
Fig.15 Haim Saadon, *Jewish Communities in the Nineteenth and Twentieth Century: Iran* (Jerusalem, 2005), colored plate between 94 and 95
Fig.16 upper left Shachar Isaiah, *Jewish Tradition in Art; The Feuchtwanger Collection of Judaica*, the Israel Museum (Jerusalem, 1971, 1981), 281 no.904.

Fig. 18 Dhamija, J. *Living Tradition of Iran's Crafts*, (Teheran, 1979), between 44 and 45.
Fig. 19 Bialer Y.L. and Fink E. p. 106 lower left.
Fig.21 upper right Ettinghausen R. Notes on the Lusterware of Spain, *Art Orientalis* I 1954 pl.6 fig.29; lower right- Gluck J. and Hiramoto- Gluck S.A, *Survey of Persian Handicraft, A Pictorial Introduction to the Contemporary Folk Art and Crafts of Modern Iran*, Teheran, New York, London 1977 p. 141.

11

The Binding of Isaac in the Work of Moshe Shah Mizraḥi

A Persian-Jewish Folk Artist in Early Twentieth-Century Jerusalem

SHALOM SABAR

INTRODUCTION

The story of the Binding of Isaac (the *'aqedah*) is perhaps the most popular biblical scene in traditional Jewish art. Ever since its first appearance above the Torah niche in the ancient synagogue of Dura Europos, dated 244/45 CE (Fig. 1),[1] the story was selected as a central theme in a long line of Jewish works of art. Over the ages many, traditional and pious meanings were attached to the story, which appeared in a surprisingly wide range of contexts, demonstrating its importance and centrality to Jews over the ages. This dramatic and moving story appears in the mosaics of two ancient synagogues (Beth Alpha and Sepphoris), in dozens

   1. For a detailed analysis of the scene in Dura, see C. Kraeling, *The Synagogue* ("The Excavations at Dura-Europos, Final Report," VIII/1) (New Haven: Yale University Press, 1956), 56–59.

of medieval illuminated Hebrew manuscripts from Europe, illustrated Passover Haggadot from the Renaissance and Baroque periods, and a great variety of other Hebrew printed books—on title pages, on printers' devices, and in the form of illustrations within the books.[2]

FIGURE 1

Detail of Torah Niche with the Binding of Isaac, Dura Europos Synagogue, Syria. 244/45 C.E.

The scene is also widespread on a variety of objects made of various materials for ritual use in the course of the yearly cycle and the life cycle,

---

2. Published studies on the topic deal mostly with the Late Antique period and the Middle Ages. See, for example, the studies of Joseph Gutmann, "The Sacrifice of Isaac: Variations on a theme in Early Jewish and Christian Art," in *Sacred Images: Studies in Jewish Art from Antiquity to the Middle Ages* (Northampton: Variorum Reprints, 1989), XIII, 115–22; idem, "Revisiting the 'Binding of Isaac' Mosaic in the Beth-Alpha Synagogue," *Bulletin of the Asia Institute* N.S. 6 (1992): 79–85. For the Sepphoris mosaic, see: Z. Weiss, *The Sepphoris Synagogue: Deciphering an Ancient Message through its Archaeological and Socio-historical Contexts* (Jerusalem: Israel Exploration Society, 2005), 141–53. For the Medieval Hebrew illuminations, see: J. Gutmann, "The Sacrifice of Isaac in Medieval Jewish Art," *Artibus et Historiae* 16 (1987): 67–89; G. Sed-Rajna, *The Hebraic Bible in Medieval Illuminated Manuscripts* (Tel Aviv: Steimatzky 1987), 34–35 and 44–48; S. Sabar, "'The Fathers Slaughter Their Sons:' Depictions of the Binding of Isaac in the Art of Medieval Ashkenaz," *Images* 3 (2009): 9–27. For 'Aqeda scenes in Hebrew printed books, see, for example: A. Yaari, *Hebrew Printers' Marks from the Beginning of Hebrew Printing to the End of the 19th Century* (Jerusalem: The Hebrew University Press Association, 1944), items nos. 46, 47, 75, 104–6.

such as circumcisers' knives, platters for redemption of the first born, illuminated *ketubbot* for weddings, and even in high relief on tombstones in the Ouderkerk cemetery of the Portuguese community in Amsterdam. The story of the *'aqedah* played an important role in synagogue decoration, and is often the only biblical theme on ritual objects, curtains for the Holy Ark and mantles for Torah scrolls.[3] Even in modern Israeli art, the story of the *'aqedah* is extremely popular, though the meaning has been dramatically altered to fit the new reality of life in a state where fathers are constantly required to "sacrifice" their best children in Israel's wars.[4] Essentially each *'aqedah* image, whether from the past or the present, reflects the ideas and ideals of the Jewish community for which it was produced.

MOSHE MIZRAḤI'S LIFE AND CAREER IN ERETZ ISRAEL

This paper analyzes the contribution to this topic by a little-known Jewish folk artist from Iran. Our subject, Moshe Shah—or as he was known in Jerusalem, Moshe ben Yitzḥak Mizraḥi (or also as Moshe Sofer Teherani)—was born in Tehran sometime before 1870.[5] Around 1890, he

---

3. Some references and specific examples are cited in n. 34, below.

4. Cf. G. Ofrat, *Aqedat-Yitzhaq ba-Omanut ha-Yisra'elit* ["The Binding of Isaac in Israeli Art"], Exhibition catalogue (Ramat Gan: The Museum of Israeli Art, n.d. [1987]) (reprinted in Ofrat, *Be-Heksher Mekomi* [Tel Aviv: Hakibbutz Hameuchad, 2004], 24–152). The same is true also for modern Israeli literature. See, for example, the studies by Ruth Karton-Blum on the subject: "The Fear of Isaac: the Akeda Myth as a Test Case in Modern Hebrew Literature" [in Hebrew], in *Mitos Ve-Zikaron*, eds. D. Ohana and R.S. Wistrich (Jerusalem: Van Leer Institute, 1996), 231–47; "'Where does this wood in my hand come from?' The Binding of Isaac in Modern Hebrew Poetry" *Prooftexts* 8 (1988): 293–310; *Profane Scriptures: Reflections on the Dialogue with the Bible in Modern Hebrew Poetry* (Cincinnati: Hebrew Union College Press, 1999) (esp. the chapter: "A Double Bind: The Sacrifice of Isaac as a Paradigm in Modern Hebrew Poetry," 15–65).

5. The basic biographical data on Mizraḥi is briefly discussed in H. Feuchtwanger, "He-Chakham Moshe Shah, z.l., Tsayyar Votiv Yerushalmi," *Yeda' Am* 4/1–2 (1956): 97–99. Dr. Feuchtwanger, a noted collector of Judaica, gathered the information from Prof. Ezra Tsiyyon Melamed, himself a Persian Jew, who knew Mizraḥi personally. On Mizraḥi and his work, see also H. Peled, "Moshe ben Yitzchak Mizrahi (Shah)" [in Hebrew], in *Omanut ve-Umanut be-Eretz Yisrael ba-Me'ah ha-Tesh'a-esreh*, Exhibition catalogue (Jerusalem: The Israel Museum, 1979), 118–24. See also, S. Sabar, "On the Difference in Attitudes towards Visual Arts between Sephardim and Ashkenazim in the Late Ottoman Empire" [in Hebrew], *Pe'amim. Studies in Oriental Jewry* 56 (1993)

immigrated to Eretz Israel, apparently together with many other Persian Jews who came to settle in the land of their forefathers, especially in Jerusalem. The Persian immigrants numbered around 230 souls in the 1890s and their number reached 1,200 in 1909.[6] They were very poor, and most of them lived in a slum neighborhood of Jerusalem, called "Shevet Tzedek".[7] However, there were some who lived in other towns, such as Safed, Hebron and Jaffa.[8]

As far as Moshe Mizraḥi is concerned, it is not clear whether he settled immediately in Jerusalem. According to one oral account—reported by a certain Mr. Levi, who was the cantor of the noted Yoḥanan Ben Zakai Sephardi synagogue of Jerusalem, and knew Mizraḥi personally—the young Persian immigrant did not live all the time in Jerusalem, but spent some years in Safed as well.[9] Levi also mentioned that, while in Safed, Mizraḥi became a disciple of the noted Turkish rabbi, Shelomoh Eliezer (called Mercado) Alfandari (born circa 1829 in Istanbul and died in Jerusalem in 1930).[10] Since Ḥakham Alfandari, who was a highly respected rabbinical authority both among the Sephardim and Ashkenazim of the "Old Yishuv," served as the chief rabbi of Safed from 1904 to 1918, this would give us the time frame during which Mizraḥi could have been active in Safed. Whether long or short, the Safed chapter in his

---

esp. 100–101; idem, "Remember Zion: Jewish Folk and Souvenir Art in the Nineteenth Century," in *From Jerusalem with Love: A Fascinating Journey through the Holy Land with Art, Photography and Souvenirs, 1799–1948*, eds. W. Lindwer and H. Pool (Amsterdam: Waanders, 2010), esp. 152–55 (in English and Dutch).

6. Cf. A. Netzer, "Aliyah and Settlement of Persian Jewry from the End of the 19th Century till the Balfour Declaration" [in Hebrew], in *Miqqedem Umiyyam: Studies in the Jewry of Islamic Countries* (Haifa: University of Haifa Press, 1981), Vol. 1, 283–84.

7. That was the "Neighborhood of Tin Huts" adjacent to Mahane Yehuda (near Agrippas Street). The names reflect the poverty of the residents whose houses were built of recycled tin. Cf. Y. Gellis, *Shekhunot bi-Yerushalayim: Parashat binyanah ve-hitpatḥutah shel ha-ʻir ha-ḥadashah shemi-ḥuts la-ḥomot* (Jerusalem: Sifriyat Rishonim, 1962), 118.

8. Cf. Netzer, "Aliyah," 286–88.

9. As reported by Levi to the late Tel Aviv collector, Mr. Yitzchak Einhorn, whose collection included many pieces of Mizraḥi's work. I am indebted to Mr. Einhorn for sharing this information with me many years ago and for his enthusiasm and encouragement to research the folk art of Moshe Mizraḥi.

10. On Hakham Alfandari, see M. D. Gaon, *Yehudei ha-Mizrach be-Eretz Yisrael* (Jerusalem: Gaon, 1937), Vol. 2, 85–6; and cf. A. David, "Alfandari, Solomon ben Eliezer," in *Encyclopaedia Judaica*, 2nd ed. (Detroit: Macmillan Reference USA, 2007), 638.

life had apparently influenced his work, and would actually explain some issues in his artistic development, as we shall see later.

Mizraḥi apparently spent most of his adult life in Jerusalem. Reportedly, Mizraḥi occupied a modest and crowded apartment near the Damascus gate in the Old City of Jerusalem, and not outside the city wall as did most of the other Persian immigrants. Mizraḥi, however, made his living in the Old City, where he opened a few years later a shop for frames and mirrors in the old Spice Market. During these years he also frequented the Old City Yeshiva "Sha'ar ha-Shamayim," learning Talmud and Kabbalah. Only in the wake of the Arab attacks on Jews in 1929 did Mizraḥi and other Jewish merchants abandon the Old City, re-establishing their business in the new city. With his family, Mizraḥi now settled in the neighborhood "Naḥalat Zion," where he apparently lived modestly until he passed away circa 1935. As many pious Jews of his time, he was buried in the venerated cemetery on the Mount of Olives, just across the Temple Mount which he loved so much.[11]

In his spare time, Mizraḥi used to make images of the Holy Sites, beloved biblical stories and Menorah tablets ("*shiviti* plaques," in Ashkenazi parlance).[12] One of his favorite techniques was reverse glass painting: the internal side of a sheet of glass was smeared with opaque paint, and after the paint dried, the desired shapes were scratched out of the dried paint and replaced with silver or gold foil.[13] This method was known among the Jewish communities of Persia and Central Asia, and Mizraḥi apparently experimented with variations of the technique. It is curious to note that according to one report, during the war years (WWI), he obtained the glass from shattered windows in Jerusalem. As the years progressed, Mizraḥi achieved a reputation as a fine and honest craftsman. Many Jews of the Old Yishuv, especially members of the Sephardi and Oriental com-

---

11. Cf. Feuchtwanger, "Moshe Shah," 99. According to a more recent report (however, without any reference), Mizraḥi died in 1940 "at a ripe age and sound of mind." Cf. S. Zekharia, *Soharim u-va'alei melakha yehudim bi-yerushalyim ha-atika ba-'avar* (*"Jewish Traders and Artisans in Old Jerusalem in the Past"*) (Jerusalem: Zur Ot, 2002), 274.

12. The largest selection of works by Mizraḥi is reproduced in *Omanut ve-Umanut* (note 5, above), figs. 66, 72, 78–79, 84–106, 108–109 (not all the works are signed by the artist, but in a future article, I hope to discuss their attribution and authenticity). Some other sources: Feuchtwanger, "Mosheh Shah," 65, 97; Sabar, "Sephardim and Ashkenazim" (note 5, above), cover illustration and fig. 22; N. Behrouzi, ed., *Jerusalem: Spirit and Matter*, Exhibition catalogue (Tel Aviv: Eretz Israel Museum, 1993), nos. 10–12 (wrongly dated), 56 and 63.

13. Cf. *Omanut ve-Umanut*, 122.

munities in Jerusalem, commissioned him to create paintings on glass of subjects they liked, amulets to protect their houses, colored lithographic prints to decorate their Sukkot, and *shiviti*-Menorah tablets for the walls of their synagogues. In fact, some old synagogues in Jerusalem still have works by Mizraḥi on their walls,[14] and on a recent trip to Jewish communities in Central Asia, I discovered that his works are still admired there to this day (see below).

AN EARLY ʿAQEDAH PANEL BY MIZRAḤI

Of the several biblical topics that appear in Mizraḥi's work (e.g., various episodes in the Book of Esther, David and Goliath), the most popular was undoubtedly that of the Binding of Isaac. To this story Mizraḥi returned many times in his career, depicting it as an independent episode or in connection with other scenes and monuments. In depicting this story, he employed all the media and techniques known to him, from hand-painted images on paper, to color lithographs and reverse painting on glass.[15]

The earliest work with this topic that can be safely associated with Mizraḥi is from the year 1901/2. It is a color lithograph preserved in the Gross family collection, in Tel Aviv (Fig. 2). According to the two bottom medallions, the page was created "Here in the holy city of Jerusalem, may it be rebuilt and established soon in our days," by "Moshe son of Isaac Teherani, a resident of the holy city of Jerusalem, may it be rebuilt." The sentiments to Jerusalem are further enhanced in the large inscription on the left border: "In the year *'in the consolations of Zion'* to the short account" (an acronym for [5]662 [=1901/2]).[16]

14. And cf. also the testimony of Feuchtwanger, "Moshe Shah," 98.

15. The total work of Mizraḥi has been never catalogued; some works are still preserved by the original owners, and others are in un-catalogued private collections. In this paper, there is no attempt to analyze every known ʿAqeda panel by Mizraḥi (or those attributed to him), but only works that add to the understanding of his ideas and artistic development. For an example of an ʿAqeda watercolor that is generally attributed to Mizraḥi but not discussed here, see J. Ungerleider-Mayerson, *Jewish Folk Art from Biblical Days to Modern Times* (New York: Summit, 1986), 135 (cf. *Omanut ve-Umanut*, 132, no. 108).

16. Dating by use of verses that express longing for Jerusalem and the building of Zion is known from a number of objects and books produced by the Old Yishuv in Eretz Israel. The title pages of books printed by R. Israel Bak, the founder of the first Hebrew print shop in Jerusalem, gives the date as an acronym of the verse "and

FIGURE 2

Moshe Mizraḥi, Binding of Isaac, color lithograph, Monsohn, Jerusalem, 1901/1902. Tel Aviv, Gross Family Collection

Many features in the lithograph are characteristic of the work of a folk artist. Firstly, the page is divided into two panels, shaped as a decorative domed house. The two panels are crowded with figures, which narrate the story in a series of consecutive episodes. The background has no importance, and save for a narrow line of grass, there is no notion of realistic space, or perspective. No figure blocks another, and only the items necessary for telling the story are depicted. Also typical of a work of folk art are the numerous inscriptions. The folk artist leaves very little to the imagination of his audience, and thus every person and even the objects are fully identified. The inscriptions have an additional function: filling every empty space with large and small letters, so that the entire

---

instruction shall come for the from Zion and the word of the Lord from Jerusalem" (Isaiah 2:3 or Micah 4:2) or "and you shall find comfort in Jerusalem" (Isaiah 66:13). In these verses, some letters are given in bold and adding them up gives the date (e.g. in the last verse 604[5] = ובירושלים, which parallels 1864). Cf. reproductions of these title pages in S. Halevy, *Sifrei Yerushalayim Harishonim* (Jerusalem: Ben Zvi Institute, 1976), 13 and 14.

field is covered—a feature known as *horror vacui* ("fear of empty space"), which characterizes Islamic art in general.

Though the upper panel depicts the central image of the *'aqedah*, the story actually begins in the bottom panel (right corner). Isaac is shown here as a middle-aged man with a black beard, dressed in a long red gown, as he carries on his back pieces of firewood tied with a rope held by his left hand, while in his right he holds an object identified as "the fire"—a kind of large torch from which stylized flames emerge. This figure clearly illustrates the verse: "Abraham took the wood for the burnt offering and put it on his son Isaac" (Genesis 22:6). However, here as in the rest of the panel, Moshe Mizraḥi demonstrates his knowledge of the Midrashic literature he learnt in the Yeshiva. Thus, Isaac is not shown as a boy, as was common in Christian art over the ages—and actually in most of the works of European Jewish art as well, which were obviously created under the influence of Christian iconography. Mizraḥi's bearded Isaac follows the Midrashic tradition which determines the age of Isaac at the time of the *'aqedah* as 37.[17]

Abraham is depicted as an elderly person with a white beard, walking in front of Isaac, armed with his knife—in accordance with the continuation of the aforementioned verse: "He himself [i.e., Abraham] took the firestone [lit., "fire"] and the knife; and the two walked off together." Judging from this verse, it is evident that Mizraḥi erroneously placed the "fire" in the hand of Isaac rather than in that of Abraham. Indeed, no Midrash known to me confirms this change of roles. Moreover, in his later *'aqedah* depictions, Mizraḥi indeed "corrects" this mistake.

In front of Abraham are seated two Oriental looking figures. According to the text inscribed behind and in front of Abraham, these are the two young men that accompany him and Isaac, whom he ordered to "Stay here with the ass. The boy and I will go up there; we will worship and we will return to you" (Gen. 22:50). The two young men are dressed as Turkish or Arab types, with typical daggers; the right one, his head covered with a red Turkish turban, smokes a hookah, while his turbaned friend smokes a long pipe. While in the Bible the two "young men" are

---

17. This tradition appears in a number of midrashim, e.g. *Gen. Rabba* 55, 4 and 5:8; *Midrash Hagadol*, Gen. 22, 3; *Seder Olam Rabba* 1. And cf. L. Ginzberg, *The Legends of the Jews* (Philadelphia: Jewish Publication Society of America, 1909–38), Vol. 1, 280.

nameless, Mizraḥi follows the Midrash and Rashi's commentary[18] and identifies them with the captions: "This is Ishmael" and "This is Eliezer."

The latter is actually guarding the large ass behind him, and the words from Gen. 22:5 "Stay here with the ass" are repeated in large bold letters. What is the reason for this emphasis on the ass? Actually, it is in the quoted words that the Turkish appearance of Abraham's servants is revealed. The Midrash explains that the servants were not capable of seeing what Abraham and Isaac could easily see in front of them, and the words עִם הַחֲמוֹר (with the ass) in the verse should be read as עַם הַחֲמוֹר (people like an ass). In other words, Abraham told them: "You are like the ass - as little as it sees, so little you do see."[19] This disparaging remark was in fact aimed against the Gentiles (Christians in particular) since antiquity,[20] and, apparently, Mizraḥi is using it here against the Ottomans ruling the Holy Land at the time.

The upper section shows the ʿaqedah itself. Half-nude, Isaac lies bound on an altar, made of bricks and supported by four pillars in its corners. This altar was curiously illustrated in reversed perspective, expanding as it recedes. Abraham on the right is anachronistically portrayed wearing a Ḥasidic tallit with black stripes, holding in his right hand the knife of a ritual slaughterer. The angel hovering above with colorful wings uses his hand to prevent Abraham from using the knife. With his other hand, the angel points at the ram caught in the thicket (on the left). Paralleling the rose bush-like thicket at right is a tree labeled "She is a tree of life to those who grasp her, and whoever holds on to her is happy" (Proverbs 3:18).

In illustrating the tree and quoting this particular verse, Mizraḥi achieves two goals that can be understood only by someone who is well versed with rabbinical teachings and their connection with the ʿaqedah. The Tree of Life reminds us of Paradise, and indeed, according to the rabbinic tradition, the ram was one of the ten extraordinary things God created at the twilight of the sixth day of creation.[21] The ram grazed in

18. Lev. Rabba 26, 7; Cf. Rashi on Gen. 22:5. Cf. Ginzberg, *Legends of the Jews*, Vol. 1, 276.

19. *Gen. Rabba* 56, 2. The midrash appears in different versions in a number of places (cf. Ginzberg, 279). On this midrash, see: J. Heinemann, "ʿAm ha-domeh le-hamor' gilgulav shel midrash eichad," *Molad* 22 (1964): 456–62.

20. Ibid., esp. 462.

21. See, for example, *Yalkut Shimoni*, Parashat va-Yera, par. 101. And cf. Ginzberg, *Legends of the Jews*, Vol. 1, 282.

Paradise, until the propitious moment came. The verse quoted also alludes to the Torah, "the tree of life"—which is epitomized in the story of the 'aqedah, being a symbol of sacrifice in the Temple and the Temple site itself, an idea which Mizraḥi would continue to develop in his future works (see below). Finally, the idea that the 'aqedah is the epitome of prayer and supplication to the Lord is enhanced by the quote from the liturgy of the New Year, which is inscribed along the exterior border ("and the binding of Isaac, [God] remember today, for the sake of the seed of our father Jacob").²²

MIZRAḤI'S PICTORIAL SOURCES

As the 'aqedah panel of Mizraḥi, as well as many other images created by him, contain figural representations, one should first tackle the problem of how could it be that a traditional Jewish artist from an Islamic land would show interest in figurative art. The fact is that, unlike their brethren in Holland, Italy or Germany, the Jews in Islamic lands followed a rather strict interpretation of the Second Commandment, which explicitly forbids "the making of graven images" (Exodus 20:4). Thus, while some European Jewish communities adopted a relatively lenient interpretation of the biblical injunction, the Jews of Islam accepted the norm in their host society, which disapproved of figurative representations in religious context (e.g., in a mosque or a Qur'an manuscript),²³ and refrained for the most part from the use of figurative representations.

---

22. The common version of this expression is "and the binding of Isaac remember today for the sake of his seed," but there are versions of the High Holiday prayer book (particularly Sephardi ones) that add the words "of Israel / of Jacob," in order to exclude the descendents of Esau, who was also Isaac's son. R. Israel Meir Cohen (the "Ḥafetz Ḥayyim," 1838–1933) criticized the emendation, saying that anyone who adds it "changes an expression that was coined by the sages and is simply in error." Cf. *Mishna Berura*, Par. 591:12. This remark reflects the popularity of the addition. In other portrayals of the 'aqeda, Mizraḥi expanded this expression even more. For example, in an unpublished plaque held in the National Museum of Samarkand, Uzbekistan, the arch on top of the plaque is inscribed with the expression: "and the binding of Isaac remember today mercifully for the sake of the seed of our Father Jacob, may he rest in peace."

23. Regarding the attitudes and approaches of early Muslim authorities towards visual art in general and figurative art in particular, cf. the classical studies: T.W. Arnold, *Painting in Islam: A Study of the Place of Pictorial Art in Muslim Culture* (New York: Dover Publications, 1965), 1–40; O. Grabar, *The Formation of Islamic Art* (New Haven: Yale University Press, 1977), 75–103. On the attitude of the Jews in Islamic lands to

Human figures do appear in Islamic art of some countries in "secular" contexts, e.g., chronicles, poetry, adventures of rulers, etc.[24] Persia was one place where such images were encouraged by the rulers (see, for example, the case of the manuscripts of the historical royal epic *Shah Nameh*), and they became widely known and popular. And from a Jewish point of view, Persia is an exception in this category as well. While in some Islamic lands a few highly exceptional Jewish works of art with figural decorations were produced on rare occasions,[25] Persia is the only Muslim land where the local Jews accepted such images as a norm, although not in every place and every period.

And again, as in Islam, figural representations do not appear in the synagogues or in Bible manuscripts written in the Hebrew language, or even in ketubbot. Rather, they are found in a relatively large group of Judeo-Persian manuscripts, containing biblical paraphrases of popular stories and heroes.[26] These were mostly composed by Jewish writers, such as the fourteenth century poet Moulana Shahin, but Persian literary tradition of biblical nature (e.g., Abd al-Rahman Jami's *Yusuf and Zulaykha*

---

painting and the visual arts, see: L. A. Mayer, *L'art juif en terre de l'Islam* (Geneva: Kundig, 1959) (English translation: "Jewish Art in the Moslem World," in *Jewish Art: An Illustrated History*, ed. C. Roth (New York: McGraw-Hill, 1961).

24. For a representative selection and discussion, see R. Ettinghausen, *Arab Painting* (Geneva: Skira, 1977).

25. For example, human figures appear in two rare *ketubbot* from San'a, Yemen: a) 1787—in the Library of the Jewish Theological Seminary, New York; b) 1794—The Israel Museum, Jerusalem. See: S. Sabar, *Mazal Tov: Illuminated Jewish Marriage Contracts from the Israel Museum Collection* (Jerusalem: Israel Museum, 1993), pl. 26; idem, "A Jewish Wedding in 18th Century San'a: The Story of the Ketubbot of the Al-Eraqi and Al-Sheikh Families—Between Tradition and Innovation," *Rimonim* 6-7 (1999), esp. 21–22 (in Hebrew), in which I maintain that the human figures may have been made under Persian influence and perhaps even by an itinerant Persian-Jewish artisan.

26. See on these manuscripts: J. Gutmann, "Judeo-Persian Manuscripts," *Studies in Bibliography and Booklore* 8 (1968): 54–76 (reprinted in *No Graven Images: Studies in Art and the Hebrew Bible*, ed. Gutmann [New York: Ktav, 1971]), 466–488); V. Basch Moreen, *Miniature Paintings in Judaeo-Persian Manuscripts* (Cincinnati: Hebrew Union College, 1985). For an important study that examines the Jewish manuscripts against the contemporary book arts in Isfahan, see A. Taylor, *Book Arts of Isfahan: Diversity and Identity in Seventeenth-Century Persia* (Malibu: J. Paul Getty Museum, 1995), esp. 31–46. Cf. also A. Amar, "Moses and Musa—Stories of Moses in the Musa Nama," in *Between Judaism and Islam in the Mirror of Art: Proceedings of the 27th Annual Conference of the Society for Jewish Art*, ed. S. Sabar (Jerusalem: Society for Jewish Art, 1996), 6–17 (in Hebrew).

romance) was employed as well. Most of these codices were copied and illustrated in the seventeenth century in Safavid provincial style, possibly in the city of Isfahan.[27] However, it is important to note that this artistic genre continued through the Qajar period in the nineteenth century. A noted example is a rich and attractive manuscript of *Yusuf and Zulaykha*, which was produced as late as 1853 by the scribe Eliyahu ben Nissan ben Eliyahu in the holy city of Mashad.[28] In the second half of the nineteenth century, just prior to Mizraḥi's emigration, it became popular to depict biblical scenes on individual pages. Gradually, this practice expanded to include decoration of objects, luxurious utensils and carpets.[29]

The Judeo-Persian manuscripts reflect Persian folk art at its best. Characteristics of this tradition are evident in Moshe Mizraḥi's work, and although it cannot be ascertained by the little information available on his youth in Persia, it is evident that he was closely familiar with this artistic genre and with Persian folk art in general. Thus, in addition to the popular technique of reverse painting on glass mentioned above (see also below), he included in his *'aqedah* panels such typical Islamic motifs as the colorful wings of the angels, or symmetrically positioned vases with large flowers in bright colors (see Figs. 2, 6, 7, 9). On the other hand, though the scene of the story of Isaac (or actually Ishmael) was extremely popular in Islamic miniature painting, including in Persia, it is not known from the aforementioned extant Judeo-Persian manuscripts.[30] Moreover, a close comparison between such episodes and Mizraḥi's *'aqedah* panels does not show any significant iconographic similarities. Given

27. Cf. Taylor, *Book Arts of Isfahan*, 31 and 32–46.

28. Preserved at the Library of the Jewish Theological Seminary of America, New York (JTS Mic 1534). The manuscript is described in Moreen, *Judaeo-Persian Manuscripts*, no. III, 22–4, 29.

29. The transition to individual pages is generally attributed to European influence on Persian art. Cf. N. Brosh & R. Milstein, *Biblical Stories in Islamic Painting*, Exhibition catalogue (Jerusalem: The Israel Museum, 1991), 31–32. Regarding Biblical images on carpets, cf. A. Felton, *Jewish Carpets: A History and Guide* (Woodbridge: Antiques Collectors' Club, 1997), 57–67, 81–93, 107, 127–28. Some of the dates suggested by the author should be amended (see below).

30. For the *'aqedah* in Islamic art, see M. Schapiro, "The Angel with the Ram in Abraham's Sacrifice: A Parallel in Western and Islamic Art," in *Late Antique, Early Christian and Mediaeval Art. Selected Papers* (New York: Braziller, 1979), 288–318; Brosh and Milstein, *Biblical Stories*, 40–43 (and see there, pp. 42–43, examples of the topic in folk Persian art of the nineteenth century); R. Milstein et. al, *Stories of the Prophets: Illustrated Manuscripts of Qisas al-Anbiya* (Costa Mesa, CA: Mazda, 1999), 120–21.

the folkloristic nature of Mizraḥi's panels, one must conclude, therefore, that the direct pictorial source for his work lies elsewhere.

In Eretz Israel of the late nineteenth century, the knowledge and interest in the story of the 'aqedah (or Sacrifice of Isaac, or *Dhabih* in Arabic) was not limited to the Jewish population, but naturally shared by Muslims and Christians as well. However, to the best of my knowledge, craftsmen working for the local (or pilgrim) Christian and Muslim populations produced in this period a relatively small number of souvenir objects and images depicting the stories of the Hebrew Bible in general and the story of Isaac-Ishmael in particular.[31] One such rare example is a Muslim lithograph, possibly printed in Jerusalem in the last quarter of the nineteenth century (Fig. 3).[32] Notwithstanding some Western influences in the treatment of figural representation and the landscape, the traditional Muslim motifs predominate—the son is wearing a blindfold, and the archangel Gabriel descends from above holding the ram in his arms.[33] The scene is accompanied by quotes from the Qur'an related to the story (37:99–108)—and from this point of view, the page shares some parallel characteristics with the work of Mizraḥi. Obviously, however, the Muslim overtones and other features (such as showing Abraham's son as a child) are far from Mizraḥi's depictions, and such a rare Muslim composition cannot be considered a direct source.

---

31. One should not exclude the possibility of competition—the popular Christian olive-wood souvenirs, for example, depicted symbols and scenes related to the Passion Christ, which attracted the attention of the Jerusalem pilgrims, while the Jewish examples emphasize the holy sites and tombs frequented by Jews. Selected Christian examples are discussed and reproduced in *Omanut ve-Umanut*, 78–83, 210–16; Sabar, "Remember Zion" (n.5, above), 168–69 (and see there on the production of the olive-wood souvenirs, 162–65).

32. Preserved in the collection of Willy Lindwer, Jerusalem.

33. For the iconography of the story in Islamic art, see the sources in note 30, above.

FIGURE 3

Ibrahim about to sacrifice Isma'il, Muslim color lithograph, Jerusalem (?), ca. late 19th c. Jerusalem, Willy Lindwer Collection

We are thus left with Jewish iconography as a possible source of influence. And as surprising as it may seem, in the "melting pot" of artistic traditions brought to Eretz Israel in the late nineteenth century, the one which apparently influenced Mizraḥi's treatment of the *'aqedah* the most is that of the Polish Hassidim. It was in Poland of the eighteenth and nineteenth centuries that the *'aqedah* was certainly the most popular biblical episode in Jewish art. The scene appears on myriad objects, including the device of a Hebrew printer, Torah Ark curtain, Torah crowns, silver buckles for Yom Kippur belts, plates for Redemption of the First Born ceremonies, silver book bindings, popular paper cuts (Fig. 4), etc.[34] Many of these objects, which were produced in the nineteenth century, display a similar composition and bear striking iconographic similarities

---

34. There is no study of the *'aqedah* on these objects, which are reproduced in many catalogues of Judaica. For example, C. Benjamin, *The Stieglitz Collection: Masterpieces of Jewish Art,* Exhibition catalogue (Jerusalem: Israel Museum, 1987), nos. 102 (belt buckle), 206 (circumcision knife), 211 (*Pidyyon ha-Ben* plate), 215 and 219 (ketuvot), 248 (book binding), 248.I (printer's device); Behrouzi, *Jerusalem Spirit and Matter,* no. 62 (papercut); W. Seipel, ed. *Thora und Krone: Kultgeräte der jüdischen Diaspora in der Ukraine,* Exhibition catalogue, Kunsthistorischen Museums (Vienna: Das Museum, 1993), nos. 3 (Torah crown), 103 (belt buckle). The colorful papercut in Fig. 4 is taken from Regina Lilentabw *Święta żydowskie w przeszłości i teraźnieiszosci* (Cracow, 1908) pl. 3. I am indebted to Piotr Gracikowski for his help in obtaining this image.

to Mizraḥi's panel. Most noteworthy is the fact that Abraham wears a Tallit—an extremely rare feature of the 'aqedah in art, but one which is natural in Polish Judaica. Notable also is the presence of the two boys, who are generally not included in this scene.

FIGURE 4

Binding of Isaac, colored papercut, Poland, late 19th century
(after Regina Lilientalowa, *Święta żydowskie w przeszłości i teraźnieiszosci*, Cracow, 1908, pl. 3)

While we do not have details on the personal contacts which Mizraḥi might or might not have had with Ashkenazi-Polish Jews, the Jewish folk art of Eastern Europe was ubiquitous and enjoyed great popularity in nineteenth century Jerusalem.[35] Immigrants brought with them their various crafts and a wide range of motifs to which they were accustomed in their homeland. Naturally, these designs were at times modified to fit the new reality of life in the Holy Land, but the basic forms and designs of each community can be still discerned. Thus, for example, a craftsman from Kolomyya (Kolomea) in Galicia carved the magnificent Holy Ark of the Ashkenazi Ari synagogue in Safed in 1857 in the same style of Arks he knew in his youth. However, the decorative animals, which are an essential part of such Arks in Galicia, are absent from the Safed Ark, since

---

35. Cf. S. Sabar, "Jewish Folk Art in Late Nineteenth and Early Twentieth Century Jerusalem and its European Sources," in *Jerozolima w kulturze europejskiej*, eds. P. Paszkiewicz and T. Żadrozny (Warsaw: Instytut Sztuki Polskiej Akademii Nauk, 1997), 481–88.

the local Hassidic community frowned upon the usage of such "graven images."[36]

'Aqedah scenes in the spirit of East European Jewish art were similarly available in Jerusalem. It was typical, for example, for a young bride to embroider this scene with colorful woolen threads on a perforated cardboard tablet (Fig. 5). As a typical folk artist, Mizraḥi had no problem "borrowing" motifs and designs, though he himself included a "warning" on some of his images, stating that "according to our holy Torah [Deut 27:17], it is forbidden to *shift boundaries* [namely, copy or sell the work of someone else]."

Mizraḥi, however, was careful in his borrowings, and usually incorporated them in a new composition or layout that was more or less his own. An example is a colorful amulet to guard the home (Fig. 6). The layout of the page, the Temple as the Dome of the Rock in the center, and the circle of saints' tombs around, are all typical of the artistic tradition of Sephardi-Italian Jews.[37] However, the four corner medallions, illustrated with four animals (tiger, eagle, deer and lion - in accordance with the saying in *Pirkei Avot* 5:20), definitely come, again, from the East European tradition, and were not generally used among the Jews of Islam.[38] Thus, unlike other folk artists in the Old Yishuv, Mizraḥi was willing to adapt any source that suited his purposes, and by so doing, created a sort of harmony between the Sephardi, Oriental, and Ashkenazi traditions.

LATER 'AQEDOT BY MIZRAḤI

Moshe Mizraḥi returned to the topic of the *aqedah* several times in his career, constantly attempting to introduce variations, new motifs and new ideas. In this aspect alone he should be considered as somewhat of

---

36. For the details of this story and an illustration of the Safed Ark, see Sabar, "Sephardim and Ashkenazim" (note 5, above), 78–91 and fig. 4. For an analysis of the decoration of relevant Torah Arks, see B. Yaniv, "Praising the Lord: Discovering a Song of Ascents on Carved Torah Arks in Eastern Europe," Ars Judaica 2 (2006): 83–102

37. Ibid., 95–98.

38. For examples of Ashkenazi objects with the "holy animals" from Eretz Israel, see *Omanut ve-Umanut* (note 5, above), 183, fig. 160; Sabar, "Sephardim and Ashkenazim," 84, fig. 20.

FIGURE 5

Binding of Isaac Tablet, perforated cardboard embroidered with color woolen threads, Jerusalem, 1866/67(?). Los Angeles, Skirball Museum.

FIGURE 6

Moshe Mizraḥi, Home Protection Amulet, color lithograph, Monsohn, Jerusalem, ca. 1920. Tel Aviv, Gross Family Collection

an exception among folk artists, who generally adhere to known traditions and schemes. Mizraḥi's naive art, however, demonstrates his growth and learning, and one may even find in it echoes to the events and ideology of the time.

In a panel dated 1912/13, also preserved in the collection of the Gross family, many of the designs found in the earlier panel recur, but a few curious ones are added (Fig. 7). Firstly, the panel is divided this time into three registers, with the new lower one depicting a story supposedly unrelated to the 'aqedah. This is the story of Eliezer and Rebecca at the well: she is shown giving water to Abraham's tired servant, behind whom ten camels stand in a neat line, none blocking the other (Gen 24:10, 16–21). The connection of this story to the 'aqedah is explained in the Midrash: Abraham sent Eliezer at this crucial point "by reason of the resolution he had taken immediately after the sacrifice of Isaac on Moriah, for he had there said within himself that if the sacrifice had been executed, Isaac would have gone hence childless."[39] Genesis Rabbah also mentions that "while he [Abraham] was still on Mount Moriah, he was informed that his son's mate had been born."[40]

FIGURE 7

Moshe Mizraḥi, Binding of Isaac, color lithograph, Monsohn, Jerusalem, 1912/13. Tel Aviv, Gross Family Collection

39. Ginzberg, *Legends of the Jews*, Vol. 1, p. 293 (see also midrashim on the mission of Eliezer); cf. *Gen. Rabba*, 57, 3.

40. *Gen. Rabba*, 57, 2. English translation: *Midrash Rabbah*, eds. H. Freedman and M. Simon (London: Soncino, 1961), Vol. 1, 504.

The upper two registers repeat for the most part the iconography of the previous panel, but display some additions. Abraham is shown, correctly this time, holding the fire, while Isaac who follows him with the wood on his back, holds an open book. This extra-biblical element comes again from the Midrash:

> And Abraham said to himself, "How shall I separate my son from Sarah his mother and offer him as a sacrifice before the Lord?" And he came into the tent, and he sat before Sarah his wife, and he spoke these words to her: "Our son Isaac is grown up, and he has not yet studied the service of God. Now, tomorrow I will go and bring him to Shem and Eber his son, and there he will learn the ways of the Lord, for they will teach him to know the Lord; and to pray to Him at all times, so that He will answer him; and to know how to serve the Lord his God."[41]

Based on this Midrash, which is not commonly illustrated, Mizraḥi chose to portray Isaac as a pious Jew, learning Torah on his way to the Yeshiva of Shem and Eber. In one of the midrashim, these two are mentioned together with Abraham and Noah as comprising the four pious men of the generation of the Tower of Babel.[42]

Mizraḥi employed this approach of expanding the details of the story in later as well as earlier panels. For example, a panel that he created a few years earlier (1907/8) combines the story with the emblems of the twelve Tribes of Israel, two pairs of lions flanking Torah crowns, flowering vases, and two additional events related to the main story (Fig. 8).[43] Here again Mizraḥi presents a mixture of the Islamic East (e.g., the vases) with the Ashkenazi West (the Tribes and lions).[44]

---

41. *Sefer Hayashar*, ed. Goldschmidt (Berlin: Benjamin Harz, 1923), 75; and cf. Ginzberg, *Legends of the Jews*, Vol. 1, 274–5.

42. Cf. A.J. Wertheimer, ed. *Batei Midrashot* (Jerusalem: Mosad ha-Rav Kook, 1952), 149.

43. In the previous literature, including that of the present author, the date of this panel is given as 1888 (see, for example, D. Bahat and S. Sabar, *Jerusalem Stone and Spirit: 3000 Years of History and Art* [Tel Aviv: Matan Arts, 1997], 142–43). This date would mean that the panel was executed by Mizraḥi before he even came to Eretz Israel, which is, of course, impossible. However, upon a recent close examination of the panel, it became evident that the Hebrew date should indeed read 668([5])תרס״ח 1907/8=), and not 1887/8= 648([5]) תרמ״ח).

44. Such symmetrical vases are common in nineteenth-century Persian art and Jewish art in Persia. For example, see a marriage contract, possibly of Mashhad Anusim, dated 1870 in D. Davidovitch, *The Ketuba: Jewish Marriage Contracts through the Ages* (Tel Aviv: Lewin-Epstein, 1979), 70, 71, pl. X (incorrectly dated).

THE BINDING OF ISAAC 273

FIGURE 8

Moshe Mizraḥi, Binding of Isaac, color lithograph, Monsohn, Jerusalem, 1907/8. Tel Aviv, Gross Family Collection

Set in square frames at the bottom corners, the two additional scenes depict an abbreviated episode of Rebecca giving Eliezer water (Mizraḥi managed to insert only one camel this time), and, on the left, an earlier event: Abraham sending Hagar and Ishmael away (Gen. 21:14). According to the Midrash, Ishmael threatened Isaac and planned to take a double inheritance, and so Abraham was forced to send him away.[45] In the context of Mizraḥi's milieu, this story may imply that Jews, and not the Arabs, are those who have the right to the land.

The idea of connecting the ʿaqedah with the Holy Land, Jerusalem and the Temple in particular, is strengthened in Mizraḥi's later work. An unsigned and undated poster-like tablet, which was discovered by this writer in a remote synagogue in Kuba (Azerbaijan), is definitely the work of Moshe Mizraḥi, and should be dated to the early 1910's (Fig. 9).[46] The familiar episodes are here accompanied at top by a register depicting Abraham ready to obey God and go on his painful journey to sacrifice his son (Gen. 22:1). This new episode is flanked by views of holy tombs and shrines in and around Jerusalem, such as the famous tombs in the Kidron Valley, overlooking the Temple Mount.

45. *Gen. Rabba*, 53; cf. Ginzberg, *Legends of the Jews*, Vol. 1, 263–4.

46. Another copy is preserved at the Magnes Collection of Jewish Art and Life, University of California, Berkeley (the source for the reproduction here).

FIGURE 9

Moshe Mizraḥi (?), Scenes from the life of Isaac, color lithograph. Jerusalem, early 1910's. Berkeley, CA., Magnes Collection of Jewish Art and Life

FIGURE 10

Moshe Mizraḥi (?), The Binding and the Temple Mount, reverse painting on glass, Jerusalem, early 20th cent. Formerly: Tel Aviv, Yitzchak Einhorn Collection

While the holy sites occupy a rather minor place in the last panel, in a reverse painting on glass, undoubtedly executed by Mizrahi, the 'aqedah appears only in the upper section, while the entire lower part is dedicated to the Temple Mount (Fig. 10). Moreover, this section takes up more space than the familiar 'aqedah scene. It is comprised of a stereotyped view of the holiest Jewish site in Jerusalem, the Western Wall, above which grow symbolic cypress trees, flanked at left by the Dome of the Rock (representing the Temple) and the Al Aqsa mosque (right), standing for "Solomon's School." In the background, behind the eastern wall of the Temple Mount, is the Mount of Olives - again shown with the Kidron Valley tombs, and the traditional tomb of Ḥuldah, the prophetess, at the top. The connection is clear: Mount Moriah, the place of the 'aqedah is identical with the Temple Mount, the location of the Holy of Holies. This connection was already made in the earliest known depiction of the 'aqedah in Jewish art, that of Dura Europos.[47] However, despite the popularity of the 'aqedah scene in art, showing it in the vicinity of the Temple was hardly known. Based on his devotion and learning, and certainly independently of the Dura precedent (the synagogue was discovered only in 1932), Mizraḥi revived this pious connection.

Looking for the reasons for this revival, one may point of course at the Midrash and Jewish tradition regarding the 'aqedah. However, Mizraḥi apparently had in mind more than that. In the latest dated work by Mizraḥi on this topic his feelings towards the 'aqedah and its significance to a contemporary Jew living in hostile Jerusalem, are fully expounded (Fig. 11). Dated 1925/26, the panel which appeared in several lithographic editions, displays the 'aqedah "sandwiched" between a large image of the Temple (top) and the Temple Mount (bottom). Flanking these scenes are two columns, embedded with many other holy sites in the land of Israel. The most significant additions are, however, the Zionist flags at top. The claim for Jerusalem, its holiness for the Jews, and the right to the land and its holy shrines, is rooted in and emanates, in the eyes of our artist, from the story of the 'aqedah and the promise given to Abraham and his seed on Mount Moriah (Gen. 22:17). Mizrahi even chose to date his work using the numerical value of the words "The place of our Temple" ([5]686=1925/26)—not just any verse glorifying Jerusalem, but

---

47. See Kraeling, *The Synagogue* (n.1, above), 58; and cf. A. St. Clair, "The Torah Shrine at Dura-Europos: A Re-evaluation," *Jahrbuch für Antike und Christentum* 29 (1986): 109–17.

words laying claim to the Temple Mount. Pious, messianic Jewish feelings are thus combined with the Zionist spirit of the time.

FIGURE 11

Moshe Mizraḥi, Binding of Isaac and the Temple Mount Tablet, color lithograph, Monsohn, Jerusalem, 1925/26. Tel Aviv, Gross Family Collection

THE INFLUENCE OF MIZRAḤI'S 'AQEDAH IMAGES

Although Mizraḥi's work is hardly known today and has been generally absent from books on the history of Israeli art,[48] his images had a

---

48. Most surveys open with an analysis of the first art school in Israel, "Bezalel" (founded by Boris Schatz in 1906). Cf. H. Gamzu, *Painting and Sculpture in Israel: The*

tremendous impact on the folk art created both in Eretz Israel and in some communities in the Diaspora. As mentioned above, his work was very popular among the Sephardim and Jews of Islam in Jerusalem. One may find his images in some houses and synagogues of the Old Yishuv to this day. As far as his 'aqedah designs are concerned, their influence went beyond mere decorations for the Sukkah or home. The printed lithographic panels provided an inexpensive and immediate source for imitations, and, directly or indirectly, inspired the creation of numerous folk art images and objects. Thus, for example, women of the Old Yishuv frequently used his designs to embroider colorful textiles, which were hung at home or given as wedding gifts (Fig. 12).[49] Noteworthy are also the Sukkah panels, issued first for the New Year, depicting the typical "Mizrahi scene:" a bearded Isaac, the Ottoman looking boys, and, in the background, a faded image of the Temple Mount (Fig. 13). In fact, several versions of this Next Year tablet are known, created by local anonymous artists (Fig. 14), some of which were still used as popular Sukkah decorations in Jerusalem of my childhood (namely, 1950s early 1960s) (Fig. 15).

Plastic Arts from the Bezalel Period to the Present Day (Tel Aviv: Eshcol, 1951), 11; R. Shechori, *Art in Israel* (Tel Aviv: Sadan, 1974), 6. Exceptional in this respect is Gideon Ofrat—in his surveys of art in Eretz Israel, he begins with a discussion of folk artists of the Old Yishuv, such as Moshe Mizrahi. Cf., e.g., D. Levita and G. Ofrat, *The Story of Israeli Art: From the Days of Bezalel, 1906 to the Present*, ed. B. Tammuz (Givataim: Massada, 1987), 12 (in Hebrew—though the single page devoted to these artists is printed in a smaller font than the rest of the chapters in the book); and much more expanded evaluation in a later book: G. Ofrat, *One Hundred Years of Art in Israel* (Oxford: Westview and the Mizel Museum of Judaica, 1998), 7–14. Ofrat sees in the art of the Old Yishuv the "pre-historic" phase in the history of art in Palestine and elsewhere describes the work of Mizrahi and his colleagues as "religious, functional art, lacking any personal expression [. . .] removed from time and lacking any awareness of the history of art" (G. Ofrat, *"Thou shalt make . . .": The Resurgence of Judaism in Israeli Art* (Tel Aviv: Zeman le-Omanut, 2003), 12 (in Hebrew; my translation). However, in this context, it is important to mention not only the importance of the 'aqedah scene and the Temple Mount in Israeli art for the Old Yishuv, as mentioned above, but also the political connection between Mizrahi's work and the riots of 1929 (see below).

49. Regarding this fashion, cf. Y. Einhorn, "Sacred and Secular Objects, their Motifs, Sources and Essence," *Omanut ve-umanut* (n.5, above), 62 (in Hebrew); Sabar, "Sephardim and Ashkenazim" (n.5, above), 98.

FIGURE 12

Binding of Isaac, linen cloth embroidery, Jerusalem (?),
early 20th cent. Formerly: Tel Aviv, Yitzchak Einhorn Collection

FIGURE 13

Follower of Moshe Mizraḥi, Rosh ha-Shanah and Sukkot Panel with the
Binding of Isaac, color lithograph, Monsohn, Jerusalem, ca. 1920s–30s.
Tel Aviv, Gross Family Collection

Mizraḥi's tablets also reached Jewish communities in the Diaspora—East and West. We noted earlier that his ʿaqedah and other iconographic themes are closely related to the biblical images imported from Poland to Eretz Israel. In the first decades of the twentieth century things were reversed - Mizraḥi's tablets were sent to Poland, obviously as Holy Land souvenirs for raising funds, and they, in turn, influenced some local works. An important example is a large *'aqedah* colored lithograph that was printed according to the inscription at bottom right by "Concordia" in Warsaw (Fig. 16). This is clearly derived from the tablet from the Mizraḥi tablet at the Magnes Collection of Jewish Art and Life (Fig. 9)—however, it is not a reprint, but a newly designed page, and the figures are definitely not of Mizrahi. We can be certain that it is not the opposite—namely, that Mizraḥi copied the Polish lithograph—because the typical Ottoman-looking figures, the holy sites around Jerusalem, etc. clearly betray the Eretz Israel provenance of the images, which must therefore have been created in the Holy Land, and then copied in the Diaspora. Moreover, the "dialogue" between Abraham and Sarah, quoted above the central image in the upper register, is taken directly from the Medieval *piyyut* dealing with the *'aqedah, et sha'arei tatzon le-hipate'ach*— the central *piyyut* recited among the Sephardim and Jews of Islam on Rosh ha-Shanah.[50]

FIGURE 14

Rosh ha-Shanah and Sukkot Panel with the Binding of Isaac, color lithograph, Jerusalem, ca. late 1930s–40s. Jerusalem, Willy Lindwer Collection

50. The *piyyut* was composed by the 12th century poet R. Judah ben Shmuel Abbas (born in Fez, Morocco). For the Medieval *piyyutim* of the Binding of Isaac, see Sh. Elitzur, "*Akedat Yitzhaq: bi-vekhi o be-simha? Hashpa'at masa'ei ha-tzlav 'al ha-sippur ha-miqra'i be-piyyutim*," *'Et ha-Daat* 1 (1997): 21–34.

In Islamic lands, Mizraḥi's tablets were mostly influential in the "Persian realm"—including his homeland Iran, as well as Bukhara, Azerbaijan and Afghanistan.[51] The most striking example of the influence of these works on the local Jewish art are several large Persian carpets—most probably produced in Kashan—which bear striking similarity to Mizrahi's panel of 1925/26 (Fig. 17).[52] In the previous literature, the assumption had been that these carpets inspired the Mizraḥi's panel (i.e., he imitated something he remembered from his childhood), rather than the opposite.[53] Indeed, the carpets bear a full Hebrew date: Friday, first of Tevet, 5640, which is equivalent to December 8, 1839 - i.e., many years before Mizraḥi came to Eretz Israel. However, even if we assume, following Felton, that later embroiders copied the entire carpet, including the date and name of the original maker, a date of 1839 is highly improbable for this type. The conventional images of the holy sites as they are depicted here were hardly known at this time in the Holy Land, and did not reach the lands of Islam before the last decades of the nineteenth century.[54] Moreover, the Zionist flags, with the Star of David in the center, made their appearance at even much later date.[55] Finally, the said day in 5640 did not fall on a Friday, but on a Sunday. Obviously, therefore, the date is a forgery, and the carpets were produced in the twentieth century—apparently

51. Items made by Mizrahi were still in use in 1992, decorating the walls of synagogues in Uzbekisten (Bukhara) documented by an expedition of the Center for Jewish Art, Jerusalem, of which this writer was a member. Cf. A Amor, "'All Readers Shall Rejoice, While Thieves Shall be Destroyed': The Visual Culture of the Bukharan-Jewish Community," in *Threads of Silk—The Story of Bukharan Jewry*, ed. D. Yeroushalm, (Tel Aviv: Beit Hatfutsot - the Museum of the Jewish People, 2013), 195–96. Amor suggests (p. 46) in the Hebrew Section) that one of these tablets is from Safed, 1900, proving that Mizraḥi was indeed in the town as early as the turn of the century (see pp. 257–58 above).

52. Five carpets from Kashan following the design of Mizraḥi's plaque are known and preserved in collections in Israel (the Israel Museum, the Wolfson Museum at Hechal Shlomo, Kibbutz Hazorea, and a private collection). For their description, cf. Felton, *Jewish Carpets* (n.29, above), 153–55, nos. 85–9.

53. See H. Peled in *Omanut ve-Umanut*, 124; Felton, *Jewish Carpets*, 185 note 289. And cf. also Ofrat, *Aqedat-Yitzhaq* (n.4, above), [n.p.]. This matter is also discussed in Ofrat's book *Be-Heksher Mekomi* (n.4, above), 25.

54. On the beginning of these images in Eretz-Israeli art cf. H, Peled, "R. Yehosef Schwarz—hoker Eretz-Yisrael ve-tzayyar," *Omanut ve-Umanut*, 110–16; Sabar, "Sephardim and Ashkenazim," 95–98 (regarding the question of Mizraḥi and the carpets cf. ibid., 101 n.73).

55. See A. Mishory, "*Le-korotav shel degel medinat Yisrael*," *Cathedra* 62 (1991): 155–71.

in Kashan where such carpets with human figures were popular in these years. Thus, they were made when Mizraḥi was already in Eretz Israel, and were most probably based on his original designs.

FIGURE 15

Rosh ha-Shanah and Sukkot Panel with the Binding of Isaac, color lithograph, Jerusalem, ca. late 1940s. Jerusalem, Shalom Sabar Collection

It is curious to note that the influence of Mizraḥi was not limited to folk art, but also extended to some artists considered as mainstream and, indeed, as pioneers of modern Israeli art. In 1924, the artist Yitzḥak Frenkel (later Frenel; 1899–1981), who was then working in Safed, created an oil painting of the 'aqedah (Fig. 18) which is clearly inspired by Mizraḥi's work.[56] Frenkel even included the identifying inscriptions above each figure in the style of Mizraḥi. According to Ofrat, Frenkel, whose style developed in a totally different way, was reacting to the folk art that he discovered as a young artist in Safed. An even more noted artist who was inspired in these years by Mizraḥi's 'aqedah was Moshe Castel (1909–1991). His oil painting on the topic, created in 1925, resembles

---

56. Cf. Ofrat, *Aqedat-Yitzhaq* (n.4, above), opening pages; idem., *Be-Heksher Me-komi* (n.4, above), 125.

both Mizraḥi's and Frankel's works (Fig. 19).[57] In the case of Castel, it was perhaps his strong Sephardi roots that attracted him to Mizraḥi's work.

FIGURE 16

Binding of Isaac and the Temple Mount Tablet, color lithograph, Concordia, Warsaw, ca 1915. Tel Aviv, Gross Family Collection.

Mizraḥi's image of the *'aqedah* and the Temple Mount had another and more unexpected influence. Against the background of the Arab-Jewish conflict during the Mandate period, one of the means used by the Mufti of Jerusalem, Haj Amin al-Husseini (1895 or 1897–1974), to arouse turbulence among the Arab residents, was to turn the Islamic sites

57. Cf. Ofrat, *Binding of Isaac in Israeli Art*; idem., *Be-Heksher Mekomi*, 125, 130. Castel also used Mizrahi's 1925/26 lithograph of the Temple-Akeda (Fig. 11) as the background for a later serigraph, entitled "Homage to Jerusalem".

of Jerusalem into important symbols of the struggle against the Jews. On Yom Kippur 1928, the British police took measures against Jews praying at the Western Wall, and the Mufti took advantage of the turmoil to spread rumors that the Jews intended to take over the Temple Mount and its holy sites. This propaganda was supported by the Arab newspapers, helping the Mufti to spread his incitement. One of the "proofs" that al-Husseini brought to demonstrate the intentions of the Jews was a photograph of popular Jewish plaques with pictures of the Dome of the Rock and the inscription "the place of the Holy Temple," or flags with the Star of David above it.[58] Evidently, one of pictures was the Mizraḥi's lithograph discussed above. It was made two or three years before these events (Fig. 11), and achieved popularity and notoriety which our artist could never have imagined.[59]

---

58. Regarding the affair of the Western Wall and the Temple Mount in the riots of 1929, cf. Y. Slutzky, "From Defense to Struggle," in *Sefer Toledot Hahaganah*, eds. S. Avigur et al. Vol. 2/1 (Tel Aviv: Misrad Ha-Bitachon, 1971), 304–11 (in Hebrew); Z. Aner. "The Struggle for the Wall," in *The Western Wall*, eds. M. Ben Dov, M. Naor and Z. Aner (Jerusalem: Ministry of Defense Pub. House, 1987), 121–37 (esp. 132–34). On this affair in detail, see Yehuda Etzion, *'Ahlot ha-Mufti ve-ha-doktor: ha-Siatḥ ha-Tziyoni-Muslemi be-nose Har ha-Bayit 'al reqa' pera'ot 1929* (Jerusalem: Sifriyat Bet-El, 2014).

59. Cf. Y. Lossin, *Pillar of Fire: The Rebirth of Israel* (Jerusalem: Shikmona Pub. Co., 1983), 163. A reproduction of the plaque appears in the book as well. In *Sefer Toledot Hahaganah*, 305, the authors write that the remarks referred to "innocent Jewish propaganda pictures, such as the 'Mizraḥ' that was produced by the Etz Ḥayyim Yeshiva already in the Turkish period, among them the traditional portrayal of the Mosque of Omar with the inscription 'the place of our Holy Temple.'" It is important to point out that this inscription, or a variation of it, is inscribed above the Dome of Rock or beneath it in many of Mizraḥi's works (such as the lithograph amulet for protecting the home and in the glass copy of the plaque—both in the Gross family collection); Cf. Behrouzi, *Jerusalem: Spirit and Matter* (n.12, above), 30–31, items 10–11.

FIGURE 17

Jewish Carpet from Kashan (?) showing the Binding of Isaac and holy sites, after 1926. Jerusalem, Wolfson Museum.

Finally, the legacy of Mizraḥi's ʿaqedah was revived by another folk artist, Shalom of Safed (1887–1980), whose work, unlike that of Mizraḥi, is widely known and has gained international recognition. The fame of Shalom of Safed is mainly attributed to his "visual innocence" and "ignorance of [past] artistic conventions."[60] However, one artist to whom Shalom of Safed owes much is clearly Moshe Mizraḥi. The latter not only preceded Shalom of Safed in many of the aspects that made Shalom's biblical images world renown, but, in the case of the ʿaqedah, also served as a direct source (Fig. 20). Thus, the earliest works of Shalom, created in the late 1950s, were colorful toys made of plywood and painted in tempera colors, which depict various scenes in the ʿaqedah: Eliezer and Ishmael

---

60. See Daniel Doron's introduction to *Images from the Bible: The Paintings of Shalom of Safed, the words of Elie Wiesel* (Woodstock, NY: Overlook, 1980), 28.

sitting with the ass, Abraham and Isaac waking to Mount Moriah, the Binding of Isaac, etc.[61] All these scenes, and a few panels created in the late 1950s, are clearly modeled after Mizraḥi's 'aqedot.

FIGURE 18

Yitzchak Frenkel, Binding of Isaac, oil on canvas, Safed, 1924 (after G. Ofrat, *Binding of Isaac*)

In conclusion, Mizraḥi's Persian roots, and his familiarity with the Judaeo-Persian visual tradition, prepared him for his occupation as a folk artist in Eretz Israel. Once he settled in the Holy Land, he was exposed to the other "imported" artistic traditions, especially of the two leading communities, the Ottoman Sephardim and East European Ashkenazim. The folk art which he locally produced colorfully represents this "mixture" of Jewish cultures. Mizraḥi's love of the Bible, particularly the story of the Binding of Isaac, led him to learn the topic thoroughly and to illustrate it numerous times, in every technique he knew. His 'aqedot images demonstrate his devotion and deep knowledge of Jewish sources. Despite their naïveté and simplicity, the attractive images clearly reflect the ideology and spirit of the time, and imply the aspirations for building the new homeland. These images gained widespread popularity and influenced the creation of folk and high art in Eretz Israel and the Diaspora.

61. Reproduced ibid., 24.

Moshe Castel, Binding of Isaac, oil on canvas, 1925
(after G. Ofrat, *Binding of Isaac*)

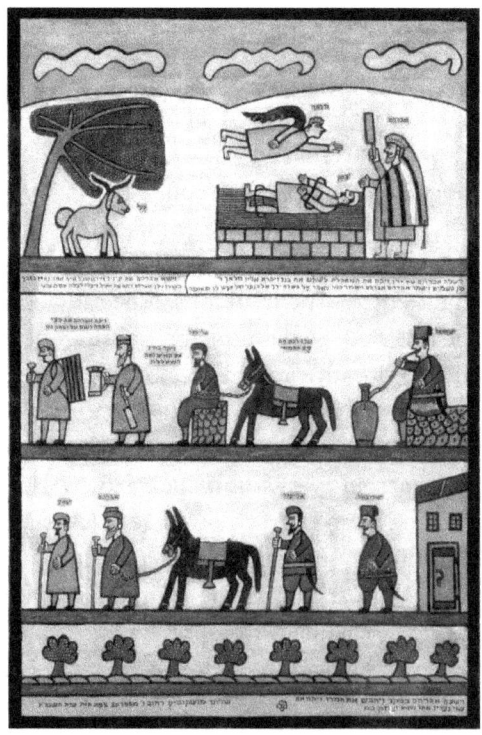

Shalom Moskovitch (Shalom of Safed), Binding of Isaac, tempera on paper,
Safed, 1958. Private Collection

12

Iranian and Jewish
Becoming Iranian American Jewish

LEAH R. BAER[1]

From 1979 to early 1981, between thirty thousand and forty thousand Jews were among the several hundred thousand Iranians who immigrated to the United States following the Islamic Revolution.[2] The challenge of adapting their heritage to an American future demanded a fundamental reevaluation of the relationship between a nation and its people as well as the attendant reconciliation of cultural and social traditions. The Jews were aware of the potential for significant changes in the features of their ancestral heritage and were determined that the disruption of continuity would not result in a loss of continuity. The American-born descendants of Iranian Jews have progressed from the status of a passive community alienated from participation in public dialogue to an Iranian American Jewish community, which, in addition to being involved with economic

---

1. Sincere thanks to Houman Sarshar, Jacqueline Soomekh, Mahnaz Farahmandpour, and Lerone Edalati for their valuable assistance with this paper. Any shortcomings are solely mine.

2. Avi Davidi, "Zionist Activities in Twentieth-Century Iran," in *Esther's Children: A Portrait of Iranian Jews*, ed. Houman Sarshar (Beverly Hills, CA: Center for Iranian Jewish Oral History; in association with The Jewish Publication Society, 2002), 258.

and academic affairs, is actively engaged in the political arena. This paper focuses on some of the experiences that the American generation encountered in their endeavor to align characteristics of their heritage to a different political environment.

The task was twofold: in addition to a different political environment, Jews from Iran were confronted with a form of Judaism incongruent with their own. The intangible symbols, images, and metaphors that defined their Judaism did not correspond with those of the established Jewish community in the United States. The challenge of harmonizing their ethnic heritage with an American ideology was compounded when they discovered that the patterns of their religious practices, which usually served as a stable, unifying core, were weakened, since they, too, had been called into question by a "foreign" Judaism rooted in the European Jewish experience. Whereas in Iran, they were a self-contained community and there was no Judaism other than their own, they found themselves in the midst of another form of Judaism, and theirs was no longer a uniquely defining characteristic.

Cultural diversity is not an unknown phenomenon for the peoples who live on the Iranian plateau. The majority of the population are followers of Twelver Shi'ite Islam with Sunni Muslims among the minority groups that include followers of Christian, Zoroastrian, Baha'i, and Jewish religious beliefs, as well as Kurdish, Turkoman, Baluchi, and Arabs among tribal organizations whose ethnic symbols are based on elements other than religion.[3] Ethnic symbols include tangible elements (artifacts) as well as intangible elements that incorporate historical data, traditional values, a network of social roles, kinship regulations, and group customs that define the cultural persuasions of the community.[4] Objective elements are the distinctive cultural features of the group that include language, territory, and usually religion; the subjective elements are the sense of kinship and community, the "we" feeling that relates to a belief in a common ancestry and group history.[5] There may be little or no objective

---

3. F. Towfiq, 'ašāyer, in *Encyclopædia Iranica*, II/7, 707–24; an updated version is available online at http://www.iranicaonline.org/articles/asayer-tribes.

4. Sudhir Kakar, *The Inner World: A Psychoanalytic Study of Childhood and Society in India* (Delhi: Oxford University Press, 1978), 2.

5. Eliezer Ben-Rafael and Stephen Shorat, *Ethnicity, Religion and Class in Israeli Society* (Cambridge: Cambridge University Press, 1991), 6, 22; also Eliezer Ben-Rafael, *The Emergence of Ethnicity. Cultural Groups and Social Conflict in Israel* (Westport, CT: Greenwood, 1982), 43.

evidence of common ancestors, but it is the group's self-perception and representation of itself that is important.⁶

In Iran, the perspective of the dominant Shi'ite society determines the parameters for the boundaries and concomitant behavioral patterns for all segments of the population. This perspective encompasses the view that earthly matters are invariably determined by Allah's will: democracy is a profanity, and, at least in theory, the government is drawn not by the will of the people but by Allah. Iranians perceive their destiny as being pre-determined with few choices: all facets of life—social, commercial, legal, political—are qualified and regulated by religious boundaries. Religion was traditionally experienced as a sociopolitical bond as well as a belief system with ethical and spiritual teachings. During the first centuries of Islam, followers of pre-Islamic religions—namely, the Jews, Christians and Zoroastrians—were granted the status of protected minorities known as *dhimmi*. They were given the right of religious freedom as well as communal autonomy in family, personal, and religious matters in return for the unequivocal recognition of Islam and the supremacy of Muslims. The degree of tolerance for *dhimmis* was neither constant nor consistent: *dhimmis* were permanent outsiders with few privileges in any part of Muslim society.⁷ Tsadik discusses the *dhimma* regulations during the eighteenth and nineteenth centuries and concludes that even with improvements in the status of some minorities following the Constitutional Revolution (1906–1911), the issue of the societal position of religious minorities persisted.⁸

A multi-phased progression for Jews to select alternatives in an attempt to improve their status was introduced during the late nineteenth century. New opportunities for schooling for Jewish children were offered through two different sources. One posed a conflict with their Iranianness, the other presented a potential compromise of their Jewishness. American and English missionaries who were active in Iran offered schooling for boys with the condition that they convert to Christianity.⁹ Despite admonitions from Jewish community leaders, some Jewish

---

6. Ben-Rafael and Shorat, *Ethnicity, Religion and Class in Israeli Society*, 6.

7. Norman A. Stillman, *The Jews of Arab Lands. A History and Source Book* (Philadelphia: Jewish Publication Society of America, 1979), 25–26, 108–10.

8. Daniel Tsadik, "The Legal Status of Religious Minorities: Imāmī Shi'ī Law and Iran's Constitutional Revolution," *Islamic Law and Society* 10 (2003): 376–408, esp. 396–403, 405–8.

9. Robin E. Waterfield, *Christians in Persia: Assyrians, Armenians, Roman Catholics*

families sent their sons to the missionary schools with the hope that an education would alleviate the oppressive restrictions. The missionaries knew that Jews were liable to unceasing persecution, extortion and contempt, and were puzzled by their intense hostility toward conversion.[10] Missionaries were aware that following conversion, the boys remained steadfast in their loyalty to their families and their Jewishness: the converts were known as "Hebrew Christians" or "Jewish Christians."[11] The converts learned English and were instructed in medical subjects; upon completion of their studies, they were awarded a diploma as medical doctors.[12] Prior to the missionary activity, the status of Jewish doctors was usually better than that of other Jews, but the availability of improved European medical technology increased the demand for quality treatment, so Jewish doctors were given an opportunity to treat more patients. Consequently, they became more tolerable members of society. Yet, in order to treat Muslim patients, in some communities, they converted or concealed their faith, but most did not renounce their Jewishness. An informant remarked "Thank G-d they needed us (Jews)," relating that her father, a doctor during the early twentieth century who converted,

---

and Protestants (London: Allen & Unwin, 1973), 112, 114–15.

10. Waterfield, *Christians in Persia*, 112–13; Reverend Albert A. Isaacs, *Biography of the Rev. Henry Aaron Stern, D.D., for More Than Forty Years a Missionary amongst the Jews: Containing an Account of His Labours and Travels in Mesopotamia, Persia, Arabia, Turkey, Abyssinia, and England* (London: Nisbet, 1886), 43–45, 49, 52–53. In addition to a desire for children to follow family religious beliefs and traditions, the hostility noted by the missionaries may have been an effort by Jewish leaders to protect an outward appearance of common purpose and harmony within the community—a matter that was essential in the presence of Muslim eagerness to convert non-believers. Lewis writes that the opportunity to convert as a means to escape degradation and humiliation "was always there and always easy, and what surprises us is not its occurrence, but its rarity." Bernard Lewis, *The Jews of Islam* (Princeton: Princeton University Press, 1984), 95.

11. Lyle L. VanderWerff, *Christian Mission to Muslims: The Record: Anglican and Reformed Approaches in India and the Near East: 1800–1938* (South Pasadena, CA: William Carey Library, 1977), 138–39. Records of forced conversions of Jewish communities, especially in the seventeenth and nineteenth centuries, relate the devotion of the converts to their Jewish identity. See Vera B. Moreen, *Iranian Jewry's Hour of Peril and Heroism: A Study of Babai ibn Lutf's Chronicle (1617–1662)* (New York: American Academy for Jewish Research, 1987), 163; by the same author, "The Status of Religious Minorities in Safavid Iran 1617–1661," *Journal of Near Eastern Studies* 40 (1981): 125; Walter J. Fischel, "Secret Jews of Persia: A Century-Old Marrano Community," *Commentary* (January 1949): 28–33.

12. VanderWerff, *Christian Mission to Muslims*, 138–39.

was outwardly a Muslim but never forgot he was Jewish, noting that food "never passed his lips" before he silently recited the appropriate Hebrew blessing,[13]

The devotion of Jews to their Jewishness is paralleled by their commitment to their Irannianness. Between 1898 and 1904, the *Alliance Israelite Universelle* established elementary schools in Iran. The goal was the preparation of students for the European perception of a useful life in a non-Jewish society; little attention was given to the teaching of Jewish subjects.[14] In Tehran, traditional families who were opposed to the curriculum protested and did not send their children to the Alliance school.[15] Soon after opening a school in Shiraz, the Alliance was asked to leave because "their curriculum was un-Jewish and their representative irreligious."[16] From the Alliance (European) viewpoint, the Jews of Iran had lost sight of their Jewish character and adopted Iranian customs and habits. They assimilated ceremonies, customs and superstitions; borrowing everything, including the lulling tone of their prayers and even adopted the Iranian way of thinking about life.[17] The Jews abandoned

---

13. Concealing one's faith is not unfamiliar to Iranians. The original motive for the phenomenon, known as *taqiyya*, was to protect the minority Shi'is from the religious and political persecution of the surrounding Sunnis. Kohlberg discusses the evolvement of an additional role for *taqiyya* associated with the esoteric nature of early Shi'ism and the related need to conceal secret doctrines from the uninitiated. Kohlberg notes the centrality of *taqiyya* in the life and thought of Shi'is and concludes that what began as a protective reaction became a tenet of faith severed from the original reasons for its development. Etan Kohlberg, "Taqiyya in Shi'i Theology and Religion," in *Secrecy and Concealment: Studies in the History of Mediterranean and Near Eastern Religions*, eds. Hans G. Kippenberg and Guy G. Strousma, Studies in the History of Religions 65 (Leiden: Brill, 1995), 345–80. See Reza Arasteh, *Man and Society in Iran*, in collaboration with Josephine Arasteh (Leiden: Brill, 1964), 40, 47–48; also Roy Mottahedeh, *The Mantle of the Prophet: Religion and Politics in Iran* (New York: Pantheon, 1985), 164.

14. Amnon Netzer. "Alliance Israelite Universelle," *Encyclopædia Iranica*, I/8, 893–895; an updated version is available online at http://www.iranicaonline.org/articles/alliance-israelite-universelle. Between 1921 and 1941 the Jewish community increased its involvement with the schools and established new schools independent of the Alliance. Ibid., 894.

15. Walter J. Fischel, "The Jews of Persia (1795–1940)," *Jewish Social Studies* 12 (1950): 119–60, esp. 145.

16. Laurence D. Loeb, *Outcaste: Jewish Life in Southern Iran* (New York: Gordon & Breach, 1977), 136.

17. Aron Rodrigue, *Images of Sephardi and Eastern Jewries in Transition: The Teachers of the Alliance Israelite Universelle, 1860–1939* (Seattle: University of Washington Press, 1993), 175–76.

everything in their practices that might be offensive to Iranian beliefs; the only thing that saved their identity from obliteration was their religion and its law, which enabled them to maintain the faith of their fathers through centuries of oppression.[18] The modes of thought and patterns of behavior assimilated from the dominant society throughout the centuries evolved into a Judeo-Persian tradition that formed the basis for Iranian Jewish identity;[19] an identity that embraced the primacy of one's religious belief commingled with elements of an Iranian cultural heritage.[20]

The Iranian Constitutional Revolution of 1906–1911 was an attempt to establish a representative government that ensured equal legal rights for all the diverse segments of the population. Those who opposed government reform argued that equal rights for all would imply religious freedom, which would be a violation of *sharia‘* (religious law); the opponents to reform further asserted that new laws had no right to tamper with the existing legal system, since Muslims and non-Muslims did not have the same rights in an Islamic nation. Reformist leaders contended that to become a modern nation, the rights of non-Muslims had to be recognized by law.[21] This was a new concept of nationality that was independent of religious belief. Even supporters of the constitution were confused by the contradictory concepts of modern secular laws and *sharia‘*.[22] The discord compromised the proposed benefits and entitlements for minority populations, and the disadvantages for non-Muslims remained irreconcilable. Nonetheless, the Constitutional Revolution introduced profound changes that provided a stepping-stone toward the modernization policies instituted by the Pahlavi regime (1925–1979).[23]

18. Ibid.

19. Lewis, *The Jews of Islam*, 78–84.

20. Daniel Tsadik, "Identity among the Jews of Iran," in *Iran Facing Others: Boundaries in a Historical Perspective*, eds. A. Amanat and F. Vejdani (New York: Palgrave Macmillan, 2012), 222.

21. Tsadik, "The Legal Status of Religious Minorities," 377–79; Janet Afary. *The Iranian Constitutional Revolution, 1906–1911. Grassroots Democracy, Social Democracy, and the Origins of Feminism* (New York: Columbia University Press, 1996), 89–115.

22. Ibid.; also, Janet Afary, "The Crucial Role of Non-Muslims in the Iranian Constitutional Revolution," in *The History of Contemporary Iranian Jews*, 2, eds. Homa Sarshar and Houman Sarshar (Beverly Hills, CA: Center for Iranian Jewish Oral History, 1997), 52.

23. The concept of nationalism compromised the traditional power and privileges of religious leaders. For the first time, non-Muslims were considered as equals of Muslim Iranians, and some religious minorities were to be granted legal rights and

The power of the Pahlavis depended upon their ability to introduce western concepts into a society governed by religious law under the powerful influence of Shi'ite religious leaders. Efforts were directed towards dissociating the economic and political arenas from the defining attributes of any particular group. The goal of the Pahlavis was to establish an Iranian identity based on a new nationalism encompassing an historical account that held that Iranians had been one of the great peoples of the ancient world for a thousand years before the rise of Islam.[24] Jews were among the peoples of the pre-Islamic world; a respondent's remark "we were there before them (i.e., Muslims)" summarized the thoughts and feelings of Iranian Jews. Religious intolerance lessened as cultural heritage, or ethnicity, became a more prominent element of national identity. There was less emphasis on religion, though not an absence of religion. An atmosphere had been created in which individuals felt freer to enjoy the celebration of their own religion. Minority populations enjoyed economic and educational privileges as well as some legal and political entitlements. A renewed self-identity evolved for the Jewish population. They sensed a revival of belonging to the modern Iran, energized by and proud of a newly discovered perception of Iranianness along with their Jewishness—not any less a Jew but a twentieth-century modern Jew with a proper national identity that also validated their religious beliefs. Jews were now perceived "as Iranians whose religious persuasion was their own private affair."[25] It is important to these people to affirm that they are something more than Jews—acceptance as Iranians implied acceptance as Jews. The Jew needs to belong, not so much for the privileges of membership as for the assurance that as a rightful resident of her country of birth or choice, she is free to be a Jew as well.[26]

The policies instituted under Pahlavi rule transformed Iran into a state with a vast and complex central government that reached into

---

included in the economic and political affairs of Iran. (Tsadik, *Legal Status of Religious Minorities*, 406). Other proposed reforms addressed issues such as land distribution, limits on the working day, and child labor (Afary, *The Iranian Constitutional Revolution*, 88). Also, though not part of the debates and demonstrations surrounding the proposed constitutional reforms, the newspaper *Iran-i-Naw* (published 1909–11) introduced European-style journalism that broke ground in its criticism of class society, anti-Semitism, and other forms of ethnic and religious prejudices (ibid., 273–74).

24. Mottahedeh, *The Mantle of the Prophet*, 312.

25. Tsadik, "Identity among the Jews of Iran," 225.

26. Leonard Gross, *The Last Jews of Berlin* (New York: Simon & Schuster, 1982), 346.

nearly every level of society.[27] As early as the 1930s, modernization policies were introduced that provided a significant step in the multi-phased progression toward an egalitarian environment enhanced by western technology. As the Pahlavi government got more involved in international business, it needed people who would not be influenced by the Shi'ite opposition and who had some knowledge of a European language, world history, and geography. Jews benefitted from the education they acquired in the Alliance schools. They were offered unprecedented opportunities and were able to acquire assets to a degree that previously had not been possible. Some were employed by the state and its institutions (such as government offices, banks, research foundations, universities, and schools); others were employed by American and European construction, manufacturing, and export-import corporations; still, others established independent businesses.

Jews now had the financial ability along with some legal right to enjoy the benefits of their successes. In the larger cities, Jews built houses and synagogues *tu khiyabun* (Pers., in the street; i.e., outside of the *mahalleh*, the term used to denote the Jewish Quarter in Iranian cities and towns), owned shops and businesses in prestigious neighborhoods, and celebrated family and community events in resplendent modern hotels. They enjoyed the comfort of central heating and cooling, owned automobiles, and followed American programs on their television sets. Yet, there remained a deficiency in the scope and latitude of Jewish association with business and professional groups. Different concepts in the political and economic areas did not signal changes in traditional beliefs. The environment did not facilitate intimate involvement or socialization with Muslims. While manufactured products and technological innovations were enjoyed across religious lines, the tenets of Islam guided Muslim-Jewish interaction. An impermeable boundary remained in place that defined the basic value system of Iranian society. There was a persistent undercurrent of popular sentiment that only Muslims were Iranian; non-Muslims were "others." The terms "Iranian" and "Jewish" were mutually exclusive.

Between the 1950s and mid-1970s, Jewish businessmen came to the United States to gain experience in manufacturing and business methods in order to enhance their economic opportunities. In addition, Jewish students were among the thousands of young Iranian men attending

---

27. Ervand Abrahamian, *The Iranian Mojahedin* (New Haven: Yale University Press, 1989), 11.

colleges and universities in America, especially in medical and engineering sciences.[28] Both the businessmen and students were usually unaffiliated with American Jewish organizations, and to most Americans, they were indistinguishable from other Iranians. The majority of them had a strong desire to return to their families and left upon completion of their work or studies, eager to be a participant in the relatively enlightened atmosphere then prevalent in the land of their heritage. A few remained for business reasons, and small enclaves of Jews from Iran began to develop in the United States. Any contact between American Jews and the Iranians was primarily business or professional with incidental socialization. Both groups were aware of the markedly different patterns of their traditions and rituals. Though there was little intermingling, networks were created that opened a path for communication between the Iranian and American Jewish communities.

In December 1978, during the turmoil that preceded the Islamic Revolution of 1979, the American Jewish Committee established contact with Iranian Jewish students to learn more about the situation in Iran and to determine how they may assist their Iranian brethren.[29] Many students were in need, perhaps more emotionally than financially; yet, they were reluctant to seek help and were apprehensive when help was offered. They did not comprehend the nature or extent of the available assistance. Moreover, they were cautious for fear of jeopardizing their families in Iran. Misconceptions arose as Americans felt that the students considered themselves more Iranian than Jewish. When several students expressed a desire to obtain a "green card" in order to remain in the United States and eventually bring their families, some of the Committee members were cynical and questioned whether their primary motive might be to participate in the "good life" in the United States. The American Jews did not recognize that Iranian Jews were devoted to their heritage, notwithstanding the alarming increase of an undercurrent of tension, along with accusations, suspicions, harassment, distrust and questions about whether Jewish loyalty to the State of Iran was compromised by faithfulness to Zionist idealism and the State of Israel. The Americans and Iranians did not understand the characteristics or the validity of each other's identity.

---

28. Leah R Baer, *Traditions Linger. Cultural Changes for Iranian Jews in the United States* (Costa Mesa, CA: Mazda, 2009), 55–56.

29. Archival documents of American Jewish Committee, Foreign Affairs Department, 165 East 56th Street, New York, NY 10022.

The relevant frame of reference for the American Jew is the comparison with the Jewish experience in Europe. The Americans were bewildered when Iranians persisted in maintaining their Iranian identity. They did not comprehend their religious brethren's nostalgia and longing for all things Iranian and were puzzled by their strange rituals and foreign ways. Other facts were also surprising to the American Jews who were—and still are—amazed to learn that Iran is home to the largest community of Jews in the Middle East outside of Turkey and Israel.[30]

Even with the notable degree of tolerance during the Pahlavi regime, the issue of Jewish religious identity did not disappear.[31] There were lingering concerns and reservations about the genuineness of social relationships. A young Jewish man felt there "was not much difference" between Muslims and himself—"all were Iranians"—yet, "down deep in his own heart," he felt his Jewishness and felt that "down deep in their hearts," his Muslim friends similarly were aware of his Jewishness. There was always the sense of "otherness," and the pragmatic option was not to reveal their Jewishness, but to feign compliance, to refrain from overt signs of Jewishness, and remain indistinct. The sense of "otherness" morphed to the American Jewish community, expressed by the first-generation immigrants as a reluctance to cultivate social relationships with American Jews or to adopt American-European Jewish traditions. Though the established Jewish community in the United States may have been willing to accept them, the Jews from Iran did not exploit the opening because the consequence appeared to be the loss of a highly valued ethnic heritage and identity. They did not leave their homeland to become assimilated with a community whose cultural attributes embrace an ethnicity incongruous with their own.

During interviews and meetings with individuals as well as groups for my initial studies, it became apparent that the Jews from Iran have a keen sense of what is "ours" and "not ours;" that is, those objects and symbols that are part of their Jewish and Iranian heritages and those

---

30. Roya Hakakian, "What Two Enemies Share," *New York TImes*, Feb. 26, 2012, http://www.nytimes.com/2012/02/26/opinion/Sunday/iran-and-israel-share-bonds.html?_r=0.

31. Tsadik relates incidents in which Jews were reminded of their religious identity, including the reportedly intentional loss of the Israeli soccer team to the Iranian team because of concern for the safety of the local Jews (Tsadik, "Identity among the Jews of Iran," 228).

things which are not.[32] The feeling of "ours" versus "not ours" and "us" versus "them" revolves around two spheres: the recognition of the philosophical differences between Judaism and other religious belief systems and the affirmation of their ethnic identity as one of the groups among the peoples who populated the Iranian plateau.[33]

The utility of communal ties is a large part of the reason for their continued existence. They are important because of their usefulness in the daily lives of people.[34] Ethnic feelings and interests are not simply a "nostalgic defense of some useless cultural artifact,"[35] the particular patterns of traditions and rituals—conveyed in the symbolic expressions of ceremonies, cuisine, and dress that differentiate one group from another—but rather, they are *ways of behaving, communicating, and thinking about human relationships, the family, the individual, and the state.*[36] There is a progression of change for those living in new circumstances where their existing patterns of social action are no longer viable. After a highly variable period of time that is rarely less than a single generation, new expressions of ethnic identity are formed or old expressions are invested with new meanings. The valued features of ethnicity are evaluated in the context of public social events rather than in the privacy of the family. Adaptations are made in activities such as rituals, ceremonies, club meetings, community dinners, periodical and book publication, and formal schooling. Other social patterns may be altered as the community is mobilized in terms of these reformulated expressions of ethnic identity. Eventually, equilibrium is achieved within the parameters of the

---

32. A respondent told of a Jewish man who was in Europe during World War II and interred in a concentration camp "even though he was Iranian and not European" (Baer, *Traditions Linger*, 95). Further evidence for the sense of "ours" and "not ours" is apparent in the archival documents at the American Jewish Committee.

33. Tsadik addresses the question of identity/ies among the Jews of Iran and concludes that religion is the "distinguishing character" of Jewish identity, which is combined with Iranian cultural elements that define ethnicity (Tsadik, "Identity among the Jews of Iran," 235).

34. Charles H. Mindel, Robert W. Habenstein, and Roosevelt Wright, Jr. "Family Lifestyles of America's Ethnic Minorities: An Introduction," in *Ethnic Families in America: Patterns and Variations,* 3rd ed., ed. by the authors (New York: Elsevier Science, 1988), 6.

35. Ibid.

36. Karen L. Plisken, *Silent Boundaries: Cultural Constraints on Sickness and Diagnosis of Iranians in Israel* (New Haven: Yale University Press, 1987), 103.

dominant society and a relatively stable tension is established between cultural identity and social patterns.[37]

The distinctive sociopolitical ideology created by the founding fathers of the United States is accepting of religious, political, and ethnic diversity, as long as the members of the different groups assume the American political creed.[38] The United States Constitution is a product of enlightenment rather than a document of doctrinal tradition. Various peoples can be accommodated within its framework, even when they are initially confronted with opposition from previously established groups.[39] This new ideology formed the framework for an American nationalism or collective identity that was transformed into what has been called "civil religion," later epitomized as the "American way of life."[40] It exemplifies values and beliefs that feature a strong future orientation with emphasis on individual achievement and equality of participatory liberties as well as the disestablishment of any official religion.[41] Although the American ideology does not include an official state religion, it does not exclude religion: the requisite freedom *of* religion does not imply freedom *from* religion. Individuals may or may not follow the tenets of their religious belief system. Furthermore, the term "equality" not only denotes equality of opportunity, but it also implies equality of respect.[42]

By the early 1980s, about twenty-five to thirty thousand Jews migrated from Iran to Los Angeles; another ten to twelve thousand settled near Great Neck, New York; smaller enclaves were in many other American cities and towns. They shopped in American supermarkets, sent their children to public schools or Ashkenazi day schools, and worshiped at Ashkenazi or Sephardi synagogues. By the late 1980s, they were establishing their own synagogues and schools; twenty to thirty Iranian synagogues are currently active in the Los Angeles area, and a dozen or more

37. Charles F. Keyes, *Ethnic Change* (Seattle: University of Washington Press, 1981), 15.

38. S. N. Eisenstadt, "The American Jewish Experience and American Pluralism: A Comparative Perspective," in *American Pluralism and the Jewish Community*, ed. Seymour M. Lipset (New Brunswick, NJ: Transaction, 1990), 49.

39. S. N. Eisenstadt, *Jewish Civilization: The Jewish Historical Experience in a Comparative Perspective* (Albany: State University of New York Press, 1992), 234.

40. Ibid., also Eisenstadt, "The American Jewish Experience and American Pluralism," 49.

41. Eisenstadt, *Jewish Civilization*, 122.

42. Seymour M. Lipset, "A Unique People in an Exceptional Country," in *American Pluralism*, 6.

are active in Great Neck. The synagogue buildings are used for social and community events, affiliated day schools (independent day schools have their own buildings), and afternoon classes for students who attend public schools.[43] The secular curriculum in the day schools is supplemented with instruction in Persian language, Iranian Jewish history and traditions, and religious studies. Iranians maintain American Jewish schools are "not for us," remarking that students are taught "what happened [during the seventeenth century] in Poland, not in Persia."[44] Some American *yeshivot* (religious schools or seminaries) introduced Iranian customs and rituals as part of the curriculum for Iranian students learning to be rabbis and teachers. Also, rabbis and community leaders are publicly recognized; in Iran, their identities were concealed because of the fear of unwanted attention from the Muslim authorities, who at times interrogated and harshly treated prominent Jews as a way of intimidating the community. Instruction continues beyond the classrooms; bilingual publications help American-born children with proficiency in Persian. Novels and history books are published for teenagers, storybooks for younger children, and picture books with captions for pre-school children. Bilingual periodicals for adults feature articles about political and social affairs, cultural events, history, and literature (short stories and poetry) as well as topics suitable for children. Also, instructional material is distributed in brochures, in pamphlets, and on websites.

Substantial changes center upon the socialization and behavior patterns of women and children. Sons and daughters are following their own interests rather than a pre-determined path in their business and professional careers; they also choose their own marriage partners. Thirty years ago, a respondent observed that the "unbelievable liberty [in America] for wives and children was puzzling... husband, wife, child do not know the limitations... kids are out late, dating, rules of the game are changing and there is family friction and conflict." Family loyalty, as well as respect for elders and others in a position of authority, are strong traits among Iranians. Traditionally, children acquired the ability to set aside self-interest and learned to cooperate in a way that insured social stability for the family and community.[45] The American ideology exemplifies values

---

43. Most public schools students attend afternoon religious school classes, some only for instruction for a Bar or Bat Mitzvah celebration.

44. Avital Louria Hahn, "Iranian Jews Blend Into Island Life," *The New York Times*, May 4, 1997, sec. 13LI, Long Island Weekly Desk, p. 1, col. 1, Late edition.

45. Kakar, *The Inner World*, 113–39. Kakar's discussion of the development of one's

and beliefs that feature equality of participatory liberties.⁴⁶ It promotes different ways of thinking about, as well as acting toward, the family and other individuals, a new cultural perspective that encourages self-indulgence rather than a sense of commitment to the community and family, fostering a way of life with an emphasis on individual achievement and self-interest, and a strong future orientation.⁴⁷ In a future-oriented society, individuals are measured in terms of potential and future productivity; there is more interest in young people than in their elders. In contrast, in past-oriented societies, individuals are measured in terms of their age and past experience. The older they are, the wiser they are thought to be, and the more respect they deserve.⁴⁸

Families are willing to adapt their traditional beliefs and conform to a modern viewpoint with regard to their daughters' future—a pattern also occurring in Iran.⁴⁹ Traditionally, for Iranian women, "their sense of self was entangled with that of their families and their communities. Their notion of self rested on the collective family identity and not on their individual selves."⁵⁰ Socializing for women centered around pious deeds that focused on the home and family rather than a public setting.⁵¹ Such ritual activities were an important way for them to keep in touch with the larger community and not feel isolated—a matter of importance

---

identity during childhood in India parallels the process in Iran since the traditional form of family organization, the extended family, is similar in both nations.

46. Eisenstadt, *Jewish Civilization*, 122.

47. Peter Homans, "Introducing the Psychology of the Self and Narcissism into the Study of Religion," *Religious Studies Review* 7 (1981): 193–99, esp. 194–95.

48. Alan Dundes, "Thinking Ahead: A Folkloristic Reflection of the Future Orientation in American Worldview," in *Interpreting Folklore* (Bloomington: Indiana University Press, 1980), 72, 75, 81.

49. Despite a regime that is hostile to a feminist ideology, similar developments emerged in Iran. Educated young women are marrying later, having children later, and having fewer children; they have more egalitarian marriages, especially with regard to decision-making on key issues. Charles Kurzman, "A Feminist Generation in Iran?" *Journal of the International Society for Iranian Studies* 41 (2008): 297–321, esp. 320. For changes in the social order in Iran, especially the role of women, see Mitra K. Shavarini, "Wearing the Veil to College: The Paradox of Higher Education in the Lives of Iranian Women," *International Journal of Middle East Studies* 38 (2006): 189–211.

50. Shavarini, "Wearing the Veil to College," 197.

51. Jewish women cultivated a meaningful religious life by turning mundane activities into sacred acts. See Saba Soomekh, "Iranian Jewish Women: Domesticating Religion and Appropriating Zoroastrian Religion in Ritual Life," *Nashim: A Journal of Jewish Women's Studies*, 18 (2009): 13–38.

in a society where women were seldom seen publicly.[52] Women are now involved in wide-reaching synagogue and community organizations, where they serve on committees along with men. They are doctors, dentists, lawyers, professors at major universities, teachers in primary and secondary schools; businesswomen engaged in real estate or owners of boutiques and fashionable specialty shops; cosmeticians who own and operate beauty salons. A few women studied at American Conservative and Reform seminaries and earned the title of rabbi or cantor. Their primary goal was to acquire an education in religious and Judaic studies rather than lead a congregation. Iranian congregations do not recognize them as religious leaders.

Educational and financial empowerment is equated with a different degree of respect for women, associated with a new level of social and intellectual esteem. A job or career signifies independence from families and husbands; women are no longer submissive, dutiful wives and mothers.[53] Some women continue their professional and business careers following marriage and motherhood. Marriages are no longer arranged by parents;[54] young people meet at high school and college events, at the synagogue, and at family or community celebrations. They date and choose their own marriage partners; most newly-married couples do not depend on their parents to provide and furnish their new homes.[55] Freedom of wives and children from traditional constraints is more readily accepted, though not without troubling consequences. It was difficult for some men to adapt to a position in the family that is perceived as humiliating or degrading.[56] Family and household authority that once was the exclusive realm of the husband and father was further compromised when parents were dependent upon their children as translators in ne-

---

52. R. A. Fernea and Elizabeth W. Fernea, "Variations in Religious Observance among Islamic Women," in *Scholars, Saints, and Sufis: Muslim Religious Institutions since 1500*, ed. Nikki R. Keddie (Berkeley: University of California Press, 1972), 400–401.

53. Shavarini, "Wearing the Veil to College," 205–7. For a detailed account of the position of women in traditional Iranian families see Farideh Goldin, *Wedding Song: Memoirs of an Iranian Jewish Woman* (Lebanon, NH: Brandeis University Press of New England, 2003).

54. Baer, *Traditions Linger*, 132–33.

55. Ibid., 182.

56. John L. Mitchell, "Iranian Jews Find a Beverly Hills Refuge: Immigrants: Khomeini's Revolution Drove 40,000 of Them into Exile," *Los Angeles Times*, February 13, 1990, Metro section, Valley edition.

gotiating business transactions such as mortgages and leases. Even mundane activities such as shopping for food, clothing, or household needs, as well as accompanying parents to the doctor to describe an illness, were tasks that children performed to help their parents. Nonetheless, the experience in interpreting thoughts and ideas between two languages and cultures in a way that is easily understood helped the children acquire skills in American social and cultural behavior patterns.[57]

An increase in the divorce rate and the more known instances of adultery may be attributed to the unprecedented freedom for women, coupled with the opportunity for children to attain their own objectives and aspirations. In Iran, divorce was not usually an option, since the societal orientation of an unwavering commitment to family and household was dependent upon an intact marriage. Protecting external appearances was a regulating ethic; family honor, prestige, and attendant social embarrassment for the individuals as well as their families were important considerations. Another significant factor was a wife's financial dependence upon her husband; it was not until the 1950s that Iranian Jewish women were awarded inheritance rights, and even then, a son was awarded twice as much as a daughter. Furthermore, in Iran, alternate arrangements for the care of children were not easily attainable. Entitlements such as alimony, child support, as well as some assets in a property settlement, were new concepts for immigrants.[58]

The incomparable educational and occupational mobility and the impact of these advantages on the possibilities of assimilation is not the focus. Rather, the focus is on what appears to be the most distinguishing aspect of the American Jewish experience: the incorporation of the Jewish people into all arenas of American life.[59] At first, many Iranian Jews were reluctant to register to vote; they preferred to stay "under the radar" and didn't want their names on lists. Even those who immigrated as children were resigned to the prevailing attitude of their parents who feared that involvement with politics and government might entail unnecessary risks.[60] Initially, involvement with the government was associated with their concern about issues that affected them such as zoning, schools, and

57. Azam Ahmed, "Children Give Voice to Immigrant Parents," *Chicago Tribune*, October 1, 2008, 25.

58. Baer, *Traditions Linger*, 140–41.

59. Eisenstadt, "The American Jewish Experience and American Pluralism," 43.

60. Rebecca Spence, "Long-Silenced Iranian Jews Find Their Political Voice," *Forward*, February 29/March 7, 2008, p. 1.

traffic. By the 1990s, they had discovered that government can be helpful; they were attending city council meetings and "participating more and more" in local political affairs. A council member remarked that Iranian Jews were "a vibrant, active community . . . [who knew] how to ask questions up front."[61] Yet, voter registration was minimal until 2000, when a significant increase was attributed to the selection of the Orthodox Jewish senator Joseph Lieberman as the candidate for vice-president.[62] In 2003 an Iranian Jew, Jimmy Delshad, was elected to the Beverly Hills (California) city council; in 2007, he was elected mayor—one of the highest-ranking Iranian American elected officials in the United States.[63] The success of Mr. Delshad was a realization that the Iranian Jewish community had a stake in the political system—that "their votes matter" and they can be effective.[64] In Great Neck, they were encouraged when an Iranian Jewess was elected to the local library board by a large margin of the vote, pleased that she won with the support of the larger community.[65]

The younger generation crossed a boundary that was impermeable to their ancestors when they became involved with the culture of the American political system. Inspired by the American ideology and the future it promised, they shed their fear of intimidation; they assumed a spirit of inquiry as well as a sense of personal responsibility, acquiring skills to enhance their lives and traditions with the privileges that symbolize the American way of life. The American generation "felt the need to contribute as new Americans and to honor our community's unique history."[66] In 2008, nearly thirty years after the Islamic Revolution of 1979, a group of young professional Iranian American Jews in Los Angeles founded "Thirty Years After" to address the issues and to institute communal changes. Within a few months, a chapter opened in New York. The goal was to add to the economic and educational achievements of their elders by encouraging involvement in political and civic affairs as well as fostering engagement with the greater American Jewish community. The organization sponsors civic action activities, programs for

61. Hahn, "Iranian Jews Blend into Island Life," 1.

62. Spence, "Long-Silenced Iranian Jews Find Their Political Voice."

63. Peter Sanders, "City Council Race Shows Changed Face of Beverly Hills," *The Wall Street Journal*, March 5, 2007, p. 1.

64. Spence, "Long-Silenced Iranian Jews Find Their Political Voice."

65. Ibid.

66. Jean Merl, "Young Iranian American Jews Look to Make a Difference in Civic Life," *Los Angeles Times*, December 27, 2014.

young people to develop leadership skills, voter registration drives, and events for members to meet candidates for political office. Thirty Years After has successfully linked pride in its ethnic heritage with participation in civic and political affairs.[67] They cultivate a dialogue that explores commonalities as well as incongruities between communities, and at the same time, undermines simplistic images and cultural misunderstandings—a dialogue that will have repercussions for other ethnic enclaves.[68]

This progression from the insularity of their parents' world is apparent in the reconciliation of elements of their ethnicity with a new sociopolitical ideology. They sponsor networking events and partnerships with American synagogues and social organizations, worship with Ashkenazi congregations, and serve on congregational boards of trustees. They also read their own periodicals, along with many different American publications; patronize their own specialty shops—grocery stores, butcher shops, restaurants, florists, beauty salons—in addition to American businesses; and continue to speak Persian and keep watch over their children (though not as strictly as their parents). Young singles, as well as families, host as many as twenty to thirty relatives and friends with Persian cuisine at Shabbat dinners. Interaction between Iranian and Ashkenazi families is increasing. There are more "mixed marriages" in which one spouse is Ashkenazi and one spouse is Iranian (intermarriage with non-Jews is relatively rare).[69] It is more common for an Iranian young woman to marry an Ashkenazi man; Iranian men are hesitant to marry an American woman, or an Iranian who has become too "westernized," who may not be able to harmonize her career with traditional Iranian responsibilities to her family and household. Most Iranians still prefer a marriage partner of their own heritage because "some of the customs and traditions are easier and the families understand each other better."[70] An intensely stressful conflict arose for some families whose children became involved with the Orthodox community: children will not eat in their parents home, they

---

67. Ibid.

68. Thirty Years After received a grant for a project to connect its own young people with those in Latino, African American, Korean, and Armenian communities. Merl, "Young Iranian American Jews Look to Make a Difference in Civic Life."

69. Marriage within families—between cousins or an uncle and niece—are not as common as it was in Iran. Also, the age difference between spouses is not as great; in Iran, it was not uncommon for a man to be ten to twenty years older than his wife.

70. Sharon Udasin, "Young Iranian Jews Now Pushing beyond Old Boundaries," *The New York Jewish Week*, Manhattan/Westchester Edition, January 2010, 29, p.1.

quarrel about Shabbat observance. It is painful when the children and grandchildren are not at family gatherings, particularly on Shabbat and holidays, or fathers cannot greet their daughters with a kiss on the cheeks or even shake their hands. The Orthodox garb is unsettling, especially when women wear wigs or cover their heads with scarves. The issue is viewed by some as a repugnant indignity, an abandonment of their heritage. In Iran, though there were differences in individual observances as well as some regional variances, there were no options based on ideology.

The American generation is aware that they stand at the critical position "where we face the inevitable reality of being the ones to take responsibility for preserving 2700 years of ancestry and heritage."[71] They feel they are experiencing the same struggle of balancing two cultures in forming an identity as their parents did. They invite their parents to some of the Ashkenazi programs; not only because they want their elders to understand their involvement with Americans, but also because they need help in reconciling an American future with the traditions and lore of an Iranian past. The twofold message to elders, "Help us define our identity and observe it as a blessing, not an obstacle to learning and growing,"[72] reflects a deep faith in cultural tradition as well as a belief that only those with firm knowledge of the past can understand and act correctly in the present. People who have been "dispossessed of their past most acutely feel the need to affirm the achievements of their ancestors," while a pursuit to form a new identity entails "reflection and selection . . . of a pattern of behavior . . . that gives authenticity and validates the self and the community."[73]

Conflict and opposition are important concepts in affecting change. They are the stimuli that prompt individuals to act (and react) in their quest for personal goals. The search for new boundaries provides an opportunity to examine a range of models for behavior, belief, and way of life that will preserve the most valued elements of their heritage.[74] A woman in her early forties who immigrated as a child related that she spent much of her young adulthood "trying to figure out who I am. I'm not really American, I'm not really Iranian . . . but I've always been

71. Udasin, "Young Iranian Jews Now Pushing beyond Old Boundaries."

72. Ibid.

73. John L. Comaroff and Jean Comaroff, *Ethnicity, Inc.* (Chicago: University of Chicago Press, 2009), 9–10.

74. Samuel C. Heilman and Steven M. Cohen, *Cosmopolitans and Parochials*, 215.

Jewish,"[75] corroborating the Iranian perspective that religion is the primary determinant of one's identity.[76] In Iran, Jews were simply known as "Yahudi" or *kalimi*,[77] or sometimes by the derogatory term "Jud." The designation "Iranian Jew" is an American phenomenon that reflects the merging of religious beliefs with ethnic heritage as an attribute of individual or collective identity. When an American-born teenager whose parents were both immigrants proudly declared, "I am Iranian," her father promptly corrected her, firmly stating, "You are American." She is an Iranian American Jew—a designation that is the bridge between her family's past and her future—a new identity that commingles traditional Iranian cultural protocols and formalities with American nationalism and its sociopolitical ideology.

Culture and religion overlap and are the means by which people assign symbolic meanings to activities, object and experiences, meanings that have something to do with values they attribute to life as a whole.[78] Social change should not be viewed as a negative phenomenon, since it focuses on the adaptation of features of an ethnic heritage into a different cultural and political system. Social instability appears less negative the more distant in time it is evaluated because the immediacy of the need for conceptual and cultural changes is usually the most challenging aspects of instability. The success of Iranian Jews in the United States, the development of Iranian Jewish institutions and activities, and the diversified patterns of participation in various spheres of American life do not assure the continuity of their collective life and creativity; neither is the fact that a pluralistic society accepts a group of individuals as a recognizable social community enough to maintain an ethnic identity.[79] An indispensable condition of ethnicity is the ability of a community to manipulate and enforce its social boundaries.[80] The Iranian American

75. Debra Rubin, "In Iran a Jew; Iranian in L.A. Author Addresses Women's Philanthropy," *Washington (D.C.) Jewish Week*, February 4, 2010.

76. Tsadik, "Identity among the Jews of Iran," 235. This observation further reveals the continuing challenges facing Iranian society with issues of its identity or set of identities in modern times (ibid).

77. *Kalimi* is the term that identifies Jews as followers of the prophet Moses, the *kalimallah*, interlocutor or communicator with God.

78. Mihalyi Csikszentmihalyi, "Social and Psychological Effects of Culture: Research Perspectives," in *Social Research and Cultural Policy*, ed. J. Zuzanek (University of Waterloo, Waterloo, Ontario: Otium, 1979), 65.

79 Eisenstadt, "The American Jewish Experience and American Pluralism," 52.

80 David Capitanchik, Review of *Ethnicity, Religion and Class in Israeli Society* by

Jewish generation is assuming the responsibility for the continuation of their heritage with loyalty and dedication.

Eliezer Ben-Rafael and Stephen Shorat in *Jewish Journal of Sociology* 34 (1992): 52.

PART 3

Modern Political History

13

The Symbolic Role of King Cyrus in Israel's Relationship with Iran

Miriam Nissimov

On November 2, 1960, there were public celebrations in Iran on the occasion of the birth of a Crown Prince, who many assumed might be named after the Achaemenid king, Cyrus.[1] On the same day Israeli Prime Minister and Minister of Defense David Ben-Gurion and Chief of Staff Lt. Gen. Haim Laskov held a press conference on the occasion of the fourth anniversary of the Sinai Campaign. Against the backdrop of a giant map, Ben-Gurion presented the security and diplomatic efforts Israel was making to "prevent the realization of Nasser's threats." Speaking about Israel's expanding ties with Turkey and Iran, he said:

---

1. Ardeshir Zahedi, the Iranian politician and diplomat who was married to Princess Ashraf Pahlavi between 1957–1964, writes in his memoir that the Shah and the Queen and a few other members in the royal family wanted to name the Crown prince Cyrus, but Shah's mother, Taj Almolok, insisted that the Prince will be named Reza, to commemorate his grandfather, Reza shah. Ardeshir Zahedi, *25 sal dar kenar-e Padeshah* (Tehran: Ataei 2002), 180. The name that was chosen for the Crown Prince was Reza and by this name his birth was celebrated in Iran; see: https://www.youtube.com/watch?v=lskNMYcvlac.

Relations with Iran have given us a lot and our relations are improving every week. Just now Cyrus was born there. But we remember the Cyrus of 2500 years ago.[2]

Two days earlier, President Yitzhak Ben-Zvi sent a congratulatory telegram to Mohammed Reza Shah Pahlavi on the birth of the Crown Prince. Israeli newspapers reported that the State of Israel would be sending the Shah an artistic, illuminated parchment scroll inscribed with select verses from the biblical books of Isaiah and Ezra in Hebrew and Farsi as gift on the occasion of the birth of Crown Prince "Reza Cyrus Ali."[3]

This article seeks to examine the image of Cyrus the Great and its place in the relationship that the State of Israel sought to establish with Iran in the 1950s and 1960s. Relations between the two countries have been the subject of books, articles and dissertations.[4] Scholars have written about the economic, the commercial, and the political, as well as the security ties. However, in the 1950s and 1960s Israel's perspective on its ties with Iran included an additional aspects which has been surprisingly overlooked.

From the time that ties were first established, Jewish and Israeli diplomats, academics, and intellectuals invested effort in grounding this relationship on a shared historical memory, namely, the figure of Cyrus the Great as he appears in the Hebrew Bible. Prominent Zionist and Israeli leaders strove to frame relations between the countries as the revival of an ancient covenant between the two peoples. The Hebrew press was captivated by reports of archaeological finds evocative of the greatness of Cyrus, which breathed life into the biblical character. In the early 1970s, Israeli academia also joined the effort and, with the assistance of research

---

2. *Ma'ariv*, 03/11/1960 (Hebrew).

3. *Ma'ariv*, 01/11/1960, *Davar* 02/11/1960 (Hebrew).

4. To name a few among the many relevant publications: Sobhani Sohrab, *The Pragmatic Entente: Israel—Iranian Relations, 1948-1988* (New York: Praeger, 1989); Tarita Parsi, *Treacherous Alliance: the Secret Dealings of Israel, Iran and the United States* (New Haven: Yale University Press, 2007); Marsha B. Cohen, *Lions and Roses: An Interpretive History of Israeli-Iranian Relations* (Ph.d. diss., Florida International University, 2007); Uri Bialer, "Fuel Bridge across the Middle East—Israel, Iran and the Eilat-Ashkelon Oil Pipline," *Israel Studies* 12 (2007): 29–67; Uri Bialer, "Between Rehovot and Tehran—Gideon Hadary's Secret Diplomacy," *Israel Studies* 17 (2012): 1–23; Doron Itzchakov, *Iran—Israel Relations 1948—1963: The Iranian Perspective* (Ph.D. diss., Tel-Aviv University, 2012) (Hebrew); Reza Zare', *Irtebat-e Nashenakhteh: Barresi-ye Ravabet-e Rezhim-e Pahlavi va Isra'eil 1327–1357* (Tehran: Mo'sseh-ye Motale'at-e Tarikh-e Mo'aser, 1384) (Farsi).

institutes focusing on pre-Islamic Iran, attempted to remind all parties of the "fruitful encounter" between the two nations.[5] The use of a common historical past, and of Cyrus the Great as the personage who symbolizes that past, was stirred by Jewish nationalist and Zionist aspirations. This article seeks to show that for Israel, ties with Iran were endowed with national-Zionist significance.

In the Zionist ideology, the figure of Cyrus and the period known as the "Return to Zion" were constitutive symbols that confirmed the right of the Jewish people to the land of Israel. Cyrus the Great was used to symbolize the historical depth of the modern return to Zion. After the foundation of the state of Israel, the relations with Iran under the Muhammad Reza Shah Pahlavi were imbued with this symbolic dimension. To better understand this dimension, we shall first discuss the position of Cyrus in the Hebrew Bible and historical memory of the Jewish people.

CYRUS IN THE BIBLE AND HISTORICAL MEMORY OF THE JEWISH PEOPLE

After the destruction of the first Temple in Jerusalem by the Babylonians in 586 BCE, many residents of Jerusalem were exiled, and the city remained desolate. The edict issued by Cyrus after he conquered Babylon in 539 BCE allowed the Jews to rebuild the Temple and reestablish its status as a cultic center. Jewish history considers this the beginning of the Return to Zion and the Second Temple period, which continued until that temple's destruction in 70 CE.[6] The biblical book of Ezra recounts the following regarding the first years of the reign of Cyrus II (559–529 BCE):

> NOW IN the first year of Cyrus king of Persia, that the word of the Lord by the mouth of Jeremiah might be fulfilled, the Lord stirred up the spirit of Cyrus king of Persia, that he made a proclamation throughout all his kingdom, and put it also in writing, saying: "Thus saith Cyrus king of Persia: The Lord God of heaven hath given me all the kingdoms of earth; and he hath charged me to build him an house at Jerusalem, which is in Judah. Who is there among you of all His people? his God be with

---

5. Shaul Shaked, *Irano-Judaica—Studies Relating to Jewish Contacts with Persian Culture throughout the Ages* (Jerusalem: Ben-Zevi Institute, 1982), Vol. 1, xiii.

6. More on the subject see: Oded Lipschiz & Manfred Oeming, eds., *Judah and the Judeans in the Persian Period* (Winona Lake, IN: Eisenbrauns, 2006).

him, and let him go up to Jerusalem, which is in Judah, and build the house of the Lord God of Israel, he is the God, which is in Jerusalem . And whosoever remaineth in any place where he sojourneth, let the men of his place help him with silver, and with gold, and with goods, and with beasts, beside the freewill-offering for the house of God that is in Jerusalem" (Ezra 1:1–4)

The edict of Cyrus the Great is also reported in Ezra 6:3–5 in Aramaic and in 2 Chronicles 36:22–23. Cyrus is mentioned by name in Isaiah 44:28 and 45:1 and in Daniel 1:21 and 10:1. There are additional references to Cyrus in the Talmud and Midrash.[7]

The historian Yaacov Shavit, in an article dealing with the place of Cyrus and the Return to Zion in the historical memory of the Jewish people throughout the centuries, distinguishes between "historical writing" and "historical memory." He observes that although Cyrus and the permission he granted to the Jews to return to Jerusalem are, indeed, preserved in the historical and religious writings of the Jews, they were pushed to the margins of the people's collective memory for many generations. Shavit shows that Cyrus' Edict and the Return to Zion were not memorialized in the Jewish calendar or liturgy despite being a formative turning point in Jewish history. The memory of Cyrus and his decree were awakened in Jewish collective consciousness during the Jewish Enlightenment movement. The figure of Cyrus served as a symbol of the "enlightened absolute ruler willing to emancipate his Jewish subjects."[8]

In the late nineteenth century, the Return to Zion became a symbol for national restoration and return under the patronage of a foreign ruler. Cyrus was mentioned in speeches given at the First Zionist Congress in Basel in 1879[9] and was even recalled by Jews who opposed the Zionist movement.[10] In November 1917, following the "Balfour Declaration," Zionist leaders hurried to draw close parallels between it and the Edict of Cyrus. Chaim Weizmann, Menachem Ussishkin, Abba Ahimeir, and

---

7. Amnon Netzer, "Some Notes on the Characterization of Cyrus the Great in Jewish and Judeo-Persian Writings," *Acta Iranica* 2 (1974): 35–52.

8. Yaacov Shavit, "Cyrus King of Persia and the Return to Zion: A Case of Neglected Memory," *History and Memory* 2 (1990): 51–83.

9. See for example: Michael J. Reimer, "The Good Dr. Lippe" and Herzl in Basel, 1897: A Translation and Analysis of the Zionist Congress's Opening Speech," *Journal of Israeli History* 34 (2015): 1–21.

10. See for example: Avigdor Lowenheim, "Herzl and the Jews of Hungary: A Discussion from 1903," *Zion* 54 (1989): 461–467 (Hebrew).

many others from the *Yishuv*[11] frequently referred to Lord Balfour as the modern Cyrus.[12] Upon his death in January 1918, one American Jewish newspaper eulogized Balfour in these words:

> Among the many romantic events accompanying the tortuous course of the world war, none, perhaps, is more romantic than the recent declaration of the British Government offering its co-operation to the Zionists in the establishment of a national home for the Jewish people upon its ancient soil in Palestine. Bridging the chasm of twenty-five centuries, it connects directly with the famous edict of Cyrus . . . .[13]

Zionist leaders did not attach Cyrus—a Persian king of antiquity— to the contemporary Iranian state. Rather, to them he was a symbol of a non-Jewish emperor who acted on behalf of the Jewish people. The repeated use of the symbol reinforced the "return" motif in Zionist ideology and shed light on its historical depth and political context, meaning that the return was made possible through the patronage of an imperial power. Zionist leaders repeatedly stressed that for assisting the Jewish people, Cyrus became known as "God's Messiah" and his name and actions were engraved in human history.

CYRUS IN THE RELATIONSHIP WITH IRAN

In the 1920s, spokespeople from the *Yishuv* continued the frequent use of Cyrus as a symbol, but not in reference to Iran. Rather, when dealing with Iranian Jewry, the Hebrew press frequently referred to Ahasuerus, Esther, and Mordecai, whom Iranian Jews believe are buried in the city of Hamadan.[14] Moreover, Cyrus was mentioned neither in reports of the

---

11. *Yishuv* refers to the Jewish community in Palestine prior to the establishment of the State of Israel. For the history of Palestine during the Mandate Years, see: Tom Segev, *One Palestine, Complete: Jews and Arabs under the British Mandate* (New York: Holt , 2000).

12. See: *The Palestine Bulletin*, Weizmann Likens Balfour to Cyrus King of Persia, 03/20/1930; *Israël*, Après la mot du grand ami du judaïsme, 03/28/1930; *The Sentinel*, A Great Name in Modern Jewish History, 04/04/1930; *Doar HaYom*, Hed Motu shel Balfur ba-Aretz, 03/20/1930 (Hebrew); *Doar HaYom*, Azkara le balfur ba-va'ad HaLumi, 03/24/1930 (Hebrew).

13. *The Sentinel*, Zionism and Religious Judaism 01/25/1918.

14. *Doar Ha-Yom*, Matzav HaYehudim beFaras, 02/16/23 (Hebrew); *Davar*, Mi Eretz Mordekhai va Ester, 03/03/1931 (Hebrew); *Doar Ha-Yom*, Matzav HaYehudim beFaras, 10/15/1933 (Hebrew); *HaMashkif*, Riza Shah Pahlavi, 08/29/1941 (Hebrew);

political situation in Iran nor in reference to its rulers.[15] In November 1925, a report headlined "Revolution in Persia" ran on the second page of the Hebrew daily *Davar*. It reported the efforts of Reza Khan Pahlavi to found a republican regime and the opposition of religious leaders to this move. Reza Khan was compared to "Kemal Pasha in Turkey" (Mustafa Kemal Atatürk), and it was noted that despite the "militant-dictatorial character" of the coup, "the government is in the hands of a man graced with the gifts of desire and intelligence who is close to the people and its needs."[16] Several months later, another article claimed:

> A new period in Persian history commenced with the ascension of Reza Khan Pahlavi to the throne, and if it encounters no obstacles erected by dark forces that use religion as a spade to dig with—Persia may well return to its former glory. The new Shah is an industrious, energetic man who strives to institute reforms in all aspects of his country's life, and controls all of the mechanisms working to awaken the ancient Persian people from it centuries-long hibernation . . .[17]

References to Cyrus in the context of contemporary Iran and its modern ruler began to appear in Hebrew newspapers in the early 1930s. The connection first appeared in articles submitted by Iranian consuls[18] or those translated from the foreign press. For example, an article titled "The Tale of Reza, the New Persian Shah who Awakened the Slumbering Cyrus," reported:

> Reza Shah Pahlavi was an ordinary army officer who, thanks to his vigor, rose to the throne of Cyrus . . . Has taken upon himself the title of Shahanshah, meaning "the king of kings," just as Darius the Great called himself in days of yore.[19]

The archaeological excavations at Persepolis made the connection between Cyrus and Iran more concrete. The excavations that began in

---

HaMashkif, Be Medinato shel Ahashverosh, 03/02/1942 (Hebrew).

15. *Davar*, HaMahpekha BeFaras, 11/18/1925 (Hebrew); *Doar Ha-Yom*, Mahpekhat Riza Khan, 12/10/1925 (Hebrew); *Doar Ha-Yom*, Paras HAKhadasha, 02/17/1926 (Hebrew); *Doar Ha-Yom*, Bikur HaKunsul HaParsi HaKellali be Eretz Ysrael, 06/19/1932 (Hebrew).

16. *Davar*, HaMahpekha BeFaras, 11/18/1925 (Hebrew).

17. *Doar Ha-Yom*, Paras HAKhadasha, 02/17/1926 (Hebrew).

18. *Palestine Post*, Decade on the Iranian Throne, 06/02/1935.

19. *Doar Ha-Yom*, 12/09/1932 (Hebrew).

1930, under the leadership of Ernst Herzfeld, were reported in Jewish newspapers around the world and in the Hebrew press in Palestine as well.[20] One Jewish periodical well-articulated the significance of these findings for the Zionist movement when writing:

> Wonderful Sculptures from the Time of Cyrus and Darius, Great Kings of Persia, Discovered
>
> When the Jews were carried off to exile in Babylon, it was the coming of the Persians that set them free from captivity. Cyrus, King of Persia, when he had invaded and conquered the Babylonian Empire, gave the Hebrews permission to return to their own country. A later king, Darius, helped them to rebuild their Temple. It is because we remember these friendly rulers, and like to think of what they did for us, that we take a special interest in the marvelous sculptures, dating from the time of Cyrus and Darius, which have been discovered a few weeks ago.[21]

The millenary celebrations honoring the Persian poet Ferdowsi were another occasion that drew attention to Iran's glorious past. On October 30, 1934, *Davar* reported, on its first page, that an event commemorating Ferdowsi was held by the Institute of Oriental Studies of the Hebrew University of Jerusalem. Speakers at the event included the renowned Orientalists Shelomo Dov Goitein and Leo Aryeh Mayer, who had returned from Iran only a few days previously. Mayer was among the scholars invited to participate in the international conference that the Iranian government organized in honor of Ferdowsi earlier that month. *Davar* was not the only newspaper that mentioned the events honoring the great poet: similar references appeared in other newspapers as well,[22] and public lectures about the "the Persian poet Ferdowsi" were delivered by Goitein.[23]

The impact these two events had on the image of Iran in the eyes of the Zionist leadership was very evident when Yitzhak Ben-Zvi, who was chairman of the National Council (*Va'ad Haleumi*) at the time, visited Iran in the summer of 1935. As he himself described it, he went to Iran to "learn about the situation of the Persian Jews, become familiar with the general situation in the country, see its antiquities, and observe its

20. *Doar Ha-Yom*, HaHafirut Be-Birat Paras HaAtika, 07/25/1933.
21. *The Sentinel*, 02/24/1933.
22. *Davar*, 10/10/1934 (Hebrew); *Doar Ha-Yom*, 10/07/1934 (Hebrew).
23. *Doar Ha-Yom*, 11/07/1934 (Hebrew).

educational, cultural, and artistic institutions."[24] In Tehran, Ben-Zvi was invited to Iran's literary association (*Anjoman-e Adabi-ye Iran*),[25] where the attendees deliberated aspects of modern Persian and Hebrew literature. There was due mention of "Cyrus, Darius, and Cambyses," and they discussed what Ben-Zvi described as "the amiable contact between the two peoples, Persian and Hebrew" in their early history.[26]

To the best of our knowledge, this was the first time that Cyrus was used as a symbol of the "friendship between the Persian and Hebrew peoples." With these comments, Ben-Zvi introduced a new dimension to the use of Cyrus as a symbol. Whereas Jewish and Zionist leaders had previously related to Cyrus as an enlightened ruler who allowed his Jewish subjects to return to their ancestral homeland, Ben-Zvi replaced the relationship between the imperial ruler and his Jewish subjects with a mutual relationship between two peoples with equal historical standing.

Two years after his visit to Iran, while in London for the coronation of King George VI, Ben-Zvi met with the chairman of the Iranian Majlis (parliament) Mirza Hassan Khan Esfandiary. The meeting was initiated by the political department of the Jewish Agency for Israel, and it was one of a series of diplomatic meetings it organized for Ben-Zvi as chairman of the National Council. At this meeting, he again related to the "traditionally friendly relations between the Jewish and Persian peoples." In his response, Esfandiary, too, spoke of the "traditionally friendly relationship between my people and the Jews since the days of Cyrus," adding that he knew that the Jewish people considered Cyrus a giant figure not only in Iranian but also in Jewish history.[27]

Prior to the establishment of the State of Israel, the main channel of communications between the *Yishuv* and Iran under the rule of Reza Shah was the Iranian consulate in Jerusalem that opened in November 1935. Consul Hasham Mukram Nourzad was well-known and liked among the

24. *Davar*, Paras—Rishmai Bikur, 08/19/1935.

25. For more on the activities of the literary Association see: Sayyed Hasan Amin, "Zendegi ve Khadamat-i Adabi va Seyasi-ye Afsar Sabzevari,'" *Mahnamh-ye Hafez* 72 (Mordad 1389 / August 2010), 22–28 (Farsi). Zahra Rostami and Morteza Fallah, Naghsh-e Anjomanhai-ye Adabi-ye Mo'acar-I daoreh-ye Pahlavi-ye Aval dar she'r-e Moacer, *Majale-ye She'rpazhohi (Bustan-e Adab) (Shiraz University)*, 4 (Winter 2014) (Farsi).

26. *Davar*, Paras, 08/19/1935.

27. *Davar*, Shlihai HaSukhnut Nifgashim im Rosh HaMemshelet Suria, 09/30/1970 (Hebrew).

diplomatic corps in Jerusalem.[28] He maintained contact with both Zionist[29] and Arab institutions,[30] lectured about modern Iran,[31] hosted receptions to mark the Shah's birthday,[32] and outlined his country's position on the question of Palestine in the local press.[33] In his public statements, the consul presented the accelerated processes of modernization and secularization underway in his country.[34] In July 1939, when Nourzad returned to Iran, the consulship was turned over to Abd-Elhassan Sadiq Esfandiary, who continued the same policy. The year after Esfandiary arrived in Jerusalem, the Zionist English-language daily *The Palestine Post* ran an article under the headline, "Modern Iran—The Creation of the Shahenshah." The article was attributed to "an Iranian correspondent" but seems to have been sent to the newspaper by Consul Esfandiary. Alongside photographs of Reza Shah, the crown prince Mohammad Reza and his wife Princess Fawzia of Egypt, the article said that the seeds of progress had been sown in Iranian society, and the ancient civilization was being reborn.[35] Newspaper reports concerning the activity of the Iranian consuls in Jerusalem, including their meetings with Zionist leaders, do not make mention of Cyrus or the "traditional friendship" between the two peoples. This absence indicated that these motifs were yet to play a role in the relationship between the *Yishuv* and Iranian officials.

The next stage in the representation of this motif in the Zionists' relationship with Iran came during World War II. Among the journalists who accompanied the British and Russian armies that conquered Iran in August 1941, there was a Jewish-Zionist reporter by the name Chaim Shoshkes. In an article headlined "In the Land of Ahasuerus," Shoshkes described his impressions of Iran. During his travels, he visited Behistun and reported with amazement on the archaeological remains there.

28. *Palestine Post* 14/06/39, p. 2.

29. Davar, HaKunsul HaIrani Be-Hanhalat Ha-Sukhnut, 11/01/1935 (Hebrew)
Davar, Le-Eimutz Kishrai HaMishar Bain Iran va Eretz Ysrael, 11/27/1935 (Hebrew).

30. *Doar Ha-Yom*, Mesiba La-Kunsul HaIrani, 11/21/1935 (Hebrew).

31. HaTsofeh, Kunsul Iran Mesaper al Artso, 06/14/1938 (Hebrew); *Palestine Post*, Iran, 06/15/38; *Palestine Post*, The New Iran, 02/28/39.

32. *Palestine Post*, Shah's Anniversary, 03/16/1937.

33. *Palestine Post*, What Iran Said, 10/28/1936; *Palestine Post*, Modification, 02/14/1939.

34. *Palestine Post*, Iran, 06/15/1938.

35. *Palestine Post*, Modern Iran, 06/18/1940.

Although archaeologists generally assign the findings there to the period of Darius, Shoshkes attributed them to Cyrus and wrote:

> We are approaching the narrow mountain pass where an impressive memorial was hewn from the rock 2600 years ago ... From a huge mass of stones a figure with a curly beard was carved, twice the natural size of a man. This is Cyrus, king of Persia, liberator of the world in his day, who freed us from the Babylonian exile ...

Referring to a monument he described as "our" Cyrus (quotation marks original) he wrote:

> For a good hour we stood before the impressive statue amazed and full of astonishment. We look proudly at Cyrus the Great, the same Cyrus who God's prophet Isaiah called the "Messiah." You certainly remember the verses—the gems....[36]

Moreover, following the conquest of Tehran, many international agencies opened offices in the city to aid the refugees flowing in from the Soviet Union. Jewish and Zionist institutions also sent delegations in order to explore the possibility of providing assistance to the multitude of Jewish refugees.[37] Writing from Iran, a member in one of the first delegations described his impressions of the country and its people with the following words:

> The Persians seem better, softer, quieter. Perhaps this is because they are more miserable and oppressed, and maybe they only seemed like that to me because they are less dangerous, more distant. I do not know their language, and perhaps [it is] because of the merit of Cyrus, who was a good king...[38]

One of the emissaries that the Jewish Agency sent to Tehran in the early 1940s was Dr. Moshe Yishai. In addition to aiding Jewish refugees and the group of Jewish children later known as "the children of Tehran," Yishai also made contact with the Jewish community of the city and became involved in organizing community institutions. On March 30, 1944, following intervention by leaders of the Jewish community, Yishai received

---

36. *HaMashkif*, Bikur bEMoshavi Ysrael BeFaras, 04/27/1942 (Hebrew).

37. Braha Havas, *Portsai HaShe'arim Me-Mizrah o-me-Yam* (Tel-Aviv: Ma'rahot, 1960), 121 (Hebrew).

38. *Davar*, BaDerkh El Gevul Rosiya, 06/12/1942 (Hebrew).

an audience with His Majesty Mohammed Reza Pahlavi, to whom he delivered the following message on behalf of the Jewish Agency:

> I have come before you today in the name of the people of Israel. The connections between our two peoples are ancient. The greatest kings who sat on this throne 2400 years ago, among them Cyrus, helped us rebuild our homeland and Temple. Now we have again returned to rebuild our homeland, and we remember well what happened at that time, and we wish to renew this relationship, and strive for positive ties.[39]

Several days later, Zionist newspapers from the *Yishuv* reported on "the diplomatic success of the Agency's emissary." The Sentinel, a Jewish paper published in Chicago, reported on "Jewish Agency presents gifts to the Shah of Iran" and the friendly relationship between the two people since the days of Cyrus.[40]

Despite these mentions, in the 1940s, prior to the establishment of the State of Israel, the figure of Cyrus continued to serve as a symbol to be attributed to an imperial ruler who graciously helped the Jewish people return to its land. For example, on April 24, 1945, one of the daily papers devoted space on its front page to reporting a memorial service held in Jerusalem for US President Franklin D. Roosevelt (1882–1945). Under the headline "Roosevelt Promised to Take on the Role of Cyrus in his Day," the article recounted the eulogy given by Rabbi Isaac Halevy Herzog, who was chief rabbi of the *Yishuv*. Herzog quoted a private conversation he had held with President Roosevelt a few years earlier, in which he had implored the president to take on the "historical role that was once filled by Cyrus" so as "to establish a new world."[41]

For Zionist leaders, the character of Cyrus the Great served to reinforce the claim of the Jews to the Land of Israel and as a foundation for its historical justification. An exchange between the Iranian ambassador to the United Nations Nasrollah Entezam (1900–1980) and David Ben-Gurion in 1947 is a clear example how each of them considered Cyrus a national asset. Entezam, who held several ministerial positions during the rule of Reza Shah, was appointed to lead the Iranian delegation to the United Nations in the early 1940s.[42] By virtue of that position, he repre-

---

39. *Ma'ariv*, Tsir Be-Lo To'ar, 05/19/50 (Hebrew).
40. *The Sentinel*, 04/13/1944 (p. 24).
41. *HaTsofe*, 04/24/1945.
42. For Nassrollah Entezam's Biography see: http://www.iranicaonline.org/articles/

sented Iran when it was selected to be a member of the United Nations Special Committee on Palestine (UNSCOP).[43] The committee visited Jerusalem in June 1947 and heard evidence from leaders of the *Yishuv*, including Chaim Weizmann and David Ben-Gurion. In an attempt to convince members of UNSCOP of the Jewish people's historical right to the land of Israel, Ben-Gurion included in his testimony quotations from the book of Ezra that report statements made by Cyrus, king of Persia. In response, Entezam said: "Your words about the Persian king who supported the Jewish people touched my heart and I thank you for them." It may be that Entezam thought that Ben-Gurion's words were intended as flattery and consideration for the Iranian representative, and he therefore thanked him for the compliment.[44]

When the State of Israel was established in May 1948 and sought the recognition of the Iranian government, the young state attempted to imbue the symbol of Cyrus with slightly different content, emphasizing the historical cooperation between the two peoples. In March 1949, under the auspices of the Foreign Ministry, *Kol Yisrael* (Israel's public domestic and international radio service) began its Farsi-language broadcasts with a speech that emphasized the importance of the relationship between "two ancient Eastern peoples in the history of the world."[45] Echoes of this idea are also evident in remarks by the Iranian envoy to Israel at the time, Abbas Siqal. In early 1949, Siqal was sent to Israel to settle property issues and the status of Iranian citizens—most of them Baha'is—who had been living in Palestine and became refugees as a result of the War of Independence. During his visit to Israel, Siqal visited with several Jewish officials and was received by the Chief Rabbis Isaac Halevy Herzog and Ben-Zion Meir Hai Uziel. During these visits, he spoke about "the traditional friendship dating from the days of Cyrus."[46] A few months later, while still working on behalf of the Iranian citizens returning to Israel from Lebanon, he again related to "the ancient historical ties between

---

entezam.

43. For a concise summary on the committee and its investigation see: William Polk, History and Betrayal: UNSCOP and Palestine, 1947, http://www.juancole.com/2014/09/history-betrayal-palestine.html.

44. *HaTsofe*, Medinat HaYehodim, 07/06/1947 (Hebrew); *Davar*, Ben-Gurion Mashiv, 07/10/1947 (Hebrew).

45. *Davar*, Erko HaMedini shel HaShidur HaParsi BeKol Ysrael, 03/17/49 (Hebrew).

46. *HaTsofe*, Konsol Iran etsel HaRav Uzi'el, 04/18/1949 (Hebrew); *Herot*, Hakarat Iran BeYsrael Teluya Be-Yishuv Ba'yat HaRekhus HaIrani, 04/19/1949 (Hebrew).

Israel and Persia" and even compared the edict of Cyrus to the Balfour Declaration.[47] Despite these declarations, it seems that Siqal did have doubts about the mutuality of the relationship between the two countries. In his response to pressure applied by Israel, which sought permission to dispatch a diplomatic envoy to Iran, Siqal wrote to the Iranian Ministry of Foreign Affairs that a precedent should not be established by allowing Israel to interfere in the affairs of Jews in other countries, and it must be clarified whether Israel is a national entity or religious entity. If Israel considers itself a national entity, meaning a nation among nations, it must be involved only in the affairs of its own citizens. If, rather, it is a religious entity, like a Vatican for the Jews, it must avoid being involved in political affairs.[48]

In March 1950, the government of Iran declared *de facto* recognition of the state of Israel. In January of that year, Siqal was returned to Iran and replaced by Reza Safiniya, who held a higher diplomatic rank. On March 26, Safiniya met with the Israeli Minister of Foreign Affairs Moshe Sharett and presented an official letter from Ali-Gholi Ardalan, who, at the time, was responsible for Iranian foreign relations. In the letter, Ardalan expressed hope that the relationship between the two countries would grow closer, in order to "promote peace, prosperity, and cooperation in the Near and Middle East."[49] Despite the covert, and possibly financial, effort invested in obtaining formal recognition from the government of Iran,[50] Israel's official response to Iranian recognition was low-key. It was not reported in newspaper headlines, and there was no official Israeli announcement of the renewal of ties with "the land of Cyrus," or "the historical friendship between the peoples," etc. For Israel, recognition was important because Iran was a Muslim country and also in the position to assist with the immigration of Jews from Iraq.[51] The "tradition of Cyrus the great" also remained unmentioned in the thank-you letter that the Sephardic chief rabbi, Rabbi Ben-Zion Meir Hai Uziel, sent to

47. Davar, HaBaha'im Hozrim, 07/17/1949 (Hebrew).

48. Gozaresh-e Mahramaneh-ye Shomareh 65 Movarkh-e 30/5/1328 az Sayqal Be Vezarat-e Kharejeh, as appears in: Ali Akbar Velayati, Iran va Tahavollat-e Felestin 1939–1979 (Vezarat-e omor-e Kharejeh: Markaz-e Chap va Entesharat, 2001) (Farsi).

49. *Davar*, Paras Hodi'a Rishmit Al Hakarata BeYsrael, 03/27/1950 (Hebrew).

50. Bialer Uri, "Between Rehovot and Tehran—Gideon Hadary's Secret Diplomacy," *Israel Studies* 17 (2012): 1–23.

51. *Ma'ariv*, Od Pirtsa BaHazit HaMuslimit Negdainu, 03/16/1950.

the government of Iran and the Shah's court.[52] Uziel simply thanked the Iranian statesman for recognizing the State of Israel.

Two years after the establishment of the State, Cyrus the Great still symbolized a ruler whose good graces facilitated the Return to Zion. Diplomatic recognition by the government of Iran was not considered part of this tradition. However, the assistance of the government of Iran in arranging the immigration of Iraqi Jewry to Israel did inspire use of this symbol. In the late 1940s, particularly following the War of Independence, the situation of Jews in Iraq worsened;[53] because of the prohibition on their leaving the country, many fled to neighboring Iran. In November 1949, because of its deteriorating relationship with Iraq, Iran threatened to deport Jews with Iraqi citizenship back to Iraq. However, as the result of the diplomatic and covert efforts invested by the State of Israel, in early February 1950, the Iranian government, headed by Muhammad Sa'ed Maraghei, announced officially that the country would continue the ancient tradition of tolerance that had characterized it for 6000 years, and it instituted an "open-door" policy regarding refugees of all religions and nationalities.[54] The Iranian government announcement was received with gratitude by Israeli officials and agencies. A few days after the announcement, at a meeting with Reza Safiniya, the Iranian envoy in Jerusalem, Rabbi Uziel warmly thanked the Iranian government and Shah, saying that it was a religious duty of all Jews to pray on behalf of the kings of Iran, thanks to whose love of humanity and sense of justice the Jewish people were redeemed from exile, regained autonomy, and rebuilt its Temple.[55] A similar message was conveyed to Safiniya by representatives of the committee of Iraqi Jewry in Israel on April 10, 1950 at a meeting arranged specifically for them to express their gratitude towards the Iranian government and Shah.[56]

---

52. The information regarding Uziel's letter is based on the report delivered by Reza Safiniya, Iran's consul to Israel, as it apperars in: Mohammad Taghi TaghiPour, *Iran va Esraeil dar Dauran-i Saltanat-i Pahlavi* (Mo'sseh-ye Motale'at va Pazhoheshha-ye Siyasi, 2015), 1.268 (Farsi).

53. For a detailed account of the Jewish community in Iraq in 1940–1950, see: Moshe Gat, *The Jewish Exodus from Iraq 1948-1951* (Portland, OR Cass, 1997).

54. *Palestine Post*, Iran Pledges Open Door to All Refugees, 02.14.1950.

55. According to Safinya's letter to Iran's Foreign Ministry as it appears in: TaghiPour, *Iran va Esraeil dar Dauran-i Saltanat-i Pahlavi*, pp. 145–147.

56. Ibid, P. 268, see also: *Palestine Post*, Members of Iraqi Jewish Committee, 04/10/1950.

The name of Cyrus also appeared frequently in contexts related to the immigration of Iranian Jews. First, the operation itself was named "Operation Cyrus,"[57] and emissaries of the Jewish Agency described their activities in light of this symbol. One of these emissaries in Tehran, Baruch Duvdevani, described the immigration from Iran as follows:

> A great thing happened this year in Persia, the ancient nation that even thousands of years ago helped us build our Temple and return our exiles, the Persian state renewed the tradition of Cyrus and allowed immigration to Israel to emerge from the underground. Today, Jews are openly leaving and in a totally legal manner returning to their country and homeland.[58]

The Jewish Agency emissaries in Iran also used this terminology in their contact with Iranian authorities. In the summer of 1951, Yehuda Datner and Baruch Duvdevani requested an audience with the Shah in order to ask his assistance with the emigration of Jews from Iran. Although their request was not granted, it was suggested to them to deliver their request to the Shah in writing. In their letter, they mentioned Cyrus the Great and the "tradition of freedom in Persia." A few days later, they received an official letter signed by Minister of Royal Court Hossein Alā, expressing the Shah's support for all humanitarian activity and instructing the Iranian Foreign Ministry to assist the activities of the Jewish Agency in Iran. The daily newspaper that reported on the story wrote that the Persian Foreign Ministry was instructed "to renew the tradition of Cyrus." Enclosing these words in quotation marks, the paper implied that they were quoted from the letter received from the Shah. Interestingly enough, however, these words were not mentioned in the letter, a photograph of which was printed next to the report.[59]

The rise of the National Front, and the appointment of Dr. Mohammed Mosaddeq as prime minister in April 1951, eventually disrupted the idyllic picture that the Jewish Agency representatives were trying to depict. In July 1951, Iran recalled its diplomatic envoy and closed its consulate in Jerusalem. Israel responded to this move with disappointment mixed with optimism that Iran had not withdrawn its recognition of Israel. *Davar* wrote that the recall of the Persian envoy from Israel should be

---

57. *Herut*, Mivtsa Kuresh, 07/03/1951 (Hebrew); *Al HaMishmar*, Mivtsa Kuresh, 07/12/1951 (Hebrew); *HaBoker*, Mivtsa Kuresh MeBirat Iran, 07/17/1950 (Hebrew).

58. *Herut*, Ketsv HaAliya Aino Madbik et HaDerisha, 07/04/1951 (Hebrew).

59. *Ma'ariv*, HaShah Tsiva Lesayi' LaAliya MiParas, 08/19/1951 (Hebrew).

seen as a moderate step between continuing proper diplomatic relations with Israel and canceling them as demanded by the Arabs.[60] For its part, Israel continued to declare its desire for normal diplomatic relations with Iran. In September 1952, the Educational Branch of the IDF devoted one of its periodic information pages to Iran.[61] Its review of the topic, entitled "Persia, Land of Petroleum and Opposites," concluded:

> Persia, despite being a Muslim nation, has diplomatic relations with Israel. It never followed the anti-Zionist and anti-Israeli policies of the Arab countries, the status of Jews there was not harmed, and they are permitted to immigrate to Israel. Since the political turmoil that began after the assassination of General Razmara, and nationalization of the petroleum fields and refineries, there has been a certain decline in Persia's attitude towards Israel, although it has not been expressed explicitly... The State of Israel is interested in proper relations with this large Muslim country, and we should hope that despite the internal weakness and the difficult political situation, the relations between our two countries will be strengthened.[62]

Although the activity of the consulate in Jerusalem was suspended, throughout the 28 months that Mosaddeq was in office, the relations between the two countries continued in various guises. The offices of the Jewish Agency continued their activity in Iran, although there was a decrease in the number of immigrants.[63] In addition, there was covert contact between diplomatic and political figures.[64] Official Israel followed the situation, and newspapers reported events in the Iranian political arena without any use of symbols related to Cyrus the Great or the ancient history of the two peoples. Approximately one month after he led the coup that toppled Mosaddeq, General Fazlollah Zahedi was asked about renewing diplomatic relations with Israel. He answered that his government was not planning to take any steps toward establishing

---

60. *Davar*, Mani'im Medinim LeSgirat Konsuliyat Paras BeYerushalaim 07/12/1951 (Hebrew); *Davar*, Paras Ve Ysrael, 07/13/1951 (Hebrew).

61. From its early days, the Education Branch of the Israel Defense Forces published a monthly information pages on various geo-political, cultural, and scientific information. These publications were aimed to offer policy explanatory pages for commanders and soldiers.

62. *HaTsofeh*, Paras—Erets HaNeft Va HaNigudim, 09/15/1952 (Hebrew).

63. Doron Itzchakov, *Iran—Israel Relations 1948—1963: The Iranian Perspective*, 112–14.

64. Ibid, 141–98.

diplomatic relations with Israel at the moment.⁶⁵ Despite this declaration, and despite the fact that only in July 1960 did Iran announce the renewal of diplomatic ties with Israel, the relationship between the two countries began to improve in 1954 and thereafter. The scale of the relationship, and the regional constraints that led to increasing cooperation between the two countries and influenced their relationship, have been discussed and analyzed in many studies.⁶⁶ However, for the Israeli use of Cyrus as a symbol for its relations with Pahlavi Iran, 1958 represents a milestone.

On December 20, 1958, the royal court announced its intention to celebrate the 2500th anniversary of the establishment of the Persian monarchy by Cyrus.⁶⁷ The Shah wanted these celebrations to be an event with international standing and recognition. In mid-February 1959, he appointed Shoja al-Din Shafa to chair the organizing committee for the celebrations. The committee worked to recruit prominent historians and archaeologists to write research papers about Cyrus and his period. Similarly, Shafa visited many countries in order to convince them to mark the event.⁶⁸ The celebrations were originally planned for September 1961 but were not actually held until October 1971. To many minds, they were a symbol of the Shah's ostentatiousness and megalomania. The motivations that propelled the Shah and his associates to initiate a celebration on such a massive scale were many, and they included a desire to display Iranian nationalism rooted in the country's pre-Islamic past, to present the current monarchy as a continuation of the grand empire recognized by the nations of the world, and to make Iran a focus of attention and an international attraction. Pahlavi Iran presented Cyrus the Great as the founder of an extensive Empire, a symbol of tolerance and a pioneer of human rights. The symbolism of this "Iranian" Cyrus had little in common with his symbolism for Jews and Israel, the ruler who facilitated the return to Zion.

Despite this, the World Jewish Congress (WJC) was one of the first organizations to respond positively to Iran's call to celebrate 2500 years of the Persian monarchy. In February 1959, as part of a mission to learn about the Jewish communities of Asia and Europe, Dr. Israel Goldstein,

65. *Herut*, Paras Lo Tehadesh Yahasayeh im Ysrael, 09/14/1953 (Hebrew).

66. See references in n.1.

67. Ruhollah Hossainiyan, Jashnha-ye 2500 Saleh-ye Shahanshahi (Chera va Cheguneh) (Markaz-e Asnad-e Enqlab-e Eslami) http://www.irdc.ir/fa/content/6058/print.aspx.

68. Ibid.

vice president of WJC and chairman of its American Board, went to Tehran and was received by Minister of the Royal Court Hosein Alā. At their meeting, Goldstein introduced himself and expressed the Jewish people's appreciation, particularly that of American Jewry, for the Shah's humanitarian policy that made it possible for Jews from Iraq, Afghanistan, and other countries to immigrate to Israel via Iran. Goldstein, who knew about the Shah's intention to mark the 2500th anniversary of Cyrus's rule, told Alā that the WJC was interested in the event because of the unique position of Cyrus in Jewish history, as a liberal king who allowed the Jews to hold high level positions in his court and permitted the Jews who were interested in doing so to return to their ancestral homeland. "We consider this current Shah as continuing in this tradition," said Goldstein.[69] The following month, on his way to visiting the Jewish community in India, Goldstein returned to Tehran. While there, he visited the Jewish communities in Isfahan and Shiraz, from where he also went to Persepolis. In his memoirs, Goldstein wrote that during his stay in Tehran, the US Embassy informed him that Hosein Alā had arranged an audience for him with the Shah. During that audience that took place on March 15, Goldstein again related to the "forthcoming 2500th anniversary of the founding of the Persian Empire by Cyrus the Great," and said:

> In Jewish history, he is remembered as a liberal ruler, liberal in the treatment of his Jewish subjects and liberal in permitting those who so desired to return to Judea in order to help rebuild the Jewish commonwealth there. We feel that Your Majesty's Government honors that tradition.[70]

Noting that he represented the WJC, which was comprised of representatives from the Jewish communities of more than 60 countries, Goldstein emphasized his organization's particular interest in the celebrations and the fact that the WJC would encourage Jews from around the world to take part in the celebrations.[71]

A few months after Goldstein returned from Tehran, the Fifth Plenary Assembly of the World Jewish Congress was held in Stockholm, Sweden. At the conclusion of the WJC Assembly, the plenary resolved to congratulate Iran and the Shah and to devote a program to the possible

---

69. Israel Goldstein, *My World as a Jew: The Memoirs of Israel Goldstein* (2 vols.; New York: Herzl, 1984), 2.21–22.

70. Ibid, 27.

71. Ibid.

participation of international Jewry in the celebrations.[72] The 2500th anniversary celebrations of the Persian monarchy were brought up also by the representative of the Iranian Jewish Community, Jamshid Kashfi. In his speech, he mentioned the name of Cyrus the Great, to which the audience responded with applause, and thanked the Shah for permitting Jews from Poland and Iraq to stop in Iran on their way to Israel.[73]

It seems to have been the decision of WJC that moved Shoja al-Din Shafa to visit Israel in October 1959. In his meeting with Minister of Foreign Affairs Golda Meir, Shafa expressed hope that the Jews would "celebrate the anniversary of Cyrus the Great who made it possible for them to return from the Babylonian captivity and help them rebuild the Temple."[74] Shafa and the committee he headed did not make any arrangements to establish an action committee in Israel but did welcome the intention of Israel and, to an even greater extent, the international Jewish community to mark the event.[75] Preparations for the anniversary, initially planned for the fall of 1961, continued vigorously; Shafa's world travels led to the establishment of action committees with the participation of senior academics, authors, artists, journalists, and radio and television stations in France, England, the United States, Turkey, Iraq, and elsewhere. Iran avoided approaching Israel directly to form a committee in honor of the anniversary, since they did not have official diplomatic relations.

Despite this, the State of Israel excitedly prepared to mark the anniversary. The press presented the celebrations as an expression of the unique historical relationship between the countries. For example, in mid-August 1960, *Davar* reported on the stamps Iran was planning to issue in honor of the Cyrus celebrations. The article stated that in a few months' time, Iran would begin celebrating the 2500th anniversary of Cyrus, "the first king of the ancient Persian Empire, the foreign king that the prophet considered the Messiah, who returned the Jewish exiles in Babylonia to their land." The article also mentioned the stamp showing a photo of the tomb of the prophet Habakkuk[76] and noted that some Iranian stamps are "somehow related to the history of Israel, based on

---

72. *Herut*, Ma Shlomam shel Yehudim Baolam, 08/14/59 (Hebrew).

73. *Ma'ariv*, Igeret MiTehran, 08/16/60 (Hebrew).

74. *Ma'ariv*, 10/27/1959 (Hebrew).

75. *Davar*, 04/08/1960 (Hebrew).

76. For a short description of the site of the tomb see: S. Soroudi, "Habaquq, Tomb of." *Encyclopædia Iranica*, http://www.iranicaonline.org/articles/habaquq-tomb-of.

historical events in the Second Temple Period."[77] Moreover, Israeli public opinion made a connection between Shah Mohammad Reza Pahlavi and the Cyrus. In August 1960, General Mohammed Deftari, at the time the chairman of the Physical Education Organization, visited Israel. Defatri was very impressed by what he saw in Israel. On his return, he said that not only politicians and public officials but also ordinary citizens in Israel wanted to express their feelings to a descendant of Cyrus the Great, the great King of Persia.[78]

While Egyptian President Gamal Abdel Nasser and his vision of Pan-Arabism were amplifying Israelis' sense of threat, Israeli public opinion was captivated by the connection between Mohammad Reza Pahlavi and Cyrus. This connection became even more concrete in October 1960 with the birth of Crown Prince and the rumor-based assumption that he will be named Cyrus.[79] Israelis considered the reports that the Shah would, sometime in the future, appoint an heir apparent who bore the name Cyrus very symbolic.[80] Israel officially congratulated the Shah on the birth of the Crown Prince and, as noted at the beginning of this article, President Yitzhak Ben-Zvi sent the Shah a gift inscribed with verses from the book of Isaiah. Moreover, the Israeli press dealt with the political impact of the birth and the symbolism of the name "Cyrus." One newspaper wrote that in light of attempts by the Kremlin and the "Egyptian dictator," who had become a "tool in the hands of Khrushchev," to undermine the stability of the royal house, the birth of the Crown Prince was an imponderable but very powerful factor for weakening hostile forces. The newspaper added that the State of Israel was interested in a friendly relationship with Persia, and "perhaps there is symbolism in the fact that the name given to the Crown Prince is Cyrus, a name that is related to Hebrew history and the return of the Jewish people from exile and the establishment of the Second Temple."[81] Reports of popular Israeli expressions of joy appeared on newspapers' front pages.[82] For example, *Ma'ariv* reported on the celebrations held by Iranian Israelis, including some who

77. *Davar*, Kever Habakuk BeBul PArsi, 08/12/1960 (Hebrew).
78. *Ma'ariv*, HaNegev Shel Paras, 08/16/1960 (Hebrew).
79. See n.1.
80. *Ma'ariv*, Malkat Paras Nikhnesa leBait Yuldot 10/31/1960 (Hebrew).
81. *Herut*, Berakhut Ysrael LeIran 11/01/1960 (Hebrew).
82. *Davar*, 11/01/60; *Davar* 02/22/1960; *Herut* 11/01/1960; *Herut*, 11/02/1960 (Hebrew).

displayed portraits of the Shah on their car windows.[83] The day after the birth, there were reports about the feelings of the new father, in which the Shah was quoted as saying that the birth of his child is the heaviest blow struck on the heads of the enemies of Allah and the Persian nation.[84]

Cyrus as a bridge between the two nations was expected to find tangible expression in early 1961, when an Israeli businessman promoted the idea of building two memorials to Cyrus, one in Ramat Gan National Park and the other in the heart of Tehran. In his travels to Iran, he attempted to recruit Jewish communal leaders and Iranian officials with whom he had business contacts for the project. He also claimed that "the brother of the Shah of Persia was enthusiastic about the idea and promised to assist in its realization."[85]

The preoccupation with Cyrus and positioning him as a symbol of the relationship between the two countries received official approval at the 1961 National Bible Conference. Held in Israel since 1952, the conferences were emblematic of the country's "emerging culture and national character."[86] They were official, gala events and attracted large crowds, including dozens of researchers and teachers.[87] The president and his wife honored the conferences with their attendance at a session, as did the prime minister and other senior ministers. The officials brought their greetings, and some even delivered scholarly lectures.[88] At the ninth conference in 1961, Prime Minister David Ben-Gurion delivered a lecture that highlighted the Bible's sympathetic attitude to Cyrus and said that it credited Cyrus with being one of the most important statesmen of his generation, who successfully established the greatest empire in only eleven years. At the conference, to which two members of the Iranian Majlis were invited, Ben-Gurion said—not without reference to the rule of the Shah and his status in the Middle East—that the success of Cyrus in establishing a large, strong, and stable empire was the result of his of

---

83. *Ma'ariv*, Psokim al Koresh, Matnat Ysrael LeShah, 11/01/1960 (Hebrew).

84. *Ma'ariv*, HaShah Kava' Lishkato BaBait Holim, 11/02/1960 (Hebrew).

85. *Herut*, Moshe Braz Maki, shtai Andarta'ot LeKoresh Melkh Paras, 03/03/1961 (Hebrew).

86. Yehuda Elitsur, "Hakinus HaArtsi HaAsiri LeTanakh," *Bait HaMikra*, Vol. 7, No. 2 (14): 1962, 168 (Hebrew).

87. *Ma'ariv*, Shivat Tsion veG'olat Ysrael, 02/28/1958 (Hebrew).

88. Elitsur, Ibid.

chivalry toward his enemies and his tolerance towards all religions, as expressed in his decisive role in the movement for returning to Zion.[89]

The conference theme and the guests from Iran led *Ma'ariv* to write that the Bible Conference had become a "demonstration of friendship between Israel and Persia."[90] *Davar* published an interview with the visitors from Iran, Majlis members Mustafa Alamouti and Muhammad Ali Moadel. The visitors described their positive impressions from their tours throughout Israel and were quoted as saying that "considering the great achievements of Israel, they are proud of being descendants of Cyrus king of Persia, who permitted the return to Zion 2500 years ago."[91]

A few months later, in August 1961, the organizers of the World Congress of Jewish Studies in Jerusalem devoted a special session to the Edict of Cyrus. Renowned Iranian scholar Ebrāhim Pourdāvoud (1885–1968) attended the congress on behalf of Tehran University.[92] President Yitzhak Ben-Zvi was among those who participated and lectured at the conference. In his speech, Ben-Zvi praised the work of Cyrus and described the connection between the Jewish and Persian peoples, saying:

> ... Two peoples with extreme longevity both met on the stage of history two centuries before Alexander of Macedonia and continued long after. Both have dealt with the ancient Greek and the Roman-Byzantine worlds, and both passed the test; both live and exist even after the two ancient worlds sunk into oblivion. Both created and continue to create human values, the inalienable assets of human civilization, even after the Arab conquest and the Crusades, and the periods of Genghis Khan and the Mamelukes. Today, we are honored to bear witness to the rebirth of fledgling Israel and modern Persia, which has renewed its youth as an eagle ... .[93]

That Cyrus became a symbol of the relationship and connection between Israel and Iran was evident in an event that brought Ben-Gurion to Tehran for a few hours. In December 1961, newspapers reported that on his way to Burma, a malfunction of his plane forced Ben-Gurion to change planes in Tehran. According to these reports, when he landed in

---

89. *Ma'ariv*, 03/27/1961 (Hebrew).

90. *Ma'ariv*, 03/27/1961, *Davar*, 03/27/1961 (Hebrew).

91. Davar, Hats'harat Yedidut Parsit Le Ysrael, 03/27/1961 (Hebrew).

92. *Third World Congress of Jewish Studies*, Jerusalem 25 July—1th August 1961, Report.

93. Y. Ben-Zvi, Koresh veTafkido BeTkomat Ysrael, *Davar*, 08/04/1961 (Hebrew).

Tehran airport, Ben-Gurion was greeted by senior representatives of the Iranian government, and the parties held "bilateral talks focusing on cultural relations and historical ties between the two countries." The newspaper added, "the axis of the conversation was, of course, Cyrus king of Persia, who allowed the return to Zion."[94]

Moreover, "the historical relationship" between the two nations was mentioned repeatedly in news stories dealing with relations between Iran and Israel. In September 1962, a few days after an earthquake in Buin Zahra, a town near Qazvin, caused 12,000 deaths and great destruction, one paper wrote:

> In addition to the general humanitarian aspect, which compels all human society, Israel feels an emotional need to supply any help the victims of the earthquake in Persia require because it is the country of Cyrus—with a tradition of friendship with the Jewish people from our first days on the stage of history—and even now continues this fine tradition in its ties with the fledgling State of Israel . . .[95]

In another article, entitled "Following Cyrus," the writer told his readers how excited he was to visit Persepolis and how the Iranian tour guide blushed when he showed him the Biblical verses that mention Cyrus.[96]

However, the use of Cyrus the Great as a symbol of the relationship between the two countries waned in mid 1960s and 1970s. Just when relations between Israel and Iran became closer and more visible, Israeli leaders and the press stopped using this symbol. Reports about visits by high rank officials lacked any reference to Cyrus or the "friendship between the two nations." In January 1963, for the first time, news about a visit to Tehran by Israeli Chief of Staff General Tzvi Tzur was publicized. "Glasses were raised to the life of the Persian army and the IDF," read a headline reporting the visit.[97] The paper noted the appreciation for the IDF that the Chief of Staff felt "in his contacts with senior Persian military officers during both meetings and the oriental-style meals." A month later, newspapers reported an unofficial visit of Foreign Minister Golda Meir to Tehran. Her associates told *Ma'ariv*, "Mrs. Meir's talks in Tehran

---

94. *Davar*, Kabalt Panim Levavit leBen Gurion BeRangun Ahar De'ga LeShlomo, 12/06/61 (Hebrew).

95. *Herut*, Ysrael Mishtatefet Be Tsa'ra shel Paras, 09/05/62 (Hebrew).

96. *Ma'ariv*, Be-'ikvot Koresh 10/09/1964 (Hebrew).

97. *Ma'ariv*, 10/03/1963 (Hebrew).

will find practical expression in relations between Israel and Persia."[98] The reports regarding Chief of Staff's visit as well as those relating to Golda Meir's visit lacked any reference to any symbolic aspects of the relationship between the two countries. The absence of this symbol was also conspicuous in reports about the coronation of the Shah in October 1967. Although these reports mentioned the 2500 years of the monarchy, "legendary oriental splendor" and even the "fair attitude towards Israel" on the part of the Shah, it did not say anything about the reign of Cyrus, or symbolism of the coronation, or anything related.[99]

The decreasing frequency of use of Cyrus the Great as a symbol for relations with Iran, despite the expansion of ties between the two countries, suggests that in these years Israel had less need for the symbol. It could be that a symbol related to the return to Zion under the auspices of an imperial ruler was less necessary because Israel felt more secure in its existence.

However, Cyrus did not entirely lose his place as a symbol for relations between the two countries, even in the 1970s. For example, he reappeared in the summer and fall of 1971, when Iran held celebrations commemorating the 2500th anniversary of Cyrus's reign. Israeli newspapers expressed disappointment that Israel had not been invited to the ceremony. In an article, entitled "Contrary to the Spirit of Cyrus," one paper protested that representatives of the people who are "the only living testimony to the contribution of Cyrus" were not invited to the ceremony.[100] In the early seventies, the Israeli academics participated in the preservation and cultivation of knowledge about the historical connections between the two nations. In the early 1970s, the Department of Iranian–Armenian Studies at the Hebrew University in Jerusalem initiated the publication of a collection of essays dedicated to Jewish Iranian history. Shaul Shaked, the distinguished scholar of Zoroastrian religion and the Sasanian Period, edited the volume and wrote in his introduction that Jewish Iranian history provides us with one of the longest and most fecund cultural encounters between two divergent cultures in human experience.[101] Although the idea for this collection was conceived when relations between the State of Israel and Iran were friendly, the

98. *Ma'ariv*, 02/06/1963 (Hebrew).
99. *Ma'ariv*, 10/27/67, *Davar*, 10/27/67 (Hebrew).
100. *Davar*, 08/13/1971, 10/28/1971, 10/29/1971 (Hebrew).
101. Shaul Shaked, *Irano-Judaica*, Vol, 1, ix.

volume was eventually published in 1982, when the political climate in both countries was less favorable for research dealing with the historical friendship between the Jews and the Iranian people.

This article sought to analyze the place that was given in the fifties and early sixties in Israel to the image of Cyrus in its relations with Iran. One important conclusion that can be drawn from this analysis is that for many in Israel, the relations with Iran were perceived as a "renewal" of the ties with Cyrus, King of Persia. In her article titled "The Bible and Israeli Identity," Anita Shapira addresses the supremacy of the Bible in modern Jewish nationalism. She writes that it endowed the young Jewish nationalism with a mythological-historical foundation to consolidate its distinctiveness around its ancestral land, serving as evidence of the "naturalness" of the Zionist solution to the Jewish problem. Shapira continues to write that The Return to Zion of the Persian era took on current relevance and was reapplied to the same landscape for the same people. Zionism seemed to be recapturing and reconstructing the drama that unfolded in the Books of Ezra and Neḥemiah.[102] This article sought to show that even if Israel's relations with Iran were established due to geopolitical considerations and Israel's need for allies beyond the circle of hostile neighboring Arab countries,[103] for Israel, the relation had a symbolic dimension, one that fed the nationalist Jewish narrative as constructed by the Zionist ideology.

---

102. Anita Shapira, "The Bible and the Israeli Identity," *AJS Review* 28:1 (2004): 13.

103. Uri Bialer, "The Iranian Connection in Israel's Foreign Policy 1948–1951," *Middle East Journal* 39:2 (1985): 292–315.

14

Jews in the Pre-Constitutional Years
The Shiraz Incident of 1905

DANIEL TSADIK

Be-karestan-e Sane' kas cheh danad,
kherad dar kar-e U hayran bemanad.[1]

THE REIGN OF MUZAFFAR al-Din Shah (r. 1896–1906) heralded a new era in the history of modern Iran: towards the end of his rule, the Shah granted his approbation for drafting a constitution and for the establishment

---

1. Shahin, *Shahin-i Turah*, ed. M. Khooban (Los Angeles: Ketab, 1999), 280. This article is dedicated to my dear friends Jubin and Natalie Meraj for their friendship and never-failing support. Deep thanks are also due to David Yeroushalmi, Houman Sarshar, Houchang Chehabi, Janet Afary, Dominic Brookshaw, the late Avraham Cohen, and the outside reader for commenting and improving this article. Special gratitude goes to my dear friends Yoni Toobian and Ilan Hayim-Poor for their tremendous support. All shortcomings are solely mine.

The archives utilized in this article are:
Alliance Israélite Universelle Library (AIU), Paris.
National Library, Jerusalem (JNL).
Metropolitan Archives (CFC=Conjoint Foreign/Jewish Committee; JBD=Jewish Board of Deputies), London.
Ministère des Affaires Étrangères (MAE), Paris.
Public Record Office (FO), London.

of a body representing the population's voice, a *majlis*, or parliament. The very promulgation of laws calling for reforms such as a parliamentary system, limitations on the Shah's authority, and constitutional government, constituted a major break with past institutions. As shown elsewhere, during the Constitutional years (1906–1911), the legal status of the Jews and some other religious minorities improved, even if only to a limited extent.[2]

Can one assume that this change in the legal status of the Jews—restricted as it was—reflected changes of the public's actual treatment toward the Jews during the days leading up to the Constitutional Revolution in 1906? To an extent, the answer is in the affirmative, and one can detect some limited glimmers of a more positive and equality-orientated approach toward the Jews.[3]

The present article argues, however, that, even if important, these subtle currents nevertheless did not reflect all of society. Many social segments generally were still harsh on the Jews. The real life situation of the Jews in the years leading up to the Constitutional Revolution was, at many times, still one of abuse and occasional persecution. To prove this contention, part I of this chapter will present some of these cases in a general fashion—from Kirmanshah, Tehran, Lar, and elsewhere, indicating their dispersion and commonality. Part II will establish some of the reasons for the attacks on Jews—not only religious, but also economic and socio-political ones, and it will also briefly suggest certain recurring paradigms surrounding it. Part III will look more closely at one case study from November 1905 in the city of Shiraz, demonstrating the situation and attempting to offer some insights as to its roots. Finally, this preliminary research will end with some concluding remarks.

---

2. D. Tsadik, "The Legal Status of Religious Minorities: Imami Shi'i Law and Iran's Constitutional Revolution," *Islamic Law and Society* 10 (2003): 406–408.

3. E.g. J. Afary, "Inqilab-i Mashrutah: Nukhustin Gam baraye Mubarazah ba Yahudi Sitizi dar Iran-i Qarn-i Bistum," *Yahudiyan-i Irani dar Tarikh-i Mua'sir*, ed. H. Sarshar (Center for Iranian Jewish Oral History: Beverly Hills, 1997), vol. 2, Persian section, 40–41. For a case of good relations between Jews and Muslims: AIU. *Bulletin Mensuel* 31 (1903): 102. Apparently written in the late nineteenth or early twentieth century, during the reign of Muzaffar al-Din Shah, the following *roman* indirectly criticizes segments of Muslim society for its killing and mistreating the Jews; see H. Vahouman (Corrector), *Juhud Kushan (Johud Koshan)* (Stockholm: Kitab-i Arzan, 1383/2005).

THE GENERAL SITUATION

In certain respects, the assassination of Nasir al-Din Shah (r. 1848–1896) and the coronation of his son, Muzaffar al-Din Shah in 1896, did not mark a new beginning for the Jews of Iran.[4] Certain themes observed during Nasir al-Din Shah's reign with reference to the Jews' position were to proceed under his son. Compared with the Jews' situation under Nasir al-Din Shah, the Jews during Muzaffar al-Din Shah's rule (r. 1896–1906) seem to have been equally mistreated and persecuted. In some locales, the days of Muzaffar al-Din Shah witnessed the worsening condition of the Jews.[5]

In Kirmanshah, the Jews' situation deteriorated in 1893. On the Hebrew date of 14 Sivan TaRNaG (May 29, 1893), the Jews of Kirmanshah suffered a major blow, as a local Shiʻi cleric accused a Jew of blaspheming the Prophet. Consequently, fourteen Jewish houses were looted and property was destroyed; the losses amounted 7,000 toman. Fearing for their money and life, some of the elderly (*zqenim*) and notables (*nikhbadim*) of the community converted to Islam.[6] They underwent other kinds of pressure as well. One example is the inheritance law: if Muslims and infidels are heirs of a person, the Muslims inherit the entire estate. The new converts applied this law. The community thus cried for help, stating that "if the skies are canvases (*yeriʻot*) and the trees are writing quills (*qolmusim*) and the seas are ink—they thus shall write the anguish

---

4. On Jews during Nasir al-Din Shah's reign, see: W. Fischel, "The Jews of Persia, 1795–1940," *Jewish Social Studies*, 12 (1950): 119–60. A. Netzer, "Qorot Yehudey Paras mi-Reshit ha Meah ha-19" in *'Edot Israel*, ed. A. Stahl (Tel Aviv: 'Am 'Oved, 1979): vol. 2, 265–71. D. Tsadik, *Between Foreigners and Shiʻs: Nineteenth Century Iran and its Jewish Minority* (Stanford: Stanford University Press, 2007).

5. Examples for the exacerbation of the Jews' plight under Muzaffar al-Din Shah: AIU: Iran.XI.E, Seneh, 5 Kislev TaRNaZ [=November 10, 1896], Sinih community to AIU. AIU. *Bullletin Mensuel*, XXIV (1896), 174. AIU: Iran. II.C.6, Teheran, TaRNaZ, received in July 1897, Tehran community to AIU. Schwarzfuchs, S, "Qehilat Isfahan Meshavaʻt le-ʻEzrah mi-KIH," *Peʻamim*, 6 (1980), 76. AIU: Iran, I.B.4, Cazran, 12 of Tishrey, TaRNaH [=October 8, 1897], Kazarun community to Baghdad. AIU: Iran. I.C.3 bis, Kachan, Adar I, TaRSaB [=February or March 1902], Kashan community to AIU.

6. AIU: Iran. II.C.4, Kermanchah, August 9, 1893, Kirmanshah community to AIU. Cohen, A. *Ha-Qehila ha-Yehudit be-Kirmanshah* (Jerusalem: Misrad ha-Hinukh ve-ha-Tarbut, 1992), 14–15. Apparently refereeing to this incident, FO 60/543, no. 100, June 14, 1893, Lascelles to FO, and memorandum by Cadogan, claims that "the Jews' complaints were exaggerated." One may assume that this and other conversion cases were possibly mostly nominal expressions of faith as a defensive mechanism.

and intensity of our exile (*galuteynu*) which, on a daily basis, grows further and further."⁷

Persecutions of Jews in Kirmanshah continued during the last days of Nasir al-Din Shah. A report from March 10, 1896, described the rise of the price of foodstuff by the governor of Kirmanshah. Conveying their discontent with this development, the population pillaged the Jewish quarter and wrecked havoc amounting 2,000 toman. "Then, they decided to massacre the Jews," and as a result, a large number of Jews embraced Islam to escape the imminent death. The composers of the letter contended that the 'ulama encouraged the new converts to mistreat their former brethren and incited the Muslims against the Jews, pushing them to loot the Jews and assault (*violenter*) their women and daughters. "The mullahs are much more influential than the Shah and his governors," claimed the Jews.⁸

Apparently, no salvage was guaranteed, and the grave situation only exacerbated in the early months of Muzaffar al-Din Shah's rule. Several months after the above dispatch, the Kirmanshah community sent letters to the Anglo-Jewish Association (AJA) in London and the *Alliance Israélite Universelle* (AIU) in Paris, probably through the AIU headmaster in Baghdad. They complained about the Jewish converts, who pressured them to join their new faith and who defamed them in the eyes of the 'ulama. The 'ulama harassed the Jews, occasionally by beating and imprisoning them—all in order to exact money from them. As usual in conversion cases, the inheritance law was enforced. The problem, however, was rooted not only in the converts, nor even solely in the 'ulama. The "authorities," who had a "great fear" of the 'ulama, did not pay heed to the Jews' "numerous appeals." Some "high functionaries," that is, the "protector of Jews," and the Head of the Gendarmerie, hindered the Jews' complaints from reaching the governor.⁹ Unable to resort to the local

---

7. AIU: Iran. II.C.4, Kermanchah, 13 [or: 17] of *mekhilan de-rahamim* [=Elul], TaRNaG [=August 25 or 29, 1893], received on September 22, 1893, Kirmanshah community to AIU. The inheritance law was abrogated on various occasions during the nineteenth century; see: Tsadik, *Between Foreigners and Shi'is*, 110, 116, 152, 232, 239.

8. AIU. *Bulletin Mensuel*. 24 (July, 1896): 101–102, Kirmanshah community to AIU, 25 Adar 5656 [=March 10, 1896]. Cohen, 15–17.

9. JBD: ACC/3121/BO2/09/009, file 2, Kirmanshah, 16 Elul, 5656 [=August 25, 1896], [Kirmanshah community] to AJA. Same is in: AIU. *Bulletin Mensuel* 24 (December, 1896): 172, probably with a mistaken date of September 16. On the office of the "protector of the Jews," see Tsadik, *Between Foreigners and Shi'is*, 50–52.

system of justice or to find redress to the wrongs committed against them, the Jews thus turned to foreign assistance, that of their European co-religionists. Their foreign brethren, in turn, activated their foreign ministries or other influential Jews such as Messrs Sassoon—a wealthy Jewish family with mercantile activity and connections with the highest administrators of Iran—on behalf of the Jews of Iran.[10]

Maltreatment of the Jews was not restricted to remote corners of Muzaffar al-Din Shah's empire. The Jews of the capital also faced certain hardships, including inability to "raise a head amongst the nations [i.e. the Muslims], even to walk two meters (*arba' amot*)" without being beaten and spat upon. Now, in the words of one Jewish dispatch, when the pious Nasir al-Din Shah had passed away, the 'ulama (*komarim*) decreed that the Jews be isolated as leprosy stricken people. They re-ordered the Jews to have patches on their clothing so as to mock them. The inheritance law was in force. In one incident, it was Muzaffar al-Din Shah who saved the Jews from a certain impending massacre and pillage.[11]

These general words seem to partially allude to the following event: In 1897, Sayyid Rayhan Allah, a Shi'i cleric, declared that the Jews must wear a red patch and have a hair style different from that of Muslims.[12] Other prohibitions included forbidding Jews from riding horses, wearing

10. JBD: ACC/3121/BO2/09/009, file 2, October 28, 1896, AJA in connection with AIU to L. Emanuel. CFC: minute book: ACC/3121/C11A/001, November 4, 1896. JBD: ACC/3121/BO2/09/009, file 2, November 13, 1896, David Sassoon to L. Emmanuel/JBD. JBD: ACC/3121/BO2/09/009, file 2, November 30, 1896, FO to CFC. MAE: Correspondance Politique et Commerciale/1897–1918 (nouvelle serie), Perse, box number 52, file: Ecoles Francais, 1897–1907; sub file: l'Alliance Israelite et les Juifs de Perse, AIU to MAE, December 15, 1896. AIU. *Bulletin Mensuel*. XXIV (December, 1896), 172–173.

11. AIU: Iran. II.C.6, Teheran, TaRNaZ, received on July 1897, Tehran community to AIU.

12. AIU: Iran.II.C.6, Teheran, May 17, 1897, Meyer Levy/Tehran to AIU. This letter with omissions is in: AIU. *Bulletin Mensuel*. 25 (June, 1897): 70–71. Cf.,: H. Sahim, "Jews of Iran in the Qajar Period; Persecution and Perseverance," in *Religion and Society in Qajar Iran*, ed. R. Gleave (London: RoutledgeCurzon, 2005), 302–3. FO 60/595, no. 14, January 28, 1898, Hardinge to FO (A biographical dictionary, page 71): "Aka Sayyid Raihan Ullah, Burujirdi—is the leader of the anti-Jewish party. Persecuted the Jews in Hamadan a year or two ago, and led the movement against them in Tehran in 1897. Resides close to the mosque of Muhammad Khan, Sipah Salar; is very learned, but not much respected by other *Mujtahid*s; has many followers among the lower classes. Age about 55." On him, see also: M. Hasan Khan, I'timad al Saltanah, *Chihil Sal Tarikh-i Iran dar Dawrah-yi Padishah-yi Nasir al-Din Shah; Al-Mathir wa-al-Athar*, ed. I. Afshar (Tehran: Asatir, 1363–1368), vol 1, 211.

socks, and leaving their houses when it rains. Their houses cannot be at the same height of Muslims', and Jewish women's trousers must have different colors for each leg. Seeking redress, the Jews turned to various avenues for help, including the important *mujtahid* Hasan Ashtiyani, who wrote to Rayhan Allah on the matter, but to no avail. Amin al-Dawlah, the Prime Minister, threatened to exile Rayhan Allah from Tehran, but the Sayyid stated he was ready to depart. Attempting to avert the imposed discriminatory laws, the Jews reportedly offered Rayhan Allah large sums of money.[13]

Apparently, on May 9, 1897, possibly sometime after Rayhan Allah's call on the Jews to accept his instructions, "a great band" of Muslims led by Rayhan Allah "attacked the Jewish quarters, pillaged the houses, dragged every Jew they could put their hands on out of their houses, brutally beat him and barbarously pulled or cut off every hair from his head and put a red patch on his clothes." They even targeted houses of influential Jews, such as Nehorai—for some time a court physician—and "dragged him and his son with cruel treatment out of his house." The son thereby "nominally" converted to Islam; "many" other Jews opted for Islam as well. Seeking to quell the situation, the government dispatched soldiers to guard the Jewish areas. Nevertheless, some Muslims still planned to rid themselves of the Jews, also by bringing the corpse of a Muslim child to the Jewish ward during the night so as to accuse the Jews of his death. As for the Jews, they felt as if "another Haman [i.e. the Biblical anti-Jewish figure] has arisen in the same land [of Iran] to exterminate the remnant of the [Jewish] despised race. We cry to Heaven for help. O Lord how long?" The Jews also called on their brethren and on England to come to their aid.[14] Another attack occurred on May 16. The tumult apparently ended following the intervention of Britain, France, the United States, and the Netherlands. Jewish European organizations and persons and the London Society for Promoting Christianity among the Jews intervened on behalf of the Jews of Tehran as well.[15]

13. MAE: Correspondance politique and commerciale/1897–1918 (Nouvelles serie), Perse, Box number 52, file: Ecoles Francais, 1897–1907, sub-file: l'Alliance Israelite et les Juifs de Perse, no. 40, May 20, 1897, French Legation/Tehran to MAE. The patch mentioned here is yellow. For a different list of restrictions: JBD: ACC/3121/BO2/09/009, file 3, May 24, 1897.

14. JBD: ACC/3121/BO2/09/009, file 3, May 24, 1897. On Nehorai Nur Mahmud: Tsadik, *Between Foreigners and Shi'is*, 11, 108.

15. AIU: Iran.II.C.6, Teheran, May 24, 1897, Meyer Levy to AIU. JBD: ACC/3121/C11/14/028, no. 70 May 26, 1897, Hardinge to FO. MAE: Correspondance Politique et

Whereas the Shah is reported on May 24 to have desired to impose on the Jews the requirement of wearing a certain "mark" with the word *"Musai,"* that is, of the religion of Moses,[16] he later on promulgated, under foreign pressure, an edict saying that "the Muslims are hereby ordered to cease their persecutions of the Jews and not to impose any distinctive sign on them. All those who mistreat our non-Muslim subjects or seek to distinguish them from others shall be severely punished."[17] By July 26, "the riots and ill treatment of Jews" "had ceased."[18]

In the years that followed, Jews were ordinarily mistreated and occasionally persecuted. In September 1897 or earlier, at Lar, for instance, where the Jewish community numbered 250 people, a certain Sayyid 'Abd al-Husayn stopped "provisions with alternative conversion or death."[19] This *mujtahid* also prohibited the Jews "on pain of death" to

---

Commerciale/1897-1918 (nouvelle serie), Perse, box number 52, file: Ecoles Francais, 1897-1907, sub file: l›Alliance Israelite et les Juifs de Perse, June 24, 1897, AIU to MAE. AIU: Iran.II.C.6, Teheran, June 28, 1897, AIU to Meyer Levy. JBD: ACC/3121/GO1/01/003, 47th Annual Report for April 1898 (London: Wertheimer, Lea, 1898). session 5655-58—1895-98. London Committee of Deputies of the British Jews, July 8, 1897, Conjoint Jewish Committee [=CFC] to FO, 34. CFC: minute book: ACC/3121/C11A/001, July 4, 1897. FO 60/583, no. 60, July 15, 1897, FO to Hardinge. JBD: ACC/3121/C11/14/028, July 16, 1897, FO to secretary of the Conjoint Jewish Committee. JBD: ACC/3121/GO1/01/003, 47th Annual Report for April 1898 (London: Wertheimer, Lea and Co., 1898). session 5655-58---1895-98. London Committee of Deputies of the British Jews, July 26, 1897, Conjoint Jewish Committee to FO, 36.

16. JBD: ACC/3121/BO2/09/009, file 3, May 24, 1897. AIU: Iran.II.C.6, Teheran, May 24, 1897, Meyer Levy to AIU.

17. AIU. *Bulletin Mensuel.* 25 (July, 1897): 86. I followed the following translation: A. Confino, "Establishment of the Alliance School in Teheran," in *Padyavand III*, ed. A. Netzer (Los Angeles: Mazda, 1999), 95. For slightly different translations: D. Littman, "Jews under Muslim Rule: The Case of Persia," *The Wiener Library Bulletin*, New Series Nos. 49/50, 32 (1979), 11 (For the French version of this article: D. Littman, "Les Juifs en Perse avant les Pahlevi," *Les Temps Modernes* 395 (1979): 1910-35; *Jewish Missionary Intelligence* (1897), 158.

18. CFC: minute book: ACC/3121/C11A/001, July 26, 1897. But, see: *Jewish Missionary Intelligence* (1897), 158 (Kirmanshah and Hamadan); Littman, "Jews," 10-11 (Hamadan).

19. Elaboration in: JBD: ACC/3121/GO1/01/003, 47th Annual Report for April 1898 (London: Wertheimer, Lea and Co., 1898). Session 5655-58—1895-98. London Committee of Deputies of the British Jews, September 3, 1897, 38. FO 60/585, no. 58, September 9, 1897, Hardinge to FO. JBD: ACC/3121/GO1/01/003, 47th Annual Report for April 1898 (London: Wertheimer, Lea and Co., 1898). session 5655-58—1895-98. London Committee of Deputies of the British Jews, February 3, 1898, Conjoint Jewish Committee to FO, 40-41. JBD: ACC/3121/C11/14/027. FO 60/596, no. 22, February 11, 1898, Hardinge to FO. FO 60/595, no. 10, February 14, 1898, FO to

"touch" the city's water reservoir, since the Jews were "unclean creatures." Furthermore, he instructed the Muslims not to have any "relations" with the Jews, causing Muslims not to interact with the Jews commercially. Answering to appeals in this regard, the Shah had Sayyid 'Abd al-Husayn exiled from Lar, but prior to his departure, the Shi'i cleric "made" all shopkeepers "swear" on the Quran "to break off all relations with the Jews." The situation only exacerbated, as the shopkeepers then demanded the Jews to return all their(?) debts to the shopkeepers. Unable to pay all debts, the Jews were given the option of conversion to Islam.[20]

Among the other Jewish communities that suffered during this time were those of Kazarun,[21] Isfahan,[22] Kashan,[23] and Urumiyyah.[24]

Other religious minorities generally shared the Jews' lot. Correspondence in the Iranian ministry of foreign affairs from the year 1318 (1900–1901) dealt with Armenians and Jews that were killed and wounded in Urumiyyah.[25] In an earlier instance, the governor of Urumiyyah instructed the execution of a Christian "in an arbitrary manner," as he

---

Hardinge. JBD: ACC/3121/A 013, minute book 13, February 20, 1898, 442–443.

20. Littman, "Jews," 11–12.

21. AIU: Iran, I.B.4, Cazran, 12 of Tishrey, TaRNaH [=October 8, 1897], Kazarun community to Baghdad.

22. Elaboration in: AIU: Iran. I.C.3, 1 Adar, year of Be-SaSON [=February 23. 1898], Isfahan community to AIU. JBD: ACC/3121/A 013, minute book 13, July 17, 1898. JBD: ACC/3121/GO1/01/003, 48th Annual Report for April 1899 (Wertheimer, Lea and Co., 1899) London Committee of Deputies of The British Jews. Session 5658-61---1898-1901, 40–42. FO 60/595, no. 67, July 19, 1898, FO to Durand. FO 60/595, no. 105, September 22, 1898, Durand to FO. AIU: Iran. I.C.3, Ispahan, TaRNaT, received on February 19, 1899, Isfahan community to AIU. A. H. S. Landor, *Across Coveted Lands* (London: Macmillan, 1902), 292: In 1901, "a Jew was murdered in cold blood a few miles from Isfahan, and his body flung into the river. Although the murder had been witnessed, and the murderer was well known, no punishment was ever inflicted upon him." See also: ibid., 294–95.

23. AIU: Iran. I.C.3 bis, Kachan, Adar I, TaRSaB [=February or March 1902], Kashan community to AIU.

24. AIU: Iran.I.B.7, Erivan, 1905/1906, Erivan community (Russia) to AIU. AIU: Iran. I.B.18, Ourmiah, month of Av, TaRSaH, received on September 19, 1905, Urumiyyah to AIU. JNL: Microfilm Center, *siman* 8276, from Urumiyyah, TaRSaU. JNL: Microfilm Center, *siman* 8276, 3 Menaḥem Av, TaRSU [=July 26 1906], from Urumiyyah community. AIU: Iran. I.B.18, Ourmiah, *rosh hodesh* Sivan, TaRSU [=May 25, 1906], Urumiyyah community to AIU.

25 *Fihrist-i Asnad-i Qadimi-yi Wizarat-i Umur-i Kharijah-yi Dawran-i Qajariyyah, 1124–1316 H.Q* (Tehran: Idarah-yi Asnad wa-Arshiw-i Wizarat-i Umur-i Kharijah Wahid-i Nashr-i Asnad, 1371), 467.

was regarded the reason for a death of a Muslim.²⁶ "Excesses" committed by the "delegates of the governor" in a Nestorian village followed.²⁷ Zoroastrians were no exception among the religious minorities. Their Muslim "oppressors" did not allow them to "wear the flowing *abba*, or Persian cloak, and restrict them to dingy yellows and browns." Although they considered to be honest people, their "touch" was viewed as defiling.²⁸ Among other disabilities imposed on the Zoroastrians were the prohibition to "ride in the towns," the obligation to "dismount if they meet any Persian of rank outside the city wall," and the prohibition to "carry umbrellas."²⁹ In some places, the Jews' situation was worse than the rest of the non-Muslim population. Thus, for instance, the Jews of Yazd indicate that the "uncircumcised Persians" of the city—apparently a reference to the local Zoroastrian community—mock the Jews, saying that their own brethren in Bombay achieved "freedom" on their behalf and exempted them for all taxes, including the poll-tax,³⁰ as opposed to the Jews' situation. Finally, Bahais were severely persecuted many times, such as in 1903.³¹

That diverse religious minorities were targeted—not only the Jews—may indicate that it is difficult to construe cases of attacks on the Jews as necessarily expressions of anti-Judaism—directed at the Jews qua Jews. The target was the other, whoever this other may have been. Furthermore, the fact that religious minorities were occasionally persecuted and ill-treated may imply that even if some social segments would increasingly espouse concepts of nationalism stripped of or with reduced religious connotations, at least some other social elements still preferred—for

26. FO 60/585, no. 93, December 22, 1897, Hardinge to FO.

27. FO 60/585, no. 100, December 28, 1897, Hardinge to FO.

28. E. C. Sykes, *Through Persia on a Side-Saddle* (London: Innes, 1898), 66, 143.

29. E. C. Sykes, *Persia and its People* (London: Methuen, 1910), 126. P. M. Sykes, *Ten Thousand Miles in Persia of Eight Years in Iran* (London: Murray, 1902), 198: Zoroastrians "are not ill treated nowadays, although still forced to wear sober-coloured clothes, and forbidden to ride in the *bazaars*."

30. AIU: Iran.II.C.8, Yezd, Heshvan, *MeAH She'ARIM* [=TaRSU= October or November 1905], Yazd community to AIU.

31. FO 60/650, no. 40, March 4, 1902, Hardinge to FO. FO 60/665, no. 3, January 6, 1903, Hardinge to FO. FO 60/665, no. 85, June 10, 1903, Hardinge to FO. FO 60/665, no. 95, June 23, 1903, Hardinge to FO. FO 60/666, no. 102, July 9, 1903, Hardinge to FO. A. Rabbani, "'Abdu'l-Baha's Proclamation on the Persecution of Baha'is in 1903," *Baha'i Studies Review*, 14 (2007), 53–67. M. Momen, *The Babi and Baha'i Religions 1844–1944* (Oxford: Ronald, 1981), 363–66.

various reasons: religious, political, economic, and social—to define a person's identity based on religious persuasion.

IMPETUS AND PARADIGMS

Various cases and incidents from the days of Muzaffar al-Din Shah demonstrate the grim situation of the Jews as described above. Reasons for the attacks were not limited to the Jews' divinely ordained second-class status of *dhimma* or to the Jews' supposed infringement on the *dhimma* by, for instance, blaspheming the Prophet, as seen above in 1893 Kirmanshah. Mundane causes can be occasionally discerned: for example, in Kirmanshah of 1896, an attempt to rebel against a local government due to its rise of prices was done on the back of the Jews.

Furthermore, mistreatment of the Jews, or attempts to discipline them along the lines of the *dhimma* coinciding with the accession of a new monarch, his anniversary, or birthday,[32] were no coincidence. The Shahs—and rulers, in general—were, in theory, the protectors of their subjects, regardless of religion. It is for that reason that an attack on minorities also constituted an attack on the Shah. At least to some extent, the Jews were occasionally merely a tool to be used by various local or national players in order to achieve a certain aim. Attacking the Jews and proving the Shah inept precisely on occasions when he desired to demonstrate his sovereignty—on his accession, anniversary, or birthday—could, for instance, remind the Shah of the significance of the Jews' assailants as well as force the Shah to come to terms with them on other fronts. Targeting the Jews was a means of rebellion against the Shah, who sought to preserve the public order.

Another possible impetus for onslaughts against the Jews was the tense economic situation. Various communities cried for pecuniary

---

32. Examples: JBD: ACC/3121/GO1/01/003, 47th Annual Report for April 1898 (London: Wertheimer, Lea and Co., 1898). Session 5655-58---1895-98. London Committee of Deputies of the British Jews, January 17, 1898, Conjoint Jewish Committee to FO, 36-37. JBD: ACC/3121/A 013, minute book 13, 440-441: "inflammatory notices had been posted in the streets and bazaars" of Tehran, "urging the inhabitants to massacre the Israelites on the anniversary of the accession of His Majesty the Shah." JBD: ACC/3121/BO2/09/009, file 3, November 18, 1897, *Kol Israel Haverim* of Tehran to AJA. AIU: Iran.XII.E.132, Teheran, Cazes, October 31, 1898, Cazes to AIU. AIU. *Bulletin Mensuel*, 26 (1898), 195. JBD: ACC/3121/G1/1/5, 56th Annual Report for October 1907 (London: Wertheimer, Lea and Co., 1907) London Committee of Deputies of the British Jews; session 5664-5667---1904-1907, 70.

support toward the end of the nineteenth century. A missive dated May 1898 from the Jews of Lar reads: "A frightful famine prevails in our country. For seven years, locusts have been devouring our crops, and the rains, vital to a region such as ours, are becoming rarer with every passing day."[33] Asserting that there has been a famine during the last two years, the Jews of Hamadan in February 1899 called on the AIU for help.[34] Rise of prices (*yoqer ha-she'arim*) was lamented in Isfahan[35] and Tehran. Even those Tehran Jews who could afford to pay for bread were not able to procure it from the gentiles, since the latter themselves also suffered during these hard times. Impoverished Jews died of hunger in the capital city.[36] *Yoqer ha-she'arim*, drought, and hunger were reported also in the Jewish community of Kashan,[37] whereas the Jews of Nihawand in 1903 still recalled the impact of the continuous famine and drought of four years earlier.[38] At least to some extent, the difficult economic situation, leading to socio-economic tensions, accounted for the gruesome attitude of some Muslims toward the Jews.

Leading the 1897 Tehran anti-Jewish campaign was Sayyid Rayhan Allah, a member of the 'ulama. Rayhan Allah was no exception among his fellow 'ulama; his approach toward the Jews reflected a broader phenomenon. As observed by a letter of the Conjoint Foreign Committee (CFC) to the Marquis of Salisbury, Secretary of State for Foreign Affairs, "these [anti-Jewish] attacks instigated by the Mollahs appear to be of a chronic character."[39] And, indeed, numerous other incidents demonstrate

33. Littman, "Jews," 11.

34. AIU: Iran. I.C.2, Hamadan, 18 Adar TaRNaT [=February 28, 1899], Hamadan community to AIU.

35. AIU: Iran. I.C.3, Ispahan, TaRNaT, received on February 19, 1899, Isfahan community to AIU.

36. AIU: Iran.XII.E.132, Teheran, Cazes, year of *'ezri me-'im Hashem 'oseh shamayim va-ares*, Kislev [=November or December 1899], Tehran community to AIU.

37. AIU: Iran.XII.E.132, Teheran, Cazes, year of *SeTeR, Seder Trumah* [=around late January or early February 1900], Kashan community to AIU. A letter from Urumiyyah, possibly from around the end of the 19th century, depicts famine and *yoqer ha-she'arim*: JNL: Microfilm Center, *siman* 36965.

38. AIU: Iran.II.E.23, Hamadan, Bassan, 22 Tevet, year of *ZMIROT* [=January 21, 1903], Nihawand community to AIU.

39. JBD: ACC/3121/GO1/01/003, 47th Annual Report for April 1898 (London: Wertheimer, Lea and Co., 1898). session 5655-58---1895-98. London Committee of Deputies of the British Jews, July 8, 1897, Conjoint Jewish Committee to FO, 34.

the role of some of the 'ulama in inciting and instigating against the Jews. In 1897, Kazarun Jews described how one religious scholar burned down their synagogues, whereas another libeled (*'asu 'alilah*) against them.[40] Aqa Najafi, the powerful *mujtahid* of Isfahan, and some other 'ulama mistreated part of the local Jews in 1897 and later on. Najafi ordered Muslim merchants not to sell the Jews clothing-related merchandise and also banned Muslims from purchasing anything from the Jews.[41] In Tehran, toward the end of 1899, 'ulama (*komarim*) instructed some Jewish merchants in the marketplace not to deal in their shops.[42] In early 1901, the preaching of a certain Shaykh Ibrahim in Tehran against shops of wine and arrack led to an onslaught against the Jewish quarter.[43] Shaykh Hadi of Kirmanshah was reported in 1904 to have instigated attacks on the Jews of the city.[44] In Isfahan of 1906, "on the formal accession to the throne of the new Shah [i.e. Muhammad 'Ali Shah]... the local clergy were forcing the Jews to wear a distinctive garb and renounce peddling ... as a result, 200 families were thrown out of work."[45]

40. AIU: Iran. I.B.4, Cazran, 12 Tishrey, 5658 [=October 8, 1897], Kazarun community to AIU.

41. Schwarzfuchs, 74–8. JBD: ACC/3121/GO1/01/003, 47th Annual Report for April 1898 (London: Wertheimer, Lea and Co., 1898). session 5655-58---1895-98. London Committee of Deputies of the British Jews, September 24, 1897, FO to Conjoint Jewish Committee, 42–43. AIU: Iran. I.C.3, 1 Adar, year of *Be-SaSON* [=February 23. 1898], Isfahan community to AIU. See also: H. Walcher, *In the Shadow of the King: Politics and Society in Qajar Isfahan, 1874–1907* (Yale University, Ph.D diss., 1999), 397–407. On Sha'ban 9, 1321 [=October 31, 1903] Aqa Najafi arrived in Tehran; he criticized the Jews for not wearing a patch (*waslah*); see: 'Abd al-Husayn Khan, Sipihr, *Yaddashtha-yi Malik al-Muarikhin* (n.p: Intisharat-i Zarin, 1368). Ed. 'Abd al-Husayn Nawai, 41.

42. AIU: Iran.XII.E.132, Teheran, Cazes, year of *'ezri me-'im Hashem 'oseh shamayim va-ares*, Kislev [=November or December 1899], Tehran community to AIU.

43. FO 60/636, no. 16, February 6, 1901, Spring-Rice to FO. AIU. *Bulletin Semestriel*, 62 (1900), 73–75. FO 60/636, no. 23, February 7, 1901, Spring-Rice to FO: "these shops [of wine and arrack] are chiefly owned by Armenians. The rioters, however, turned their attention to the Jews, the Armenian being largely under Russian protection."

44. AIU: Iran, II.C.4, Kermanchah, July 18, 1904, Masidy to AIU. H. Kirmanshachi, *Tahawwulat-i Ijtima'i-yi Yahudiyan-i Iran dar Qarn-i Bistum* (Los Angeles: Ketab, 2007), 334, 336, 338, 340.

45. JBD: ACC/3121/G1/1/5, 56th Annual Report from October 1907 (London: Wertheimer, Lea and Co., 1907); London Committee of Deputies of the British Jews; session 5664–5667—1904-1907, 70.

However, the ʿulama as a body of clerics or individual ʿulama were not inherently anti-Jewish.[46] Even if, apparently, the majority of the ʿulama of the 19th and early 20th century seem to have been critically harsh on the Jews, there were certain cases that demonstrate the opposite. Some of the ʿulama—apparently a minority—were supportive and protective of the Jews. A few examples would suffice to demonstrate this fact. Described as a "lover of the Jews" (*ohev Israel*), one of the ʿulama (*komarim*) of Urumiyyah, sought in the year of TaQSU (1835/6) to save the local Jewish community from a blood libel accusation.[47] When Urumiyyah Shiʿis attacked Sunnis in the early 1880s and killed two Jews because they allegedly sold "powder and shot to the Kurds," the Jewish quarter was saved from an imminent attack by the *Shaykh al-Islam*, who called the authorities.[48] In 1893, whereas many of the Jews of Isfahan were thrashed in the bazaars, supposedly at the beset of Aqa Najafi, the Isfahan *imam jumʿah* (a government appointed prayer leader at the main mosque of every city) "who lives in the Jewish quarter, assisted" the Jews "in the utmost."[49] Sayyid ʿAbd al-Majid abused the Jews of Hamadan in 1893,[50] but some years later, he is said to have preached—for his own reasons—to his followers that no harm is to be done to the Jews. Upon his death, the representative of AIU lamented the loss and remembered him as defending the Jews in "difficult moments."[51] The Tehran powerful cleric, Hasan Ashtiyani, mentioned above, is one example of a Shiʿi religious scholar who was occasionally sought by the Jews for protection. Another one was the *mujtahid* Hajji Aqa Muhammad of Hamadan.[52] Landor remarks in 1902 how, when the "head Mullah" of Tehran died, "the entire male Jewish community marched in the funeral procession—an event unprecedented... in the annals of Persian Mussulman history. The head Mullah, a man of great wisdom and justice, had, it was said, been very consider-

---

46. Examples of ʿulama who protected the Jews in Safawid times: V. B. Moreen, *Iranian Jewry's Hour of Peril and Heroism* (New York and Jerusalem: American Academy for Jewish Research, 1987), 65, 73-74, 90, 92, 98, 129-132.

47. *Ha-Levanon*, Year 8 (1872), 274.

48. *Jewish Chronicle*, February 4, 1881, 13b.

49. FO 60/543, no. 96, June 12, 1893, Lascelles to FO. For another case where the *imam jumʿah* of Isfahan helped the Jews: FO 60/595, no. 105, September 22, 1898, Durand to FO, enclosure by Aganoor, September 3, 1898.

50. Tsadik, *Between Foreigners and Shiʿis*, 165-66, 168.

51. AIU. *Bulletin Mensuel* 28 (1900), 212, 214. AIU: Iran.II.E.23, Hamadan, Bassan, January 23, 1902, Bassan to AIU.

52. AIU. *Bulletin Mensuel* 29 (1901), 58.

ate towards the Jews and had protected them against persecution."[53] Aqa Sayyid 'Abdallah b. Aqa Sayyid Isma'il Bihbihani from Tehran—"very well educated" in Muslim theology and father of the "chief" religious scholar at Bushihre—was viewed in 1902 as "a great friend of the Jewish nation . . . He does not permit Mohammedans to persecute the Jews, who receive help from him in every way possible."[54] Even Aqa Najafi, usually notorious for his anti-Jewish proceedings,[55] was at their side at least once against ill-treatment they suffered in Shiraz in 1906; "it is needed," he is reported to have asserted, to remind Muslims that the "Jews must be *protégés*" of Islam.[56]

Religion figured in the 'ulama's attitude toward Jews, no doubt. Nevertheless, religious ideology and worldview could be utilized differently at different occasions—to impose restrictions on the Jews, or, vice versa, to resort to religious protective measures towards the Jews—all to meet different goals, needs, and interests. No less significantly, motivations other than the imposition of religious ideology and worldview were at the root of the approach of all the 'ulama towards the Jews: economic, social, and political. As for those 'ulama who incited against the Jews, the reasons for their anti-Jewish activity ranged from pure desire to enforce Islam's approach to religious minorities, to wishes to gain fame, influence, and followings, to even more worldly aims: to challenge rival 'ulama who shielded the Jews, to pose a threat to the local or national authorities, or to gain economic advantages for the 'ulama or their followers. These 'ulama's attitude toward dealing with the Jews, and other religious minorities for that matter also stemmed from the 'ulama's general intervention in various issues of national and local significance, only one of which was the Jewish or minority issue. This intervention was another avenue through which to increase the 'ulama's power.[57]

Jews would seek to improve their situation by appealing to the local administration. Thus, for example, Jews would petition the Iranian

---

53. Landor, 115–116.

54. *Jewish Missionary Intelligence* (1902), 184. On him, see: FO 60/595, no. 14, January 28, 1898, Hardinge to FO (A biographical dictionary, p. 69).

55. Tsadik, *Between Foreigners and Shi'is*, 137–41, 144–48.

56. AIU: Iran.I.C.3, Ispahan, May 3, 1906, Lahana to AIU.

57. Examples from Nasir al-Din Shah's reign are in: Tsadik, *Between Foreigners and Shi'is*. On the "increasing power" of the mullahs: FO 60/583, no. 109, December 21, 1897, FO to Hardinge.

minister of foreign affairs regarding their molestation.[58] At the same time, incidents from the days of Muzaffar al-Din Shah show the above paradigm by which outside succor was occasionally in need to attempt alleviating the Jews' generally unfortunate position. Asking for pecuniary support for their synagogue, the Jews of Gulpaygan, for instance, wrote to Paris and succinctly depicted their sorrows at the hands of the gentiles.[59] The sojourn of an AIU representative in a certain place and his establishing a school of the AIU was occasionally to ameliorate the political and social condition of the indigenous Jews. In the Jewish quarter of Tehran, an AIU school was established in 1898. Upon learning that the Paris headquarters of the AIU called its Tehran man, Joseph Cazes, to return back to France, the Jews of Tehran wrote several letters to the AIU, calling on them to let Cazes remain in the capital city. In one of these missives, dated September 1900, one of the heads of the community, Rabbi Abraham b. Aqa (*Aghah*) Baba, writes in an obviously exaggerated fashion— but still one that reflects the importance of Cazes—that if Cazes leaves Tehran, it is as if the AIU "killed six thousand souls" of Jews. "The 'ulama, ministers, deputies, and *hamon ha-'am* (masses) think" that Cazes is the Jews' "head and officer." The writer reports that "*hamon 'am* are afraid" of Cazes, "and half of our exile (*galut*) ... has diminished" due to him. If Cazes leaves Tehran, the writer warned, the Jews will be in "danger of their lives (*sakanat nefashot*) ... and our exile will increase and expand manifold (*yrbeh ve-yfros kifley kiflayim*)."[60] Such wording exemplifies the importance of Cazes but also that of the AIU in general in providing

---

58. E.g., *Fihrist-i Asnad-i Qadimi-yi Wizarat-i Umur-i Kharijah*, 577.

59. JNL: Manuscripts and Archives Dep., 40. 199, 273, file *igrrot sh'adarim*, no exact date, but under Muzaffar al-Din Shah, Gulpaygan community to Paris and Baron de-Hirsch.

60. AIU: Iran.XII.E.132, Teheran, Cazes, 3 of Tishrey, year of *ASTeR* [=September 26, 1900], Tehran community to AIU. On Cazes, see also: AIU: ibid, 8 of Tishrey, year of *ASTeR* [=October 1, 1900], Tehran community to AIU. AIU: ibid, 12 of month of *Rahamim* [=Elul], year of *SeTeR* [=September 6, 1900], Tehran community to AIU. AIU: ibid, 13 Heshvan, year of *ASTeR* [=November 5, 1900], Tehran community to AIU. AIU: ibid, 22 Heshvan, TaRSA [=November 14, 1900], Tehran community to AIU. Indeed, some of the letters focus on the specific figure of Cazes as the source of the amelioration of the Jews' plight. On another case, from Hamadan: AIU: Iran. I.C.2, Hamadan, 18 Tevet, TaRSA [=January 9, 1901], Hamadan community to AIU. AIU: Iran.II.E.23, Hamadan, Bassan, 4 Shvat TaRSaB [=January 12, 1902], Hamadan community to AIU. On another case, from Sinih: AIU: I.B.23, Seneh, 23 Heshvan, TaRSU [=November 21, 1905], Sinih community to AIU.

protection for the local Jews. The following 1905 Shiraz case partially reflects this and some of the above tendencies and paradigms.

SHIRAZ: A CASE-STUDY

The city of Shiraz, southern Iran, had eleven quarters: five *Haydari*, five *Ni'mati*, and one Jewish.[61] The Jews were visible in the city's landscape: one estimation has Shiraz Jews in 1903 at 5,000 out of 50,000 people (10%). Their professions were diverse and included: peddlers, masons, goldsmiths, merchants, merchants of wine, musicians, druggists, butchers, and physicians, among other pursuits.[62] At least some of these vocations were viewed as socially despised or illicit according to Islam, thus either forbidden to or abhorred by Muslims. This, in turn, rendered the Jews, who were engaged in these vocations, as essential players in the economy.

The Jews of Shiraz, as other Iranian Jews and non-Jews suffered from eruptions of famine, disease, periods of drought, or other natural catastrophes. Around March 1898, the Jews were reported to have fasted and prayed for rain, which thereafter arrived.[63] In a letter received on May 15, 1898, the community writes that due to the locust attacks of the past 8 years, the prices of foodstuffs run high; the situation worsened due to the lack of rainfall. The signatories of the letter thus asked the AIU to send them money.[64]

The Jews, additionally, suffered from attacks that targeted them specifically. Around 1897/8, the Jews of Lar, and also those of nearby Shiraz, were "persecuted by the evil decrees that are being continually issued against them . . . Every means is taken to deprive them of the bare

---

61. H. Fasai, *Farsnamah-yi Nasiri* (Tehran: Muassasah-yi Intisharat-i Amir Kabir, 1367), 908, 1091, 1134. Fariwar, M. *Hadith-i Yak Farhang*, ed. G. Cohen (Los Angeles: Mortazavi, 2007), 36.

62. AIU. *Bulletin Mensuel*, 31 (1903): 104–5, 108–9 (including women's professions); AIU. *Bulletin Mensuel*, 32 (1904): 31–2; L. Loeb, *Outcaste: Jewish Life in Southern Iran* (New York: Gordon & Breach, 1977), 82.

63. S. Sirjani, ed., *Waqayi'-yi Ittifaqiyyah* (Tehran: Nuwin, 1362), 541 (March 2, 1898); *Padyavand II*, ed. A. Netzer (Los Angeles: Mazda, 1997), English section, 150.

64. AIU: Iran.I.C.1, Chiraz, 2 Nisan, TaRNaH [=March 25, 1898], Shiraz community to AIU.

necessities of life." Some of the Shi'i 'ulama were apparently behind this abuse. Discriminatory laws were applied, such as the Shi'i inheritance law.[65]

Cases from 1899 demonstrate that like other minorities, Jews of Shiraz would sometimes be harmed due to certain quarrels or disputes they had with others, not always because they were Jews per se. For instance, the Jewish *mutrib* (musician; entertainer) Mulla Aqa was beaten and robbed because of his refusal to perform at a certain occasion.[66] In another incident, his Jewish boy dancer was kidnapped and brought to the house of Hajji Sayyid 'Ali Akbar—the celebrated 'Ali Akbar Fal Asiri (d. 1901) that was known for his role in the tobacco upheavals of 1891/2 and for his ruthless attacks against the Jews of Shiraz in the 1890s—so as to cut his *zulf* (hair locks; side curls). This case, however, seems to have been at least partially rooted in Mulla Aqa's refraining from bringing his boy dancer to a certain performance earlier on,[67] not necessarily exclusively in an attempt to apply Muslim law upon a Jew by forcing him to cut his hair so as to distinguish him from Muslims.

Yet, some mistreatment would at least ostensibly derive from what was perceived as Jewish trespassing of Muslim sensitivities—that is, it stemmed from a religious reason related to the Jews' different religious orientation. Thus, in 1900, a performance of a Jewish *mutrib* near the Mushir al-Mulk mosque caused Aqa Mirza Muhammad 'Ali, who used to pray at the mosque, and his followers to arrive, beat the *mutrib*s, and hurt the people of the house.[68]

In May 1902, the Jews were abused at the instigation of Sayyid 'Ali Muhammad, a son of the aforementioned Sayyid 'Ali Akbar Fal Asiri.[69] In August, a Jewish peddler was killed on the road; the government investigated the case and found that the muleteer, who took the Jew, and another person killed the Jew. Consequently, Nasr al-Dawlah, a son of

---

65. JBD: ACC/3121/C11/14/027, no date, probably from Bushihr community to JBD.

66. Sirjani, *Waqayi'-yi Ittifaqiyyah*, 597–598 (May 11, 1899); *Padyavand II*, 152.

67. Sirjani, *Waqayi'-yi Ittifaqiyyah*, 588 (November 8, 1899); *Padyavand II*, 151–52. Apparently the same case: Fariwar, *Hadith*, 209–211. On 'Ali Akbar: Tsadik, *Between Foreigners and Shi'is*, 132–36, 140, 153, 183, 189.

68. Sirjani, *Waqayi'-yi Ittifaqiyyah*, 616 (July 26, 1900); *Padyavand II*, 153.

69. AIU: Iran.XIV.E148, Teheran, May 30, 1902, Levy Nissim to AIU. AIU. *Bulletin Mensuel*, 30 (1902): 90–91.

the influential Qawam al-Mulk, imprisoned the muleteer and sent for the other person.[70]

A report from 1903 mentions the anti-Jewish preaching of a certain Sayyid Sharif, but also the noble sentiments of the local *imam jum'ah* toward the Jews. The *imam jum'ah*'s approach, however, is depicted as an exception in the regular situation of the Jews, whereby every now and then a Jew would be assassinated.[71] Following a certain event, the Jews were allowed to produce alcohol and carry it only to Tehran, Bushihr and elsewhere, but were prohibited from vending it to Muslims in the city; if they sell it to Muslims the seller's house will be demolished.[72] Another case was related to the Jewish *mutrib*s: the governor, 'Ala al-Dawlah, instructed them to offer a report of every party (*majlis*) at which they work during the nights. They did not accept this, and fearing of 'Ala al-Dawlah they stopped working in the nights; most of them left with their bands toward Bushihr and Baghdad.[73]

Other forms of pressure on the Jews were reported in 1904: 'Ala al-Dawlah forbade wineries from selling 'araq and wine to Muslims. Realizing that persons who got drunk misbehaved, and that they bought their 'araq from Jews, 'Ala al-Dawlah ordered the beating of Fath Ilayalih, the deputy (*naib*) of the Jewish quarter.[74] 'Ala al-Dawlah's approach may have been rooted in his desire to enforce the *shari'ah*—prohibiting the selling of intoxicating beverages to Muslims, but at least equally, also in his attempt to maintain order in the city. The following case reflects more the desire to upkeep order and tranquility than an attempt to bother the Jews: due to the Jews' holiday of 'Umar (*'ayd-i 'Umar-i Yahudiha*)—most probably a reference to the Jewish festival of Purim—and as a sign of joy the Jews shot guns a lot. To those who did not know that, however, the shooting caused dread and anxiety. Salar al-Sultan, the acting governor and a son of Qawam al-Mulk, as a result, prohibited the Jews from firing the guns anymore.[75]

During the year 1323 (1905–1906), some in the Fars province thought to impose on the Jews a distinctive dress code. In the same time,

70. Sirjani, *Waqayi'-yi Ittifaqiyyah*, 681 (August 7, 1902); *Padyavand II*, 154.

71. AIU. *Bulletin Mensuel* 31 (1903): 110–12.

72. Sirjani, *Waqayi'-yi Ittifaqiyyah*, 714–715 (July 28, 1903); *Padyavand II*, 154–55. Related issue: AIU. *Bulletin Mensuel*, 32 (1904): 30–35.

73. Sirjani, *Waqayi'-yi Ittifaqiyyah*, 719 (September 22, 1903).

74. Sirjani, *Waqayi'-yi Ittifaqiyyah*, 728 (22 January, 1904); *Padyavand II*, 155–56.

75. Sirjani, *Waqayi'-yi Ittifaqiyyah*, 730 (17 February, 1904); *Padyavand II*, 156.

the Jews of Shiraz built a tomb in the ilk of Muslims' tomb. "People," i.e. Muslim inhabitants, in turn, destroyed it. The government intervened and received a pledge from the Muslims who lived in the area to rebuild the grave.[76] The above incidents may well indicate the general situation of the Jews of Shiraz in the years leading up to 1905.

To somewhat soften the above impression, two points should be borne in mind. First, even if they were generally a degraded portion of society, the Jews were still part of society. As already mentioned, they would provide larger society with vital necessities, occasionally functioning as musicians and producers of alcohol, both in demand by various social segments. Additionally, some evidence indicates that the Jews were—even if only to an extent—part of society in times of sorrow as well as on happy days. Jewish *mutrib*s entertained the public at the birthday of the Shah.[77] Even more significantly, the community fasted and prayed for rain in times of need,[78] in addition to parrticipating—along with the rest of the populace— in protests against the governor on the issue of the rise of the bread price.[79]

Second, to provide us with a better perspective on the situation of the Jews, it should be noted that other religious minorities in Shiraz and its surroundings were also occasionally targeted in different ways, for various reasons—religious, social, economic, and political. In 1899, reportedly to make a name for himself, Mulla Ahmad, the prayer leader of one of the local mosques, encroached upon a house of a Muslim who befriended a Zoroastrian (*gabr*) and welcomed his Zoroastrian friend at his home. The mulla was thereafter to be deported to Bushihr but returned at the request of the *imam jum'ah*.[80] In 1902, a traveling Armenian who was beaten died in Kazarun.[81] Those suspected of Babi or Baha'i leanings were

---

76. Sipihr, *Yaddashtha*, 171 (also on the issue of dress with reference to Kirman Zoroastrians), 281.

77. Sirjani, *Waqayi'-yi Ittifaqiyyah*, 716 (August 25, 1903); *Padyavand II*, 155.

78. Sirjani, *Waqayi'-yi Ittifaqiyyah*, 541 (March 2, 1898); *Padyavand II*, 150.

79 Sirjani, *Waqayi'-yi Ittifaqiyyah*, 664 (Dhu al-Qa'dah 27, 1319=March 7, 1902). This case might be related to the following: FO 60/652, no. 20, March 23, 1902, Hardinge to FO. See also Zahir al-Dawlah, *Khatirat wa-Asnad-i Zahir al-Dawlah*, ed. I. Afshar (Tehran: Kitabha-yi Jibi, 1972), 160–161 where Hamadan Muslims and Jews petitioned together the Shah regarding the hunger. On the Hamadan Jews petitioning on their own: ibid, 205.

80. Sirjani, *Waqayi'-yi Ittifaqiyyah*, 582 (September 7, 1899).

81. Sirjani, *Waqayi'-yi Ittifaqiyyah*, 678 (July 10, 1902). For a case where a Christian beat a Sayyid's wife: ibid, 687 (October 12, 1902).

sometime imprisoned, exiled, or killed. In 1903, the encouraging preaching of Aqa Mirza Ibrahim Mujtahid to kill Babis caused excitement, and a revolt almost broke out. As a result, ʿAla al-Dawlah sent some Babis out of the city, including the famous Malik al-Mutakallimin.[82]

∽

By 1905, the relationship between the Shiraz Jews and the outside world was rather solid. The AIU, for instance, seems to have assisted the Jews to purchase land in Shiraz.[83] The AIU was also discussing with the Shiraz Jews their share in the sponsoring of an AIU teacher.[84] This cooperation proved instrumental not only in the economic and educational spheres but also in the political arena as well, as seen in the following incident.

Sometime in June 1905, some Jews of Shiraz were attacked and massacred by parts of the Muslim population.[85] Upon learning about this event from the AIU school in Shiraz, the Paris headquarters of the AIU turned to the French Ministeʿre des Affaires Étrangeʿres (MAE), asking for intervention on behalf of the Jews and the AIU personnel in Shiraz.[86] And, indeed, the MAE telegraphed its Chargé d'Affaires in Tehran, asking him to take steps in favor of the Shiraz Jews.[87] By June 23, G. Grahame, the British Consul in Shiraz, had already asked the British, French, and Italian ministers in Tehran to intervene on behalf of the Jews. He also suggested seizing the moment and addressing the Shah, who was visiting Europe at that time; the Shah should be petitioned on the issue of Iran's Jews, mainly those residing in Shiraz.[88]

Around a week later, responding to the inquiries of the MAE, the French Chargé d'Affaires in Tehran recounted that he had already asked

82. Sirjani, *Waqayiʿ-yi Ittifaqiyyah*, 707-708 (May 28, 1903). See also: ibid, 642 (May 23, 1901), 713 (July 28. 1903).

83. AIU: Iran. I.E.14, Chiraz, 22 Tevet, TaRSaD [=January 10, 1904], Shiraz community to AIU.

84. AIU: Iran. I.E.14, Chiraz, March 3, 1904, Shiraz community to AIU.

85. On this case: AIU. *Bulletin Mensuel*, 33 (1905), 94-100. AIU: Iran. I.C.1, Chiraz, received by AIU on June 17, 1905, Shouker to AIU.

86. MAE: Coresspondane Politique et Commerciale/1897-1918 (nouvelles serie), Perse, Box number 53, File: Ecoles Francais: 1905-1907, sub-file: Ecoles Israeʾlites en Perse, June 7, 1905, AIU to MAE.

87. Ibid, June 7, 1905, MAE to Chargé d'Affaires. Ibid, June 10, 1905, MAE to AIU.

88. AIU: France, XXXV.B.320. a. file "Mme Brandon-Salvador," June 23, 1905, Grahame to [probably Mme Brandon-Salvador]. In the past, the Shah received a delegation of the AIU for an audience: AIU. *Bulletin Mensuel*, 30 (1902): 98-99.∽∽∽

the governor of the province of Fars, Prince Shuʻaʻ al-Staltanah, to take the Jews under his protection and to put an end to the threats and violence of the *mujtahid*s against them. Nevertheless, new data indicated that the Jews were still under fire—one being killed, others wounded, and houses being looted. The Jews were additionally forced to wear a distinctive patch (*rouelle*).[89]

Contemplating the condition of the Jews in Iran in general and the cause of their misery, the French Chargé d'Affaires wrote that the Jews were "considered here according to all titles as eternal foreigners (*éternels étrangers*)." Elaborating on this point, he indicated that the Iranian ministry of foreign affairs has the authority over the Jews and other foreigners. Jews were, furthermore, judged in a tribunal "for judging issues between Europeans, Armenians and Jews, but not between Muslims and Jews: no jurisdiction exists that can legally recognize such a process [of judging between Muslims and Jews]."[90] At first glance, this quote may possibly purport that no clear law was enforced in addressing Jewish-Muslim cases, which reflected the disorganized nature of the state of affairs. The quote may actually mean that the state generally did not intervene in the process of judging between Muslims and Jews, as it was Muslim law—including the *dhimmah* regulations—that addressed such issues and was applied in such cases; therefore, there was no need in a special tribunal.

In any event, in some instances, Jews were addressed as *dhimmi*s, while in others, they were taken care of by the Iranian ministry of foreign affairs. Both avenues proved unsatisfactory for the Jews: they could occasionally be abused and repressed because they were *dhimmi*s, second class subjects under Islam, whereas in other cases, they could face mistreatment because they were regarded as foreigners.

The Jews would face attacks, however, not just because of their *dhimmah* status or foreign orientated administrative affiliation. The time was ripe for such attacks, as they would go unchecked due to the inability or disinterest of the local authorities in addressing problems. A British critical assessment viewed the contemporary governor of Fars, Shuʻaʻ al-Staltanah, the second son of the Shah, as "vicious, cruel, tyrannical, and incompetent ... savage, and the fact that he suffers from epilepsy, syphilis, maniacal pride, and a variety of other ailments, renders him," so

89. MAE: Coresspondane Politique et Commerciale/1897–1918 (nouvelles serie), Perse, Box number 53, File: Ecoles Francais: 1905–1907, sub-file: Ecoles Israeʻlites en Perse, July 1, 1905, Chargé d'Affaires to MAE.

90. Ibid.

provides the report, "not only undesirable but even dangerous as a ruler" under whose government "anarchy and the insecurity of the roads" prevailed.⁹¹ "Condition of Shiraz and Fars has been steadily getting worse for some months owing to cruelty and tyranny" of Shu'a' al-Staltanah who "has now gone to Europe." The Vizier "now administering the province is equally bad," argues a British report. This state of affairs was apparently at the root of "serious riots" that erupted and threatened "to spread over the province."⁹²

One may argue that one way to look at the anti-Jewish attacks is by contending that the weakness and incompetence of the government invited onslaughts against the Jews due to various religious, political, economic, and social reasons. Another way is to argue that the attacks against the Jews were first and foremost an avenue through which the rioters demonstrated against the government; the Jews, according to this analysis, were just a tool, and an easy one, in achieving more general aims. In retrospect, the analysis viewing persecution of Jews as rooted solely in their different religious orientation or in their being somewhat related to or perceived as related to foreign interest is erroneous. This is demonstrated in the following event of the same year of 1905, again in Shiraz.

At 10 A.M of November 15, 1905, Veneziani, an Italian teacher at the AIU school in Shiraz rushed to the British Consulate, informing Grahame, the British Consul, that a "rabble" was demolishing a house in the Jewish ward, "beating and pillaging." The house that had been just completed was "about the same" height as the opposite one, apparently owned by a Muslim. Ostensibly attempting to implement one of the *dhimmah* regulations that stipulated that *dhimmi*s are forbidden to build high buildings or buildings taller than those of the Muslims,⁹³ Mullah Sayyid Muhammad, a son of the famous Sayyid 'Ali Akbar Fal Asiri (d. 1901), dispatched people to destroy the Jewish house. The Jewish owner who had turned to the Sardar (i.e. the Vizier, the current acting governor of Fars) was now willing to demolish his own house, but the Vizier forbade him, intimating that this Jews' hands "would be chopped off" if he did so. The Jewish house was not the main issue at stake; rather, it was a power

---

91. FO 60/700, no. 237, November 1, 1905, Grant-Duff to FO.
92. FO 60/701, no. 155, November 20, 1905, Grant-Duff to FO.
93. Tsadik, "Legal Status," 400–401.

struggle between the Vizier and Mullah Sayyid Muhammad, each side seeking local support of different persons or groups. It was a "popular movement . . . directed against the Sardar [i.e. the Vizier], the Jews being merely a pretext."[94]

That same day, November 15, the British Consul Grahame sent a telegraph to E. Grant-Duff, the British Chargé d'Affaires in Tehran, claiming that "an anti-Jewish agitation is now raging," and that Muslims demolished a Jewish house and were "pillaging and beating Jews."[95] In another telegraph that same day, he added that the "disturbance was instigated by the clergy." He speculated that "it is possible that the town authorities were in connivance, for, though, they were apparently forewarned, they took no precautions." According to Grahame, there was "no doubt" that the riot was "aimed at the Vizier."[96] A day later, he indicated that the "movement is increasing and is now openly directed against the Vizier." As common in times of protest, shops closed, and the 'ulama sent a telegram to the Prime Minister, elaborating on their "grievances;" according to Grahame, "discontent" was "deep" and soldiers guarded the streets.[97]

Reacting to the data on the destruction of a new Jewish house, the looting of shops, and the wounding of two Jews, Grant Duff thus turned to Mushir al-Dawlah, the minister for foreign affairs, asserting that he hoped "for the sake of" the Iranian government's "good name," that it would not permit the Jews to be "ill-treated." Delicately pressuring and threatening Iran, he briefly mentioned the "abominable and inhumane treatment that the Jews have lately received in Russia" and that "excited the indignation and scorn of the civilized world."[98]

On the same day, November 16, the Jewish quarter was attacked, but soldiers "repulsed" the attack. Syyaid Muhammad, "the instigator" of the events, offered the British Grahame to end the attacks on the Jews in return for Grahame's intervention on behalf of the "oppressed people of Fars." At the same time, probably as means to pressure Grahame, a "mob," including some "armed" *luti*s,[99] or ruffians, attacked Jewish houses, only

94. FO 60/700, no. 254, December 3, 1905, Grant Duff to FO, enclosure: November 18, 1905, Shiraz News.
95. Ibid., enclosure: no. 82, November 15, 1905, Grahame to Grant Duff.
96. Ibid., enclosure: no. 83, November 15, 1905, Grahame to Grant Duff.
97. Ibid., enclosure: no. 84, November 16, 1905, Grahame to Grant Duff.
98. Ibid., enclosure: November 16, 1905, Grant Duff to Mushir al-Dawlah.
99. Ibid., enclosure: November 18, 1905, Shiraz News.

to face the fire of Cossacks and soldiers. The result was three Muslims killed and ten others wounded.[100]

In Tehran, responding to Sayyid Muhammad's suggestion, Grant Duff maintained that he would endeavor to "have the present Vizier removed" but that Grahame would not be able to "intervene officially" on Sayyid Muhammad's behalf.[101]

The players in the attack on the Jews were the "mob," *luti*s, and some of the 'ulama. In attacking the Jews, the "mob" and *luti*s would obviously gain from the possible booty. As for the 'ulama, Sayyid Muhammad took the lead in the attacks. One may conjecture that, at least partially, there were some mundane interests at his instigation. Attempting to force the government to pay heed to problems related to the government of Fars through the persecution of the Jews, he, in fact, seems to have at least partially been interested in securing a following for himself. Seeking to inherit his dead father's position, he sought to establish a name for himself. This was more so the case as he was not "a person of high rank or good reputation among the local clergy." Those high ranking 'ulama who participated in the movement did "so in a somewhat half-hearted way, perhaps judging that its success may create a rival reputation at the expense of their own, its failure compromise their dignity."[102]

The following day, November 18, crowds of people gathered in some mosques and elsewhere, shops were "still closed," but without "active disturbances."[103] On November 20, the situation was perceived as "somewhat critical." A Jewish woman was killed, and an onslaught on the Jewish quarter was foreseen. Grahame, who was unable to shield the Jewish quarter, asked Veneziani to gather women and children to Veneziani's house, where they would be guarded by the Indian cavalry (*sowar*s) of the British.[104]

In Tehran, Grant Duff informed Mushir al-Dawlah of this development, indicating that since "the local authorities are incapable of adequately protecting either foreign interests or the Jewish inhabitants," he considered Graham's above action "necessary."[105] Mushir al-Dawlah,

100. Ibid., enclosure: no. 85, November 17, 1905, Grahame to Grant Duff.
101. Ibid., enclosure: no. 56, November 17, 1905, Grant Duff to Grahame.
102. Ibid., enclosure: no. 115, November 18, 1905, Grahame to Grant Duff.
103. Ibid., enclosure: November 18, 1905, Shiraz News.
104. Ibid., enclosure: no. 88, November 20, 1905, Grahame to Grant Duff. FO 60/701, no. 157, November 22, 1905, Grant-Duff to FO.
105. FO 60/700, no. 254, Grant Duff to FO, December 3, 1905, enclosure:

who responded on the same day, maintained that since instructions were given and measures were taken to maintain "peace" in Shiraz, the actions taken by Grahame were "beyond the sphere" of his "duty;" Mushir al-Dawlah was convinced that Grant Duff would order Grahame to "leave" the Jews "alone," because the Iranian Government was "more justified in protecting the lives and property of its own subjects."[106] Grant Duff's response was strongly worded: "Not only shall I not withdraw the Indian *sowars* from M. Veneziani's house, where the Jewish women and children are in refuge, but, should the riots at Shiraz continue, I shall be compelled to advise His Majesty's Government to strengthen the Consular guard at Shiraz by the immediate dispatch of British Indian infantry from [the Iranian city of] Bushire [i.e. Bushihr]."[107] The incident threatened to exceed the bounds of a local outrage against the Jews or the local authorities and become a broader dispute over interstate relations. It was obviously a question of prestige and sovereignty of the two states, but no less importantly, it was a struggle over the question of protection: were the Jews to be protected by their own government or by a foreign power? This case demonstrates, to some extent, the erosion of the local *dhimmah* protective measures and the simultaneous emergence of outside protection, whether of Jewish bodies such as the AIU or foreign powers such as the British. As a process that began during the latter part of the nineteenth century, the Jews—and with them, Iranians in general—were gradually being incorporated into a transnational setting.

On November 21, shops were "still closed." The governor, Salar al-Sultan, promised that the Jews would be safe.[108] That same day, Grahame ordered the *sowars* to withdraw from Veneziani's house. Later, he suggested to Veneziani that he send the refugees back to their homes "as soon as possible."[109] On November 27, the "agitation" seemed to Grahame as over "for the present."[110]

Nevertheless, on December 1, the 'ulama and the merchants petitioned the Prime Minister, specifying certain "grievances," including the heavy taxation, and requesting "justice." At the same time, there were

---

November 21, 1905, Grant Duff to Mushir al-Dawlah.

106. Ibid., enclosure: November 21, 1905, Mushir al-Dawlah to Grant Duff.

107. Ibid., enclosure: November 22, 1905, Grant Duff to Mushir al-Dawlah.

108. Ibid., enclosure: no. 90, November 21, 1905, Grahame to Grant Duff.

109. Ibid., enclosure: no. 94, November 25, 1905, Grahame to Grant Duff.

110. Ibid., enclosure: no. 95, November 27, 1905, Grahame to Grant Duff. On this incident: AIU. *Bulletin Mensuel*, 34 (1906), 16–7.

reports "from many districts" on the prevailing "unrest."¹¹¹ Around a week later, the Jews of Shiraz were still complaining of beatings and threats of imminent killing.¹¹² Some time later, both Zill al-Sultan, the governor of Isfahan, and Aqa Najafi intervened on behalf of the Jews. Aqa Najafi even contended that Muslims should know that Jews must be protected (*protégés*) by Islam.¹¹³

Such an episode, as elaborated above, may have partially encouraged some of the Jews to depart from Shiraz. In 1810, some Shiraz Jews—rabbis and others—arrived in Safed, Palestine.¹¹⁴ In 1815, Jews left Shiraz for Palestine via Bushihr, Iraq, and Damascus. Some remained in Damascus, while others proceeded to Safed and elsewhere in Palestine.¹¹⁵ In 1884, several dozens of families left Shiraz for Palestine.¹¹⁶ The family of Refael Hayim ha-Cohen left Shiraz on 26 Tamuz, TaRaN (July 14, 1890),¹¹⁷ whereas in the month of Tevet TaRNaB (January, 1892), some 120 Jewish families—mostly from Shiraz and some of Zarqan—arrived in Palestine.¹¹⁸ Miryam Sar-Shalom and one of her brothers left Shiraz and arrived in Palestine in 1906,¹¹⁹ while Michael R. Barkhurdar (later, Bar-Osher) left Shiraz and immigrated to Israel in 1950.¹²⁰ While the reasons for each wave or individual emigration varied, it was at least occasionally rooted in the attempt to elevate the Jews' misfortunes by movement to other, believed-to-be more forthcoming places.

---

111. FO 60/700, no. 254, December 3, 1905, Grant Duff to FO, enclosure: no. 96, December 2, 1905, Grahame to Grant Duff.

112. AIU: Iran.I.C.1, Chiraz, 10 Kislev, [TaRSU=December 8, 1905] Shiraz community to AIU.

113. AIU: Iran.I.C.3, Ispahan, May 3, 1906, Lahana to AIU.

114. A. Cohen, *Qol Qara va-Elekh* (Tel-Aviv: Dalyah, 2000), 13.

115. R. H. Ha-Cohen, *Avanim Ba-Homah* (Jerusalem: R. H. Ha-Cohen, 1970), 48. Note that this sources and the previous one may be speaking of the same wave of emigration, but differ on its exact date.

116. Cohen, *Qol Qara va-Elekh*, 7, 13, 22, 24.

117. Ha-Cohen, *Avanim Ba-Homah*, 7.

118. Ha-Cohen, *Avanim Ba-Homah*, 48.

119. H. Besalel, *Pirqey Hayim shel Hanah Besalel le-Beyt Bushihri* (Jerusalem: Sur-Ot, 2004), 18.

120. A. Bar-Osher, ed., *Ner Le-Michael* (Jerusalem: Bar-Osher family, 2007), [4].

CONCLUSION

The Iranian Jews' position in the pre-Constitutional years was affected by various factors, including: the heritage of the Islamic worldview (i.e. viewing the Jews as a *dhimmah* community), the Jews' administrative position placing them under the jurisdiction of the Iranian ministry of foreign affairs, the government's attitude, and the Jews' economic status, which often relegated them to despised professions. Nor was this all. Outside players, such as Jewish foreign organizations and foreign powers began intervening on behalf of the Jews already during the nineteenth century, thereby posing not only as a threat to Iran's sovereignty and prestige but also introducing foreign orientated concepts of protection that had an increasing impact on the Jews' lives.

No doubt, the Jews did not fair well in Shiraz, but neither did some other segments of society. Incompetent and extortionate administration would prove a burden on Jews and non-Jews alike. In this regard, the Jews were just another group to suffer in a complicated setting.

Having said that, Jews during the pre-Constitutional years were occasionally mistreated due to their *dhimmah* status, their perceived connection to foreign lands, or for economic reasons. Jews were often perceived as dogs[121] or as impure,[122] thereby rendering them worthy of restrictions and abuse. Such mistreatment could be carried on when the government was weak or not interested in curbing the anti-Jewish proceedings. However, these were not the only reasons at the root of anti-Jewish attacks. At times, Jews were attacked due to other reasons, namely, they served an easy tool in anti-regime protests. Not all anti-Jewish events stemmed from religious or ideological hatred, or even economic competition; occasionally, specific socio-political motivations were at the root of such a treatment, which, to some extent, should be viewed only as "nominally directed against the Jews,"[123] or as "pseudo-anti-Jewish."[124]

The situation of the Jews in early twentieth century Shiraz was not uncommon in other parts of Iran. Although around the same time, there

---

121. E.g AIU: Iran,I.B.18, Ourmiah, month of Av, TaRSaH, received on September 19, 1905, Urumiyyah to AIU.

122. Landor, 295: "The Jew is looked upon as unclean and untrustworthy by the Persian, who refuses to use him as a solider, but who gladly employs him to do all sorts of dirty jobs which Persian pride would not allow him to do himself."

123. FO 60/700, no. 254, December 3, 1905, Grant Duff to FO.

124. Ibid, enclosure: November 18, 1905, Shiraz News.

were Jews who had good relations with their Muslim neighbors, such as the community of Zarqan[125] or that of Nihawand,[126] such cases seem to have been the exception rather than the rule. Jews of various other places, such as Urumiyyah,[127] Kirmanshah,[128] Gulpaygan,[129] Isfahan,[130] or Tehran,[131] faced attacks or inimical incitement. C. Anet, who visited Iran around 1905, writes:

> Living in the midst of a fanatical and hostile population, Jews in Persia are reduced to the last extremity of degradation. Nearly all trades are forbidden to them; everything they touch is considered defiled. They cannot even live in the house of a Mussulman. There is very little justice in Persia for anybody—for the Jews there is none at all. Every possible exaction is practised on them; nobody takes their part; and they live in appalling poverty, while their moral and physical degradation is beyond description.[132]

If a strongly worded a statement, this passage still conveys at least some truth. The Shiraz incident thus mirrors, to an extent, the life of Iranian Jews on the eve of the 1906 Constitutional Revolution.

125. AIU. *Bulletin Mensuel*, 31 (1903), 102.

126. AIU: Iran.I.C.2, Hamadan, March 5, 1903, Bassan to AIU. AIU. *Bulletin Mensuel*, 34 (1906), 162–3: including grand ʿulama who speak with good terms on the Jews.

127 AIU: Iran.I.B.7, Erivan, 1905/1906, Erivan community (Russia) to AIU. AIU: Iran. I.B.18, Ourmiah, month of Av, TaRSaH, received on September 19, 1905, Urumiyyah to AIU. JNL: Microfilm Center, *siman* 8276, from Urumiyyah, TaRSaU. JNL: Microfilm Center, *siman* 8276, 3 Menaẖem Av, TaRSU [=July 26 1906], from Urumiyyah community. AIU: Iran. I.B.18, Ourmiah, *rosh ḥodesh* Sivan, TaRSU [=May 25, 1906], Urumiyyah community to AIU.

128. AIU: Iran, II.C.4, Kermanchah, July 18, 1904, Masidy to AIU: including abuse and ill-treatment by a certain member of the ʿulama.

129. AIU: Iran.I.C.3, Ispahan, June 25, 1905, Lahana to AIU.

130. AIU: Iran. VIII.E.84, Ispahan, received on July 23, 1905, [probably to AIU]: indicating that they are in *galut* and *saʿar*, exile and sorrow.

131. AIU: Iran.XVI.E, 160, Teheran, August 20, 1905, Mme Rosanis to AIU. AIU: Iran.XVI.E, 160, Teheran, September 12, 1905, Mme Rosanis to AIU.

132. C. Anet, *Through Persia in a Motor-Car*, trans. M.B. Ryley (London: Hodder & Stoughton, 1907), 221. C. Anet, "Les Écoles Israélites en Perse," *L'universe Israélite*, 61 (1905): 467.

*

The revolution improved, to a certain extent, the legal status of those religious minorities acknowledged by Shi'i Islam as compared to their legal status according to Shi'i law. On the one hand, certain revolutionary enactments provided equality before the law, abrogated the *jizyah* tax, and prescribed the principle of representation for Armenians, Nestorians, Zoroastrians, and Jews in the *majlis*. On the other hand, other enactments simultaneously consisted of discriminatory elements towards religious minorities, such as the stipulation that only a Muslim can be a minister. As a result of this incongruity, religious minorities should not be regarded as equals under the law of the revolution.[133]

Following the revolution—due to the revolution or other reasons—the situation for some Jews improved in certain places. There is evidence of fair treatment toward the Jews.[134] Zahir al-Dawlah, the governor of Hamadan in 1324 (1906–1907), reports that Jews in Hamadan were thankful that "now the Jews are much more comfortable and more free than any [other] time (*khayli rahat-tar wa-azad-tar az har zamani*)."[135] Still, other Jews feared the unknown consequences of the triumphant revolution. Thus, for instance, about 100 families of crypto-Jews of Mashhad left the city to Constantinople precisely because of the constitution. The constitution was seen as what would increase the power of the 'ulama, thereby forcing the Jewish converts to become Muslims "in something more than in name, as they are at present."[136] In retrospect, the revolution did not bring about the complete cessation of the harsh attitude towards the Jews or other religious minorities.[137] While in need of further substantiation, one may argue that, in addition to the aforementioned reasons for anti-Jewish treatment, Jews were attacked in the constitutional era, at least in part, by those elements—including some of the 'ulama—that, for religious, social, economic, and political motivations, rejected the

133. Tsadik, "Legal Status," 406–8. Of relevance is: Kirmani, N. *Tarikh-i Bidari-yi Iranian* (n.p: Agah, 1357), vol. 2, 35.

134. E.g., A. Netzer, "Yahudiyan-i Shiraz dar Sal-i 1910." In *Padyavand II*, ed. A. Netzer (Los Angeles: Mazda, 1997), Persian section, 265–66, English section, 186.

135. Zahir al-Dawlah, *Khatirat*, 160.

136. *Iran; Political Diaries, 1881–1965*, ed. R. Burrell (Archive Editors, 1997), vol. 3, 52.

137. E.g., H. Levi, *Tarikh-i Yahud-i Iran* (Tehran: Kitab Furush-i Birukhim, 1960), vol. 3, 830–831, 850.

constitutional order. Exemplifying their discontent with the constitution, they harmed the Jews, who, according to part of the constitutional enactments, were regarded as beneficiaries of the constitution. In this, they, in fact, might have attempted to thwart the existing constitutional order and were sending out a message to the constitutionalists that they were not going to give up their vested interests without a fight.[138]

At any rate, J. G. Wishard critically asserts in 1908 that "much of the persecution that has fallen upon" the Jews "is of their own making,"[139] apparently due to the vocations of some Jews, for instance, wine and arrack production and vending of "spurious" coins. It is noteworthy, nevertheless, that in some cases, Islamic culture and customs as well as socially accepted mores and beliefs encouraged Jews to incline toward certain vocations that were forbidden to adherents of Islam or toward those socially detested. In any event, even Wishard grants that "upon them [i.e. the Jews] has been visited, as upon no others, the hatred of Hagar's descendants," or that the Jews are "despised, beaten without cause by any one who chooses to do so, downtrodden and oppressed."[140] Other sources seem to verify this impression. An observer from 1909 says, "the Jews of Persia are a miserably poor, degraded class of people. Their lot is a very hard one; despised and oppressed by the Muslims, hated and cursed by all, their life is not enviable."[141] In the same year, the Jews of Kirmanshah were looted, some butchered, while many wounded.[142] Shiraz Jews were severely targeted on October 30, 1910: twelve of them were killed and around fifty "seriously injured," while generally all of the community was plundered and "stripped of everything they possessed." A scene capturing the spirit of the event depicts the following:

> An unlucky woman was wearing gold rings in her ears. A soldier ordered her to surrender them. She made haste to comply and had taken off one of the rings and was trying to remove the

---

138. This is not to say that elements associated with the constitution did not occasionally target Jews; the Bakhtiyaris in 1909 are one example for this. See J. Afary, "From Outcastes to Citizens; Jews in Qajar Iran," in *Esther's Children*, ed. H. Sarshar (Beverly Hills: The Center for Iranian Jewish Oral History, 2002), 171.

139. J. G. Wishard, *Twenty Years in Persia; A Narrative of Life under the Last Three Shahs* (New York: Revell, 1908), 171.

140. Wishard, 171, 173.

141. M.E. Hume-Griffith, *Behind the Veil in Persia and Turkish Arabia* (London: Seeley, 1909), 29.

142. Cohen, 19–21. Kirmanshachi, *Tahawwulat*, 340–347.

other when the impatient fanatic found it more expeditious to tear off the ear-lobe together with the ring."[143]

Indeed, by 1910, the Jews of Iran were "looked down upon and persecuted.[144] This situation led some of the Jews to view their lives in Iran as *galut*, or exile. Addressing her son in 1911 subsequent to his cursing and stoning by non-Jewish boys in Kashan, the Jewish mother told him that they lived in "exile" (*galut*) and that this is the "fate (*goral*) of the Jews."[145]

It is against this background that the slow but noteworthy improvement of some of the Jews' social and economic situation during the Pahlavi era—under Reza Shah (r. 1925–1941) and mainly under his son Muhammad Reza Shah (r. 1941–1979)—should be examined, assessed, and appreciated. Indeed, certain aspects of the Jews' supposed "exile" were to diminish; the "fate" of at least some of the Jews was to transform under the Pahlavis.

---

143. Littman, "Jews," 12–13. Although various social elements (some *lutis*, Sayyids, men of the Qashqai tribe, certain soldiers; general men, women, and children) were involved in the attack on the Jews, certain Muslims provided assistance to the Jews in its aftermath, including: Qawam al-Mulk ("the temporary governor"), "a wealthy Muslim lady," Mirza Ibrahim (a high ranking Shi'i cleric), the *imam jum'ah*, and Nasr al-Dawlah. 'Aqili, B, *Ruz Shumar-i Tarikh-i Iran az Mashrutah ta Inqilab-i Islami* (Tehran: Nashr-i Guftar, 1372), vol. 1, 77. Netzer, "Yahudiyan-i Shiraz," 259–280. Loeb, *Outcast*, 33. Kirmanshachi, *Tahawwulat*, 366.

144. Sykes, *Persia and its People*, 128.

145. D. Omid, *Emunah we-Tiqwah* (Jerusalem: Mena☒em, 1981), 11.

15

The Concept of Tyranny in Anti-Israeli Discourse in Contemporary Iran

Agnieszka Erdt

ORIGINS OF ANTI-ISRAELI DISCOURSE IN THE CONTEXT OF GENERAL IDEOLOGICAL REORIENTATIONS IN CONTEMPORARY IRAN

The origins of identifying Israel with the concept of tyranny date back to the last decades of the nineteenth century. This is the period of the development of Zionism, which led to increasing Jewish migration to Palestine and, subsequently, to the creation of Israel in 1948. The Israeli-Palestinian conflict, escalating throughout the twentieth century, became one of the most important events affecting the attitudes of many Iranians, political leaders, and clerics toward Israel.

In Iran, it coincides with the end of the reign of Qajars (1794–1925) and the succession of the Pahlavi dynasty (1925–1979). Although Iran has never been formally colonized by any of the Western powers, the presence of Western countries in Iran—their political, military, economic, and cultural domination over the country since the mid-nineteenth century—was unquestionable. The Qajar Shahs had to resist increasing military and economic pressures from Russia and Great Britain. A detailed discussion of this issue goes far beyond the subject and volume of this paper.¹ Nonetheless, some major events should be mentioned: war between Iran and Russia in 1828, resulting in Russia taking over South Caucasus; the war with Great Britain in 1856–1857, after which Iran had to renounce its claims to Heart; the creation of the Persian Cossack Brigade in 1879, the only modern military unit, trained and controlled from Petersburg; and granting Russia and Britain many legal and economic privileges,² which resulted in Iran's reliance on loans offered by both countries. All this proved a major weakness of the Qajar state. The Anglo-Russian rivalry, however, spared Iran from colonization by one of these countries.

The penetration of Iran by Western powers resulted in confronting Iranians with Western technology and innovations of the Industrial Revolution, along with new intellectual trends. It proved to have a major impact on the intellectual life of Iran. A new class of Westernized intelligentsia began to take shape. They became particularly active during the Constitutional Revolution of 1905–1911 (Pers. Mashrutah).³ Most scholars agree that the revolution was largely a result of the intellectual impact of the West on Iran and an attempt to modernize it according to

1. An account of the Qajar history and society can be found in: *Qajar Iran: Political, Social, and Cultural Change, 1800–1925*, ed. E. Bosworth and C. Hillenbrand (Edinburgh: Edinburgh University Press, 1983); N. R. Keddie, *Qajar Iran and the Rise of Reza Khan, 1796–1925* (Costa Mesa, CA: Mazda, 1999); N. R. Keddie, *Modern Iran: Roots and Results of Revolution* (New Haven: Yale University Press, 2006), 22–57; E. Abrahamian, *A History of Modern Iran* (New York: Cambridge University Press, 2008), 8–62; E. Abrahamian, *Iran Between Two Revolutions* (Princeton: Princeton University Press, 1982), 9–49. On religion and society, see: H. Algar, *Religion and State in Iran, 1785–1906: The Role of the Ulama in the Qajar Period* (Berkeley: University of California Press, 1969); *Religion and Society in Qajar Iran*, ed. R. Gleave (London: RoutledgeCurzon, 2005); Monica M. Ringer, *Education, Religion, and the Discourse of Cultural Reform in Qajar Iran* (Costa Mesa, CA: Mazda, 2001).

2. The biggest one was that obtained by a British aristocrat, William Knox D'Arcy in 1901. It gave the British a sixty-year concession to explore for oil in the entire country except for five provinces around the Caspian Sea. Pursuant to the agreement, the vast majority of oil company's profits ended in the pocket of the British.

3. On the Constitutional Revolution see: E. Abrahamian, *A History of Modern Iran*, 50–101; N. R. Keddie, *Modern Iran: Roots and Results of Revolution*, 58–72 (covers period of 1890–1914); M. Bayat, *Iran's First Revolution: Shi'ism and the Constitutional Revolution of 1905–1909* (New York: Oxford University Press, 1991). Among works in Persian, the most accurate and comprehensive is still A. Kasravi's *Tarikh-i Mashrutah-yi Iran* (Tehran: Negah, 2003). For English translation see: A. Kasravi, *History of the Iranian Constitutional Revolution: Tarikh-e Mashrute-ye Iran*, vol. I, trans. E. Siegel (Costa Mesa, CA: Mazda, 2006).

European models. Even though some scholars suggest that the ideals of the revolution were neither limited to the dominant narrative of Western modernity nor influenced solely by European intellectual trends,[4] the dominant desire of the constitutional revolution was, as A. Mirsepassi calls it, "reconciliation through capitulation":

> The dominant trend in this movement called for the imposition of the Western narrative of modernity in Iran. This resulted in a cultural capitulation and a concession of inferiority to European ideas. It would be mistaken to view this as an accidental side-effect of accepting modernity. Rather, the cultural capitulation to the West was proclaimed with intellectual and political pride, and the liberal modernists of the time who theorized it eagerly claimed credit for the proclamation. The inability of the Mashruteh movement to be critical of Western ideas was problematic and came to be known as "the paradox of the Mashruteh discourse."[5]

It should be noted, however, that already before the Constitutional Revolution, in the end of the nineteenth century, another answer to Iran's ills had emerged. It was pan-Islamism, with its leading figure, Sayyid Jamal al-Din "al-Afghani" (1838–1897). As noted by Vali Nasr, this political activist and ideologue was more interested in formulating a response to Western domination than theology.[6] Afghani laid the foundations of the modern politicized Islam and advocated establishing a supranational state of all Muslims. Despite this, however, the next decades after the Constitutional Revolution were a period of rapidly increasing political and intellectual dependency on the West. After the overthrow of the Qajar dynasty, Reza Khan (reg. 1925–41) came to power. To a large extent, his rule may be interpreted as a consequence of Iran's "cultural capitulation" to Western patterns of modernity. The former commander of the Cossack brigade started the process of building a state based on a centralized bureaucracy and a strong army. Yet, when Reza Khan established a new dynasty, he chose to call it the Middle Persian name "Pahlavi."

---

4. See: A. Mirsepassi, *Intellectual Discourse and the Politics of Modernization: Negotiating Modernity in Iran* (Cambridge: Harvard University Press, 2000), 55–61; M. Tavakoli-Targhi, *Refashioning Iran: Orientalism, Occidentalism, and Historiography* (New York: Palgrave, 2001), 1–17.

5. Mirsepassi, *Intellectual Discourse and the Politics of Modernization*, 61.

6. V. R. Nasr, *The Shia Revival: How Conflicts within Islam Will Shape the Future* (New York: Norton, 2006), 103.

Thus, his vision of Iran was founded, on the one hand, on modernization and Westernization of Iran, and on the other hand, on emphasizing the greatness of "Aryan" Iran. This resulted, among other things, in changing the country's official name from Persia to Iran in 1935. During the Second World War, the Shah proclaimed Iran as a neutral country, but Great Britain and the USSR were afraid of Reza Khan's pro-Nazi sympathies. Following Germany's invasion of the Soviet Union, Great Britain and the Soviet Union became allies. They invaded Iran in 1941, and forced the monarch to abdicate in favor of his son Muhammad Reza (reg. 1941–1979).

The second Pahlavi Shah of Iran carried on the pro-Western policies of his father, and Western powers continued to interfere with the internal affairs of Iran. The United States gradually replaced the position of Great Britain. This became evident in 1951, when the nationalist Prime Minister Muhammad Mossadeq (1882–1967) pushed for the nationalization of the British-led oil company, and two years later, the CIA played an active role in overthrowing his government. It was a tough lesson for Iranians, and the growing distrust and hostility toward the United States date back to that event. The period of 1953–1979, between eliminating the nationalist opposition of Mossadeq and the victory of the Islamic Revolution, were times of authoritarian rule by Muhammad Reza Pahlavi. Washington actively supported the Shah. His reign was dependent on the help of Western countries. On the other hand, in his rhetoric, Muhammad Reza Pahlavi appealed even more strongly than his father to the glory and grandeur of ancient Iran. This grandeur was to be demonstrated by the lavish celebration of the 2500th year of Iranian monarchy, organized in Persepolis.

Not all Iranians, however, were as supportive of the West as the Shah. Over time, they became increasingly critical of the West and realized the negative aspects of its ubiquitous presence in Iran. From the 1950s on, more radical reactions crystallized, and Iranians' response to the West became similar to the reactions of nationals in countries with a colonial past. First of all, it resulted in the emergence of nativistic movements, calling for rejection of Western domination and revival of authentic Iranian culture. This was to be achieved on the basis of Islam or nationalism.[7] Harbingers of this critical attitude toward the West were

---

7. There is a large collection of literature on intellectual debates in 20th century Iran. See the account in: A. Gheissari, *Iranian Intellectuals in the 20th Century* (Austin: University of Texas Press, 1998), M. Kamrava, *Iran's Intellectual Revolution*

two Iranian intellectuals, Sayyid Fakhr al-Din Shadman (1907–1967) and Ahmad Fardid (1909–1994). The turning point, however, was the clandestine publication of an essay "Gharbzadigi" (Westoxication) by Sayyid Jalal Al-i Ahmad in 1952, a passionately written account of Iranians' cultural passivity and uncritical imitation of Western models. The following years comprised of a period of increasingly virulent criticism of the Westoxication and formulation of programs and ideologies. The discourse was started by a group of lay thinkers, among whom most prominent in the 1970s was 'Ali Shari'ati (1933–1977). He called on Iranians to realize their auto-alienation (Pers. *az khud biganagi*; a term borrowed by Shari'ati from Marx) and to return to the self, which, for him, was synonymous with a revival of politicized Islam. The lay intellectuals were followed by a group of Shi'ite clerics-turned-ideologues, including Ayatollah Muhammad Husayn Tabataba'i (1903–1981), Ayatollah Murtaza Mutahhari (1920–1979), Ayatollah Sayyid Mahmud Taliqani (1911–1979), and Ruhullah Khomeini. Their position was much less complicated than that of the lay thinkers. As S. A. Arjomand points out, "the clerical ideologues were not particularly tormented by ambivalence toward the West and were more securely grounded in the Shi'i tradition they wanted to save."[8] Khomeini and his supporters made the well-known phrase "Neither East nor West," one of the main slogans of the revolution. It reflected the program to found the new Islamic Republic of Iran exclusively on Islam. Both the East, mainly identified with the Soviet Union and socialism, and the United States, identified with capitalism, were considered equally threatening to the newly established republic and its ideals. Following the collapse of communism, the slogan to com-

---

(Cambridge: Cambridge University Press, 2008). On the discourse of authenticity, nativity, and the West see: M. Boroujerdi, *Iranian Intellectuals and the West. The Tormented Triumph of Nativism* (Syracuse: Syracuse University Press, 1996); M. Tavakoli-Targhi, *Refashioning Iran, Orientalism, Occidentalism, and Historiography* (New York: Palgrave, 2001); N. Nabavi, *Intellectuals and the State in Iran: Politics, Discourse and the Dilemma of Authenticity* (Gainesville: University of Florida Press, 2003). On religious conservatives and Islamic revivalism, see: H. Dabashi, *Theology of Discontent* (New York: New York University Press, 1993). On modernity, see: A. Milani, *Lost Wisdom: Rethinking Modernity in Iran* (Washington: Mage, 2004); A. Mirsepassi, *Intellectual Discourse and the Politics of Modernization: Negotiating Modernity in Iran* (Cambridge: Harvard University Press, 2000); F. Vahdat, *God and Juggernaut: Iran's Intellectual Encounter with Modernity* (Syracuse: Syracuse University Press, 2002).

8. S. A. Arjomand, "The Reform Movement and the Debate on Modernity and Tradition in Contemporary Iran," *International Journal of Middle East Studies* 34 (2002): 721.

bat the U.S. hegemony in the region had become fundamental in Iranian foreign policy. It mostly meant that Palestinians could enjoy more support and interest from Iranian politicians. Yet again, the pro-Palestinian, anti-Israeli rhetoric became significantly enhanced when the Palestinian movements became Islamic, which was indicated by the outburst of the first Intifada and the creation of Hamas in 1987. Nowadays, when analyzing Iranian propaganda, it is sometimes difficult to identify who is considered the greater evil. The United States are called the Great Satan (originally due to close relations with the Shah), while Israel is sometimes depicted as a dog on their leash (Pers. *sagha-yi dastamuzah-yi Imrika*) or their puppet. Often, however, the opposite happens: the United States are depicted as a toy in Israeli hands. Many contemporary politicians, including Mahmud Ahmadinejad and 'Ali Khamenehi, suggest that the West is controlled by the Israeli lobby and governed by guilty conscience for the crimes of the Holocaust.[9]

Here, I can proceed to a brief account of how Iranian politicians, clerics, and ideologues have perceived Zionism and the State of Israel. Overall, it might be said that it reflected their reactions to the West and general ideological re-orientations that took place in twentieth-century Iran.

During the Qajar reign, in the late nineteenth and early twentieth century, the Palestinian issue and Zionism did not attract a lot of attention in the foreign policy of Iran. As noted by an Iranian researcher on Iranian-Israeli relations, A. M. Haji Jusifi, the only case when Palestine appeared in Iranian politics was the situation of Iranian Jews, their migration to Palestine, and the situation of Iranian nationals living in Palestine:

> In general, it can be said that until the rise of the Zionist government, the Palestinian issue did not enjoy great importance in Iranian foreign policy. Even if Palestine occasionally gained some attention, it was due to the fact that the Jews inside the country addressed some requests, they became problematic to the Iranian government, or if the presence of Iranians in Palestine demanded such an interest.[10]

---

9. See: *Parah-yi Tan-i Islam dar Ayinah-yi Haqiqat: Filistin wa-Rezhim-i Sahyiunisti dar Nigah-i Rahbar-i Mo'azam-i Inqilab-i Islami* (Tehran: Muisisiyyah-yi Farhangi Qadr-i Vilayat, 2003), 75; 85–86.

10. A. M. Haji Jusifi, *Iran wa-Rezhim-i Sahyunisti az Hamkari ta Manazi'i* (Tehran: Intisharat-i Danishgah-i Imam Sadiq, 2003), 81.

Iran officially recognized the state of Israel in 1950. However, only a year later, the Prime Minister Muhammad Mussadiq closed the Iranian consulate in Jerusalem and moved it to Amman, which was intended to prevent further Israeli-Iranian cooperation. But it did not last long, and after the overthrow of Mussadiq in 1953, the Shah gained full control over the politics of Iran. Since then, the Israeli-Iranian entente developed intensively.[11] The main reason for the close Israeli-Iranian cooperation was the existence of mutual strategic interests—the entente took shape within the framework of anti-Arab "periphery doctrine." Both countries also hoped to obtain additional benefits. For Israel, the existence of the Jewish Diaspora in Iran and the Iraqi Diaspora, for whom Iran was a transit route for migration, was important. Moreover, Israel looked forward to the opening of the Iranian raw-materials market, as well as benefits from the provision of military assistance to Iran. For Iran, an important impulse for strengthening relations was the possibility of acquiring new technologies from Israel. The Iranians also hoped that Israeli influence in Washington would help to strengthen U.S.-Iranian relations. Another important factor was the desire to deepen cooperation with Israeli security services. All these gave rise to the formation of Iranian-Israeli entente. Most of the guidelines were implemented in subsequent years. Israel developed large-scale economic activity in Iran, selling products, pursuing agricultural, and construction investments. Iran, in turn, sold oil to Israel. The countries continued bilateral diplomatic cooperation. No less important was the military cooperation. It included mainly the purchase of military hardware and secret service cooperation. Thanks largely to the help of Israeli intelligence specialists, SAVAK (National Intelligence and Security Organization) was established in 1957.

The Iranian clergy adopted quite a different position. Since the beginning of the Jewish-Palestinian conflict, Shi'ite clerics supported the Palestinians and issued fatwas condemning any actions empowering the Zionists. Leading Iranian clerics opposed projects to create a Jewish state, and when it happened, consistently refused to recognize the legitimacy of Israel. As pointed out by 'Ali Akbar Wilayati, there was no change in the position regarding Palestine in circles of Shi'ite clergy since the 1930s,

---

11. There have been only two thorough publications on this subject. One of them is Sohrab Sobhani's *The Pragmatic Entente: Israeli–Iranian Relations, 1948–1988* (New York: Praeger, 1989). More recent is Trita Parsi's *Treacherous Alliance: The Secret Dealings of Israel, Iran, and the United States* (New Haven: Yale University Press, 2007).

and many clerics enunciated it very clearly.¹² The most important voice was a fatwa issued in 1934 by Muhammad Husayn al-Kashif al-Ghita (1877–1953), the leader of the Shi'is in Najaf. It was a historic fatwa, and many of today's Iranian ideologues still invoke it. One of them is 'Ali Khamenehi, who maintains that al-Ghita was one of the first religious leaders to recognize the Islamic character of the Palestinian struggle.¹³ Al-Ghita called for a jihad against the Zionists settling on Palestinian lands and called selling land to the Zionists injustice, *zulm*, committed against Islam and its followers:

> Is there a greater injustice than that when a person breaks and tramples the rights of both his ancestors and grandchildren? You can also say what kind of injustice is greater than this when a man tramples on the truth of his sanctities and religion, and diminishes the principles of the Quran.¹⁴

The most characteristic feature of the early claims of Shi'ite clerics was their emphasis on issues of economic and moral injustice, committed, in their opinion, both by Zionists and those Palestinians who were ignoring religious obligations, rather than political struggle against foreign powers. The latter kind of discourse can be found for the first time after proclamation of Israel's independence in 1948. It caused a significant radicalization of the position of the clergymen. One of them was Ayatollah Kashani (1882–1962), a cleric who was considered the main Iranian opponent of the Zionists in the 1940s and 1950s and was renowned for his extreme views, founded on opposition to tyranny, despotism, and colonialism. Many followers and disciples of Ayatollah Kashani remained under the influence of his anti-Israeli rhetoric. The most famous among them was Sayyid Mujtaba Navab Safavi (1925–1955), disciple and close associate of the Ayatollah, founder of the Fadayan-i Islam (Devotees of Islam Organization). In 1953, he was delegated by Kashani to represent the Iranian clergy at the first General Islamic Congress for Jerusalem. According to reports from participants of the congress, Navab Safavi was a fiery speaker and a staunch supporter of the Palestinian issue. In one of his speeches during the congress, he claimed:

12. 'A. A. Wilayati, *Iran wa-Masalah-yi Filistin bar Asas-i Asnad-i Wizarat-i Umur-i Kharijah* (1275–1316 sh./1897–1938 m.) (Tehran: Daftar-i Nashr-i Farhang-i Islami, 1999), 163.

13. *Parah-yi Tan-i Islam*, 125.

14. *Baygani-yi Asnad-i Wizarat-i Umur-i Kharijah, sal-i 1313, kartun-i 12, dosyah-yi 21*, in: 'A. A. Wilayati, *Iran wa-Masalah-yi Filistin*, 165.

Look what this bunch of scoundrels with support and intrigues of superpowers has done to us. But when Muslims unite, when they rise up, like they did in the days of the greatest glory of Islam, what can governments of the United States, Great Britain, or Russia possibly do?[15]

A breakthrough in the perception of Israel and its presence in the Middle East was made by Ruhollah Khomeini. He may have influenced that perception among Iranians more than anyone else. Khomeini was the most trenchant Iranian opponent of the presence of Israelis in Palestine, who identified their rule with the idea of tyranny. His anti-Israel standpoint was evident since the early 1940s but gathered full momentum in the early 1960s, along with the growing cooperation within the Israeli-Iranian alliance. The leader of the Islamic Revolution introduced a new element to the anti-Israeli discourse. He combined opposition to colonialism and superpowers with harsh political attacks against the Iranian-Israeli entente (thereby criticizing both Israel and the Shah). Khomeini was certainly aware that friendly relations between Muhammad Reza Pahlavi and Israel provoked a constantly growing discontent among many Iranians. A report sent to the Iranian embassy in Tel Aviv mentions what a journalist of the Israeli newspaper *Maariv* saw on the streets of Tehran:

> This journalist reports about demonstrations and discontent caused by the close relations between Iran and Israel. He also mentions slogans like "Shah is a Jew" and changing the name of the Pahlavi dynasty to "Papa Levi."[16]

The close relations between Muhammad Reza Shah and Israel spawned great hostility among Iranians toward the Shah and his domestic actions. Iranians perceived the Shah as a stranger, one of *them*, somebody whom anthropologists call the "Other." As I will show in the second part of this paper, the strangeness attributed not only to the Shah but also to the Zionists and Israel as well is one of the most important, indispensable features of a tyrant, *zalim*. Khomeini used the anti-Israel sentiment

---

15. 'A. A. Wilayati., *Iran wa-Tahawulat-i Filistin* (1317–1357 sh./ 1939–1979 m.) (Tehran: Markaz-i Asnad wa-Khadamat-i Pazhuhishi-yi Vizarat-i Umur-i Kharajah, 2005), 250.

16. *Guzarish-i shumarah-yi 1107/m muwarakh-i 4.4.1352 az Ibrahim Teymuri bah vizarat-i umur-i kharijah, bah naql az ruznamah-yi „Maariw," namayandigi-yi Tel Aviv, sal-i 1350-55, kartun-i 3, parvandah-yi 122_2* in: 'A. A. Wilayati, *Iran wa-Tahawulat-i Filistin*, 264.

to mobilize the masses against the Pahlavi regime. As the former foreign minister of Iran 'Ali Akbar Wilayati notes, "In fact, the fight against Zionism and Israel was the common link among all the fighters."[17]

Anti-Israel sentiments gained an institutional framework after the victory of the Islamic Revolution in 1979. In the years following the proclamation of the Islamic Republic of Iran, not only within the circles of Shi'ite clergy, but also evident in official statements by politicians and leaders, both lay and religious, Israel began to be described mainly in the context of oppression, *zulm*. Tyranny, previously also associated with the Shah, became exclusive of Israel. This was followed by many anti-Israel actions. In February 1979, the Israeli embassy in Tehran was closed. In March, an office of the Palestine Liberation Organization (PLO) was opened in place of the former Israeli embassy. Yasser Arafat and the son of Ayatollah Khomeini, Hujjat al-Islam Sayyid Ahmad Khomeini, were invited to the ceremony. Not incidentally, Yasser Arafat was the first foreign visitor to visit Iran after the revolution. In this manner, the importance of the Palestinian issue in Iranian foreign policy was symbolically underlined.

The ideological claim that the Islamic Revolution is a sharp cessation in Israeli-Iranian relations and that it simply marks the definite end of them is represented by the vast majority of Iranian officials. Although some scholars rebut such ideological explanations as simplistic and far from being accurate,[18] the main subject of this paper is the official anti-Israel discourse centered around the concept of tyranny, and for that reason, it is worth quoting an example of this omnipresent claim, here made by 'Ali Akbar Wilayati:

> One of the main objectives and principles of the Islamic Revolution and the Islamic Republic of Iran has been the struggle against tyranny and colonialism, and the support of anti-colonial and liberation movements. From this perspective, it is clear that Iran cannot accept any oppression or injustice. This

---

17. 'A. A. Wilayati., *Iran wa-Tahawulat-i Filistin*, 264.

18. Parsi, for example, argues, "the current enmity between the two states has more to do with the shift in the balance of power in the Middle East after the Cold War and the defeat of Iraq in the first Persian Gulf War than it does with the Islamic Revolution in 1979. Though the Iranian revolution was a major setback for Israel, it didn't stop the Jewish State from supporting Iran and seeking to improve its relations with the Khomeini government as a counter to Israel's Arab enemies." T. Parsi, *Treacherous Alliance: The Secret Dealings of Israel, Iran, and the United States* (New Haven: Yale University Press, 2007), xi [Preface].

is regardless of whether this applies to Iran or other Muslim countries. Supporting ideals of the oppressed Palestinians and opposition to the Zionist regime and its biggest ally, the United States, has been one of the main slogans of the Islamic Revolution and the Islamic Republic of Iran.[19]

To date, two comprehensive works on the history of the Iranian-Israeli relations have been published. The first, Sohrab Sobhani's *The Pragmatic Entente: Israeli-Iranian Relations, 1948–1988*, was published more than two decades ago, and it is devoted to relations between the two countries in the geopolitical context of the Middle East. Another work is Trita Parsi's *Treacherous Alliance: The Secret Dealings of Israel, Iran, and the United States*. It covers the period from the creation of the State of Israel in 1948 to present times, and it is based on 130 interviews the author conducted with Iranian, Israeli, and American officials and analysts. As Parsi admits, he focused on "geopolitical forces and developments rather than on ideology, fleeting political justifications, or simplistic Manichean perspectives."[20]

I believe, however, that a study focused on Iranian culture and its intellectual history is also needed. Such studies can shed some light on the country's political culture and can help to understand its development and the reactions of the society. Culturally grounded notions, like the notion of tyranny, are very clear for most Iranians and evoke certain emotions and attitudes, so they can be successfully used in propaganda to shape Iranians' attitudes toward Israel. Moreover, claims emphasizing the continuity and permanence of Iranian culture enjoy unceasing popularity and are widespread among Iranians, ordinary citizens and scholars alike. This opinion is expressed, i.a., by Fereydoun Hoveyda, the former Iranian ambassador to the United Nations under the Shah (1971–1978), who notes that the transmission of Ancient mythology to kids still plays a great role in molding their minds and emotions from the earliest days of childhood. In his book *The Shah and the Ayatollah: Iranian Mythology and Islamic Revolution*, Hoveyda analyzes aspects of the 1979 revolution from the perspective of Iranian mythology. He maintains that he has found "many points in the events that led to the fall of Muhammad Reza

---

19. 'A. A. Wilayati, *Iran wa-Tahawulat-i Filistin*, 189.
20. T. Parsi, *The Treacherous Alliance*, xi (Preface).

Shah and the ascent of Ayatollah Khomeini that can be explained only by the impact of old mythology on Iranians' mind-sets.[21]

So far, however, there has been no comprehensive research analyzing the history of Iranian-Israeli relations in the context of the discourse and its key concepts. There is also no separate study on the concept of oppression in Iranian culture. Of course, many scholars acknowledge the great importance of this idea in Islam, particularly in Shi'ism, but only some references in works on other subjects can be found. For instance, Taghavi notes that the concept of tyranny appeared in the socio-political thought of Social Theists, Iran Freedom Movement, and Navabi's *Fada'iyan-e Islam*.[22] It is also worth noting here H. Ram's article, in which he analyzes how utilization of "the Karbala paradigm," the mythologized martyrdom of Imam Husayn (a concept closely connected to the notion of *zulm*), enhanced the process of homogenizing the image of the hostile (Western) Other and shaping the dichotomy between him and the Injured (Iranian) Self in revolutionary Iran.[23]

Therefore, my goal is to show how one of the most distinct concepts in Iranian culture was employed against Israel in order to perpetuate enmity between the two states. I analyzed primary sources that have not yet been discussed in the context of the concept of oppression. The authors are leading politicians, clerics, and political analysts, including Ruhullah Khomeini, 'Ali Khamenehi, Mahmoud Ahmadinejad, and 'Ali Akbar Wilayati, who is the author of a study on the history of the Iranian-Israeli relations spanning from the late nineteenth century to the 1979 revolution. Another group of sources are publications on the Israeli-Palestinian conflict, written by Iranian scholars and researchers. Even though their objectivity and reliability are sometimes questionable, they represent interesting material for a cultural analysis. The last group of primary sources consists of popular and somewhat controversial publications, such as the Protocols of the Elders of Zion, propaganda brochures, daily newspapers, and other materials of that sort published in Iran. In addition, I rely also

---

21. F. Hoveyda, *The Shah and the Ayatollah: Iranian Mythology and Islamic Revolution* (Westport: Praeger, 2003), ix (Preface).

22. S. M. A. Taghavi, *The Flourishing of Islamic Reformism in Iran. Political groups in Iran (1941–1961)* (London: RoutledgeCurzan, 2005), 46, 77–78, 102–3.

23. H. Ram, "Mythology of Rage: Representations of the 'Self' and the 'Other' in Revolutionary Iran," *History and Memory* 8/1 (1996): 67–68. The term "Karbala paradigm" was coined by M. Fisher in his study *Iran from Religious Dispute to Revolution* (Cambridge: Harvard University Press, 1980).

on visual material: anti-Israeli cartoons and official graffiti and murals that can be found throughout Iran.

THE ISRAEL-PALESTINE-IRAN TRIAD

In this part, I argue that the concept of oppression employed in anti-Israeli discourse since the 1960s, particularly due to Khomeini, gained a wider meaning embedded in the politico-cultural paradigm. This paradigm consists of three basic terms or model characters: the tyrant, the oppressed and the one combating tyranny. In anti-Israeli discourse, these model characters are projected onto Israel, Palestine and Iran, respectively. I will also present in detail how Iranian ideologues and politicians depict these three countries. Finally, I will show that these models come from narratives found in all (pre)Islamic Iranian culture, particularly in the ancient mythology and Shi'ism. They have constantly recurred over the centuries, and various rulers have been described within this model. In the twentieth century alone, several rulers and countries can be enumerated, including Saddam Husayn and the Ba'ath party, Anwar Sadat, Muhammad Reza Pahlavi, the United States. After 1979, however, Iranian leaders and ideologues have employed this paradigm primarily when referring to Israel.

Israel = Tyrant

Israel's tyranny has been described in two ways. First of all, Israel is directly called the symbolic names of oppressors. Hence, Khamenehi compares Israel to the Pharaoh. Israel is an oppressor because, as Khamenehi asserts, it suppresses the Muslim inhabitants of Palestine. To stay in power, he continues, Israelis need to involve a huge apparatus of oppression. This allows them to force others to obey:

> Let God and His pious servants cut the hand that signed the first agreement with Israel and clutch their black earthly life and its otherworldly fate with the Pharaoh.[24]

H. Wa'izi presents Israel as the one who supports the Pharaoh and cooperates with him. He asks:

---

24. Ibid., 149.

> Why did they [Jews] always live in a strategic alliance with the Pharaohs of their times and [act against] the disadvantaged?[25]

Iranian ideologues see a parallel between Israeli policies in Palestine and the Umayyad rule. According to Khomeini, Israelis, just like the Umayyads, went astray and violated principles of faith and ethical standards. Moreover, they spread heresy. Therefore, it is essential to combat them:

> Gentlemen, you should know that today's danger to Islam is no smaller than in the Umayyad era. With full force the apparatus of oppression helps Israel—a sect which descended from the right path and leads others astray.[26]

More often, however, Israel is attributed a set of characteristics and behaviors, which are logical entailments of the narratives about tyranny that I will discuss at the end of this paper. One of them is strangeness. Iranian ideologues and politicians often describe people and authorities of Israel as false, illusory (*ja'li*), and alien (*biganah*). Ayatollah Khamenehi argues that it stems from the fact that Israelis are a random group of people who migrated from different parts of the world and seized lands that, until then, were inhabited by its indigenous population. The supreme leader of Iran defines Israelis as dangerous adventurers, criminals, and people seeking profit. He claims they do not represent any moral values and are familiar with only political intrigues and deceits. According to Khamenehi, Israelis are not a true nation; thereby, even the U.S. government is more predestined to rule, as it is founded on a nation. In his speech during a visit to Mashhad in 1996, Khamenehi remarked:

> Of course, the Zionist government in occupied Palestine is dirtier than America. Why? Because after all, the American government is founded on a nation. While principally the Israeli usurper is not founded on any nation! The nation that lived in this land is now fugitive! Israel was founded on tyranny and genocide, lies and deceit.[27]

---

25. H. Wa'izi, *Nabard-i Nabarabar: Rawand-i Zuhur wa-Suqut-i Rezhim-i Sahyiunisti* (Tehran: Surush, 2004), 3.

26. *Filistin wa-Sahyunizm. Dar Justiju-yi Rah az Kalam-i Imam. Az Bayanat wa-I'limiyah-yi Imam-i Khomeini az Sal-i 1241 ta 1361* (Tehran: Intisharat-i Amir Kabir, 1984), 42.

27. *Parah-yi Tan-i Islam*, 37.

M. Ahmadinejad expresses a similar opinion. In one of his speeches, he stated that the Israeli government was created by the Western powers and then forced upon Palestinians:

> Israel is a product of the British, brought up by the Americans, and with their help commits crimes in the region.[28]

Ahmadinejad also suggests that because of its strangeness and falsehood, to be understood as a lack of identity based on historical ties with Palestine, Israel has no culture. Those who possess it are the Palestinians: fair, indigenous inhabitants of the Palestinian lands. Israel operates as a state only by armed force, whose proper functioning is ensured by the United States:

> The Zionist regime has no philosophy of existence and therefore is an occupier. They perform acts of tyranny and murder, have no culture or civilization, and lean solely on military strengths ...[29]

As noted by H. Ram, the oppressive Other in the discourse of revolutionary Iran has been identified primarily as the West.[30] Furthermore, Western countries are accused of imperialism directed against the oppressed nations of the East. Therefore, Israel—as an agent of their interests in the Middle East—is also described as imperialistic. Iranian politicians and ideologues link Israeli imperialism with a conspiracy, which was allegedly hatched by Jews in early twentieth-century Europe. The authors of anti-Israeli publications derive such beliefs from *The Protocols of the Elders of Zion*, which has been officially disseminated in Iran since 1979.[31] One of its editions, issued by the Islamic Propaganda Organization,[32] provides an introduction warning Muslims about the dangers imposed by the Jews on all Muslim countries, the full text of 24 protocols and a map of planned conquest, demarcating the territory of Greater Israel from the Nile to the Euphrates. The credibility of the *Protocols* is not officially questioned in Iran. Conversely, many authors derive their claims

28. www.etdweb.blogfa.com/post-966.aspx.
29. www.irannewsagency.com/index.php?news=2826.
30. H. Ram, "Mythology of Rage," 84.
31. For example: *Jewish Conspiracy. The Protocols of the Learned Elders of Zion*, Tehran: Islamic Propaganda Organization, 1985).
32. Islamic Propagation Organization was founded in 1981 on the initiative of Khomeini. It was intended to promote Islam and the ideals of the Islamic Revolution and to fight ideologies such as capitalism and communism.

from this publication. They assert that success of the conspiracy would guarantee Zionists power over the world:

> The World Zionist plan has been developed in 24 chapters and 24 protocols. Its aim is to create a central authority over the world, led by the Zionists. According to this four-step plan, Orthodox Russia, Catholic Europe, the Vatican and finally Islam—due to various deceits—were supposed to gradually lose their greatness so that World Zionism could take control of the world.[33]

Wa'izi argues that over the last hundred years, Zionists have managed to fulfill all the stages, except for the last. Therefore, they moved to Palestine, the heart of the Muslim world.[34] Ayatollah Khamenehi also refers to the *Protocols*. He states that even though Zionists rarely use the name of Greater Israel directly, their intentions have not changed. This is evident from the intensity of armament and ceaseless combat readiness that has no real justification—Palestinians are not a threat to Israel, as they have too small a military capacity.[35] R. Khomeini, too, repeatedly referred to the idea of Israeli imperialism, even though he rarely cited the *Protocols* directly. However, the frequently repeated phrase about boundaries of Israel, stretching from the Nile to the Euphrates, proves that he also was influenced by the theories drawn from this fraudulent apocrypha. For instance, Khomeini warned of the threat that Israeli imperialism poses to Islam and Muslim countries during al-Quds Day in 1980:

> Israel, this seed of corruption, will not be satisfied with Jerusalem, and if it is given an opportunity, all Muslim countries will be in danger.[36]

A year later, on the same occasion, Khomeini called on Muslims to unite against the imperialist ambitions of Zionists:

> When Israel saw that nations came out against each other, and the government of Egypt is its companion and brother, as is Iraq, it started to move forward step by step. Rest assured that if you show weakness, they will want to come to the Euphrates. They say that everything is their property.[37]

33. H. Wa'izi, *Nabard-i Nabarabar*, 21.
34. Ibid., 21–43.
35. Ibid., 184.
36. *Filistin wa-Sahyunizm*, 130.
37. Ibid., 132.

Another characteristic of Israel as a tyrant is its infidelity, which has repeatedly been described by Iranian authors. It is close to a definition of tyranny that can be found in the *Qur'an*. Ideologues infer it from the fact that the state of Israel was established on the basis of secular Zionist ideology. Therefore, they continue, Israelis utterly alienated themselves from God and disposed of all moral principles. Ayatollah Khamenehi stresses that Israel, looking solely for material benefits, performs acts of tyranny without scruples. He spoke about it in one of his sermons, preached in 2002:

> They attacked mosques and churches in Bethlehem. They refused to permit ambulances there. They declined provision of food and medicine to people who were injured. They shot at ambulances.[38]

All politicians and ideologues, however, separate Jews from Zionists. Moreover, many ideologues stress that the righteous and God-fearing Jews, as well as representatives of other religions living in Israel, are persecuted and oppressed by the secular and sinful Zionists. Iranian authors often employ references to Judaism to show the extent to which Zionists have abandoned the ideals and values of Judaism. Khomeini frequently returned to this topic. In one of his speeches from 1979, he formulated the following position:

> We separate Jews from Zionists. They are not a part of the People of the Book. Uprising against the arrogant is the way of Moses (PBUH), and this is completely contrary to the Zionist program. Zionists cling to the arrogant, they are their spies and servants and act against the disadvantaged. The way of Zionists is absolutely opposite the teachings of Moses, who, like other prophets, was a simple commoner and rose up against Pharaoh and his power in order to liberate people from the domination of arrogance. Zionists are linked to the arrogant and act against the disadvantaged. These are a certain number of Jews, who were deceived, and came there [to Palestine] from different parts of the world and maybe even now they regret it. They regret that they came there because everyone who goes there and sees what they are up to, what genocide they are responsible for, and what connections they have with America, cannot stand the fact that the tribe, which says that it comes from the Jewish community, is acting against the teachings of Moses. We know

38. *Parah-yi Tan-i Islam*, 94.

that the account of the Jewish community is not the same as Zionists' account. With the latter we are in conflict and our opposition is based on the fact that they are hostile to all religions. They are not Jews. They are political people who operate under the name of the Jews. Jews also burn with hatred for them; all people should hate them.[39]

Ahmadinejad also refers to the secular character of Zionism. It is one of the main slogans of his anti-Israel speeches. The former Iranian president says that Israelis became oppressors as they wiped out religion from their lives. In his speech during a visit to the United States in 2006, he claimed:

> Fundaments of tyranny are in polytheism. Alienation from the only God is the core of all forms of oppression and corruption that has been taking place in today's society ... The existence of racial discrimination, humiliation of peoples because of their skin color, their ethnicity or religion and terrorism are results of this process.[40]

According to Iranian ideologues, Zionists are hostile to other religions because they are afraid of the strength that religion gives people. It was first pointed out by R. Khomeini in the early 1960s. He claimed that Israel is in alliance with the Pahlavi regime to weaken religion in Iran. Khomeini explained many of the political events by way of Israel's enmity toward religion. For example, he related shutdown of a Qur'anic school *Fayziyyah*[41] with instructions allegedly given by Israelis to Muhammad Reza Pahlavi. In his speech on this occasion he appealed:

> Israel does not want the *Qur'an*, Muslim *ulama*, Islamic precepts or scholars in this country. Israel with the hands of its black agents destroyed the *Fayziyyah* school, destroyed us, and you, my nation. They want to seize your economy, destroy your commerce and agriculture, and appropriate your wealth. Israelis with the hands of their agents want to remove those things that are an obstacle for them. The *Qur'an* is an obstacle, so it

---

39. *Filistin wa-Sahyunizm*, 29–30.

40. www.ariadata.ir/MyModule.aspx?Type=Modules&Module=NewsModule&CodePar=2104&Act=ShowNews.

41. In June 1963, Khomeini delivered his historic sermon against the Shah, after which the authorities closed the *Fayziyyah* school, brutally pacified people gathered there, and arrested Khomeini. A year later, he was forced to leave Iran. These events are known as the insurrection of the 15th of Khordad (the 5th of June 1963).

should be removed, the clergymen are an obstacle, they should be defeated, the *Fayziyyah* school and other scientific centers are an obstacle, they should be destroyed, students of theology will possibly become an obstacle in the future, so they should be broken, thrown from the roof, should be smashed into dust so that Israel can fulfill its interests. The Iranian government offends us by following the objectives and plans of Israel.[42]

Harassing members of other religions and ethnic groups is, as argued frequently in Iranian anti-Israeli discourse, another manifestation of Zionists' profanity. To prove it, Iranian authors go back to the history of Zionism. Waʿizi asserts that Zionists use the Jewish belief of a chosen people in a deliberately fraudulent manner. He argues that after the emergence of political Zionism, Jews began to manifest their superiority over others and disseminate originally religious claims that Jews are a chosen people in order to gain control over other nations. Moreover, they started to identify religious superiority with racial superiority:

> Zionists, with their claims of racial and tribal superiority, called Palestine their promised land and demanded bringing a Jewish nation into existence and formation of Israel in the Promised Land ... After more than a century that has passed since the official and public announcement of the program of world Zionism, this word has become a synonym of racism, occupation, tyranny and injustice, exploitation, dictatorship, tricks and occupation of territories belonging to other countries, as well as imperialism and desire for power.[43]

Israelis are regarded as racists by most Iranian ideologues. Khamenehi compares methods used by Israelis in Palestine with the methods used by racists in other places around the world, like in South Africa in the era of apartheid:

> You can see how world politics is conducted with the use of force and tyranny and how it disregards human rights. The oppressed Palestinians are expelled from their houses. A group of racists with financial resources and political oppressors use tyranny, oppression, cruelty, and racial discrimination against the Palestinian nation. What happened in Palestine out of racist motives has its counterpart in few places in the world, such as South Africa. But in South Africa, the problem was black or

---

42. *Sahifah-yi Nur*, v. I, 644 in: *Sahifah-yi Imam* (Tehran: 2001 [CD-ROM]).
43. H. Waʿizi, *Nabard-i Nabarabar*, 12.

white color of skin, and here we are dealing with the problem of Jewish and non-Jewish race.[44]

Such claims are expressed not only by the leading ideologues and political leaders but also, in recent years, by Iranian media. In February 2006, the popular newspaper *Hamshahri* announced an international Holocaust cartoon contest. Later on, the winning works were published in a separate album. Most of the participants alluded to the racism of Israelis. Their works showed Palestinians as victims of Israeli ethnic cleansing, and a many authors suggested that Israel has been committing a second Holocaust. The winning work shows construction of the security fence separating Israeli territories from the West Bank. The author attached to the fence a photo showing a ramp and gate to a concentration camp. The runner-up was a work showing a man standing by the same fence and stretching out his hands in despair. He has a Palestinian keffiyeh on his head but wears a prisoner's striped uniform from Nazi concentration camps.[45]

Another strategy to discredit Israelis used in anti-Israeli propaganda is showing their connection with other, equally oppressive, countries. Reasons for Israel's close cooperation with them seem understandable and natural. Together, they can effectively act against the oppressed. Iranian authors claim that history is full of examples of Israel's friendship with other persecutors of innocent peoples. Depending on the political situation, Israel's partners may change. This is because Israel forms alliances with whomever they can at a given time, depending on what best serves its interests. Iranian politicians argue that Zionists are led only by a desire to expand their power and by the need to harass innocent people. As long as the Shah ruled Iran, he remained the greatest ally of Israel. Khomeini made it one of the key arguments in his criticism of the Shah, calling both tyrants. For example, in 1978, a year before the victory of the revolution in Iran, he stressed:

> One of the reasons that have put us in opposition to the Shah was his support for Israel. I have always repeated in my speeches that the Shah cooperated with Israel since the very beginning of its existence, and even when the war between Israel and Muslims reached its climax, the Shah also sold oil captured from

---

44. *Parah-yi Tan-i Islam*, 27.

45. *Holocaust. Hulukast. Asar-i Barguzidah-yi Awalin Namayishgah-i Beyn al-Melali-yi Kartun wa-Karikatur-i Hulukast* (Tehran: Khanah-yi Karikatur, 2007).

Muslims to Israel. This was one of the reasons for my opposition to the Shah. The Muslim nation of Iran has never supported Israel and because of that, it was a target for attacks and tyranny of the Shah.[46]

Although in 1979, the regime of the Shah collapsed, and the new Islamic authorities immediately manifested their hostility towards Israel, the idea of Israel's sinister alliance with other oppressors remained alive in Iran. However, Iranians have focused on the relationship linking Israel with the United States. Iranian leaders condemn these relations with equal firmness. ʿAli Khamenehi, in a speech marking the end of Ramadan in 1995, said:

> It is clear that this cancerous tumor, which is still evolving, is the Israeli usurper and Zionism. But the hand that helps them is the global leader of arrogance—that is, the U.S. government.[47]

Iranian thinkers, in their deliberations on the idea of tyranny, not only describe Israel as a tyrant, but also devote much effort to analyzing its fate. This corresponds to a concept that can be found in the Qurʾan, where a detail not found in the Old Testament appears. In the holy book of Islam, God punishes the Pharaoh with death for his idolatry and tyranny directed at the faithful. This apposition of Pharaoh's fate is characteristic to the concept of *zulm* in the Qurʾan, where it is presented mainly from an eschatological perspective. The fate of anyone who commits injustice is clear: it is eternal damnation. Contemporary ideologues express belief that Israel, too—like every oppressor—is doomed to punishment. This punishment will be inevitably imposed on Israel by God, but even before then, by Palestinians, if they remain faithful to Islam and steadfast in the fight. According to Iranian ideologues, it is inevitable because Israel's existence is solely material, which gives no assurance as to its duration. On the contrary, it is sure to pass. Ayatollah Khamenehi described it as follows:

> Unlike the superficial observers, who look at U.S. support for Israel and consider this matter [i.e., the destruction of Israel] impossible, [we say] it is possible, and it will be achieved. Great powers do not last forever. Material powers are here one day, the next day they are gone.[48]

---

46. *Filistin wa-Sahyunizm*, 177.
47. *Parah-yi Tan-i Islam*, 33.
48. Ibid., 203.

According to the supreme leader of Iran, Israel, like any other power not based on religion, will eventually be defeated. Khamenehi reiterates that tyrannical rule is easily perishable, for it has no divine legitimacy, and one can be absolutely sure that the fate of tyrants is sealed. In his speeches, he often refers to Islamic eschatology, reaching for quotes and references to the Qur'an:

> No one should doubt that this bad tree, which is "uprooted from above the earth and has no stability," will have no basis and duration. No one should doubt that truth will prevail, and Palestine will return to the body of Islam.[49]

M. Ahmadinejad, too, often recalls the story of the Pharaoh and asserts, on this basis, that the fate of Israel is already known. Moreover, he suggests that Israel is a Nimrod or Pharaoh of our times. Therefore, just like the Pharaoh, who relied on injustice and violence, Israel, also, will be harshly punished:

> Heavenly tradition is based on defeating tyrants, oppressors, and the selfish, and on the victory of the God-fearing and the pious. Also, today, the world's tyrants are not excluded from the fate of Pharaohs and Nimrods. Their states are built on occupation, aggression and plunder of nations' riches.[50]

According to the previous president of Iran, even though punishment on the Judgment Day is inevitable, everyone should pursue justice in the world. Ahmadinejad suggests that there should be a referendum in Israel in which every rightful inhabitant of Palestine, regardless of religion or ethnicity, would take part, including groups of Christians and non-Zionist Jews living in Palestine. Ahmadinejad argues that they have the same right to decide about the fate of these lands as the Muslim majority. Together, then, they should decide upon the future shape of Palestine.[51]

---

49. Ibid., 256. This is a reference to Sura Ibrahim, ayats 25–28: "Dost thou not see how Allah sets forth the similitude of a good word? *It is* like a good tree, whose root is firm and whose branches *reach* into heaven. It brings forth its fruit at all times by the command of its Lord. And Allah sets forth similitudes for men that they may reflect. And the case of an evil word is like *that of* an evil tree, which is uprooted from above the earth and has no stability. Allah strengthens the believers with the word that is firmly established, both in the present life and in the Hereafter; and Allah lets the wrongdoers go astray. And Allah does what He wills."

50. www.tiknews.net/display/?ID=69308&page.

51. www.irannewsagency.com/index.php?news=2826. In fact, the Iranian president

Palestine = the Oppressed

Another concept related to the concept of *zulm* is the oppressed, *mazlum*. For contemporary Iranian thinkers, this term is now epitomized by Palestine. In fact, one can observe that when Iranian ideologues talk about Palestine, they use a reversed discourse to that of the oppressor. In this reversed discourse, Palestinians are portrayed in a simplistic manner, as a complete antithesis of Israelis. Phrases such as "the oppressed Palestinian people," *millat-i mazlum*, oppressed Palestine, *Filistin-i mazlum*, are constantly repeated. Iranian newspapers are filled with detailed descriptions of suffering and persecution that Palestinians have to endure, with words of sympathy for the victims and condemnation of the perpetrators. They are accompanied by images of desperate mothers, martyrs, who suffered heroic death at the hands of Israeli soldiers or children living in refugee camps. The image of Palestine that emerges from contemporary Iranian discourse is the image of a land where, for more than a hundred years, tyranny that cannot be compared to injustice committed elsewhere has continued to take place.

As Wa'izi suggests, since the beginning of the twentieth century, Palestine has been a field of uneven battle, the scene of a conflict between the world's tyrants and the oppressed, tormented Palestinians. In his view, the oppression of the Palestinians is an undeniable fact, and even superpowers, with their deceits falsifying the truth, could not hide that.[52] 'Ali Khamenehi, too, presents this dichotomy, saying that the oppressive Israel and the oppressed Palestine constitute an inextricable problem in which the ideals they represent, such as good and evil, justice and injustice, are contrasted with each other:

> The point is that, on the one hand, the manifestation of bloodthirstiness, ferocity, predacity, and disregard for any human standards, rights, and values (that is, the Zionist army), and on the other hand, the manifestation of the heroic resistance of the oppressed (the oppressed Palestinian people), stood against each other.[53]

---

repeats what 'Ali Khamenehi formulated in one of his speeches, see: *Masalah-yi Filistin wa-Sahyunism. Rahnamudha-yi Hazrat-i Ayatollah Khamenehi, Maqam-i Mu'azam-i Rahbari* (Tehran: Daftar-i Risaniha-yi Markaz-i Amuzish wa-Pazhuhish),122.

52. H. Wa'izi, *Nabard-i Nabarabar*, 1.
53. Ibid., 95.

For the supreme leader of Iran and many other contemporary politicians, such as 'A. A. Wilayati or M. Ahmadinejad, the Palestinian-Israeli conflict is the main problem of the modern world. 'Ali Khamenehi states:

> The most important issue today is the issue of Palestine, which for the last 50 years, was the most serious problem of the Muslim world and perhaps the most important problem of humanity. We talk about suffering, exile, and oppression of a nation, conquest of the entire country, and creation of cancerous growths in the heart of the Muslim world, where East meets West. We talk about permanent tyranny, which has now been affecting two generations of Palestinians.[54]

What then makes Palestinians the perfect embodiment of oppression? Analysis of pro-Palestinian discourse shows that the feature most often invoked is the religious identity of the Palestinian liberation movement. As I have shown, Iranian clergy has always supported the Palestinians, but ever since Palestinian movements gained religious character (especially after the outburst of the first Intifada in 1987), support for the ruling Shi'ite clergy in Iran has gained its momentum. Iran proclaimed itself the spiritual precursor for Hezbollah and Hamas. Therefore, in contemporary pro-Palestinian discourse, one can find multiple religious references. Ayatollah Khamenehi compares Palestinians to the biblical David and allusively mentions his victory over Goliath.[55] In his view, the faith of Palestinians, who desire to end tyranny and establish justice in its place, will prove to be stronger than any material force that remains powerless before religion:

> The fight that the Palestinian nation began today is not a fight of one army against another, where we could say, those have fewer tanks and the others have more. It is a battle of bodies and souls of people who are not afraid of death. Each devoted young man who rises against the usurper regime threatens it no less than an entire army. Tanks, missiles, airplanes, or Apache helicopters are no longer an answer for such a person. When someone is not afraid of death and is prepared to sacrifice in the name of God and wants to fulfill his duty, he becomes the greatest danger to the unjust rulers of this world. You have seen that Americans analyzed their chances of succeeding against those young people who want martyrdom. But I say that any analysis

---

54. *Parah-yi Tan-i Islam*, 23–24.
55. Ibid., 174.

does not make sense. The desire for martyrdom clearly does not come from emotions. It rises from the faith in Islam, the Judgment Day, and the Hereafter. Wherever there is true Islam, arrogance is in danger. Arrogance is forced to fight Islam to rule over Palestinians...[56]

Iranian authors also indicate that the Palestinian resistance movement has a national character. Therefore, they present Palestinians as a united nation, sharing a common goal—the struggle against Israel. Iranian politicians protest against perceiving liberation movements fighting in Palestine as scattered groups with different goals and programs. Khamenehi argues that the strength of the Palestinians, apart from Islam, comes from a sense of community and national unity. He stressed this in one of his speeches in 2001:

> Palestinians are a strong nation, and it showed. Palestinians proved that they have power of resistance, and their motivation is profound. Without a doubt, they will crush the bloodshedding invaders.[57]

Iran = the One who Opposes Tyranny

According to Iranian ideologues, Iran has always been the epitome of one who combats tyranny, *zulmsitiz*. They talk about it in terms of obligation, arguing that in today's world, there are particularly disadvantaged nations that need help, such as Afghanis, the Lebanese, and especially Palestinians. Iranians are the ones who can come to their rescue. They have always acted against oppression; Iranian history and mythology is full of heroic events that prove Iranians' longing for justice and struggle for its restoration. Khomeini made this claim a principle in Iranian foreign policy. Ayatollah Azari Qumi elaborates on this in his work on Khomeini's key political concepts. Azari Qumi stresses that Khomeini's entire foreign policy was based on one *ayat* prohibiting Muslims from remaining under the rule of nonbelievers.[58] Furthermore, Azari Qumi highlights that "Islam has a mission of promoting global justice and negation of tyranny

---

56. Ibid., 129.
57. Ibid., 244.
58. A. Azari Qumi, *Khat-i Imam wa-Wizhegi-yi An* (Qum: Dar al-'Ilm, no year), 12. The ayat he mentions is IV: 141.

and arrogance."⁵⁹ He also mentions that Khomeini clearly separated the group of the oppressed from another seemingly similar group of the disadvantaged. The latter, *mahrumin*, are the poor, the disabled and the hard working who are deprived of sufficient means in life. Azari Qumi assures that while Khomeini was also concerned with them, his main focus was, however, on the second group, *mustaza'fin*. This group consists of the oppressed, *mazlumin*, the exploited, *estethmarshudigan*, and those who are in captivity.⁶⁰ The special importance that Khomeini gave to the oppressed, Azari Qumi argues, was evident from his appeals to Arab countries to join forces in a common struggle, as well as his initiatives to enhance pan-Islamic solidarity. R. Khomeini reiterated that Iran should be a model for other Muslim countries to follow:

> Iran serves as a model for all countries. Possibly, also in the other world, God will make Iran an argument for those who have settled down with tyranny, submitted to the usurper and have not risen.⁶¹

Khamenehi, too, called Iran the vanguard of the struggle for justice.⁶² He spoke about Iran's duty to defend the oppressed:

> The main duty of Muslims, apart from readiness to protect Islam and the collective identity of Muslims, is to defend the oppressed nations, which became suppressed by the hand of rage, arrogance, and sin, which imposed the most severe conditions of life. The oppressed Palestinians are undoubtedly an example of such a nation.⁶³

According to the supreme leader of Iran, Iranians' objection to the situation of Palestinians manifested itself particularly strongly after the victory the 1979 revolution through the immediate breaking of all relations with Israel. Today, it is evident from the continuing steadfastness of Iranians, which gave new impetus to the Palestinian fight:

> Zionists imagined that they could finally breathe calmly, but then they saw that there is a place in the world where, thanks to the blessing of the banner of Islam and its rule, thanks to

---

59. Ibid., 13.
60. Ibid., 27.
61. *Filistin wa-Sahyunizm*, 149.
62. *Masalah-yi Filistin wa-Sahyunism*, 41.
63. Ibid., 102.

the blessing of people's faith in the Quran, in its principles and verses, thanks to the courage and resistance against superpowers and arrogance, the nation and the government persisted in their resistance. They cried one voice that the usurper Zionist regime should be thrown out of Palestine. It was thanks to the persistence of the Iranian nation, government, and the system of the Islamic Republic of Iran that blood in the drying veins of the Palestinian movement began to move again, and young Palestinians—that is, the third generation—have discovered the true revival and continued their movement in the Islamic shape.[64]

Ahmadinejad, too, describes Iran's unique position—its leadership in the fight against tyranny—in a metaphorical way full of religious references. He uses the metaphor of a caravan, which refers to an idea that leads humanity, one that animates the noble tasks to be fulfilled by mankind:

> One day, this caravan appeared in Noah's movement and his ark of salvation, then in the movement of Moses against the Pharaoh and breaking sorcerer's spells. Once again, it was manifested in the battle of Jesus against the apostates and tyrants. Yet, another time, in the form of [the battles of] Badr, Uhud, Khaybar, Hunajn and, finally, in the form of the seal of noble prophets, Prophet Muhammad (PBUH), and, in its climax, this caravan appeared in Karbala.[65]

Ahmadinejad refers here explicitly to Imam Husayn. According to the president of Iran, the entire history of mankind culminated in the events of Karbala. Ahmadinejad regards the battle of Karbala and the martyrdom of Husayn as the most important events in the world's history. In his view, Iran today best fulfills Husayn's mission, or as Ahmadinejad puts it, Iran today is the leader of the caravan. He claims that for decades, the world has been watching how Iran pursues its mission:

> Once, this caravan appeared in the time of the [Islamic] revolution, once again during the eight-year holy war [Iranian-Iraqi war], and now it has appeared in the steadfastness of the Iranian nation against the dictatorial powers and idolaters.[66]

---

64. Ibid., 110.
65. www.tiknews.org/display/?ID=56680
66. Ibid.

According to Iranian politicians, to fulfill the obligation to fight tyranny, one should precisely recognize the enemy. Hence, they claim that Iranians should closely monitor the actions of Israel and analyze its current and past deeds. As expressed by 'Ali Wilayati, they also have an obligation to publish the results of their investigations. Wilayati is the author of a publication that examines Iranian policy towards Israel, and this is how he explains the purpose of writing the book:

> ... a clear recognition of Zionists and their crimes has the importance of political necessity to Muslim nations. For us Iranians, this recognition has a magnified importance. Because, among all Muslim countries, Iran is, without false modesty, the strongest and the state most determined to protect the interests of Muslims and oppose the enemies of Islam. Bearing this in mind, Israel explicitly shows its hatred for the Islamic Republic of Iran and does not refrain from any opportunity to strike at Islamic Iran. For this reason, perhaps the best way to learn about this insidious enemy is to analyze his actions, when during the unfavorable, sinister bind of the Pahlavi regime with the West, reached over to meddle in the national interests of Iran.[67]

As pointed out by many Iranian politicians, one of Iran's basic obligations is to remind the world about the oppression of Palestine. According to the president of Iran, this is not an easy task because Western countries defend the interests of Israel and do not allow anyone to speak the truth, including their own citizens. Moreover, Ahmadinejad asserts that nobody dares to tell the truth about Israel's tyranny and the oppression of Palestinians because the media are controlled by Zionists and the allied powers. All decisions are made behind closed doors. International organizations are also controlled by Western powers. According to Ahmadinejad, this is a major cause of helplessness in the international community, keeping it from resolving the problems of Iraq and Palestine:

> Why [is] anyone who in today's world opposes the Zionist regime in the slightest is immediately accused of terrorism, while those who have power and strength never mention the oppression of Palestine?[68]

Iranian leaders denounce other strategies used by Israel. They claim that one of them is what they call *mazlumnamai*. They understand it as

---

67. 'A. A. Wilayati, *Iran wa-Tahawulat-i Filistin*, XVII–XVIII (Introduction).
68. Ibid.

the creation of a false, exaggerated image of oppression of Jews. This applies both to the Holocaust and the Palestinian attacks on Israeli citizens today. As stated by Waʻizi, the aim of this strategy is to trick the powers, mainly Britain and the United States, and persuade them to support the State of Israel. It is worth noting that all the leaders and researchers dealing with the Palestinian issue repeat statements concerning the alleged Jewish *mazlumnamai*. One of them is Ayatollah Khamenehi:

> The most advanced media are used in order to establish a lie in place of pure truth! With help from the most famous artists, they try to prove—just imagine—oppression of Zionists. This is the most ridiculous thing you can say in the contemporary world! Zionists are shown as oppressed, while it is they who introduced the powerful and enduring tyranny in a part of the world.[69]

According to Iranian ideologues, the other purpose for which Israel uses the tactic of *mazlumnamai* is gaining a moral explanation for its oppressive rule. Hajji Jusifi explains that it is to justify the unlawful seizure of Palestine.[70] Ahmadinejad also shares this opinion. In many of his speeches, he emphasized that Israelis exaggerate the scale and impact of anti-Semitism, calling the Holocaust a fairy-tale told by people who pretend to be the chosen people whom God had promised to return to the Promised Land. It is precisely on this claim that Ahmadinejad founded his denial of the Holocaust and called for revision of history. He argues that if the Holocaust actually took place, Western countries should give Iran permission to undertake an independent study. Ahmadinejad also challenges the credibility and objectivity of Western scholars. He presented such an opinion in an interview for British television in 2007:

> If the Holocaust is a historical fact, it should be allowed to examine it. It is possible that afterwards new problems emerge. Lack of permission for research is suspect.[71]

---

69. *Parah-yi Tan-i Islam*, 246. There are programs on Iranian television intended to expose the Zionist stategy of creating the image of its own oppression. In these programs, films are analyzed from a perspective of topics related to Jews. Selection of scenes and their analysis is to prove that Zionists created a type of a Jewish hero whose numerous misfortunes and failures elicit the American audience's pity. Thereby, they exert influence on popular culture in the United States and create positive attitudes toward Israel in American society.

70. A. M. Haji Jusifi, *Iran wa-Rezhim-i Sahyunisti*, 108.

71. www.irannewsagency.com/index.php?news=2826.

Another concept linked to the notion of *zulmsitizi* is Muslim unity. This was particularly stressed in Khomeini's speeches, and he returned to it repeatedly. Muslims should unite, Khomeini argued, to effectively fight for justice. He expressed it in a well-known phrase, which can be seen in various graffiti across Iran:

> If Muslims were united, and each of them poured a bucket of water, Israel would be carried by flood.[72]

Khomeini returned to the phrase many times but said it first during a meeting with the foreign minister of Syria, which took place in August 1979, shortly after the victory of the revolution. According to R. Khomeini, united Muslim forces would not only be able to overcome the tyranny of Israel but also effectively prevent injustice affecting any of the states. On the eve of the Iranian revolution, Ayatollah Khomeini called Yasser Arafat for unity and mutual support:

> As far as the Palestinian issue is concerned, we have always been against the Shah, Israel, and their allies; we spoke with you [in] a common voice and announced Israel's acts of tyranny to the nations. Now, when Iran is trodden by boots of the Shah's executioners, surrounded by tanks and cannons; Israeli soldiers are killing defenseless Iranians with machine guns on the streets of Tehran - speak one voice with our oppressed nation and transmit our voice to the world through your media.[73]

Ayatollah Khamenehi took up Khomeini's idea of Muslim solidarity. He asserts that the continued lack of solidarity among Muslim countries in the fight against tyranny is the cause of failure for Islamic states in their struggle against oppressors and superpowers. Iran's supreme leader points out that Muslim countries act in isolation. Therefore, they perceive themselves as too weak to oppose the oppressive powers and, as a result, see themselves forced to take part in negotiations with Israel. Khamenehi insists, however, that all negotiations in which Israel is treated as an equal party in the conflict and a host of Palestine, is also an act of tyranny against Palestinian people. Khamenehi assessed the peace conference in Madrid as follows:

> You can now see what the situation in the world is. This conference, which was held today in Madrid and during which

---

72. *Filistin wa-Sahyunizm*, 126.
73. Ibid., 120–121.

decisions were made, is a manifestation of dictatorship directed against the Muslim nations and the great tyranny against Palestinian people.[74]

Iranian ideologues emphasize that Iran's opposition against tyranny cannot be restricted to alarming and incitement. Khomeini argued that the contempt for tyranny must be incessantly manifested. Iran should act, being the vanguard of the movement against oppression. That includes all forms of activity, including provision of material assistance. Therefore, Khomeini, as the first political leader, decided that the means to help Palestinians should be obtained from religious sources. This includes various forms of charity, such as *zakat* and *sadaghe*.[75] Thus, since the 1980s, money collected in this way has been spent to fund Palestinian organizations.[76]

Khomeini recognized another way to combat tyranny, which is the political use of the pilgrimage to Mecca, *hajj*. He believed that Muslims should treat it as an opportunity to demonstrate the capabilities of the Islamic world, its unanimity, and its strength. Khomeini insisted that *hajj* was to be a time of intensified meditation over the oppression of Palestine and an opportunity to link the Palestinian issue with the whole of Islam.[77] This idea was later developed by Ayatollah Khamenehi:

> During the *hajj*, Muslims should consider this issue [oppression of Palestine], engage in it, and—after setting proper modes of action—start to act accordingly.[78]

According to Iranian ideologues, the special role in anti-Israeli policies is reserved for the celebration of al-Quds Day, which is celebrated on the last Friday of Ramadan. It was established by Khomeini and had an unusual importance to him, as shown by the quantity of speeches which explained its meaning and character in detail. Khomeini emphasized that Quds Day should encompass all the ideas associated with the concept of

---

74. *Parah-yi Tan-i Islam*, 156.

75. *Zakat*—the annually giving of one's possession allocated to charity, its amount is caltulated on the basis of material possessions. In Shi'ism it is 5% of possession surplus wealth; *sadaqah*—all other types of financial or material assistance beyond the mandatory, intended for the needy.

76. *Filistin az Didgah-i Imam Khomeini* (Tehran: Muisisiyyah-yi Tanzim wa-Nashr-i Asar-i Imam-i Khomeini, 1999), III (Introduction).

77. For more on this subject see ibid., 145–55.

78. *Parah-yi Tan-i Islam*, 146.

zulmsitizi. Khomeini insisted that Quds Day is a time when all the Muslim nations unite and show their solidarity by organizing demonstrations and marches. This was intended, in his view, to show willingness and readiness to fight. Khomeini believed that Quds Day is actually the prelude to an uprising, a massive levy of people opposing tyranny. During this day, the goals, ideals, and capabilities of Muslims may be presented. Khomeini pointed out that these goals are not limited solely to the liberation of Palestine but also concern the fight against tyranny and injustice that affects all Muslims:

> Quds Day is a global day. It is not exclusive to the city of Quds. It is a day of confrontation between the disadvantaged and the arrogant, confrontation between the oppressed nations and the superpowers. It is a day when the disadvantaged should mobilize against the arrogant and show them their place. It is a day when hypocrites and intriguers are distinguished from those who are truly devoted.[79]

The Zulm Paradigm

As I have already suggested, the triad in which Israel, Palestine, and Iran are described may already be found in the mythology of ancient Iran. It developed throughout almost all historical periods. The essential stages of this development were marked by important political and cultural transformations. Thus, the oldest mentions of tyranny can already be found in the Avesta, the holy book of a set of dualistic beliefs of ancient Iran. Following the advent of Islam, the indigenous Iranian concept of tyranny merged with the Islamic notion of *zulm*. This concept appears in the Quran on numerous occasions and with different meanings. Close investigation of the term in the Quran goes far beyond the scope of this study; nonetheless, one of the most important meanings—crucial for this study—will be mentioned later on. It can be found in the history of Pharaoh and Moses' fight against him. However, the biggest influence on the contemporary understanding of *zulm* was Shi'ism. The idea of combating oppression was associated with the martyrdom of the imams. The fight against tyranny and martyrdom in the name of justice has become one of the most characteristic features of Shi'ism. In spite of all these transformations, however, a recurring pattern—a pattern that forms the *zulm*

---

79. *Filistin az Didgah-i Imam Khomeini*, 134–135.

paradigm—can be traced. This is particularly evident when comparing mythological and Shi'ite narratives.

In the beginning of this narrative, we see times of justice, peace and harmony. Tyranny does not exist. In both traditions, just rule stemmed from the fact that it was based on divine foundations. In mythology, Yima, later known as Jamshid,[80] is the symbol of a just ruler. During his reign, the world was harmonious, and for hundreds of years, it was not blighted by disease, war, or death. This was so because Jamshid owned *farr*,[81] the divine glory that guaranteed legitimacy of rule and was a sign of divine sanction. This corresponds with a similar image of times of justice, undisturbed by tyranny, found in the Shi'ite tradition. It relates to the rule of cousin and son-in-law to Muhammad, 'Ali ibn Abi Talib, over the Islamic Caliphate (656–661). Shi'ites believe that Prophet Muhammad anointed 'Ali as his only legitimate successor.[82]

However, both narratives describe a moment in the history of the world when injustice first occurred. In the case of Jamshid, it happened when the ruler committed blasphemy by comparing his majesty and power to the grandeur of Ahura Mazda. As a result, the Divine Glory legitimizing his rule until then left him. He became a usurper and tyrant, and the world filled with injustice and oppression. With Jamshid's loss of *farr*, previously unknown phenomena appeared, such as war, disease, crime, and injustice. In the Shi'ite tradition, too, a crime terminated the times of justice. However, it was not committed by 'Ali but by his political opponents. As the Shi'a believe, 'Ali's inalienable rights to rule were unjustly taken away. This happened after the death of the Prophet, when the *umma* split into groups rivaling for succession: Sunnis and Shi'ites. Finally, this battle for power was won by a close companion of the Prophet, Abu Bakr from the tribe of Quraysh. 'Ali was being kept from any

---

80. A few myths about Yima can be found in the *Avesta*. He is a great king ruling in the golden age of the world. Yima saves living creatures from extinction by sheltering them underground for the winter.

81. *Farr* (old-Persian *khvarnah*) was a divine glory. It was hereditary, passed both in paternal and maternal lineage. It might leave a ruler due to his misconduct.

82. It happened during the farewell pilgrimage to Mecca in 632 in a place called the pond of Khumm. According to the hadith of Khumm, the Prophet delivered a sermon in which he declared: "Of whomsoever I had been master, Ali here is to be his master. O Allah, be a supporter of whoever supports him (Ali) and an enemy of whoever opposes him." The Shi'a believe it to be an appointment of 'Ali by Muhammad as his successor. See: M. H. Tabatabai, *Shi'ah dar Islam* (Kitabkhanah-yi Buzurg-i Islami, 1974), 232–40.

decisions and consequently murdered. Followers of Shi'ism interpret this as an act of tyranny, *zulm*, against the rightful successors of the prophet. According to Shi'ites, the caliphate of Abu Bakr was an act of injustice not only to 'Ali but also to God. It was a violation of the divine justice, *'adl*, manifested in the decision of Muhammad. This act, and, consequently, the caliphate of Abu Bakr and his two successors, 'Umar and 'Uthman, was a usurping of power. The deprivation of 'Ali's rights ended the reign of justice and started an era in which *zulm* became an inalienable principle of the world. According to the Shi'ite tradition, tyranny will exist until the emergence of the last imam, who will restore order and justice. Until then, mankind will have to suffer its consequences.[83] As one scholar of the Shi'ite tradition put it:

> But in reality, we must say that the tyranny, oppression, and corruption that pervades the modern world are the result of the huge injustice committed 14 centuries ago after the death of Muhammad (PBUH) by the enemies of religion to the saint family [the household of the Prophet](. . .).[84]

As a consequence of these events, a tyrant appears. In mythology, the paradigm is a king named Zahak. His reign became a symbol of oppression and injustice, usurpation of power from the hands of the rightful kings. This was because Zahak lacked *farr*, which, as hereditary, remained in the royal lineage. Therefore, it could belong only to Iranians

83. Contemporary ideologues, while speaking about the situation in Palestine, often refer to this understanding of tyranny as a constant feature of the world. Khomeini argued that the tyranny of Israel is nothing more but a consequence of earlier, equally oppressive reigns: "There were many movements and numerous revolutions in the world. But usually, they replaced one tyrant with another. There was no just movement. Quite the opposite, they destroyed one oppressive regime to replace it with another form of tyranny." See: *Sahifah-yi Nur*, vol. XIII, 137 in: *Sahifah-yi Imam*, Tehran [CD-ROM]. 'Ali Khamenehi, too, places the tyranny of Israel in a broad context. His speeches show that the spiritual leader of Iran sees the current situation in Palestine as a result of past events. According to him, tyranny affects the defenseless, tormented peoples: "The world is dark and filled with oppression. The nations are alone and need support." See: *Parah-yi Tan-i Islam*, 223. An Iranian scholar, H. Wa'izi, also places Israel's tyranny in a broader context. According to Wa'izi, Palestinian struggle for liberation is not only a struggle of Muslims or Arabs against Jews, but it is also a struggle of man against tyranny. Wa'izi believes that Israel's victory over Palestinians would be tantamount to accepting the oppression of mankind. See: H. Wa'izi, *Nabard-i Nabarabar*, 1–2.

84. M. M. Rastgu, "Az Ruzi ke Amir al-Mu'minin Alayhu as-Salam Khanah-nishin Shud, Dunya pur az Zulm-u-Sitam Shud," *Khurshid-i Makkah*, no. 39, (February/March 2005): 38.

or be acquired through marriage. Zahak, however, was a stranger (in *Shahnamah*, he came from Arabia, whereas in *Avesta*, from Babylon). It is an important detail in the context of the tyranny concept. It proves that ancient Iranians conceptualized the distinction between themselves and others. This distinction corresponded with the division between good and evil and in the context of power and authority—justice and tyranny. As noted by B. Lincoln, although Pahlavi texts say that all people are descendants of Gayomard, this egalitarian vision is distorted by the fact that only Iranians remained where they lived at the beginning, while other nations dispersed across the world in the times of Hushang and Taz. These were times of division between Iranian kings and Western enemies. B. Lincoln noted, "such of his [Taz's] descendants as the text deigns to mention were scoundrels, monsters, and usurpers."[85]

Islam, too, provides many examples of tyrannical rulers. The Qur'an provides a story of the Pharaoh. Iranian researchers point out that the Pharaoh became "one of the most important manifestations of tyranny, injustice, and rebellion against God."[86] The Pharaoh is a timeless paradigm of a sinner and idolater as well as an oppressor. His idolatry equaled his tyranny, which was manifested in tormenting Israelites, the just monotheists.[87] In Shi'ism, the tyrant is epitomized by Umayyad Yazid ibn Mu'awiya.

The last element of both the mythological and Islamic narratives is a struggle against oppression by defenders of lost justice. In Iranian mythology, this was symbolized by the blacksmith Kaveh, who organized an uprising against the tyranny of Zahak. As a result, Zahak was overthrown, and justice returned, as Feridun, the rightful descendant of the royal family, regained power. In the Qur'an, the fight against tyranny, as I have already mentioned, is exemplified by stories of prophets.[88] According to one of the hadithes, Muhammad also strongly condemned any kind of injustice and oppression, and he commanded to fight it:

---

85. B. Lincoln, "Human Unity and Diversity in Zoroastrian Mythology," *History of Religions* 50 (2010): 12.

86. "Far'un," *Nasim-i Vahi*, No. 9, (November/December 2007), can be found online at: www.hawzah.net/Hawzah/Magazines/MagArt.aspx?id=62662.

87. *Qur'an*, XXVIII: 4.

88. Surahs VIII and XI contain the stories of Noah, Salih, Hud and Shu'ayb; Surah XIV—the story of Abraham, Sura VII and XXI—enumerates virtually all unjust peoples and their righteous prophets; and finally Surahs X, XX, XXVI and XXVIII—include stories of Moses and the Pharaoh.

When people face an oppressor, and do not stop him from committing tyranny, let them fear God, who will punish them painfully in hell.[89]

An analogous concept of combating tyranny exists in Shi'ism. As Shi'ites believe, 'Ali had never accepted injustice committed against him by his enemies. For some time, he left the political scene but finally returned to fight for justice. He was defeated and killed. His martyrdom was later repeated by all the imams. According to Shi'ite tradition, they all died trying to restore justice. Among them, the perfect embodiment of this struggle was Husayn, the second son of Ali and Fatima. He was defeated by the army of the then-caliph Yazid ibn Mu'awiya in the battle of Karbala on the 10 of Muharram of 680, on a day called *'Ashura*. The Shi'a believe that Husayn was sure of his death at the hands of enemies and therefore decided to become a martyr fully and consciously.[90] This conscious willingness to sacrifice is the most important element that shaped the concept of *zulmsitizi*. Husayn became a symbol of the oppressed, *mazlum*; Yazid—the epitome of a tyrant; and Karbala—a kind of "narrative archetype," a mythologized event that formed a cultural paradigm. Throughout the ages, the Karbala paradigm stressed Husayn's defeat, which, in turn, "reinforced political passivity, acquiescence and submissiveness among the Shi'a."[91] In the 1960s, however, as H. Ram pointedly observes, Shi'ite clergy altered the understanding of the Karbala paradigm. One of the first religious scholars to do so was Salihi Najaf-Abadi. In his book *Shahid-e Javid* (The Immortal Martyr), he tried to establish that Imam Husayn's defeat was far less important than his heroism, and therefore, Shi'ites should abandon quietism and passivity and present a more active attitude.[92] Indeed, this new understanding of the Karbala paradigm now seems to be prevalent. Contemporary clerics tried to reinterpret the understanding of Karbala and argued that the fight against tyranny took the form of an organized and deliberate movement, and consequently, led to the downfall of the Umayyad caliphate.[93] Recent history, especially the 1979 revolution and Iran-Iraq War, has shown that

---

89. A. Q. Payandah, N*ahj al-Fasahah*, (Tehran: Jawidan, 1983), 834, in: 'A. A. Babasifri, „Zulmsitizi dar Shi'r-i Shi'ah," *Shi'a-shinisi*, No. 18 (V), (Summer 2005): 112.

90. M. H. Tabatabai, *Shi'ah dar Islam*, 279.

91. H. Ram, "The Mythology of Rage," 70.

92. *Ibidem*, 73–74.

93. 'A. A. Babasifri, „Zulmsitizi dar Shi'r-i Shi'ah," 116.

this new understanding can be easily applied and transformed into action. Ideologues of the Islamic Revolution of 1979 often referred to it. M. Mutahhari, one of the main leaders of the Islamic Revolution and a prominent religious scholar, argued:

> Islam tells us: the most honorable and the highest *jihad* is the one in which a person facing an oppressor breathes with justice and tells about it. Elsewhere, I wrote how much this short sentence has created heroism in Islam. If the religious principle of hatred and discord against tyranny will meet with [the actual] oppression, then religion will be able to sow the seed of revolution among its followers.[94]

Of course, also in their anti-Israeli propaganda, contemporary ideologues refer to this activist understanding of the Karbala paradigm, which implies the obligation to resist tyranny. Depending on the rhetorical needs, they activate some or all elements of this paradigm: the tyrant, the oppressed, and the one fighting against tyranny. It should be stressed, however, that what I have been trying to prove here it is not limited only to the Shi'ite narrative of Karbala but also includes Qur'ani, and especially mythological parallels upon which the Shi'ite narrative was based.

CONCLUSION

The main aim of this paper was to show that utilization of the concept of tyranny in anti-Israeli discourse does not differ much from what is known from the (pre)-Islamic tradition. Indeed, one of the most striking features of the concept of tyranny is its enduring existence. It seems, however, that Israel's identification with *zulm* is invoked and stimulated from above rather than it coming from below as a spontaneous expression of societal attitudes (or at least of the majority of them). However, there are situations where a novel utilization of the *zulm* concept emerges from authentic dissension of the society against somebody or someone. For example, this could be seen after the 2009 presidential election, when protesters employed the concept of tyranny against the ruling regime. During the post-election unrest, one could find cartoons on the Internet showing Khomeini with two snakes at his shoulders, a clear reference to Zahak. Mir Husayn Musawi, the defeated candidate, explicitly expressed an opinion that failure to respect the election result is the establishment

---

94. M. Mutahhari, *Piramun-i Inqilab-i Islami* (Tehran: Sadra, 1993), 56.

of tyranny.⁹⁵ The protesters accused political leaders of usurpation of power, lies, and violation of justice. Moreover, some of the clergy that supported the protesters referred to the concept of tyranny as well. A group of reformist and dissident clerics from Qum, known as the *Association of Teachers and Researchers of Qum (Majma'-i Mudarisin wa-Muhaqiqin-i Howzah-yi 'Ilmi-yi Qum)*, called people who were killed or wounded the oppressed who follow the path of Imam 'Ali and asked the Council of Guardians to respect the election results.⁹⁶ On the other hand, the authorities maintained the current interpretation of the discourse on tyranny, which binds it with the West. Therefore, Ahmadinejad accused the protesters of being controlled by Western countries.⁹⁷ This was to show the strangeness of the protesters, which is, as I have shown, tantamount to their lack of legitimacy.

All of this shows that despite the existence of geopolitical and strategic interests, resulting in the hostility of Iranian regime toward Israel, one cannot fully understand all the perplexities of Iranian reactions to Israel merely by resorting to political explanations. It also shows that tyranny is by no means conceived as inherent or tied to Israel. Propaganda about the culturally motivated paradigm of tyranny is designed primarily for the top-down mobilization of the society and can be viewed as an attempt to shape desired reactions.

---

95. http://www.bbc.co.uk/persian/iran/2009/06/090613_bd_ir88_mousavi_statement.shtml.

96. http://www.radiofarda.com/content/f3_guardianscouncil/1769255.html.

97. http://www.president.ir/fa/?ArtID=17235&term=انتخابات.

Index

Aaron (biblical), 137
Abarg, 67, 80–82, 84–87, 89, 91, 96, 106
Abba (Rav), 93
Abba Ahimeir, 314
Abbas Judah Samuel, 153–54
Abbas Siqal, 322
Abbas son of 'Ali, 245
Abd al-Hussayn, Sayyid, 342–43, 348
Abd al-Rahman Jami, 264
Abdallah b. Aqa Sayyid Isma'il Bihbihani, Aqa Sayyid, 349
Abda-Yahu son of Baraka-Yama, 9
Abdullah Burujirdi Hamadani, Akund Mullah, 183
Abraham (biblical), 11, 51, 56, 131, 261–62, 266, 268, 271–73, 275, 279, 285
Abraham b. Aqa Baba, 350
Abu Bakr, 399–400
Abual Hasan, 192–193
Achaemenid (Empire), ix, xii, 3, 5n., 6, 7n., 8n., 9–12, 14, 16–17, 19, 35, 41–42, 45, 311
Adashir I, 58
'adl, 400
Adur, 108n.
Adur Farnbay I Farokhzadan, 53
Afghanistan, 46, 213, 237, 250, 280, 328
Agasi, Shim'on Aharon, 122
Aggadah, 53

Agha-yi b. Mullah moshe b. Mullah Avraham b. Mullah Shabbatai, 179
Aharon bar Hasin, 148
Ahasuerus, 14n., 20, 315, 319
Ahmadinejad, Mahmud, 372, 378, 381, 384, 388, 390, 393–95, 404
Ahriman, 29–30, 54
Ahura Mazda, 29, 38, 399
a-kar, 104, 109–10
a-kār, 89–90
Akbar Wilayati, 'Ali, 373, 376, 378, 394
Al Aqsa, 275
Ala, Hossein, 325
Alamouti, Mustafa, 332
Albo, Joseph, 125
al-Dawlah, Ala, 353, 355
al-Dawlah, Amin, 341
Alekseevich, Vladimir, 141
Alexander of Macedonia, 30n., 332
Alfandari, Shelomoh Eliezer (Mercado), 257
Ali, 243, 249, 399–400, 402
Ali Akbar (Fal Asiri), Hajji Sayyid, 352
Ali Muhammad, Sayyid, 352
Aliyat Moshe le-marom (Ascension of Moses), 153–54
Allah, 289, 331, 388n., 399
Alliance Israelite Universelle (also Ki'ach, "Kol Israel Haverim"), 174–77, 179, 202–3, 291, 336n., 339

INDEX

al-Quds, 382, 397
al-Sultan, Salar, 353, 360
al-Sultan, Zill, 361
al-Yahudu, 10
America/American, 289, 290n., 294–306, 315, 328, 348n., 377, 380–81, 383, 390, 395n.
American Jewish Committee, 295, 297n.
Amin al-Husseini, Haj, 282
Amman, 373
Ammonites, 131
Amsterdam, 256
Anahita, 52
Anatolia, 3, 213
anatomy, 64
angel, 25–26, 31, 33, 110, 112–13, 129–32, 136–37, 262, 265–66
Angel of Darkness, 25–26
Anglo-Jewish Association, 174, 339
Angra Mainyu, 29, 37–38
Anjoman-e Adabi-ye Iran, 318
Ankara, 213
anti-Arab, 373
Antiochus I of Commagene, 29
apartheid, 385
Apex, 237, 242–43, 245
Apocrypha, 6, 21, 28, 41n., 55
apostasy, 57–58
Aqa Muhammad, Hajji, 348
Aqedah, see Binding of Isaac
Arafat, Yasser, 376, 396
Aramaic, 7, 16, 18n., 35, 45–46, 112, 118n., 145–46, 149, 166, 225, 230, 314
araq, 353
archaeology/archaeologist, 7, 312, 316, 319–20, 327
Ardalan, Ali-Gholi, 323
Aristotle (Aristotelian philosophy), 123, 126
Ark/Heikhal, 215, 232–35, 244, 256, 267–68, 393
Aryan, 370
Asarah haruge malkhut (Ten Martyrs of the Kingdom), 153

Ashkenazi, 204, 257–58, 268–69, 272, 285, 298, 304–5
Ashtiyani, Hasan, 341, 348
Ashura, 245–46, 402
Asiatic Museum of the Imperial Russian Academy of Sciences, 141
Assi, 96–97
assimilation, 302
Association of Teachers and Researches of Qum, 404
Assyria, 14, 230, 231
authority, 15, 49, 93–94, 99, 192, 257, 299, 301, 337, 356, 382, 401
Azerbaijan, 237, 273, 280
Azulay, Hayim Joseph David, 143, 160–61

Ba'ath party, 379
Babai b. Lutf, 146
Babel, 52, 209, 272
Babi, 354–55
Babolsar, 228
Babylon/Babylonia, 4, 8, 49, 52, 59, 61, 66, 78, 114, 118, 120, 188, 313, 317, 329, 401
Babylonian, 4, 5, 9, 11, 14, 16, 37, 46, 48, 52, 59–60, 62, 66, 78, 80, 90, 93, 99, 108–10, 114, 117–21, 185, 225–26, 230–31, 313, 317, 320, 329
badge, 184
Baha'i, 176, 178–80, 187, 190, 211, 288, 322, 344, 354
Bahram, 226
Balaam, 131–32, 139
Balfour Declaration, 177, 179, 225, 314–15, 323
Baluchi, 288
Bani-Srayel, 53
baqqasha, 153–54
Basel, 314
Bassan, Isaac, 175, 183–84
Bassan, Yitzhak, 175, 183–84
bat qol (divine voice), 132
Bat-Shemuel, Rachel, 173
bazaar, 348

Behistun, 16, 319
Beit Menahem, 176
Belial, 26, 31–33, 37–39, 45
ben Gabirol, Solomon, 153–54, 156, 158
Ben-Gurion, David, 311, 321–22, 331
Benjamin b. Misha'el, 144, 147–48
Ben-Mashiach, Shimon, 176n.
Ben-Zvi, Yitzhak, 312, 317–18, 330, 332
Berlin, Meir, 205
Beroukhim Booksellers, 216
Beth Alpha, 254
Bethlehem, 383
Bible, 11, 17, 28, 55, 115, 123, 131, 133, 166, 177, 261 264, 266, 285, 312–13, 331–32, 335
Binding of Isaac, 153–54, 157, 160–61, 254–55, 259, 260, 263, 265–71, 273–79, 281–82, 284–86
Bishapur, 226–27
blood libel, 185, 348
body, 62–64, 66–82, 85–86, 90–91, 98–100, 102–3, 116, 129, 135
Bombay, 205–6, 344
Book of Ardashir, 157
Brauer, A. I., 206
Bucharim, 176
Buddhists (shaman), 49, 58
Buin Zahra, 333
Bulgaria, 212
Bundahisn, 110, 112–18
Burma, 205, 332
Burning Bush, 115, 138

Caliphate, 399–400, 402
capitalism, 371
cartoon, 379, 386, 403
Caspian Sea, 228, 368n.
Castel, Moshe, 281, 286
Caucasus, 368
Cazes, Joseph, 350
Central Asian Republic, 46
Chicago, 321
children (Jewish), 289, 320

children of righteousness, deceit, 25–26, 27n., 33
choice (freedom of), 28, 32–34, 40, 44–45
Chosen Ones, 13
Christian, 175, 261–62, 266, 288–90, 341, 343, 388
Chronicles, Book of, 6, 17, 314
Church, 46, 219, 383
civil religion, 298
Cohen Tzedek, Shlomo, 184
Cohen, Israel Meir (Hafetz Hayyim), 263n.
Cohen, Rafael Hayim, 188
colonialism, 374–76
Committee of Persian Jews in Jerusalem, 191
communism, 371, 381n.
Communist, 214
community, 6, 8, 10–11, 13, 24, 49, 56–58, 94, 122, 174–75, 177, 179, 181, 193, 205–6, 208, 211, 239, 251, 256, 268–69, 338–39, 344, 362–63, 391
Community Rule, 25–27, 31–33, 38, 39
community, Jewish, 11, 94, 216, 232, 287–89, 320, 328–29, 342, 346, 348, 350, 352, 354, 365, 384
Conjoint Foreign Committee, 336n., 346
conspiracy, 381–82
Constantinople, 364
Constitutional Revolution, 289, 292, 337, 363, 368–69
conversion, 57–58, 122, 128, 178, 180n., 183–84, 187, 290, 338n., 339, 342–43
corpse, 62, 71–73, 75–76, 79, 82–83, 99, 103–4 341
Cossack, 359, 368–369
Council of Guardians, 404
creation (ex nihilo), 26, 38, 54–56, 112, 133, 174
Crusades, 332

culture, 6, 10, 12, 17, 35–36, 47, 58, 59–60, 78, 80, 91, 107, 109, 115, 124, 181, 199–201, 250, 285, 287–88, 292–93, 296–300, 302–6, 318 331, 334, 365, 367, 369–70, 373, 377–79, 381, 398, 402
custom, 56, 60, 211, 245, 247n., 288, 291, 299, 304, 365
Cylinder, Cyrus', 4–5
Cyrus, 3–7, 15, 17, 176, 225, 311–35

Dadestan-I Denig, 52
Dahag, 51–53, 56
Damascus, 205, 361
Damascus Document, 34, 39–40
Daniel (biblical), 6–8, 14n., 15–16, 19n., 35, 163–64, 314
Darius, 15n., 16, 316–18, 320
Darmesteter, James, 111
Datner, Yehuda, 325
Davar, 316–17, 325, 329, 332
David b. Laya, 158
Daxsta, 34
Dead Sea Scrolls, 21, 24, 30, 35, 36, 40
deceit, 24–28, 36, 51
Dedication of Temple, 7
defecation, 63, 73–74, 79–82, 99
Deftari, Mohammed, 330
deku, 9
determinism, 28, 33
Dhabih, see Binding of Isaac
dhimmi, 289, 356–57
di Trani, Moses b. Yosef, 122
Diaspora, 6n., 11–13, 16, 19n., 22, 121–22, 231, 277–79, 285, 373
Dick, Isaac Meir, 143, 163
dictatorship, 385, 397
digestion process, 62–67, 69–81, 85–86, 89–92, 94–102, 105–6
Dinkard, 50–53, 55–56
divine omniscience, 24–25
divine Providence, 133
divine wisdom, 53, 123, 127
divorce, 48, 302

Do'ar HaYom, 177
doctor, 173–74, 290, 301–2
Dome of the Rock, 236, 269, 275, 283
dress code, 353
dualism (cosmic, social), 24, 26–28, 30, 32–34, 39, 45, 54
Duff, E. Grant, 358
Dura Europos, 254–55, 275
Duvdevani, Baruch, 325

East Anatolia, 213
egalitarianism, 294, 401
Egypt, 5–6, 205, 216, 221, 319, 330, 382
Einhorn, Yitzchak, 274, 257n., 278
Eleazar, 74, 76, 96–97
elementary schools, 291
Elephantine, 5, 6
Eliezer, 264, 271, 273, 284
Eliezer Hayyim b. Abraham, 143, 160
Elijah, 112, 113, 151, 152
Elisha b. Samuel, 163–64
Eliyahu b. Ha-Mullah Menashe, 148
Eliyahu b. Yishaq, 153
Eliyahu Bavli, 158
Eliyahu ben Mordechai Halevy, 173
Eliyahu ben Nissan ben Eliyahu, 265
Elyashar, Yaakov Shaul, 173
Enlightenment, 188, 298, 314
Entezam, Nasrollah, 321
equality, 298, 300, 337, 364
Erzincan, 213
Eschatology; eschatological age, 26, 37, 39, 40, 45, 387–88
Esdras, 6, 14n., 20n.
Esfandiary, Abd-Elhassan Sadiq, 319
Esther (book), 19–23, 43, 175, 184, 194, 211, 229, 259, 315
ethics, 25–26, 81, 289, 380
ethnicity/ethnic symbols, 10, 46, 106, 288, 293, 296–98, 304–6, 384–86, 388
Euphrates, 62, 381–382
Evil Spirit, 38, 52–54, 173
Exegesis, 53, 86–87, 93, 124, 126

Exile, 4, 10, 17–23, 37, 185, 188, 209, 231, 313, 317, 320, 324–25, 329–30, 339, 341, 343, 350, 355, 366, 390
exorcist, 16
Ezekiel, 4, 19, 162, 207
Ezra (biblical), 6–8, 13–17, 313–14, 322, 335

Fadayan-i Isalm, 374
faith, 34, 37, 40–41, 50–51, 55–58, 108, 121–26, 128, 133–34, 176, 179, 180, 183, 187, 192–93, 290–92, 339, 380, 387, 391, 393
Fakhr al-Din Shadman, Sayyid, 371
faleshood, 33, 381
family, 142, 171–76, 180, 193, 204, 207–8, 258, 289, 294, 297, 299–302, 304–6
famine/drought, 173–74, 346, 351
Fardid, Ahmad, 371
farr, 399–400
Fars, 3, 222, 353, 356–59
Farsi, 177, 199, 211, 312, 322
fatwa, 373–74
Fayziyyah, 384–85
feminism, 300n.
Ferdowsi, 317
Feridun, 401
fire, 48, 61–62, 72, 81–82, 85, 89, 109–119, 210, 212, 261, 272
Fire altar, 108
Fire temple, 109–10
Firkowicz, Abraham, xiii, 141
Freiman, A. A., 141, 143
French, 111, 163, 175–78, 183, 355–56
Frenkel, Yitzhak, 281, 285
Fundamentalism, 40n., 43–45, 182

Gabriel, 112, 113, 266
Galen, 63–67, 73, 90–91, 95, 99, 106
Galicia, 268
Galilean, 98
Gandhi, 205
Gaon, Moshe David, 179
Gathas, 27–28, 30, 32, 34, 40–42, 45

Gayomard, 401
Gendarmerie, 339
General Islamic Congress for Jerusalem, 374
Genesis Rabbah (midrash), 271
gentile, 32, 262, 346, 350
Geonic literature, 53
Gharbzadigi (Westoxication), 371
Ginsburg, I. I., 141
Gittin, 34n., 48, 109
God, 5, 13–21, 23, 25, 26, 29, 31–34, 38–40, 47, 49, 55–58, 124, 126–32, 134, 136, 139, 177, 189, 193, 198–99, 207, 209, 210, 220, 226, 262–63, 272–73, 313–14, 320, 379, 384, 387, 388, 390, 392, 395, 400–402
Gogusasp, 84–85
Goitein, Shelomo Dov, 317
Golden Calf, 135, 137
Goldstein, Israel, 327–28
Goliath, 259, 390
government, 35, 127, 174, 179, 182, 184, 188, 200, 202, 289, 292–94, 302–3, 315–17, 322–24, 326, 328, 333, 337, 341, 345, 348, 352, 354, 357–60, 362, 370, 372, 375, 380–82, 387, 393
Graeco-Roman culture, 59–60, 62, 106,
graffiti, 379, 396
Grahame, G., 355
grammar, 160–61, 163–64
Great Neck, 298–99, 303
Great Satan, 372
Guide for the Perplexed, 134–36
gullet, 95–97
Gulpaygan, 350, 363
Gushnasp, 117

Habakkuk, 329
habar, 109
Ha-cohen, Rahamim Melamed, 188
Ha-Cohen, Refael Hayim, 361
Hadi, Shaykh, 347
Hafiz, 144, 146, 151

410 INDEX

Haftarah, 177
Hagar, 273, 365
Haggai, 5, 6
hajj, 397
Halakha, 53, 111
Halevy, David, 176
Halevy, Menahem Shemuel (Mollah Menahem; Monsieur Menahem),
Halevy, Mordechai, 172–73, 176
Halevy, Shemuel Mordechai, 173
Halevy, Yaakov, 176
Halevy, Yocheved, 174–75
Hamadan, 171–77, 179–85, 187–90, 193, 197–205, 211, 228–30, 315, 346, 348, 364
Haman, 10, 49, 341
Hamas, 372, 390
Hamburg (manuscript), 93
hamsa, 215, 249
Hanina b. Teradyon, 115
Hanukkah, 109
Hanukkah lamp, 236
ha-Oreah, 143, 163–64
Hasham Mukram Nourzad, 318–19
Hassidim, 267
Havdalah, 149, 236n.
Haydari, 351
Hebrew, 35, 77, 112, 120–21, 124, 142–48, 149–51, 153–54, 156–57, 159, 160–66, 173, 175, 177–79, 182, 188, 190, 192, 197–97, 203–5, 211–12, 216, 228, 230, 233, 255, 264, 266–67, 280, 291, 312–18, 330,
Hebrew printer, 267
Hebron, 257
Hehalutz, 110
Hellenistic period, 41, 43
heritage, 118, 287–88, 292–93, 295, 296, 304–7, 362
Herzog, Yitzchak Isaac Halevy, 204, 208, 321–22
Hevrat Me'orerei Yeshenim, 177–178
Hezbollah, 390
Hida, See "Azulay, Hayim Joseph David"

Hindus (braman), 49
Histadrut Haluzei Ha-Mizrachi, 204
hixr, 80–82, 85–86, 89, 99
holiness, 85, 197, 210, 275
Holocaust, 372, 386, 395
Holy of Holies, 275
Holy Spirit, 132
Hovevei Yehsurun, 178
Hoveyda, Fereydoun, 377
Hovot Yehudah, 120–21
Huldah, 275
Husayn, Imam, 378, 393, 402
Husayn, Saddam, 379
Hushang, 401
Hussayn, 245

ibn Abi Talib, 'Ali, 399
ibn Mu'awiya, Yazid, 401–2
Ibrahim b. Mullah Abu'l Khayr, 152, 155, 160–61
Ibrahim Mujtahid, Aqa Mirza, 355
Ibrahim, Shaykh, 347
ideology (Zionist), 198, 199, 207, 313, 315, 335, 383
Ifra Hormiz(d), 47
Iliyaziyaoff, Ya'qov, 166
immersion (ritual), 69, 71–72, 79, 103
imperialism, 381–82, 385
Imrani, 150, 153, 155, 157–58, 166
India, 205–6, 328
Indian, 52, 110n., 359–60
infidelity, 383
ingestion, 62–63, 69, 73, 77, 80–81, 90–91, 94, 97, 99
inheritance law, 338–40, 352
Institue of Oriental Manuscripts, 140–43
Institute of Oriental Studies, 141, 317
Internet, 403
intestines/me'ayim, 63, 65, 72, 95, 97, 99
Intifada, 372, 390
Iran Freedom Movement, 378
Irani, Eliyahu Kohen b. David, 143
Iranian Jewish Committee, 187

Iranian Minsitry of Foreign Affairs, 323, 343, 356, 362
Iran-Iraq War, 402
Isaiah, 4, 6, 14, 15, 39, 260n., 312, 314, 320, 330
Isfahan, 160–61, 216–23, 243–44, 265, 328, 343, 346–48, 361, 363
Ishmael, 262, 265–66, 273, 284
Islam, 29, 40, 50, 51, 121–22, 124, 127–28, 134–35, 139, 172, 178, 183, 187, 192–93, 246, 261, 263–64, 269, 272, 277, 279, 280, 282, 289, 292–94, 313, 327, 338, 339, 341, 348–49, 351, 356, 361–62, 369–72, 374–75, 378–80, 382, 384, 387–88, 391–94, 396–98, 401
Islam, Shi'ite, 183, 245, 288, 364–65
Islamic Propagadna Organization, 381
Islamic Revolution, 287, 295, 303, 370, 375–77, 403
Israel Defense Force, 326, 333
Israel Museum, 242, 252
Israel, God of, 16, 26, 314
Israel, Land of, 8, 39, 109, 172, 178–79, 185, 189–91, 197, 202, 205, 207, 256–57, 266–67, 275, 277, 279, 285, 321–22
Israel, People of, 39, 131, 134, 137, 188, 190, 199, 201, 207, 211–12, 272
Israel, State of, 176, 216, 222, 228, 232, 242, 252, 256, 295–96, 311–13, 318, 321–25, 326–35, 361, 367, 372–92, 394–98, 404
Israeli, 222, 228, 256, 276, 281, 311–12, 330, 334
Israelite, 14, 17, 124, 209, 216, 221
Istanbul, 212–13, 215, 257
Ivas Emuna, 242–43

Jacob b. Mordecai of Fulda, 143, 156
Jadid al-Islam, 193
Jalal Al-I Ahmad, Sayyid, 371
Jam, 54, 56
Jamal al-Din "al-Afghani", Sayyid, 369
Jami, 54, 151
Jamshid, 223–25, 399
Jephtah, 131
Jerusalem, 11, 15–16, 19, 20n., 21, 22, 51, 53, 176–77, 189, 192, 204–5, 207–9, 212, 215–16, 223, 229, 232, 236, 256–60, 266–84, 313–14, 317–18, 319, 321–22, 324–26, 332, 373–74 382
Jewish Agency for Israel, 318, 320–21, 325–26
Jewish apocalyptic literature, 14, 17
Jewish text/literature, 4, 16–17, 42/43
Jonah, 131
Joseph, 54, 103n., 104
Joseph b. Isaac, 155
Jospippon, 159
Judah, land of, 313–314
Judeans/Judea, 4–5, 8, 10, 18, 23, 31–32, 35, 41–43, 328
Judeo-Iranian, 121
Judeo-Persian, 140–67, 264–65, 292
Judges (book of), 130
Judgment Day, 388, 391
Judith (book), 6
Jusifi, Hajji, 395

Kabbalah, 110n., 258n.
kaddish, 176
kaf yad, 247–48
Kamal, Yishaq, 150, 155
Karaite movement, 99
Karbala, 245, 249, 378, 393, 402, 403
Kartir, 49–50, 57
Kashan, 162n., 280–81, 284, 338n., 343, 346, 366, 374n.
Kashani, 374
Kashfi, Jamshid, 329
Kaveh, 401
Kazarun, 338n., 343, 347, 354
Keren Hageula, 178
Keren Hayesod, 178, 199, 205
Keren Kayemet LeYisrael, 178

Kermanshah, 172–73, 202, 229–30, 337–39, 342n., 345, 347, 363, 365
Ke-tapuah be-'ase ha-ya'ar (Like an Apple Among the Trees of the Forest), 153
Keter Malkhut, 153–54, 156, 158
ketubbah (marriage contract), 243, 244, 272n.
Khamenehi, 'Ali, 372, 374, 378, 389–90
Khodayadad, 150, 152, 155, 160–61
Khomeini, Ahmad, 376
Khomeini, Ruhullah, 371, 378
Khudaydad ha-Kohen, 150
Kidron Valley, 273, 275
King George VI, 318
Kings, book of, 8, 112, 167, 220
kinnot, 163–64
Kohen b. Mullah Hayim Jamula, 150
Kohut, Alexander, 110–11
Kol Yisrael, 322
Kolomyya/Kolomea, 268
Kremlin, 330
Kuba, 273
Kurdish, 288
Kuuirinta, 52
Kuusi, Matti, 216
Kyrgyzstand, 3

Lar, 337, 342–43, 346, 351
Laskov, Haim, 311
Lavon Affair,
Lebanon, 205, 322
Leipzig (manuscript), 110
leniency, 83–84, 105–6
Letter of Tansar, 58
Levant, 3
literacy, 120
liturgy, 209, 263, 314
locust attack, 351
Lohrasp, 53
London, 178, 184, 189, 192, 253, 318, 339
London Society for Promoting Christianity, 341
Los Angeles, 252, 270, 298, 303
lutis, 358–59

Maariv, 330, 332–33, 375
Mabit, See "di Trani, R. Moses b. Yosef"
Madrid, 396
Magen David/Shield of David, 229, 233, 235, 245n.
Mahoza/Ctesiphon, 47, 94
Maimonides, 74, 96, 122–25, 128–29, 133–39
Majlis, 318, 331–32, 337, 353, 364
Malakhi (prophet), 6
Malik al-Mutakallimin, 355
Mandean, 46
Manichean, 29, 46, 49–50, 377
Manuscript, 45, 75–77, 93, 140–43, 165n., 180n., 192, 203, 211, 244, 255, 263–65
Mardan-Farrokh, 54–56
Marquis of Salisbury, 346
marriage, 60, 173, 243, 299, 300n., 301–2, 304
martyr; martyrdom, 150, 378, 389–91, 393, 398, 402
Mashhad, 160, 187, 364, 380
Mashrutah, 368
Matbet, Kefil, 200
Mayer, Leo Aryeh, 317
medicine, 63, 66, 173, 383
Medomah, 67, 80–82, 86–87, 89, 91, 99, 106
Meir, Golda, 329, 333–34
Melkiresa, 26, 31
Melki-sedeq, 31
Menog, 30, 36–37, 40, 53
Me'orer Yeshenim, 177–79
Mesopotamia, 4, 8, 10, 16–18, 46, 202, 205
Messiah, 159, 315, 320, 329
Meyer, Jacob, 204
Middle Persian, 29, 36, 41, 54, 56, 57, 59, 61, 79, 84, 110, 369
Midrash, 59, 93, 114, 152–54, 166, 221, 261–62, 271–73, 275, 314
Midrash Abba Gurion, 114
military (cooperation, hardware), 7, 333, 367–68, 373, 381–82
minaret, 213, 236

INDEX 413

Minhat Shemuel, 174, 176
Ministe're des Affaires Etrange 'res, 336n., 355
miracle, 117, 119, 126, 136
Miriam (biblical), 137
Miriam and Her Seven Sons, 150, 153, 155
Mirza Hassan Khan Esfandiary, 318
Mishnah, 59, 60, 63, 66–68, 70–76, 78–80, 83, 90–91, 93–94, 99, 102–6, 122, 125, 135, 159
Mithra, 226–227
Mizrachi (organization), 178, 205–6, 208
Mizrachi, Hanina, 181, 188
Mizrah, 283n.
Mizrahi, Moshe /Moshe Shah, 256–57, 260, 261, 265, 270–71, 273–74, 276, 278, 284
modernization, 292, 294, 319, 370
money, 178, 190, 203, 213, 338–39, 341, 351, 397
Monotheism, 28, 33, 44, 53, 55n., 401
Montefiore, Moses, 143, 163–64
Mordecai (biblical), 9, 21, 22, 211, 229, 315
Mordechai VeEsther BeShushan HaBira, 184
Mosaddeq, Mohammed, 325–26
Moses, 51, 120, 134–39, 153, 154, 162–63, 264, 306n., 342, 383, 393
Mossadeq, Muhammad, 370
Mount Ararat, 214–15
Mount Carmel, 113
Mount Moriah, 271, 275, 285
Mount of Olives, 258, 275
Mount Sinai, 134–35, 138–39
Muhammad (prophet), 128, 175, 192–93, 236, 393, 399–401
Muhammad ali Moadel, 332
Muhammad 'Ali, Aqa Mirza, 352
Muhammad Hassan Bahari, Aqa Shaykh, 175
Muhammad Husayn al-Kashif al-Ghita, 374
Muhammad Husayn Tabataba'i, 371

Muhammad Sa'ed Maraghei, 324
Muhammad, Sayyid, 357–58
Mujtaba Navab Safavi, Sayyid, 374
mukhammas, 146
Mulla Ahmad, 354
Mulla Aqa, 352
Munich Olympic Games, 212
Murasu, 8
Murtaza Mutahhari, 371
Musawi, Mir Husayn, 403
Mushir al-Dawlah, 358–60
Mushir al-Mulk, 352
Musibat-nama (Book of Calamity), 150, 152–53, 155, 158
Muslim, 29, 50, 121, 123, 127, 134, 172–73, 175–77, 182–84, 189–90, 192–93, 197, 203, 205, 213, 220, 222, 232–33, 236, 237, 264, 266–67, 288–94, 296, 299, 323, 326, 338–44, 346–47, 349–59, 361, 363–66, 369, 375, 377, 379, 381–82, 384, 386–88, 390–92, 394, 396–98
mustaza'fin, 392
mutrib, 352–54
Muzaffar al-Din Shah, 336–40, 345, 350
Mystery, 35
mythology, 53, 117, 377–79, 381, 391, 398–401

Nabi Samuel, 175
Nadan, 34
Nahalat Zion, 258
Nahsir, 34
Naiza-ka, 34
Najaf, 374
Najaf-Abadi, Salihi, 402
Najafi, Aqa, 347–49, 362
Najara, Israel, 144, 147–51, 160
Najasah, 184
names, Babylonian, 9
narrative texts, 31
nasa, 62, 80–82, 84–86, 89, 99
Nasir al-Din Shah, 338–40, 349n.
Nasr al-Dawlah, 352, 366n.
Nasr, Vali, 369

Nasser, Gamal Abdel, 330
Natan the Babylonian, 114
Natan'el, 150
National Bible Conference, 331
National Front, 325
National Library of Russia, 140–41, 165
nationalism, 49, 293, 298, 306, 327, 335, 344, 370
NATO, 213
Nazi, 370, 386
Nazoreans (nazara), 49
Nebuchadnezzar (Boxt-Narse), 15, 17, 53, 112, 114n.
Neharde'a, 62
Nehemiah (biblical), 6–8, 11, 13–17, 19n., 335
Nehorai, 341
Ne'ilah, 193
Neo-Babylonian Empire, 4, 9
Netherlands, 341
Netzer, Amnon, 120n., 122, 143, 212, 231n.
Nihawand, 346, 363
Nile, 381–82, 221, 232
Ni'mati, 351
Nimrod, 388
Nippur, 8, 9, 10

occupation, 385, 388
Ohrmazd, 29–30, 55, 81–83, 113
Old Avesta; Avestan text; Avesta; Avestan Yasna, 27, 29n., 34, 41–42, 52, 54, 59, 62, 79–82, 86–87, 113, 116, 398, 401
Old Testament, 387
Old Yishuv, 257–59, 269, 277
On the Natural Faculties, 64
Operation Cyrus, 325
Oral Torah, 94
organ, 65, 97
Ottomans, 262
Ouderkerk cemetery, 256

Pahlavi, 36, 40–41, 89, 99, 327, 366–67, 369–70, 375–76, 401
Pahlavi regime, 292–294, 296, 384, 394

Pahlavi Videvdad, 79, 81
Pahlavi, Mohammed Reza Shah, 214, 312–13, 316, 321, 330, 366, 370, 375, 379, 384
Pahlavi, Reza Khan, 316
Palestine Liberation Organization, 376
Palestine Post, 319
Palestine; Palestinian, 319, 322, 361, 367, 372–83, 385–98,
pallate, 96, 98–99
Pan-Arabism, 330
Paradise, 81, 83, 213, 262–63
Paris, 173–75, 339, 350, 355
Parokhet (curtain), 232–34, 256, 267
Parsi, Trita, 373n., 377
Parthian, 43, 116
Passover, 106, 145
Passover Haggadot, 255
Pazand, 54
periphery doctrine, 373
Persepolis, 223–24, 316, 328, 333, 370
Persian Board of Education and Culture of Hamadan, 199
Persian monarchy, 327, 329
Persian-English Proverbs, 216
Petersburg, 141–42, 368
Pharaoh, 379–80, 383, 387–88, 393, 401
philosophy, 129
physiology, 54, 64
Pir Bakran, 216, 220–21
piyyut, 279
Poland, 267–68, 279, 299, 329
polemic, 54, 56–58, 123–24, 127, 134–35, 139
politics, 20, 43, 302, 372–73, 385
polytheism, 384
Popova, Irina F., 142
portyokesan, 86
Pourdavoud, Ebrahim, 332
Prayer of Nabonidus, 16
predestination, 28–29
priest, 21, 48–49, 57–58, 71, 87, 103, 185, 191, 251
Priestly Benediction, 251

priestly tradition, 87
Prince of Light, 25–26, 31, 33
Princess Fawzia, 319
Propaganda, 16, 213, 283, 372, 377–78, 381, 386, 403–4
Prophecy, 126–39
prophet, 5, 15, 21, 39, 51, 125–39, 165, 175, 188, 209, 275, 320, 329, 338, 345, 383, 393, 399–401
prophetic plentitude, 130
Protocols of the Elders of Zion, 378, 381
proto-Esther, 43
Psalm, 4, 209
Pseudo-Daniel literature, 7
Pumbedita, 94, 103n., 104
Purim, 353
purity laws, 51, 61–62, 67–72, 76, 78–81, 83–85, 90, 104, 184

Qajar, 172n., 203–4, 265, 340n., 347n., 365n., 367–69, 372
Qawam al-Mulk, 353
Qazvin, 215, 333
Qi☒☒a-yi haft barādarān (Story of the Seven Brothers), 150, 152, 155
Qom (also Qum), 216, 404
Qumran, 7, 21, 24–28, 31–45
Qur'an, 123, 139, 263, 266, 236, 343–74, 383–84, 387–88, 393, 398, 401

R. Judah, 104
R. Judah b. Bathyra, 72, 74, 76
R. Papa, 93, 96
R. Yohanan, 66, 95–98
Ra"N (R. Nissim), 137
Rabbah, 48, 63, 91–94, 99, 102–4
rabbinic literature, 59, 91, 115
rabbis, 20n., 59–63, 66–70, 78–80, 83, 85–86, 90, 94, 96, 109, 112, 118, 120, 299, 361
racism, 385–86
Rahamim b. Hakham Eliyahu 'Ofer Bavli, 160
Ramadan, 387, 397

Ramat Gan, 331
Rammi b. Hamma, 101
Ramsar, 228
Rashi, 100, 262
Rava, 47, 63, 91, 93–94, 99, 101–6
Rayhan Allah, Sayyid, 340–41, 346
Rebecca (biblical), 43, 271, 273
Redemption of the First Born, 256, 267
Reines, Yitzchak Yaacov, 178n.
religious identity, 47, 50, 296, 390
religious intolerance/discrimination, 183, 187, 293
Res, 35
Resh Galuta/Exilarch, 48
resurrection, 37, 126
Return to Zion, 188, 204, 207, 209, 313–14, 324, 327, 332–35
revelation, 130–31, 136, 138
Reza Cyrus Ali, 312
Reza Shah, 318–19, 321, 366
righteousness, 22–23, 25–26, 33, 39, 57, 83, 85
rimonim, 238
ritual bath, 71
ritual objects, 231–32, 236, 239, 249–52, 256
ritual slaughterer, 262
Rome; Hram, 48, 53
Roosevelt, Franklin D., 321
Rosh Hashanah, 192
Ruach (rwh), 36–37, 40, 45
Rumi, 151
Russia, 140–42, 165, 176, 178, 319, 358, 367–68, 375, 382

Saadi, 222
Sabbath (Shabbat), 48, 109, 163–64, 304–5
Sadat, Anwar, 379
Safavid, 265
Safed, 122, 257, 268, 281, 284, 285, 286, 361
Safiniya, Reza, 323–24
sage, 125, 130, 151, 181, 198
Salemann, Carl, 162
Samuel (Talmudic sage), 60–62, 93, 104

Sansan, 150
Sar-Shalom, Miryam, 361
Sasanian (Empire), 46–50, 57, 63, 87, 89, 91, 106, 108–9, 116, 118–19, 230, 334
Sassoon, Messrs, 340
SAVAK (National Intelligence and Security Organization), 373
Schorr, Joshua Heschel, 110, 113
sectarian, 21, 26–27, 31, 39, 42–43, 45
Sefer Agron (Book of Lexicon), 166
Sefer Ben Gorion, 159
Sefer ha-Melisah, 166
Sefer Harkhal, 159
Sefer Shoshannat Ya'qov, 143, 156
Selihot, 175
seminary, 299, 301
Sepphoris, 254
Sha'ab el Ammer, 243
Shabbatai, 145
Shabbetai Zevi, 122
Shah, 4, 174, 178, 228, 311n., 312, 316, 321, 324–25, 327–31, 334, 336, 339, 342–43, 345, 347, 354–56, 370, 372–73, 375–78, 384, 386–87, 396
Shah Abbas Hotel, 219–20
Shahid-e Javid, 402
Shahin, 157, 162–63, 165, 264, 336n.
Shahnamah (or Shahnameh), 220, 401
Shalom of Safed, 284, 286
Shapur, 47, 49, 226–27
sharia, 292
Shari'ati, 'Ali, 371
Sharif, Sayyid, 353
Shekhina/Divine Presence, 112–13
Shelomoh bar ha-Rav Shemuel, 166
Shelomoh Siman Sa'ir Balkh Berkaha Kohen ha-Zaken, 163
Shemuel b. Yosef ha-rofe, 162
sheretz, 91
Sheshbazzar, 9
Shi'is, 175, 183, 185, 189, 193, 348, 374, 378–79, 398, 400, 402
Shim'ayinon b Hakham Eliahu 'Ofer, 160
Shimon b. Laqish/Resh Laqish, 95–98
Shim'on bar Yohai, 151
Shiraz, 187, 192, 203, 222–27, 239, 242, 291, 328, 337, 349, 351–52, 354–55, 357, 360–66
shiviti (plaques), 234, 258–59
Shkand Gumanik Wizar, 50, 54
Shohet, Yitzhak b. Mullah Avraham, 145
Shoja al-Din Shafa, 327, 329
Shoshani, Ezra, 177 188
Shoshendokht, 48
Shoshkes, Chaim, 319–20
Shu'a' al-Staltanah, 356–57
Simhat Torah, 151
Simkhat Ha-regel, 143, 160–61
sin, 24, 26–27, 31–33, 37, 57, 61, 81–83, 86, 193, 392
Sinab, 35
Sinai Campaign, 311
Sippar, 4
Sivas, 213
Siyah ha-Sadeh (Musings of the Field), 143, 160
Social Theists, 378
socialism, 371
society, Iranian, 294, 319
society, Muslim, 172, 289
Sofia, 212
Sohrab Sobhani, 377
soldier, 182–83, 326n., 341, 358–59, 389, 396
Solomon (biblical), 17, 275
Solomon b. Samuel of Urgench, 166
Soncino, 72, 93, 95, 97
South Africa, 385
Soviet Union, 320, 370–71
spice container, 236
St. Petersburg, 140–42
stamps, 329
Stockholm, 328
Sukkah, tractate, 102
Sukkah (booth), 277
Sukkoth, holiday of, 229
sunni, 245, 288, 348, 399

supreme leader, 380, 388, 390, 392, 396
Susa, 10, 11, 20, 49n.
Sweden, 212, 328
synagogue, 177–80, 192–93, 205, 216, 219, 231n., 232, 239, 251–52, 254–57, 259, 264, 268, 273, 275, 277, 280n., 294, 298–99, 301, 304, 347, 350
Syyaid Muhammad, 358

Tabriz, 215, 243
tafsir, 157, 167, 211
Takht-e-Jamshid, 223–25
Taliqani, Mahnud, 371
tallit, 262, 268
Talmud, 53, 63, 67, 86, 132, 166, 184n., 192, 211, 230, 258, 314
Talmud, Babylonian, 46–48, 59, 73, 75–80, 89–93, 95, 97–99, 102, 105–7, 108–19, 226
Talmud, Palestinian, 78, 90, 98–99
talmudist, 89, 93
taqiyya, 291n.
technology, 290, 294, 368
Tehran, 173, 182–85, 188, 214, 216, 230, 234, 256, 291, 318, 320, 325, 328, 331–33, 337, 341, 346–50, 353–55, 358–59, 363, 375–76, 396
Temple Mount, 258, 273–75
Temple; Second Temple, 5, 7, 15, 18–19, 36–37, 40–42, 61, 118, 263, 269, 273, 275, 283, 313, 317, 321, 324–25, 329–30
Tish'a be-'Av, 163–74, 182n.
The Dadestan-I Menog-I Xrad, 30, 53
The History of the Jews of Persia from the completion of the Talmud until Today, 211
theodicy, 38
Thessaloniki, 212
Thirteen Principles of Faith, 122, 124

Tobit, 6, 21
Toharot, 83
tomb, 194, 216, 221–22, 225, 229, 236, 248, 269, 273, 275, 329, 354
Torah, 51n., 94, 126, 133–35, 162–64, 175, 177–78, 244–45, 249, 251, 254, 263, 269, 272
Torah case, 235, 237–42, 245, 251
Torah crown, 267, 272
Torah curtain, 233–34, 267
Torah finial, 236, 238, 243, 245, 251
Torah pointers, 242–44, 247, 249–51
Torah scrolls, 115, 232, 249, 256
Tosefta, 59, 63, 66–67, 70, 73, 75–78, 90, 92, 106
Tower of Babel, 272
Treatise of the Two Spirits, 24, 32, 36, 45
Tree of Life, 262–63
Tribes of Israel, 272
truth, 25–28, 33, 36, 48, 55, 138, 374, 388–89, 394–95
tumah, see "defecation"
Turkey, 296, 311, 316, 329
Turkoman, 288
Two Spirits, 24–28, 32, 36, 42, 45
tyranny/depotism, 357, 367, 374–81, 383–85, 387, 389–404
Tzur, Tzvi, 333

ulama, 339–40, 346–50, 352, 358–60, 364, 384
Umayad Yazid ibn Mu'awiya, 401
umma, 399
United Nations, 321–22, 377
United Nations Special Committee on Palestine (UNSCOP), 322
United States, 287–88, 294–96, 298, 303, 306, 329, 341, 370–72, 375, 377, 379, 381, 384, 387, 395
Ur, 11
Urumiyyah, 343, 348, 363
Ussishkin, Menachem, 314
Uthman, 400

Uziel, Ben-Zion Meir Chay, 208, 322–23
Va'ad Haleumi/National Council, 191, 204, 317
Vaad Ha-Sephardim, 204
Vaiiu, 52
Vatican, 323, 382
Vatican (manuscript), 93
Veneziani, 357, 359–60
Videvdad, 61, 79–81
violence, 183–84, 356, 388
Visions of Amram, 31–32, 44
vomit, 63, 67, 71–72, 76, 80–82, 85, 87, 90, 96–97, 103–4

War of Independence, 322, 324
War Scroll, 26, 32–34, 42
Washington, 370, 373
Weizmann, Chaim, 314, 315n., 322
West Bank, 386
Western Wall, 275, 283
wine, 347, 351, 353, 365
women, 22, 176, 179, 201, 216, 230, 239, 277, 299–302, 306, 339, 341, 359–60
World Congress of Jewish Studies, 332
World Jewish Congress, 327–28
World War I, 179, 189
World War II, 287n., 319

Yahudi/kalimi/Jud, 306
Ya'qov b. Mullah Shelomo b. Mullah 'Abdullah b. Mullah Eliyahu b. Mullah Qandin b. Mullah Inayat, 142, 154
Yasna, 27–32, 44, 113
Yazdgird, 48
Yehud, 4n., 5–8, 11, 13–14, 20–21, 23, 42
Yehudah ben Elazar (RIBA), 120, 125–39

yibbum, 173
Yishai, Moshe, 320
Yishuv, 257–58, 269, 277, 315, 318–19, 321–22
Yitzhaq b. Eliyahu, 147
Yom Kippur, 154, 156, 180, 193, 219, 267, 283
Yonathan b. Mullah Moshe Kohen, 166
Yosef b. Yishaq, 158
Yugoslavia, 212
Yusuf Yahudi, 146, 151

Zahak, King, 400
Zahedi, Fazlollah, 326
Zahir al-Dawlah, 364
zakat (or sadaghe), 397
Zarqan, 361, 363
Zechariah (prophet), 5
Zerubbabel, 5n., 9, 14–15n., 20n.
Ziara, 246
Zion, 178, 188, 193, 209–10, 245, 259, 332
Zionism, 184, 197–99, 204, 207, 232, 275–76, 280, 295, 312–15, 317–21, 324, 327, 332–35, 365, 372–76, 380–89, 392–95
Zionist Assembly, 184, 188–89, 192
Zionist Congress, 314
Zionist Union, 178–79, 184, 189, 196, 211
Zoroastrianism, 24, 27–31, 33–34, 37–41, 43–45, 46–52, 54–58, 60–63, 67, 73, 77n., 78–81, 85–97, 90–91, 94, 97, 99, 105–6, 108–18, 226, 288–89, 334, 344, 354, 364
Zoroastrische Studien, 110
Zuckermandel, 75
Zurvanism/Zurvanite heterodoxy, 29–30

www.ingramcontent.com/pod-product-compliance
Lightning Source LLC
Chambersburg PA
CBHW071225290426
44108CB00013B/1297